MARKETING CHALLENGES

CASES & EXERCISES

THIRD EDITION

Christopher H. Lovelock
International Institute for Management Development (IMD)

Charles B. Weinberg
University of British Columbia

Optional Personal Computer Software
Robert E. Krider
John D. Claxton
Charles B. Weinberg
University of British Columbia

McGRAW-HILL, INC.

New York • St. Louis • San Francisco • Auckland • Bogotá • Caracas •
Lisbon • London • Madrid • Mexico • Milan • Montreal • New Delhi •
Paris • San Juan • Singapore • Sydney • Tokyo • Toronto

This book was set in Times Roman by Monotype Composition Company.
The editor was Bonnie K. Binkert;
the production supervisor was Richard A. Ausburn.
The cover was designed by Keithley & Assoc.
Project supervision was done by The Total Book.

MARKETING CHALLENGES, Cases and Exercises
International Editions 1993

Exclusive rights by McGraw-Hill Book Co. - Singapore for manufacture and export. This book cannot be re-exported from the country to which it is consigned by McGraw-Hill.

1 2 3 4 5 6 7 8 9 0 KKP KKP 9 8 7 6 5 4 3

P/N 038802-4
PART OF
ISBN 0-07-911577-2

Library of Congress Cataloging-in-Publication Data

Marketing challenges: cases and exercises / Christopher H. Lovelock,
    Charles B. Weinberg. - 3rd ed.
        p.   cm. - (McGraw-Hill series in marketing)
    Includes bibliographical references.
    ISBN 0-07-911577-2 (set)
    1. Marketing - Case studies.   2. Marketing - Problems, exercises, etc.
    I. Lovelock, Christopher H.   II. Weinberg, Charles B.   III. Series.
    HF5415.M29747   1993
    658.8-dc20   92-38991

When ordering this title, use ISBN 0-07-112513-2

Printed in Singapore

ABOUT
THE AUTHORS

Christopher H. Lovelock and Charles B. Weinberg, who wrote the text and prepared more than half the cases in *Marketing Challenges*, have been working together since they first met on the faculty of the Stanford Graduate School of Business in 1972. They have continued their collaboration through numerous articles and a total of seven books, including *Public and Nonprofit Marketing*, and its companion volume, *Public and Nonprofit Marketing: Cases and Readings* (both published by The Scientific Press, South San Francisco, 1989, 1990).

Christopher H. Lovelock, a Massachusetts-based consultant and writer, is also a member of the visiting faculty at the International Institute for Management Development (IMD) in Lausanne, Switzerland, where he was a full-time visiting professor from 1990 to 1992. He also served as Professor at the Harvard Business School for eleven years and has taught at Stanford, Berkeley, and MIT. He is author or coauthor of more than fifty articles and ten books, including *Services Marketing* (Prentice-Hall, Englewood Cliffs, N.J., 1991). A native of Great Britain, Dr. Lovelock obtained a B. Com. and an M.A. in economics from the University of Edinburgh. After working in advertising in London and in corporate planning in Montreal, he went on to obtain an M.B.A. from Harvard and a Ph.D. from Stanford. In 1984, he received the *Journal of Marketing*'s Alpha Kappa Psi Award for his contribution to advancing marketing practice.

Charles B. Weinberg is Alumni Professor of Marketing at the Faculty of Commerce and Business Administration, University of British Columbia (UBC). Previously, he taught at Stanford University, the London Business School, and New York University. He has been actively involved in the development of distance-education marketing courses in such diverse settings as the Canadian Centre on Philanthropy and the Open Learning Institute of Hong Kong. He won a University Teaching Prize in 1991, the UBC Commerce Alumni Teaching Award in 1987 for innovations in teaching, and the Killam Research Prize in 1986. A widely published researcher, he also serves on the editorial boards of *Marketing Management* and *Marketing Science*. He has been actively involved in managing and advising nonprofit organizations and has served as Vice President of Marketing for the Vancouver Symphony Orchestra. He grew up in New Jersey and earned a Sc.B. from Brown University, an M.B.A. from Harvard, and a Ph.D. from Columbia.

ABOUT THE CONTRIBUTORS

Francis Aguilar is Professor of Business Administration, Harvard University.

Kimberly A. Bechler is a Research Associate, IMD.

Martin Bless is a Research Associate, IMD.

Thomas V. Bonoma is Professor of Business Administration, Harvard University.

David Carter-Whitney is an M.B.A. graduate of the University of British Columbia.

Bruce H. Clark was formerly a Research Assistant at the Harvard Business School.

John D. Claxton is Associate Professor of Marketing, University of British Columbia.

Frank Conley is an M.B.A. graduate of the University of Virginia.

Cornelius A. deKluyver is Professor, George Mason University.

Jim Dooley was formerly at the University of Seattle.

Gerald J. Eskin is Professor, University of Iowa.

Paul W. Farris is Professor of Marketing, University of Virginia.

Thomas F. Funk is Professor, University of Guelph.

Katherine Gallagher is Assistant Professor, Memorial University of Newfoundland.

E. Gimpel is affiliated with the University of Guelph.

Jonathan Guiliano is an M.B.A. graduate of the University of Virginia.

O. Guindo is affiliated with the University of Guelph.

David H. Hover is a Research Associate, IMD.

Peter T. Hutchison is an M.S. graduate of Stanford University.

Per V. Jenster is Professor, IMD.

Kamran Kashani is Professor, IMD.

Robert J. Kopp is Assistant Professor, Babson College.

Robert E. Krider is a doctoral student, University of British Columbia.

Gordon H.G. McDougall is Professor, Wilfrid Laurier University.

William F. Massy is Vice President of Business and Finance and Professor of Business Administration, Stanford University.

Penny Pittman Merliss was formerly a Research Associate at the Harvard Business School.

Joyce Miller is a Research Associate, IMD.

David B. Montgomery is Robert A. Magowan Professor of Marketing, Graduate School of Business, Stanford University.

James E. Nelson is Associate Professor, Marketing Department, University of Colorado.

John R. Oldland is Associate Professor of Business Administration, Bishop's University.

Don E. Parkinson is an M.S. graduate of Stanford University.

Grant N. Poeter is an M.B.A. graduate of the University of British Columbia.

Craig R. Pollack is a B. Com. graduate of the University of British Columbia.

Richard W. Pollay is Professor of Marketing, University of British Columbia.

J. Carter Powis was formerly a Research Associate, IMD.

Kenneth Shachmut is an M.B.A. graduate of Stanford University.

Kenneth Simmonds is Professor of Marketing and International Business, London Business School.

Douglas Snetsinger is Associate Professor, Marketing Division, University of Toronto.

Susan Spencer is affiliated with the University of Toronto.

Marika Taishoff is a Research Associate, IMD.

Shirley F. Taylor is Assistant Professor, Queen's University.

Nancy Trap is an M.B.A. graduate of the University of Virginia.

Dominique Turpin is Professor, IMD.

Sandra Vandermerwe is Professor, IMD.

William L. Weis is Professor, Albers School of Business, University of Seattle.

William R. Woolridge is Assistant Professor, University of Massachusetts.

To Our Children
Timothy and Elizabeth Lovelock
and
Beth & Geoff Taubman and Amy Weinberg

CONTENTS

PREFACE

As the title *Marketing Challenges* suggests, marketing is both a demanding and exciting field. In preparing the third edition of this book, we sought to capture the breadth and depth of marketing management in the modern world. In particular, global challenges—both problems and opportunities—increasingly confront marketing managers. Consequently, we have developed an extensive set of international cases written with North American students in mind. More than one-fourth of the cases in this book are set outside North America.

Overall, of the forty-six cases in this edition, about half are new to *Marketing Challenges* and have been carefully classroom tested. In addition, six that appeared earlier have been given improved classroom value through pruning or other revisions. As noted, many of the new cases address challenges and increasing pressures from international competitors in both home and foreign markets. The new cases include marketing decisions faced by a number of high-technology companies on the one hand and well-known, branded consumer products firms on the other. A number of the new cases reflect societal and environmental concerns. The optional computer software, now distributed directly to the instructor, is even more user friendly than before.

As in the previous editions, we've tried to select a mix of cases that would embrace a broad cross section of industries and products. The cases are set in both service and manufacturing organizations, ranging in size from small entrepreneurial start-ups to giant multinational corporations, and selling to individual consumers as well as to industrial or institutional purchasers. The environment is usually that of for-profit companies but also includes some public and nonprofit situations.

The book is divided into ten parts, each focusing on a different aspect of marketing management—although there is, of course, some overlap among the parts. Each part begins with a textual introduction, followed by a number of cases or other exercises.

Complementing the textual notes is a glossary of selected marketing and management terms in Appendix 1. To help students understand some of the basic financial analyses required in marketing, Appendix 2 presents a short note on financial and economic analysis in marketing, as well as a set of exercises.

The first edition of this casebook broke new ground by presenting an optional package that enabled students to undertake computer-assisted analysis of many of the materials. The computer aids, formatted to be compatible with *Lotus 1-2-3*, are designed to reflect a marketing management viewpoint. Details of how to use the optional software are provided in Appendixes 3 and 4. However, we do want to emphasize that data in all the cases and exercises in this book can be analyzed without the use of a computer.

More than half of the cases are drawn from the collections of the business schools at Harvard, the International Institute for Management Development (IMD), Stanford, and the University of British Columbia. The balance was prepared by contributors from a wide variety of institutions. Our thanks are due to the individual authors, who are acknowledged in ''About the Contributors,'' as well as on the title page of each case. We wish to thank Professor Gordon H. G. McDougall of Wilfrid Laurier University not only for allowing us to include his cases but also for providing valuable assistance in other aspects of the book. Similarly, we thank Professor Sandra Vandermerwe of IMD for her valued contributions. We extend our appreciation to the copyright holders for permission to reproduce their materials. In addition, we are grateful to the management of the many organizations—sometimes disguised—whose willingness to share experience and data made case development possible in the first place.

John D. Claxton played a major role in the development of the optional computer disk that accompanies this book. We wish to recognize his commitment to innovation in teaching and express our deep gratitude to him for his participation in the development of this work. We also thank Robert E. Krider for his significant role in preparing the revised version of the disk for use with the third edition.

A great many people have assisted in the preparation and publication of *Marketing Challenges*. We're particularly grateful to Rosalea Dennie, who capably and cheerfully typed and managed the word processing of innumerable drafts of this book and its accompanying instructor's manual. Our thanks are due, too, to Josiane Cosendai for her assistance. We're also very appreciative of the important role played by the editorial and production staffs at McGraw-Hill, Inc., especially for the assistance given by Bonnie Binkert and Annette Bodzin.

We owe the following instructors—adopter and nonadopter alike—a debt of gratitude for their evaluation of the manuscript. Their thoughtful comments and helpful suggestions contributed greatly to the finished version of *Marketing Challenges: Cases and Exercises*, third edition: Kim Corfman, New York University (Stern School of Business); David E. Hartman, University of Virginia; Michael V. Laric, University of Baltimore; W. Glynn Mangold, University of Louisville; Jay M. Mower, University of St. Thomas; Robert S. Stevens, Northeast Louisiana University; John B. Stewart, University of Miami; and Ron Stiff, University of Baltimore.

Finally, we want to thank our many former students in both university and corporate settings. Over the years, their critical and enthusiastic classroom discussions have helped us sharpen and refine many of the cases, serving to remind both of us that much of the challenge and satisfaction of case teaching comes from the interaction between students and instructors.

Christopher H. Lovelock

Charles B. Weinberg

ANALYZING AND LEARNING FROM CASES

Unlike methods of instruction that use lectures and textbooks, the case method of instruction does not present students with a body of tried-and-true knowledge about how to be a successful manager. Instead, it provides an opportunity for students to learn by doing.

As a student, you may find that dealing with cases is very much like working with the actual problems that people encounter in their jobs as managers. In most instances, you'll be identifying and clarifying problems facing the management of a company or nonbusiness organization, analyzing qualitative information and quantitative data, evaluating alternative courses of action, and then making decisions about what strategy to pursue for the future.

You may enjoy the process more—and will probably learn more—if you accept the role of an involved participant rather than that of a disinterested observer who has no stake, or interest, in resolving the problems in question.

The goal of case analysis is not to develop a set of ''correct'' facts but to learn to reason well with available data. Cases mirror the uncertainty of the real-world managerial environment in that the information they present is often imprecise and ambiguous. You may perhaps be frustrated that there is no one right answer or correct solution to any given case. Instead, there may be a number of feasible strategies management might adopt, each with somewhat different implications for the future of the organization, and each involving different trade-offs.

If you're using this book in a course or seminar, you'll be exposed to a wide range of different management situations within a relatively short time. As a result, the cases presented in this book will collectively provide a much broader exposure to marketing-related business problems than most managers experience in many years on the job.

Recognizing that managerial problems are not unique to a particular institution (or even to a specific industry) forms the basis for developing a professional approach to management.

CASES AND THE REAL WORLD

It's important to recognize that even though case writers try to build realism into their cases, these cases differ from real-world management situations in several important respects. First, the information is prepackaged in written form. By contrast, managers accumulate their information through memoranda, meetings, chance conversations, research studies, observations, news reports, and other externally published materials—and, of course, by rumor.

Second, cases tend to be selective in their reporting because most of them are designed with specific teaching objectives in mind. Each must fit a relatively short class period and focus attention on a defined category of management problem within a given subject area. To provide such a focus—and to keep the length and complexity of the case within reasonable bounds—the writers may need to omit information on problems, data, or personnel that are peripheral to the central issues in the case.

In the real world, management problems are usually dynamic in nature. They call for some immediate action, with further analysis and major decisions being delayed until some later time. Managers are rarely able to wrap up their problems, put them away, and go on to the next "case." In contrast, discussing a case in class or writing an analysis of a case is more like examining a snapshot taken at a particular point in time—although sometimes a sequel case provides a sense of continuity and poses the need for future decisions within the same organization.

A third, and final, contrast between case analyses and real-world management is that participants in case discussions and authors of written case reports aren't responsible for implementing their decisions, nor do they have to live with the consequences. However, this doesn't mean that you can be frivolous when making recommendations. Instructors and classmates are likely to be critical of contributions that aren't based on careful analysis and interpretation of the facts.

PREPARING A CASE

Just as there is no one right solution to a case, there is also no single correct way of preparing a case. However, the broad guidelines outlined in "Preparing a Case" may help familiarize you with the job of case preparation. With practice, you should be able to establish a working style with which you feel comfortable. The guidelines on initial analysis and on developing recommendations should also serve you well for preparing written case reports or case-based exams.

Initial Analysis

First, it's important to gain a feel for the overall situation by skimming quickly through the case. Ask yourself:

- What sort of organization does the case concern?
- What is the nature of the industry (broadly defined)?
- What is going on in the external environment?
- What problems does management appear to be facing?

An initial fast reading, without making notes or underlining, should provide a sense for what is going on and what information is being presented for analysis. Then you'll be ready to make a very careful second reading of the case. This time, seek to identify key facts so that you can develop a situation analysis and clarify the nature of the problems facing management. As you go along, try to make notes in response to such questions as:

- What decisions need to be made, and who will be responsible for making them?
- What are the objectives of the organization itself and of each of the key players in the case? Are these objectives compatible? If not, can the problems be reconciled or will it be necessary to redefine the objectives?
- What resources and constraints are present which may help or hinder attempts by the organization to meet its objectives.

You should make a particular effort to establish the significance of any quantitative data presented in the text of the case, or, more often, in the exhibits. See if new insights may be gained by combining and manipulating data presented in different parts of the case. But don't accept the data blindly. In the cases, as in real life, not all information is equally reliable or equally relevant. On the other hand, case writers won't deliberately misrepresent data or facts to try to trick you.

Developing Recommendations

At this point in the analysis, you should be in a position to summarize your evaluation of the situation and to develop some recommendations for management. First, identify

---

PREPARING A CASE: A BRIEF OUTLINE

I. Initial fast reading
- No notes
- Get a feel for what's going on
- Think about major problems and forces present

II. A second careful reading
- Make notes identifying:
  - Organizational objectives
  - Nature of problem(s)
  - Key facts
  - Key decisions
- Evaluate and analyze case data

III. Development of recommendations
- Identify alternative courses of action to meet objectives
- Consider implications of each action
- Provide recommendations, supported by analysis

---

the alternative courses of action that the organization might have. Next, consider the implications of each alternative, including possible undesirable outcomes, such as provoking responses from stronger competitors. Ask yourself how short-term tactics fit with longer-term strategies. Relate each alternative to the objectives of the organization (as defined or implied in the case, or as redefined by you). Then, develop a set of recommendations for future action, making sure that these recommendations are supported by your analysis of the case data.

Your recommendations won't be complete unless you give some thought to how the proposed strategy should be implemented:

- What resources—human, financial, or other—will be required?
- Who should be responsible for implementation?
- What time frame should be established for the various actions proposed?
- How should subsequent performance be measured?

Small-Group Discussions

The best results in the early stages of case preparation are generally achieved by working alone. But a useful step, prior to class discussion, is to discuss the case with a small group of classmates. (In some instances, you may find yourself assigned to a small discussion group or you may be required to work with others to develop a written report for possible group presentation.)

These small groups facilitate initial testing of ideas and help to focus discussion on the main considerations. Within such a discussion group, present your arguments and listen to those of other participants. Except in the case of group projects, the aim of such a meeting is not to reach a consensus, but to broaden, clarify, and redefine your own thinking—and to help others do likewise.

Effective management of a business involves adjusting corporate resources to the changing character of the marketplace; this is different from just applying knowledge about what works and what doesn't work in management. Accordingly, the focus of small-group discussions should be on analysis and decision making: What are the facts? What do they mean? What alternatives are available? What specifically should management do? How and when?

CLASS DISCUSSIONS

Courses taught by the case method emphasize inductive learning, with conceptual frameworks and strategic guidelines developed from the analysis of a variety of real-world situations. This approach contrasts sharply with the deductive approach to learning used in lectures where the concepts are presented first and must then be applied to actual situations.

Role of the Instructor

In class, you may find that the role played by an instructor using the case method usually differs significantly from that of a lecturer. The instructor's role in case discussions is often similar to that of a moderator—calling on students, guiding the discussion, asking questions, and periodically synthesizing previous comments. Teaching styles vary, of course, from one case instructor to another.

Many professors like to begin the class by asking a student to ''lay out'' the case, which may involve your being asked to identify key problems and opportunities, to present some preliminary data analysis, and perhaps to outline a possible plan of action.

Some instructors assign study questions in advance to help students with their case preparation; but others feel it is more realistic (albeit more demanding) to let students define for themselves how they should approach each new case.

Responsibilities of Participants

Instead of being a passive note taker, as in lecture classes, you'll be expected to become an active participant in class discussions. Indeed, it's essential that you participate; for if nobody participates there can be no discussion! If you never join in the debate, you'll be denying other participants the insights that you may have to offer. Moreover, there's significant learning involved in presenting your own analysis and recommendations and debating them with your classmates—who may hold differing views or else seek to build on your presentation. But don't be so eager to participate that you ignore what others have to say. Learning to be a good listener is also an important element in developing managerial skills.

Occasionally, it may happen that you are personally familiar with the organization depicted in a case. Perhaps you are privy to additional information not contained in the case, or perhaps you know what has happened since the time of the case decision point. If so, keep this information to yourself unless, and until, the instructor requests it. (This advice also holds true for written reports and case exams.) There are no prizes for 20/20 hindsight; injecting extra information that nobody else has is more likely to spoil a class discussion than to enhance it.

Learning comes through discussion and controversy. In the case method of instruction, participants must assume responsibility not only for their own learning but also for that of others in the class. Thus, it's important for students to be well prepared, willing to commit themselves to a well-reasoned set of analyses and recommendations, and receptive to constructive criticism. Students unwilling to accept this challenge are likely to find the case method aimless and confusing. On the other hand, if you do accept it, we're confident that you'll experience in the classroom that sense of excitement, challenge, and even exasperation that comes with being a manager in a real-world situation.

EXAMPLE OF A CASE ANALYSIS

There is no universal formula for analyzing cases, but there *are* ways to learn how to do better case analyses. The introductory note ''Analyzing and Learning from Cases'' provides suggestions on how to approach case analysis.

The textual notes at the start of each section provide a review of the major issues in each section's cases and exercises. However, you should always remember that management problems don't come in neatly classified fashion. Therefore, cases almost always raise multiple issues and students must recognize that identifying problems and establishing priorities are important parts of case analysis.

To help you become accustomed to the nature of case analysis, we have provided on the following pages a short case (Western Products, Inc.), a student's written analysis of that case, and an instructor's critique of the student's report.

Western Products, Inc.

Charles B. Weinberg

George Norrin, the major owner of Western Products, Inc., of Portland, Oregon, faced an important decision. Should the company, for the first time in its 35-year history, begin a large advertising campaign?

The advertising campaign, if begun, would focus on the company's chain saw products. Western Products marketed a variety of power tools—pneumatic drills, generators, concrete vibrators—to the industrial and construction markets in the three Pacific states—Washington, Oregon, and California—and in the western provinces of Canada.

Western had entered the chain saw business 15 years ago when one of Mr. Norrin's closest friends, Jim Dagan, decided to retire. Mr. Dagan had owned a small company which manufactured and marketed chain saws. Mr. Dagan asked his friend if he was interested in buying the company, Dagan Power Saws. The two men quickly worked out a reasonable price. Mr. Dagan was still a passive partner in the company and received 10 percent of the profits from the chain saw division of Western Products. Now chain saws accounted for 42 percent of Western's sales and 48 percent of the company's profits (see *Exhibit 1*).

MARKET BACKGROUND

While no precise data were available, Western estimated it held about a 15 percent market share in its market area for gasoline-powered chain saws. It was the fourth largest manufacturer of gasoline-powered chain saws in its region.

Gasoline-powered chain saws were sold to loggers, farmers, large land owners (companies and institutions), and homeowners—primarily casual users with many trees on their land. The last market appeared to be something of a growth market. The logger market was quite cyclical, rising and falling with the boom-and-bust cycle which seemed to characterize the forestry industry.

At the time that Dagan Power Saws was purchased, three-fifths of its sales were made through a distributor, Excelsior Sales, which owned a number of retail outlets and acted as a wholesaler to many other retail outlets throughout the west. It was Excelsior's wholesaling system that allowed Western to achieve distribution in both

EXHIBIT 1
WESTERN PRODUCTS INC. INCOME STATEMENT
(In Thousands)

Sales		$ 4,233
Cost of goods sold		
Materials	$ 1,901	
Shipping	278	
Labor	962	3,141
Contribution		$ 1,092
Manufacturing overhead	$ 630	
Administrative expenses	151	
Sales and marketing	138	919
Net profit (before tax)		$ 173

the United States and Canada. All sales to Excelsior carried Excelsior's own brand names. The Excelsior name was used for sales through its own stores and the Harter brand name for sales through other companies. (The Harter brand name was solely owned and controlled by Excelsior.) Overall, Excelsior accounted for 59 percent of Western's chain saw sales; this percentage had been virtually constant over the past 15 years. Mr. Norrin thought that his relationship with Excelsior was excellent.

Mr. Norrin and his chief assistant, Kara Smith, regularly called on all major forestry companies, other companies and institutions that were likely to be buyers of gasoline-powered chain saws or involved in land-clearing operations, operators of lumber yards and building supply distributors, and occasionally large retailers themselves. However, Mr. Norrin and Ms. Smith were not able to visit many of the dealers who sold chain saws. For example, of the 53 dealers in the state of Washington who sold Dagan brand chain saws, they had only called on 19 in the most recent year. Most dealers sold several brands of chain saws, but many limited themselves to two or three brands. All sales in these markets (41 percent of the chain saw business) were made under the Dagan brand name. The majority of these sales were made through wholesalers and retailers.

The company also participated each year in a number of agricultural fairs, such as the Pacific National Exhibition in Vancouver, and sponsored log-rolling and other contests. However, the company had never advertised either in trade journals to reach dealers or in magazines that might directly reach the people who were the buyers and users of chain saws.

Western manufactured a variety of chain saw models, but they differed primarily in the length of the chain saw blade and horsepower. Trade association surveys showed that a number of other features were important to users. Weight of the chain saw, ease of controls, whether it had a gas protector, and the warranty were important to consumers, with safety being a critical—although unspoken—concern to many. The Dagan chain saws were at least as good as the major competitors on all these dimensions and had a slight weight advantage when compared with other chain saws. That is, for any given horsepower and blade length, the Western saw would weigh slightly less than competing brands. However, this weight advantage was very difficult to notice unless someone worked with a chain saw for a period of time.

A typical chain saw had a retail price of $500. Excelsior received a 30 percent discount on this price, as did most other distributors and wholesalers to whom Dagan sold. On average, Excelsior or other wholesalers would take one-third of this discount (i.e., $50) and the retailer would receive the remaining two-thirds (i.e., $100).

Of Dagan's revenues, 48 percent represented materials (including preassembled components), 22 percent represented labor, and the remainder was contribution to overhead and before-tax profit. Because Excelsior picked up the chain saws from the Dagan factory, there were no shipping expenses.

THE ADVERTISING PROPOSAL

Two years ago, Mr. Norrin had hired Kevin Style as marketing manager for Dagan chain saws. Mr. Style, who held a bachelor's degree in business administration, paid for his college education by working as a logger in the summers. After graduation, he worked for five years as a sales representative with James Faucets, a major marketer of plumbing fixtures, and then for two years as associate sales manager at the company's head office.

Mr. Style felt that Dagan could substantially increase sales of its own brand of chain saws if it achieved a greater presence in the marketplace. He felt that name brand recognition would increase the company's sales, both because dealers would be more inclined to mention the brand to their customers and because customers would be more inclined to specify—or at least recognize—the Dagan brand name.

Recently, a trade journal had published the results of a market survey about how individuals bought power tools. Although Mr. Style could not determine what portion of the buyers were professionals (such as loggers or carpenters) and what portion were homeowners, he still felt the results were helpful. The magazine had sent out a questionnaire to 1,200 recent buyers of power tools and had received 800 replies. The main results of the survey are shown in *Exhibit 2*. In brief, Mr. Style noted that the findings showed that 57 percent of buyers had a brand of power tool in mind before buying it and that 44 percent said that the dealer had quite a bit or a great deal of influence on the brand that was purchased. He felt that these results supported his contention that advertising could pay off for Western.

Mr. Style interviewed a number of ad agencies about the possibility of handling the Dagan account. After extensive discussion, he hired the Summit Advertising Agency to represent his company and prepare an advertising plan. He negotiated a one-year contract with a flat fee of $5,000 to the agency. He did this rather than pay a commission on advertising dollars spent, because he didn't want the agency to have an incentive to recommend advertising expenditures just to increase its earnings.

Summit recommended that advertising would be an excellent investment for Dagan. However, they believed that if the Dagan brand name were to achieve recognition, a few small space ads would not do much. Rather, the agency suggested that full-page ads should be used on a frequent basis. Summit had conducted some research and had identified a set of magazines and local papers that most loggers read, two trade

EXHIBIT 2
EXCERPTS FROM SURVEY OF RECENT BUYERS OF POWER TOOLS COSTING
MORE THAN $100

How much time did you spend thinking about purchase?	
Less than 1 week	4%
1 week to 1 month	15%
1 month to 3 months	41%
More than 3 months	40%

How familiar were you with the product before you bought it?	
Very familiar	28%
Somewhat familiar	43%
Not too familiar	29%

Did you have a brand in mind before your first visit to a dealer?	
Yes	57% (40% said they bought this brand)
No	43%

How great was the dealer's influence on your purchase?	
Considerable	44%
Some	18%
Hardly any	15%
None	23%

Source: Recent trade publication.

journals that reached most retailers and wholesalers in Dagan's market area, and three magazines that targeted the do-it-yourself homeowner who might make use of a chain saw. As shown in *Exhibit 3,* Summit proposed spending $45,000 on this campaign (of which 15 percent, the commission that the media paid to Summit, would be rebated to Dagan). A key advertising point would be Dagan's lighter weight.

Mr. Style thought this was an excellent proposal and heartily endorsed it. An expenditure of this magnitude would require the approval of Mr. Norrin, not only because of its size but because of its novelty for this company.

EXHIBIT 3 SUMMARY OF SUMMIT ADVERTISING PROPOSAL

Market target	Media description	Intensity	Cost
Retailers and wholesalers	Two monthly trade journals: *Lumber Wholesaler & Retailer* and *Store Management*	Six ads per year in each magazine	$16,400
Homeowners	Three magazines aimed at do-it-yourselfers: *Popular Crafts, Western Homeowner,* and *Canadian Homes*	Ads in two issues of each magazine during heavy selling season	$18,500
Loggers	Local newspapers and magazines, e.g., *Forestry Workers' News*	One to four ads in selected newspapers and magazines	$10,100

STUDENT ANALYSIS OF WESTERN PRODUCTS, INC.

Issue: *Should Western begin a large advertising campaign for its chain saw products?*

Discussion

Mr. Style thinks that Western can substantially increase sales of Dagan brand name chain saws by undertaking a major advertising campaign in Western's market area. Although Mr. Style's past work experience provides him with knowledge of marketing procedures, he has not fully considered the implications of his proposal. At James Faucets, Mr. Style's prior employer, Mr. Style sold products in a market with many direct competitors (assumed). At Western, Mr. Style is selling products in a market with direct and indirect competitors (including Excelsior with Excelsior and Harter brand names, see *Exhibit 4*). By increasing advertising for Dagan chain saws, and therefore causing an increase in sales of Dagan chain saws (assumed), Excelsior's chain saw sales, under both brand names, will likely suffer. This could serve to tarnish the "excellent" relationship that currently exists between the two companies, and that has apparently existed for the past fifteen years, as evidenced by the fact that Excelsior has continually accounted for approximately 60 percent of Dagan chain saw sales over the past 15 years.

If the relationship does become tarnished, Western has more to lose than gain by operating independently of Excelsior. Excelsior's distribution channels allow Western

EXHIBIT 4   DIRECT AND INDIRECT COMPETITORS

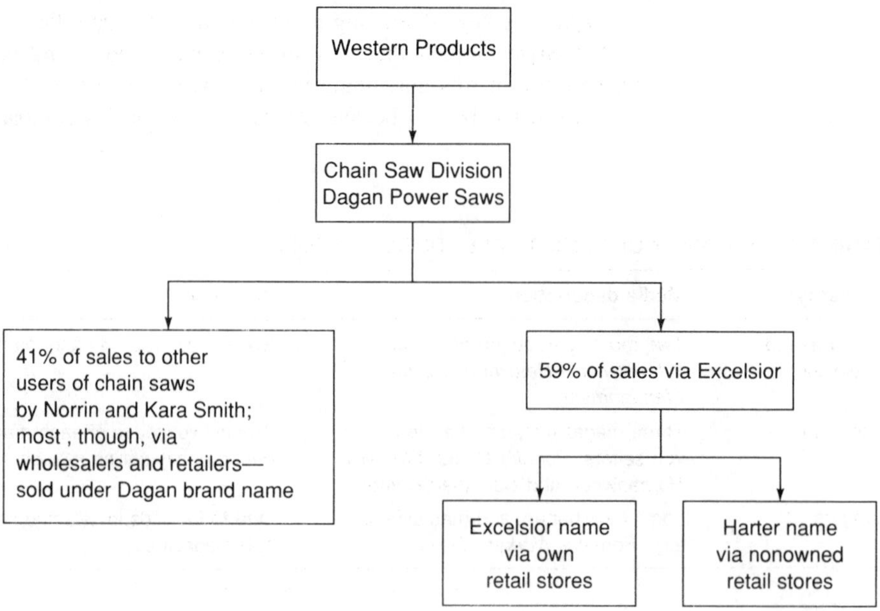

to sell its products in western states and provinces. Also, as indicated by the power tool buyer survey, many consumers tend to purchase well-known brand name products. To capitalize on this fact, Western needs to have a well-established name through which to sell its products, something that Excelsior provides because of its large distribution channels. And because of the influence retailers have on purchases, also indicated by the survey, Excelsior again has a strong influence on Western's sales. Finally, because most of Western's sales are currently through retailers and wholesalers, who require the same margins as Excelsior, Western saves nothing in lower margins to dealers by not selling through Excelsior. In fact, Western saves money by selling to Excelsior because Excelsior absorbs the delivery costs of the chain saws, as shown in *Exhibit 5*.

Therefore, assuming that there are presently no threats to Western by Excelsior to stop selling Dagan chain saws under the Excelsior and Harter brand names, increasing advertising to try to increase Dagan chain saw sales could cannibalize Excelsior's sales of Dagan chain saws and jeopardize the excellent relationship that currently exists between the two companies and, in the long run, cause Western to lose its powerful distribution channel that accounts for about three-fifths of its chain saw sales.

Alternatives

1. Proceed with advertising plans.
2. Propose co-op advertising with Excelsior for Excelsior's brand names in areas where Dagan brand name chain saws are not heavily promoted by Western.

Analysis of Alternatives

1. Proceeding with advertising plans could weaken the relationship between Western and Excelsior and cause Western to lose or jeopardize its powerful distribution channels.
2. Proposing co-op advertising with Excelsior for Excelsior's brand names would allow Western to magnify its advertising dollar and perhaps increase sales for chain saws in areas in which Mr. Norrin and Ms. Smith do not make strong attempts to sell Dagan chain saws.

Recommendations

Propose to Excelsior that co-op advertising for Excelsior brand name chain saws be undertaken in areas in which Western does not heavily promote Dagan chain saws.

Closing Note

If Western does decide to advertise, either with or without Excelsior, the increase in sales of chain saws required to pay for the advertising will give Western an idea of the feasibility of the proposal. As indicated in *Exhibit 5*, to pay for an advertising cost of $43,250 Western would have to have an incremental increase in chain saw sales of 412 under the Excelsior name or 601 under the Dagan name. These numbers would represent a 1.7 percent and 2.5 percent increase in market share (out of a total market of 23,700 chain saws), respectively.

EXHIBIT 5   FINANCIAL ANALYSIS

Revenue to Western per unit		
Retail price		$500
Discount (30%)	$150	
Wholesaler margin (⅓ of 30%)	50	
Retail margin (⅔ of 30%)	100	150
Revenue to Western/chain saw		$350

Western's current unit sales	
Percentage of market	15%
Total dollar sales	$4,233,000
Percentage revenue from chain saws	42%
Chain saw revenue	$1,777,860
Chain saw price	$500
Approximate number of chain saws sold—Western total ($1,777,860 ÷ 500)	3,555
Chain saws sold via Excelsior (59%)	2,100
Chain saws sold direct by Dagan	1,455
Total chain saw market (3,555/0.15)	23,700 units

Contribution per chain saw				
	Dagan name		**Excelsior name**	
Revenue/chain saw		$350		$350
Materials (48%)	$168		$168	
Labor (22%)	77		77	
Shipping (see below)	33		0	
		278		245
Contribution/chain saw		$ 72		$105

Calculation of shipping cost per chain saw sold under Dagan name	
Western's total shipping costs	$ 278,000
Western's total revenue	$4,233,000
Total chain saws sold	3,555
Chain saws sold via Dagan name	1,455
Price per chain saw	$ 500
Revenue generated via Dagan chain saw sales (1,455 × $500)	$ 728,000
Dagan chain saw revenue as percentage of total revenue ($728,000/$4,233,000)	17%
Approximate shipping costs/Dagan chain saw (17% × $278,000/1,455)	$ 33

Advertising costs	
Flat fee	$ 5,000
Proposed spending	45,000
15% returned to Western	(6,750)
Total advertising cost	$ 43,250
Extra chain saw sales required to cover advertising cost	
Under Dagan name ($43,250/$72)	601 units
Under Excelsior name ($43,250/$105)	412 units

INSTRUCTOR CRITIQUE OF STUDENT ANALYSIS OF WESTERN PRODUCTS, INC.

Overall Evaluation

Your analysis of the advertising campaign issue is thorough and clear. You should have widened the scope of your analysis to capture some of the more subtle issues: Is Western Products too dependent on Excelsior? What are the relative merits of advertising and personal selling? What market segments should be pursued?

Issue Identification

Your statement of the issue is clear and concise. However, you didn't develop a statement of the broader problems facing the company. Remember that what people think is the problem is often only a symptom of the real problem. In this case, Mr. Norrin was focusing on whether to advertise the Dagan brand of chain saws. You should have asked yourself why Mr. Norrin was even considering this change. After all, Western Products was not in any kind of obvious trouble. There must have been a good reason for contemplating an investment like this. Was the market changing, making new forms of communications necessary? Did existing channels of distribution need to be supplemented? Was personal selling no longer feasible or effective?

Among the case facts to be considered to help in identifying key issues are:

- Only 41 percent of sales are under the Dagan brand name.
- Mr. Norrin and Ms. Smith lacked the time to call on a majority of other dealers and distributors.
- Brand preference is important to buyers.
- Dealers exert considerable influence on buyers.

Always question whether what seems to be the issue actually is. Often, the problem goes deeper.

Your flowchart in *Exhibit 4* was very useful in clarifying the pattern of chain saw sales and Western's relation with Excelsior.

Situation Analysis

You did not do a thorough situation analysis. It is usually a good idea to do one, because it helps you organize in your own mind a lot of information that sheds light on the issues in the case. It also makes explicit the assumptions under which you are operating and lets you know what you *don't* know.

A situation analysis would have revealed, for example, that Western Products' relationship with Excelsior may be a mixed blessing. In your analysis, you do a very good job explaining the advantages of the relationship, but you overlook the associated threat. Western Products' dependence on a single major distributor puts it in a vulnerable position. That puts the advertising question in a different, more favorable light—not only might an advertising campaign generate some ''pull'' demand, it might also reduce Western Products' vulnerability. However, you did a good job in recognizing that the impact of Dagan's ad campaign on relations with Excelsior must be considered in making a decision.

Alternatives

Given your identification of issues, your list of alternative courses of action is fine. For completeness, it should have included the option "Do nothing different." However, even more critical, you should have considered the alternative of hiring an additional salesperson. The case mentions that the executives don't have the time to call on all the accounts, and the market research data show that the dealer's influence is important in the purchase process.

The second alternative you propose (co-op advertising) is particularly good because it goes beyond what has been suggested in the case; a creative solution like this is a big plus.

Analysis of Alternatives

Your analysis of the alternatives you suggested is concise. It is important to state the criteria against which you are evaluating the alternatives. To a certain extent you did this, but only in your "Closing Note." You seem to evaluate the alternatives against different criteria. For example, what is the incremental financial cost of each alternative? What are the incremental financial benefits? What are the nonfinancial costs and benefits? These criteria should have been the logical result of your situation analysis. You need to examine each alternative systematically, so you can see exactly how well each one does on each criterion. Then, if new information changes the firm's priorities—for example, if the relationship with Excelsior sours—it is easier to see how the alternatives now stack up.

You economic analysis of the advertising alternative was good. You generally made reasonable assumptions to evaluate the financial impact of the proposed advertising plan. It's a good idea, as you did, to translate the numbers into a market share target. For a company with a current market share of 15 percent, an incremental market share gain of 2.5 percent is a considerable challenge.

In your analysis, you might note that the $5,000 fee to Summit Advertising is already committed for this year, so it is not an incremental cost and would not be appropriate for the break-even analysis. You were generally quite careful in your analysis, and it was correct to recognize the 15 percent rebate on media costs.

You should not be convinced too early that a particular alternative is superior. Avoid the temptation to try to find the one "right" answer. Look at each possibility in as balanced a way as possible. For example, the alternative of co-op advertising still leaves Western Products very much dependent on Excelsior.

Recommendation

Your recommendation is clear and actionable. However, you could have been more specific by making recommendations that would address such issues as these: What rate should be used to share the co-op ad costs? What's the budget? What is the likely outcome?

Organization of Report

You might have used a more formal approach or framework in your "Analysis" or "Discussion" section. As mentioned earlier, you did not do a situation analysis. Consider using subheadings such as:

- Consumer/buyer analysis
- Market segmentation
- Environmental analysis
- Company versus competition—strengths and weaknesses.

While these categories may not always be appropriate, they help the reader to understand the presentation. Further, the categories may help you to organize your thoughts and analysis. As one example, under "Buyer Analysis," you might consider: How important is advertising in the buying decision for a chain saw? How important is personal selling? Are potential buyers aware of the Dagan brand name? The Excelsior brand name?

As well, the "Closing Note" catches the reader by surprise. This note should be presented earlier in the discussion so that the merits of your recommendations can be assessed.

To Recap

You have done a good job of examining one aspect of the case. If you had applied the same creativity to other issues and had approached the case more systematically, yours would have been a superior case analysis.

MARKETING CHALLENGES

CASES AND EXERCISES

PART ONE

The Nature of Marketing

E very reader of this book has been an active consumer for years, evaluating and purchasing a wide array of products from competing suppliers. The cases and exercises in this book place the reader in a different role, that of the marketing manager in a diverse group of organizations, responsible for helping to develop, price, and distribute their products and encouraging customers to purchase them.

In a purchase, the customer offers something of value (typically money, but also time and personal effort) in exchange for the value represented by the product. Managing and facilitating these transactions lies at the heart of marketing management. Success in this endeavor requires an understanding of how individuals and organizations make decisions relating to purchase behavior and how this behavior may be influenced.

Historically, the study of marketing emphasized the purchase and sale of physical goods in the private sector of the economy. The greatest sophistication was achieved in consumer packaged goods, with attention later being directed to marketing consumer-durable and industrial goods. Today, the situation is different in that marketing expertise is now also highly valued by managers of service firms (whose output accounts for over half the gross national product of the United States). In the public and nonprofit sectors, too, there is widespread interest in developing a stronger marketing orientation among organizations as diverse as disease prevention agencies, transit authorities, museums, and performing-arts programs. Most nonbusiness organizations market services, but some sell goods through retail stores or mail-order catalogs, and many promote social issues and behavior patterns—such as conserving scarce resources and voting in political campaigns. In this book, we will use the term *product* in its genetic sense to include goods, services, and social behaviors.

1

MANAGEMENT AND CUSTOMER PERSPECTIVES

Success in developing a marketing program for any type of product requires the ability to understand both management and customer perspectives. The organization attempts to achieve profitability through the sale of its products (public and nonprofit organizations may seek to achieve social as opposed to *financial* profits and thus need to attract gifts or tax revenues to help cover their costs); customers are interested in what the product will do for them.

At one level, the marketing process is used by the organization to develop an overall product-market strategy. Decisions must be made on which customers to serve with what products in order to meet organizational goals. Such decisions must be made in light of the company's resources and with regard to future as well as current market conditions. This perspective reflects the costs and benefits accruing to the marketer. At a second level, the marketing process is used to develop detailed marketing programs that reflect a good understanding of the needs of final customers and intermediary organizations. Managers should be asking: What specific combination of product features, delivery systems, pricing, and information dissemination will lead a specific customer (or group of customers) to purchase a specific product from us rather than from a competitor—or not at all?

The materials in this casebook are concerned with both levels of the marketing process. This dual focus requires, first, careful analysis and evaluation of each organization's product-market strategy. Is this strategy realistic and sound in the light of environmental trends, market characteristics, customer needs, and competitive activities? What modifications, if any, are required? Rarely is there one obvious strategy or plan. Widely varying solutions to a marketing problem may be appropriate, depending on the manager's knowledge and assessment of current and future conditions, creativity in generating plans of action, willingness to take risks, and judgment about the resources available and the goals to be met. Moreover, some strategies may be more difficult to implement than others. Although case analysis and discussion do not allow for actual implementation, likelihood of successful implementation is an important criterion in assessing a strategy. Different strategies are, of course, likely to have different consequences down the road.

Developing a specific marketing plan emphasizes the second level of the marketing process, since here the focus is on resolving a particular marketing problem or taking advantage of a specific opportunity. A critical part of most marketing plans is using special skills (or "distinctive competences") that will make the firm particularly effective in its chosen product-market, relative to its competition. Developing a marketing plan usually proceeds in the following manner:

1. Identify and define the problem or opportunity.
2. Establish the marketing goals to be met.
3. Analyze relevant data on the market, customers, intermediaries, competitors, and other relevant environments.
4. Develop alternative approaches and plans of action.

5. Analyze the economic implications of alternative strategies as these relate to costs, revenues, and anticipated volumes. Consider other relevant criteria.
6. Use these analyses to select and justify a specific plan of action.

MARKETING TOOLS AND CONCEPTS

The cases in this first section of the book introduce various analytical tools and conceptual frameworks that are central to the development of marketing strategy. These include marketing analysis, market segmentation, buyer behavior, competitive analysis, and role of intermediaries. Many marketing decisions can be broken down into several elements that are collectively referred to as the *marketing mix*. These elements include product policy, pricing, distribution, and communication (for example, personal selling, advertising, and promotion).

Market Analysis

Central to the development of any marketing program is information on market size, structure, and dynamics. From this information, managers can gain insights into the performance of existing products relative to the competition and into the prospects for existing or proposed products in the future.

Among the most significant questions that the manager should seek to answer are:

- How large is the market for the product in question?
- Is it growing, shrinking, or static?
- What are the major forces influencing the level of demand for this product?
- Can the market be broken down into segments? If so, what are the most useful bases for segmentation?
- At what stage in the product life cycle is this market? Are we dealing with a new-product category that is growing rapidly, a mature and well-established one, or an old-product category for which demand is falling?
- Is demand consistent over time, or does it fluctuate sharply in response to random or cyclical factors?
- Who are the competitors serving this market? What is the basis of competition? Where is the competition vulnerable?

Market Segmentation

The concept of market segmentation is implicit in decisions on what customer groups to serve and on how to combine marketing variables to appeal to a particular group of potential customers.

Market segmentation is based upon the following propositions:

1. Not all customers are alike—many customers (or institutional purchasers) differ from one another in marketing-relevant ways.

2. Segments of consumers can be identified and isolated within the overall market according to such factors as their personal characteristics, geographic location, lifestyles, the needs they seek to satisfy, their buying behavior, and levels of usage of the product in question.

Most marketing organizations find themselves operating in "mass markets" of thousands or even millions of customers and prospective customers. Market segmentation represents a middle way between a strategy of market aggregation, in which all customers are treated similarly, and market disaggregation, in which each customer is treated uniquely. The goal is to combine the efficiencies of economies of scale with the attention to personal concerns that comes from focusing on the needs of individuals who share certain important characteristics. Effective marketing strategy requires an explicit choice of which segments to serve.

Buyer Behavior

How does a customer decide to buy a product and then go about purchasing it? Managers need to understand buyer behavior before they can move to strategy development. Some purchases are impulsive acts by individuals, such as buying a magazine at a supermarket checkout counter. Other purchases entail more time and planning, whether they represent the decision of an individual or a group. Large purchases in a family or institutional setting may involve several members who may act as a type of buying committee. Such a group is sometimes known as a decision-making unit, since its members arrive at the purchase decision collectively, even though a single individual may take responsibility for making the purchase or placing the order.

Individuals or decision-making units are often influenced in their purchase decisions by advice or information from other parties. Friends and relatives, for instance, may encourage or discourage a particular course of action, such as buying a new car. Large organizations may have a formal buying committee which is responsible for selecting a vendor or choosing which product to buy. Moreover, corporate executives outside the buying committee may influence the product "specs" in one way or another or impose requirements that specify which manufacturers and service suppliers represent approved vendors.

Although analysis of one's personal experiences in buying consumer goods and services may offer useful insights, it is unwise to generalize too broadly from these. Other people may approach similar purchases in different ways. The buying behavior of industrial firms and other institutions is frequently somewhat different from that of household purchasers, the former involving substantially larger volumes, unfamiliar product categories, and formalized procedures for decision making.

A general set of questions for understanding buyer behavior might include:

- Who initiates the buying process?
- What events or factors stimulate a need to purchase?
- What are the constraints associated with the decision?

- Is this a one-time or repetitive purchase situation?
- What criteria are used to evaluate alternative products?
- How are these criteria set? Which criteria are most important and how will they change over time?
- Whose opinions influence the evaluation of alternative purchases?
- Who makes the final buying decision, and does any one individual have effective veto power?
- Who implements the actual purchase transaction?
- Who uses the product once the purchase has been made?

Competitive Analysis

Actions taken by competitors play a major role in determining whether a particular marketing program will be successful. At the outset, analysis of the market should identify and evaluate the relative strength of current competitors, using the following criteria:

- How long has each competitor been active in the market?
- What is its market share in both volume and financial terms?
- And has this share been rising or falling over time?
- Does each competitor appeal to a broad cross section of customers, or does it pursue a "niche" strategy, targeting its product(s) and marketing programs at one or more market segments?
- What are key strengths and distinctive competences of each competitor?

Determining the current competitive situation, however, is not sufficient. Any manager who presumes, without good evidence, that competing organizations will continue their present strategies into the future is most unwise. Marketers need to know enough about each competitor—its financial situation, marketing strengths and weaknesses, people resources, short- and long-term objectives, potential for innovation, cost structure, and management values—to predict, with reasonable accuracy, how it is likely to respond to new initiatives.

Role of Intermediates

Marketers of both consumer and industrial products may find it necessary, or simply advantageous, to delegate certain marketing functions to independent intermediaries. Thus, the design and execution of advertising campaigns are frequently contracted out to advertising agencies. Similarly, credit financing may be arranged through a financial institution such as a bank or credit card company. The most important use of intermediaries concerns the physical distribution of goods and the delivery of services (sometimes through franchising or the use of electronic channels for financial and information services). A major advantage of using intermediaries rather than doing the work oneself is that it substitutes variable costs for fixed overheads and semivariable costs.

Organizations that choose to market through intermediaries—such as wholesalers, retailers, distributors, brokers, or agencies—are looking for leverage. In return for a portion of the final selling price, the original marketer gets the intermediary to offer customer benefits like greater convenience, expert advice, added service features, and one-stop shopping for related products. Additionally, the intermediaries may take full or partial responsibility for selling, advertising and promotional efforts, credit, and display. In some instances, selected intermediaries may receive exclusive rights to distribute a specific product, as in franchising or exclusive dealerships. In other instances a qualified intermediary may be permitted to act as a distributor for the product in question.

Marketers should always remember that intermediaries are independent organizations which are free to enter into an agreement, or not, with primary suppliers of goods and services. The alternative for the marketer is to integrate vertically and operate its own distribution system—a strategy that is much more common in the service sector than in manufacturing, particularly for consumer goods. Some distributor relationships are highly structured, as in franchising, and give the original marketer a significant degree of control. In other relationships, as with a small manufacturer selling through a well-established retail chain, the power lies more strongly with the retail chain.

In certain respects, analyzing current and prospective intermediaries is analogous to customer analysis. Intermediaries can be segmented according to a variety of factors (size, target market, geographic location, hours of operation, and so forth). Their involvement with competitors' products can be studied. An analysis can—and should—be made of how an intermediary makes decisions on whether or not to distribute particular goods and services, what criteria its management employs in making such decisions, and which individuals compose its decision-making unit. Finally, consideration should be given to what advantages might be gained over competitors by improving the margins provided to intermediaries, offering advertising and promotional assistance, providing market research data, and increasing contact with relevant managers.

The Marketing Mix

Putting together a marketing plan requires the manager to make strategic decisions in several important areas, which are collectively known as the marketing mix:

1. The product
2. The distribution and delivery system through which products are made available to customers
3. The price at which the product is sold
4. The communications by which prospective customers are informed about the product and encouraged to buy it

Many people mistakenly equate marketing solely with communication activities—advertising, promotion, public relations, and personal selling. Viewed from the perspective of the marketing mix, we can see that the scope of the marketing function is considerably broader.

The marketing mix provides a very useful organizing framework for strategy development. First, product characteristics must be designed with reference to both customer needs and the requirement to differentiate the product from competing alternatives. Second, choices must be made on how to get the product delivered to the customer through physical or electronic channels. Third, a price must be set that will, at projected sales volumes, enable the marketer to cover costs and generate the level of profit desired. This price must also be set with reference to the prices of competing products and the ability and willingness of prospective customers to pay. Credit arrangements may be necessary to bring the product within reach of many would-be customers. Finally, the marketer must evaluate the most cost-effective ways of communicating with customers to tell them (or remind them) about the product and encourage them to buy it. This involves decisions about messages, advertising media, personal selling efforts, publicity and public relations, point-of-sale information, labeling, signing, and instructional materials. While this sequential approach may be a helpful first step, all marketing mix elements are ultimately interdependent and the marketing plan must recognize these interdependencies.

CONCLUSION

Marketing is the most externally directed of all the management functions, focusing on customers, intermediaries, competitors, and market dynamics. Successful marketers need to adopt multiple perspectives. They must understand the strengths and weaknesses of both their own organizations and those of their competitors, recognizing the goals that each seeks to achieve. They must also be able to see the world from the viewpoint of prospective customers and intermediaries, in terms of the needs that each seeks to satisfy and the criteria that they employ in evaluating alternative suppliers.

The first task of marketing is to establish an overall product-market strategy to meet organizational objectives. The second task is to develop a marketing plan, including detailed substrategies for each element of the marketing mix. Decisions must be made on the features that the product should possess, how it is to be delivered to customers (should intermediaries be used?), how it is to be priced, and what information should be communicated through what media to potential customers. Each of these decisions must be oriented toward the needs and characteristics of the market segments at which the product is targeted. Managers should also take into account the strategies directed at each segment by competing organizations to assess how much of a threat they represent. Sound plans should anticipate and counter or finesse competitive efforts. The third and final task—which is critical to the ultimate success of any plan—is to have the cooperation of all involved. The challenge is to persuade the organization to commit the necessary resources to the product and ensure that all managers, personnel, and intermediaries understand their roles in helping to implement the plan.

The Chevrolet Corvette

Frank Conley
Nancy Trap
Paul W. Farris

In mid-1983 Chevrolet introduced a new, redesigned, version of the Corvette. Simultaneously the price was increased and an advertising campaign comparing Corvette to imported sports cars, primarily Porsche, was begun. Initial sales were strong, but by early 1986 sales were down 25 percent from the same period in 1985. The April 14, 1986, issue of *Autoweek* (p. 3) reported, "Corvette and Fiero production will be cut significantly this month to stem a stockpile of sports cars, which are selling slower than predicted according to General Motors. Second-shift production at the Bowling Green, Kentucky Corvette plant will be eliminated." The Corvette's advertising support appeared to have been reduced from 1983–1984 levels, but special lease rates and financing plans were offered in late 1985 and early 1986.

The time was appropriate for addressing several important questions. What was the proper strategic role for Corvette within G.M. and Chevrolet? How important was advertising in fulfilling that role? What kind of advertising and promotion program would be appropriate? How useful would price pro-motions be? Finally, what kind of advertising program should be used?

GENERAL MOTORS AND THE AUTOMOTIVE INDUSTRY

In 1985 it was estimated that 16 percent of private, nonagricultural workers in the United States were employed in the manufacture, distribution, maintenance, and commercial use of motor vehicles.[1] Some 52.8 percent of all households owned two or more cars. In households with incomes of $40,000 or more, 87 percent owned two or more cars and 43 percent owned three or more cars.[2] The net sales of G.M., Ford, Chrysler, and American Motors accounted for 3.9 percent of the 1983 Gross National Product.[3] Of the U.S. auto manufacturers, G.M. was by far the largest, dominating the 1985 new-car market with six of the top ten selling cars in the country.

---

[1] Public Affairs Division of Motor Vehicle Manufacturers' Association of the United States, Inc., *Facts and Figures '85.*

[2] U.S. Department of Transportation, Federal Highway Administration, *Highway Statistics 1984.*

[3] *Ward's Automotive Yearbook*, 46th ed., Harry A. Stark, ed. (1984).

In recent years the U.S. auto industry had faced major market competition from foreign manufacturers. "Voluntary" quotas slowed import penetration in 1984, but imports still accounted for 23.5 percent of total U.S.-market automobile sales.

Recent Developments at G.M.

In response to an increasingly competitive environment, G.M. had recently reorganized five former autonomous car divisions into two groups, the Oldsmobile-Buick-Cadillac group and the Chevrolet-Pontiac-G.M. group. This reorganization reflected a concern of G.M. that historic divisional distinctions between Chevrolet, Pontiac, Oldsmobile, Buick, and Cadillac had become blurred. (The problem was compounded by the fact that many of G.M.'s cars looked alike.)

Two acquisitions, Hughes Aircraft Company and Electronic Data Systems, provided access to leading-edge technologies as G.M. began to design its auto lines for the twenty-first century. The hope was that the aerospace technology would be adapted in automotive areas ranging from computer-integrated manufacturing to futuristic car dashboard displays. In 1986 G.M. also bought Group Lotus Cars, a British automobile engineering and production firm known for state-of-the-art automotive technology in racing cars.

New ventures for G.M. included a G.M.-Toyota join venture that produced the new Chevrolet Nova, and the Saturn project that would produce G.M.'s first new make since the 1930s. Additionally, G.M. imported and marketed cars from three foreign companies.

Chevrolet

Chevrolet sold several different models of passenger cars and a line of trucks. Each model came in a variety of options and prices. In 1985 the Cavalier was the number one selling car in America, and the Celebrity and Caprice were third and seventh, respectively. (See *Exhibit 1* for Chevrolet model line sales and *Exhibit 2* for a brief description of these models.)

EXHIBIT 1
CHEVROLET MODEL LINE SALES

Model	1984 units	1985 units
Cavalier	377,466	431,031
Chevette	164,917	129,927
Camaro	202,172	199,985
Celebrity	322,198	363,619
Citation	92,174	43,667
Monte Carlo	115,930	112,585
Corvette	34,024	37,956
Other Chevrolet	258,902	280,800
Total Chevrolet	1,565,143	1,600,200
Total G.M.	4,587,508	4,607,458

Chevrolet sales were especially subject to swings in the economy, perhaps because the cars were priced lower than other G.M. cars of the same body type. In 1983 Chevrolet Motor Division General Manager Robert Stempel commented, "The last people who stop buying new cars are rich people, and the last people out of work are rich people. That 10 percent unemployment is a helluva lot more important to me at Chevrolet than it is at a lot of upscale car companies."[4]

SEGMENTATION OF THE SPORTS CAR MARKET

Segmentation of the automobile market was complex. Individuals considered economic, status/image, comfort, and performance factors in making a purchase decision and segments often overlapped. See *Exhibit 3* for an example of a market map depicting the position of various models. Even the sports car market could be further segmented. (See *Exhibit 4* for product and price data.)

Economy sports cars were mass-produced and generally constructed from sub-assemblies taken from the manufacturer's parts bin and then modified and assembled to increase the overall performance of the final product. The *Grand Turismo* (GT) class of sports cars seated four people and had superior performance and handling characteristics. The *high-*

---

[4] "Marketing the '83s," *Ward's Auto World*, October 1982.

EXHIBIT 2   THE 1986 CHEVROLET LINE

Chevette: An inexpensive subcompact with standard four-speed manual transmission, rack-and-pinion steering, fully reclining bucket seats, and rear hatch with fold-down rear seat. Available in two models: two-door coupe and four-door sedan. Price: $5,280

Cavalier: America's best selling compact for three years running. Standard features included front-wheel drive with rack-and-pinion steering, four-speed manual transmission, and V-6 engine. Options included sunroof, choice of Delco-Bose music systems, and rear luggage carrier. Thirteen models available including convertible sedan and wagon. Price: $7,600

Celebrity: America's best selling mid-size car. Standard features were front-wheel drive with rack-and-pinion steering, V-6 engine with electronic fuel injection, and cloth interior. Models included coupe, sedan, and wagon body types. Wide variety of options allowed for personally "customized" car. Price: $15,000

Camaro: America's best selling 2 + 2 sports coupe came standard with V-6 multi-port fuel-injection engine, five-speed manual transmission, power steering, sports suspension, rally wheels, and rear hatch. Available options included: Delco-Bose wrap-around music system, electric rearview mirror controls, and rear window louvers. Camaro had long received "hand-me-down" Corvette technology, and the Iroc Z28 was available with a Corvette engine option. Camaro races were becoming increasingly popular. Four models to choose from. Price: $10,400

Caprice: Full-size car offered standard V-6 engine with electronic fuel injection and three-speed automatic transmission, rear-drive power steering, and 20.9 cubic feet of luggage space. Model selection included Brougham and Classic series in sedan and wagon body types. Many options available for personalized customizing. Price: $11,400

Monte Carlo: Full-size rear-drive automobile with full coil suspension, power steering and brakes. Standard features included three-speed automatic transmission, electronically fuel-injected V-6 engine, and cloth bench seat with center arm rest. Available in luxury sport and super sport models. Price: $11,700

Corvette: Performance sports car with standard features including a V-8 engine with tuned-port fuel injection in a choice of four-speed manual with overdrive or four-speed automatic transmissions, vehicle anti-theft system, Bosch ABS II anti-lock brake system, corrosion-resistant fiberglass body, targa roof, air conditioning, and electronic instrument cluster. Options available included leather seats, Delco-Bose stereo system, and performance handling package. Also available in convertible model. Price: $28,500

---

performance sports cars were usually produced in relatively small numbers and often had a racing heritage. These cars generally had much higher resale values than others and were looked at by some as investments.[5] (Peter Shutz, CEO Porsche, paid $8,500 for a 1976 Corvette, and three years later sold it for the same price when he moved to Europe.) High-performance sports cars also could be viewed as a subset of the *luxury-car market*. (*Exhibit 5* gives demographics for buyers of selected models.)

G.M. was expected to launch its ultra-luxury two-seat convertible, the Cadillac Allante, in the beginning of 1987. The Allante, designed by Pininfarina, the Italian firm responsible for many Ferrari models, was scheduled for low-volume production and a price

tag of $50,000. Industry analysts believed that G.M. was hoping the Allante would provide a "halo" effect for the Cadillac, helping to update and differentiate its product image. The car had been premiered on the television series "Dallas," in Fall, 1986, replacing a Mercedes Benz 450SEL that had been driven by J. R. Ewing the previous season.

HISTORY OF THE CORVETTE MODELS

1953–1955

Years ago this land knew cars that were fabricated out of sheer excitement. Magnificent cars that uttered flame and rolling thunder from exhaust pipes as big around as your forearm, and came towering down through the white summer dust of American roads like the Day of Judgement . . . today, they have an inheritor—the Chevrolet Corvette. (1955 Corvette ad copy)

---

[5] David E. Gumpert, "Porsche on Nichemanship," *Harvard Business Review*, March/April, 1986.

EXHIBIT 3 MARKET MAP

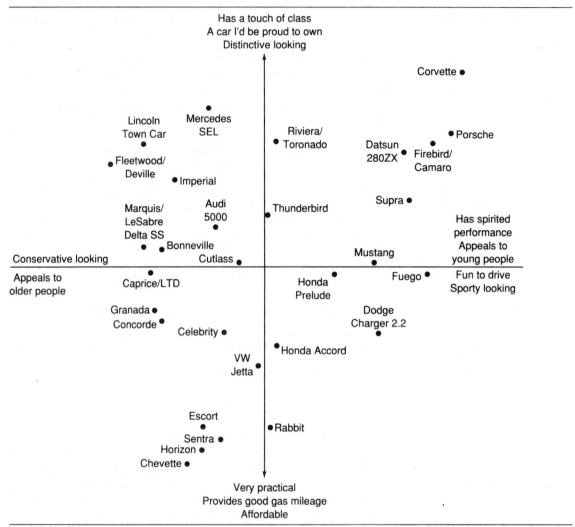

Source: Modified version of the Opinion Survey Center, Inc. using sampling of 12,000 responses as printed in "Marketing the '83's," *Ward's Auto World,* October 1982.

The Corvette "dream" car was introduced to the public at the 1952 Motorama Show, and the fiberglass-bodied, two-seat convertible was the hit of the show. Chevrolet began regular production of the car in 1953, and limited the production run to 300 cars that were sold to people who qualified as "VIPs"—political figures, movie stars, business executives, and preferred customers (*Exhibit 6*). Unfortunately,

the VIPs weren't impressed by a sports car that had pop-in plastic windows, leaked in rainstorms, had an anemic six-cylinder engine with an uncivilized two-speed Powerglide automatic transmission, and was slower than a well-tuned Cadillac or Oldsmobile.[6]

[6] Auto Editors of Consumers Guide, *Corvette, America's Sports Car* (New York: Beekman House, 1984).

EXHIBIT 4   PRODUCT AND PRICE DATA FOR SELECTED SPORTS CAR MODELS

Model	Wheel base, in.	Length, in.	Weight, lb.	Horse-power	Price	U.S. sales 000s	U.S. sales, % of prod.	No. of U.S. dealers
Corvette	96.2	176.5	3,280	230	$24,891	38.0	81.0	5,050
Ferrari 308 GTBi	92.1	174.2	3,250	230	54,300	N/A	N/A	42
Mazda RX7 Turbo	95.7	168.9	2,850	182	14,145	53.8	N/A	767
Nissan 300ZX Turb	99.2	178.7	3,255	228	17,699	67.4	N/A	1,101
Jaguar XJ SC	102.0	187.6	4,025	295	32,250	3.8	N/A	167
Porsche 944	94.5	168.9	2,900	147	21,440	16.7	N/A	317
Porsche 911	89.5	168.9	2,750	200	31,950	5.9	N/A	317
Porsche 928S	98.4	175.7	3,540	288	50,000	2.6	N/A	317

Source: Road & Track and *Motor Trend* magazines, 1986 issues; *Automotive News Market Data Book,* 1985, 1986.

EXHIBIT 5
1984 NEW-CAR BUYER DEMOGRAPHICS

Car make	% Male	Median age, years	% Married	Median HH income, 000s
Chevrolet	56	41	65	33.4
Corvette	85	38*	59	59.2
BMW	65	35	58	61.0
Jaguar	64	44	80	100.0+
Mercedes-Benz	68	46	76	87.5
Porsche	78	36	62	81.2

*In 1981, "median age" and "income" for Corvette owners were 33 years and $33,000, respectively.
Source: Automotive News, New Car Buyer Demographics, April 1984.

EXHIBIT 6
CORVETTE PRODUCTION DATA FOR SELECTED YEARS*

Year	Total Corvette production, 000s	Total Chevrolet production, 000s	Chevrolet Corvette, % of Chevrolet	Chevrolet, % of domestic production
1953	0.315	1,447	0.02	24
1958	9.3	2,367	0.39	40
1963	21.5	2,303	0.93	30
1968	28.3	2,148	1.31	24
1973	34.5	2,334	1.47	24
1978	46.8	2,347	1.99	26
1982	25.4	1,004	2.52	20
1984	28.2	1,294	2.18	19
1985	46.3	1,626	2.85	19

*No 1983 model was produced.
Source: Ward's Automotive Yearbook, 46th ed., Harry A. Stark, ed. (1984).

1954's production run of 3,640 cars ended with a surplus of 1,500 new Corvettes. Rumors circulated that the car would be scrapped, but the Corvette's salvation occurred in two forms: First, Ford, Chevrolet's major competition, came out with the Thunderbird, a two-seat "personal" car that brought out G.M.'s competitive spirit. Second, a 45-year-old German-trained enthusiast, race driver, and designer named Zora Arkus-Duntov began his 20-year association with the Corvette as its head of engineering. For 1955 the production run was 674 cars with a new V-8 engine that improved the Corvette's performance.

1956–1962

Even in Turin [Italy] no one has fuel injection! Sí, è vero. But the really fantastic item about the new Corvette is not the fuel injection engine, the new fourspeed gearbox, the slingshot acceleration or the pasted to the road stability. It is the fact that the Corvette above all other high performance sports car in the world, is a true dual-natured vehicle. It is a genuine luxury car and a sports car, both wrapped in one sleek skin. . . . (1957 Corvette ad copy.)

The second generation of Corvettes received a major body change, but Chevrolet had to determine if the Corvette was to remain a sports car or forge into Ford Thunderbird territory as a "personal" luxury car. The 1956–1957 Corvettes seemed to appeal to both markets. In 1956 Corvettes took the Sports Car Club of America (SCCA) "C" Production Championship, and in 1960 four Corvettes were entered in the international Le Mans Twenty-Four-Hour Endurance Race. The car was continually refined both mechanically and stylistically. By 1962 *Motor Trend* was saying, "This is an exciting high performance automobile with real hair on its chest—the type of car that only true enthusiasts will appreciate."

1963–1967

Corvette is America's one true sports car—has been for years. But Corvette is also two body styles. Five engines and three transmissions available. Plus enough other equipment you can order to make any kinds of sports car you want. For aficionados, there's the snarly Corvette. Ordered with a 375 horsepower Ramjet, fuel injected V8. . . . For boulevardiers, there's the plush Corvette, ordered with power brakes, steering and windows, tinted glass. . . . (1965 Corvette ad copy.)

The third-generation Corvette was derived from a G.M. styling exercise and was dubbed the Corvette "Stingray." It came in convertible and fastback coupe configurations and had many optional features. The car was available with a variety of engines, the most powerful approaching 500 hp. Lasting only five years, this model was the most short-lived of the Corvette body styles, but its timeless styling has made it the most popular model with car collectors and enthusiasts.

1968–1979

Here it is. It's not really a whole lot different looking. But in 17 years we've never changed it just to change it. . .It's still a car that's built for the person who drives for the sheer excitement of it. . . . No, it isn't a hard-core sports car. There are too many nice things about it. No, it isn't the smoothest riding car you'll find. But then again it won't rattle your bones. What it is is a new Corvette. It's refined for 1970. (1970 Corvette ad copy.)

The fourth generation of the Corvette was introduced in 1968, and the "Vette" had gone through some drastic changes. Corvette production was reduced to 21,801 units in 1971 from the 1969 high of 38,762, which allowed Chevrolet Division General Manager John DeLorean to place emphasis on improving the car's slipping quality control. The 1970s ushered in the era of government regulation. Corvette's performance steadily declined with the addition of catalytic converters and the unleaded-gasoline mandate. Its horsepower reached a low of 165 in 1975. A T-Top removable roof was introduced in 1968, offering "top down" motoring without the hassles. Subsequently, Corvette convertibles waned in popularity and were discontinued. In spite of these changes and the oil shortages and economic downturns of the 1970s, Corvette sold well. The entire 1975 Corvette production of 38,465 cars was sold out by March, and 1976 production jumped to 46,558.

Because 1978 was the Corvette's 25th anniversary, it was chosen as the pace car for the Indy 500.

1980–1983

In this ever changing world some things endure. A fine red wine, soft smoke on an autumn evening. A walk along the seashore. And Chevrolet Corvette. Now 26 years young. And still America's only true production sports car. . . . But beyond the machinery, there is the dream—Corvette and the open road. (1980 Corvette ad copy.)

In 1980 Chevrolet sent the Corvette to the fat farm so it wouldn't suffer an EPA ''gas guzzler'' tax. The car lost 280 lbs., and aerodynamic styling changes were added to improve fuel economy. The only engine available was a 305 cu. in. V-8, and the option of manual transmission was discontinued. All models sold were automatics. One industry observer commented that the Corvette had become a car for upwardly mobile secretaries. Even though the Corvette had lost much of its performance, it remained popular with the public and the motoring press. *Road & Track* pointed out in its November 1982 issue, that the Corvette remained a car whose function was on par with its form: "No matter how much luxury, electric seats, remote mirrors, or teddy bear hide velour interior you pack into a Corvette, the basic honesty of the car rises above its own image."

THE "NEW" CORVETTE

Now that the skeptics have been silenced, we can get down to business. The most important piece of business concerning the new Corvette. Performance. And in tests on G.M.'s proving grounds, conducted by professional drivers, the new Corvette performs beautifully. (1984 Corvette ad copy.)

There was no 1983 Corvette, as production was shifted to a plant built specifically for producing the new Corvette model (it had 50 percent more production capacity than the old plant). The fifth-generation Corvette was a radical change and showcased G.M.'s latest developments in suspension, braking, and electronic engine control while still remaining true to the basic Corvette layout: front engine/rear wheel drive and fiberglass body, a two-seat, high-performance sports car.

The new Corvette had a pop-off targa roof and a 350 cu. in. V-8 engine. It featured new technology in the use of fiberglass springs and alloy castings in the suspension system, digital and LED display instrumentation, and electronically controlled fuel injection and overdrive. Its price of $23,835 represented a 73 percent over 1982. For 1985, improvements to the fuel-injection system increased power, and in 1986 an Anti-Lock Braking System (ABS) and an improved Anti-Theft System were added. The ride was substantially softened through adjustments to the shock absorbers, and torsional steering shake was reduced with the addition of restrictors in the power steering lines. The convertible model was reintroduced in 1986, at a $4,518 premium over the base sticker price of $27,502. (See *Exhibits 7* and *8* for prices and estimates of maintenance costs, respectively, for selected models.) A *New York Times* article in the July 26, 1983, issue wondered whether the new Corvette has not been priced out of its traditional strength, the youth-oriented market, and into one of

EXHIBIT 7   1986 DEALERS' STICKER PRICES, 000s

	Corvette*	Porsche 944	Porsche 944 Turbo	Porsche 928S	Datsun 300ZX Turbo
Base car	$27.5	$24.5	$29.8	$52.0	$20.8
Average price paid†	23.4	24.1	N/A	N/A	N/A

*Price could vary on a Corvette depending on the time of year the car was purchased, whether the car was bought off the lot or ordered, and purchaser's negotiating skill. Other cars' prices were believed to be *relatively* firm.
†N.A.D.A. Official Used Car Guide.
Source: Casewriter's survey of Charlottesville, Virginia, car dealers, April 1986.

EXHIBIT 8 MAINTENANCE-AND-REPAIR COST COMPARISON

Maintenance parts	Average replacement*	Cost of Replacement			
		Corvette	Porsche 944T	Nissan 300ZX	Mazda RX7
Exhaust system	70,000 mi	$ 413	$ 425	$ 164	$ 180
Engine tuneup cost		90	160	160	100
Clutch	N/A	270	892	117	160
Sport shocks	60,000	360	517	685	344
Factory engine	100,000	3,900† (New)	5,246 (New)	5,153 (New)	1,000 (New)
Car warranty, Months/miles		36/36,000	24/unlimited	12/12,000	12/12,000

*Longevity of parts depends greatly on driver use and maintenance. The average vehicle was driven 10,300 miles per year.
†With multi-port fuel injection.
Source: Casewriter's survey of dealers.

the older professionals. . . . The article went on to say, "For G.M., the Corvette represents only a small part of the company's auto output . . . but the Corvette's real value, analysts say, is its ability to lure curious customers into showrooms."

Corvette Advertising

The advertising campaign that introduced the 1984 Corvette was lavish and technically oriented. Chevrolet ran multipage spreads in magazines touting the advanced technology and engineering that were incorporated in the newest generation of Corvettes and stressing its high-performance characteristics. The advertising budget was the highest in the car's history. Chevrolet spent $7,778,900 on the 1984 Corvette—compared to a previous high of $285,300 in 1977. (See *Exhibits 9* and *10* for data on advertising budgets and magazine media respectively.)

The comparison campaign was launched with TV and print ads. The cars compared to the 1985 Corvette ($26,703 price as tested) were the Lamborghini Countach, Porsche 944, Porsche 928S, Ferrari 308 GTSi, and Lotus Turbo Esprit. They ranged in price from $26,121 to $103,700 and were tested on a 0–60 mph acceleration, braking from 60–0 mph, time through a slalom course, and lateral acceleration on a skid pad. The United States Auto Club (USAC)

certified the testing, and the Corvette scored first in two of the tests and second and third in the remaining two tests. The scoring system that was used allotted six points for first place, five for second, etc. The Corvette was declared the overall winner in the comparison with a score of 21 points. The $103,700 Lamborghini placed second with 18 points.

. . . Corvette, Ferrari, Porsche, Lotus, Lamborghini. They're Europe's exotic few. And they don't let just anyone into their club. But in the case of the Chevrolet Corvette, they really didn't have a choice. In independent tests conducted by the United States Automobile Club, Corvette was the overall winner. (1985 Corvette Comparison ad copy.)

EXHIBIT 9
ADVERTISING DOLLARS SPENT BY CORVETTE AND COMPETITION, MILLIONS

Car make	1983	1984	1985	1986
Corvette			$ 7.8	$ 2.2
Jaguar XJS		$ 1.3	3.9	2.0
Nissan 280/300 ZX	$ 6.7	7.0	11.9	15.5
Nissan (total)	36.3	48.9	54.7	60.1
Mazda RX7	3.1	9.7	6.1	13.1
Porsche (total)	6.0	8.0	6.4	2.8

Source: Leading national advertisers.

EXHIBIT 10 THE CHEVROLET CORVETTE: MAGAZINE ADVERTISING,* 1983

Magazines	Corvette, 000s	Datsun 280ZX 000s	Porsche 911, 000s	Porsche 928S, 000s	Porsche 944, 000s	Readership		
						Median age	Median income, 000s	% College graduates
Architect's Digest	$ 133.5			$ 56.8		N/A	N/A	N/A
Business Week	350.0	$162.6	$ 156.1	117.1	78.1	39.4	25.2	46.9
Car & Driver	31.4	115.6	57.3	111.5	26.7	29.6	18.3	19.9
Food & Wine	62.3			129.3	71.4	39.4	16.3	32.2
Fortune	300.9		207.7			37.7	28.8	55.2
Newsweek	925.8	55.8	151.1	226.7	151.1	36.4	18.3	34.0
Road & Track	67.2	95.6	48.8	95.6	73.0	29.4	19.9	29.8
Science Digest	79.2					36.4	17.6	31.0
Science 83	110.0					36.2	17.7	44.5
Smithsonian	265.5			64.7		43.4	20.1	45.3
Sports Illustrated	913.6	60.2	60.2			32.8	18.6	24.8
Time	382.2		451.4	334.3	255.7	36.0	18.3	31.8
Travel & Leisure	142.1					45.7	25.1	36.8
Esquire		86.4	83.4	90.1	64.6	35.2	17.6	39.1
Golf		32.5				42.6	22.3	37.4
Los Angeles		19.6				N/A	N/A	N/A
Money		69.0		67.0		37.3	22.8	41.9
New Yorker		69.9	40.6	40.6	40.6	41.7	23.2	51.7
Playboy		118.6	118.6	118.6		31.1	17.9	19.6
Sports News		32.7				33.7	18.9	27.5
TV Cable		3.6				N/A	N/A	N/A
Inc.			40.1	85.3	42.6	36.4	25.2	58.4
Forbes			64.6	142.8		42.1	27.8	57.7
Signature			22.5	22.5		N/A	N/A	N/A
USN & WR			103.8	196.1	103.8	42.1	21.2	32.6
Dun's Business				25.6	22.5	N/A	N/A	N/A
Gourmet				46.9		N/A	N/A	N/A
Penthouse				37.0	34.0	29.4	17.6	15.6
Sunset				54.3		44.2	20.3	34.5
Tennis				32.7		29.7	16.5	32.4
Texas Monthly				47.4	11.3	N/A	N/A	N/A
Town & Country				41.7		40.2	17.5	34.7
Venture				43.4	24.6			
Total†	$4,084.6	$944.1	$1,605.3	$2,298.9	$1,031.6			

*Higher dollars per ad usually indicate layouts were used.
†Not all magazines are listed, therefore totals and individual entries may not agree.
Source: The PIB/LNA Magazine Advertising Analysis for 1983. Simmons 1983 Study of Media & Markets in Home Audiences.

The comparison campaign was continued in 1986, when Corvette made the Bosch ABS II antibraking system a standard feature on the car and then compared the braking characteristics of the Lamborghini Countach, Ferrari 308 GTSi, Porsche 944, Lotus Turbo Esprit, and Corvette on a rainslick curve. The Corvette was the only car to demonstrate the ability simultaneously to stop and steer the curve under maximum braking conditions. Once again it was proclaimed "Corvette, A World Class Champion" against a collection of European exotic cars.

Promotion and Racing Activities

The Chevrolet Division of G.M. published *Corvette News* quarterly and sent it free to purchasers of new Corvettes for three years (thereafter $18 for three years). The 30-page, full-color, glossy magazine kept Corvette owners informed on new Corvette model developments, news of Corvettes on the race track, and do-it-yourself repairs. *Vette Magazine, Vette Vues, Corvette Fever*, and *Keep'in Track* were the titles of four independently published monthly magazines devoted exclusively to Corvette enthusiasts.

There were over 700 organized Corvette clubs in the United States and Canada and a few in Europe. These clubs were federated under the National Council of Corvette Clubs. Club activities included car shows, rallies, slalom races, drag races, and social gatherings. A separate Corvette organization was the National Corvette Restorers Society, organized for people dedicated to restoring older Corvettes to "original" condition.

John Pierce, a member of Chevrolet's Special Products Group explained in the Summer 1985 issue of *Corvette News*, "Our policy is to develop the hardware and technology necessary to win and make sure it's properly represented in competition. We [Chevrolet] figure if we can put together a winner, then there'll be a demand for a better mousetrap." The group's efforts resulted in privately owned Corvette GTPs (Grand Touring Prototypes) participating in the IMSA (International Motor Sports Association) GT's circuit that visited 17 U.S. cities in the 1985 racing season.

For the second race of the 1986 season, the Corvette GTP car qualified but retired early due to mechanical failure. At the fourth race, Road Atlanta, the Corvette's second appearance was greeted with skepticism: "if they last . . ." (from the Ford folk); "if they live. . ." (the Porsche persons); "They can't run that fast in the race . . ." (Jaguarists).[7] The Corvette's first victory in the Road Atlanta race broke Porsche's string of 16 consecutive IMSA wins.

In another race series, Showroom Stock, Corvettes dominated. These races pit stock production cars against machines of similar performance capability. The Chevrolet Camaro was also promoted in a series of races in which professional drivers competed in modified Camaros capable of 200 mph speeds.

In 1986 the new Corvette roadster was chosen to be the Indianapolis 500 pace car. Chevrolet also developed a futuristic car, the Corvette Indy, that was shown on the 1986 Automobile Show circuit. Built by Lotus, the Indy was a showcase of technology to be used in the next generation Corvette—mid-engine, four-wheel drive, and four-wheel steering.[8]

The value of racing to an automobile's image was difficult to assess. Many sports cars, including Corvette, were featured in ads for tires, auto stereo systems, other accessories and unrelated products. For example, a Corvette was the grand prize in a toothpaste coupon sweepstakes and in numerous other promotions and contests.

Distribution

The Corvette was sold by the Chevrolet network of over 5,000 Chevrolet dealers in the United States. (Porsche, for example, had only 330 authorized dealers.) Some dealers, especially those near large population centers, were known for selling many Corvettes. However most small dealers rarely stocked Corvettes and sold only for special orders. To help those dealers with less experience learn to sell the

---

[7] Sylvia Wilkinson, "Hand Grenades One and Two," *Autoweek*, April 14, 1986.

[8] George Damon Levy, "Corvette Indy," *Autoweek*, January 20, 1986.

"new" Corvette, Chevrolet implemented a special dealer training program for 1986. Corvette mechanics also received special training.

Often the Corvette occupied a prominent place on the showroom floor and "Register-to-win a Corvette" campaigns were used by Chevrolet to increase dealer traffic.

THE COMPETITION

Porsche

Porsche was a family-owned European company known for its product quality. In recent years Porsche had introduced new models aimed at new segments. Notable successes were the 944 and 928. Standard company policy was to keep production levels just below the demand level.[9] From 1980 to 1985 Porsche sales grew 56 percent.

Schutz, CEO of Porsche, stated in the 1986 March/April issue of the *Harvard Business Review* that

our customers are people who place high expectations on themselves. And they expect no less from the companies and people with whom they associate . . . As a result, in positioning our company we have to strive to be what these people are as individuals. That means, among car companies, we have very high goals. And we have to pursue those goals virtually without compromise.

He considered Porsche competition to come from two sectors: luxury discretionary items, such as sailboats and airplanes, and other automobile manufacturers. He believed that Porsche 944's competition included Corvette, Pontiac Fiero, and certain Japanese cars; the 928's competition came from Jaguars, Ferraris, Mercedes Benz large coupes, and the Cadillac Allante; that the 911 had no competition; "It drives like no other car and sounds like no other car."

In its advertising, Porsche concentrated on the thoroughness and competence of its cars. The ads appeared to be aimed at people who weren't familiar with Porsche and told a story about the company's

engineers, the cars they had designed, and the constant development of Porsche cars being done on the world's most demanding racing tracks. Early in 1986 Porsche began a series of lavish magazine spreads, some as many as 12 pages each. Magazines in the campaign included *Business Week, Time*, and *Newsweek.*

Shutz said Porsche supported cars in international sports car racing for three reasons:

First, it is probably the single most effective way to do our advertising and public relations. It gets us free space in the auto enthusiasts' magazines. The second factor is the contribution that it makes to our technical development . . . the most important . . . is the contribution that racing makes to our corporate culture. The racing activity is highly visible, and it has a couple of characteristics that I find extremely valuable in achieving the kind of quality we want.

He added, "Racing is an opportunity for us to demonstrate our competence, to demonstrate the state of technology with which we're building their [the public's] automobile."[10]

Porsche's bi-monthly magazine, *Christophorus*, continued articles on Porsche race activities and recent developments, art, travel, and books. The "They Drive Porsche" section read like a "Who's Who" and carried pictures of world-class athletes, royalty, V.I.P.s, and race car drivers with their Porsches. Among those featured in the August 1985 issue were Olympic swimming champion Michael Gross, King Carl XVI of Sweden, and a prominent West German physician. Typical advertisers in the magazine were high-quality clothing and accessory manufacturers, jewelers, and European airlines.

In August 1984, as Porsche's distribution contract with Volkswagen of America was about to expire, Peter Schutz, chief executive of Porsche AG, created a new distribution plan to abolish dealers and replace them with agents who would order the cars as they were sold. Instead of keeping inventories, the agents would be supplied by 40 company centers. Two Porsche warehouses would operate in the United States, one in Reno, Nevada, and one on the East

---

[9] Op. cit.

[10] Gumpert, "Porsche on Nichemanship."

Coast. Three weeks after the announcement of the new distribution system, Shutz abandoned it; he stayed committed only to severing Porsche's U.S. link to Volkswagen.[11]

Nissan

In recent years Nissan's (originally Datsun) 240Z model had increased in size, weight, and price. During this time it had evolved from an "economy" sports car to something more like a GT car. A change in image resulted.

Those in marketing who ply their trade with demographics describe the 300ZX purchaser as one who is not as concerned with ultimate performance as with the "image" of performance. To the Nissan engineers this means a suspension system whose main priority is ride comfort, not cornering power of balance. Under the hood it means a priority on smooth, docile power characteristics rather than serious horses—which might require too much driver attention, detracting from image-enhancement time. To paraphrase Nissan television advertising: "You may never need this kind of performance, but knowing it's there is awesome."—*Motor Trend*, January 1986.

Nissan advertising for the 300ZX stressed that it was the best "Z" car ever, technically advanced with a plethora of functional electronic wizardry. The ads did not mention any performance statistics or measurements for the car.

Mazda

With the second generation of the very successful RX-7 introduced in 1986, Mazda continued to emphasize the advanced technology and engineering of its sports car model. The ads were dominated by written copy and had technical drawings of components as well as a cut-away view of the car's mechanicals. Mazda also ran ads in car-enthusiast magazines concerning the RX-7's successful racing career. Mazda's evolution was somewhat similar to that of the Datsun (now Nissan) "Z" series. It was initially

built and priced to compete in the "economy" sports car segment, but successive generations became heavier and more expensive with more "standard" options. Recent models were thought by some to resemble the Porsche 944 in appearance.

PRESS REACTIONS TO THE NEW CORVETTE

May 1983: Motor Trend tested the Ferrari 308 GTSi, Porsche 928S, Jaguar XJS, and the 1984 Corvette on a race track to determine the best-handling production car available in America. The Corvette was "markedly superior in every handling category and stands alone at the top of the heap. . .the Vette is now something it has never been; a world class performer." *Motor Trend* also voted the Ferrari the most sexually appealing car and the Jaguar "one to live with day in and day out." Corvette's appeal as a "daily runner" was diluted by its harsh riding characteristics,[12] but it was the choice for "the hardest-charging backroad burner money can buy." The Porsche 928S—"by any clear-headed standard, may be the best car in the world."

August 1983: Road & Track did a "comparison test" of the Corvette, Ferrari 308GTBi Quattro-valve, Porsche 944, and Porsche 928S. They saw the new Corvette as G.M.'s effort "to build sophistication and high technology into a package that still embodies traditional Corvette values. . .the car is still the bargain leader in its high-roller performance class." In performance tests the Corvette was on par with the competition and best in the lateral acceleration and slalom course speed tests. In "Cumulative Ratings—Subjective Evaluations" (points awarded for performance, comfort/controls, and design/styling), the Corvette scored 420 points, Ferrari 451 points, Porsche 928 482 points, and Porsche 944 482 points. The staff's price-independent choice was Ferrari, and the price-dependent choice was the Porsche 944.

November 1985: Motor Trend compared the improved 1986 Corvette to the just released Porsche

---

[11] David B. Tinnin, "Porsche's Civil War with Its Dealers," *Fortune*, April 16, 1984.

[12] The ride was substantially softened in subsequent model years.

944 Turbo. The Corvette was the fastest from 0–70 mph; the Porsche was faster than 70–90 mph in covering the quarter mile and in top speed. The Corvette won the braking, skid pad, slalom, and road course portions of the testing. In conclusion, the testers stated, "Pressed to make a choice between these two exceptional GT's, we'd probably opt for the Corvette. But the final choice lies in individual tastes and driving habits. There's a lot of hot rod in the Vette. A lot of flash and American brashness. The turbo Porsche is understated elegance. Quiet, confident, and subtle. Whichever approach reflects your individual driving habits and ego is the one you'll swear is the hands-down winner and the only logical choice. Just make sure you bring plenty of green stuff."

April 1986: Road & Track's latest testing of the Corvette involved taking it to Italy and running it over a 1,000-mile course of autostradas, city streets and country roads that once made up the famous Mille Miglia Race, competed on in 1927–1957. Other cars included in the test were European versions of the Alfa Romeo GTV 6/2.5, Jaguar XJS Cabriolet, Nissan 300ZX Turbo, and the Porsche 944 Turbo. In this test of cars driven by a group of famous ex-race car drivers, the questions posed were: "If the Mille Miglia were held today, in what order would the cars finish?" and "Which car would you choose for a vacation tour of the Mille Miglia route?" The drivers scored the first question: Corvette 23, Porsche 22, Alfa 13, Nissan 12, and Jaguar 5. They scored the second question: Porsche 25, Corvette 17, Alfa 13, Nissan 11, Jaguar 9.

A summary of *Motor Trend* performance data is contained in *Exhibit 11*. See the appendix to this case for definitions of technical terms used in the industry.

EXHIBIT 11   1986 PERFORMANCE COMPARISON OF SELECTED SPORTS CARS

Manufacturer & model	0–60 mph, sec	1/4 mile, sec	Top speed, mph	Braking, 80 mph, ft	Slalom, mph	Skid pad, G's	Interior noise, 70 mph, DBA	MPG
Corvette Coupe	5.8	14.4	154	243	58.9	.91	77	19.0
Alfa Romeo Spider	10.4	17.6	103	288	58.4	.77	93	23.8
Ferrari 308 GTBi	6.8	15.2	142	262	58.0	.81	80	16.0
Jaguar XJS HE	7.8	15.6	148	276	56.6	.73	72	13.5
Mercedes Benz 380SL	10.9	18.4	110	277	54.2	.70	74	19.0
Mazda RX7 GXL	8.5	16.5	119	267	62.0	.83	N/A	N/A
Nissan 300 ZX Turbo	7.4	15.7	133	249	62.8	.80	73	17.0
Porsche 944	8.9	16.6	123	256	62.5	.86	72	22.1
Porsche 944 Turbo	6.0	14.6	155	255	62.8	.90	72	19.4
Porsche 911 Cabriolet	5.7	14.3	130	266	59.8	.80	79	18.6
Porsche 928S	6.3	14.5	162	247	57.9	.83	71	16.3

Source: Motor Trend's Performance Summary.

Technical Terms

Tests Used in Performance Comparisons

Skid Pad Test: Measured the cornering ability of a car in a steady state. Cars that generated numbers of greater than .8 g force had a stiff suspension and harsh riding characteristics on surfaces rougher than a smooth race track.

Slalom Test: Measured a car's cornering ability in transient maneuvers as it wove through a course of eight pylons spaced at 100-ft. intervals.

Braking Test: Measured the minimum distance required to come to a full stop from a stated speed. Typically tested from 60 to 80 mph.

Innovations in Automobile Technology

Braking

Anti-Lock Braking System (ABS): Disc brake calipers had an electronic sensor that prevented brake lock up in panic stops. This innovation resulted in better stopping power and eliminated loss of control (skidding).

Suspension

Dynamic Suspensions: Being developed so that electronic sensors could detect road conditions, allowing a car's suspension components to react.

Active Suspensions: Sensors monitoring load-influenced flex in the rear suspension to adjust the rear wheel suspension automatically.

Driver Adjustable Suspensions: Allowed the driver to alter the stiffness of a car's shock absorber to increase a car's handling performance or ride characteristics.

Engine

Turbocharging: A method of increasing a car's horsepower output by increasing the air flow into the engine's combustion chambers.

Intercooling: Creating a denser charge and increasing the horsepower of a turbocharged engine by cooling the air charge of a turbocharger.

Fuel Injection: A system, usually electronic, that controlled and injected fuel directly into the combustion chamber.

McDonald's: The Greening of the Golden Arches

Sandra Vandermerwe
Marika Taishoff

Go away. We don't want your garbage: we've got no place to put it, and enough pollution problems already so don't think you can just burn it.

We don't want companies which kill rain forests to raise cattle.

Sure, your hamburgers might take five minutes to eat, but your packaging will take the earth several centuries to digest.

These were just some of the comments that Peter Oehl, Director of Environmental Affairs for McDonald's Germany, continued to see in the papers with growing frequency since the late 1980s. They came from city councillors, governmental ministers, and environmental demonstrators alike. He reflected:

The problem of paper litter and waste has been haunting us for almost 20 years. We can't seem to win: we tell people that we don't purchase beef raised on rain forest land, but it doesn't seem to make the slightest bit of difference. We tell them we're doing more about recycling than most other companies, but look at what happens. . . . What do they expect us to do?

He spoke as the company geared up for the opening of its first store in what had previously been East Germany. A "grand opening," as McDonald's employees called it, was always a major event for the company, and everyone involved tried to make certain that all the right local notables, celebrities, and press be present. It was to be carried out in the way that McDonald's, the American fast food giant, knew best—with marching bands, much fanfare, balloons, lights, and the famous "arches." The restaurant staff had also been geared up, ready to handle the eager and curious customers who were expected to stream in on that cold day in December 1990.

MCDONALD'S FORMULA

After World War II, Richard and Maurice McDonald were having trouble staffing their San Bernardino, California carhop restaurant. Recalled Dick McDonald:

We said, 'Let's get rid of it all.' Out went dishes, glasses and silverware. Out went service, the dishwashers and the long menu. We decided to serve just hamburgers, drinks and french fries on paper plates. Everything prepared in advance, everything uniform. All geared to heavy volume in a short amount of time.

When Ray Kroc, a milkshake multi-mixer salesman, came across the McDonald brothers' diner in 1954, he was astounded: "This little drive-in had people standing in line. The volume was incredible." Together with the two brothers, he began to sell franchises, and in 1955 the first of the Golden Arches opened for business.

McDonald's launched the fast food industry. During the 1970s, it grew at an average of almost 30% annually, a growth rate which was propelled by increasing the number of units by an average annual rate of 15%, extending store hours to include breakfast, expanding the menu and concurrently the check size, and adding new services such as the Drive-Thru window. All a customer had to do was pull up, order, and eat the already prepared food on site or, simpler still, take it away in handy, throwaway cartons and packaging. Individual disposable wrappings soon replaced the large refillable dispensers for ketchup, mustard, dressing, salt, pepper, and sugar.

The tight standards which the company insisted on were expressed by its motto, "QSCV"—quality, service, cleanliness, value. The McDonald's training center, "Hamburger University," was established to ensure that all employees be uniformly trained to apply these quality criteria in all behind-the-counter operations and counter procedures. In addition to quality, the company's strategy focused on quick service at affordable prices. Buns, french fries, and meat patties were delivered in large corrugated containers, salads came pre-packaged, and the bulk of the kitchen work was limited to deep frying according to standardized procedures. McDonald's employees did not wait on tables or wash dishes; they flipped hamburgers and worked the check-out counters. Customer waiting time had to be kept to a carefully determined minimum, so the burgers and fries were prepared in advance and kept as warm and moist as possible for peak hour crowds. The art was not just to be able to prepare a burger in one minute, but to be able to serve it in no more than ten; otherwise, it had to be thrown away.

The company's growth surged throughout the 1970s and 1980s, and McDonald's became as recognizable a feature of America as Disneyland. The hamburger chain, which spent over 6% of its total sales on advertising, was among the most advertised single brands in the world. Almost one million dollars a day was spent on television spots. In any given year, 96% of American consumers ate at a McDonald's, and the chain served 7% of the US population every day.

Worldwide Growth

Between 1979 and 1989, the company's systemwide compound annual growth rate was 12%, of which US sales accounted for 10% and international sales 19%. It was not long before the arches began to appear on the international landscape as well. By 1989, international sales constituted 30% of total sales. Of the 11,500 outlets worldwide, 8,000 were in the US. By the end of the 1980s, McDonald's was the largest restaurant chain in Britain, Germany, Canada, Australia, and Japan; it was the most successful American retailer in the international market, and the largest owner of retail property in the world.

In 1990, too, despite predictions of a slowdown in the fast food industry, the company posted record earnings, increasing its worldwide sales to $18.76 billion from $17.33 billion.[1] Although sales per store in the US diminished somewhat, and quarterly earnings growth was not as dramatic as in the previous decade, this was more than offset by the strong growth in overseas operations. McDonald's was now the largest food service organization in the world.

Although fast food competitors soon came on the scene, McDonald's stayed ahead with over 30% of the market. During the 1980s, the two major competitors, Wendy's and Burger King, each closed about 150 restaurants annually, while McDonald's was opening a new one every 17 hours. The company viewed any establishment which sold food—quick service eating establishments, mom and pop stores, take-outs, pizza parlors, coffee shops, convenience

---

[1] For simplicity, all financial data have been converted to US dollars. Exchange rates at the time were approximately $1.00 = DM1.70 = SFr1.45 = £0.58).

food stores, delis, supermarket freezers, and microwave ovens—as competition.

GARBAGE AND ENVIRONMENTAL ISSUES

Despite instructions, which were in place almost from day one of the company's existence, that restaurant crews pick up all paper wrappings, napkins, soda goblets, and other typical fast food remnants within a one block radius of each establishment, the litter around the stores quickly accumulated. By the 1970s, this situation stoked the anger of conservationists, such leading US consumer advocates as Ralph Nader, and environmental lobbies which conducted a series of analyses to determine the source of the waste, as well as where and how it was destined to ultimately end up.

When such groups wanted to know "How many trees have to be cut down just to end up as street litter afterwards?" it was a prelude to the debate which would emerge a decade later about McDonald's role in the deforestation of the Brazilian rain forest.

From Paper to Plastic Packaging

In 1976 the company decided to switch to a polystyrene packaging, which was more cost effective than paper. Polystyrene, a rigid transparent thermoplastic with excellent electrical and physical insulating properties, was a lightweight material derived from petroleum and natural gas by-products. McDonald's contracted SRI (an international research institute) to perform an environmental impact study in the United States comparing paper packaging with the proposed polystyrene plastic packaging.

SRI analyzed the two packaging alternatives from a variety of aspects, ranging from source to disposal: the amount of energy to manufacture, resource depletion, weight and volume in landfills, and potential for recycling. Based on these criteria, the study concluded:

1. There appears to be no supportable basis for any claim that paper-related products are superior

from an environmental standpoint to plastic related ones, including polystyrene.
2. The weight of existing evidence to date, for which there is no countermanding data, indicates that the favorable true environmental balance, if any, would be in the direction of the plastic related product.

Based on these findings, beginning in 1977 McDonald's started using polystyrene instead of paper wherever possible, especially for its beverage cups and goblets, sandwich containers, and clamshell hamburger containers. The company believed that it was not only behaving ecologically, but that its customers would also get improved products and service; polystyrene retained heat, moisture, and freshness better, and was "cleaner" than paper, since it stopped grease spills. Shortly thereafter, foam plastic accounted for 75% of McDonald's total plastic use; plastic forks, knives, and spoons, cup and salad bowl lid covers, and coffee stirrers accounted for the remaining 25% of plastic used.

During the 1980s, the environmental movement began to gather steam. Waste was measured, litter was scrutinized, and fingers continued to point. As the number of hamburgers sold each year at McDonald's increased, so too did the consumer protest over the amount of packaging waste. In the US the company's marketing people soon had to deal with the bags of letters reproaching the company for its role in garbage production. Schoolchildren began sending boxes of the foam clamshell back to the firm with notes blaming it for littering streets, choking waste bins, and cluttering landfills.

Cost Initiatives and Environmental Repercussions

The accelerating rise in US per capita solid waste generation led to an equally steep drop in available landfill space: In 1975 there were 18,500 landfills sites; less than a decade later only 6,000 remained, and it was estimated that only half of those would be operative by the mid-1990s. In most countries in Europe, the situation was even worse by the end of the 1980s, with most landfills closed and recourse to incineration contraindicated due to air pollution effects.

To minimize the use of resources and reduce waste and pollution, McDonald's took several initiatives:

- In 1978, the weight of sandwich wrap was reduced, resulting in a packaging reduction of three million pounds a year.[2]
- In 1981, the large fry box was redesigned, lowering packaging weight by 600,000 pounds per year.
- Corrugated dividers were removed from cup packaging, thus saving two million pounds of paper.
- In 1983, the heavy paper-foam hot cup was replaced by a light foam-only cup, a packaging reduction of more than a million pounds a year.
- In 1984, the thickness of the foam sandwich container was reduced by 28%, saving three million pounds in packaging.
- Shaving the straws by 25% saved two million pounds of packaging.

---

[2] One pound (lb) = 0.45 kilograms (kg).

- In 1987, two years before being required by international legislation, McDonald's instructed its suppliers to cease using chlorofluorocarbons (CFCs) as an expansion agent in the manufacture of polystyrene foam cups.
- In 1989, a new Coke distribution system was initiated; rather than shipping the soft drink mix in cartons to all the outlets, the syrup was pumped directly from delivery trucks into tanks in the restaurants, thereby saving two million pounds of packaging.

These measures, together with some others, helped the company in the US reduce the amount of its packaging waste by over 24 million pounds within the space of a decade. (Refer to *Exhibit 1* for US waste stream composition, and *Exhibit 2* for a breakdown of waste at a McDonald's outlet in the US.)

McDonald's became the largest user of recycled paper in the restaurant industry worldwide, spending $60 million a year on recycled paper for its two billion tray liners and napkins, and for its 500 million

EXHIBIT 1
US WASTE STREAM COMPOSITION
(by weight)

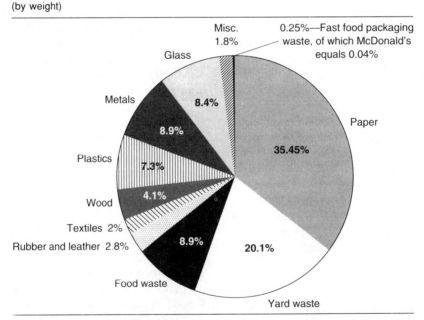

Source: Adapted from Franklin Associates Ltd., 1989. Reprinted in "McDonald's and the Environment" (McDonald's publication, 1990).

EXHIBIT 2
MAJOR SOURCES OF WASTE AT MCDONALD'S—USA

Paper

Plastics

Food waste

11%

7%

34%

6%

Non–McDonald's
waste

8%

Liquids

34%

Corrugated

Source: Adapted from *Wall Street Journal,* April 17, 1991.

"Happy Meal" boxes. The company's 1989 Annual Report, which focused on the environment, was printed entirely on recycled paper generated from the paper waste of its offices and outlets worldwide.

Extensive advertising budgets were allocated by marketing for communicating these initiatives to customers. A campaign was also launched which categorically denied any responsibility for the destruction of the Brazilian rain forest: nowhere in the world, consumers were informed, did McDonald's purchase beef which had been raised on rain forest land. Similar campaigns were intended to exonerate the firm from damage to the ozone layer.

The Plastic Dilemma

Plastics continued to be singled out as major culprits in the US landfill shortage problem, since, in contrast to yard waste and papers, both organic in nature, plastics were synthetic and were not biodegradable in landfills.

In the United States, a billion pounds of polystyrene were produced annually for the food service packaging industry; McDonald's purchased 75 mil-

lion pounds of it. Once dumped, polystyrene accounted for one-quarter of one percent of landfill volume. The 4,000 pounds of polystyrene waste generated annually by each fast food restaurant was equal to one-seventh of one percent of total waste.

McDonald's justified its continued use of polystyrene to customers and environmental interest groups through PR, marketing, and advertising campaigns, concentrating on:

- *Recyclability:* Polystyrene was 100% recyclable and could be made into a variety of products such as serving trays, carpet fibers, insulation board, video cassettes, park benches, and garbage bins.
- *Separability:* Wax-coated paper, the suggested alternative to polystyrene, was not a good idea, McDonald's countered, because the wax and the paper would have to be separated before recycling.
- *Biodegradability:* Refuting the biodegradability arguments used by those who supported paper-based packaging, findings at the University of Arizona revealed that paper in a landfill, with no exposure to air, water and micro-organisms, would not readily decompose and, in fact, the process could take decades.

- *Energy efficiency:* Paper mills consumed more energy and produced more waste water than foam manufacturing plants did, according to a study by the US Environmental Protection Agency.
- *Sanitation:* A study by the American Public Health Association confirmed that reusable plates, cups, and utensils were much less sanitary than disposable products.
- *Incineration:* Polystyrene foam was safer and less expensive to incinerate than paper since, when incinerated, it produced harmless, non-toxic ash, carbon dioxide, and water.

The fact that polystyrene did not decompose was also considered a positive factor, since, chemically inert, it could not create dangerous toxins in the decomposition process. Also, although foam packaging appeared bulky, 90% was air, which compressed easily in a compactor or under the weight of a landfill. Using a study by the German Society for Research into the Packaging Market, the company stated that alternatives to plastic packaging would result in a 404% increase in the weight of waste thrown into landfills, and 256% in the volume of such waste.

Critics still pointed out that the manufacturer of plastics depended on nonrenewable resources, i.e., on oil and petroleum, while paper was based on a renewable resource. Moreover, they added, while paper recycling was a well-established practice with a growing market demand, this was not the case for plastics; most plastics were simply being dumped. Plastics were more difficult to recycle; only 1% were being recycled in the US, and 5% in Europe. The comparative figures for paper recycling were 25% in the US, and 45% in Europe.

McDonald's realized that in order to be truly committed to the environment, it would have to do more than just say so. Some firm steps would be needed, but it could not take them all alone, and suppliers would have to become even more involved.

Working with the Suppliers

In 1989, in response to mounting consumer pressure, McDonald's instructed its more than 700 suppliers worldwide that, if they wished to continue to do business with the firm, they would have to adapt their products and packaging to the new and increasingly rigorous environmental standards which the company had now staked its image on and assumed responsibility for.

These suppliers ranged from agricultural, livestock and dairy products, to drinks manufacturers, and to paper, corrugated, and plastics suppliers. In the US, the environmental directives were aimed almost exclusively at packaging suppliers. The new requirements that suppliers had to fulfill ranged from using corrugated boxes with at least 35% recycled content, through the directive that the thickness of foam containers be reduced by 29%, and the weight of plastic straws and sandwich wrappers be another 20% lighter. The same directives were applied in Europe, where agricultural suppliers were also requested to use fertilizers and pesticides which were environmentally safe.

In late 1989 McDonald's, together with eight leading plastics suppliers—including Amoco, Mobil, and the major polystyrene manufacturer Dow—announced a trial program to begin collecting polystyrene food containers from 450 New England restaurants in the US. The program, the initial cost of which was $16 million, was intended to eventually become national in scope.

The plastics producers formed a new company that would purchase a recycling facility and build others across the United States; McDonald's subsidized the collection and hauling costs. The goal was to recycle, by 1995, at least 25% of the one billion pounds (45,000 metric tonnes)[3] of polystyrene used in food services packaging. In order to make the plan work, restaurant patrons were asked to dispose of their plastic containers separately in specially marked baskets. The separate handling of the plastic packaging and the education of customers was estimated to cost each store $400 a month.

Back to Paper

Despite these initiatives, consumers continued to write letters and complain to the company about its waste, and pressure continued to escalate. Ralph

---

[3] 1 metric tonne (1,000 kg) = 2,200 lb.

Nader stated blatantly that grassroots environmental groups were not convinced that McDonald's was serious about creating a better environment, and the American conservationist group, Friends of the Earth, said that if the chain were really serious, it would give customers the choice of eating from a real plate.

In August 1990, in a dramatic move, the company signed an agreement with the Environmental Defense Fund. The EDF, a Washington-based public policy group, established itself as a major lobbying organization representing consumers' environmental concerns in 1972 when it succeeded in banning the insecticide DDT from the American market. Now the EDF and McDonald's would create a joint task force to study the solid waste problem and arrive at mutually acceptable solutions. The EDF task force members were allowed to analyze purchasing data and were given free access to McDonald's operations and to suppliers' factories. They also had stints as fry cooks and bun flippers.

It took three months for the first recommendation to be drafted by the EDF and accepted by McDonald's. As part of a package of 42 recommendations intended to reduce waste by over 80% at the 11,500 outlets within a few years, polystyrene would, after 15 years of use, be abandoned and the company would revert to paper packaging.

McDonald's acknowledged that its decision had been open to considerable debate, especially since there was no conclusive scientific evidence to substantiate it. The bottom line, the company explained, for the drive back to paper was that there were still customers who did not understand that plastic was recyclable. The customer, the company underscored, always came first at McDonald's and always would come first. Since the customer did not feel happy about plastics, the company would stop using it.

The firm's participation in the polystyrene recycling program was halted, and McDonald's purchasing department now had to look to suppliers who could design and deliver efficient paper-based packaging. Marketing's efforts were geared both at attracting such suppliers, as well as informing the American public of the company's new move.

The directive would be effective immediately in its US stores, with international operations expected to follow. While country managers were allowed some leeway in adapting the new standards to their specific market requirements, it was expected that they would abide by the directive from headquarters unless circumstances were so market specific as to warrant a different approach.

MCDONALD'S GERMANY

Shortly after city officials throughout Germany began urging McDonald's to switch from disposable to reusable packaging, Peter Oehl received the news from headquarters to revert to paper. He knew he was in trouble. He was stunned by the company's decision to switch from plastic to paper, which had been the cause of so much trouble in the past 15 years. He also knew that he would not only have to justify such a radical switch to the German public, but would also have to find a practical solution about what to do with the paper after its use as packaging. And even if he abided by the US directive, how long would it be until the municipal and consumer pressure again mounted to demand a move to reusables? In any event, the European, and especially the German, situation had always been different from the one in the US.

When McDonald's opened its first German restaurant in 1971, it recognized the tradition-bound nature of restaurant service in Europe and so veered away from its standard interiors and menus. If offered chicken, and even played with the idea of serving bratwurst. In Germany, hamburgers were associated with natives of Hamburg, but not with meat. Beer was on the menu, too, and the somber wood-paneled interiors resembled German "bierkellers."

However, that look had discouraged families from going inside, and it was not until the outlets were located in downtown areas, and standardized in appearance with a menu identical to the one in America, that the chain began to prosper. Creative and humorous advertising concepts were used to deflect criticism that American eating habits were denigrating German culture. By 1990, McDonald's was the leading restaurant operator in Germany, with 330 outlets, annual sales of over $580 million (DM 1 billion), and major plans to be the first fast food operator in the former East Germany.

The Challenge for McDonald's Germany

A lot had been riding on the creation of the post of Director of Environmental Affairs, which the Board of Directors offered Peter Oehl in 1988. Over 80% of German consumers were willing to pay more for environmentally sound goods, and incidents were frequent where "Green" groups, as a protest against needless waste, would rip the packaging off products in supermarkets. (Refer to *Exhibit 3* for an illustration of what comprises German household waste.)

Although the Green party in Germany was a political minority, its policies and principles on ecological issues were quickly adopted by all the mainstream parties. Environmental legislation in Germany reflected this popular sentiment. Of all the members of the Organization for Economic Corporation and Development (OECD), the Germans spent the highest percentage of their gross domestic product (GDP) on environmental protection policies.

Packaging had been a special target of this legislation. By requiring distributors and retailers to be the ones to manage the problems of waste caused by consumer goods packaging, the German government effectively put the cradle-to-grave approach to product management into practice.

The lack of landfill space was common everywhere in Germany, but it was especially acute in some regions, which led to the creation and enforcement of stringent waste management requirements:

• There were 200 German cities that planned to prohibit the use of disposable packaging, in restaurants and for take-out, if the municipality had to deal with the waste which ensued.

• In other cities, the municipal authorities planned to prohibit landfilling outright except when necessary, with the burden of proving such necessity falling on the waste producer. Under such a system, if the big generators of waste—hospitals, train stations, stadiums, airports, hotels, and restaurants—needed to use a landfill, whose costs were expected to more than double by 1992, the authorities would first

EXHIBIT 3   GERMAN WASTE STREAM COMPOSITION
(by weight)

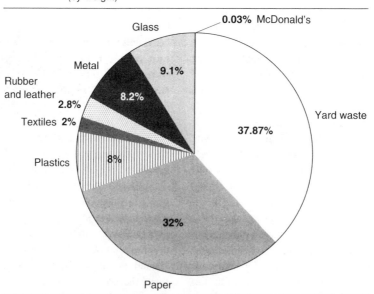

Source: Adapted from *Statistisches Bundesamt,* 1987. Reprinted in "Das McDonald's Umweltprogramm: Wertstoffrückgewinnung" (McDonald's Publication, 1990).

have to be satisfied that the material in question could not be recycled.

- Other municipal areas threatened to drastically hike—by as much as 1,600%—their fees for separating unseparated trash.

- Some cities simply refused to grant companies such as McDonald's operating licenses unless they could be satisfied beyond any doubt that the company would be able to handle its waste problem on its own, without recourse to municipal landfills or incineration.

On the day Oehl received the directive to move back to paper, he was more convinced than ever that if McDonald's were to switch its image from an "enemy of the earth" to a "caring company," it would have to look well beyond the present situation and take a leap ahead in time to anticipate the consequences, and payoffs, of its current actions. As he gazed out the window at the new "Hamburger University," which was still under construction at McDonald's Munich-based German headquarters and which was intended, like its American prototype, to imbue all McDonald's employees with the company's standards of quality and operational principles, he thought:

By the time that building is finished, I'll make certain that all the graduates know more than just what a recyclable plastic is. What I want is for them to understand, and have the courage to apply, the kinds of changes that will be necessary. And this means starting right from the beginning of the process, making sure that our cattle are "happy cows" living under the right conditions, through to the ingredients in our food and the processes we use in the kitchen, all the way to making sure that every bit of waste we create can be used and reused again and again, eventually as bio-gas to fuel our stores.

Closing the Loop

The leap ahead in time that the German situation required, Oehl knew, meant more than switching from plastic to paper or even from a disposable plate to a reusable one. Ideally, he envisaged that 100% of the material which remained on site after original use—organic, paper, and plastic—to be recyclable,

reusable, or convertible into energy: in other words, capable of being transformed into valuable goods.

Forty-four percent of McDonald's waste was kitchen waste, 14% was plastic, and 42% paper. (Refer to *Exhibit 4* for a breakdown of waste in McDonald's Germany.) If the company were to achieve the zero waste scenario that Oehl intended, these materials would first have to be collected and separated. Then, through an integrated separation and recycling process, remade and reused, either in their original forms—as packaging, for example—or as a new product—a waste bin, for instance, remanufactured from McDonald's plastic waste, or leftover shortening treated and then reused by the cosmetics industry.

Based on his discussions with specialized waste engineering firms and other experts, a five-step process would be necessary if the amount of waste destined for landfills or incinerators were to be reduced to almost zero:

1. The packaging material used for delivering the buns, meat patties, and condiments to each restau-

EXHIBIT 4
MAJOR SOURCES OF WASTE AT MCDONALD'S—GERMANY

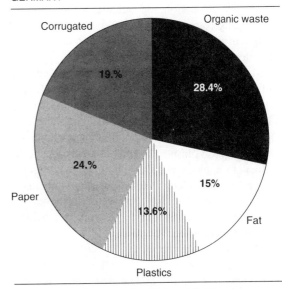

Source: Adapted from "Das McDonald's Umweltprogramm: Wertstoffrückgewinnung" (McDonald's Publication, 1990).

rant, as well as the packaging the restaurant used for its own meals, would have to be standardized.

2. Unnecessary packaging, both for in-house and takeaway sales, would have to be reduced.

3. Customers and/or McDonald's employees would have to separate those materials, such as cardboard, plastics, and metal cans, for which existing collecting and recycling systems were available.

4. The remaining waste mixture—primarily paper, small plastic items, and food—would then be treated in an integrated system in which the plastic would be chemically broken down to be recycled, and the paper and organics processed into compost and bio-gas.

5. Ultimately, these new raw materials could be re-used within the restaurant chain itself as a source of construction material, road gravel, and energy sources for stores.

Oehl found two firms which, if they worked together, could make the system feasible: BTA, a small Munich-based waste engineering firm which had developed a process to separate plastics and other lighter material from paper and organic waste, and then convert that paper and organic waste into compost while effectively creating bio-gas as an alternative source of energy; and Belland, a Swiss plastic engineering company which had already spent $50 million in an attempt to develop and produce a group of water-soluble plastic polymers.

McDonald's Germany had already invested $1.7 million in developing a project with Belland to find a plastic with built-in separability and recyclability suitable for use in all consumer packaging. The idea, Oehl reasoned, was to seek out the "chemical fingerprints" in those plastics. The major advantage of the Belland technology was that it built a breaking point into the polymer chain which allowed easy chemical separation from the other materials. If this could be applied to consumer packaging as well, it would be the key to cost-effective recycling.

Oehl was aware that it was much harder to take chemicals apart than it was to combine them. But, he also knew that, as the crucial first step in closing

the loop on waste, this separation process warranted more than an advertising expense. It required investment and commitment.

The BTA technology was based on the use of micro-organisms which could transform liquid organic waste into bio-gas which, once purified, could be used as a source of energy—one-third to meet the needs of the process itself, with the remaining two-thirds sold to third-party markets as energy. The solid organic waste, as well as paper, would be transformed into almost heavy metal-free compost suitable for landscaping and gardening.

For such a circular system to work, a BTA plant with an attached Belland recycling unit would need 20,000 metric tonnes of waste annually; McDonald's generated 15,000 tonnes. There was only one test-plant site in Germany and, taking into consideration the costs and time involved in the logistics, Oehl reasoned that 15 fully operating plants would have to be constructed throughout the country, within a 150-kilometer (30-mile) radius of each major city, at a total cost of $150 million. He began negotiating with other major waste producers, including hospitals, airports, stadiums, hotels, and restaurants.

In Germany, the average cost to handle one metric tonne of waste in a landfill in 1990 was $120; to incinerate a tonne would cost $150. The cost of hauling a tonne of waste to either a municipal landfill or incineration site was $77. All these prices were expected to at least double within the next two to four years. The estimated processing cost per tonne of waste using the McDonald's/Belland/BTA system was expected to be approximately $150. The price of hauling the waste depended heavily on how many plants could be constructed and how their distribution service network could be designed.

RESPONDING TO THE AMERICAN DIRECTIVE

It was clear to Oehl, as he re-read the memo announcing the move back to paper, that he would have to think things through very carefully before making a recommendation to his management. Abiding by the

US decision, attempting to opt out, or looking for other solutions involved weighing the various pros and cons:

After all [observed Oehl], the German market is so different from the American one, and we've already spent so much money and effort on environmental R&D in plastics. My solution could be even more cost effective than the existing one if we could involve the other fast food chains and some other industries, and so create economies of scale.

On the other hand, one of the key factors for our world-wide strength and reputation is the consistency of our products and services everywhere. Would marketing be able to sell the idea to customers who were so anti-plastic? What if it costs more? Consumers may say that they'd pay more for "green" products, but would they be willing to pay more for a Big Mac if the new packaging ends up costing more?

There are some people in the company who say we should take a lower profile on the environment. According to them, we've already gotten ourselves into enough trouble without being able to please anyone. McDonald's should just stick to making and selling fast food and avoid any risky ideas, especially since US quarterly earnings figures are down. . . .

I *know* that constantly looking for Green-friendly packaging alternatives is the kind of halfway measure which can never work in the long term. We must be able to deliver the same kind of uncompromising excellence in the environmental arena as we do with our hamburgers and our in-store service.

Customers have always come first for the company, and making certain that they are happy is a prime corporate objective. Should customers drive the decision on this one? Maybe once and for all we simply have to do the things we believe are right, even if it means that our customers will be unhappy for a while.

And if I decide not to abide by headquarters' decision, how will I be able to explain it to them?

Hurricane Island Outward Bound School

Bruce H. Clark
Thomas V. Bonoma

Tell yourself, while 50 feet above a quarry on a one-foot-long, one-inch-wide cliff, being held up by a single rope, that you're not scared, but rather having fun. Capability becomes a state of mind, depending on how focused and committed you are. These are not challenges of you conquering the cliff, but of trust conquering fear. Do you trust the person holding your safety line? Or, rather, do you trust yourself?

—*Student*

I learned that I am a strong person, that even when I'm almost dead sure I can't do something, I can. Now I'm ready to hold out my hand—like my instructors held out their hands—and pull up someone who needs help. Ready to give my friend who is discouraged a hug. Ready to recognize the people I can rely on and those I can't.

—*Student*

To serve, to strive, and not to yield.

—*Outward Bound motto*

Philip Chin sketched out ideas in a notebook as the small commuter plane he had ridden from Boston approached Owls Head Airport. Behind Owls Head

lay the town of Rockland, Maine (population 8,000), home to the headquarters of the Hurricane Island Outward Bound School (Hurricane), where Chin was director of marketing.

Hurricane was one of the U.S. schools in the Outward Bound movement. Outward Bound had pioneered a rigorous form of "experiential" education that placed groups of students in wilderness settings to develop self-confidence, teamwork, and respect for the environment.

In early October 1986, the summer crowds in Penobscot Bay were largely gone; the quiet waters below Chin's plane sported only a few fishing boats at anchor. Soon the fall weather would settle in, closing Owls Head two days out of three and thus requiring a two-hour drive to Portland for reliable air service. Now, operationally, the school was slowing down, while administratively the nonprofit organization's pace was quickening. The school was well into its 1987 planning process.

Chin had been at Hurricane for only eight months. He had been brought to Maine from New York City especially for his marketing experience. A Wharton MBA, he had worked in marketing management at General Foods, Doubleday Book Clubs, and PepsiCo. He had spent the last five years as a new-venture and marketing consultant. Except for the controller, Joe Adams, Chin was the only senior manager at Hurricane who had not risen from the course development and instruction side of the school.

As director of marketing, Chin was responsible for the organization's 1987 marketing plan. The 1987 plan would be his first for Hurricane. Aside from choosing the most productive tactics on which to spend a very limited marketing budget, Chin had to be certain that any marketing initiative would accurately reflect the unique character and concerns of Hurricane Island Outward Bound.

OUTWARD BOUND HISTORY

The first Outward Bound school was established by Kurt Hahn in 1941. Originally the headmaster of a German boarding school, Hahn was jailed in 1934 for his outspoken criticism of Adolph Hitler. He escaped to Scotland and continued his work in education, developing a system of interrelated athletic and educational standards for teenage boys. This system became the foundation for the first Outward Bound course and school, in Wales. During and after World War II, the Outward Bound concept spread rapidly; in 1986, there were more than 30 chartered Outward Bound schools around the world.

The first U.S. Outward Bound school was chartered in 1962 in Colorado, followed immediately by the Voyageur school in Minnesota. Hurricane was founded in 1964. In 1965, these three schools collaborated to found a national coordinating body—Outward Bound, Inc., also known simply as "National." National was a nonprofit institution responsible for chartering new schools and supporting the Outward Bound movement in the United States. While the schools were independently organized and managed, they agreed to abide by certain joint policies established by National. National also conducted fundraising, publicity, and advertising campaigns for Outward Bound as a whole. To support these activities, each member school paid franchise and marketing fees to National. Franchise fees went toward safety and curriculum work; marketing fees paid for Na-

tional's marketing campaign, and were based on the level of activity National conducted for each school. Beyond these activities, the confederation of schools was quite loose.

Each school was governed by a board of trustees, similar in function to a board of directors. The schools' trustee chairs comprised National's Outward Bound Executive Committee (OBEX), which ruled on issues of national concern to Outward Bound.

HURRICANE ISLAND OUTWARD BOUND SCHOOL

Most of the Outward Bound schools, while offering a variety of courses, specialized in one area. Hurricane Island was the sea school. Founder and school president Peter Willauer's work in education and sailing led him to envision an outdoor classroom on the ocean. While working at a private school, he began to piece together the philosophy, funding, and board members for Hurricane. After enlisting volunteers to construct the Hurricane Island site in the summer of 1964, Willauer enrolled and graduated the school's first group of students in 1965.

The early years of the school were lean. In the mid-1980s, Vice President for Development Pen Williamson recalled "a little summer-sailing school" struggling for existence in Boston. In 1971, the school moved to new headquarters in Rockland. Over the next decade, Hurricane expanded dramatically, both in facilities and in number of staff and students. It was not until the 1980s, however, that rapid growth seemingly began to outstrip the ability of the organization to manage it. (See *Exhibit 1* for a financial summary of Hurricane's performance.)

Through 1985, Hurricane had never broken even on an operating basis. Instead, the organization relied on contributions to make up the difference between tuition revenues and expenses. In the early 1980s, the trustees became concerned as the organization accumulated a series of large operating deficits. Peter Willauer seemed particularly stretched in his dual role as chief executive officer and chief fund-raiser. Hank Taft, formerly president of National, noted that

EXHIBIT 1
STATEMENT OF ACTIVITY, 1982–1985 ($000)

	1982	1983	1984	1985
Support and revenue				
Tuition				
Public courses	$1,563	$2,013	$2,445	$2,672
Special programs	485	744	944	1,284
Subtotal	2,048	2,757	3,389	3,956
Outside support				
Operating contributions	418	883	789	732
Support from National	0	68	85	66
Other	169	191	256	200
Subtotal	587	1,142	1,130	998
Total support and revenue	2,635	3,899	4,519	4,954
Expenses				
Cost of sales				
Public courses	1,442	1,851	2,264	2,395
Special programs	425	644	793	1,054
Depreciation	95	138	73	84
Subtotal	1,962	2,633	3,130	3,533
Operating expenses				
Administration	421	543	639	697
Marketing	346	319	293	319
Development	131	135	188	173
Student aid	333	467	486	323
Depreciation	49	51	63	71
Other	104	81	37	0
Subtotal	1,384	1,596	1,706	1,583
Total expenses	3,346	4,229	4,836	5,116
Operating surplus (deficit)	(711)	(330)	(317)	(162)
Net capital additions*	1,028	177	60	962
Excess (deficiency) to funds	317	(153)	(257)	800
Fund balances end of year	2,148	1,995	1,738	2,538
Balance sheet items				
Total assets	3,522	3,650	3,635	3,981
Total liabilities	1,374	1,655	1,897	1,443

Source: Hurricane Island Outward Bound School.
*Includes capital contributions, gain (loss) on sale of property and equipment, and net investment activity.

burnout from this dual role was common for school directors; Willauer was the only school founder in the country who was still running his school.

Like most of the Outward Bound schools, Hurricane had a very active group of trustees. Thirty-six men and women sat on a half-dozen committees, which met monthly to monitor and aid the school's management. Most trustees were successful businesspeople, and all had been on at least one Hurricane course.

In late summer 1985, management and the trustees agreed on a new organizational structure, giving Willauer some relief on the operating side of the organization. They created the office of vice-president to take over day-to-day operating responsibilities. Vice presidents Bob Weiler and George Armstrong shared these tasks, freeing Willauer to focus on strategic direction and fund-raising. (See *Exhibit 2* for Hurricane's organization chart.)

In 1985, the operating deficit became smaller, and 1986 found the school in the midst of its busiest year ever. By year's end, some 3,700 students would spend over 70,000 student program days (SPD)[1] in over 50 courses at any of 13 sites in Maine, Florida, New York, New Hampshire, and Maryland. Control-

---

[1] One student program day: one student in a course for one day.

EXHIBIT 2   ORGANIZATION CHART

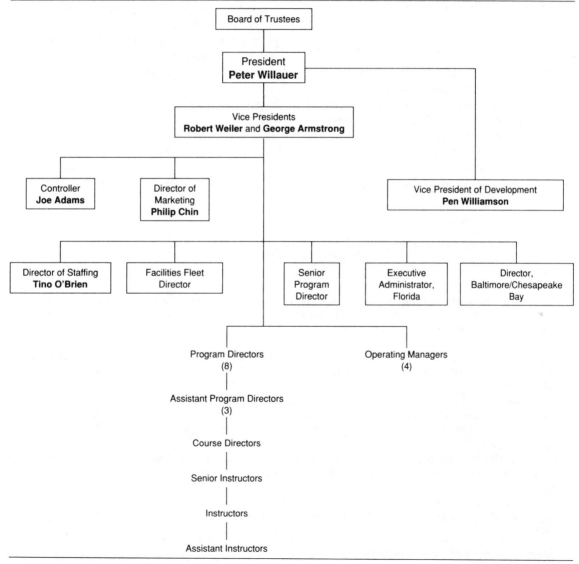

Source: Hurricane Island Outward Bound School.

ler Joe Adams predicted that in 1986, the school would break even for the first time, and accumulate record revenues of just over $5 million. Still, finances were a high management priority. The school required a sound financial base to continue its growth.

Course Offerings

The mission of Hurricane Island Outward Bound is providing safe, challenging, educational experience in a wilderness setting, carefully structured to improve self-esteem, self-reliance, concern for others, and care for the environment.

—Mission Statement

The school's offerings were divided into two segments: (1) special programs, administered by vice president George Armstrong, and (2) public courses, directed by vice president Bob Weiler. Special programs were courses that the school ran by contract for specific groups, often through government agencies. Among the populations served in this manner were Vietnam veterans, emotionally and developmentally

handicapped youth, juvenile delinquents, and substance abusers. In 1985, special programs accounted for 23% of Hurricane's students, 32% of student program days, and 33% of tuition revenues.

All other students enrolled in public courses. The marketing department worked almost exclusively with public courses (special programs were more the result of contract negotiations). Public courses were divided into four segments by location and activity: Maine Sea, Florida Sea, Winter Land, and Summer Land. (See *Exhibit 3* for descriptions of the segments and *Exhibit 4* for recent attendance trends. *Exhibit 5* gives the most recent projections for 1986 financial performance from the marketing department.)

Course length ranged from 3 to 101 days. All courses were carefully constructed to provide challenges while ensuring safety. Both the course directors and an active Trustee Safety Committee rigorously monitored course activities and instructors. In addition, the school required U.S. Coast Guard certification for all sailing instructors, and land instructors were certified by the state of Maine as "Maine

---

EXHIBIT 3   COURSE DESCRIPTIONS

I. Public Courses

Maine Sea Program
   Sailing courses run from May through September. A 30-foot open pulling boat becomes the base for lessons in seamanship, navigation, sailing, rowing, ecology, and survival on land and sea. Includes segments on rock climbing and the Hurricane Island ropes course. Based in Penobscot Bay, Maine.

Florida Sea Program
   Sailing courses run from November through April. Content similar to Maine Sea, but conducted in the tropical wilderness of the Florida Keys. Includes extensive swimming and snorkeling to explore the ecology of the Keys. Based in the Great Heron Wildlife Preserve, Florida.

Summer Land Program
   Canoeing, backpacking, white water rafting, bicycling, and "multi-element" courses run from May through September. Most courses include rock climbing, wilderness camping, and expedition-planning skills. Based in Maine and New York.

Winter Land Program
   Winter mountaineering courses run from December through March. Activities include cross-country skiing, snowshoeing, backpacking, and winter camping. Based in Maine and New Hampshire.

II. Special Programs and Populations
   Ongoing programs have been developed for a wide range of audiences, including Vietnam veterans, substance abusers, troubled youth, schools, and corporations. These customized programs use many of the facilities and activities of the public courses.

Source: Hurricane Island Outward Bound School.

EXHIBIT 4 ATTENDANCE BY COURSE AREA, 1981–1985

	1981		1982		1983		1984		1985	
	Students	SPDs*	Students	SPDs	Students	SPDs	Students	SPDs	Students	SPDs
Public Courses										
Maine Sea program	1,016	18,432	938	16,849	1,091	19,439	1,208	21,409	1,120	18,088
Florida Sea program	183	2,095	249	3,097	230	3,287	275	4,315	289	4,658
Winter Land program	120	1,017	244	2,711	231	1,970	184	1,612	190	1,611
Summer Land program	157	2,771	289	4,304	372	6,141	441	5,599	645	8,700
Other	92	1,343	236	5,724	319	7,824	366	8,056	363	8,169
Subtotal public courses	1,568	25,658	1,956	32,685	2,243	38,661	2,474	40,991	2,607	41,226
Special Programs	474	8,686	726	13,060	1,596	15,134	1,264	16,525	760	19,137
Total enrollment	2,042	34,344	2,682	45,745	3,839	53,795	3,738	57,516	3,367	60,363

Source: Hurricane Island Outward Bound School.
*Student program days.

Guides." As a result, the school had never had a fatality despite the often strenuous nature of course activities.

In each course, participants were organized into "watches" of up to 12 students and one or two instructors. The watch was the basic unit of instruction; watch members performed most of their activities as a group. In the early part of a course, instructors concentrated on teaching the skills necessary for course activities; they assumed no prior experience. Once student skills were adequate, the instructors began allowing the group to perform activities with less direct supervision, intervening only in the event of trouble. The climax of most courses was Solo, when the watch broke up and individuals spent anywhere from several hours to three days alone in the wilderness, except for daily visits from an instructor.

Although learning wilderness survival skills was an important part of each course, more important was learning to work with a group under often trying circumstances and gaining self-confidence and the ability to trust fellow watch members. For this reason, the school had lately begun running short courses for groups of managers who desired this kind of experience. The courses, called the Professional Development Program (PDP), were very successful—158 executives attended in 1985—leading to expanded activities in 1986. Hurricane's marketing

department was responsible for PDP in addition to regular public courses.

Marketing at Hurricane

For a long time, marketing consisted of opening our doors at the beginning of the summer and closing them at the end. More people came every year. Then in 1979 that didn't work anymore; our enrollment dropped. And 1980 was the same.

—*Bob Weiler, Vice President*

Marketing did not exist as a formal function at Hurricane before 1980. The school's major promotion tool then was group presentations: instructors and managers went out to schools and other institutions to talk about the Outward Bound experience. In most cases, Hurricane arranged presentations reactively. A request for a presentation would come in, and whoever wanted to go and give the talk would do so.

One result of the late 1970s' enrollment dip was the upgrading of the marketing function. In 1981, Hurricane hired Ted Rodman as the school's first marketing director. The Trustee Marketing Committee advocated and won a marketing budget equal to 10% of projected public course revenues. (The committee felt this percentage was an average figure for the business world.) The budget included salaries

Course	Student capacity	SPD capacity	Tuition	Students	SPD	Revenue
Maine Sea						
HI 26-day	100	2,600	$1,600	64	1,664	$102,400
HI 22-day	596	13,112	1,225/1,425	386	8,492	541,650
HI 11-day	240	2,640	900	152	1,672	136,800
HI 6-day	120	720	600	57	342	34,200
Sea Kayak 7-day	40	280	700	36	252	25,200
Sea Kayak 14-day	20	280	1,000	18	252	18,000
Contracts/Groups	90	990	809	85	935	68,765
Subtotal	1,206	20,622		798	13,609	$927,015
Florida Sea						
FL College 22-day	10	220	$1,200	8	176	$9,600
FL 22-day	10	220	1,200	8	176	9,600
FL 14-day	180	2,520	1,000	104	1,456	104,000
FL 8-day	200	1,600	800	72	576	57,600
Contracts/Groups	20	160	500	18	144	9,000
Subtotal	420	4,720		210	2,528	$189,800
Summer Land						
Maine Chall. 26-day	192	4,992	$1,600	128	3,328	$204,800
Long Jrs. 28-day	144	4,032	1,700/1,800	126	3,528	223,400
Juniors 22-day	72	1,584	1,300	66	1,452	85,800
Rafting 6-day	105	630	600	90	540	54,000
Summerland 22-day	120	2,640	1,300	92	2,024	119,600
Summerland 9-day	160	1,440	800	105	945	84,000
Cycling 22-day	40	880	1,300	16	352	20,800
Cycling 9-day	100	900	800	46	414	36,800
Dynamy 22-day	48	1,056	700	42	924	29,400
Contracts/Groups	36	288	500	32	256	16,000
Subtotal	1,017	18,442		743	13,763	$874,600
Winter Land						
Winter College 22-day	12	264	$1,000	8	176	$8,000
Winter 22-day	12	264	1,000	6	132	6,000
Winter 9-day	60	540	800	24	216	19,200
Winter 6-day	100	600	600	34	204	20,400
Gould 8-day	84	672	400	72	576	28,800
Subtotal	268	2,340		144	1,304	$82,400
Managers						
Career Dev. 4-day	96	384	$500	80	320	$40,000
Maine Sea 8-day	116	928	950	84	672	79,800
Land 6-day	20	120	750	16	96	12,000
Contracts/Groups	60	360	1,200	50	300	60,000
Subtotal	292	1,792		230	1,388	$191,800
Other						
Summer 64-day	24	1,536	$3,200	20	1,280	$64,000
Florida 78-day	24	1,872	3,800	16	1,248	60,800
Florida 80-day	24	1,920	3,800	17	1,360	64,600
Jrs. 15-day	180	2,700	900/950	162	2,430	150,400
Maine directive	154	4,312	1,800	127	3,556	228,600
Florida directive	110	3,080	1,800	82	2,296	147,600
Instructor training	36	3,612	3,800	21	2,107	79,800
Subtotal	552	19,032		445	14,277	$795,800
Public Course Total	3,755	66,948		2,570	46,869	$3,061,415

Source: Hurricane Island Outward Bound School.

for the marketing and public relations departments, the National meeting fee, and funds for marketing and public relations (PR) campaigns.

Rodman had previously operated his own direct-mail and graphic design firm, and he transferred the skills he had developed there to Hurricane. He championed what he called "volume marketing," which consisted of major direct-mail campaigns whose yields could be accurately predicted. He concentrated on new advertising creative work, market segmentation, and positioning.

The primary direct-mail price for marketing was the school course catalog. Produced once every two years, it was a glossy, 24-page, full-color magazine describing the school and the various programs it offered. Prospective students could get more information by writing the school or calling its toll-free number. In either case, they received an application and course schedule, which provided additional details about the courses and their exact dates. Students then applied for specific courses on specific dates, listed alternate preferences, and enclosed a nonrefundable $25 application fee. Upon receipt of the application, the admissions department sent the student an enrollment package that included comprehensive information on clothing, travel, and any other requirements for each course. The package also included a 4-page medical form. All students were required to have a physical exam before being accepted in a course.

The admissions department encouraged students to return the enrollment forms as quickly as possible. Along with the completed forms, students sent a nonrefundable $100 enrollment fee. This fee reserved a spot for the student in a specific course. Tuition was due in full 60 days before the beginning of the course, or with the enrollment fee if the student was applying later. If a course was oversubscribed, the admissions department placed students on a waiting list. If a student was not admitted to the course by two weeks before the course's beginning, he or she was given the option of getting a tuition refund or having the money credited to a future course. Noting the length of the admission process, Chin remarked, "Enrollment is not an impulse buy."

Supplementing the Hurricane catalog was the Na-tional course catalog, which described all five schools' offerings, organized by activity. Inquiries to National were routed to the appropriate school.

In 1984 and 1985, Ted Rodman, controller Joe Adams, and the Marketing Committee began a re-evaluation of the school's pricing. As Adams put it, "We know we can always sell a course if the price is low enough. Can we sell it at a price where we cover our costs?" Public course tuition in 1986 ranged from $400 to $3,800 per student, depending on the length and nature of the course. Approximately 20% of students received substantial support from Hurricane's financial aid program as part of the school's commitment to serving the underprivileged. Marketing allocated financial aid to help support appropriate levels of female and minority participation in Outward Bound.

Marketing under Ted Rodman received mixed reviews from other Outward Bound managers. Public course enrollment did recover strongly in the 1980s, and the curriculum shifted to a more profitable mix of courses. Others also appreciated Rodman's feel for visuals; his catalogs featured stunning photography. They further credited him with developing an accurate forecasting system for overall public course enrollment.

Still, some staff members were uneasy with the idea of "marketing" the school. Most people who worked for Outward Bound did so because they were dedicated to the concepts behind and experiences offered in the courses. Those who ran the courses feared that marketing would "tell them what to do," or distort the concepts. When formal marketing first came to Hurricane, director of staffing Tino O'Brien recalled, "We spent a good deal of time educating our marketers in the reality of what Outward Bound was."

In September 1985, Rodman left to become marketing director for a local ski area. Vice president George Armstrong took over his duties until Philip Chin arrived in February of 1986.

1986 Marketing Efforts

The 1986 marketing plan was based on four strategic initiatives: (1) segmenting markets, (2) developing

EXHIBIT 6
1986 PRICING, 22-DAY MAINE SEA COURSE

Starting date	Ending date	Tuition	Student capacity	Actual students
5/16/86	6/6/86	$1,225	72	12
5/26/86	6/16/86	1,225	72	12
6/12/86	7/3/86	1,425	72	48
6/14/86	7/5/86	1,425	48	46
7/9/86	7/30/86	1,425	48	46
7/11/86	8/1/86	1,425	72	70
8/5/86	8/26/86	1,425	68	64
8/8/86	8/29/86	1,425	72	70
9/5/86	9/26/86	1,225	72	18

Source: Hurricane Island Outward Bound School.

new pricing, (3) changing the course mix, and (4) assigning financial aid dollars to low-demand areas.

Hurricane made a concerted effort to segment the markets it served and assign priorities to the segments. Analysis of historic enrollment patterns revealed that some parts of the population dominated the school's student body. Given management beliefs that Hurricane's market penetration was low in all areas, the school decided to target those groups with which it had had the most success in the past.

Demographically, the organization identified 14- to 19-year-olds as its primary target, with 20- to 35-year-olds next. Geographically, the school gave first priority to the northeastern United States, which it defined as the six New England states and New York. Second priority went to the mid-Atlantic states (New Jersey, Pennsylvania, Delaware, and Maryland), plus Florida. In addition, to these segments, the marketing department identified six buying groups within the demographic and geographic markets whom it felt the school could successfully address: (1) high school and college students, (2) "juniors" (ages 14 and 15), (3) municipal and agency contacts (for special programs), (4) young professionals, (5) corporations, and (6) Hurricane course alumni.

The school also developed a differential pricing scheme, both to maximize revenue and to smooth demand. Hurricane raised prices on introductory and adult courses, but tried to keep prices competitive on "mature" courses like Maine Sea. The school lowered prices on certain off-peak courses (September

through May) to encourage enrollment at those times, although tuition differences between identical courses rarely exceeded 15%. (See *Exhibit 6* for an example of a differential pricing schedule.)

Hurricane continued to examine the profitability and popularity of its courses, shifting the mix to build more revenue and better utilize existing facilities. In many cases this involved shortening less profitable courses or reducing the number of times they were offered. This increased capacity for other, more profitable courses.

Finally, the school used its scholarship program to support Maine Sea and to build off-season demand. Hurricane targeted scholarship-subsidized groups for such efforts, as this was more manageable than attempting to coordinate individual-aid programs.

Tactically, these strategic moves were translated into a number of marketing initiatives over the course of the year, including experimenting with two new sales tools. The first was a direct sales recruiter, who gave presentations to educational institutions, civic groups, trade associations, and business groups. The school especially hoped to increase high school student enrollments, and supported the recruiter, a former course director from Hurricane, with a direct-mail campaign to principals of public and private high schools.

The marketing department's second innovation was a telemarketing campaign aimed toward prospective students who had applied but not yet enrolled. Members of the admissions department staff called these students to discuss the Outward Bound experience as part of a larger effort to improve the school's response to inquiries about courses.

Following the 1985 PDP experience, Hurricane expanded its effort to reach corporations. Chin and Bob Weiler made most of the sales calls, as both had had experience working in major corporations. By summer's end, Hurricane had completed contracts with the Gillette Company, Citicorp, Corning Glass, MCI, Xerox, and General Electric, among others.

The school also continued its advertising and direct-mail effort in 1986, mailing over 35,000 pieces in four major campaigns and a series of smaller efforts, which included the high school mailing mentioned earlier.

1987 Considerations

Nobody's in this to make money. Everybody's involved in a tremendous educational process. Beyond that, you want to run it well.
—Hank Taft, former president, National; former Marketing Committee chair, Hurricane

The overall goals for the school were continued growth and financial stability. With those guidelines in mind and a very limited budget, Chin had to develop and support marketing tactics that would help the school realize two strategic objectives: (1) maintain school leadership within the Outward Bound system, and (2) build off-season business.

Maintaining School Leadership Defining Outward Bound's competition was extraordinarily difficult because of the diverse markets the school served. For juniors, the competition could be summer camp. Vacations, summer jobs, and other wilderness experience organizations beckoned college students. Corporate training was a fragmented, high-growth industry that was becoming more competitive.

The one constant in all of these markets was the presence of the other Outward Bound schools in the United States. Although National's policies restrained cutthroat competition on territory and advertising, there was a usually friendly rivalry among the five schools. Hurricane was the largest of the five in terms of SPDs, while Colorado enrolled the most

students. Between them, the two schools controlled approximately 70% of the system's business. Leadership in the system was a source of pride to staff members, and the school strove to maintain it.

Building Off-Season Business In talking with managers, it was apparent that marketing's most important objective was to build off-season business. Each year, Hurricane served well over half of its students in June, July, and August. Marketing Committee chair Bill End noted, "Selling the summer is not the trick for marketing. You could probably do nothing and sell out this period." Building business in the "shoulders" around the peak season, however, seemed to be where marketing could truly add value.

The dramatic seasonality of Hurricane's student population affected every aspect of the school's operations. The biggest problem was staffing the courses. Tino O'Brien, in an office wallpapered with huge charts depicting staffing requirements for every course at the school, spoke with feeling: "It's a totally untenable, high-risk situation with staffing. We need fully trained, fully committed staff for two months." The school's inability to offer year-round positions to instructors hamstrung recruiting efforts. "It affects both quality and safety," added O'Brien. George Armstrong agreed. He noted that over half the school's expenses were labor-related, and that simply hiring people for the summer and then laying them off in the fall was not viable because the immediate labor supply was tight.

Results in this area had been unsatisfactory. Off-season pricing and skewing scholarship funds to off-peak courses had proven unable to offset the fact that most juniors, high school students, and college students were simply unable to attend courses during the academic year. And Hurricane's Florida base was too small to provide a winter counterweight to courses based in the Northeast.

Marketing Options

The 1987 marketing expense allocation was $308,000. Of this, $125,000 was dedicated to payroll for current staff; $40,000 covered the Outward Bound National marketing fee; $39,000 was for other marketing programs, including advertising and the school's direct-mail campaign; $15,000 was for public relations, trade shows, and other sales promotions; and $35,000 was for two new staff positions, an assistant marketing manager and a new public relations/production coordinator. This left $54,000 for discretionary 1987 marketing programs. Chin already had a number of proposals on which he could spend the money.

1. Expand "Alumni in Marketing" Network
Chin thought the "Alumni in Marketing" (AIM) network might prove the most cost-effective and least controversial of any of the proposals he was considering. More than 25,000 people had taken Hurricane courses in the last 20 years, and the school had a solid alumni mailing list that it used for fund-raising and public relations activities. Managers throughout Hurricane were enthusiastic about the network in principle, but were uncertain about how to use the alumni resouce.

Chin identified two ways alumni could help marketing. The first was to identify interested groups and individuals to whom the school could direct its efforts. Alumni often had access to schools, professional associations, and other institutions through which they assembled audiences for group presentations. The second way alumni could help was to take part in the presentations by doing publicity, helping with logistics, and providing testimonials.

Experiments with alumni volunteers in 1986 had been very successful. Charlie Reade, the direct sales recruiter, had coordinated alumni efforts in the course of making his presentations. Two direct-mail campaigns for leads had been successful enough to warrant repeating them in 1987. But Chin was uncertain how enthusiastically he should push this network, as he had no clear idea of how many alumni would want to volunteer. If too few were interested, the effort in reaching them might be wasted. If too many were interested, administering the network would rapidly become complex. The latter situation seemed more likely than the former. If AIM took off, Chin might have to hire someone to manage it, which he calculated would cost at least $20,000 per year. Even with a manager dedicated to the network, coordination

of effort among marketing, sales, and hundreds of alumni would be a substantial task. If volunteers were overutilized, they might tire or reduce donations on the grounds that they were already giving their time. If they were underutilized, they might lose enthusiasm for the network or even the school. Chin felt that careful management of both operations and volunteers' expectations would be critical.

If successful, the AIM network could be a great asset to all phases of marketing. In the future, selected alumni might be able to make their own presentations under Hurricane supervision. Some managers estimated that over half of all public course inquiries came from word of mouth; getting alumni talking about and working for Hurricane in a new way could boost these referral enrollments. And well-managed participation would be bound to generate renewed enthusiasm for the school, perhaps adding to the donor base and generating repeat business.

Unfortunately, Chin foresaw problems in tracing revenues generated by AIM. Like public relations, the benefits generated through AIM would mostly be intangible: better organization for presentations, more word-of-mouth advertising, greater enthusiasm.

Given the response to 1986 tests, Chin felt that expanding a network of volunteers would require hiring a manager over the course of the year. He did not want to cut into Charlie Reade's valuable sales time with extensive administrative duties. Assuming they hired someone in spring 1987, the cost would be about $15,000 for the 1987 budget.

2. Build Corporate Professional Development Program (PDP) "PDP raises emotions at the school," Chin commented. "It raises concerns with the program [course development] people. It raises joy with Joe Adams."

In the early PDP work Hurricane had done, the school had presented itself as an alternative to traditional in-house training. The goal was to put managers together under adverse conditions and watch them respond. The PDP course focused on leadership, team building, stress management, communication, and goal setting. Usually, the Outward Bound experience was mixed with a more traditional training presentation. For example, General Electric's group came to Rockland for a seminar and a three-day course before reporting to GE's New York training center for four weeks of in-house work.

The 1986 experience with PDP had been very positive. Although there was no formal feedback mechanism to collect information from the companies involved, informal follow-up elicited numerous positive comments. Responses from human resource professionals at the companies suggested that managerial participants showed a greater sense of confidence, were better at meeting deadlines, and had stronger presentation and communication skills than they had had in the past.

In addition to benefiting the participants, the program could be extraordinarily profitable for the school. Chin felt that Hurricane could charge corporate clients more, perhaps as much as $200 per SPD, and that $75 per SPD was an appropriate overall goal for public courses. (Adams estimated that the direct cost to Hurricane of one SPD was $45. The remaining $30 in the goal covered fixed overhead.) Also, corporations were more likely to fill off-season courses because executives often took vacations in the summer.

Finally, Chin felt there was moral justification for expanding PDP. "Businesspeople need to learn compassion. We hide behind titles and systems rather than confronting emotional and moral issues." Chin noted feedback that suggested the experience of seeing peers surpass their limits was transferred to the workplace. Managers became more open and able to cope with emotions. Chin felt that such managers would be stronger assets not only to their companies, but also to their communities.

Other Hurricane managers had mixed feelings about the program. Vice president George Armstrong listed three criteria he considered when looking at new course proposals:

First, does it fit what the organization is all about? Second, does it make money? Third, does it fit the schedule? If we can develop a three-day managers' course that meets those goals, I say let's do as many as we can.

Some felt that PDP was precisely *not* what the organization was all about. Former Marketing Committee chair Hank Taft remarked, "I think we owe it to the underprivileged to serve them, even though managers can benefit."

Tino O'Brien noted that staffing such courses was sometimes difficult. "We have a lot of young, idealistic instructors, and it's hard to get them excited about serving rich people." Still, he continued, "the objection to them is mostly theoretical. Once the instructors get out with them on a course, they usually enjoy it." Personally, Tino said, he felt that school should run some PDP courses as long as PDP did not drive the organization. He added dryly, "Executives are people, too."

In general, Chin felt, the school needed to strike a balance on PDP. The school could not go very heavily into corporate programs without endangering its donor base. Most managers believed that donors might contribute less to Hurricane if the school seemed to be moving away from its mission to serve youth and the underprivileged.[2] Also, PDP courses were not as operationally flexible as the average Hurricane offering. Once established, schedules could not be changed; groups of managers could not be shifted to different dates or courses. Chin recalled the time when a late-summer demand surge had hit the school, and Hurricane had to scramble to serve all of its students, particularly the corporate clients. He remembered painfully, "There were situations this summer where we mobilized an extra effort to serve the people who paid."

Chin thought the best way to expand PDP was to hire a recruiter specifically for the program. "In the past, we have been reactive. We want to put resources to our opportunities." Chin envisioned a coordinated marketing approach, beginning with a PDP-specific brochure. The brochure would be mailed to the vice presidents of human resources at *Fortune* 500 companies and other identified prospects in the Northeast,

---

[2] In 1985, donors provided $732,000 in contributions for operations and $956,000 in contributions for property, plant, equipment, and other capital items.

and followed up first by phone and then in person by the PDP recruiter.

The mailing alone would cost about $1,000; adding a PDP recruiter would cost as much as $30,000 once travel and other expenses were factored in. In return, Chin hoped to realize about $200,000 in gross revenue. In any case, it did not seem feasible for him and Bob Weiler to continue making these sales calls as the complexity of other parts of their jobs grew, so he would have to develop a staffing solution anyway.

3. Expand Direct Sales Recruitment In 1986, Hurricane's sales force consisted of two ex-instructors: Charlie Reade, who recruited for public courses, and Holly Miller, who was in charge of special programs. Previously, instructors and managers had gone out on an ad hoc basis, but the school felt that it would benefit from a more systematic approach to direct recruitment. Reade and Miller had begun full-time organized recruiting in 1986, with much success. The school projected that recruiting would generate 17% of 1986 applications and 20% of 1986 enrollments. Demand for group presentations was rising. The school estimated that it would make over 50 presentations in the first three months of 1987.

Many managers considered face-to-face presentations the most effective way for the school to approach prospective students. Presentations had changed with the advent of full-time recruiters. Chin explained that the biggest change management had made was to encourage recruiters to ask for applications or a contract on the spot, whereas in the past they had merely given the informational presentation and asked people to call if they were interested. Chin felt "asking for the order" had made a greater difference in the success of the recruiters, but it had been controversial. Recruiters were unaccustomed to that style. Chin remarked, "It began to smack of commercialism to some people. That worried them."

Rather than add more full-time recruiters, Chin was considering expanding the use of "sub-recruiters." Sub-recruiters would address specific segments, such as high school students. They would work under short-term contracts with specific performance objectives like the number of presentations made or the number of organizations contacted. Hurricane managers hoped that they might be able to provide off-season work to course instructors by making them sub-recruiters; another leadership school put all its instructors "on the road" every fall. Hurricane's sub-recruiters would work under the supervision of the full-time recruiters. Chin estimated that adding two sub-recruiters would cost $9,000 in 1987.

4. Build Telemarketing Capabilities In 1986, the admissions department experimented with calling prospective students after they had applied but before they had enrolled. Students seemed to enjoy speaking with someone from the school, especially given the high levels of anxiety some had about course activities. Chin and others believed that students who were contacted would be more likely to enroll, although tracking on the initial experiment had been inadequate to determine this conclusively.

Unfortunately, the admissions department could not provide full-time telemarketers. Chin believed that hiring good telemarketers for Hurricane would be a tough job. Candidates needed to have both good selling skills and sufficient program knowledge to answer student's questions.

One alternative to full-time telemarketing would be an extended test. Chin envisioned calling 500 to 1,000 prospective students who had applied but not yet enrolled. By setting up a careful response-tracking system, the school could determine whether a further investment was warranted. It was difficult to determine the cost of all this. Even using part-time people to start, payroll and phone costs would escalate rapidly. Chin had tentatively allocated $6,000 for an extended test in 1987.

Alternatives: Pricing and the Course Mix

Given the amount of money Chin had available, he could not fund all four of the programs outlined above. One way of getting around this problem was to find ways to make the school's courses more profitable, thus providing more funds for marketing programs.

In addition to the differential pricing schedules

developed in 1985 and 1986, the school's prices in general had increased at a pace of about 15% per year for the last two years. Raising prices again had been discussed in 1987 planning meetings. Joe Adams was in favor of another price increase; the school average was still below his goal of $75 per SPD. Others were not so sure. Hurricane had reached what Chin called "the $2,000 barrier" on a number of popular courses. He was uneasy about raising prices any higher for these courses. It was unclear how much selective or general price increases would affect demand, or what they might do to marketing's overall contribution to profit.

Another way to raise course profitability would be to alter the course mix further. The effect would be easier to trace, though implementation would be more difficult. Course mix was the area in which course managers and the marketing department were most likely to clash. While it was relatively easy to expand activities in a profitable course, it was much more difficult to cut back on an unprofitable one. Because of the school's nonprofit mission, many managers believed firmly that profitability was not a valid criterion for judging the worth of a course. Courses were more likely to be eliminated for safety reasons or for lack of students. In addition, many courses had been championed by individuals who were dedicated to the segments their courses served. The Vietnam veterans' course in the special programs area, for example, had been created, funded, and marketed primarily through the efforts of an ex-Green Beret colonel. Further, certain courses were strongly identified with the organization as a whole. The Marine Sea courses, for example, were part of the school's history and original mission. Despite the significant overhead expense of maintaining the 18 large boats used in them, there was no question that Marine Sea would continue to be integral to Hurricane's operations.

Evaluating Marketing Tactics

Three numbers appeared at the head of virtually every planning document for marketing at the school: the number of students served, the number of SPDs, and total revenue. Different interested parties, however, placed different emphases on these numbers. On one side, the "business-oriented" managers and many of the trustees were most concerned with the revenues that public courses generated. The financial crisis of the early 1980s had convinced them, above all, that the school had to break even on its operating revenues and expenses. Two of their long-term goals were to reduce the school's debt burden and to purchase certain properties critical to its operations; therefore a surplus of revenues over expenses would be even better.

On the other side, many of the "course-oriented" managers and donors were more concerned with serving as many deserving students as possible. They tended to focus on number of students and SPDs. For them, marketing's job was to "fill the courses." Beyond students and SPDs, these people watched such measures as the proportion of students receiving financial aid, and the demographic characteristics of students, including age, sex, and race. While they knew that obtaining funds was important, they were worried that marketing and finance concerns might drive the organization away from its original mission of serving youth and the disadvantaged. Growth seemed far more worthwhile than debt reduction.

Each of the four marketing initiatives proposed had strengths and weaknesses relative to the tension between financial concerns and service concerns. Direct sales and telemarketing, for example, were targeted approaches that allowed the school to solicit populations with desirable demographic traits, such as minority groups. They could also be used to concentrate on filling specific courses. AIM was less controllable and measurable—who the tactic reached depended on which alumni volunteered and what their contacts were. PDP was focused and profitable, but some felt it was aimed at the wrong target market.

Beyond all this, Chin was concerned about how accurately the school would be able to link results to *any* initiative. Despite the admissions department's heroic effort to organize student data, Hurricane often had no idea why a given student enrolled. (See *Exhibit 7* for a rough forecast of 1986 results by marketing tactic.) Chin was dedicated to developing better

EXHIBIT 7   PROJECTED RESULTS BY MARKETING TACTIC, 1986

	National marketing*	Direct sales	Direct mail	Other/ unknown	Total
Applications[†]	1,100	600	340	1,500	3,540
Conversion rate	60%	85%	75%	75%	72%
Students enrolled	660	510	256	1,125	2,551
Revenues	$792,000	$612,000	$307,200	$1,350,000	$3,061,200
Direct cost	$39,000	$68,500	$26,250	na	$295,000

Source: Hurricane Island Outward Bound School.
*Inquiries about Hurricane courses generated by National (Outward Bound, Inc.) marketing.
[†]Approximately 1 of every 15 inquiries about all Outward Bound courses generated by National eventually converted to applications. Approximately 1 of every 8 inquiries Hurricane generated internally converted to applications. Hurricane received about 27% of all applications generated by National.

marketing information systems at the school (which was one reason he wanted an assistant marketing manager aboard), but this would require changing procedures in marketing and admissions, and he was not sure what the financial or organizational costs of these changes would be.

Finally, there were the three marketing objectives staring at him from the front page of his notebook. With all the other plan goals, these were the real ones: delivering 2,700 students, 47,800 SPDs, and—perhaps most important—$3.4 million in revenues while staying within his budget and balancing the interests of management, donors, trustees, instruction staff, and, ultimately, the students.

On the one hand, Chin felt the school was slowly becoming more "businesslike" due to the demands of growth. On the other hand, as Hank Taft had remarked before he retired in September, "Nobody's in this to make money." Changing the way Outward Bound concepts were marketed could change other things about the organization as well. Chin wondered if there were other ways to reach his goals that he had missed. As his plane landed at Owls Head, he snapped his notebook shut, but the questions remained.

Winkleman Manufacturing Company

Jim Dooley
William L. Weis

In a recent staff meeting, John Winkleman, president of Winkleman Manufacturing Company, addressed his managers with this problem:

Intense competitive pressure is beginning to erode our North American market share in handheld digital multimeters (DMMs). I have documented 11 large orders that have been lost to Backman and Winston within the past three months. On an annual basis this amounts to nearly 10,000 units and $1.5 million in lost opportunities. Within the last 18 months, at least 16 serious competitors have entered the market. Two-thirds of these DMMs have continuity indicators. The trend is the same for European and Japanese markets as well. Our sales of handheld DMMs in fiscal year 88 is forecast to grow only 1.7 percent. According to Dataquest projections, the handheld DMM market will grow 20.9 percent for the next five years. I think that figure is conservative. Our competitors are gaining attention and sales with added features, particularly at the present time with continuity indicators. Since a new Winkleman general-purpose, low-cost handheld is two years from introduction, it is important that something be done to retain the profitable position of market leader in our traditional direct and distributor channels. Next meeting I want some ideas.

Winkleman Manufacturing, a major electronics manufacturer in the Northwest, produced a variety of products. The three products that most concerned Mr. Winkleman were the Series A handheld digital multimeters (DMMs). As an innovator in the field of handheld DMMs, Mr. Winkleman had seen his business flourish in recent years. But now, with his three most successful products in the late stages of maturity and the economy in slow growth, times were not looking as rosy.

The three multimeters of concern were model numbers 1010, 1020, and 1030. These three models formed a complementary family line. The 1010 was a low-cost unit containing all standard measurement functions and having a basic measurement accuracy of 0.5 percent. The 1020 offered identical measurement functions but had an improved basic measurement accuracy of 0.1 percent. The top of the line was the 1030. In addition to a basic accuracy of 0.1 percent, the 1030 offered several additional features, one being an audible continuity indicator. *Exhibit 1* provides sales and projected sales for the three models.

At the next staff meeting, one of the newer management team members, Dave Haug, presented his ideas for tackling the lost market problem:

EXHIBIT 1
SELECTED SALES AND PROJECTIONS, IN NUMBER OF UNITS

Model	Last year actual	Current year forecast	Percentage change
1010	37,455	35,500	−5.5
1020	67,534	61,800	−8.4
1030	25,602	35,500	+39.0
Total	130,591	132,800	+1.7

What we need is a face-lift of our existing product line to hold our position over the next two years. Changes in color, a new decal, some minor case modifications, and most important an audible continuity indicator in the 1010 and 1020 should give us two more years of product life to tide us over. We can call this Series B to retain continuity in switching from the old to the new. As my analysis indicates, Winkleman's decline in 1010/1020 sales could be reversed and show a modest increase in market share over the next two years with the inclusion of the Series B features [*Exhibit 2*]. Discussions with large-order customers indicate that Winkleman could have won 40–60 percent of the lost large orders that were mentioned at our last meeting if our entire handheld family features audible continuity. As you well know, the popularity of continuity indication has been confirmed in several other studies conducted over the past two years.

An estimate of sales of Series B has been generated from inputs from field sales, distribution managers, and discussions with customers. Conservative estimates indicate the sales of Series B will increase 6.9 percent above current Series A levels, with a marginal revenue increase of $1.5 million list and assuming the same list prices as

the Series A models. During this current period of slow economic growth, the market is becoming increasingly price sensitive. I am aware that our normal policy dictates multiplying the factory cost by three for pricing purposes and that the added factory cost of an audible continuity indicator is $5.00; but for income purposes we should not tack this on to the current prices. My analysis indicates that an increase of $5.00 would reduce incremental sales by 20 percent and an increase of $10.00 would reduce incremental sales by 80 percent.

We should also consider fixed costs. Our fixed costs this year were 25% of total factory costs. These costs will remain the same next year no matter what models or what volumes we sell.

Also remember that we must pay for some nonrecurring engineering costs (NRE) [*Exhibit 3*]. These must come out of our contribution margin—which at Winkleman is calculated by taking the total dollar sales less the 28 percent discount to distributors less factory cost for those units. I believe that increasing these prices will reduce our margins significantly, hindering our ability to cover the NRE, let alone make a profit. Therefore I propose we go ahead with Series B and hold the line on prices.

EXHIBIT 2   SERIES A AND B—PROJECTED COMPARISON

Model	Unit price	Series A, units	Series B, units	Change, percentage	Total sales (change)*
1010	$139	35,500	40,000	4,500 (+ 12.6%)	$ 5.56 (+ .63)
1020	179	61,800	66,000	4,200 (+ 6.8%)	11.81 (+ .75)
1030	219	35,500	36,000	500 (+ 1.4%)	7.88 (+ .11)
Total		132,800	142,000	9,200	$ 25.25

*Dollars in millions.

EXHIBIT 3
ENGINEERING COSTS AND SCHEDULE

The objectives for Series B, models 1010, 1020, and 1030 are:
   All case parts molded in medium gray
   New decal for all units
   Pulse-stretched beeper for 1010 and 1020
   Rubber foot on battery door
   Positionable bail
   Manuals updated as necessary
For these objectives, NRE costs will be:

Manual (updated schematics for 1010, 1020, along with instructions for operation of beeper; model number and front panel changes for all units)	$ 3,500
Battery door mold (add three units)	12,000
Battery door foot die	3,000
Decal	1,900
Bail improvement	8,600
Photo lab	250
PCB fab (prototypes)	500
Engineering labor (25 man-weeks)	81,000
Hard model run	6,000
Total	$116,750

Dennis Cambelot, a longtime Winkleman employee, spoke up with a comment on Dave's proposal:

Dave, I think this Series B idea shows a lot of potential, but pricewise you are way out of line. We have always added the standard markup to our products. We make quality products, and people are willing to pay for quality. The only thing your fancy M.B.A. degree taught you was to be impractical. If you had gotten your experience in the trenches like me, your pricing theories would not be so conservative, and this company could make more money. And forget about the fixed cost stuff.

At the close of the meeting, Mr. Winkleman asked that each manager consider the Series B proposal. He directed that this consideration include: (1) whether or not to adopt the B series; (2) if yes, at what price level; and (3) alternative suggestions.

Evergreen Paper Co.

David Carter-Whitney
Richard W. Pollay
Charles B. Weinberg

We are fighting to show that all recycled paper is not the same.

　　　　　　　　Paul Stewert, Evergreen Paper Co.

In Spring 1991, Paul Stewert, Janet Pierce and Dan Patterson, the owners of Evergreen Paper Co., a wholesaler of printing, writing and other fine papers, were discussing what direction the company's marketing activities should take. In the previous two years Evergreen had successfully introduced recycled paper products to the Portland, Oregon area and subsequently had gained over half a million dollars in sales without engaging in formal marketing activities. Recently, the company had faced increasing challenges from the four large paper wholesalers that dominated the local paper market and from a number of small firms competing for a similar client base. Stewert, Pierce and Patterson had to decide what action, if any, the company should take to defend and/or build its share of the rapidly growing recycled paper market.

THE COMPANY

Evergreen was founded in December 1988 by Pierce and Stewert in response to the lack of recycled paper in Portland. Although both were social workers with limited business experience, they decided to start their own paper wholesale company in order to make "environmentally responsible" paper products available. Patterson joined the company a year later.

As environmentalists, Stewert, Pierce and Patterson promoted products that helped to preserve the forests and reduce pollution *(Exhibit 1)*. This meant only marketing "least impact" paper products which were primarily composed of recycled waste and which were also non-chlorinated and unbleached. In addition, Evergreen participated in attempts to lobby city, state and federal governments both to buy recycled paper and to set higher standards for the percentage of recycled and post-consumer fibers that were legally required before a paper product could be called "recycled." Stewert, who served as Evergreen's marketing manager, was definite about what made Evergreen unique: "We have an environmental, not a commercial focus to our business." This focus influenced the products that the company marketed and was fundamental to all decisions the staff made.

EXHIBIT 1
BENEFITS OF RECYCLING PAPER
(100% recycled fiber content)

- Each ton of recycled paper produced saves about 17 trees.
- Each ton of recycled paper produced requires about 4,102 kwh less energy than virgin paper production.
- The manufacture of recycled paper requires 7,000 gallons less water per ton compared to non-recycled paper.
- Manufacturing recycled paper reduces overall emission of air pollution by 60 pounds per ton of paper produced.
- For every ton of recycled paper produced, landfill is reduced by three cubic yards.

Source: PIMA Journal, June 1990, p.50.

THE ENVIRONMENT AND PAPER ISSUES

The recent increase in environmental awareness was accompanied by an increase in "green" marketing which sought to appeal to environmental concerns. This had a strong impact on the marketing of paper, a highly visible product.

In the mid-1980s, the U.S. Environmental Protection Agency (E.P.A.) published a guideline requiring that to be called "recycled," paper had to contain a minimum of 50% recycled material.[1] The stated objective of the guidelines was "to reduce the amount of paper entering the solid waste stream." However, the guidelines did not distinguish between pre- and post-consumer waste, and therefore many brands of recycled paper actually did divert any post-consumer waste from landfill. The majority of paper currently being produced and marketed as "recycled" just met, but did not surpass, the minimum standards for content.

Another concern of environmentalists was the use of chemicals in the production of paper. The by-products of paper pulping included (1) sulphur-dioxide, a leading cause of acid rain, and (2) aluminum salts, which were highly toxic to certain fish. In order to produce white paper, pulp was chlorine bleached, which also produced an array of toxic chlorine compounds called organochlorines. Between five and eight kilograms of these organochlorines were discharged into nearby water sources per ton of pulp bleached. About 300 organochlorines in pulp mill effluent were identified as being carcinogens (cancer-causing) or mutagens (causing chromosomal damage), the best-known being dioxin.

Recycling itself raised environmental problems. In order to create white paper from recycled waste, the previously used paper had first to be de-inked, a process that created toxic waste from the ink. Although most recycled papers were bleached white for cosmetic purposes, some mills were now producing unbleached paper which had a cream or gray color. By not bleaching or de-inking, these mills not only reduced toxic discharges but also lowered their energy consumption by eliminating one stage of production. Environmental groups, and the people at companies like Evergreen, were strongly opposed to the continued use of chlorine-bleaching and encouraged the use of unbleached products.

[1]Recycled paper was measured by two standards: the amount of recycled material it contained and the amount of post-consumer material it contained. "Recycled material" referred to the amount of waste recovered from any source, and included both pre-consumer and post-consumer waste. Post-consumer waste referred to material that had completed its life cycle as a consumer item and would have been disposed of as solid waste. It included old newspapers, magazines, office waste paper and used corrugated containers. Most of this waste traditionally ended up in garbage dumps. Pre-consumer waste referred to paper and wood products generated in production which never reached the consumer. This category included bindery trimmings, unused printed material, obsolete stock, mill ends and sawdust. Traditionally, the majority of this material was recycled.

The Fine Paper Industry and Recycling

Fine paper was produced in mills throughout the United States, and around the world; often one manufacturer owned several mills producing different types of paper. Large-volume wholesale merchants bought paper directly from mills, but smaller dealers generally bought through paper brokers. Evergreen bought some of its paper directly from mills and some through brokers, but paid a relatively high price because of the small volumes it purchased. Stewert estimated that Evergreen paid 10–20% more than its large competitors for some identical paper products.

Fine paper was a broad term describing printing, writing and business communication papers. Copying paper and computer printouts were included in this category, newsprint and yellow kraft papers were not. Fine paper could be recycled into newsprint, but newsprint could not be upgraded into fine paper.

EVERGREEN'S CURRENT ACTIVITIES

Evergreen was a wholesale company, marketing products with higher recycled and post-consumer fiber content than were available from its competitors *(Exhibit 2)*. The company's activities were divided into three areas:

1. Evergreen was the only wholesaler in Portland for many high-percentage recycled papers. These paper products were sold to companies, governments and non-profit organizations.
2. Evergreen contracted with other companies to convert blank, flat paper into retail products like

---

EXHIBIT 2   EVERGREEN PAPER CO. PRODUCT LIST

FINE PAPER (with matching envelopes if needed):

Review—Natural color, 100% recycled fiber, not secondarily bleached or de-inked
Ecopaper—Not quite white, 100% recycled, 50% post-consumer, non-chlorine bleached
Tropical—Cream or gray, 100% post-consumer fiber, not de-inked
Vibrant—Sandstone color, 60% recycled, 30% post-consumer, unbleached, de-inked without chemicals
Premium copy—White, 50% recycled, 10% post-consumer, for use in high speed copiers and laser printers
White copy/bond—White, 50% recycled, 10% post-consumer
Sycamore colored bond—Various colors, 50% recycled, 10% post-consumer
Bellbrook Laid—White or ivory, 50% recycled, 25% post-consumer
Medallion—White, pewter or denim, 50% recycled, 10% post-consumer
Passport—Gypsum, amethyst, rose quartz or coral sand, 50% recycled, 25% post-consumer
Speckletone—5 colors, 85-100% recycled, 10-20% post-consumer

Most papers were available in 16 lb., 20 lb., 24 lb. or heavier sheets. The weight was a measurement of the thickness of the paper. For example, 20 lb. was a standard weight for photocopiers, while 80 lb. was often used for covers of publications.

FILE FOLDERS:

Legal or letter size—brown, 100% recycled

COMPUTER PAPER:

News—100% post-consumer, 18 lb.
Standard white—50% recycled, 10% post-consumer, 15 or 20 lb.
Review—100% recycled, unbleached, 20 lb.

RETAIL PRODUCTS:

Brite writing pads—Canary yellow or natural gray, 100% post-consumer newsprint, no chlorine bleaching
Evergreen writing pads—100% recycled unbleached fiber, lined or unlined
Evergreen stationary sets—85–100% recycled fiber
Review looseleaf filler—100% recycled fiber, not secondarily bleached or de-inked
Evergreen gift wrap—made from Vibrant minimum packaging to reduce waste
Presentation folders—made from Passport papers

---

stationery pads, looseleaf filler, fine stationery kits and wrapping paper. These products were sold either directly to stores that requested them, or through a distributor that serviced various natural food retailers.

3. Evergreen's staff also supported activities and projects that complemented their environmental concerns. These activities included lobbying governments, donating paper to particular projects, or placing advertising in environmental magazines as a form of donation.

As the first company to market recycled paper in Portland, Evergreen received a substantial amount of free publicity from the local media in the form of interviews and articles. Subsequently, Stewert relied on word-of-mouth publicity and the occasional print advertisement. These ads were placed in various Portland business and computer magazines in an effort to reach businesses and printers. Some ads also appeared in environmental newspapers and magazines; however, this was mostly an effort to support groups with similar environmental objectives. Stewert believed that the advertising had not paid for itself, because most of Evergreen's new business was through the growth of traditional channels. As result, in January 1991, the company stopped advertising. Evergreen did not try to reach individual consumers who bought small quantities of paper from retail outlets.

In May 1990, the company moved into an office with a warehouse which allowed for a larger inventory and quicker filling of orders. With the move, operating expenses had risen from $2,500 per month to almost $10,000 per month. In its first full year of operation, Evergreen sold $450,000 of paper products, primarily fine, printing paper. Sales for the current fiscal year, ending July 31, 1991, were estimated at $650,000 *(Exhibit 3)*. Evergreen's sales were primarily to small businesses and non-profit organizations (55%), although sales also occurred to various governments (20%), some departments at the local universities (5%) and a few larger companies (20%). *Exhibit 4* shows the potential of various types of accounts to Evergreen.

EXHIBIT 3
PRO FORMA 1991 INCOME STATEMENT

Sales	$650,000	
Cost of goods sold	520,000	
Gross profit		130,000
Operating expenses		
Salaries	82,000	
Advertising	9,000	
Rent	21,000	
Office overhead	2,000	
Delivery expense	1,200	
Depreciation	2,100	
Total operating expenses		117,300
Operating income		$12,700

EXHIBIT 4
SELECTED MARKET SEGMENTS AND THEIR ESTIMATED DEMAND FOR PAPER

	Number in Portland	Average order	Orders per year
Public schools	274	$ 600	2
Churches/synagogues	317	300	3
Small businesses	thousands	500	6
Stationers	88	1200	12
Universities	24	1000	12
Photocopy stores	65	1500	12
Non-profit organizations	180	800	4
Unions	80	500	6

The Portland Market

Wholesalers in the Portland market sold approximately $150 million of fine paper annually. The rapid growth in demand for recycled paper made it difficult to estimate accurately the size of the market or relative market shares. By counting the number of truckloads of recycled paper being purchased by Portland firms from one of the major producers, Stewert estimated that Evergreen's market share for recycled paper dropped from 100% in December 1988 to 0.5% at present. Nevertheless, Evergreen's sales increased by 50% in the last year, indicating that the growth in demand for recycled paper was phenomenal.

A manager from one of the large wholesale firms "guesstimated" that the industry was currently selling $14 million of recycled paper annually in Portland, representing around 15% of total sales. Other marketing managers in the industry expected that recycled fine paper would grow to no more than 25% of the total market because of the limited supply of post-consumer and other recycled fiber.

Printers were the largest customers of the major wholesale companies, accounting for approximately 60% of all fine paper sales. The remaining 40% was sold to businesses, institutions, governments and stationers. For example, the City of Portland used approximately 20 million sheets per year, representing approximately $500,000 in sales. The state and federal governments were also major consumers of fine paper.

COMPETITION

Large Wholesalers

Prior to 1988, no wholesale company was distributing recycled paper in the Portland market. However, after Evergreen's successful first year and the increase in environmental awareness of consumers, all the major companies introduced various lines of recycled products. It appeared that the large companies had not increased market share by introducing recycled products, but were merely holding customers who might otherwise purchase from another source.

The fine paper market in Portland was dominated by four large wholesale companies, the two largest each holding about a 33% market share. Prairie Paper, one of the two largest firms, estimated that 75% of its sales were to printers and organizations, like telephone companies, that did their own printing. Sales people also encouraged companies to request a particular Prairie paper with desired characteristics from printers as part of their order. Stationers and governments each accounted for approximately 10% of Prairie's sales.

An active sales force was essential to the operations of the larger companies. Sales people established relationships with purchasing agents from governments, universities and larger companies and thereby created a barrier to new companies, like Evergreen. Prairie equipped sales people with a variety of promotional materials, including brochures and samples of various papers displayed in a compact folder.

Small Competitors

Recently, a number of small companies had begun to compete with Evergreen for the smaller market niches. One company, Nature's Choice, started as a mail order company to consumers but found it hard to survive and entered the wholesale business as well. Another company performed a consulting function for businesses, helping them to "go green"; one obvious way to go green was to use recycled paper. Evergreen supplied some of their needs, although the company also bought from competitors. A new competitor called "The Recycled Source" began to manufacture writing pads and stationery sets much like those sold by Evergreen. To date, The Recycled Source had not started a wholesale operation.

MARKETING ACTIVITIES BY EVERGREEN

Identifying Potential Markets

In July 1990, John Grant was hired on a one-year contract to set up a marketing program and get it rolling. Grant left Evergreen in December for personal reasons, having created data bases for clients in five target sectors: (1) stationery and gift stores,

(2) printers, (3) small businesses, (4) corporations, and (5) government.

Stationery and gift stores were of particular interest to Stewert because they would reduce the company's dependence on wholesale activity. It was expected that, as the large companies introduced additional lines of recycled paper, the wholesale market would become increasingly competitive. However, retail sales had not progressed as well as Evergreen's staff had hoped, and wholesale markets had remained consistently strong.

In the fall, Grant opened about 30 stationery store accounts, but few sales resulted. Stewert acknowledged that Evergreen had not provided any promotional support to these accounts in the form of point of purchase displays or advertising, but hoped to attack these problems in the near future. "Weber's," a local stationery store that strongly promoted recycled paper products, sold over $3000 of recycled paper each month, about half of which was bought from Evergreen. Evergreen had established a good relationship with the owner and several times a year sent free samples of new products to Weber's. Stewert believed that stationery store accounts had enormous potential, but was unsure of how to proceed. Portland had roughly one hundred stationers.

Printers bought the greatest quantities of fine paper, and as a result this area of the market was highly competitive and dominated by the large companies. Frequent service from salespeople and discount pricing were used by the major companies to maintain their business with printers. When Evergreen first started, printers were reluctant to deal with a new, unknown company which did not offer trade pricing (discounts). Because printers were unwilling to deal with them, Evergreen sold some paper directly to customers who took it to their printers. The printing companies objected to this activity because they were losing 10–30% on the sale of paper for these jobs. As Stewert noted, "They want us to sell only to them, but they don't buy from us because they are married to their traditional suppliers. We are the rough edge elbowing our way in there."

Evergreen had one line of paper, Review, which came in rolls and sheets and was suitable for printing.

Although Review was an excellent product with superior recycled content, there was a limited supply and as a result the large wholesale companies chose not to market it. Nevertheless, Stewert was concerned that, if Evergreen sold to too many printers, the large companies could respond by outbidding Evergreen for the scarce supply of Review.

Recently, two printers began to deal with Evergreen on an ongoing basis. One printer placed a purchase order for a six-month supply. The other steadily increased its orders for Review. These two printers provided Evergreen with $5000 to $6000 in monthly sales.

One area of disappointment for Evergreen was a distribution agreement with Sunset Distributors, a health food broker which placed its retail products in co-ops and health food stores. Although these outlets reached people who were environmentally conscious, there had been several problems which meant that anticipated monthly sales of $10,000 had not materialized. The first several months in the fall of 1990 yielded sales of $4,000 but orders had dwindled since then.

Selling to retailers through Sunset increased the price of the paper to the final purchaser by about 33%, making the paper very expensive for many consumers. (*Exhibit 5* shows the relative mark-ups at each level of distribution for two of Evergreen's retail products.) Stewert recognized that some sales difficulties were due to the fact that paper was not typically purchased in a health food store. In addition, it did not get displayed or featured prominently, either by Sunset (which is primarily a food broker) or by the health food stores.

Sunset and the health food stores wanted Evergreen to provide promotional support for its products to improve sales. Evergreen was considering developing point-of-purchase displays in conjunction with a local designer who had similar environmental interests. Alternatively, Evergreen could pay for advertising space in Sunset's catalogue to draw attention to its products. However, Stewert was unsure of how much money to invest in this project, and did not want to "throw energy and money where there was no chance of return."

EXHIBIT 5 PRICING AND MARGINS FOR TWO OF EVERGREEN'S RETAIL PRODUCTS

	Fine stationery sets			Lined writing pads		
Cost to Evergreen		$4.30			$1.05	
Evergreen price range*	$5.30		$4.80	$1.30		$1.20
(% Evergreen markup)	(23%)		(12%)	(24%)		(14%)
Wholesaler's price		$6.55			$1.50	
(% Wholesale markup)	(24%)		(36%)	(15%)		(23%)
Retail price		$9.99			$3.39	
(% Retail markup)		(53%)			(126%)	

*Evergreen sold to wholesalers who bought a small volume of products (e.g., fine stationery sets) at a price of $5.30 for a mark-up of $1.00 (23% of $4.30). To wholesalers who bought a large volume of fine stationery sets, Evergreen sold at a price of $4.80 for a mark-up of $0.50 (12% of $4.30).

Pricing

Evergreen charged a 30% margin (mark-up on cost of goods sold) on the smallest quantities sold. For larger orders, Evergreen charged a 12% margin on some products. This was a vulnerable area, Stewert admitted, because competitors like Prairie bought much larger volumes at lower prices. On identical papers, Evergreen paid 10–20% more than Prairie both because of having to purchase through a broker and because of the low volume of their orders. Once these prices were passed on to the consumer, Evergreen was at a serious disadvantage, as is shown in *Exhibit 6*.

The price gap was widened when standard white paper, which was still Prairie's "bread-and-butter" product, was compared to Evergreen's Review, which accounted for 66% of Evergreen's total sales. Evergreen charged $13.95 per thousand sheets, and discounted back to $10.45 per thousand for 20 cartons or more (5000 sheets per carton). By contrast, Prairie's best-selling product was plain, non-recycled white paper. Prairie sold it for $8.93 per thousand sheets and discounted it to $8.04 (10%) for orders over 10 cartons.

Tropical was the only paper which Evergreen sold at a lower price than Prairie. However, despite its high content of post-consumer fiber, this paper was an unattractive yellow color and was known to per-

form poorly in laser printers and photocopiers. It was believed that Prairie used this paper to bolster the breadth and environmental quality of its recycled paper line, but discouraged its purchase by charging a relatively high price.

EXHIBIT 6
COMPARISON OF PRICES CHARGED BY EVERGREEN AND PRAIRIE
(Prices per 1000 Sheets)

Product	Evergreen	Prairie
Standard white (0%, 0%)*		
1 Ctn.	—	$ 8.93
20 Ctns.	—	8.04
Review (100%, 0%)		
1 Ctn.	$13.95	—
20 Ctns.	10.45	—
Recycled white (50%, 10%)		
1 Ctn.	$12.35	$ 9.72
20 Ctns.	10.45	8.75
Tropical (100%, 100%)		
1 Ctn.	$15.00	$16.82
20 Ctns.	11.25	15.14
Bellbrook Laid (50%, 25%)		
1 Ctn.	$17.15	$16.95
20 Ctns.	16.25	15.25

*Recycled fiber, post-consumer fiber.

Other Markets

Prior to Christmas, Stewert sold five cartons of paper to one outlet of "The Copy Place," a local chain of photocopy stores, but had not heard anything from the store since. Photocopy stores used an enormous amount of paper on an ongoing basis, but traditionally had not purchased recycled paper. There were approximately 65 photocopy stores in Portland.

Stewert believed that Evergreen had a strong market position with non-profit organizations, but had not focused on expanding this segment. Portland had approximately one hundred and eighty non-profit organizations concerned with environmental, social justice and health issues. In addition, Portland was home to the offices of roughly eighty unions. Many unions were very active in supporting environmental causes. Finally, Evergreen serviced some churches and synagogues which each purchased about 10 cartons per year. There were approximately three hundred churches and synagogues in the area.

Sales Force Considerations

"I had planned to start actively pursuing sales on a full-time basis this winter, but there just was not enough time," Stewert said. Although he would have liked to hire five sales people to use the data base left by Grant, Stewert recognized that the company's resources were limited, and a failed, large-scale sales effort could bankrupt Evergreen.

Stewert identified several problems that had to be addressed in order to establish a sales policy. Up to this point, Stewert, Pierce and Patterson had each been drawing $18,000 per year, which was probably not enough to hire experienced sales help. They would be willing to pay someone more than themselves, but that person would have to generate enough sales volume to pay his or her own way in several months. Stewert had considered the use of straight commission or some combination of salary and commission, but this would require greater role definition in the office because a commissioned employee would not want the salaried employees handling sales at his or her expense. As Stewert said, "We knew that something had to be done about sales, but we'd

been hoping that the right person would just walk through the door."

Evergreen's promotional material currently consisted of a four-page price list, a two-sided information sheet discussing some of the issues surrounding the use of recycled paper, and a set of $3'' \times 4''$ samples of the various papers sold by the company. Regular retail customers, like Weber's, were sent samples of new products as they were introduced.

FUTURE PLANS

Stewert noted that Evergreen currently was marketing six lines of white paper that have 50% recycled content because people demanded these products and the company could not survive without the sales. However, by the end of 1991, Evergreen planned only to market paper products that were 100% recycled and unbleached.

In addition to making this shift, Stewert also hoped to reduce Evergreen's reliance on too few products for the majority of its sales. Approximately 60% of Evergreen's sales were accounted for by products made of Review, and another 20% were from the 50% recycled products that the company hoped to phase out.

The staff of Evergreen also believed that other markets in the Pacific Northwest had not been serviced well and that these represented potential growth areas. However, with the current three-person staff there were not sufficient resources available to allow broader efforts.

Evergreen planned to continue its involvement in lobbying activities seeking to encourage governments to increase their requirements for a paper to be classified as "recycled" to 80% recycled material (including also higher amounts of post-consumer waste than currently required). If these levels were not attained in federal legislation, it was hoped that other levels of government could be persuaded to require them as a standard for any recycled paper.

Stewert admitted that there had been environmental "fads" before which died out after several years and that the recent recession had slowed the momentum for environmental change. Nevertheless, he was convinced that Evergreen was selling recycled paper products that were superior to what was available previously and that the demand for such products would continue to grow.

As Stewert, Pierce and Patterson talked, it was evident that there were disagreements over whether or not to hire sales people, what market segments to pursue, what products to carry and what other promotional activities to engage. in that also supported their environmental agenda. However, they all realized that they had to reach some decisions soon or else they might miss opportunities offered in this rapidly changing market.

PART TWO

Market Selection

M arket selection, along with product policy, is one of the central elements of marketing management. *Product-market choice*—what products to offer to which markets—is at the core of every organization's strategy. In this section of the book, we focus primarily on the choice of which markets to serve; the following section emphasizes decisions on which products to offer. However, these two decisions are often closely interrelated, since different markets may have different needs, and not all products (or specific formulations of a particular product) will appeal to all markets.

Several companies in the same industry may make sharply different market selection decisions. To illustrate, one cosmetics firm may concentrate on developing highly advertised cosmetics sold in department stores at high prices to a style-conscious, upscale market, while another cosmetics firm devotes its efforts to women who prefer the convenience and advice obtained from a sales representative who brings product samples to the customer's own home. A third company may concentrate on budget-minded individuals who shop in discount stores. Each firm, by choosing a different market target, is simultaneously making a decision about the marketing skills and resources required to succeed, the nature of competition likely to be encountered, the potential for growth and profitability to be obtained, and the threats and opportunities to be met in the external environment.

It is critical that managers carefully choose the markets in which their firm will compete (see *Exhibit 1*). Failure to do so may result in the firm's efforts being scattered by attempting to be all things to all people—rarely a successful strategy. It may also result in lost opportunities to enter newer markets or too much emphasis on old markets which are declining, unprofitable, or crowded with other competitors. An organization's success is dependent on the opportunities available in the market or market segments it selects, as well as on how effectively it competes in those markets.

EXHIBIT 1
FRAMEWORK FOR MARKET SEGMENTATION, TARGETING, AND POSITIONING

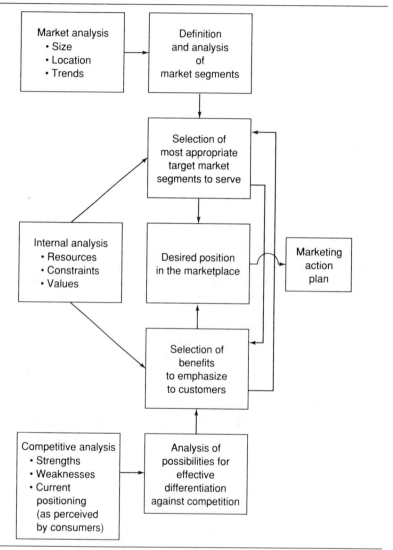

Source: Based upon an earlier schematic by Michael R. Pearce.

OPPORTUNITY ANALYSIS

An early step in market selection is identification and analysis of the opportunities available to the enterprise. *Opportunity analysis* involves identifying markets of good size and growth potential. The competitive structure of the prospective market should allow for profitable entry, while the environmental threats and opportunities should be within the organization's capabilities. Opportunity analysis requires the organization to match its own strengths and weaknesses against the requirements for success in each market it is contemplating entering. When a company's own particular strengths match the key success requirements of a particular market opportunity, then the company is likely to have a differential advantage—or "distinctive competence"—which will allow it to become successful in that market if it can design and implement a sound strategy. Quite often, of course, a firm will be strong on some of the key success factors and weaker on others. At the same time the firm may also be uncertain as to what actions current and future competitors are going to take. Proper balancing of risks and rewards is an important managerial function: excellent decision making is required to identify the best marketing opportunities available.

MARKET DEFINITION AND TARGETING

In many instances, the entire market is too broad to serve as a useful basis for analyzing opportunities. The answer is to look for ways of subdividing the overall market in order to determine where the best chances of success may lie. This is where the concept of market segmentation comes in.

Segmentation plays two basic managerial purposes. The first is *market definition*—helping the organization identify and select those segments within the overall marketplace that offer the best opportunities for meeting the organization's objectives, and therefore represent an appropriate target for marketing efforts. The second purpose is *target marketing*—helping the manager direct marketing activities at the target markets that have been selected. This activity may require making further subdivisions within the target population and then developing several coordinated marketing programs tailored to these target market segments.

Market Definition and Selection

How should a manager get started on the process of defining and selecting markets? Often there are broad and obvious divisions within the market for a given product category. In many instances, the same basic product may be sold to both industrial and household purchasers. Smoke detectors, for example, are required by law in most new buildings and are purchased in bulk for this purpose by electrical contractors. But many homeowners also buy smoke detectors, either as a retrofit in an older home or to replace an existing detector that is no longer functioning. Builders' supply stores might be used to reach the first two markets, with electrical outlets supplying the first and third markets, and additional distribution to the third market taking place through hardware stores, department stores, and mass merchandisers.

Another way of subdividing the market for the same product might be on the basis of geography. A firm might be faced with the choice between deeper penetration of a regional or national market in which it is already active versus moving into new regions or countries—a move involving not only significant start-up costs but also, perhaps, ongoing differentiation of the strategies used in each major market area.

A third type of market selection decision might focus on different uses of the same product. Consider the trucking firm which has historically concentrated on transporting packaged goods for delivery to supermarkets. If it wants to expand its sales by delivering perishable foods, it will have to invest in new types of equipment, including refrigerated trucks, to serve that market (even though the buyer is the same). Higher prices may be needed to compensate for the extra cost, but how will competitors respond to a new market entrant? Will they provoke a price war?

In evaluating alternative markets, the manager must find answers to a series of questions:

- Which markets will fit best with our organization's skills, resources, and current product line?
- Which are large enough and have sufficient growth potential to offer our firm the chance of achieving the sales volume identified in organizational objectives?
- Which markets are at risk of being eroded by new technological, legal, or social developments?
- In which markets can a sustainable competitive advantage be obtained?
- What costs will be incurred in operating in each market, given the competitive situation and the need for sales and advertising efforts?
- In which markets will distributors be most receptive to our sales approach and our established ways of doing business? What is our corporate and product reputation among both distributors and end users in each market?
- To what extent will our marketing mix strategies need to be modified to compete effectively in each alternative market—and do we want to make such modifications?

Target Marketing

When one or more markets have been selected, the manager will need to undertake a detailed analysis of buyer characteristics, needs, and product usage behavior in a search for possible ways of further segmenting the chosen markets. In some instances, the most efficient approach is to pursue a policy of undifferentiated marketing that involves using the same marketing strategy without modification for all prospective buyers. But in highly competitive markets, further segmentation may yield opportunities to differentiate the firm's marketing approach from that of competitors. There are a wide variety of possible ways of segmenting a market, as shown in *Exhibit 2*. Two broad groupings are user characteristics versus user responses.

User characteristics include demographics, geography, and psychographics. The first two are usually easier to identify than the third, which includes less "obvious" factors such as personality and attitudes. A fourth category, benefit segmentation, seeks to group prospects according to the different types of

EXHIBIT 2
MAJOR SEGMENTATION VARIABLES AND SELECTED SUBDIVISIONS

User characteristics

Demographic and
socioeconomic segmentation
  Age
  Sex
  Marital status
  Family size
  Composition of household
  Household or individual income
  Occupation
  Education level
  Religion
  Race or ethnic background
  Language spoken
  Physical characteristics
  State of health

Geographic segmentation
  Nation
  Region of country
  Specific political jurisdiction (state or
    province, county, district, city, town)
  Neighborhood or community
  Size of city or metropolitan area
  Urban versus rural areas
  Population density
  Type of climate
  Nature of terrain

Psychographic segmentation
  Personality factors
  Lifestyle
  Quality of marital and family relations
  Attitudes
  Interests and avocations
  Personal ambitions
  IQ
  Level of motivation
  Loyalty and commitment

Benefit segmentation
  Benefits sought
  Costs or problems avoided

User Responses

Segmentation by product-related
behavior
  Frequency of use
  Amount used on each occasion
  Method of use
  Expenditures on related products
  Taking of prior qualifying steps
  Timing of use
  Location of use
  Circumstances or purpose of use
    ("occasion segmentation")
  Attitudes toward use
  Perceptions of product characteristics
  Knowledge of product features

Sensitivity to marketing variables
  Response to product modifications
  Price sensitivity
  Access to retail outlets
  Response to communications
    variables

benefits that they hope to obtain from the product in question, as well as the types of problems they hope to avoid.

User response variables attempt to group prospects according to product-related behavior and sensitivity to different marketing variables. Research may indicate that these variables are related to user characteristics. For instance, elderly consumers may purchase certain medications in large quantities; households in hot, humid climates are more likely to buy air conditioners and use them extensively; families who pursue an outdoor lifestyle may watch less television.

The basic challenge in segmentation is to select one or more segmentation variables that will be appropriate for use in a specific context. Most markets can be segmented in numerous different ways. Which should the manager select? Three broad criteria should always be used to evaluate any given segmentation scheme:

1. *Size:* Is the segment large enough or sufficiently important to merit the time and costs of separate marketing attention?
2. *Compatibility:* Are the marketing skills and techniques needed to serve a specific segment compatible with the organization's resources, style, and values? What would it take to redirect an organization to serve a new market segment, and what would be the impact on its existing business?
3. *Accessibility:* Are the target segments readily identifiable within the chosen market (for instance, among middle-income men aged 25 to 39, which ones are especially health conscious), and how can we reach them? Two basic strategies can be used: controlled coverage seeks to zero in on the population of interest; customer self-selection, by contrast, relies on broad-based marketing efforts containing a specific appeal to which target customers are expected to respond by self-selecting.

CONCLUSION

The process of market selection consists of:

1. Dividing the overall market into meaningful groups for purposes of identification and analysis
2. Selecting those groups on which the organization should concentrate its efforts
3. Developing specific marketing programs to appeal to each of the chosen market targets

A firm need not confine its efforts to just a single market segment but may choose to target several market segments, approaching each segment with a differentiated marketing strategy.

Since the objective of market selection is to compete in areas where the organization can expect to enjoy some competitive advantages, it is important for management to analyze the market in ways that will best reveal the opportunities available to the firm and the threats that may be faced. As was illustrated in the example of the cosmetics industry, firms may use different bases for segmenting a market and select their own unique segments on which to concentrate.

Market selection is a critical decision at all levels of an organization. It determines the types of customers that the firm will serve and often the specific geographic locations in which the firm will make its products available. These factors, in turn, serve to determine the nature of the competition that the company will face as well as the types of marketing intermediaries (distributors, advertising agencies, retailers) with whom it may choose to work. Sound decisions on market selection should set the basis for the firm's success. Less carefully thought-out decisions can expose the firm to competitive perils and environmental threats that endanger achievement of organizational objectives.

TenderCare Disposable Diapers

James E. Nelson

Tom Cagan watched as his secretary poured six ounces of water onto each of two disposable diapers lying on his desk. The diaper on the left was a new, improved Pampers, introduced in the summer of 1985 by Procter & Gamble. The new, improved design was supposed to be drier than the preceding Pampers. It was the most recent development in a sequence of designs that traced back to the original Pampers, introduced to the market in 1965. The diaper on his right was a TenderCare diaper, manufactured by a potential supplier for testing and approval by Cagan's company, Rocky Mountain Medical Corporation (RMM). The outward appearance of both diapers was identical.

Yet the TenderCare diaper was different. Just under its liner (the surface next to the baby's skin) was a wicking fabric that drew moisture from the surface around a soft, waterproof shield to an absorbent reservoir of filler. Pampers and all other disposable diapers on the market kept moisture nearer to the liner and, consequently, the baby's skin. A patent

attorney had examined the TenderCare design, and concluded that the wicking fabric and shield arrangement should be granted a patent. However, it would be many months before results of the patent application process could be known.

As soon as the empty beakers were placed back on the desk, Cagan and his secretary touched the liners of both diapers. They agreed that there was no noticeable difference, and Cagan noted the time. They repeated their "touch test" after one minute and again noted no difference. However, after two minutes, both thought the TenderCare diaper to be drier. At three minutes, they were certain. By five minutes, the TenderCare diaper surface seemed almost dry to the touch, even when a finger was pressed deep into the diaper. In contrast, the Pampers diaper showed little improvement in dryness from three to five minutes and tended to produce a puddle when pressed.

These results were not unexpected. Over the past three months, Cagan and other RMM executives had compared TenderCare's performance with ten brands of disposable diapers available in the Denver market. TenderCare diapers had always felt drier within a two- to four-minute interval after wetting. However, these results were considered tentative because all tests had used TenderCare diapers made by RMM personnel by hand. Today's test was the first made with diapers produced by a supplier under mass manufacturing conditions.

ROCKY MOUNTAIN MEDICAL CORPORATION

RMM was incorporated in Denver, Colorado, in late 1982 by Robert Morrison, M.D. Sales had grown from about $400,000 in 1983 to $2.4 million in 1984 and were expected to reach $3.4 million in 1985. The firm would show a small profit for 1985, as it had each previous year.

Management personnel as of September 1985 included six executives. Cagan served as president and director, positions held since joining RMM in April 1984. Prior to that time he had worked for several high-technology companies in the areas of product design and development, production management, sales management, and general management. His undergraduate studies were in engineering and psychology; he took an M.B.A. in 1981. Dr. Morrison currently served as chairman of the board and vice-president for research and development. He had completed his M.D. in 1976 and was board certified to practice pediatrics in the state of Colorado since 1978. John Bosch served as vice-president of manufacturing, a position held since joining RMM in late 1983. Lawrence Bennett was vice-president of marketing, having primary responsibilities for marketing TenderCare and RMM's two lines of phototherapy products since joining the firm in 1984. Bennett's background included an M.B.A. received in 1981 and three years' experience in groceries product management at General Mills. Two other executives, both also joining RMM in 1984, served as vice-president of personnel and as controller.

Phototherapy Products

RMM's two lines of phototherapy products were used to treat infant jaundice, a condition experienced by some 5 to 10 percent of all newborn babies. One line was marketed to hospitals under the trademark Alpha-Lite. Bennett felt that the Alpha-Lite phototherapy unit was superior to competing products because it gave the baby 360-degree exposure to the therapeutic light. Competing products gave less complete exposure, with the result that the Alpha-Lite unit treated more severe cases and produced quicker recoveries. Apart from the Alpha-Lite unit itself, the hospital line of phototherapy products included a light meter, a photo-mask that protected the baby's eyes while undergoing treatment, and a "baby bikini" that diapered the baby and yet facilitated exposure to the light.

The home phototherapy line of products was marketed under the trademark Baby-Lite. The phototherapy unit was portable, weighing about 40 pounds, and was foldable for easy transport. The unit when assembled was 33 inches long, 20 inches wide, and 24 inches high. The line also included photo-masks, a thermometer, and a short booklet telling parents about home phototherapy. Parents could rent the unit and purchase related products from a local pharmacy or durable medical equipment dealer for about $75 per day. This was considerably less than the cost of hospital treatment. Another company, Acquitron, Inc., had entered the home phototherapy market in early 1985 and was expected to offer stiff competition. A third competitor was rumored to be entering the market in 1986.

Bennett's responsibilities for all phototherapy products included developing marketing plans and making final decisions about product design, promotion, pricing, and distribution. He directly supervised two product managers, one responsible for Alpha-Lite and the other for Baby-Lite. He occasionally made sales calls with the product managers, visiting hospitals, health maintenance organizations, and insurers.

TenderCare Marketing

Right now most of Bennett's time was spent on TenderCare. Bennett recognized that TenderCare would be marketed much differently than the phototherapy products. TenderCare would be sold to wholesalers, who in turn would sell to supermarkets, drugstores, and mass merchandisers. TenderCare would compete either directly or indirectly with two giant consumer goods manufacturers, Procter & Gamble and Kimberly-Clark. TenderCare represented considerable risk to RMM.

Because of the uncertainty surrounding the marketing of TenderCare, Bennett and Cagan had recently sought the advice of several marketing consultants. They reached formal agreement with one, a Los Angeles consultant named Alan Anderson. Anderson had had extensive experience in advertising at J. Walter Thompson. He also had had responsibility for marketing and sales at Mattel and Teledyne, specifically for the marketing of such products as IntelliVision, the Shower Massage, and the Water Pik. Anderson currently worked as an independent marketing consultant to several firms. His contract with RMM specified that he would devote 25 percent of his time to TenderCare the first year and about 12 percent the following two years. During this time, RMM would hire, train, and place their own marketing personnel. One of these people would be a product manager for TenderCare.

Bennett and Cagan also could employ the services of a local marketing consultant who served on RMM's advisory board. The board consisted of twelve business and medical experts who were available to answer questions and provide direction. The consultant had spent over twenty-five years in marketing consumer products at several large corporations. His specialty was developing and launching new products, particularly health and beauty aids. He had worked closely with RMM in selecting the name TenderCare, and had done a great deal of work summarizing market characteristics and analyzing competitors.

MARKET CHARACTERISTICS

The market for babies' disposable diapers could be identified as children, primarily below age three, who used the diapers, and their mothers, primarily between ages eighteen and forty-nine, who decided on the brand and usually made the purchase. Bennett estimated that there were about 11 million such chil-

dren in 1985, living in about 9 million households. The average number of disposable diapers consumed daily in these households was thought to range from 0 to 15 and to average about 5.

The consumption of disposable diapers was tied closely to birth rates and populations. However, two prominent trends also influenced consumption. One was the disposable diaper's steadily increasing share of total diaper usage by babies. Bennett estimated that disposable diapers would increase their share of total diaper usage from 75 percent currently to 90 percent by 1990. The other trend was toward the purchase of higher-quality disposable diapers. Bennett thought the average retail price of disposable diapers would rise about twice as fast as the cost of materials used in their construction. Total dollar sales of disposable diapers at retail in 1985 were expected to be about $3.0 billion, or about 15 billion units. Growth rates were thought to be about 14 percent per year for dollar sales and about 8 percent for units.

Foreign markets for disposable diapers would add to these figures. Canada, for example, currently consumed about $0.25 billion at retail, with an expected growth rate of 20 percent per year until 1990. The U.K. market was about twice this size and growing at the same rate.

The U.S. market for disposable diapers was clearly quite large and growing. However, Bennett felt that domestic growth rates could not be maintained much longer because fewer and fewer consumers were available to switch from cloth to disposable diapers. In fact, by 1995, growth rates for disposable diapers would begin to approach growth rates for births, and unit sales of disposable diapers would become directly proportional to numbers of infants using diapers. A consequence of this pronounced slowing of growth would be increased competition.

COMPETITION

Competition between manufacturers of disposable diapers was already intense. Two well-managed giants—Procter & Gamble and Kimberly-Clark—accounted for about 80 percent of the market in 1984 and 1985. Bennett had estimated market shares at:

	1984	1985
Pampers	32%	28%
Huggies	24	28
Luvs	20	20
Other brands	24	24
	100%	100%

Procter & Gamble was clearly the dominant competitor with its Pampers and Luvs brands. However, Procter & Gamble's market share had been declining, from 70 percent in 1981 to 50 percent currently. The company had introduced its thicker Blue Ribbon™ Pampers recently in an effort to halt the share decline. It had invested over $500 million in new equipment to produce the product. Procter & Gamble spent approximately $40 million to advertise its two brands in 1984. Kimberly-Clark spent about $19 million to advertise Huggies in 1984.

The 24 percent market share held by other brands was up by some 3 percentage points from 1983. Weyerhaeuser and Johnson & Johnson manufactured most of these diapers, supplying private-label brands for Wards, Penneys, Target, K-Mart, and other retailers. Generic disposable diapers and private brands were also included here, as well as a number of very small, specialized brands that distributed only to local markets. Some of these brands positioned themselves as low-cost alternatives to national brands; others occupied premium ("designer") niches with premium prices. As examples, Universal Converter entered the northern Wisconsin market in 1984 with two brands priced at 78 and 87 percent of Pampers' case price. Riegel Textile Corporation's Cabbage Patch diapers illustrated the premium end, with higher prices and attractive print designs. Riegel spent $1 million to introduce Cabbage Patch diapers to the market in late 1984.

Additional evidence of intense competition in the disposable diaper industry was the major change of strategy by Johnson & Johnson in 1981. The company took its own brand off the U.S. market, opting instead to produce private-label diapers for major retailers. The company had held about 8 percent of

the national market at the time and decided that this simply was not enough to compete effectively. Johnson & Johnson's disposable diaper was the first to be positioned in the industry as a premium product. Sales at one point totaled about 12 percent of the market but began to fall when Luvs and Huggies (with similar premium features) were introduced. Johnson & Johnson's advertising expenditures for disposable diapers in 1980 were about $8 million. The company still competed with its own brand in the international market.

MARKETING STRATEGIES FOR TENDERCARE

Over the past month, Bennett and his consultants had spend considerable time formulating potential marketing strategies for TenderCare. One strategy that already had been discarded was simply licensing the design to another firm. Under a license arrangement, RMM would receive a negotiated royalty based on the licensee's sales of RMM's diaper. However, this strategy was unattractive on several grounds. RMM would have no control over resources devoted to the marketing of TenderCare: the licensee would decide on levels of sales and advertising support, prices, and distribution. The licensee would control advertising content, packaging, and even the choice of brand name. Licensing also meant that RMM would develop little marketing expertise, no image or even awareness among consumers, and no experience in dealing with packaged-goods channels of distribution. The net result would be that RMM would be hitching its future with respect to TenderCare (and any related products) to that of the licensee. Three other strategies seemed more appropriate.

The "Diaper Rash" Strategy

The first strategy involved positioning the product as an aid in the treatment of diaper rash. Diaper rash is a common ailment, usually lasting two to three weeks before being cured. Although some infants are more disposed to diaper rash than others, most babies are affected at some point in their diapered lives. The ailment is caused by "a reaction to prolonged contact with urine and feces, retained soaps and topical preparations, and friction and maceration" (Nelson's *Text of Pediatrics,* 1979, p. 1884). Recommended treatment includes careful washing of the affected areas with warm water and without irritating soaps. Treatment also includes the application of protective ointments and powders (sold either by prescription or over the counter).

The diaper rash strategy would target physicians and nurses in either family or general practice and physicians and nurses specializing either in pediatrics or dermatology. Bennett's estimates of the number of general or family practitioners in 1985 was approximately 65,000. He thought that about 45,000 pediatricians and dermatologists were practicing in 1985. The numbers of nurses attending all these physicians was estimated at about 290,000. All 400,000 individuals would be the eventual focus of TenderCare marketing efforts. However, the diaper rash strategy would begin (like the other two strategies) where approximately 11 percent of the target market was located—California. Bennett and his consultants agreed that RMM lacked resources sufficient to begin in any larger market. California would provide a good test for TenderCare because the state often set consumption trends for the rest of the U.S. market. California also showed fairly typical levels of competitive activity.

Promotion activities would emphasize either direct mail and free samples or in-office demonstrations to the target market. Mailing lists of most physicians and some nurses in the target market could be purchased at a cost of about $60 per 1,000 names. The cost to print and mail a brochure, cover letter, and return postcard was about $250 per 1,000. To include a single TenderCare disposable diaper would add another $400 per 1,000. In-office demonstrations would use registered nurses (employed on a part-time basis) to show TenderCare's superior dryness. The nurses could be quickly trained and compensated on a per-demonstration basis. The typical demonstration would be given to groups of two or three physicians and nurses and would cost RMM about $6. The California market could be used to investigate the

relative performance of direct mail versus demonstrations.

RMM would also advertise in trade journals such as the *Journal of Family Practice, Journal of Pediatrics, Pediatrics,* and *Pediatrics Digest.* However, a problem with such advertisements was waste coverage because none of the trade journals published regional editions. A half-page advertisement (one insertion) would cost about $1,000 for each journal. This cost would be reduced to about $700 if RMM placed several advertisements in the same journal during a one-year period. RMM would also promote TenderCare at local and state medical conventions in California. Costs per convention were thought to be about $3,000. The entire promotion budget as well as amounts allocated to direct mail, free samples, advertisements, and medical conventions had yet to be decided.

Prices were planned to produce a retail price per package of 12 TenderCare diapers at around $3.80. This was some 8 to 10 percent higher than the price for a package of 18 Huggies or Luvs. Bennett thought that consumers would pay the premium price because of TenderCare's position: the pennies-per-day differential simply would not matter if a physician prescribed or recommended TenderCare as part of a treatment for diaper rash. "Besides," he noted, "in-store shelf placement of TenderCare under this strategy would be among diaper rash products, not with standard diapers. This will make price comparisons by consumers even more unlikely." The $3.80 package price for 12 TenderCare diapers would produce a contribution margin for RMM of about 9 cents per diaper. It would give retailers a per-diaper margin some 30 percent higher than that for Huggies or Luvs.

The Special-Occasions Strategy

The second strategy centered around a "special-occasions" position that emphasized TenderCare's use in situations where changing the baby would be difficult. One such situation was whenever diapered infants traveled for any length of time. Another occurred daily at some 10,000 daycare centers that accepted infants wearing diapers. Yet another came every evening in each of the 9 million market households when babies were diapered at bedtime.

The special-occasions strategy would target mothers in these 9 million households. Initially, of course, the target would be only the estimated 1 million mothers living in California. Promotion would aim particularly at first-time mothers, using such magazines as *American Baby* and *Baby Talk*. Per-issue insertion costs for one full-color, half-page advertisement in such magazines would average about $20,000. However, most baby magazines published regional editions where single insertion costs averaged about half that amount. Black and white advertisements could also be considered; their costs would be about 75 percent of the full-color rates. Inserting several ads per year in the same magazine would allow quantity discounts and reduce the average insertion cost by about one-third.

Lately Bennett had begun to wonder if direct mail promotion could instead be used to reach mothers of recently born babies. Mailing lists of some 1–3 million names could be obtained at a cost of around $50 per 1,000. Other costs to produce and mail promotional materials would be the same as those for physicians and nurses. "I suppose the real issue is, just how much more effective is direct mail over advertising? We'd spend at least $250,000 in baby magazines to cover California while the cost of direct mail would probably be between $300,000 and $700,000, depending on whether or not we gave away a diaper." Regardless of Bennett's decision on consumer promotion, he knew RMM would also direct some promotion activities toward physicians and nurses as part of the special-occasions strategy. Budget details were yet to be worked out.

Distribution under the special-occasions strategy would have TenderCare stocked on store shelves along with competing diapers. Still at issue was whether the package should contain 12 or 18 diapers (like Huggies and Luvs) and how much of a premium price TenderCare should command. Bennett considered the packaging and pricing decisions interrelated. A package of 12 TenderCare diapers with per-unit retail prices some 40 percent higher than Huggies or

Luvs might work just fine. Such a packaging/pricing strategy would produce a contribution margin to RMM of about 6 cents per diaper. However, the same pricing strategy for a package of 18 diapers probably would not work. "Still," he thought, "good things often come in small packages, and most mothers probably associate higher quality with higher price. One thing is for sure—whichever way we go, we'll need a superior package." Physical dimensions for a TenderCare package of either 12 or 18 diapers could be made similar to the size of the Huggies or Luvs package of 18.

The Head-On Strategy

The third strategy under consideration met major competitors in a direct, frontal attack. The strategy would position TenderCare as a noticeably drier diaper that any mother would prefer to use anytime her baby needed changing. Promotion activities would stress mass advertising to mothers using television and magazines. However, at least two magazines would include a dollar-off coupon to stimulate trial of a package of TenderCare diapers during the product's first three months on the market. Some in-store demonstrations to mothers using "touch tests" might also be employed. Although no budget for California had yet been set, Bennett thought the allocation would be roughly 60:30:10 for television, magazines, and other promotion activities, respectively.

Pricing under this strategy would be competitive with Luvs and Huggies, with the per-diaper price for TenderCare expected to be some 9 percent higher at retail. This differential was needed to cover additional manufacturing costs associated with TenderCare's design. TenderCare's package could contain only 16 diapers and show a lower price than either Huggies or Luvs with their 18-count packages. Alternatively, the package could contain 18 diapers and carry the 9 percent higher price. Bennett wondered if he really wasn't putting too fine a point on the pricing/packaging relationship. "After all," he had said to Anderson, "we've no assurance that retailers or wholesalers would pass along *any* price advantage TenderCare might have due to a smaller package. Either one or both might instead price TenderCare near the package price for our competitors and simply pocket the increased margin!" The only thing that was reasonably certain was TenderCare's package price to the wholesaler. That price was planned to produce about a 3 cent contribution margin to RMM per diaper, regardless of package count.

Summary of the Three Strategies

When viewed together, the three strategies seemed so complex and so diverse as to defy analysis. Partly the problem was one of developing criteria against which the strategies could be compared. Risk was obviously one such criterion; so were company fit and competitive reaction. However, Bennett felt that some additional thought on his part would produce more criteria against which the strategies could be compared. He hoped this effort would produce no more strategies; three were plenty.

The other part of the problem was simply uncertainty. Strengths, weaknesses, and implications of each strategy had yet to be given much thought. Moreover, each strategy seemed likely to have associated with it some surprises. An example illustrating the problem was the recent realization that the Food and Drug Administration (FDA) must approve any direct claims RMM might make about TenderCare's efficacy in treating diaper rash. The chance of receiving this federal agency's approval was thought to be reasonably high; yet it was unclear just what sort of testing and what results were needed. The worst-case scenario would have the FDA requiring lengthy consumer tests that eventually would produce inconclusive results. The best case could have the FDA giving permission based on TenderCare's superior dryness and on results of a small-scale field test recently completed by Dr. Morrison. It would be probably a month before the FDA's position could be known.

"The delay was unfortunate—and unnecessary," Bennett thought, "especially if we eventually settle on either of the other two strategies." In fact, FDA approval was not even needed for the diaper rash

strategy if RMM simply claimed (1) that TenderCare diapers were drier than competing diapers and (2) that dryness helps treat diaper rash. Still, a single-statement, direct-claim position was thought to be more effective with mothers and more difficult to copy by any other manufacturer. And yet Bennett did want to move quickly on TenderCare. Every month of delay meant deferred revenue and other postponed benefits that would derive from a successful introduction. Delay also meant the chance that an existing (or other) competitor might develop its own drier diaper and effectively block RMM from reaping the fruits of its development efforts. Speed was of the essence.

FINANCIAL IMPLICATIONS

Bennett recognized that each marketing strategy held immediate as well as long-term financial implications. He was particularly concerned with finance requirements for start-up costs associated with the California entry. Cagan and the other RMM executives had agreed that a stock issue represented the best option to meet these requirements. Accordingly, RMM had begun preparation for a sale of common stock through a brokerage firm that would underwrite and market the issue. Management at the firm felt that RMM could generate between $1 and $3 million, depending on the offering price per share and the number of shares issued.

Proceeds from the sale of stock had to be sufficient to fund the California entry and leave a comfortable margin remaining for contingencies. Proceeds would be used for marketing and other operating expenses as well as for investments in cash, inventory, and accounts receivable assets. It was hoped that TenderCare would generate a profit by the end of the first year in the California market and show a strong contribution to the bottom line thereafter. California profits would contribute to expenses associated with entering additional markets and to the success of any additional stock offerings.

Operating profits and proceeds from the sale of equity would fund additional research and development activities that would extend RMM's diaper technology to other markets. Dr. Morrison and Bennett saw almost immediate application of the technology to the adult incontinent diaper market, currently estimated at about $300 million per year at retail. Underpads for beds constituted at least another $50 million annual market. However, both of these uses were greatly dwarfed by another application, the sanitary napkin market. Finally, the technology could almost certainly be applied to numerous industrial products and processes, many of which promised great potential. All these opportunities made the TenderCare situation that much more crucial to the firm: making a major mistake here would affect the firm for years.

Health Systems Inc.

Penny Pittman Merliss
Christopher H. Lovelock

Kelly Breazeale, vice president of Health Systems Incorporated (HSI), a Boston-based consulting firm, tilted his chair back from his desk, gazed at his calendar and shook his head. The airline tickets on his left meant another trip to Michigan this week. The neat 18-inch stack of papers placed in a corner by his secretary was an insistent reminder of the "Certificate of Need" required before the State of New Hampshire would approve the construction project planned for the Mary Hitchcock Medical Center in Hanover, N.H. Heaped at the back of his desk was a pile of notes for the 55-page hospital consolidation proposal due to be presented in suburban Woburn, Mass., on Thursday afternoon. It occurred to him suddenly that by skipping lunch and dinner for four days, a consultant could add one extra eight-hour working day to his week. Just as he was mulling over the consequences of this rather austere regimen, there was a knock at the door.

"Morning, Kelly." Bob DeVore, HSI's president,

stuck his head in the doorway. "I finished reading the Baptist Hospital report—it looks OK to mail. And I've arranged a meeting next week to discuss possible locations for our new office. We also need to talk about how we market HSI and how a branch office would affect our marketing. Can you give it some additional thought over the weekend?"

COMPANY BACKGROUND

Health Systems Inc. (HSI) had been founded in 1970 by Robert DeVore, an architect, and Robert Bland, a venture capitalist, who had been classmates at college. The partners split almost half of the stock of the new venture between themselves and agreed that DeVore, because of his architectural experience and entrepreneurial inclination, would serve as chief executive officer; Bland took the title of executive vice president in charge of project management, serving as consultant to health-care construction projects. Their goals, DeVore recalled, were threefold: to have fun, to make money, and to make a social contribution in health-care planning and policy.

DeVore and Bland were convinced that market analysis, project and operating cost models, and elaborate forecasting could be applied to public and nonprofit health-care projects as well as to private sector construction. But they also recognized the unique needs of health-care facilities in design, capital construction, and financing. Originally HSI was organized to offer design, engineering, construction, and financial expertise in a single package; unfortunately, such broad positioning resulted in a severe competitive handicap as the firm found itself competing against both architects and contractors for jobs. As DeVore himself later remarked, describing the company's early struggles: "We made the classical marketing error of running in 20 different directions at 20 different times."

As contracts began to flow into the firm, DeVore made a crucial decision: HSI was not in the business of architecture. Design would be subcontracted in the future, as would a few smaller services originally offered by the company. Government regulation of health care was mushrooming, especially in Massachusetts, and DeVore was convinced that the firm's future lay in management, financial planning, and construction cost control. By the end of its first decade of operations, the company employed 15 professionals and 9 supporting staff. The backgrounds and experience of HSI professionals varied widely, ranging from hospital administration to real estate development to health-care regulation.

Organization

The Management, Planning, and Financial Services (MPFS) Group, headed by Kelly Breazeale, was the fastest-growing segment of the company. Among the services offered by MPFS were strategic planning, multi-institutional work (involving mergers, consolidations, or sharing of facilities between two or more institutions), and financial feasibility studies (often projecting the results of planned expansion or cutbacks in services). Facility master planning, another MPFS service, included marketing studies as well as operations and management analysis. Certificates of Need (CON) were also handled by this group. The CON process, a series of lengthy regulatory hearings designed to curb unnecessary hospital spending, was

a legal prerequisite in many states to hospital construction, expansion, or introduction of new services.

Marketing studies produced by MPFS could lead to long-range planning projects for the same clients; a CON contract frequently followed. The CON jobs in turn could produce projects for HSI's Project Management Group. In general, Breazeale noted, "Any small-scale specialty study can lead to a long-term relationship with a client." Current MPFS work included joint planning and consolidation studies for the Choate and Symmes hospitals, near Boston. By year end, HSI expected to bill almost $350,000 on this project. Breazeale saw it not only as a major income producer but as an opportunity for the firm to offer innovative solutions to some of the key problems facing hospitals. MPFS had recently completed a long-range market plan for Episcopal Hospital in Philadelphia. This project was considered important as an entree for HSI to the Philadelphia market; it had already produced an invitation to compete for planning work at another hospital.

The Project Management Group, headed by Bob Bland, handled management, financing, and construction of building projects for hospitals, nursing homes, clinics, and other health-care facilities, including doctors' offices and institutional garages. Among other tasks, Bland and his consultants assisted clients in the selection of architects, engineers, and general contractors; established detailed project cost models; submitted frequent reports describing progress toward performance standards and work deadlines; and advised clients in the preparation of documents for regulatory agencies. Projects ranged from a small office building for Goodall Hospital in Sanford, Maine, to a $32 million ambulatory care center for the Massachusetts General Hospital (MGH) in Boston.

The ongoing MGH job was the largest in HSI's history. It had been awarded following a CON project for MGH. DeVore had personally supervised this initial project, which he regarded as a watershed in HSI's development. By planning an ambulatory care center for one of the most prestigious medical centers in the country, DeVore believed HSI had achieved visibility and credibility in addressing a problem that would be faced by almost every major medical center. The CON study for MGH had led directly to similar CON-project management work for Tufts-New England Medical Center, also in Boston. A later recommendation from an MGH administrator had helped HSI win a substantial contract for a feasibility study and strategic plan for ambulatory care at the University of Michigan Medical Center. HSI expected to be competing for project management of the satellite clinic that the MPFS Group had subsequently recommended for Michigan. *Exhibit 1* shows a divisional breakdown of HSI projects according to fees received in the last four months of the most recent fiscal year.

THE HEALTH-CARE CONSULTING ENVIRONMENT

Health care, once the province of apothecaries, snake oil salesmen, and village healers, had become the third largest industry in the United States.

Following the enactment of Medicaid and Medi-

care in the mid-1960s, the government share of total expenditures for personal health care began to increase sharply. Federal and state interest in controlling health-care spending rose simultaneously. In states like Massachusetts where regulation had reached an advanced stage, hospitals were subjected to state and federal investment controls, rate-setting by state commissions, utilization review (to prevent unnecessary or overly long hospital stays) by federally sponsored Professional Standards Review Organizations (PSROs), and a variety of other checks on independent decision making. (See *Exhibits 2* and *3* for data on hospital size, location, and regulation.) HSI consultants considered Connecticut, Maryland, Massachusetts, Michigan, New Jersey, New York, Ohio, and Washington the nation's most heavily regulated states. By comparison, a state like Florida, which ranked very low in state support for Medicaid, was relatively "wide open."

The cost and complexities of health-care administration placed a premium on top management skills. One industry journal predicted that "operations research modeling, trade-off analysis and decision

EXHIBIT 1   DOLLAR VALUE OF FEES ON HSI PROJECTS FOR LAST FOUR MONTHS OF FISCAL YEAR

| Client category | Management, Planning, Financial Services Division | | | | | Project Management Division |
	Strategic planning	Multi-institutional work	Financial feasibilities	Certificates of need	Facility master planning	
Large teaching hospitals, 400 + beds	133				17	386
Community hospitals, 150–400 beds	70	149	6	89		40
Small hospitals, 50–150 beds	16			37		46
Government work	3					
Hospital-based physicians						9
Community physicians' offices	8					12
Neighborhood health centers				9		
Nursing homes	1			15		18
Total	231	149	6	150	17	511

Source: Company records.

EXHIBIT 2 U.S. COMMUNITY HOSPITALS: REGIONAL ANALYSIS*

U.S. census division[†]	Total hospitals	Number of beds						Perceived level of regulation[‡]
		6–99	100–199	200–299	300–399	400–499	500+	
New England	379	142	90	52	41	19	35	1
Middle Atlantic	820	167	211	161	86	47	148	1
South Atlantic	1,014	405	256	137	78	50	88	3
East North Central	1,076	368	271	152	93	73	119	2
East South Central	543	289	128	45	21	26	34	4
West North Central	898	567	153	54	36	26	62	3
West South Central	961	592	196	71	28	23	51	4
Mountain	446	296	68	31	29	8	14	4
Pacific	878	439	217	101	50	32	39	2

*Excludes veterans' and other government hospitals, psychiatric hospitals, convalescent (long-term) hospitals, TB hospitals, and hospital units of nonhospital institutions.
[†]States composing these regions are indicated in *Exhibit 3*.
[‡]Varies from 1 (stringently regulated) to 4 (loosely regulated).
Source: HSI.

game-playing will become commonplace in hospital decision making ... supplemented by the use of outside consultants as task complexity increases."

Competitive Activity

Competitors could be divided into three major groups. First, large general management consulting or accounting firms with branches throughout the U.S.; second, specialized health-care consulting firms offering at least one of the services offered by HSI; and finally, for-profit hospital management and ownership firms.

Health care, initially disregarded by many large consulting firms because it had been viewed as a service function managed by nonprofit institutions, had begun to attract considerable interest from general management consultants. Arthur D. Little (ADL), headquartered in Cambridge, Mass., was particularly active in the field. ADL was the nation's largest management consultant, with over 2,500 employees. The firm maintained an international consulting practice in health care and in recent years had published numerous reports on the industry. A typical project was the development of an entire system of hospitals in Brazil. Booz, Allen and Hamilton, the

second largest American management consultant, based its health and medical services in Chicago.

Specialization in consulting was underlined by the growing importance of big accounting firms.

Bob DeVore felt that only ADL and Booz, Allen offered the firm any real competition in providing creative, contemporary solutions to clients' problems. Even so, DeVore commented,

They lack the follow-through in project management that we offer. It's also an advantage that they're not really interested in the small hospitals. We're not in a position yet to compete regularly with Booz or ADL on a national basis, but we can regionally. By selectively focusing our market efforts, I'll know more about that market than anyone else. HSI will do more homework and apply more principals' time to the job. Actually I love to compete with these guys, because they charge huge fees and we can creep right underneath them. Our close ratio against the big firms is better than 70%—but we compete against them selectively, not all over the country.

DeVore considered the potential threat of the big accounting firms and general management consultants more serious than the challenge posed by any of the specialized health-care consulting groups.

In evaluating competition among the specialized groups, several HSI consultants identified the Tri-

EXHIBIT 3 UNITED STATES CENSUS REGIONS AND DIVISIONS

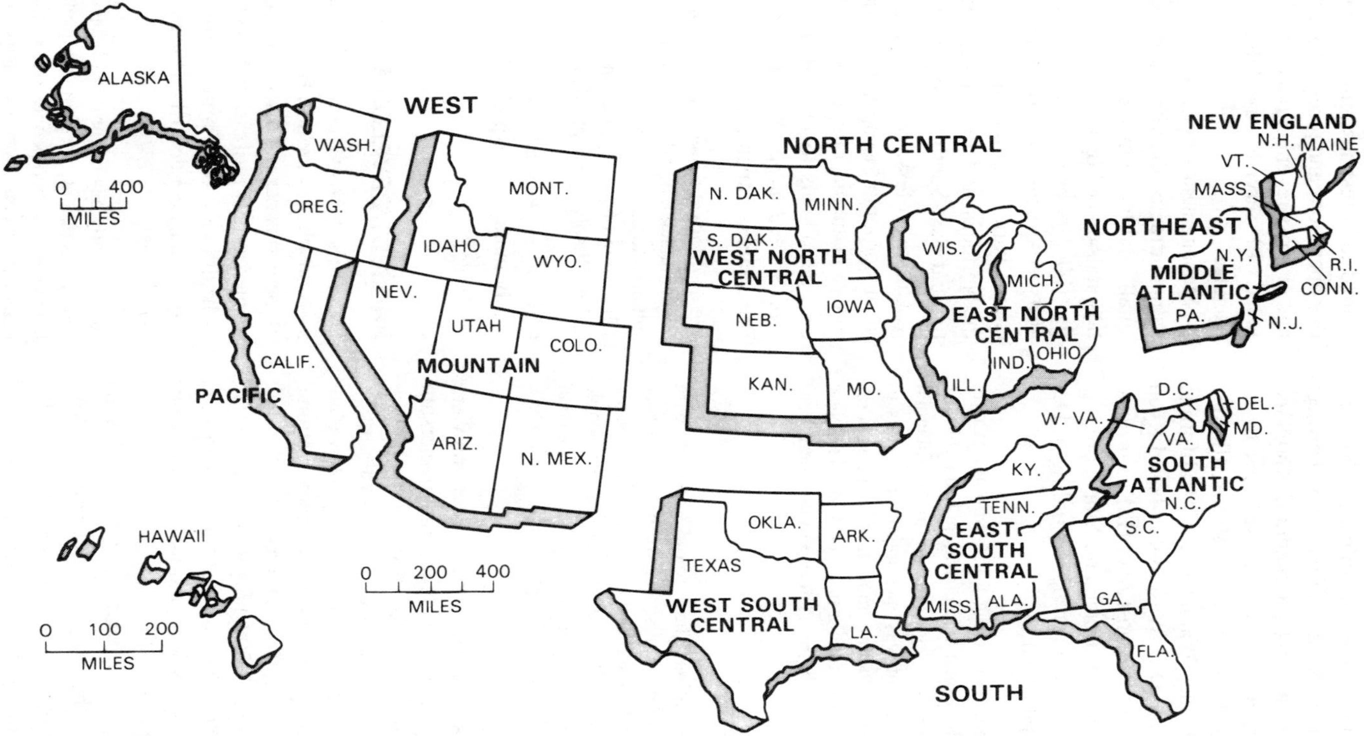

Source: Department of Commerce

Brook Group as their most significant rival. Tri-Brook, unlike most of the other firms, offered project management as well as strategic planning, CON assistance, merger studies, and other services to its clients. It maintained offices in Oak Brook, Illinois; Birmingham, Alabama; Walnut Creek, California; and near Washington, D.C. Washington-based Ryan Advisors also duplicated almost all of HSI's services, and had branch offices in Rome and Singapore.

Most of the firms in this group, according to De-Vore, had been established by

... the old-line hospital consulting firms, who did exactly what the doctors and hospital administrators wanted in the days when there were no regulators or tough financial modes and the government was encouraging hospitals to expand. I don't consider them competitors in the spheres where HSI operates. TriBrook, for instance, closed its New England offices because the regulatory environment here is too tough.

Breazeale disagreed:

I think they *are* competition. They are old-line firms with traditional solutions to problems, and we beat them routinely, but that is not to say that they're not competition. Potential clients respond very well to very senior people who've really been around—they don't always realize that the solutions that were good 20 years ago don't work anymore.

The final factors in the competitive equation were the for-profit hospital management and ownership corporations. Originally investor ownership of hospitals had been limited primarily to small, local groups, often established by doctors; as costs rose and planning and regulation became more complex, national management and ownership chains were formed. One thousand of the 7,000 hospitals in the U.S., accounting for 108,000 of the nation's 1.4 million beds, were owned by local or national organizations and operated for profit.

Through management contracts, typically lasting two to five years, the hospital management firms provided purchasing, cost-saving, and revenue-producing assistance to some 300 independent hospitals (triple the number managed five years earlier). Under the usual contract, the management corporation as-

sumed total responsibility for the hospital's day-to-day operations and received a fee based on a percentage of gross revenue, plus incentive. One major firm listed 40 services available in its management package.

Management services—as well as outside ownership—attracted the interest of a significant portion of small- and medium-sized hospitals. Almost 40% of hospitals owned by national for-profit chains were in the 100–199 bed category; only 2% contained over 400 beds. The proportion of hospitals owned by chains varied significantly by region, being low in the Northeast and high in the Mountain, South Atlantic, and East-South Central regions.

Unlike professional consulting firms, the management corporations advertised their services vigorously, in media ranging from professional health-care periodicals to local daily newspapers and the *Wall Street Journal.* Appraising their relation to HSI, Breazeale commented:

We do different things. Most of our business is in helping clients understand what problems they have and tailoring solutions to those problems. Health-care management firms sell a solution. "The solution to your problem is, hire us and we'll solve your problem."

HSI did occasionally compete for projects at privately managed hospitals, but such invitations were unusual.

PROJECT DEVELOPMENT AT HSI

DeVore's intensive personal contacts and reputation as a consultant were still HSI's most important source of new business. This personal network was augmented as new professionals with their own contracts in health care were brought into the firm. One HSI project manager described the evolution of a proposal as follows:

A job usually begins for us with a letter or phone call from a potential client, presenting a problem. We respond by having at least two people, one of them a potential project manager or better yet a principal in the firm, set up an appointment and go to see them and find out informally what's on their minds. That's really a marketing strategy in two ways: one is to leave an impression with them of how we do business; the other is to show them that we're there to find out more than just what was in the letter.

If the results of that visit appeared promising, the future project manager would write a draft of a proposal, send it to the client, and follow up with a second personal visit, asking for reactions. HSI took preliminary work very seriously; it was not unusual to invest heavily up front in developing a major proposal, "custom-tailored to clients 100%."

After the second visit the proposal was rewritten and resubmitted, and the HSI project manager returned for another visit, this time often accompanied by a junior member of the staff. Negotiations followed: a client group, for example, might feel that they couldn't afford HSI's assistance on the whole project and would ask for advice on how to do one or more segments themselves. Following final revisions, a formal presentation to a board or governing committee was required in 80% of HSI's jobs. Community hospitals usually recruited both their board and their administrators locally. The board of a major academic medical center, in contrast, consisted of well-known business, professional, and public leaders drawn from across the nation.

Usually the company was allowed 1–2 hours to present a proposal, frequently in a highly pressured situation where competitors' presentations preceded and followed HSI's. Communication skills were considered an essential part of the consultant's job, according to Breazeale:

One of the goals of the firm is to hire 100% presentable people: we don't want people who only sit in their office and crank around numbers. Everyone who's hired in the firm is hired with the notion that they either are currently or are capable of becoming a project manager—articulate, carrying themselves well, and relating well to other people. We don't have people who are not capable of client relationships.

Proposals had five major elements. First, HSI's understanding of the client's problem, as constructed from interviews and conversations. Second, the scope of the effort, including an analysis of possible solutions. Third, a detailed time schedule; sometimes

a critical path schedule. Fourth, the resumes of the people who would work on the project. (These included descriptions of previous jobs.) The final component was an estimate of fee. Project work was subdivided in detail and hours of work in each job category were figured for each participant, then multiplied times that person's hourly rate. What the client saw was a flat fee, stating that HSI would do the job in a certain time for a certain amount. Said one manager:

I think that makes an incentive contract; it forces us to look at the market, and say if we go there with a $100,000 fee, that's way out of the league of this particular institution. We can also look at it and say, this is a risky deal, or market conditions ought to make that a more expensive study. In that case we could go from $100,000 to $120,000 without touching the scope of the job.

Depending on how well they knew the client, the HSI team tried to follow up a presentation before a decision was made. These calls and letters were considered a marketing device, to show the firm's continued interest and willingness to change if a presentation had not met the client's needs. The time elapsed from first contact with a client to a signed contract usually exceeded four months.

Professional Lifestyle

The typical project lasted 5–7 months, though complex or highly regulated contracts could require 1–2 years. It had been company policy never to locate consultants at a local office; all business was conducted out of the HSI office in Boston. Kelly Breazeale was not sure whether HSI's lack of branch offices had caused the firm to lose business:

I accept the notion that we are so successfully competitive in New England because we live here and we understand it better. I find it difficult to believe that you can understand an area and carry out successful, indirect, informal marketing when you don't live there. I can also say that none of us like the idea of making 40 round trips to Michigan in order to do a project the way we want to do it. So our desire to set up a branch office is motivated as much by our need to do the work in a *manner* we deem satisfactory as it is by our need to get the work.

The average HSI project manager or senior consultant worked about 55 hours a week. Because of the firm's regional base, even project managers rarely spent more than 6 nights a month away from home. Breazeale estimated that about 40% of his time was spent on "billable" projects, either in planning jobs for which he had primary responsibility or in informally helping others bring their projects along. Approximately 30% of his average week went to marketing: conferring with his staff, developing proposals, making presentations, and meeting with prospective clients. General administration of the MPFS Group and recruitment and support of new consultants accounted for the remainder of his time. HSI had no formal recruitment or training program.

Breazeale enjoyed the variety and intellectual stimulation of the constant problem-solving which consulting required. His feelings were shared by the other senior members of the firm—each of whom, shaped by his own temperament, also saw disadvantages to the job. DeVore's entrepreneurial zest made it very difficult for him to settle down to desk work; he wanted new continents to conquer. For Bland there was a disconcerting aspect to consulting—the need to jump constantly from one set of problems to another. It often occurred to him, he said, that it might be pleasant to work for one institution with one set of problems, one environment, one kind of politics—facing questions that could be known and anticipated.

Communication Efforts

Many professional service firms marketed their skills aggressively through brochures, advertisements in trade journals, and seminars. But more traditional, established members of the profession argued that, "People find us, we don't find them." On DeVore's personal insistence, HSI paid for no advertisements or professional listings. Business came solely through referrals, and it was still a point of pride to DeVore that the company had "never made a cold call." He refused to join either of the two major professional organizations in his field:

They're a marketing device for old-timers. Some people have told me that joining might help HSI establish a base outside New England, but I don't want any identification with that group. If I get in their pack I'm one of them, and then I'm one of twenty.

DeVore felt that his refusal to join was not just a philosophy but a marketing strategy in itself: "HSI's uniqueness is an absolutely essential part of its image." Though very wary of any promotional schemes that might demean HSI's professional status, DeVore was not opposed to promotion if appropriately conducted. He made it a point to speak frequently before groups of hospital administrators and other professionals who might provide contacts. "Marketing is an area where I lack some sophistication," he admitted. "I need to learn more about it."

When a new associate joined the HSI staff, he or she often wrote letters to friends and colleagues announcing the news and including an HSI brochure. At present, there was some debate in the office as to how far the marketing efforts of a professional group like Health Systems could go.

PLANNING COMPANY GROWTH

HSI's senior staff generally agreed that, as Bob Bland put it, "the health care environment is so tightly knit that we can only do so much work in Boston—even in Massachusetts—before we run into conflict-of-interest problems from serving so many competing institutions." (*Exhibit 4* indicates HSI's activities in the New England market.) But Bland urged caution in any expansion, since he was concerned that HSI might spread itself too thin and sacrifice quality. Already his Project Management Group was turning down jobs, and he had almost no time available for recruiting.

One option open to the company was acquisition. DeVore had looked at two smaller health care consulting firms on the East Coast, but was not enthusiastic about the idea.

The firms that were buyable that I knew about were either old-line firms that were declining, or their offshoots. I did not want the association of any of those old-timers or their derivatives. I don't like what they do—besides, I can't

EXHIBIT 4   HSI ACTIVITIES IN THE NEW ENGLAND MARKET

	Total hospitals		Hospitals by bed size			HSI projects by bed size			Total HSI beds
	No.	Beds	50–150	150–400	400 +	50–150	150–400	400 +	
Massachusetts (by county)									
Eastern counties (including Greater Boston)*									
Essex	21	3,709	11	9	1	1	2	1	1,267
Middlesex	37	11,452	10	22	5	3	7	1	3,458
Suffolk	36	10,339	12	16	8	2	4	5	4,584
Norfolk	21	3,024	4	7	0	1	1	0	262
Plymouth	9	2,519	5	2	2	0	1	0	322
Bristol	9	2,227	3	3	3	0	1	0	220
Central and western counties									
Worcester	24	4,720	12	9	3	0	1	0	226
Franklin	2	285	1	1	0	1	1	0	285
Hampshire	8	2,673	4	1	3	0	0	0	0
Hampden	11	2,963	5	4	2	0	0	0	0
Berkshire	5	836	3	2	0	0	0	0	0
Cape Cod and the islands									
Barnstable	3	400	2	1	0	0	0	0	0
Nantucket	1	50	1	0	0	0	0	0	0
Duke's	1	80	1	0	0	0	0	0	0
Maine	50	5,577	37	11	2	4	2	1	1,326
New Hampshire	30	4,352	19	10	1	2	2	0	679
Vermont	16	2,246	12	3	1	1	0	0	100
Rhode Island	19	4,837	8	7	4	0	0	1	494
Connecticut	51	15,132	19	19	13	1	2	1	1,386

*Figures include five projects at mental health care facilities, accounting for 3,674 beds.
Source: Company records.

market-differentiate myself in one breath and then be a businessman and buy them out in the next breath.

Others in the firm had pointed out the problems of acquiring bad staff, as well as good, when a whole firm was purchased. Currently, the greatest general interest centered on opening an HSI branch. Washington, Atlanta, Philadelphia, Cleveland, and Detroit had all been mentioned as possible sites.

One senior consultant strongly favored Atlanta.

Atlanta is a boom town. The whole state of Georgia is just getting started—and has lots of growth potential. Labor and materials are still fairly cheap. Housing projects down there are two-thirds to three-quarters the cost of jobs in New England. Atlanta is the metropolis and sophisticated

hub of the whole Southeast—but as far as housing development or health care goes, it's just beginning to have and handle the kind of problems we've been dealing with up here. In Boston our competition is fierce—but there's a drastic drop in the competitive level of expertise out of state. I say let's maximize that advantage while it lasts.

Breazeale disagreed:

Where we're likely to do poorly is in places where our style and Boston-based credibility are not a factor. I'd like to see us have a chance to reestablish these roots quickly in any move—that's why I support a relatively similar environment like Philadelphia or Washington.

Breazeale felt it important that the firm consider a third expansion site simultaneously with a second;

he didn't want HSI to pin itself geographically into a corner that might make further expansion difficult.

DeVore as yet was undecided. He preferred to think of possible expansion sites as spheres of influence or regional medical networks rather than specific cities. Just as HSI's Boston office reached out to New England and upstate New York, he felt that a Washington office, for example, could reach out to suburban Maryland and Virginia, Philadelphia, and national projects. Alternatively,

... through an Atlanta office HSI could move north to Kentucky and Tennessee, where the local mining industry could provide a lot of projects related to both health care and housing. Ohio is also a real possibility; seven cities of over one million population, decaying urban areas, hospitals located downtown. I think regulation is moving fast into Pennsylvania; a location there could take full advantage of a Boston-type market.

Offices west of the Mississippi had not yet been considered. New York City was dismissed as a "nightmare," whose health-care regulation was so intricate and so area-specific that it would not be profitable to locate a regional office there. "New York City and the rest of New York State are completely different regulatory spheres," said one HSI consultant.

Market Positioning

Another subject of internal debate was the problem of positioning. Most HSI professionals were well aware of views similar to those expressed by an industry observer:

The health-care consulting firm seeking to survive against the giants moving into the field is going to have to position itself very carefully. The key is to target the kinds of hospitals most likely to need its services, identify the size and location of the jobs it can most successfully bid for, and concentrate its efforts on those jobs.

DeVore, in contrast, insisted that HSI had a mission to serve a wide range of institutions—small rural hospitals as well as large academic medical centers. (See *Exhibit 5* for the scope and distribution of recent HSI projects.) Breazeale went further:

What motivates people at HSI is interesting work, having fun, the thrill of discovery. Much of our work will always be "typical" projects, which are not much fun for the high-caliber people once they've learned how to do them. Variety and growth are absolutely essential.

A recent disappointment suffered by the company in rural northern Maine had brought the issue of positioning to the fore. Seven small hospitals seeking a long-range plan had asked HSI and two competitors for presentations. Follow-up phone calls indicated a favorable response to HSI's proposal—but after ten days there was still no word from the hospitals. HSI made four more phone calls. In each case the company was told that its proposal was too expensive—though each respondent conceded that HSI had the best proposal, the best staff, and the best chance of success on the project. Further investigation uncovered a second explanation for HSI's failure: the hospital decision makers did not want to risk real change. Apparently what had been desired was a pro forma study, and the winning proposal had come from a 73-year-old freelance consultant whose ideas for change promised to be essentially cosmetic.

The experience had led to an internal debate: Should HSI bid at all in a situation where the company might appear too high-powered for the client? What would this mean for DeVore's desire to meet the needs of rural and smaller hospitals as well as the needs of major national medical centers? As a former hospital administrator himself, Breazeale was well aware of the arrogant image sometimes presented by consultants. One expert in the field had pointed out that each group of clients had its own "absorption capacity"—its own limit to the scope, pace, and range of innovation it could absorb from a consultant. To what extent, he wondered, should HSI be modifying its image for individual clients? How would a move to a new geographic area affect the answer to that question?

DeVore listened to Breazeale's concerns with interest and added several of his own. "Our problem," he declared at the meeting called to discuss HSI's expansion, "is to devise a marketing strategy for the next three years that will maintain an annual growth target of 30%. It seems to me that we have several

EXHIBIT 5 GEOGRAPHIC DISTRIBUTION OF HSI PROJECTS IN PROGRESS AT YEAR'S END
(Number of Ongoing Projects Inside and Outside New England at Year End)

Client category	Management, Planning, Financial Services Division											
	Strategic planning		Multiinstitutional work		Financial feasibilities		Certificates of need		Facility master planning		Project management	
	NE	Other	NE	Other	NE	Other	NE	Other	NE	Other	NE	Other
Large teaching hospitals, 400 + beds	2	1†							2	1†	1	1§
Community hospitals, 150–400 beds	5		2		1		6				3	
Small hospitals, 50–150 beds	2						1				2	
Government work	1											
Hospital-based physicians											2	
Community physicians' offices	1										3	1‡
Neighborhood health centers							1					
Nursing homes	1						2				1	
Annual totals	12	1	2		1		10		2	1	12	2

NE (New England) = Maine, New Hampshire, Vermont, Massachusetts, Connecticut, and Rhode Island.
† = Philadelphia
‡ = Baltimore
§ = Cincinnati
Source: Company records.

important questions to answer. What kind of image do we want to project? What kind of client do we want to serve? Where are those clients located? And, within the constraints imposed by our professional status, how can we convince those clients to choose HSI?"

Curtis Automotive Hoist

Gordon H.G. McDougall

In September 1990, Mark Curtis, president of Curtis Automotive Hoist (CAH), a Canadian company, had just finished reading a feasibility report on entering the European market in 1991. CAH manufactured surface automotive hoists, a product used by garages, service stations, and other repair shops to lift cars for servicing. The report, prepared by CAH's marketing manager, Pierre Gagnon, outlined the opportunities in the European Community and the entry options available.

Mr. Curtis was not sure if CAH was ready for this move. While the company had been successful in expanding sales into the United States market, Mr. Curtis wondered if this success could be repeated in Europe. He thought, with more effort, that sales could be increased in the United States. On the other hand, there were some positive aspects to the European idea. He began reviewing the information in preparation for the meeting the following day with Mr. Gagnon.

CURTIS AUTOMOTIVE HOIST

Mr. Curtis, a design engineer, had worked for eight years for the Canadian subsidiary of a U.S. automotive hoist manufacturer. During those years, he had spent considerable time designing an above-ground (or surface) automotive hoist. Although Mr. Curtis was very enthusiastic about the unique aspects of the hoist, including a scissor lift and wheel alignment pads, senior management expressed no interest in the idea. In 1980, Mr. Curtis left the company to start his own business with the express purpose of designing and manufacturing the hoist. He left with the good wishes of his previous employer who had no objections to his plans to start a new business.

Over the next three years, Mr. Curtis obtained financing from a venture capital firm, opened a plant in Lachine, Quebec, and began manufacturing the marketing hoist, called the Curtis Lift (*Exhibit 1*).

From the beginning, Mr. Curtis had taken considerable pride in the development and marketing of the Curtis Lift. The original design included a scissor lift and a safety locking mechanism that allowed the

EXHIBIT 1   EXAMPLES OF AUTOMOTIVE HOISTS

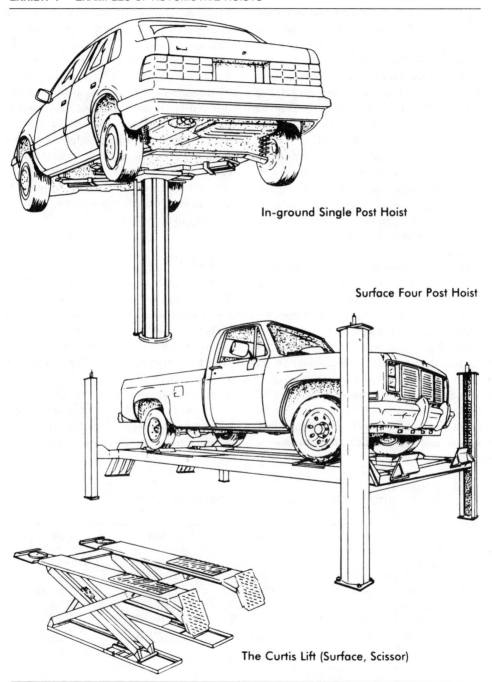

In-ground Single Post Hoist

Surface Four Post Hoist

The Curtis Lift (Surface, Scissor)

hoist to be raised to any level and locked in place. As well, the scissor lift offered easy access for the mechanic to work on the raised vehicle. Because the hoist was fully hydraulic and had no chains or pulleys, it required little maintenance. Another key feature was the alignment turn plates that were an integral part of the lift. The turn plates meant that mechanics could accurately and easily perform wheel alignment jobs. Because it was a surface lift, it could be installed in a garage in less than a day.

Mr. Curtis continually made improvements to the product, including adding more safety features. In fact, the Curtis lift was considered a leader in automotive lift safety. Safety was an important factor in the automotive hoist market. Although hoists seldom malfunctioned, when they did, it often resulted in a serious accident.

The Curtis Lift developed a reputation in the industry as the "Cadillac" of hoists; the unit was judged by many as superior to competitive offerings because of its design, the quality of the workmanship, the safety features, the ease of installation, and the five-year warranty. Mr. Curtis held four patents on the Curtis Lift including the lifting mechanism on the scissor design and a safety locking mechanism. A number of versions of the product were designed that made the Curtis Lift suitable (depending on the model) for a variety of tasks, including rustproofing, muffler repairs, and general mechanical repairs.

In 1981, CAH sold 23 hoists and had sales of $172,500. During the early years, the majority of sales were to independent service stations and garages specializing in wheel alignment in the Quebec and Ontario market. Most of the units were sold by Mr. Gagnon, who was hired in 1982 to handle the marketing side of the operation. In 1984, Mr. Gagnon began using distributors to sell the hoist to a wider geographic market in Canada. In 1986, he signed an agreement with a large automotive wholesaler to represent CAH in the U.S. market. By 1989, the company sold 1,054 hoists and had sales of $9,708,000 (*Exhibit 2*). In 1989, about 60% of sales were to the United States with the remaining 40% to the Canadian market.

INDUSTRY

Approximately 49,000 hoists were sold each year in North America. Typically, hoists were purchased by an automotive outlet that serviced or repaired cars including new car dealers, used car dealers, specialty shops (for example, muffler shops, transmission, wheel alignment), chains (for example, Firestone, Goodyear, Canadian Tire), and independent garages. It was estimated that new car dealers purchased 30% of all units sold in a given year. In general, the specialty shops focused on one type of repair, such as mufflers or rustproofing, while "non-specialty"

EXHIBIT 2
CURTIS AUTOMOTIVE HOIST—SELECTED FINANCIAL STATISTICS
(1987–1989)

	1987	1988	1989
Sales	$6,218,000	$7,454,000	$9,708,000
Cost of sales	4,540,000	5,541,000	6,990,000
Contribution	1,678,000	1,913,000	2,718,000
Marketing expenses*	507,000	510,000	530,000
Administrative expenses	810,000	820,000	840,000
Earnings before tax	361,000	583,000	1,348,000
Units sold	723	847	1,054

Source: Company records.
*Marketing expenses in 1989 included advertising ($70,000), four salespeople ($240,000), marketing manager and three sales support staff ($220,000).

outlets handled a variety of repairs. While there was some crossover, in general CAH competed in the specialty shop segment and, in particular, those shops that dealt with wheel alignment. This included chains such as Firestone and Canadian Tire as well as new car dealers (for example, Ford) who devote a certain percentage of their lifts to the wheel alignment business and independent garages who specialized in wheel alignment.

The purpose of a hoist was to lift an automobile into a position where a mechanic or service person could easily work on the car. Because different repairs required different positions, a wide variety of hoists had been developed to meet specific needs. For example, a muffler repair shop required a hoist that allowed the mechanic to gain easy access to the underside of the car. Similarly, a wheel alignment job required a hoist that offered a level platform where the wheels could be adjusted as well as providing easy access for the mechanic. Mr. Gagnon estimated that 85% of CAH's sales were to the wheel alignment market to service centers such as Firestone, Goodyear, and Canadian Tire and to independent garages that specialized in wheel alignment. About 15% of sales were made to customers who used the hoist for general mechanical repairs.

Purchase Behavior

Firms purchasing hoists were part of an industry called the automobile aftermarket. This industry was involved in supplying parts and service for new and used cars and was worth over $54 billion at retail in 1989, while servicing the approximately 11 million cars on the road in Canada. The industry was large and diverse; there were over 4,000 new car dealers in Canada, over 400 Canadian Tire stores, over 100 stores in each of the Firestone and Goodyear chains, and over 200 stores in the Rust Check chain.

The purchase of an automotive hoist was often an important decision for the service station owner or dealer. Because the price of hoists ranged from $3,000 to $15,000, it was a capital expense for most businesses.

For the owner/operator of a new service center

or car dealership the decision involved determining what type of hoist was required, then what brand would best suit the company. Most new service centers or car dealerships had multiple bays for servicing cars. In these cases, the decision would involve what types of hoists were required (for example, in-ground, surface). Often more than one type of hoist was purchased, depending on the service center/dealership needs.

Experienced garage owners seeking a replacement hoist (the typical hoist had a useful life of 10 to 13 years) would usually determine what products were available and then make a decision. If the garage owners were also mechanics, they would probably be aware of two or three types of hoists but would not be very knowledgeable about the brands or products currently available. Garage owners or dealers who were not mechanics probably knew very little about hoists. The owners of car or service dealerships often bought the product that was recommended and/or approved by the parent company.

COMPETITION

Sixteen companies competed in the automotive lift market in North America: four Canadian and twelve United States firms. Hoists were subject to import duties. Duties on hoists entering the U.S. market from Canada were 2.4% of the selling price; from the U.S. entering Canada the import duty was 7.9%. With the advent of the Free Trade Agreement in 1989, the duties between the two countries would be phased out over a ten-year period. For Mr. Curtis, the import duties had never played a part in any decisions: the fluctuating exchange rates between the two countries had a far greater impact on selling prices.

A wide variety of hoists were manufactured in the industry. The two basic types of hoists were in-ground and surface. As the names imply, in-ground hoists required that a pit be dug "in-ground" where the piston that raised the hoist was installed. In-ground hoists were either single post or multiple post, were permanent, and obviously could not be moved. In-ground lifts constituted approximately 21% of total lift sales in 1989 (*Exhibit 3*). Surface lifts were

EXHIBIT 3
NORTH AMERICAN AUTOMOTIVE LIFT UNITS SALES, BY TYPE
(1987–1989)

	1987	1988	1989
In-ground			
Single post	5,885	5,772	5,518
Multiple post	4,812	6,625	5,075
Surface			
Two post	27,019	28,757	28,923
Four post	3,862	3,162	3,745
Scissor	2,170	2,258	2,316
Other	4,486	3,613	3,695
Total	48,234	50,187	49,272

Source: Company records.

installed on a flat surface, usually concrete. Surface lifts came in two basic types, post lift hoists and scissor hoists. Surface lifts, compared to in-ground lifts, were easier to install and could be moved, if necessary. Surface lifts constituted 79% of total lift sales in 1989. Within each type of hoist (for example, post lift surface hoists), there were numerous variations in terms of size, shape, and lifting capacity.

The industry was dominated by two large U.S. firms, AHV Lifts and Berne Manufacturing, who together held approximately 60% of the market. AHV Lifts, the largest firm with approximately 40% of the market and annual sales of about $60 million, offered a complete line of hoists (that is, in-ground and surface) but focused primarily on the in-ground market and the two post surface markets. AHV Lifts was the only company that had its own direct sales force; all other companies used (1) only wholesalers or (2) a combination of wholesalers and a company sales force. AHV Lifts offered standard hoists with few extra features and competed primarily on price. Berne Manufacturing, with a market share of approximately 20%, also competed in the in-ground and two post surface markets. It used a combination of wholesalers and company salespeople and, like AHV Lifts, competed primarily on price.

Most of the remaining firms in the industry were companies that operated in a regional market (for

example, California or British Columbia) and/or offered a limited product line (for example, four post surface hoists).

Curtis had two competitors that manufactured scissor lifts. AHV Lift marketed a scissor hoist that had a different lifting mechanism and did not include the safety locking features of the Curtis Lift. On average, the AHV scissor lift sold for about 20% less than the Curtis Lift. The second competitor, Mete Lift, was a small regional company with sales in California and Oregon. It had a design that was very similar to the Curtis Lift but lacked some of its safety features. The Mete Lift, regarded as a well-manufactured product, sold for about 5% less than the Curtis Lift.

MARKETING STRATEGY

As of early 1990, CAH had developed a reputation for a quality product backed by good service in the hoist lift market, primarily in the wheel alignment segment.

The distribution system employed by CAH reflected the need to engage in extensive personal selling. Three types of distributors were used: a company sales force, Canadian distributors, and a U.S. automotive wholesaler. The company sales force consisted of four salespeople and Mr. Gagnon. Their main task was to service large "direct" accounts. The initial step was to get the Curtis Lift approved by large chains and manufacturers and then, having received the approval, to sell to individual dealers or operators. For example, if General Motors approved the hoist, then CAH could sell it to individual General Motors dealers. CAH sold directly to the individual dealers of a number of large accounts including General Motors, Ford, Chrysler, Petro-Canada, Firestone, and Goodyear. CAH had been successful in obtaining manufacturer approval from the big three automobile manufacturers in both Canada and the United States. As well, CAH had also received approval from service companies such as Canadian Tire and Goodyear. To date, CAH had not been rejected by any major account but, in some cases, the approval process had taken over four years.

In total, the company sales force generated about 25% of the unit sales each year. Sales to the large "direct" accounts in the United States went through CAH's U.S. wholesaler.

The Canadian distributors sold, installed, and serviced units across Canada. These distributors handled the Curtis Lift and carried a line of noncompetitive automotive equipment products (for example, engine diagnostic equipment, wheel balancing equipment) and noncompetitive lifts. These distributors focused on the smaller chains and the independent service stations and garages.

The U.S. wholesaler sold a complete product line to service stations as well as manufacturing some equipment. The Curtis Lift was one of five different types of lifts that the wholesaler sold. Although the wholesaler provided CAH with extensive distribution in the United States, the Curtis Lift was a minor product within the wholesaler's total line. While Mr. Gagnon did not have any actual figures, he thought that the Curtis Lift probably accounted for less than 20% of the total lift sales of the U.S. wholesaler.

Both Mr. Curtis and Mr. Gagnon felt that the U.S. market had unrealized potential. With a population of 248 million people and over 140 million registered vehicles, the U.S. market was over ten times the size of the Canadian market (population of 26 million, approximately 11 million vehicles). Mr. Gagnon

noted that the six New England states (population over 13 million), the three largest mid-Atlantic states (population over 38 million), and the three largest mid-eastern states (population over 32 million) were all within a day's drive of the factory in Lachine. Mr. Curtis and Mr. Gagnon had considered setting up a sales office in New York to service these states, but they were concerned that the U.S. wholesaler would not be willing to relinquish any of its territory. They had also considered working more closely with the wholesaler to encourage it to "push" the Curtis Lift. It appeared that the wholesaler's major objective was to sell a hoist, not necessarily the Curtis Lift.

CAH distributed a catalogue type package with products, uses, prices, and other required information for both distributors and users. In addition, CAH advertised in trade publications (for example, *Service Station & Garage Management*), and Mr. Gagnon travelled to trade shows in Canada and the U.S. to promote the Curtis Lift.

In 1989, Curtis Lift sold for an average retail price of $10,990 and CAH received, on average, $9,210 for each unit sold. This average reflected the mix of sales through the three distribution channels: (1) direct (where CAH received 100% of the selling price), (2) Canadian distributors (where CAH received 80% of the selling price), and (3) the U.S. wholesaler (where CAH received 78% of the selling price).

Both Mr. Curtis and Mr. Gagnon felt that the company's success to date was based on a strategy of offering a superior product that was primarily targeted to the needs of specific customers. The strategy stressed continual product improvements, quality workmanship, and service. Personal selling was a key aspect of the strategy; salespeople could show customers the benefits of the Curtis Lift over competing products.

THE EUROPEAN MARKET

Against this background, Mr. Curtis had been thinking of ways to continue the rapid growth of the company. One possibility that kept coming up was the promise and potential of the European market. The fact that Europe would become a single market in 1992 suggested that it was an opportunity that should at least be explored. With this in mind, Mr. Curtis asked Mr. Gagnon to prepare a report on the possibility of CAH entering the European market. The highlights of Mr. Gagnon's report follow.

HISTORY OF THE EUROPEAN COMMUNITY

The European Community (EC) stemmed from the 1953 "Treaty of Rome" in which five countries decided it would be in their best interest to form an internal market. These countries were France, Spain, Italy, West Germany, and Luxembourg. By 1990, the EC consisted of 12 countries (the additional seven were Belgium, Denmark, Greece, Ireland, and the Netherlands, Portugal, and the United Kingdom) with a population of over 325 million people.[1] In 1992, virtually all barriers (physical, technical, and fiscal) in the EC were scheduled to be removed for companies located within the EC. This would allow the free movement of goods, persons, services, and capital.

In the last five years many North American and Japanese firms had established themselves in the EC. The reasoning for this was twofold. First, these companies regarded the community as an opportunity to increase global market share and profits. The market was attractive because of its sheer size and lack of internal barriers. Second, in 1992, companies that

---

[1]As of September 1990, West Germany and East Germany were in the process of unification. East Germany had a population of approximately 17 million people.

were established within the community were subject to protection from external competition via EC protectionism tariffs, local contender, and reciprocity requirements. EC protectionism tariffs were only temporary, and would be removed at a later date. It would be possible for companies to export to or establish in the community after 1992, but there was some risk attached.

MARKET POTENTIAL

The key indicator of the potential market for the Curtis Lift hoist was the number of passenger cars and commercial vehicles in use in a particular country. Four countries in Europe had more than 20 million vehicles in use, with France and West Germany having the largest domestic fleets of more than 30 million vehicles followed by Italy and the United Kingdom (*Exhibit 4*). The number of vehicles was an important indicator because the more vehicles in use meant a greater number of service and repair facilities that needed vehicle hoists and potentially the Curtis Lift.

An indicator of the future vehicle repair and service market was the number of new vehicle registrations. The registration of new vehicles was important as this maintained the number of vehicles in use by replacing cars that had been retired. Again, West Germany had the most new cars registered in 1988 and was followed in order by France, the United Kingdom, and Italy.

Based primarily on the fact that a large domestic market was important for initial growth, the selection of a European country should be limited to the "Big

EXHIBIT 4
NUMBER OF VEHICLES (1988) AND POPULATION (1989)

| Country | Vehicles in use (000s) | | New vehicle registrations (000s) | Population (000s) |
	Passenger	Commercial		
West Germany	28,304	1,814	2,960	60,900
France	29,970	4,223	2,635	56,000
Italy	22,500	1,897	2,308	57,400
United Kingdom	20,605	2,915	2,531	57,500
Spain	9,750	1,750	1,172	39,400

Four" industrialized nations: West Germany, France, the United Kingdom, or Italy. In an international survey companies from North America and Europe ranked European countries on a scale of 1 to 100 on market potential and investment site potential. The results showed that West Germany was favoured for both market potential and investment site opportunities while France, the United Kingdom, and Spain placed second, third, and fourth respectively. Italy did not place in the top four in either market or investment site potential. However, Italy had a large number of vehicles in use, had the second largest population in Europe, and was an acknowledged leader in car technology and production.

Little information was available on the competition within Europe. There was, as yet, no dominant manufacturer as was the case in North America. At this time, there was one firm in Germany that manufactured a scissor-type lift. The firm sold most of its units within the German market. The only other available information was that 22 firms in Italy manufactured vehicle lifts.

INVESTMENT OPTIONS

Mr. Gagnon felt that CAH had three options for expansion into the European market: licensing, joint venture, or direct investment. The licensing option was a real possibility as a French firm had expressed an interest in manufacturing the Curtis Lift.

In June 1990, Mr. Gagnon had attended a trade show in Detroit to promote the Curtis Lift. At the show, he met Phillipe Beaupre, the marketing manager for Bar Maisse, a French manufacturer of wheel alignment equipment. The firm, located in Chelles, France, sold a range of wheel alignment equipment throughout Europe. The best-selling product was an electronic modular aligner that enabled a mechanic to utilize a sophisticated computer system to align the wheels of a car. Mr. Beaupre was seeking a North American distributor for the modular aligner and other products manufactured by Bar Maisse.

At the show, Mr. Gagnon and Mr. Beaupre had a casual conversation in which each explained what their respective companies manufactured, they ex-

changed company brochures and business cards, and both went on to other exhibits. The next day, Mr. Beaupre sought out Mr. Gagnon and asked if he might be interested in having Bar Maisse manufacture and market the Curtis Lift in Europe. Mr. Beaupre felt the lift would complement Bar Maisse's product line and the licensing would be of mutual benefit to both parties. They agreed to pursue the idea. Upon his return to Lachine, Mr. Gagnon told Mr. Curtis about these discussions, and they agreed to explore this possibility.

Mr. Gagnon called a number of colleagues in the industry and asked them what they knew about Bar Maisse. About half had not heard of the company, but those who had, commented favorably on the quality of its products. One colleague, with European experience, knew the company well and said that Bar Maisse's management had integrity and would make a good partner. In July, Mr. Gagnon sent a letter to Mr. Beaupre stating that CAH was interested in further discussions and enclosed various company brochures including price lists and technical information on the Curtis Lift. In late August, Mr. Beaupre responded stating that Bar Maisse would like to enter a three-year licensing agreement with CAH to manufacture the Curtis Lift in Europe. In exchange for the manufacturing rights, Bar Maisse was prepared to pay a royalty rate of 5% of gross sales. Mr. Gagnon had not yet responded to this proposal.

A second possibility was a joint venture. Mr. Gagnon had wondered if it might not be better for CAH to offer a counter proposal to Bar Maisse for a joint venture. He had not worked out any details, but Mr. Gagnon felt that CAH would learn more about the European market and probably make more money if they were an active partner in Europe. Mr. Gagnon's idea was a 50-50 proposal where the two parties shared the investment and the profits. He envisaged a situation where Bar Maisse would manufacture the Curtis Lift in their plant with technical assistance from CAH. Mr. Gagnon also thought that CAH could get involved in the marketing of the lift through the Bar Maisse distribution system. Further, he thought that the Curtis Lift, with proper marketing, could gain a reasonable share of the European market. If that happened Mr. Gagnon felt that CAH was likely to make greater returns with a joint venture.

The third option was direct investment where CAH would establish a manufacturing facility and set up a management group to market the lift. Mr. Gagnon had contacted a business acquaintance who had recently been involved in manufacturing fabricated steel sheds in Germany. On the basis of discussions with his acquaintance, Mr. Gagnon estimated the costs involved in setting up a plant in Europe at: (1) $250,000 for capital equipment (welding machines, cranes, other equipment), (2) $200,000 in incremental costs to set the plant up, and (3) carrying costs to cover $1,000,000 in inventory and accounts receivable. While the actual costs of renting a building for the factory would depend on the site location, he estimated that annual building rent including heat, light and insurance would be about $80,000. Mr. Gagnon recognized these estimates were guidelines but he felt that the estimates were probably within 20% of actual costs.

THE DECISION

As Mr. Curtis considered the contents of the report, a number of thoughts crossed his mind. He began making notes concerning the European possibility and the future of the company.

- If CAH decided to enter Europe, Mr. Gagnon would be the obvious choice to head up the "direct investment" option or the "joint venture" option. Mr. Curtis felt that Mr. Gagnon had been instrumental in the success of the company to date.

- While CAH had the financial resources to go ahead with the direct investment option, the joint venture would spread the risk (and the return) over the two companies.
- CAH had built its reputation on designing and manufacturing a quality product. Regardless of the option chosen, Mr. Curtis wanted the firm's reputation to be maintained.
- Either the licensing agreement or the joint venture appeared to build on the two companies' strengths; Bar Maisse had knowledge of the market and CAH had the product. What troubled Mr. Curtis was whether this apparent synergy would work or would Bar Maisse seek to control the operation.
- It was difficult to estimate sales under any of the options. With the first two (licensing and joint venture), it would depend on the effort and expertise of Bar Maisse; with the third option, it would depend on Mr. Gagnon.
- CAH's sales in the U.S. market could be increased if the U.S. wholesaler would "push" the Curtis Lift. Alternatively, the establishment of a sales office in New York to cover the eastern states could also increase sales.

As Mr. Curtis reflected on the situation he knew he should probably get additional information—but it wasn't obvious exactly what information would help him make a "yes" or "no" decision. He knew one thing for sure—he was going to keep his company on a "fast growth" track—and at tomorrow's meeting he and Mr. Gagnon would decide how to do it.

Asian Food Importers of America

Katherine Gallagher
Charles B. Weinberg

"Well, I'm still not convinced that we should get into the Korean honey market," said Gerald Tong, one of two executive vice-presidents of Asian Food Importers of America. "We've built a $15 million business by doing what we know best, importing Asian foods into North America. I can see that exporting Canadian honey to Korea has potential, but is it sound enough for us to go ahead with now?''

"Gerald, we built this business by taking risks," said Bonita Woo, the firm's other executive vice-president. "The marketing plan is well researched and the time to move is now. If anything, I think the plan is too cautious. I admit that it'll take several years until it's profitable, but it's a real opportunity. Pardon the pun, but it's a 'honey' of a deal."

Michael Chan, president and founder of Asian Food, felt it was time to make a decision. A year earlier, his young cousin, David Chan, who operated the Canadian arm of the business, out of Vancouver, British Columbia, had become convinced that exporting Canadian honey to South Korea was a great opportunity. Now, in early February 1988, David Chan had just presented the marketing plan he and

his staff, with the help of outside consultants, had spent considerable time putting together.

"Okay, let's review this one more time," said Michael Chan. "Let's meet Monday morning at 8:00 a.m. and go through all the details again. We'll stay as long as necessary to reach a decision. Can you clear your schedules for Monday?"

COMPANY BACKGROUND[1]

Asian Food Importers of America was a San Francisco firm specializing in the import, distribution and wholesaling of foods from Asian Pacific countries. It employed about 50 people in its San Francisco head office, and branch offices were located in several Asian cities, including Seoul, Hong Kong, Taipei, Bangkok and Jakarta. United States offices were located in several cities, including New York, Chicago and Los Angeles. There was also a Canadian office in Vancouver, and plans were in place to open another office in Toronto to serve the large Asian market there. (See *Exhibit 1* for a financial statement.)

---

[1]Some corporate data in this case are disguised. Unless otherwise noted, all figures are in U.S. dollars.

EXHIBIT 1   ASIAN FOOD IMPORTERS OF AMERICA: FINANCIAL SUMMARY OF OPERATIONS (000's)

	1982	1983	1984	1985	1986	1987*
Net sales	$6,920	$8,079	$9,611	$12,672	$13,652	$14,701
Cost of product sold	5,363	6,249	6,997	8,638	9,270	9,820
Gross profit	1,557	1,831	2,614	4,034	4,383	4,881
Marketing, administrative, and general expenses	900	1,082	1,579	2,562	2,798	3,133
Operating income	657	749	1,035	1,472	1,585	1,748

*In 1987, sales of imports of food products to North America (86.2% to the U.S., 13.8% to Canada) were $11.4 million (78% of total sales), sales of imports of non-food products were $2.9 million (20%), and sales of exports of all products were $0.3 million (2%). The import of food products accounted for 85% of operating income, the import of non-food products accounted for 13% of operating income, and exports accounted for 2% of income. The percentages for both sales and income had remained virtually unchanged (within +/− 2%) over the past three years.

Asian Food Importers of America started modestly twenty years earlier when Michael Chan, then a recent immigrant from Hong Kong, began importing Chinese specialty foods to sell in his grocery store in San Francisco's Chinatown area. Asian Food had grown steadily, although it had experienced a few setbacks. In its first few years, overly optimistic estimates of market potential for some items led to losses. It also had intermittent problems with getting suppliers to provide consistent product quality; occasionally, lapses in product quality had been very costly. However, during the 1980s, increasing numbers of Asian immigrants in the U.S.,[2] as well as greater acceptance of and curiosity about Asian cultures in the Caucasian population, had led to market growth for many Asian food imports.

In 1985, the company had opened an office in Vancouver, run by Michael Chan's cousin David, who had received an MBA from the University of British Columbia the year before, after emigrating from Hong Kong in 1979. David was only 28 in 1988, but he had done a good job building business in Canada. While Michael Chan was pleased with David's aggressive approach, he sometimes worried

that his young cousin was inclined to do things too quickly.

Asian Food's management had lately been investigating opportunities for exporting North American products. Over the years, they had built an extensive network of contacts in Asia. Many of these, in appreciation for the job that Asian Food had done in selling their products in the U.S. and Canada, had expressed a willingness to reciprocate in their home markets. This seemed like a worthwhile opportunity. Also, Michael Chan believed that it would be prudent to balance the company's risks and vulnerability by being both an exporter and an importer. When David Chan heard about this new direction for the company, he suggested that Canadian honey be considered for export to Korea. Since the U.S. was a net importer of honey, it did not seem worthwhile to consider the export of U.S. honey when Canadian honey was readily available. David's enthusiasm and hard work had resulted in the marketing plan Asian Food's management was presently considering. Honey was the first product to be seriously considered for export.

CANADIAN HONEY

Honey is a sweet, sticky substance made by honeybees from the nectar of flowers. According to a recent market research survey, almost 80% of Americans claim to be users of honey; it is perceived as a whole-

[2]A change in the immigration laws in 1965 allowed for a higher quota of immigrants from the Eastern Hemisphere than the Western. The two largest sources of immigrants were the Philippines (first) and China (second).

some, natural food. Honey consists mostly of glucose and fructose, although there are also traces of proteins and vitamins.

The two forms of honey, liquid and solid, do not differ in content. Conversion between liquid and solid forms and back is easily accomplished by temperature changes. There are also two types of honey, pasteurized and unpasteurized. In pasteurized honey, yeasts, which might ferment the honey, have been killed by heat.

The flavor of the honey depends on the flowers from which the honeybees collect nectar. For instance, honey from alfalfa and clover is golden-colored, with a light smell and taste; buckwheat honey is dark-chocolate colored and has a very strong smell. Honey from different flowers can be mixed to get special characteristics. In addition, flavors such as strawberry or cream can be added to the honey.

There were four grades of Canadian honey, unimaginatively labelled No. 1, No. 2, No. 3 and No. 4, with No. 1 honey being the highest quality. The grade depended on the honey's color, smell, taste, water content, total sugar content, amount of crystallization, stickiness, and so on. "Good" honey should be golden-colored, the smell and the taste should be "good," specific gravity should be 1.4 or higher, the total sugar content should be high (the less saccharase—a sugar compound—the better), and the honey should crystallize very well at room temperature. Stringent government regulations controlled the quality of Canadian honey.[3]

THE KOREAN HONEY MARKET

When they first considered exporting honey to Korea, David Chan's group outlined what they believed the firm's strengths and weaknesses would be in this market. They saw three main strengths. First, Asian Food was in a strong financial position, with retained earnings of several million dollars. Second, the company's experience dealing with Asian food concerns had given them "connections" in most Asian countries, including Korea. Finally, there was an existing infra-structure in place to ensure the efficient movement of food products. Of particular importance were the shipping, customs brokerage, and telecommunications networks.

These strengths were balanced by two serious weaknesses. First, the company had no experience exporting to Korea. Even though Asian Food had done some limited exporting to Japan, the planning group recognized that Korean culture and the business environment there were somewhat different. Second, Asian Food was a trading house—the middleman—not the producer. It therefore had little control over suppliers, especially with respect to such crucial factors as quality, quantity, and packaging technology. The positive relationships with its Asian suppliers that Asian Food had developed and cultivated over the years had meant that this had largely ceased to be a problem on the import side of the business, but the reliability of Canadian honey suppliers was unknown.

What was known, however, was quite a bit about the Korean honey market. A few months earlier, David Chan had organized an extensive review of the situation. A Korean consultant had collected data on Korean attitudes toward honey, as well as the regulatory situation.

Korean Consumers

Koreans traditionally regard honey, not as a food, but as a medicinal substance. It is thought to be both a source of vigor and a "miracle medicine" that sustains good health. For instance, honey is used after medical operations to speed recovery. Diluted with hot water, it is said to cure a hangover. More commonly, sliced ginseng is pickled with honey and eaten a couple of times a day to maintain good health. Although western medicine has not demonstrated that it has any curative or preventative properties, Koreans maintain that honey is an invaluable instrument of preventative medicine.

Canadian honey was perceived to be of higher

---

[3]Canadian regulations required at least 78% sugar content and allowed no saccharase, no artificial sweeteners, and no artificial colour in honey. Up to 18.6% moisture was allowed.

quality and lower cost than the domestic product. According to data collected by David Chan's assistant, Canadian honey was one of the most popular gift items sent by Korean immigrants to their relatives back home. Many Korean visitors to Canada bought 20 to 30 kilograms of honey to take back to Korea.

In Korea, honey was bought at numerous herb stores or honey specialty stores, usually by women—not for themselves, but for their husbands, fathers-in-law, and mothers-in-law—in their role as guardians of family health.[4] Korean shoppers did not seem to have confidence that domestic honey was "pure." Several shoppers were overheard querying shopkeepers, "Is it pure honey? I hope I'm buying real (pure) honey this time." Wealthy Koreans sometimes went as far as seeking out farmers to find "real" honey, often at very high prices.

Demand and Supply

Even given the lack of consumer confidence in the product, there was strong demand for honey in Korea, and research led David Chan's group to believe that demand would increase. At the same time, it seemed likely that the domestic supply of honey would not keep up with demand.

In 1988, there were about 41 million people in

Korea.[5] In 1986, the last year for which there were figures, per capital consumption of honey had increased to about 0.45 kilogram from 0.20 kilogram in 1979. In comparison, consumption in the Canadian province of British Columbia, where David Chan's Vancouver office was located, was about 1.2 kilogram per person, typical for North America.

David Chan believed that Korean demand for honey would continue to increase. He saw three reasons for the expansion of the market. First, Koreans appeared to be becoming more health conscious. Expenditures on food and beverages as a percentage of total household expenditure had decreased from 48.1% in 1980 to 44.6% in 1985 while medical and health-related expenditures had increased from 3.9% in 1980 to 4.3% in 1985. Second, honey was becoming more affordable. The average monthly earning power of workers was increasing while the per unit price of honey was decreasing (*Exhibit 2*). Finally, David Chan anticipated that, as they used it more frequently, Korean consumers would start to consider honey a food, rather than just a medicinal substance.

The growing demand for honey in Korea was not being met by domestic production. In 1986, total

---

[4]Korean tradition called for a woman to put the needs and desires of her in-laws and husband ahead of those of her own.

[5]Major cities were the capital, Seoul (population 10 million), Busan (3.5 million), Taegu (2 million), and Incheon (1.3 million). The population growth rate was about 1.25% and population density was 419 per square kilometre. Recently the government had recommended that families have only two children, and imposed penalties on families with more children. Koreans were well-educated: almost everyone finished high school, and most went to university.

EXHIBIT 2
KOREAN EARNINGS AND PRICE OF HONEY (IN WON)

	1982	1983	1984	1985	1986
Average Monthly Income per Worker	245,981	273,119	296,907	324,283	350,965
Price of Honey per Kilogram (at Farm)	9,700	10,104	10,090	10,052	9,827
Price Ratios (%)	3.8	3.6	3.3	3.1	2.8

Note: In 1986, $1.00 = 880 Won

domestic honey production was only 18.5 million kilograms (*Exhibit 3*). There were several reasons for low honey production. First, the average Korean honey farmer kept only about 9 hives. Beekeeping was rarely a farmer's primary occupation; it tended to be a sideline or hobby. Second, unit production per hive was low. This was a result of scarcity of source-flowers due to widespread rice farming (rice does not produce source-flowers), short blooming seasons for what source-flowers there were, and the fact that the time of greatest source-flower bloom coincided with heavy rains, preventing bees from collecting nectar. Finally, many Korean beekeepers were still using "non-improved" bees, which are not highly productive.

It was David Chan's contention that the supply of domestic honey would only increase marginally and might even decrease or become uneconomical in the next few years. As Korea's population increased, more and more farmland was being developed for urban use. As honey production is heavily dependent on the availability of land, geographical environments, and proper weather conditions, this decrease in farmland would limit or decrease honey production.

Price

As one might expect in a situation of excess demand, honey in Korea was not cheap. The price ranged from $10 to $100 per kilogram. Honey at the lower end of the price range had recently been introduced in grocery and department stores by a food processing company, Dong Seo Foods, as one of its food lines. Honey at the higher end of the price range was supposedly collected from the honeycombs of wild bees, and was sold either at herbal medicine stores, at honey specialty stores, or directly by farmers. The bulk of Korean honey was sold through herbal medicine stores and honey specialty stores.

Distribution

Although no one firm dominated the distribution system, the wholesale herbal medicine distributors, which supplied herbal medicine stores, were major players. Major competitors were the domestic honey producers, who often sold honey (as a medicine) directly to customers, to herbal medicine stores in the cities, or to the Agricultural Co-op.

Recently, several Korean food companies, such as Dong Seo Foods, had started marketing honey through domestic food channels. Dong Seo Foods was well known in the Korean food processing industry. They bought their honey directly from domestic producers, processed, packaged, and labelled it, then sold it through large food stores. The product was not high quality, as was typical of most Korean honey. Other distributors sold honey through department stores.

Regulatory Changes

Until 1987, honey could be imported only by firms approved by the Ministry of Agriculture, or by the Head of the Agriculture Co-op with permission from

EXHIBIT 3
NUMBER OF KOREAN HONEY FARMS AND PRODUCTION

	1982	1983	1984	1985	1986 (Est.)
Farms (000's)	51.9	54.5	53.2	51.5	52.8
Hives (000's)	395	444	451	467	475
Production (mil. kg)	14.13	15.98	16.24	16.81	18.45
Growth rate of production	N.A.	13%	2%	4%	10%

the Ministry of Agriculture. There was a 25% tariff. At the end of 1987, however, a trade surplus, coupled with political pressure from the outside, notably the U.S., prompted the Korean government to relax certain import restrictions. As a result, honey imports were allowed, but for hotel use only, and imported honey was required to have a sugar content of at least 78%, higher than the 76% required for the domestic product.

The consultant hired by David Chan reported that Korean consumer groups were complaining that the price for honey was too high. Indications were that import restrictions on honey would be relaxed soon. The consultant also expected that eventually the government would eliminate the protection of domestic honey production, since honey was not the main source of income for honey farmers, and they were relatively inefficient. This move would be consistent with recent de-regulation in the wine industry, where the government had announced its intention to open up 40% of the market within two years. If and when this happened, Korean importers might consider several countries. The major producers of honey were: the U.S.S.R. (190 million kg), China (150 million kg), the U.S.A. (91 million kg), Mexico (47 million kg), Canada (38 million kg), and Australia (27 million kg).

Although the U.S.S.R. and China were the biggest producers, under the present administration, it seemed unlikely that the Korean government would encourage substantial imports from Communist countries. Mexico and Australia were major producers but did not have as much political clout as Canada, due to the Korean trade surplus with Canada. The U.S. was also a large producer, but domestic production was insufficient for export—the U.S. was a net importer of honey. Therefore, Asian Food's expectation was that the Korean government would look favorably at Canadian imports of honey.

CANADIAN HONEY IN THE KOREAN MARKET

David Chan's group believed that Canadian honey was superior to Korean honey in several ways. The Canadian government imposed higher quality specifications than the Korean government.[6] Canadian honey contained less moisture, more total sugar, and finer particles. Many Canadian brands of honey exceeded the minimum specifications. In contrast, Korean honey production practices were not regulated. Beekeepers often added sugar to the honey to increase volume.

Second, the flavor of Canadian honey was preferred to that of Korean honey. In Canada, alfalfa, clover, buckwheat, and fruit tree blossoms are the main source-flowers. These produce better-tasting honey than do the source-flowers commonly found in Korea. In addition, lower levels of air pollution in Canada and a longer collection season (due to the absence of a rainy season) contribute to better taste.

Canadian honey also had a price advantage. The lowest priced honey in Korea retailed for $11 per kilogram, far above the average retail price of $6 in Canada. As shown in *Exhibit 4*, Asian Food could be very price competitive because the basic cost was only $3.70 for high quality honey landed in Korea.

Supplier Decision

Asian Food had a choice of a number of suppliers of Canadian honey. It had tentatively decided on Bee Star, the largest honey supplier in Canada. It collected honey from farmers, then processed and packaged it for wholesalers. Bee Star also did some promotion in Canada and the U.S.

Bee Star was already exporting honey to more than twenty countries, so the brand was well recognized internationally, including Japan. Bee Star had shown an interest in expanding its market in association with Asian Foods, and it seemed clear that they could consistently supply honey for export. Moreover, Bee Star would agree to give Asian Foods an exclusive license for Korea provided minimum quantities (to be specified in contract negotiations) were ordered each year.

---

[6]Korean government specifications required the sugar content to be at least 76%, allowed up to 21% moisture and saccharase up to 7%. No artificial sweeteners nor artificial colors were allowed.

EXHIBIT 4
EXPORT COST ANALYSIS

Honey price/kg	Description
$2.75	Wholesale price at Vancouver port ($2.60 to $2.90)
0.13	Shipping cost; 12 (1 kg) jars/case, 1000 cases in a container
0.14	Insurance, custom fees, etc.
0.68	Tariff; 25% of invoice price
$3.70	Price at the Korean port

Note: The wholesale price is for Canada No. 1 white honey (Alfalfa-Clover).

In order to take advantage of the positive reputation of Canadian honey, packaging and labelling would emphasize the origin of the "Canadian" product and the "purity" of the honey. Consequently, the product would be packaged and sealed in Canada, and labelled "Sealed in Canada."

MARKETING PLAN

Michael, Gerald, and Bonita had all agreed that the Korean honey market was worthy of further investigation. Consequently, David Chan had been put in charge of a three-person team to develop a marketing plan. The basic planning assumptions were that Asian Food Importers of America was to enter the Korean honey market, supply of Canadian honey was viewed as assured, and no more than $500,000 would be invested. The following consists of the main points from the four phase plan that the team developed.

A FOUR PHASE MARKETING PLAN

The first phase (hotels) deals with the current situation, where we can only import honey for use in hotels under current import regulations. In this stage, efforts will be focused on hotels to develop goodwill with the government and gain a foothold in the Korean market.

The second phase (hotels and medicine) will go into action when the Korean government opens the honey market and relaxes import restrictions. (Some restrictions may still apply.) At this stage, consumers

still consider honey as a medicine rather than food. The main strategy is to build sales in the medicine market and eventually obtain dominance in this market segment. At the same time, a minor thrust into the food market will be attempted.

The third stage (medicine and food) will come into effect when consumers' attitudes toward honey change. In this phase most consumers will have undergone a cultural change and consider honey as food, rather than medicine. Although honey-as-medicine sales will remain strong, the food market will grow considerably. The main strategy is to hold and maintain the medicine market segment and to build the food market segment.

The fourth stage (food) will be reached when the abundance of honey turns it into a commodity. Similar to the current situation in North America, Koreans will have sufficient income to purchase honey as a regular item. The strategy in this phase is to hold and maintain profits, in the face of anticipated competitive pressures. At the present time, this phase of the marketing plan would not be developed.

Phase I

Environment. There are several significant aspects of the market to consider. This will be the first time Canadian honey will have been introduced to Korea for commercial purposes. Many Koreans have tasted Canadian honey, but it was as a souvenir of travel or a gift from relatives who had emigrated to

Canada. In addition, Canadian honey will not be available directly to Koreans, because all imported honey will be used only in hotels. We need to consider the special business environments of this phase.

On the legal side, there is an import restriction at this time: honey can be imported for hotel use only. We expect this to change, but it will likely be done step-by-step because of pressure from Korean honey producers.

In terms of market size, there are roughly 300 hotels in Korea, with about 160 concentrated in the four largest cities: Seoul, Busan, Taegu, and Incheon.

Although there is no major importer at this time, the threat of competition from other Canadian sources, as well as Australia, needs to be kept in mind. The strongest selling point for Canadian honey is the image of Canada as a big, unspoiled, natural country. In addition to foreign competitors, there are several local honey companies like Dong Seo Food and Han Yang Food. Since the local honey price is very high, if Asian Food introduces Canadian honey at a low price, we expect the competition will give up the small hotel market.

Product. The main consumers of honey in Korean hotels will be foreigners, we will offer only high quality liquid honey (Canada No. 1 White), because most foreigners prefer it. This will not only please foreigners, it will also give us a small foothold with Korean consumers, as Koreans with high incomes are also an important segment of the hotel market. This is very important, because we plan to import Canadian honey for consumer use in the next phase.

We have decided against introducing other forms of high quality honey during this phase, since the goal is simply to gain a strategic foothold in Korea in anticipation of the next phase. Profitability is not a major goal in Phase I.

Price. We will charge the lowest price possible in order to get into more hotels, thereby allowing more Koreans to be exposed to Canadian honey. The low price of Canadian honey, which Koreans might take as a signal of low quality, will not be known to potential consumers, since the hotels will mark it up, so it should not have a negative impact on the image of Canadian honey.

The lowest price for break even is $6 per kilogram (*Exhibit 5*). We do not know the likely price of other imported honeys, but transportation and other related costs will be similar to ours. As for production costs in Australia, we believe that they are about the same

EXHIBIT 5
DERIVATION OF BREAK EVEN PRICE (3 year average)
(Before lobbying costs)

Cost /kg (at Korean port)		$3.70
Annual sales (kg)	(80 hotels at 500 kg/hotel) =	40,000 kg
Cost of goods sold	(40,000 × $3.70) =	$148,000
Administration and promotional costs		$92,000
Total cost		$233,000
Approximate minimum price	$240,000 / 40,000 =	$6/kg

Assumptions:
1) Average hotel purchase = 500 kg/yr
2) Market size and share (at end of phase I): 160 hotels in 4 cities × 50% = 80 hotels
3) Incremental personnel costs = $40,000
   Office rental = $20,000
   Set-up costs (written off over 3 years) = $17,000
   Sampling program (average over 3 years) = $ 5,000
   Recipe book = $10,000
   Total: $92,000

as ours. We could price as much as $4 per kilogram more and still be substantially below current Korean prices.

Distribution. At present, honey used in hotels bears the brand name of the distributor, such as Dong Seo or Han Yang. The main focus of Dong Seo and Han Yang is coffee and various drinks, respectively; honey is not their chief interest. They gather honey directly from producers, process it minimally, and then distribute it through their own channels. The larger hotels purchase honey directly from the company-owned distribution agency but the smaller hotels usually buy at nearby supermarkets. The quality of this honey is lower than Canadian honey, and the price is considerably higher.

Our strategy for distribution is to set up our own office with two salespeople in Seoul. This location has been chosen because it is the political, economic, cultural, and social center of Korea. It also has one third of the total hotels in the nation. Once the Seoul office has been established, we will use it as a base to open direct channels to hotels in other main cities.

Promotion. We will pursue three different promotion strategies. The first is person-to-person and door-to-door. This is possible because the hotel market is limited in terms of location and number. Main targets will be restaurant managers and/or cooks. A close relationship between a salesperson and a manager (and/or a cook) is a very important factor for sales in Korea, and we need to establish and maintain good relationships. Our second strategy is to distribute free samples to hotels. Because we are certain that Canadian honey is of much better quality than the local product, as well as lower in price, we feel this will be a good way to establish relationships with the hotels. The sample will be the same in size and shape as the honey that we will be selling. The salespeople will carry these samples with them when they visit the hotels.

Third, we will print and distribute recipe booklets which also tell the Canadian honey story. The booklets will give hotel cooks new ideas for using honey, and can also be used in the consumer phases.

Marketing Budget. We can allocate up to $500,000 for this phase, which we believe will last about three years. We estimate that this will be sufficient to set up and operate the Seoul office. One manager, currently based in Korea, will be responsible for the initial business and two salespeople will be employed locally. At this time, we have no plans to send additional people to Korea. Space adjacent to our current offices in Seoul is available. Incremental personnel costs will be $40,000 annually and office rental (and related expenses) will be $20,000 annually.

Set-up costs are estimated to be roughly $50,000: $30,000 for two cars and $15,000 for furniture and fixtures. Another $5,000 is allocated for other expenses, such as handling charges.

The cost of the sampling program is expected to be $10,000 (at most) in the first year, and minimal thereafter. The recipe booklet will cost $10,000 in each of the three years. We feel it is important to update the recipe books on a regular basis.

The major portion of the budget for this phase will be allocated to government lobbying. We estimate it at up to $225,000 ($75,000 for each of three years).

Timing. Asian Food will start exporting Canadian honey to Korea in January 1989. We expect to concentrate on Seoul in the first year and gradually expand to Busan, Taegu, and Incheon. The Phase I strategies will be continued until the Korean government opens up the honey market. Although we cannot pinpoint when this will be, we do not anticipate that it will be more than three years, given Korea's current trend toward a more open market.

Marketing Action Plan. The three goals are: (1) take 50% of hotel restaurant market in the four major cities by the end of three years, (2) open the market as soon as possible, and (3) accumulate experience. Two potential problems exist: (1) Korean honey producers may resist the government's opening of the market. The strength of their resistance will be an important determinant of the timing of the lifting of import restrictions. Thus the Korean government must be cultivated in a careful (and silent) way.

(2) Other exporters will see, and go after, the same opportunity.

Phase II

Environment. With import restrictions removed, the potential for the honey market is huge. The food market will be larger than the medicine market. At this time, the medicine market is over $200 million annually. Consequently, in this phase, we will begin to target consumers. We expect substantial market share and commensurate profits. At this stage, special business environments become crucial.

First, we anticipate that the Korean government will not open the market completely, chiefly because of political pressure from honey producers and the possibility of a swing in public opinion against opening agricultural markets to international competition. On the other hand, the precedents in Korea point to a more open economy. Furthermore, the loosening of agricultural trade restrictions are expected to be a major issue in the 1992 General Agreement on Tariffs and Trade (GATT) negotiations in which most countries would participate. Our main concern is the size of the honey quota and the way it will be allocated among various countries. We are guessing that the size of the initial quota will be 5% of local production and that the allocation will be based on previous trade volumes in other goods. This puts us in a good position.

We expect that local honey production will reach 22 million kilograms per year by 1992, up from about 18 million kilograms in 1986, and honey imports will reach 1.1 million kilograms per year. The value of the Korean honey market (local and imported) is estimated to be roughly $231 million a year, at retail; the imported honey market will be about $11 million a year (based on $10 per kilogram).

Consumer behavior must also be considered. The traditional Korean view of honey is as a medicine or health tonic. Although we believe this attitude can be changed so that consumers view honey as food, such a change will take time to accomplish. That is the overriding goal of Phase II. Closely related to this is the need to ensure consistently high quality.

Because honey has been so expensive and quality has been so low, the reputation of the honey trade is poor: hence the Korean proverb that "the father does not believe the son in the honey trade."

Another important aspect of consumer behavior is that housewives purchase the honey. This must be taken into account in all strategies. We have made contacts with a leading Korean market research firm. They are prepared to, and capable of, doing a major market research survey of consumers, but advise against doing so until a year before we are ready to enter the consumer market directly.

There will be powerful local competition from companies such as Dong Seo Food and Han Yang Food.

Product. Until recently, Koreans have been unfamiliar with liquid honey. Whenever they think of honey, Koreans imagine creamy honey. One food company started distributing liquid honey at a low price a few years ago, but the introduction was unsuccessful, because creamy honey is so well established as a medicine.

Thus, in this phase, we will export two different kinds of Canadian honey. For hotels, liquid honey will still be provided, but creamy honey will also be available. For the consumer market, creamy honey will be offered, except for department stores, where liquid honey will also be available. No matter what the form, market, or channel, the Canadian honey we export will be the premium product.

Packaging will differ in the hotel and consumer markets, in order to allow us to charge different prices. It is crucial that honey will be labelled and sealed in Canada for authenticity.

Price. For the hotel market, we will continue the previous pricing policy, for two reasons. First, profit from the hotel market is negligible no matter what the price, and, second, our high quality image will be reinforced if our product is widely available in hotels.

For the consumer market, we plan to charge a premium price, equivalent to at least $11 per kilogram (in today's dollars). The important thing in the

Korean honey trade in Korea is, as mentioned before, authenticity. The higher price will reassure customers that quality is high. Furthermore, under quota restrictions, products with higher prices are more profitable.

Distribution. Channels for the hotel market will continue as set up.

During this phase of the marketing plan, we will begin distributing Canadian honey to consumers through herbal medicine dealers. We will focus on the largest four cities, because under a 5% import quota, distribution to the smaller cities will be less profitable, given the higher costs of reaching these markets.

The department store channel will be a second focus. It is not unusual for department stores in Korea to sell imported or gourmet foods in a special section of the store. Since it is recognized in Seoul that the department stores deal with the high quality and expensive commodities, it is consistent with our product strategy to place Canadian honey here. In addition, through this channel, we will be able to monitor changes in the perceptions of honey (as a medicine or as a food). This will become an important factor in Phase III.

We will avoid supermarkets at this stage, because the honey in supermarkets is inexpensive and therefore incompatible with our high quality image.

Promotion. We will, at this stage, establish one more office with two salespeople in Busan, the largest port and second largest city in Korea. The Seoul office will be in charge of the northern part of the country and the Busan office will take care of the south.

We are also considering three advertising strategies. The first is advertising through herbal medicine periodicals. There are over 3,000 herbal medicine clinics in Korea, and the influence of the herbal medicine doctor is strong. Advertisements in these periodicals will be based on a chemical analysis of honey, and we expect that herbal medicine doctors will begin recommending Canadian honey to their patients.

We will also advertise in women's magazines, because women make most honey purchases. The

high quality and the authenticity of Canadian honey will be emphasized.

Finally, recipe booklets will be distributed to department store customers. These booklets will be similar to those used for hotels in Phase I. Here we intend to introduce the idea that honey is a food, and show housewives how to use it.

Marketing Budget. During Phase II, we expect to become profitable. For setting up the Busan office, we will allocate the same amount of money as for the Seoul office and have similar staffing policies. Additional sales assistants will be hired in both cities as necessary to provide sufficient market coverage. We anticipate that all personnel costs (including salary and expenses) will be 10% of sales.

Lobbying of the government will also be necessary, to encourage either the complete opening of the market or a larger quota. But the government lobbying at this stage will be at a lower rate, but protracted. Thus we allocate $50,000 annually for ten years.

The cost of the advertising program can only be roughly estimated. Personal selling will be strongly supported by the advertising strategies described above. We budget advertising at 5% of sales, though market research will be undertaken to better understand the response to differing advertising strategies.

Timing. In the first half of Phase II, we will concentrate on medicinal use of honey, but in the second half, the focus will shift to honey as food.

Marketing Action Plan. The goals of Phase II are: (1) establish 50% market share of the 5% import quota, (2) maintain and enhance a high quality image, (3) convince Korean consumers that honey is also a food, (4) continue to open the market, and (5) make a profit, with full recovery of costs, by 1995.

Phase III

Phase III will begin when the market is open. While we can set the general direction of Phase III, all numbers are highly speculative. In brief, being successful at Phases I and II will put us in the position of being able to pursue a highly profitable competitive strategy that late entrants will have difficulty in matching.

Environment.   Phase III of the marketing plan will be reached when consumers perceive honey as a food rather than as a medicine. We think that this change is inevitable, based on the theory of "cultural convergence." That is, as Koreans interact more with the West, they will adopt more Western attitudes, including the attitude that honey is a food. This effect will be hastened by increasing supplies of honey.

Despite the expected demand increase in the food market and the decrease in the medicine market, the medicine market will still remain relatively large compared with the food market during this phase of the marketing plan. In the long run, the traditional medicine market is not of much interest to us, but as a service, high quality honey will continue to be sold through medicine stores in a market maintenance mode.

The general market condition will be "growth." As honey changes from being a medicine to being a food, the volume of sales is expected to increase rapidly. Early converts to the food market will influence other consumers to use honey as a food, accelerating demand. This market condition is expected to persist for between two and five years before growth in demand flattens.

We anticipate an intense competitive situation. Although foreign competition will be minimal (probably only temporarily) due to the exclusive marketing agreements secured in Phase II of the marketing plan, domestic producers of honey are expected to put up an intense fight for market share. The government, more specifically the Korea Trade Commission, will likely take measures to protect the approximately 50,000 honey farmers. Import quotas or tariffs may be imposed, but probably only to help farmers adjust to the new market realities. The Korean government will recognize that Korea does not have a comparative advantage in the production of honey, and that it would be more efficient and economical to import in the long run. As long as the government restricts

imports, the price level will be maintained at a relatively high level, and the target market will continue to be high and middle income families.

Product.   In the food market segment, only medium quality (Canada No. 2 and No. 3) honey will be sold; Canada No. 1 will be reserved for the medicine market.

Price.   In the medicine market, the target retail price will be considerably higher than that of domestically produced honey. The profit margin is difficult to estimate because the tariff rate during this phase is unknown. However, a minimum 20% profit margin is require to cover the potential risks in a declining market.

In the food market, the retail price will likely be set at parity with domestic honey. Since the quality of Canadian honey is superior, at parity pricing, it will be a better value. Parity pricing also prevents accusations of dumping, which might provoke the Korean government to invoke protectionist measures. We see here why it is important to have secured the exclusive rights or agreements for honey distribution, so that we can maintain an orderly growth, minimizing disruptive competition from other foreign competitors in this sensitive phase of growth.

Distribution.   In this phase, because of the large volume (about 6 million kg) of honey to be distributed, we will require a warehouse—either our own or a joint venture with a large local distributor—near a seaport. The number of sales representatives will be increased in order to deal with the larger number of customers. The exact number of sales reps will depend on the number of customers we have. As a rule of thumb, each customer should be called on at least once every two months.

In the medicine market, the traditional herbal distribution system will continue to be followed.

In the food market, the traditional food distribution system is far too complex to be used. Currently, food passes through at least five distribution steps before it reaches a retailer. The large number of small wholesalers in the Korean food distribution system makes the servicing of all wholesalers unwieldy. Therefore, in this phase only department stores, supermarkets and the larger distributors will be used. Our honey will not be retailed through grocery stores, as it is in North America; this channel will be left to local producers, should they want to pursue this opportunity (an unlikely eventuality). This distribution plan is congruent with the goal of targeting only the upper-middle income segment of population which tends to frequent department stores and the supermarkets.

Promotion. In the medicine market, the promotion strategy will remain the same as in the previous phase.

In the food market, magazine advertising, introductory discount coupons, and posters in department stores will be used in an awareness campaign. In this phase, promotions will be aimed at middle and high income earners, as the price of honey will still be relatively high.

Budget. The total size of the honey market is (crudely and very conservatively) projected to be at least equal to the current market size:

Market = Current Domestic Production × Wholesale Price
= (18.5 million kg)($6/kg)
= $111 million

The targeted market share is between 30% and 60%. With a wholesale margin of 15%, the projected annual profit will be $5 million as summarized in the following table:

	Minimum	Maximum
Market size	$111 million	$111 million
Market share	30%	60%
Annual sales	$33 million	$67 million
Margin	15%	20%
Contribution	$5 million	$13 million

It should be noted that the operating profit calculated above does not include the expected growth in demand prior to and during Phase III. Therefore, the projected profit will be more accurate near the beginning of the phase; towards the end of the phase, market size is expected to increase but operating margins are expected to shrink.

THE MONDAY MORNING MEETING

At precisely 8:00 a.m. on Monday morning, Michael Chan called the meeting to order. "We've all had a chance to review David's marketing plan. I think we agree that he and his team have done a very thorough job, and should be congratulated.

"Obviously, the honey market in Korea has great potential, despite the fact that it is closed to foreign imports at this time. It seems pretty clear that the Koreans will relax the import restrictions in the near future. It is also pretty obvious that if we want to benefit from this situation, we have to act immediately to gain first mover advantage before other competitors step in. But I have to be honest. I'm not in favor of this plan."

There was silence in the room. The management team at Asian Food waited for the boss to elaborate. They all thought the plan, while it had its weaknesses, was viable, and it certainly was consistent with the strategic direction they wanted to take.

Michael Chan paused, and then continued, "This company has always operated with the highest ethical standards. Sometimes it has cost us money. But I believe that in the long run, doing the right thing makes good business sense. Can we and should we go into another country and convince the people to change centuries of tradition? Can we and should we try to change cultural values so that we can make a profit?"

Bonita Woo almost choked on her coffee. "Don't you think you are being a little melodramatic, Michael?" she asked.

Gerald Tang, who had never been in favor of the idea of exporting honey to Korea, had nevertheless been impressed with David's plan. He knew David would put up a good fight for it. Gerald thought it was going to be an interesting meeting.

PART THREE

Product Policy

A n organization's choice of products to offer and markets to serve influences all the other elements in the marketing program. Product policy decisions center on what goods and services the business should offer for sale and what characteristics these should have. These decisions involve matching the resources and goals of the company with market opportunities—hence the close link between market selection and product planning. Product decisions, therefore, require careful analysis of existing and potential products relative to the characteristics of both the market and the organization.

Appraising the need for changes in the product line is a continuing process, reflecting the dynamic nature of the marketplace as well as changes in the nature and resources of the company itself. One objective should be to eliminate or modify products which no longer satisfy consumer needs or fail to contribute significantly to the company's objectives. Another set of objectives relates to adding new products or product features which will meet consumer needs better, enhance the firm's existing product line, and improve utilization of present resources. Complacency in product management in the face of a dynamic, competitive environment is a sure road to ruin.

PRODUCT POSITIONING

To compete effectively in any given market a company must position its products appropriately relative to:

1. The needs of specific market segments
2. The nature of competitive entries
3. Its own strengths and weaknesses (*Exhibit 1* provides a listing of how product positioning can help management).

111

EXHIBIT 1
PRINCIPAL USES OF POSITIONING IN MARKETING MANAGEMENT

1. Provides a useful diagnostic tool for defining and understanding the relationships between products and markets by indicating
   a. How the product compares with competitive offerings on specific attributes
   b. How well the product performance meets consumer needs and expectations on specific performance criteria
   c. The predicted consumption level for a product with a given set of performance characteristics offered at a given price
2. Identifies market opportunities for
   a. Introducing new products
      (1) What segments to target
      (2) What attributes to offer relative to the competition
   b. Redesigning (repositioning) existing products
      (1) Appeal to the same segments or to new ones
      (2) What attributes to add, drop, or change
      (3) What attributes to emphasize in advertising
   c. Eliminating products that
      (1) Do not satisfy consumer needs
      (2) Face excessive competition
3. Aids making other marketing mix decisions to preempt or respond to competitive moves, for example
   a. Distribution strategies
      (1) Where to offer the product (locations, types of outlet)
      (2) What customer service to provide
   b. Pricing strategies
      (1) How much to charge
      (2) What billing and payment procedures to employ
   c. Communication strategies
      (1) What target audiences are most easily convinced that the product offers a competitive advantage on attributes important to them
      (2) What messages; which features should be emphasized

An effective product positioning strategy requires careful analysis of market segments and an evaluation of how well competitors are meeting the needs of specific segments. Tylenol's successful positioning, for instance, is based on its ability to bring pain relief without the use of aspirin. Sometimes positioning, or repositioning, represents a deliberate attempt to attack another firm's product and take away its market share; in other instances, the objective is to avoid head-to-head competition by appealing to alternative market segments whose needs are not presently well served by existing products.

Product positions often reflect not only intrinsic product characteristics but also the image created by promotional strategies, pricing decisions, and choice of distribution channels. For instance, the Cadillac name carries different connotations for car buyers than does Chevrolet, although both are products of General Motors. Similarly, hotel corporations such as Holiday Inns may sometimes use different names to differentiate their luxury hotels from their budget motor inns. These are examples of selective use of alternative brand names in multibrand companies to achieve a desired image. As an alternative to physical modification of an existing product, firms sometimes elect to *reposition* the product simply by revising such marketing mix elements as advertising and promotion, distribution strategy, pricing, or packaging. However, a revision of the entire mix, including product features, may also accompany a repositioning strategy.

Analysis of competitive offerings involves not merely a review of product features and other marketing mix strategies but also an evaluation of competitive advertising *content*. The image generated by advertisements and the nature of the slogans employed may constitute a major positioning tool, especially for "commodity-type" products such as beer, cigarettes, or airline travel.

PRODUCT-MARKET FIT

Bright ideas for new products cannot always withstand objective scrutiny. Among the questions to be asked under the broad category of product-market fit are the following:

* Does the market need the benefits offered by our (proposed) product?
* How well do competing products satisfy customer needs?
* Is there an opportunity to expand primary demand?
* Will our product be perceived as equal or superior to existing products?
* Is the market large enough to support a new entry?
* Have we the skills and resources needed in this market?

If the answer to one or more of these questions is negative, managers should be very wary of proceeding further.

PRODUCT-ORGANIZATION FIT

Even if good opportunities exist for a new or repositioned product, this does not necessarily mean that the company should offer such a product. Unless there is a good "fit" between the proposed product and the firm's needs and resources, the net result of a "go" decision may be harmful or, at best, suboptimal.

The company must also consider how well the product matches the organizational mission and its impact on the firm's financial situation. Questions should be asked about the product's fit with other resource inputs, such as labor availability, management skills, and physical facilities. Other issues include the proposed product's impact upon the market position of other goods and services marketed by the company and its consistency with the firm's existing image. An evaluation should also be made of the feasibility of using the existing sales force, advertising media, and distribution channels or service delivery systems and of the consequences of introducing new alternatives.

PRODUCT DECISIONS

Virtually all manufacturing firms and service organizations produce a variety of different products. Policy decisions, therefore, may be approached from three possible levels:

1. Individual product items.
2. Product lines, namely a group of products which are related in the sense of satisfying a particular class of need, being used together, possessing common physical or technical characteristics, being sold to the same customer groups through the same channels, or falling within given price ranges.
3. The product mix, which comprises all products offered for sale by an organization. Although a particular product item—or even an entire product line—may not be profitable in itself, it may contribute to the well-being of the firm by enhancing the overall product mix.

Product mix decisions should reflect not only market factors and corporate resources but also the underlying philosophy of company management. Most organizations are faced with several options over time. Some choose to pursue a policy of diversity; others prefer to concentrate their efforts on a narrow mix offering a limited number of products in only a few sizes and varieties to a small set of targeted market segments. A diversified product mix reduces risk by spreading it across many different product lines, usually in different markets. Poor performance by one product or in one market should not have a drastic effect on overall performance. For the same reason that it reduces risk, however, a diverse product mix puts a ceiling on returns. A very successful product in a diversified mix will have much less of an impact than if it were part of a narrow, specialized mix.

Product strategy choices should be determined by management's long-run objectives concerning profit levels, sales stability, and growth, as modified by personal values and attitudes toward risk taking. Market opportunities determine the upper limits for potential profitability. The quality of the marketing program tends to determine the extent to which this potential is achieved.

The Product Life Cycle

It is important to recognize that new products and markets eventually mature and that different strategies are required over time. Many managers find it useful to divide a product's life cycle (*Exhibit 2*) into four stages:

1. *Introduction:* A period of typically slow growth in sales volume following the launch of the product. At this point, an innovative organization that is the first to market the product may have the field to itself. However, extensive communication efforts are often needed to build consumer awareness.
2. *Growth:* Demand for the product begins to increase rapidly, reflecting repeated use by satisfied customers and broadening awareness among pro-

EXHIBIT 2   PRODUCT LIFE CYCLE

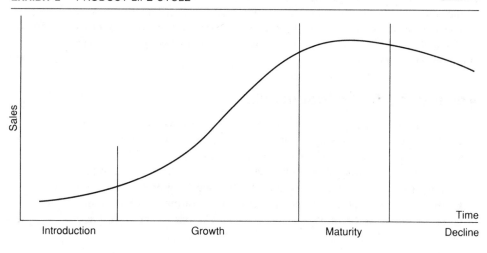

spective customers who now try the product for the first time. Competition develops as other organizations introduce their own versions, transforming a single product into a product class of competing brands.

3. *Maturity:* This is often an extended period during which sales volume for the product class stabilizes and astute marketers seek to position their own product offerings in ways that will differentiate them from those of competitors. Often this stage is characterized by market share battles. However, fad and fashion products may have very short life cycles in which demand grows extremely rapidly, peaks briefly, and then goes into sudden and precipitous decline.

4. *Decline:* Sales volume for the product class declines as a result of environmental forces such as changing population profiles, changing consumer preferences, new legislation, or competition from new types of products that meet the same generic need. Some competitors, anticipating the death of the entire product class, kill off their own entries in the market.

The product life cycle concept suggests marketing strategies tailored to the life cycle stage the product is in. However, the product life cycle concept should not be employed without question. The life cycle of a product class often seems so long as to be meaningless. Further, in evaluating the relationship between marketing strategy and the product life cycle, it is questionable whether the life cycle for a particular product or product class is an inevitable, independent force to which companies must adapt their marketing efforts, or whether marketing strategy can change the course of the life cycle.

Nevertheless, in order to manage its product mix effectively, every firm needs to have a sense of where its individual products stand in terms of their respective life cycles. It is particularly important to understand the life cycle of the product class in which individual offerings compete. Failure to do so can result in such mistakes as launching a new product when the product class is moving into decline or introducing an innovative product without sufficient communication support.

Adjustments to the Product Mix

While the "ideal" product mix will vary from one business to another and may be hard to define, the following situations may indicate a suboptimal mix of products: chronic or seasonally recurring excess production capacity; a high proportion of profits coming from a small percentage of product items; competitors taking the initiative in markets; and steadily declining profits or sales.

Changes in product policy designed to correct any of the above situations or otherwise improve the firm's profitability can take one of the three basic forms:

1. Product abandonment, involving discontinuing either individual items or an entire line. Management issues include questions of how quickly to abandon a product (immediate discontinuance vs. a preannounced phase-out period) and how to handle after-sales service and spare parts for durable goods.
2. Product modification, involving changes in either tangible or intangible product attributes. It may be achieved by reformulation, redesign, repositioning, and addition or removal of certain features.
3. New-product introduction, involving the generation, development, evaluation, and introduction of new products or product lines. Managers need to be clear in their own minds whether a new product is designed to *replace* an existing product or to be a new addition to the line.

New Product Development

Designing and marketing new products is vital to a company's health. The new product development process should proceed systematically through a series of steps, beginning with a review of corporate objectives and constraints and continuing through to product introduction. *Exhibit 3* summarizes these steps in diagrammatic form. The starting point is an assessment of (1) company and marketing objectives and constraints and (2) a situation analysis including information on the current and anticipated market, the competitive situation, and other environmental factors. With this information, management can establish objectives for new products and develop suitable criteria for evaluating new product ideas.

Exhibit 3 lists other stages in the new product development process. First is the generation of new product ideas, since without this stage the rest of the process cannot exist. In idea generation, it is important to ensure that the source of new ideas comes from both market needs (e.g., single-serving food

EXHIBIT 3   NEW PRODUCT DEVELOPMENT PROCESS

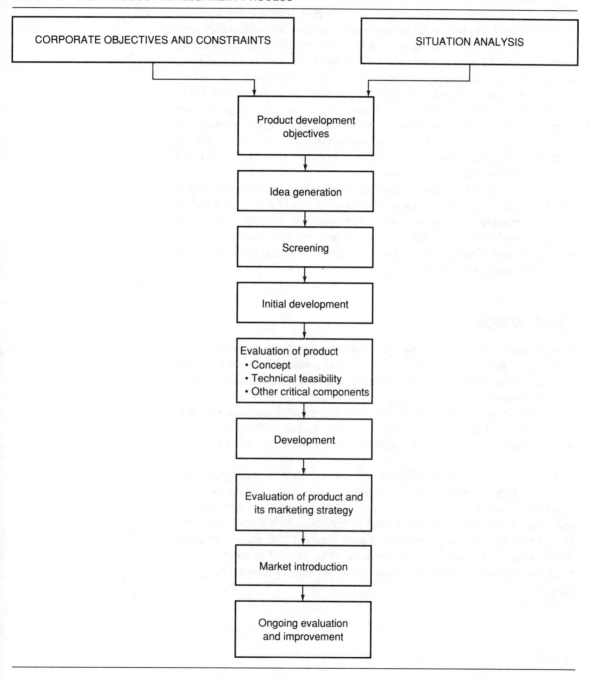

containers) as well as technological advances. Throughout the development process, there is a continuing interchange between evaluation and development. A company must set criteria that balance the risk of rejecting an idea that could become successful against accepting a project that later fails. As the financial commitment to the project increases, the evaluation becomes more extensive. In the early stages, ideas may just be checked to see if they meet new product development objectives and are within the company' capabilities. Profitability analysis becomes a critical part of the evaluation process. Later stages involve carrying out full scale evaluations of a product and its marketing strategy and may include test-marketing for consumer goods and services. At this critical stage, the concept is translated into reality—including how the product will be priced, distributed, and communicated.

The last stages of the new product development process involve market introduction and ongoing evaluation and improvement of the product and its marketing program. Management must recognize that its work is not done even if the product is successfully launched. Changing market needs, competitive thrusts, and technical developments all place continual pressure on the company to progress even further.

CONCLUSION

Product policy decisions are ongoing, reflecting the changing nature of the marketplace. Because an organization's choice of products has such important implications for every facet of the business, it tends to be of great concern to top management.

Product decisions are directly linked to market selection decisions. Without sound analysis of market needs and the development of a strong positioning strategy against competitors in targeted markets, products are unlikely to succeed.

The resources of the firm, the corporate objectives established by management, the characteristics of existing and potential markets, the nature of the competition, and the existing product mix are all factors to be considered in making product policy decisions. It must be remembered, however, that virtually all products eventually lose their market appeal. Firms must abandon or modify products that are no longer competitive or that fail to serve a market need, and develop an effective system for developing and introducing new products.

The Cochlear Bionic Ear

Sandra Vandermerwe
Marika Taishoff

"It's mystifying," Mike Hirshorn muttered, gazing out at the bright June light across the Rhine to Germany, which was just visible from the Swiss-based European headquarters in Basel. "Our system works better than any other surgical procedure. We have a failure rate of 1%. No other kind of surgery offers that sort of result. Why aren't we selling more?" By June 1990 Hirshorn, CEO Worldwide, was getting increasingly concerned about the drop in sales of the Cochlear hearing implant device.

Hirshorn had been with the Australian-owned company since its inception, and had experienced all the ups and downs of getting regulatory approval and carving out an entirely new market. As one of the original members of the project team, he had helped take the ear implant invention of a university professor and transform it into a commercially viable product for the profoundly deaf.

"Look," he declared, "we've managed to get rid of 3M, our biggest competitor. But still we've only succeeded in selling 3,500 units worldwide. Do you realize there are another 50,000 adults out there, if

not more, who need us? Yet we can't seem to break through!"

After a brief silence Brigette Berg, CEO for Europe, responded. "Maybe we just have to face the fact that the market is smaller than we think. The only place we're still growing is in Europe, and that's only because new countries are finally beginning to include us in their health coverage schemes." Brigette had set up the Basel office in 1987 to market and distribute the Cochlear hearing system, the most technologically advanced in the world.

She went on. "Maybe we should stop worrying about volumes. After all, we've got 90% of the market in the US and 60% in Europe and the best product in the world. Why shouldn't the market be prepared to pay more for it? It makes more sense to me to consider raising the price." She looked across at Dennis Wheeler, CEO-North America, for a reaction.

"Perhaps in Europe, where most countries just fix quotas and aren't that price sensitive," Dennis said quickly. "But then we'll risk losing the 25% of the US market which depends on government support. In my opinion, if we want to stay ahead of the competition, we've got to bring down the price even if it means finding ways to cut back on spending."

"We've got to be careful there, Dennis," Mike

119

replied. "I would hate to hold back now. There's no way we can survive without opening up the market. Which means we must invest in marketing our implant better. At the moment, 95% of our potential customer base still doesn't even know we exist."

COCHLEAR'S BACKGROUND AND FINANCIAL PROFILE

In 1979, after ten years of researching the possibility of implanting hearing devices into the cochlea, or inner ear, Professor Graeme Clark, head of the Department of Otolaryngology at the University of Melbourne, Australia, looked for an industry partner to help further his project. The Australian government, seeking to encourage a high-tech development, called for tenders from companies able to perform a market study and write a development cost plan for commercialization. Nucleus Limited, a local company specializing in cardiac pacemakers and diagnostic ultrasound imaging equipment, won the tender.

Nucleus quickly put together a project team to engineer the product's evolution. This entailed three tasks: development of the product itself, filing the necessary patents, and developing a strategy. By September 1982, they were ready to perform the first implant which proved to be a huge success. The following year, Nucleus Cochlear Pty Limited set up in Sydney to handle the new innovation's research and development, manufacturing, and sales. The first US implant took place in 1983 and, in the following year, the US subsidiary Cochlear Corporation was established outside Denver, Colorado.

Real momentum began two years later when the US Food and Drug Administration (FDA) gave its approval. Only when this had been granted would US health insurers provide coverage for the product and the surgical procedure necessary to implant it. Unit sales in the US increased from 409 in 1987 to 596 the following year, although they decreased to 553 in 1989. In that same year, Cochlear produced and began clinical tests on the world's first inner ear implant for children.

Cochlear began to cultivate the European market

in 1986, and in 1987 set up an office, Cochlear AG, in Basel, Switzerland. Although European countries did not have regulatory bodies such as the FDA for medical devices, the FDA's opinion was regularly adopted by the European medical authorities. By 1989, when the national health systems in certain countries began to reimburse patients in full or on a quota basis, the company's European position strengthened, with 198 units sold that year. This led to worldwide growth from 1988 to 1989 despite the decrease in US unit sales.

In an attempt to open up the Japanese market, a four-man operation called Nihon Cochlear was established in Tokyo in 1988; the company was the only player in that market. Clinical tests had been in progress since 1986 with 17 implants completed to date. However, FDA was not valid there and a governmental import license, which Cochlear was waiting for, had to be obtained. The Japanese trials cost $1.5 million. In order to get the import license, Cochlear had to provide implants free of charge.

The company reached financial breakeven for the first time in 1986. Beginning in 1987 profits improved steadily, and in 1988 Cochlear became a cash generating unit for its parent company, Nucleus. In 1987, R&D expenditure increased significantly while operating expenses decreased as a percentage of sales. During this time, the sales and promotion expenses remained constant at 80% of general and administration expenses. The worldwide promotion budget was steady at half a million dollars a year.

The cost of goods was maintained at a relatively low level in order to fund research and clinical support. Salesforce expenses were about 25% of the sales expense budget. The policy of allocating 15% of sales revenue to R&D was exceeded in 1989 due to the urgency of bringing out a new speech processor and a fall in anticipated sales volume. As a guideline, the company tried to spend 15% of its R&D budget on applications research for other developments. Any additional R&D expense had to be cleared by Nucleus, which insisted on a 20% return for all investments. (Refer to *Exhibit 1* for unit sales and financial data.)

EXHIBIT 1
UNIT SALES AND FINANCIAL DATA

Unit sales	1987	1988	1989
(*including clinical trials*)			
USA	409	596	553
Worldwide	574	798	839
Dollar sales (*excluding upgrades*)			
Worldwide (in $ millions)	8.7	13.0	14.2
R&D (in $ millions)	1.1	2.3	3.2
General and administration expenses (in $ millions)	5.9	7.1	7.0
Promotion expenses	0.6	0.6	0.6
Cost of goods sold	constant	constant	constant

ON DEAFNESS AND BEING DEAF

There were two categories of deaf people, about equal in size: "postlingually" deaf (deaf as a result of illness, age, or accident after having learned to hear) and "prelingually" deaf (deaf at birth). The hearing-impaired market was comprised of the *profoundly deaf* and the *severely deaf.*

Severely deaf people could be helped, to a greater or lesser extent, by a hearing aid which amplified sound. Paying approximately $1,000, the customer bought this device after consulting a doctor or by going directly to a hearing aid retailer. These retailers, who were very commercialized, tended to regard Cochlear as a competitor and, therefore, a threat. Research showed that less than 20% of the people who needed a hearing aid actually bought one and, of those who did, only 50% used it. The rest put it in a bottom drawer either because it "failed to help," or because it "looked bad" and "made their handicap too evident."

People whose hearing problems were not being satisfactorily improved by hearing aids could have become a market for implants. But, as long as they could hear at all, such consumers were usually not prepared to risk surgery. In addition, they tended to mix frequently with profoundly deaf people and, thus, had an important influence on them as well as in the political arena.

Research was commissioned to assess the extent of the deaf phenomenon. It was estimated that in developed countries approximately 500,000 *adults* worldwide were profoundly deaf, and that another 500,000 were severely deaf. Applying the rule of thumb for high-tech medical markets, it was assumed that the US accounted for roughly half of this amount.

Ordinary devices such as hearing aids were useless for the profoundly deaf, as the inner ear had become so damaged that surgical intervention was necessary. In ascertaining the real size of the profoundly deaf market, Cochlear took into account psychological and medical factors. Many people who became deaf early in life did not consider themselves "sick" and, therefore, saw no need for surgery. People with heart problems had no choice; without surgery they could die. But, typically, deaf people would try to live with their deafness.

Many potential users were wary of the concept of

an ear implantation, especially of having an electronic device inside the body. One piece of research showed that over 40% of potential users were against the idea of "having wires in their head," "were afraid of doctors and hospitals," or "saw the procedure as far too risky to justify."

Cochlear therefore estimated that only about 10% of the profoundly deaf, or about 50,000 patients worldwide, were possible implant candidates. Apart from this backlog, the data suggested that another 3,000 new cases occurred each year worldwide. In 1990 there were about 10,000 profoundly deaf *children* in the Western world, with approximately 1,200 new cases per year. As of that time, only 50 children had been recruited to the clinical trials in the US. These trials showed good results, particularly for the postlingually deaf and for children implanted very early in life. While deaf children had to go to special schools, those who had had the Cochlear implant could often attend normal schools, although teachers had to be briefed and trained.

Generally, deaf people tended to be less well off economically than those with normal hearing; Cochlear assumed that about 10% were able to fund the implant themselves. Widely dispersed geographically, there were deaf people in all age categories, although 25% of the profoundly deaf were over 65 years of age.

DECISION MAKING AND INFLUENCES FOR HEARING IMPLANTS

The decision-making process for an ear implant could be complex, as there were many actors and influences well beyond just the end user. These included doctors, regulatory authorities, families, insurance companies, deaf associations, and the media.

The Medical Community

Typically, patients would visit a doctor about a hearing problem. He or she would refer them to audiologists or ear-nose-and-throat (ENT) surgeons in hospital implant centers, where they would then be examined to see if they were suitable candidates for an implant operation.

The characteristics of patients and doctors differed in the US, Europe, and Japan. American patients tended to be litigation prone and self-directed in their decisions. Although they were concerned about the implant's appearance, the prime consideration in their decision making was whether and how much it would improve their earning potential. American specialists characteristically offered patients options rather than dictating what had to be done. European deaf patients were more influenced by the surgeon, were not as litigation minded, and the quality of life was more pivotal in their decision making than were professional prospects. They were somewhat swayed by the look of the device, although less so than Americans. Since the main motive for Japanese patients was to cure the problem, they tended to do as their doctors told them.

Doctors in America tended to adopt new medical technologies before those in other countries, and so, despite the stringency of the FDA, the US was always considered the most important market. In fact, it was taken for granted that, in order to succeed worldwide, a firm first had to become established there.

Of the 7,000 American ENT specialists, who were predominantly self-employed or worked for free enterprise hospitals, 200 fitted Cochlear devices in the implant centers, of which 100 did so at least once a year. The doctor was strongly influenced by the need to make a profit, while the hospital hoped to at least break even. Audiologists, a profession unique to the United States, would diagnose hearing loss as well as fit hearing aids and speech processors. The doctor and audiologist worked closely with the patient before, during, and after the operation diagnosing, fine-tuning the system, and counseling and training.

Private or government insurance covered most Americans, with 60 private health insurers providing coverage for about 75% of those insured; the government welfare programs, Medicare and Medicaid, insured the rest. These reimbursement schemes invariably fell a few thousand dollars short of the average $30,000 necessary for the product and procedure. It was then either left to the patient to find the money, or for the hospital to agree to carry the shortfall. Of the 200 US hospitals which purchased the product, about half funded the shortfall either for reasons of prestige or for furthering medical research.

Most European surgeons, typically affiliated with state-run universities and hospitals, were not as profit oriented as the American doctors. Although held in high esteem, they were subject to "hospital politics" and were more conservative and slower to adopt new innovations. The more adventurous, who had sufficient decision-making experience and were influential politically, tended to be in their sixties. Since audiology was not usually a separate specialization in Europe, all diagnosis and fitting was done by the surgeons themselves. Of the 2,500 European ENT specialists, 40 regularly implanted and fitted the device.

In Japan, surgeons also worked primarily at state-run hospitals, which were often poorly funded. These hospitals lacked audiologists, and only a small number of surgeons specialized in ear surgery. Ear surgeons were usually university professors with high status but conservative in outlook and slow to adopt innovations. The more aggressive doctors tended to be in their sixties, but those with political influence were the 80 year olds. As of mid-1990, eight surgeons had been involved in clinical trials in Japan.

Because of the changes which were anticipated as a result of 1992, regulatory medical bodies similar to the FDA, but less well funded, were expected to emerge in Europe. After six years of lobbying by Cochlear, the UK's Department of Health and Social Security decided in 1990 to fund 100 units per year for three years. With Sweden beginning in 1983 and Norway in 1986, Scandinavia sponsored about 20 units per year. Workers' disability insurance covered relevant cases in Switzerland. Germany, which accounted for 60% of all European units sold, was the only country whose medical insurance system provided 100% coverage to anyone who needed the implant. In the remaining European countries, implants were funded by research and charity institutions, and were decided on a case-by-case basis.

The Deaf Community

Deaf peoples' associations were organized on state, national, and worldwide levels and although membership was limited to 10,000–20,000, their influence was widespread. In certain cases, Germany for instance, families were part of the lobby for government support. Some associations or charities, such as the Royal National Institute for the Deaf in the UK, were continuously lobbying on behalf of the deaf to obtain more funding from the national health system.

Encouragement from families and friends of potential patients to seek help and undergo surgery depended largely on whether those families and friends were also hearing impaired and part of the strong "non-hearing" communities which were growing worldwide.

The "deaf pride" movement had become a powerful force in the 1980s with various factions. Extremists went so far as to suggest that Cochlear was experimenting with deaf peoples' brains. Mainstream members emphasized that deaf people constituted an ethnic community with their own languages and culture. Many were opposed to any pressure or opportunity for individuals to hear. They claimed it was better to have perfect communication with sign language than imperfect communication with an implant which they said relegated them to the status of second-class citizens in the "speaking" world. There were as many sign languages as languages and, because of increased mobility and the rapid internationalization of deaf associations, a move was on to develop a global version.

During the 1980s, public awareness about deaf pride had grown. The film *Children of a Lesser God* had raised public consciousness on an emotional level because it dealt with the philosophic issue as to whether profoundly deaf people should *want* to change. At that time, there was also widespread media coverage of the Washington-based Gallaudet University exclusively for the deaf where students could follow a full university program in sign language. Public interest in this institution was enhanced when students protested over the nomination of a "non-deaf" president, forcing him to resign.

THE COCHLEAR HEARING IMPLANT SYSTEM

The Cochlear implant was named after the *cochlea*, a part of the inner ear about the size of a pea and shaped like a snail shell. *Cochlea,* in fact, was the Greek term for "snail shell" which was what the product implant resembled. (Refer to *Exhibit 2* for a illustration of its technical characteristics.)

People could become profoundly deaf either at birth or later in life due to injury or an illness such as bacterial meningitis or mumps. The inner ear had a multitude of sensory cells, or hair cells, each one connected to the hearing nerve which transmitted sound in electrical messages to the brain. Profoundly deaf people lacked or had lost such sensory cells.

Hearing aids amplified sound. This instrument was only adequate for the "hard of hearing" or, in some cases, the severely deaf. The Cochlear "Bionic Ear" was for the profoundly deaf who could not hear at all. Micro-electronic engineering had been adapted to the latest research on hearing physiology to produce a high-tech system which consisted of five parts,

EXHIBIT 2   TECHNICAL CHARACTERISTICS

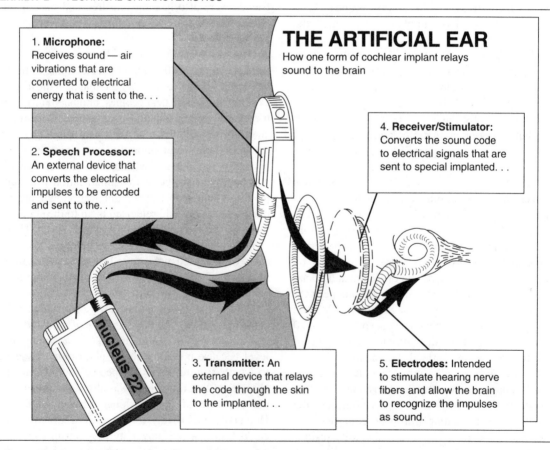

1. **Microphone:** Receives sound — air vibrations that are converted to electrical energy that is sent to the. . .

2. **Speech Processor:** An external device that converts the electrical impulses to be encoded and sent to the. . .

3. **Transmitter:** An external device that relays the code through the skin to the implanted. . .

THE ARTIFICIAL EAR
How one form of cochlear implant relays sound to the brain

4. **Receiver/Stimulator:** Converts the sound code to electrical signals that are sent to special implanted. . .

5. **Electrodes:** Intended to stimulate hearing nerve fibers and allow the brain to recognize the impulses as sound.

Note: Speech processor can be placed in a pocket or clipped to a belt.

all of which were necessary to enable the deaf person to hear:

The *directional microphone* (fastened onto the ear) picked up sounds, converted them into electrical energy impulses which were sent to the speech processor.

The *speech processor* (resembling a Walkman and worn externally on a belt, shoulder pouch, or in a pocket) was a computer that selected the most important electrical impulses needed for hearing noises and words, coded them and sent them to the transmitter.

The *transmitter* (placed behind the ear) relayed the coded noises and words through the skin to the receiver/stimulator in the implant.

The *implant* itself (surgically placed in the bone behind the ear) consisted of a *receiver and electrodes*. The receiver, comprised of an integrated circuit with more than 1,000 transistors (similar to those in a pacemaker), converted the codes into electrical signals and sent them to the electrodes. The electrodes, which substituted for the damaged sensory "hair cells," electrically stimulated the hearing nerve fibers, and thus allowed individuals to hear a variety of high and low sound pitches which were subsequently transmitted to the brain to be deciphered. (Refer to *Exhibit 3* for illustrations of the product in use.)

Cochlear was the only company to have a 22-channel electrode. Unlike the original 1-channel unit, the multichannel device enabled more sounds to be heard and could be fine-tuned for a particular pitch and loudness by the surgeon, thereby catering to the individual hearing needs of each patient. But, no matter how much customizing was done, people who had become deaf could not hear in the same way as before the impairment. They would hear new sounds which had to be correlated with ones they had heard in pre-deaf years. This process was like learning to speak a foreign language, and it took, on average, three months of training and practice. For children, this process was even longer. It could take years for those who were born deaf to be able to hear and speak.

Despite Cochlear's technological superiority, it remained impossible to predict before a surgical operation how each individual patient would respond. Research showed that about 50% of patients who had the operation were eventually able to understand speech without lip reading, and could even use the telephone. The remaining 50% benefited as well, but to significantly varying degrees—from the worst cases, where only noises and warning signals were audible, to those who could follow speech only by lip reading. The result depended on each individual—the state of the ear as well as the brain's learning capacity—neither of which could be assessed at the outset.

Research and Manufacturing

All R&D in Australia was done by 25 people. R&D was grouped into three areas: implant technology, electronic engineering, and mechanical design. Aware that many patients would be hesitant to undergo successive surgery because of improvements in technology, Cochlear's R&D team deliberately designed its first implant version in 1982 with much more capacity than the speech processor could then handle. The idea was to enable the patient's hearing ability to be improved at some future date, without having to undergo further surgery, by updating and modifying the speech processor.

Since then, most R&D efforts had gone into improving the speech processor, with rewarding results. In the first six months of 1990, the firm sold $4 million worth of upgrades and modifications to its existing customer base. Every new model or improvement of an existing model had to go through the FDS approval procedure. New product development could not be heavily publicized because users would put off any buying decision when they anticipated a model change, which caused serious inventory problems.

All manufacturing was done in Sydney. Using a manual process with extensive computer testing, the

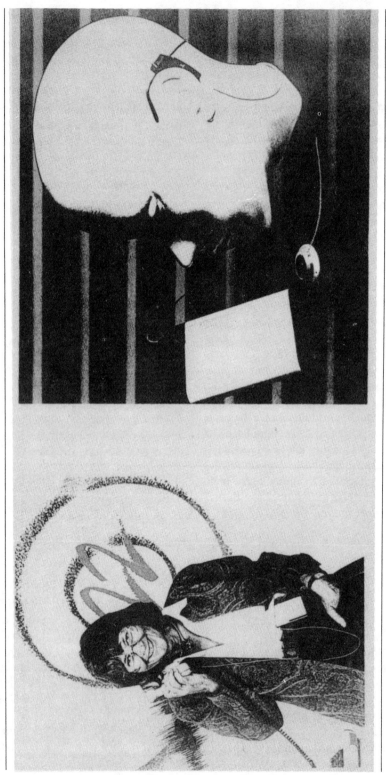

EXHIBIT 3 ILLUSTRATIONS OF PRODUCTS IN USE

50 highly skilled and specially trained plant workers produced approximately 1,400 systems annually, but there was capacity for twice that amount. The components used were very specialized and tended to come from single-goods suppliers worldwide. A constant stock was kept to eliminate delays in the event of problems in the suppliers' market and in order to get bulk prices.

There were two main areas in Cochlear's factory: the section where the implant was made under "clear room" procedures, and the non-environmentally controlled area where the speech processor "externals" were made. For the implant, subassembled parts were first manufactured and then put together in small batches of 20–30 units. The entire cycle, which required using microscopes, would take at least three months. Discrete electrical components and custom-integrated circuits were soldered onto circuit boards. The external parts of the system were made using standard assembly techniques similar to those used by any small volume, high-tech electronics equipment manufacturer.

Improving reliability of the units and the performance of the system were key priorities. It required ongoing upgrading of the electrode manufacturing methods. Although the staff generated many ideas, 99% of them could not be used because of the difficulties of working with an item as small as .6mm in diameter.

Over the years, Cochlear looked at three other applications for its technology: implantable hearing aids, tinnitus, and functional electrical stimulation (FES). In 1986 it seemed that hearing aids had considerable synergy with its product. However, after having spent $1 million up to 1989, the company decided that the technology, marketing, manufacturing, and profit margin formulas were too different to warrant further investment. In 1989, Cochlear started work on the treatment of tinnitus ("ringing in the ears" syndrome), a condition experienced by 1 in 7 people. By mid-1990, half a million dollars had been spent. A large investment would have been necessary to perfect an FES device, an implant which electronically stimulated the nerves of paraplegics. Cochlear carried out some R&D, but decided, after losing a tender to supply the US Department of Veterans Affairs, to give the FES only low level research support.

Overview of Cochlear's Competitive Position

The American multinational 3M had entered the market at approximately the same time as Cochlear, with a lower technology product that the company believed would yield a similar hearing benefit. As 3M's price was one-third lower than Cochlear's, 3M initially dominated the market. Once Cochlear entered, however, the US firm gradually lost market share and faded from the scene late in 1989.

Although there were five major players in the worldwide market, Cochlear was the only one with FDA approval. The others—Hochmair, Hortmann, Symbion, and Minimed—were all developing similar devices and intended to get the required approval. Because some European doctors protested that Cochlear was making too much money, one or two university medical schools in Europe, including the University College of London, developed their own low-budget version of the implant. Although such hearing systems, distributed only through the universities' clinics, were only one-tenth the price of Cochlear's device, they were not regarded as sufficiently reliable to pose a serious competitive problem.

While Cochlear was confident, given its 3,500 satisfied patients worldwide and the FDA stamp, that it had a clear competitive advantage, the company constantly monitored the competitive strength of the main manufacturers, using four criteria:

1. Organization, size and professionalism;
2. Technology;
3. Clinical benefit and effectiveness;
4. Safety.

Neither the Hochmairs, an Austrian team, nor Hortmann of Germany were considered serious opponents by Cochlear, given their lag in the important categories of clinical benefit, effectiveness, and safety. However, the two American firms, Symbion and Minimed, were both perceived as potential threats to future sales.

Symbion, a firm associated with the University of Utah, was in the clinical trial stage. It had managed to produce a unit which, while using a much lower level of implant technology, nonetheless achieved the same hearing performance, and at the same price, as Cochlear's device. Symbion's accomplishment was due to putting considerably more effort into the speech processor than into the implant. A plug which connected the microphone headset to the implant by penetrating the skin created both an aesthetic and a safety disadvantage as the passageway could permit infection to enter the inner ear and the brain. It was considered a flexible product, however, because any kind of stimulation could be used whereas the Cochlear device only allowed radio wave transmission.

Affiliated with the well-known University of California at San Francisco medical school, Minimed began its research in 1966. Although its device had only 16 channels, Minimed's performance could potentially be as good as Cochlear's due to its capacity to better represent certain non-speech sounds. Be-

cause of problems with its micro-chip technology, the company had not yet been able to begin clinical trials needed to receive FDA approval and medical coverage. There were rumors that the problem would soon be solved and by 1991 Minimed would be making clinical trials.

The company annually analyzed market share. With doctors eager for more players to enter the field, Cochlear had, in making its projections for 1990 and 1991, factored in the entry of Minimed and a growth in market share for Symbion. (Refer to *Exhibit 4* for market shares from 1982–1989 and projections for 1990.)

Cochlear's Marketing Strategy

Cochlear treated the ear implant market as a single one. The logic was that the medical profession and deaf associations were linked internationally through medical conferences and medical journals.

The product was identical worldwide. All units

EXHIBIT 4   MARKET SHARE AND 1990 PROJECTIONS

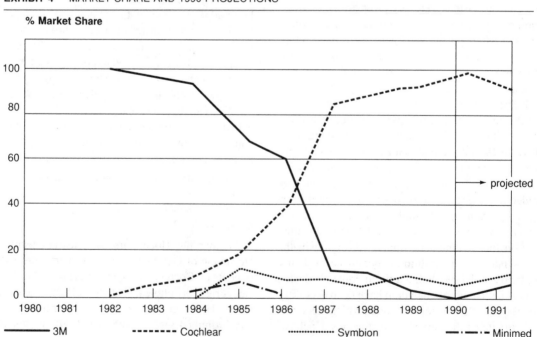

and promotional material clearly identified the Cochlear brand name and logo, and the 22-channel feature was used extensively to differentiate the product as the one with maximum clinical benefits.

Cochlear decided early on that it could not devote equal time and resources to both aesthetics and performance. Convinced that the latter would be the more important criterion for the market, the company decided to position itself as the most technologically sophisticated and clinically superior.

In early 1990, market research confirmed what top management had suspected: Performance was more important than either price or appearance. This survey, which was intended to gain a better understanding of the needs and wants of the implant market, was conducted among 14 Cochlear implant patients, 11 audiologists, a surgeon, and the director of an implant center in one of the US hospitals which fitted Cochlear devices. The results revealed that implant patients considered performance to be the most important factor. In fact, on a scale of 1–10, performance was ranked 8 out of 10, price 5, and appearance 3.

These people were extremely happy to be able to hear and, if given a choice, would have opted for an implant system that allowed them to hear speech, music, and environmental sounds over one where the external units were either cordless or worn behind the ear, but offered lower performance. Nevertheless, the patients did acknowledge that a segment of the deaf market would consider a Cochlear implant if a behind-the-ear system became available, and would probably accept a lower performance level to get a device so small and unobtrusive.

Cochlear had given some thought to the cosmetic appeal of its external units, particularly the speech processor. Initially, it had been made from plastic pipe, then from stainless steel and, in September 1989, a more contemporary design was developed using molded plastic.

For three months after surgery, patients had to return to the hospital or the doctor for training; checkups were then repeated annually. The non-usage rate of all implant patients worldwide was 1%. For the very few patients who experienced a problem with

their unit, there were doctors trained by Cochlear to "troubleshoot." If a unit proved faulty, it was sent back to the regional office for repair. While the implant was guaranteed for five years, it was expected to last a lifetime. The speech processor had an average breakdown time of three years, and each system had a three-year warranty. Hospitals had to maintain adequate supplies of spare units at all times to avoid any risk that the patient could be incapacitated due to a faulty product.

A premium price strategy was deliberately used and strictly maintained in order to highlight the Cochlear system's unique technology. The average $30,000 cost to patients included the Cochlear system as well as all hospital and surgical expenses. On average, the Cochlear device was priced at $17,000 for both adults and children, although it was slightly more in Europe and even higher in Japan. The figure was three times the price of the 3M model when it had been on the market. Symbion's price was equal to Cochlear's, and it was rumored that Minimed would enter clinical trials at the same price level. Hochmair and Hortmann were priced in the middle range.

Cochlear distributed its products directly in three regions—Denver, Basel, and Tokyo—each one headed by its own CEO reporting to the Sydney head office. The salespeople, clinically trained audiologists and engineers, called on doctors and hospitals. They were supported by a team of clinical experts who advised, counseled, and handled any problems that arose, using clinical support centers in each region. These support centers would also work with patients who wanted an implant but were unsure how to handle the finances or apply for insurance. Every office also maintained a technical service team, reimbursement specialists, and 2–3 marketing people to organize conferences, handle PR and prepare brochures.

In the US, some private audiologists who had fitted and tested hearing devices would leave their own practices and, on a part commission basis to help cope with the workload, sell Cochlear implants. Some extra audiologists in hospitals were funded by Cochlear. In Europe, where the ENT surgeon was also the audiologist, the Basel-based European headquarters oversaw all sales except for the UK, Scandinavia, and Israel, which were handled in London. Any direct selling by doctors would have been regarded as unethical in Europe. In Germany, Cochlear managed to persuade one of the largest hearing aid retailers to stock its cables and spare batteries.

Upgraded units became an important part of Cochlear's marketing activities. The $4 million in sales in 1990 was achieved by reaching users through doctors and offering a special reduction in price (from $6,000 to $4,000) if a decision were made by a particular date. The upgrade was introduced and launched at a promotional event hosted on a river boat. This event was followed by direct mail and by papers presented at conferences by doctors who had experienced improved performance during clinical trials. Most patients paid for their own new units in the US because the insurance companies refused to pay. In Europe, they were funded by the national health systems.

Publicity was aimed at patients and doctors. Initially, the novelty of the implant innovation made it relatively easy to get media attention and, on the whole, newspapers, radio, magazines, and TV provided reasonable coverage, particularly of successful cases. Although no formal market research had been done, the Cochlear top team estimated that company awareness worldwide was 70–80% among ENT surgeons, and around 5% among potential users.

The company encouraged medical and scientific journal articles about its product and occasionally paid doctors' travel expenses when they delivered papers at conferences. The system was exhibited at major worldwide medical conferences, while local community forums and meetings with education departments and school authorities were routinely organized. Because it could be considered unethical to directly approach such supporting charities as the Rotary Club, Cochlear provided information only when needed.

Promotional material was distributed to doctors, hospitals, audiologists, and hearing aid retailers to enable them to respond to queries. Post-operative instructional booklets were provided for patients, and a newsletter was sent out from each sales office to doctors, to the existing patient base as well as to local family self-help events. Lectures were given to any deaf association on request, and papers were presented at conferences on deafness whenever possible. Inevitably, though, these activities engendered a certain amount of antagonism, such as walk-outs or other forms of protest from "deaf pride" members in the audience.

AT THE MANAGEMENT MEETING

Mike Hirshorn continued talking. "The FDA is on the verge of giving us the go-ahead for children. That's a market worth another 10,000 units provided we do the job right. Parents will do anything to help their children, so I expect that market to be much easier and quicker to penetrate than it was for adults."

He stood up and walked to the window watching the last rays of sunshine disappearing over the horizon. "For a start, we could increase our salesforce. That way, we could break into new territories and increase the call rates with existing doctors."

"What about the additional costs?" Brigette Berg enquired.

"It's not a big deal," Hirshorn answered. "Even if we doubled our salesforce worldwide, we would only have to sell 15% more units. The Sydney factory can easily handle the extra volumes."

"We could, of course, use the capacity to make a cheaper second model instead," Dennis Wheeler suddenly suggested. "Maybe then we could get into some new countries like Turkey, Greece, the Middle East, and Southeast Asia. Come to think of it, that could also push up our numbers in the States and maybe even in Europe."

"That would ruin our image," Berg responded. "If we want to keep our position, we have to stick to making the highest performance quality even if it means raising our price. Isn't there a section of the US market that could take a price hike, Dennis?"

"Yeah, maybe 10%, max 20% but of the privately insured market," Wheeler replied hesitantly. "Don't forget, though, that this may be exactly what Symbion and Minimed are waiting for—to grab market share."

Hirshorn listened carefully. He knew that he would soon have to recommend to his board ways to maintain profitability despite sagging sales and more threatening competition. He agreed that Cochlear's future hope was its hearing technology. But, somehow the company had to get that technology used and appreciated.

B.C. Packers

Craig R. Pollack and
Charles B. Weinberg

In February 1989, Dr. David McIvor, General Manger of the Export Canned Sales Division of British Columbia Packers Limited, was considering whether his division should launch a canned cat food product in the Canadian cat food market. Some categories in this market had experienced impressive growth in recent years, but Mr. McIvor recognized that competition was increasing; for his company to compete successfully he knew that B.C. Packers would have to enter the market fairly quickly or not at all.

COMPANY BACKGROUND

B.C. Packers was founded in 1923 as a private company. In 1984, it was purchased by George Weston Limited—a publicly traded multi-billion dollar conglomerate. B.C. Packers is best known for its canned tuna and salmon products; the company's Canadian product line includes the Cloverleaf, Rupert, Bumble Bee, and Paramount brands. Cloverleaf is the market leader in both canned salmon and tuna, holding more than a 35% market share in both markets. Sales for

Some of the data in this case are disguised. Copyright © 1990 by Charles B. Weinberg. Revised 1992. All figures are in Canadian dollars.

the Fisheries Division of Weston Resources (which includes B.C. Packers) for 1987 and 1988 were $564 million and $573 million respectively. Operating income for 1987 and 1988 was $42 million and $32 million respectively.

In the early 1980s, B.C. Packers entered into a joint venture agreement with the Philippines government, opening a canning facility in that country under the name of the Mar Fishing Company. The Philippines operation supplied canned fish products to various overseas markets as well as manufacturing a canned cat food product. The cat food, called "Lovely," had been produced for several years and was sold only in Japan.

CANADIAN CANNED CAT FOOD OPPORTUNITY

Management at B.C. Packers had been considering the possibility of entering the Canadian cat food market for a few years. The domestic cat food opportunity arose primarily because B.C. Packers was looking for more profitable alternatives for the fish by-product that was generated in the processing of their canned salmon and tuna. Currently, B.C. Packers either sold this by-product in bulk as fish meal (a commodity for which the firm just covers its costs) or as a cat food for the Japanese market. While selling a well-known brand of cat food in Japan had proved to be fairly profitable for B.C. Packers, competition was very heavy in this market. Also, the Philippines plant had a considerable amount of excess capacity in which to process the fish by-product; Mr. McIvor felt that it was unlikely that B.C. Packers could generate enough sales in Japan to utilize all the excess capacity.

In addition to B.C. Packers' successful experience with selling a branded, advertised cat food in Japan, there were other reasons that Mr. McIvor felt that marketing a cat food product in Canada might be viable for the firm. The reasons included: there has been a considerable rise in the number of cats as household pets in North America over the last five years due to changing socio-demographic factors; B.C. Packers had an established network of brokers throughout Canada that distributed their canned salmon and tuna products; B.C. Packers was highly regarded by the Canadian retail trade; and Weston could provide product research support for a B.C. Packers cat food product.[1] Based on B.C. Packers' experience in Japan, and the strength of Weston's research labs, Mr. McIvor was confident that his firm could formulate cat foods that were equal to that of any major cat food manufacturer and superior to many.

While Mr. McIvor recognized that these were quite compelling reasons, he realized that he needed more information about the Canadian cat food market before he could commit the firm to introducing a product. Consequently, Mr. McIvor formed a three-person management team to carry out a study of the Canadian cat food industry. The team took two months to research, write and submit a report to Mr. McIvor. After looking at the report in detail, Mr. McIvor felt he had a good understanding of the market.

---

[1] Many of the major North American cat food manufacturers utilized large product research facilities in an attempt to gain a competitive advantage over their competition.

THE CAT FOOD INDUSTRY

According to the report, the 1989 Canadian total cat food sales at retail prices were forecast to be $325 million. Grocery store sales were placed at $250 million (an increase of 7% over 1988) while the remaining $65 million in sales would be generated by specialty pet food stores. Cat food sales through specialty stores were estimated to be growing at a rate of 10% annually.

Within the cat food category, total cat food sales for 1989 in grocery stores by type were forecast as follows:

Canned	60.9%	$158.3 million
Dry	30.8%	80.1 million
Semi-moist	8.1%	21.1 million
Snacks	0.2%	0.5 million
TOTALS	100%	$260.0 million

Specialty store sales of canned cat food were forecast at $30 million.

The management team further broke down the canned cat food category in terms of the products' promoted images. The canned cat food found in grocery stores was classified into three distinct classes: Gourmet, National and Price (including store) brands. See *Exhibit 1* for a "store check" summary of some products from each brand category.

The gourmet class, less than two years old in Canada, consisted of "extravagantly" flavored canned cat food sold at a premium price. These brands were targeted to consumers who placed a "higher value" on their cats, and therefore, were willing to spend more on a product that they believed to be superior. Although the flavor offerings provided improved palatability, gourmet products were not necessarily nutritionally superior. Nevertheless, consumers might buy these brands due to their perception that gourmet products were of higher quality. Examples of such brands were Fancy Feast and Whiskas Supreme. Flavors of Fancy Feast, which was sold in 85 gram cans, included whitefish & tuna, salmon feast, tender beef, and cod, sole & shrimp. The flavors of Whiskas Supreme included tuna & whitefish, salmon & crab, chicken & game, and tur-

EXHIBIT 1   RESULTS OF CANNED CAT FOOD STORE CHECK

Brand	Category	# of Flavors	Sizes	Regular price	Feature price
Fancy Feast	Gourmet	9	85g	0.69	0.59
Whiskas Supreme	Gourmet	10	105g	0.69	0.59
Whiskas	National	12	170g & 380g	0.79, 1.33	0.62, 1.09
9-Lives	National	13 +	170g	0.49	0.39
Kal Kan	National	9	170g & 383g	0.68, 1.09	0.58, 0.99
Miss Mew	National	10	170g	0.62	0.49
Dr. Ballards	National	3	397g	1.09	0.99
Pamper	National	13 +	170g & 380g	0.69, 109	0.59, 0.99
President's Choice	Store	6	170g & 397 g	0.49, 0.89	N/A
No Name (Super-Value)	Store	6	170g & 397g	0.43, 0.86	N/A

key & giblets. The average retail price of the gourmet brands was $0.69 per can.

National brands came in a variety of beef, poultry, and seafood flavors that were competitively priced. They were targeted towards the average consumer encouraging brand loyalty and offering a low risk purchase through strong brand awareness. Miss Mew, 9-Lives, Puss 'n Boots, and Kal Kan were examples of national brands. Most of the dollar sales for national brands were accounted for by the 170 gram can size, which had an average retail price of $0.59.

Price brands, which included supermarket and generic brands, offered a limited selection of flavors, and competed primarily on price. On average, they were sold at a retail price of $0.49 per 170 gram can. Virtually no advertising effort or promotional support was invested in these brands.

According to industry sources, the 1989 expected grocery outlet market shares (and sales) of each class of canned cat food were as follows:

Gourmet brands	12.5%	$ 19.8 million
National brands	72.5%	$114.7 million
Price brands	15.0%	$ 23.8 million
TOTALS:	100.0%	$158.3 million

Although the bulk of sales in the cat food market was generated via the national brands, industry ex-

perts all noted a polarization trend in the market. It appeared that the fastest growth was occurring in the gourmet category with an estimated growth of 50% per annum during its initial two years on the market.[2] Similarly, the price brands experienced a strong growth of 17% during the same two year time frame. These polarized segments cannibalized the national segment which experienced an 8% decrease in dollar sales during 1987–1988.

RETAIL DISTRIBUTION CHANNELS

There were two primary retail distribution channels for pet foods. Grocery stores (supermarkets, superettes, convenience stores, and all other food stores) accounted for more than 75% of total pet food sales. Pet food was very important to the grocery trade, as it was the second largest product category in terms of dollar sales in supermarkets.

The second type of retail distribution channel consisted of specialty pet food stores, which were expected to account for an estimated $30 million (retail) of canned cat food sales in 1989. In addition to

---

[2] Gourmet cat food products in the United States, which have been on the market for three to four years longer than their Canadian counterparts, experienced a growth rate of 50% during their first two to three years but then experienced considerable decline. In 1987, the U.S. gourmet cat food market grew at a 5% to 12% rate—the range was due to conflicting figures from different industry experts.

carrying a variety of gourmet, national, and price brands, these stores had the exclusive rights to sell premium brands which were positioned as highly nutritious products. Examples of premium brands were Pro Plan and Science Diet. These brands were usually purchased by owners whose pets were either competitive "show pets" or had some kind of nutritional deficiency. Specialty store owners said that these premium brands accounted for a sizable portion of their sales, probably exceeding 30%. Gourmet brands were also said to do well in specialty stores, although somewhat below the level of the premium brands. National and price brands made up the remainder of their sales. Detailed data were not available on the share of market held by the various brands in these stores. Most major brands, however, were stocked by these stores.

PET FOOD MANUFACTURERS

Canadian cat food manufacturers can be divided according to the type of product they produce into national/gourmet, premium, or price brand producers.

National/Gourmet Manufacturers

Manufacturers in this category included firms that produced either or both a national or gourmet cat food. The leaders among the national brand manufacturers included: Nestle (Miss Mew), Effem (Whiskas and Kal Kan), Quaker Oats (Puss 'n Boots and Pamper) and Starkist (9-Lives). The major gourmet brand producers were Nestle (Fancy Feast) and Effem (Whiskas Supreme). (Many of the gourmet and national firms were widely diversified into other grocery product lines.) Virtually all the products in this category were available in numerous flavors. Many national brands were backed by annual million dollar (or more) advertising and promotion campaigns, while some gourmet products were also supported by large expenditures. Manufacturers in this category offered special deals and discounts to consumers and the trade at various times during the year. For example, in a one month period two major brands were offering trade promotions—one at 8% off and the other at 20% off the wholesale price if specified volume and display requirements were met. Another

brand was offering consumers one can free if two cans were purchased. Two brands had just finished offers of free gifts (e.g., a calendar with pictures of cats) if a sufficient number of labels were sent to the company.

Premium Manufacturers

Leaders in the premium cat food segment included Hill's Pet Products (Science Diet), Martin Feed Mills (Techni-Cal) and Ralston Purina (Pro Plan). The dominant pet food manufacturer in the Canadian premium pet food segment, named IAMS, did not compete in the canned cat food market. Its pet food line included products in the dry dog and cat food market. In addition to being sold in specialty outlets, premium products were also available in veterinary clinics. Cat food manufacturers in this category pursued a serious commitment to research and development; their products were positioned as highly nutritious. Marketing support typically included limited advertising in trade journals, and various training and nutritional programs for veterinarians and specialty retailers.

Price Manufacturers

Price brands were manufactured by various regional manufacturers. Price products were lower priced, had minimal advertising support, and had a smaller number of flavor offerings. Manufacturing these brands was not a particularly difficult task and there were a number of potential suppliers. In addition, supermarket chains that wanted to offer a private brand of pet food could easily arrange for a contract packer to produce whatever quantities were needed.

BUYER PROFILES

The time available to the management team had not permitted them to carry out a consumer survey. Nevertheless, they compiled their own profiles of Canadian cat food buyers using industry sources, trade periodicals, and some previously collected market data. The four major segments are described in *Exhibit 2.*

Shoppers who bought at grocery stores typically

EXHIBIT 2   PROFILES OF CANADIAN CAT FOOD BUYERS

Premium Buyers:	upper income, professional, specialty store shopper, nutritionally oriented, very pet health conscious, pure-breed cat owner, regular veterinarian visits, strong attachment to cat.
Gourmet Buyers:	generally women age 35 and over, affluent, upper income, large grocery store shopper, personification of cat as a baby substitute, typically single cat owner, spoils cat after working all day, perceives high price to be quality, identifies with luxury image.
National Buyers:	generally women 25–54, somewhat price sensitive, low-risk purchaser, conservative, some brand loyalty, perhaps multiple cat owners, family oriented.
Price Buyers:	budget-constrained, price sensitive, possibly multiple cat owner, buys in volume, cat may have a smaller role in the household.

shopped once a week and bought 7–10 cans at a time. Specialty store shoppers usually bought twice as much and shopped two to three times a month. Specialty food store buyers were believed to make most of their purchases at one store, but not necessarily always of the same brand. Among national and gourmet brand purchasers, there was believed to be a considerable amount of brand switching. Some buyers (or at least their cats) were thought to be loyal to flavors rather than to brands.

PET FOOD CERTIFICATION

The nonprofit Canadian Veterinary Medical Association (CVMA) offered the only third party nutritional quality assurance program for pet foods in Canada. Established in 1976, the CVMA was a very well respected, credible association. However, not all pet food companies in Canada chose to have their products certified by this organization. This could be attributed to many factors, including the fact that certification was a voluntary process, and that gourmet and some national brands did not want to be "associated with" the price brands that obtain certification.[3]

_____
[3] CVMA's fee for certification was about $8000 for the initial listing (per flavor) and $5000 per year (per flavor) to monitor the product.

OTHER FACTORS

As Mr. McIvor read the management team's report, some other factors that seemed important to him as they pertained to the Canadian pet and cat food industries were:

- It was difficult to secure substantial distribution for many new pet food products as competition for store shelf space was intense.
- Some of the larger pet food companies utilized direct sales forces (versus brokers) in order to gain better exposure for their products with retailers.
- The pet food industry was characterized by competitive, aggressive pricing strategies; retailers frequently received products at discounts ranging from 8% to 20% off the wholesale price. Over a year, these discounts typically averaged 4% of a manufacturer's sales.
- Most grocery stores carried two to three price brands of which one was usually a store brand.
- Nestle's national brand "Friskies" cat food, which was number three in canned cat food sales in the USA, was expected to be introduced in Canada in 1990.
- As a result of the Canada/USA Free Trade Agreement, competition in the Canadian pet food industry might increase because of imports of U.S. products by Canadian brokers and wholesalers.
- During the period of 1983 to 1987, the cat popula-

tion in Canada increased 4.6% in total as compared to a 5.8% decrease in the dog population. The various factors contributing to this trend were: (1) people moving into smaller dwelling units due to higher housing land costs—cats were viewed as more appropriate pets in smaller living quarters; (2) a rise in urbanization—cats seemed to function better in less space than many dogs; (3) changes in the family—more women entering the work force and spending less time at home caring for the family and pets—cats tended to require less care than most dogs.

CONSIDERING THE CAT FOOD OPPORTUNITY

While Mr. McIvor felt that the management team's report was informative and helpful, he still had some hesitations about entering the Canadian canned cat food market. Mr. McIvor voiced his concerns to his superiors and together they decided that Mr. McIvor, and his export division staff, should develop a business plan; the firm would use the plan as its basis for deciding whether B.C. Packers should enter the canned cat food market. In developing the business proposal, Mr. McIvor was especially concerned with the question of which product class market, if any, B.C. Packers should enter. While Mr. McIvor had many factors to consider, he recognized that a profitability analysis of each option would help him with his decision. In order to do this, Mr. McIvor estimated the contribution margins that B.C. Packers would likely achieve from each class. His estimates, before advertising and trade discounts, were a 57% contribution margin (on B.C. Packers' price) for gourmet brands, 48% for national brands, and 37% for generic brands. Mr. McIvor based these estimates on the average prices manufacturers were currently receiving for their products. Gourmet brands were sold by manufacturers for an average price of $11.50 per case of 24 cans (85–105 grams sizes). National and price brands were typically sold in larger can sizes (170 grams and 380 grams). For national brands, manufacturers typically realized $9.24 for a case of 24 (170 grams) cans. Manufacturers of generic

brands typically sold their product to retailers at a price of $7.25 for a case of 24 (170 grams) cans. Mr. McIvor felt that, initially, B.C. Packers would use those prices, depending on the product class.

After estimating the firm's prices and contribution margins, Mr. McIvor recognized that the promotion and advertising requirements needed for each product class should be included in the calculations. Mr. McIvor had asked B.C. Packers' advertising agency to estimate what would be required to succeed in the cat food market. Trinka James, the account manager, suggested that an expenditure of $650,000 would be required to achieve 10% of the gourmet market, but she said her estimate of share could be off by ±3%. She also said that the national brand market was much tougher. At least twice as much advertising and promotion would be needed to be heard above the clutter and even so only a fraction of the national market could be gained. She noted that one established national manufacturer had spent more than a million dollars and only achieved a 5% share (of the national market) in the first year. Less spending would be needed in subsequent years. Incremental marketing, general, and administrative costs would also be incurred. For this project, these items were estimated to be $150,000. (If B.C. Packers' cat food sales exceeded $2 million, these costs would likely rise by another $50,000.) Additionally, trade discounts had to be factored into any decision.

The fish processing plant in the Philippines had sufficient excess by-products to supply B.C. Packers with up to 800,000 cases (24 cans, 90 grams each) per year. (Chicken and beef, to make a complete product line, would be purchased from other divisions of the company.) Beyond that, an investment of $250,000 would be required to expand plant capacity.

Mr. McIvor knew that a number of other questions and issues also needed to be resolved. Several of the more pressing ones were the following:

- Could B.C. Packers secure shelf space in retail outlets? This was an extremely important consideration as securing adequate shelf space was critical to the success of any packaged good product. Obtaining shelf space depended on many considerations including the number of competitors in the product category, a company's reputation within the packaged goods industry, the ability of a sales-person/broker to sell a product to a retail buyer, trade allowances provided by the brand, ad support behind the product, and the track record of the brand in other stores. Mr. McIvor wondered which product category would allow the firm to gain the most shelf space.

- How much money should B.C. Packers allocate for consumer promotions? Mr. McIvor not only wanted to know how much money the firm should spend on promoting and advertising a product during its introductory year, but also how much they should spend against a brand over the first three to five years. Also, Mr. McIvor wondered what media vehicles the firm should utilize in promoting a cat food. It appeared that many national and gourmet brands spent considerable amounts on television and print advertising. Current advertising spending by competitors was not known.

- What would be an appropriate package size? Currently, the plant in the Philippines has the equipment to manufacture a 90 gram can—the size of B.C. Packers' canned salmon and tuna products. If a gourmet line was to be introduced, this package size would be chosen. However, a product for the other categories would require a larger size can. (There would be a one-time cost of $20,000 for each new can size.) Another option was to package the cat food in a can with a pull-tab top that was shaped so that the can would then serve as the cat's feeding dish. This package would only be viable if B.C. Packers targeted the gourmet market where the small can size was comparable to a single meal for a cat. Adopting this option would involve a one-time cost of $50,000 for machine retooling, but would also add an estimated $0.60 to B.C. Packers' cost per case.

- Mr. McIvor had tentatively decided to use his current brokers to distribute the new cat food product if it were introduced. The brokers, who would be paid a 5% commission on sales (at the wholesale price), could cover both the supermarket and specialty store channels. However, he wanted to think again about the advantages and disadvantages of B.C. Packers' hiring its own salesforce. The biggest benefit of hiring and training its own salesforce was that B.C. Packers would receive maximum exposure for the cat food product as brokers usually sold the products of numerous firms. The main disadvantage of using a salesforce was that sales-people were not as cost efficient as brokers at lower volume levels. In addition, salespeople would require a partially guaranteed salary (at least initially) while brokers would be paid strictly on a commission basis.

While Mr. McIvor recognized that there were many difficulties to overcome, he did not want to let a profitable opportunity slip away. With these thoughts in mind, he began to prepare the business proposal.

The Parker House

Robert J. Kopp
Penny Pittman Merliss
Christopher H. Lovelock

Yervant Chekijian, group director of operations for the Classic hotels division of Dunfey Hotels, didn't mince words. "Business at the Parker House has never been better—but our biggest challenge may be right around the corner."

Robert McIntosh, general manager of the Parker House, Boston's oldest hotel, watched as Chekijian picked up a newspaper clipping dated April 1979 and headlined, "Hotels Bring Jobs to Boston, Tax Money to State."

"This story in the *Globe*," he continued, "confirms what we've suspected for some time—that within five years, as many as five or six brand new hotels may open within three miles of the Parker House. Business travelers in this town are going to have more atriums, swimming pools, and king-size beds than they know what to do with. Our mission statement outlines the market position we want for the Parker House; now we need to establish how each department of the hotel will contribute to that position."

McIntosh nodded in agreement. "We'll need more than old-world charm to hold on to our market share," he observed. "What we're really talking about is competition-proofing the Parker House."

HISTORY OF THE PARKER HOUSE

The Parker House, the oldest continuously operating hotel in America, opened on October 8, 1855, and was immediately popular with Bostonians and visitors alike. Charles Dickens, the most popular English novelist of the nineteenth century, was a regular visitor to the Parker House during his American tours and in 1867 described it to his daughter as "an immense hotel, with all manner of white marble public rooms. I live in a corner high up and have hot and cold bath in my bedroom." Dickens was unusually well qualified to judge the merits of his bath, having fallen into it fully dressed one night after enjoying the Parker House wines.

The founder of the hotel, Harvey Parker, was a former stableboy from Maine who began his career in the hospitality industry by operating a moderately priced lunchroom in Boston's Courthouse Square. After opening his new hotel, Parker directed his energies toward food and beverage development and was

139

the first hotelkeeper in the world to offer a formal American plan: lodging plus three meals daily at a single price. His French chef, hired for $5,000 in a day when many hotel cooks earned about $500 annually, created lavish banquets that brought additional fame to the hotel; Boston cream pie was first served at the Parker House, and the soft, crustless Parker House rolls created by the hotel's German baker were shipped as far west as Chicago.

Refurbished and enlarged throughout the nineteenth century, the Parker House was almost totally rebuilt in 1927. Constructed from yellow-gray brick, the 14-story building stood on the corner of Tremont and School streets, both busy, narrow thoroughfares in the heart of Boston. The Boston Common, a large public park established as a cow pasture by the Puritans, was two blocks away.

Although the exterior of the Parker House resembled an office building more than a grand hotel, the wood-paneled lobby with its rich carpeting, framed 18th century engravings, and ornate brass elevator doors created an aura of elegance which was reflected in the handsome first floor dining room and the other public rooms on the second floor. In 1927 the newly built hotel contained a total of over 550 guest rooms and suites, and throughout the 1920s and 1930s continued to attract the rich and famous.

But the following decades were not kind to the hotel. During the 1950s and 1960s Boston's waterfront and many of the downtown streets which bordered it fell into decay, and new shopping and commercial areas grew up in the suburbs and the Back Bay. With its main entrance tucked away on a narrow side street and its facade growing darker with age, the Parker House failed to catch the eye of many tourists and corporate travelers. By 1969, occupancy was down to 35 percent, and the former grand old lady of Boston had fallen into bankruptcy.

The Parker House was brought back to life in 1969 by Dunfey Family Hotels, a privately owned, regional lodging chain which at that time operated 11 hotels and inns in the northeast U.S. The company was founded in 1954 by six Dunfey brothers and their mother. To finance further expansion following the purchase of the Parker House, the Dunfey family

sold the company to Aetna Life Insurance in 1970. Five years later, Jon Canas, formerly head of international marketing for the Sheraton Corporation, joined the company as vice president of sales and marketing. In 1976, Aer Lingus, the national airline of Ireland, acquired Dunfey from Aetna and arranged to lease the hotel properties through a subsidiary. Throughout these changes of ownership, Jack Dunfey remained chief executive officer of Dunfey Hotels Corp.

Initial Renovations

In February 1973, as a major step in their effort to revive the Parker House, the Dunfey's hired Yervant Chekijian, who had managed the prestigious Mayflower Hotel in Washington, D.C., as general manager. Chekijian arrived in Boston to discover a city in renaissance. The huge Prudential Center, a network of apartments, shops, hotel, and plazas built on former railroad yards in the Back Bay area of Boston, had ignited redevelopment in 1959. Next came Government Center, a 60-acre project planned by I.M. Pei, which transformed shabby Scollay Square into an open plaza surrounded by two large government office towers, a sweeping curve of retailing and office space, and other government buildings. The focal point of the project was a dramatically modern City Hall, which one architectural critic considered "as fine a building for its time and place as Boston has ever produced." Nearby was Boston's financial district, where banks and other financial firms were building new 30- and 40-story office towers.

Dunfey management could see that the Parker House's location now offered the hotel a distinctive advantage over its major competitors. Built in a day when many business travelers in the city still preferred to walk to their destinations, the Parker House was closer to Boston's corporate, legal, and financial offices than any other hotel in town. Three rapid transit stations lay within a five-minute walk; Logan Airport was only 2½ miles away, and could be reached by taxi in half the time it took to travel there from any other downtown hotel. Although the Parker House did not have its own parking garage, guest parking was available within one block.

Impressed by the hotel's distinguished history, the Dunfeys saw a chance to rebuild its dominant position by catering to corporate and professional travelers and discriminating tourists rather than large groups of conventioneers. They knew that much individual business was booked locally, since travelers frequently relied on those whom they were visiting to make lodging arrangements. The key to rebuilding wide demand for the Parker House, they decided, was reestablishing the hotel's image within Boston itself.

The first public area of the Parker House to be renovated in 1973 was The Last Hurrah, an informal bar and restaurant in the basement, created from a former grillroom. The Last Hurrah offered moderately priced drinks and meals and, later, one of the only live swing bands in Boston. Decorated with photographs depicting figures from Boston's colorful political past, The Last Hurrah soon attracted a loyal lunch and after-work following from City Hall, the state legislature, and the financial district.

Total renovation of most of the Parker House guest rooms and corridors was the second stage of the repositioning of the hotel. During 1973–74 walls were stripped, repainted and repapered; new furniture and carpets purchased; new bathroom fixtures installed and bathtubs reglazed; and new lighting and mirrors added. Additionally, the entire hotel was rewired and individual heating and air-conditioning controls (costing approximately $2,500 per room) were installed in each bedroom. "Not one piece of old furniture was left in the renovated rooms," Chekijian recalled. "Our objective was to create a first-class facility that would not offend any top-of-the-line traveler; by adding a very high level of service to this new physical plant, we could then market the Parker House as a luxury hotel."

In 1975, Dunfey management renovated the hotel's once-elegant dining room, used as a meeting room since 1969. Reopened as Parker's Restaurant, it was furnished with overstuffed sofas and large wingback chairs, its brown and beige color scheme accented by spectacular floral arrangements. Its warm atmosphere and mixture of French and American cuisine soon made Parker's one of the most popular fine restaurants in town: readers polled by *Boston* magazine considered it one of the top ten in the city and felt that Parker's service was second only to that of the Ritz. Bostonians were particularly fond of Parker's Sunday brunch; diners were served from a buffet line as a harp played softly in the background. Adjoining Parker's Restaurant was Parker's Bar, which had been transformed into a quiet, luxurious piano lounge.

"This was the key to our repositioning effort," Chekijian commented. "It's important to sell a dining room to the local community, since local residents, not those who are visiting, usually make dining decisions. We saw the dining room as a window onto us for the community, and we wanted to create a room which would define the hotel."

The total cost of renovations through 1975 exceeded $5 million. The following year, the south wing of the hotel, which had been closed off since 1969, was completely renovated at a cost of $500,000, adding another 51 guest rooms and giving the Parker House a total of 546 rooms. Occupancy rose from 52 percent in 1973 to 83 percent in 1976, when Chekijian was promoted to a new position at Corporate Headquarters.

By 1979, the only restaurant to remain substantially unrenovated was the Revere Room, a 108-seat coffee shop serving breakfast and lunch. A holdover from Dunfey's early days at the hotel, when management had instituted a colonial theme, the Revere Room was prominently located near the Tremont Street entrance. It offered fast, reasonably inexpensive meals in what management conceded was a rather dull and conventional setting.

THE DUNFEY ORGANIZATION

The rising popularity of the Parker House mirrored the growing success of the Dunfey corporation as a whole. Revenues had doubled since 1977, when Jon Canas became executive vice president. Chainwide occupancy rates leaped from 56 percent in 1975, below industry average, to a projected 76 percent in 1979. By late 1979, the company, now known as Dunfey Hotels, owned or managed 23 hotels and inns. These properties were divided into six distinct groups, among which was the Classic hotels division, consisting of the Parker House, the Ambassador East in Chicago, and the Berkshire Place in New York City.

The Dunfey Management Process

The character of Dunfey inns and hotels varied widely; within the Boston area alone, Dunfey-managed facilities included a 275-room executive inn and a 120-room suburban motor inn in addition to the Parker House. Accordingly, the corporation made it a point to maintain clear distinctions in planning, pricing, and promotion between the Classic hotels and other Dunfey properties.

The foundation of the Dunfey management process, established by Jon Canas, was the annual mission statement developed for each hotel. Responsibility for this detailed planning document was shared between corporate marketing and operations executives and the Executive Operating Committee (EOC) of each individual property. The Parker House EOC included Robert McIntosh, general manager; the director of sales; the resident manager for food and beverage; the resident manager for rooms; and the personnel director. Working closely with Yervant Chekijian, they attempted, through the mission statement, to specify what kind of customer, at what time of year, at what rate, was most desirable for the hotel. After this "ideal business mix" (IBM) had been determined, objectives could be set for the rooms division and the food and beverage division, capital needs established, and a marketing plan designed.

Through this marketing plan, based on the mission statement, detailed strategic blueprints covering four-month and twelve-month periods could be devised for each hotel. Essential to the plan in each case was a supply/demand analysis for each major revenue-producing area (rooms, banquets, a la carte operation, lounges). Such a study showed demand by market segment; it also analyzed the features of the competition and the hotel's competitive advantages and disadvantages vis-a-vis the needs of each market segment. The mission statement expressed the desired market position of the hotel; the supply/demand analysis provided data through which a plan designed to achieve that position could be constructed.

THE CLASSIC HOTELS

Each Dunfey Classic hotel was considered a unique facility with a character and tradition all its own. This individuality was reflected in the hotels' decorating schemes: Manhattan's Berkshire Place, acquired in 1978, was furnished in a sophisticated contemporary mixture of marble, plants, oriental rugs, and over-stuffed furniture; the decor of Chicago's Ambassador East, acquired in 1977, blended 18th century antiques with contemporary accessories; and the Parker House evoked a wood-paneled comfortable club.

Like the Parker House, the Ambassador East and the Berkshire Place were restorations of old, centrally located hotels. Such restorations were advantageous to Dunfey for several reasons. It was faster and less expensive (on a per-room basis) to restore an old hotel than to construct a new one. In the long run this could produce a relative cost advantage for Dunfey Classic hotels challenged by newly constructed competitors. Moreover, the location of such hotels—in the heart of the downtown business district—was often difficult for a new property to duplicate.

The history and physical facilities of the Classics also created an atmosphere which many Dunfey executives felt was missing in more modern hotels. As the company's newsletter stated:

Our Classic hotels have a tangible quality and an intangible ambience . . . much like an older, cultured, grand lady whose very presence exudes charm, sophistication, and prestige. We believe that many travelers seek an escape, an oasis from the sterile sameness of some national hotel chains. Even in the newer, plush megastructures of modern hotels, there is the risk of being lost in a sea of convention-eers, of experiencing impersonal service. We know there is a growing market for hotels where guests are treated as individuals in distinctive settings.

On the other hand, hotels constructed during an era when guests frequently traveled with their servants generally had many bedrooms considerably smaller than those offered by more modern competitors; 50 rooms at the Parker House, for example, were too small to include a full bathtub and contained only showers. Even after renovation, the rooms of older hotels tended to vary widely in size and location, a potential source of annoyance to guests charged the same rates for "different" rooms. Repair and maintenance costs were higher than for new hotels.

Pricing Policy

As Jon Canas described it, "pricing is the exteriorization of your marketing position"; with this philosophy in mind, Classic hotel rates were customarily set to fall within the top 10 percent of local competition. Local rates could also be an inhibiting factor: al-

EXHIBIT 1

THE PARKER HOUSE: OPERATING STATEMENTS

1979 Budget vs. 1978 Actual

	1978	1979 (budgeted*)
Dept. Revenues		
Rooms	$ 6,273,078	$ 6,865,270
Food	2,829,678	3,078,900
Beverage	1,454,066	1,560,600
Food & bev.—misc. income	53,852	59,100
Telephone	251,655	259,480
Valet & guest laundry	39,677	34,700
Other income	16,129	11,400
Check room	5,149	11,500
Operated dept. revenues	10,923,554	11,880,950
Profit (or Loss)		
Rooms	4,682,429	5,198,601
Food & beverage	824,007	962,096
Telephone	(153,007)	(122,730)
Valet & guest laundry	13,209	11,880
Check room	(9,952)	(5,070)
Operated dept. profit	5,356,686	6,044,777
Other income	16,129	11,400
Gross operating income	5,372,814	6,056,177
Deductions		
Administrative & general	701,310	657,214
Marketing	371,769	471,854
Energy costs	695,385	815,961
Property operation	531,079	892,617
Total deductions from inc.	2,299,543	2,837,646
House profit	3,073,750	3,218,531
Commercial rental**	190,479	173,580
Gross operating profit	3,263,750	3,392,111
Property tax & fire ins.	813,544	712,000
Operating rentals***	59,379	59,640
Operating profit	2,390,827	2,620,471
Depreciation and amortization	1,342,000	1,435,000
Hotel earnings	1,048,827	1,185,471

*"Budgeted" amounts were a low estimate for financial purposes and did not represent what was expected of management.

**Derived from shops approached through the Parker House lobby.

***Cost of rented color television sets in rooms.

Source: Company records.

though Parker House management felt that the hotel's high average occupancy rate had given them substantial pricing leverage, Boston hotel rates in general were much lower than those in New York. Yervant Chekijian summarized the situation as follows:

Right now, at the Parker House, we're running $53–65 single and $65–75 double. Personally, I'd like to see these rates brought closer to parity with New York, where the Berkshire, for instance, is charging $85 single. But local custom heavily influences pricing. In Chicago, when a number of hotels began offering substantial discounts to their corporate customers, we had to lower rates at the Ambassador East to match competition.

On the other hand, continuing inflation in construction and furnishings costs meant that rates charged by new hotels generally had to be set higher than prevailing rates in the same area. The average rate for Massachusetts hotels in 1979 was projected to reach about $42. Discussing this figure, Chekijian noted:

The average rate, even for a luxury hotel, can appear surprisingly low. It's important to remember that heavy seasonal and day-of-the-week variations give a hotel much flexibility in discounting. The average room rate is thus the result of sales to many different market segments at significantly different rates.

According to Dunfey management, any hotel operating at 85 percent room sales efficiency or above needed a rate increase. Room sales efficiency (RSE) was a standard used throughout Dunfey Hotels to measure the occupancy-price performance of an operation in which substantial discounting was common; RSE was defined as the ratio of total room sales revenues achieved during a specific period divided by the sum of the maximum revenues that could have been obtained if all available rooms had been sold at full (or "rack") rates during the same period. For example, if occupancy was 90 percent and the average room rate obtained was 90 percent of the full rate, the RSE would be 81 percent.

Room sales accounted for close to three-fifths of the hotel's departmental revenues in 1978 (*Exhibit 1*); because the incremental costs of room rental were relatively low, the hotel's high occupancy meant a substantial profit margin in that department—72 percent in 1978. The margin for food and beverage, by contrast, could be as low as 18 percent. The Parker House's earnings, like the earnings of every Dunfey hotel, returned to the corporation for distribution.

Advertising and Sales Efforts

National and major regional advertising for each Classic hotel was supervised by Dunfey's director of advertising and public relations, who was based at the head office in Hampton, N.H. In addition to placing ads of individual Classic properties in such periodicals as *The New Yorker* and *Forbes (Exhibit 2),* the advertising department was developing an advertisement which would promote the Classic hotels as a group in such print media as *Business Week, Sports Illustrated,* and *Time.* Total national advertising for the Classics was budgeted at about $784,000 for 1979.

As well as creating demand for rooms at the three Classic properties, the promotional campaign was designed to meet two other objectives: first, to create awareness of Dunfey Classic hotels as a group in order to pave the way for expansion of the division in other key metropolitan areas; and second, to establish a favorable institutional image for the corporation as a whole. Obtaining management contracts for prime properties from third-party owners was a continuing part of Dunfey's plan for expansion.

Local advertising for the Parker House was supervised by Bob McIntosh, working with the hotel's director of sales, and was used primarily to promote Parker's Restaurant and The Last Hurrah (*Exhibit 2*). A Boston public relations firm also worked closely with McIntosh in achieving local visibility for the hotel. Sales department expenditures totalled $371,769 in 1978, of which 52 percent went to salaries and wages, 38 percent to advertising, and 10 percent to sales and promotions. Newspaper advertising, which totalled about $51,000 in 1978, was budgeted at almost $130,000 in 1979.

Although most hotels segmented their guests into two or three categories (tourists, corporate travelers,

EXHIBIT 2

EXAMPLES OF PRINT ADVERTISING BY THE PARKER HOUSE, 1978–79

Advertising in National Print Media.

For People Who Appreciate the Classics.

Classic Accommodations   Classic Service

In Boston

PARKER HOUSE

A DUNFEY CLASSIC HOTEL

Tremont & School Sts. Boston. MA 02107   617/227-8600
Reservations 800-228-2121

PH

Advertising in Boston-Area Print Media.

A lot of Boston restaurants are simply replicas of Boston's best.

There is only one great Boston night spot with authentic turn-of-the-century atmosphere, delicious traditional fare, moderate prices, free garage parking by valet, no cover charge and nightly dancing to the delightful sound of the Winiker Swing Orchestra.

The others can only try their best.

At The Parker House
Dining/Dancing/Sunday Brunch
Tremont & School Streets/
Boston/Reservations
227-8600

Local Advertising.

and groups), the Parker House identified eleven major segments. The three most important—individual professionals and executives, corporate groups, and professional or special-interest associations—were contacted regularly by the Parker House sales staff. The hotel did not have space to accept large conventions. "Customers contribute to the atmosphere or hotel experience," declared one Dunfey executive. "You should choose your clientele selectively to match your mission."

Two Parker House salespeople represented the hotel's Executive Service Plan (ESP) sales effort, targeted toward individual business travelers; they had a weekly quota of 40 sales calls to Boston-based organizations. According to McIntosh, no other hotel in the city carried out an equivalent direct sales campaign. In a further effort to attract ESP guests, who were always charged rack rate, the hotel offered an unlisted telephone number for reservations, larger rooms, express check-out, complimentary newspapers, and free weekend accommodations for an ESP guest's spouse. Other Parker House sales representatives solicited business from associations and groups in or near Boston. Obtaining bookings from companies, associations, and tour groups outside the Boston area was the responsibility of Dunfey's corporate sales department.

The Parker House Rooms

In May 1979, the 546 Parker House guest rooms were divided into the following eight categories:

| | | **Daily Rate** | |
Room Type	Number	Single	Double
Patriot	36	$ 35	(none)
Airline	117	47	(none)
Standard	151	53	$ 63
Deluxe	168	57	67
Top of the Line	23	65	75
Mini-Suites	33	75	85
Suites	17	75	$110
Deluxe Suite	1		210

Rooms were classified according to size, location (i.e., whether the room had an outside view), and quality of furnishings and appointments. The hotel's 36 Patriot rooms were the smallest it offered, accommodating only single occupancy, and were located in the interior of the building, overlooking a central airshaft. These rooms were sold at a substantial discount to government employees; similar, somewhat larger rooms were sold, by annual contract, to airline personnel. Standard and Deluxe rooms were larger than Patriot rooms, possessed an outside view, had better quality furniture, and contained such amenities as color television and an AM-FM clock radio. Top of the Line rooms were more spacious still and had king-sized beds. Suites consisted of one or more very large rooms—often constructed by combining two smaller rooms—with superior appointments; many suites had kitchen facilities such as a sink or wet bar.

In addition to its guest rooms, the Parker House contained a variety of facilities for meetings, including three small "board rooms" accommodating 8–15 people; ten meeting rooms accommodating 25–200; and one ballroom accommodating 350. Duplicating machines, blackboards, and audiovisual equipment were available to groups at a small fee. Opening off the main lobby were a gift shop, a bank, a small shop selling newspapers, magazines, and sundries, and an Aer Lingus ticket office. A barber shop was located on the basement level. Laundry/valet service, airport limousines, and rental cars could all be requested through the hotel's front desk.

Occupancy rates at the Parker House, in keeping with the upward trend enjoyed by the city's hotels at large, had risen sharply in recent years. However, Dunfey executives realized that these figures were averages, in which the high weekday occupancy balanced out significantly lower weekend levels. As the corporation's director of sales explained:

The Parker House is favored with a very heavy demand on Monday, Tuesday, and Wednesday nights. Management still has to stretch the Sunday night arrivals that are staying through the week. On Thursday, Friday, and Saturday nights, the hotel is not favored with a tremendously high turnaway. The ideal, of course, would be to have people coming in on Sunday, checking out Friday, and followed by a heavy weekend influx. That's still not true for the Parker House.

At the same time, the hotel had also shown an improvement in room sales efficiency. Published room rates at the Parker House had risen at least once each year; the most recent increases had been posted on December 1, 1977; September 1, 1978; and April 1, 1979. *Exhibit 3* shows occupancy rates; room sales efficiency index; and room, food, and beverage sales figures at the Parker House for calendar 1978 and early 1979.

THE BOSTON HOTEL MARKET

The average occupancy rates for Boston hotels had been considerably higher than the national average for a number of years (*Exhibit 4*). The city offered many diverse attractions to visitors: in addition to its status as a financial and commercial center, the Boston area boasted the greatest concentration of colleges and universities in the world, including both Harvard University and the Massachusetts Institute of Technology. Known as the "Medical Mecca" of the United States, Boston was also home to the Massachusetts General Hospital and a host of other renowned medical centers and research institutions. The Museum of Fine Arts and the Boston Symphony Orchestra were world famous, and the area's many colonial historic sites also attracted a substantial number of tourists.

A major Atlantic seaport, Boston had a very accessible airport and one of the most extensive public transportation systems in the U.S. But driving in the city could be difficult; many downtown streets followed the meandering patterns of colonial cow paths, and parking was scarce and expensive. Driving was particularly a problem in winter, when heavy snow falls and illegally parked cars (Bostonian drivers, according to a *New York Times* article, were notorious scofflaws) rendered some streets almost impassable. The city's most pleasant season, many felt, was fall, when tourists flocked to the area on their way to view autumn foliage.

EXHIBIT 3 SELECTED PERFORMANCE MEASURES AT THE PARKER HOUSE, 1978–79

Period	Room nights	Occupancy rate (%)	Room sales efficiency (%)	Room sales ($)	Food sales ($)	Beverage sales ($)
Total 1978	160,062	80	68	6,273,077	2,829,678	1,454,066
January 1978	11,565	68	53	411,868	194,618	106,487
February	11,402	75	59	418,806	177,638	105,908
March	12,944	77	63	489,657	247,263	141,023
April	13,710	84	72	541,328	250,043	120,689
May	13,863	82	70	547,462	242,681	119,742
June	13,598	83	71	545,280	220,276	105,067
July	12,638	75	63	496,233	168,230	81,632
August	15,081	89	76	598,732	217,394	101,655
September	14,516	89	76	577,712	254,965	125,853
October	15,495	92	79	623,768	316,894	142,092
November	13,659	84	75	573,061	260,021	135,576
December	11,591	69	56	449,170	279,655	168,162
January 1979	13,244	78	61	522,829	234,525	132,179
February	11,741	77	60	463,630	208,382	118,915
March	14,809	87	73	624,512	275,125	154,401
April	14,527	89	80	661,863	280,206	139,566

Source: Company records.

EXHIBIT 4 AVERAGE HOTEL OCCUPANCY RATES IN BOSTON BY MONTH, 1965–78

	1965	1966	1967	1968	1969	1970	1971	1972	1973	1974	1975	1976	1977	1978	Weighted Average 1965–77
January	61.9	59.3	69.8	68.7	62.6	58.6	53.3	53.8	59.7	53.9	49.8	51.4	56.6	59.3	57.8
February	65.0	63.7	73.0	75.0	70.8	60.8	57.8	58.3	57.0	58.1	51.6	54.8	57.2	64.1	61.1
March	67.9	66.4	75.5	78.9	73.1	66.7	62.6	68.0	63.3	68.0	55.1	62.9	65.7	73.5	70.2
April	69.6	71.3	82.3	79.6	80.5	80.1	66.7	78.3	71.1	72.6	68.5	69.8	74.8	80.3	73.9
May	66.0	79.6	78.9	84.2	79.5	71.9	69.4	68.5	73.0	76.1	75.6	74.9	76.1	83.6	74.7
June	68.6	80.7	83.4	82.4	83.1	77.4	72.2	78.3	78.5	80.8	74.7	81.7	81.8	87.6	78.7
July	56.7	67.5	75.0	73.1	74.6	63.5	66.9	67.3	67.4	69.9	61.7	72.3	67.8	76.8	68.0
August	65.3	76.0	82.0	80.2	77.8	77.6	75.3	67.3	72.6	78.1	68.3	76.9	78.3	87.1	75.3
September	73.1	82.0	88.0	80.9	80.6	74.2	77.2	75.6	76.5	73.9	74.2	80.4	84.8	90.1	78.4
October	77.4	91.0	85.5	90.1	85.4	81.6	83.9	87.7	84.8	82.3	83.7	84.1	88.6	89.9	85.1
November	65.5	71.5	72.2	72.3	67.1	62.5	63.0	69.1	64.2	62.4	62.0	59.6	67.6	75.1	65.8
December	50.0	53.6	56.6	52.4	58.3	51.3	47.3	51.9	50.3	43.9	43.4	55.1	52.8	58.7	51.1
Total	66.7	72.2	76.8	76.5	74.4	68.9	66.4	68.9	68.3	68.3	64.1	68.9	71.2	77.1	69.9
National averages	71.3	72.2	74.6	73.6	73.3	67.6	64.1	65.0	66.3	65.8	62.5	65.9	67.7	N.A.	

Source: Cited in *Hotel and Convention Center Demand and Supply in Boston,* Boston Redevelopment Authority, March 1979, p. IV-4.

EXHIBIT 5 CURRENT HOTEL STOCK AND PROJECTED DEMAND IN DOWNTOWN BOSTON BY CLASS AND MAJOR USE, SPRING 1979

	Class A Luxury hotel rooms			Class B Moderately priced hotel rooms			Class C Inexpensive hotel rooms			Totals		
	Current Stock	1985 Demand*	1985 Stock*	Current Stock	1985 Demand*	1985 Stock*	Current Stock	1985 Demand*	1985 Stock*	Current Stock	1985 Demand*	1985 Stock*
Business Visitor	2,169	3,845	4,019	1,003	1,536	1,487	211	302	221	3,393	5,683	5,727
Tourist	518	1,321	1,123	599	1,342	949	296	642	296	1,413	3,305	2,368
Convention	1,294	2,487	3,894	720	1,234	720	105	148	105	2,119	3,869	4,719
Total	3,981	7,653	9,036	2,322	4,112	3,156	622	1,092	622	6,925	12,857	12,814

*Projections.
Source: Boston Redevelopment Authority study, 1979.

The city had not always been so popular; between 1930 and 1955, not a single new hotel room was built in Boston. Between 1930 and 1960, the city posted a net decrease of 4,938 hotel rooms. Although construction resumed during the 1960s, many hoteliers put aside plans for expansion following the recession of 1974–75.

With a restricted supply of hotel rooms, the city's economic revival pushed occupancy rates steadily higher (*Exhibit 4*). In 1978, average occupancy rates exceeded 80 percent during six months out of twelve, reaching a peak of 90 percent in September and October. Since weekend occupancy tended to drop sharply, this meant that many hotels were fully booked Monday through Thursday for several months of the year.

The supply/demand imbalance in Boston had reached what many city officials described as a crisis by early 1979, when two major national organizations called off plans to hold conventions in the city, citing lack of space. Hynes Auditorium, located in the Prudential Center, was Boston's only major convention center and contained only 150,000 feet of floor space; although Boston was the eighth largest population area in the nation, 30 other cities could accommodate larger conventions. It was estimated that the loss of major conventions, plus straight business and tourist turnaways, was costing the city and state $30 million annually.

Despite Boston's severely limited convention facilities, convention visitors composed 31 percent of local hotel guests in 1978. Tourists accounted for 20 percent, and business travelers, 49 percent. Business demand was expected to reach 5,683 rooms by 1985, a 67 percent increase over 1978.

According to a recent study conducted for the mayor of Boston by the Boston Redevelopment Authority (BRA), the city was noted for possessing an unusually large concentration of what the BRA defined as "luxury" hotels. More than half of the town's 6,925 rooms were classed as luxury by the BRA; one third were classed as moderately priced; and less than ten percent were categorized as inexpensive. *Exhibit 5* presents the BRA's analysis of Boston's hotel stock by class and major use.

Competition

Visitors to Boston could choose from approximately a dozen major hotels, as well as several lesser ones, located within a three-mile radius of the central city (*Exhibit 6*). The Boston hotel stock was positioned to absorb the cream of hotel demand, leaving the adjacent metropolitan region to accommodate the overflow of convention delegates and tourists (an additional 2,883 rooms were located outside the city in Cambridge and other suburbs).

McIntosh and Chekijian agreed that the Parker House's most significant competitors were the Ritz Carlton, the Copley Plaza, and the Hyatt Regency (the latter located across the river in Cambridge). Built in 1927 by a Harvard graduate who for decades admitted guests according to his evaluation of their social status, the Ritz never suffered the temporary decline that blighted the Parker House. Ninety percent of its guests were repeat visitors, and though its dining room was felt to have slipped somewhat in recent years, it was still considered one of the best restaurants in town. After its owner's death in 1961, the Ritz had been sold to a local real estate investor, and several senior employees resigned in the ensuing years, stating, it was reported, that the hotel's rigorous standards had declined. (One chef, for example, expressed indignation over the presence of frozen food in the kitchen.)

Nevertheless, the Ritz remained a formidable competitor. Its Back Bay location, between Newbury Street and Commonwealth Avenue, was some distance from Boston's congested financial center, but very convenient to the city's shops, theatres, and galleries; the public rooms and many guest rooms offered a fine view of the Boston Public Garden, situated across the street from the hotel's main entrance. Guest rooms were also equipped with working fireplaces, and the hotel's average ratio of 0.7 rooms per staff member was the lowest in town (*Exhibit 7*). Although one industry expert interviewed by *Boston* magazine in 1977 considered the Ritz somewhat "tired looking," he nevertheless declared that "if there were a list of great hotels in the United States, and a hotel in Boston had to be on it,

EXHIBIT 6   LOCATION OF MAJOR EXISTING AND PROPOSED HOTELS IN THE BOSTON AREA, 1979

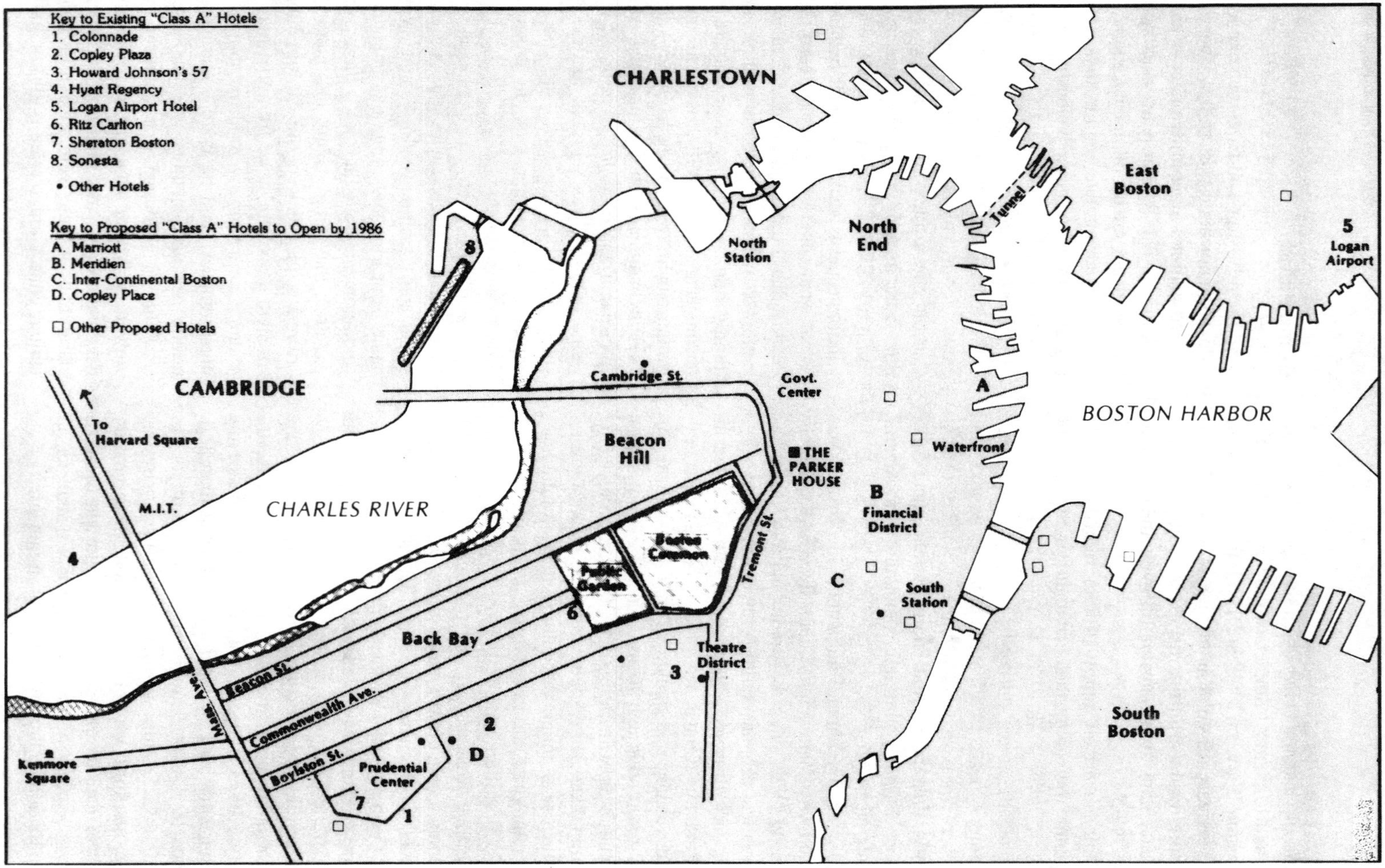

Key to Existing "Class A" Hotels
1. Colonnade
2. Copley Plaza
3. Howard Johnson's 57
4. Hyatt Regency
5. Logan Airport Hotel
6. Ritz Carlton
7. Sheraton Boston
8. Sonesta
• Other Hotels

Key to Proposed "Class A" Hotels to Open by 1986
A. Marriott
B. Meridien
C. Inter-Continental Boston
D. Copley Place
□ Other Proposed Hotels

CHARLESTOWN

East Boston

Logan Airport

BOSTON HARBOR

South Boston

North End

Waterfront

Financial District

South Station

Govt. Center

THE PARKER HOUSE

Theatre District

Tremont St.

Beacon Hill

Cambridge St.

Boston Common

Public Garden

Back Bay

Prudential Center

CHARLES RIVER

CAMBRIDGE

M.I.T.

To Harvard Square

Kenmore Square

North Station

Commonwealth Ave.

Boylston St.

Mass. Ave.

Tunnel

EXHIBIT 7   CHARACTERISTICS OF HOTELS COMPETING IN THE CENTRAL BOSTON MARKET

Hotel	Opening date	Number of rooms	1979 Price range		Class*	Major use**	Employees	Rooms per employee	Permanent residents
			Single	Double					
Boston Park Plaza	1927	1100	$32–42	$38–50	B	C	375	2.1	0
Bradford Hotel	1927	322	24	29	C	T	70	4.6	7
Children's Inn	1968	82	31	33	B	B	75	1.1	0
Colonnade Hotel	1971	306	58–64	66–72	A	B	260	1.2	0
Copley Plaza Hotel	1912	450	41–58	49–66	A	B	420	1.1	4
Copley Square Hotel	1895	160	28–32	32–38	B	T	45	3.6	15
Essex Hotel	1900	300	21–27	27–32	C	B	45	6.7	60
Fenway Boylston	1956	94	29	37	B	B	50	1.9	0
Holiday Inn	1968	300	41	45	B	B	175	1.7	0
Howard Johnson's 57	1972	400	44	52	A	B	225	1.8	0
Howard Johnson's Kenmore Square	1963	178	30–32	38–42	B	B	130	1.4	0
Hyatt Regency (Cambridge)	1976	478	45–73	58–68	A	B	600	.8	0
Lenox Hotel	1900	220	34–46	40–54	B	C	140	1.6	0
Logan Airport Hilton	1975	600	42	52	A	B	270	2.2	0
Midtown Motor Inn	1961	161	42	49	B	T	90	1.8	0
Parker House	1927	546	53–65	63–75	A	B	432	1.3	0
Ramada Inn-Logan	1972	209	39	47	B	B	150	1.4	0
Ritz-Carlton Hotel	1927	250	60–75	65–75	A	B	350	.7	8
Sheraton Boston	1965	1428	35–58	59–70	A	C	1000	1.4	1
Sonesta Hotel (Cambridge)	1963	200	48–52	53–60	A	B	150	1.3	1

* Class: luxury (A), moderate (B), inexpensive (C).
** Major use: tourist (T), business visitor (B), and convention (C).
Source: Boston Redevelopment Authority study, 1979; Cambridge hotel data added separately.

the Ritz is the only Boston hotel that would make it." A tower extension to the Ritz was presently under construction and scheduled to open in 1981. This addition would add 50 new rooms and a ballroom to the hotel; the remainder of the tower would be divided into condominiums.

Discussing the Hyatt Regency, opened in 1976, Yervant Chekijian commented:

Although the Cambridge location is a bit isolated and thus somewhat of a disadvantage, this is our toughest competition. They have a unique physical plant, the freshest rooms, and a beautiful view of Boston across the Charles River. Food and beverage is very good, and there is a wide selection of room configurations in the hotel. They are well managed and have the highest rates in town, as well as a national identification. All in all, a customer who doesn't like the Parker House will probably go to the Hyatt Regency.

The Hyatt offered visitors a swimming pool, a revolving rooftop restaurant, and an exotic lobby described by one local journalist as

. . . nothing short of spectacular, a soaring brick atrium built on the scale of a railroad station . . . the main attractions here are four glass-enclosed elevators that glide aloft to the revolving Spinnaker lounge and swoop swiftly down to a thrilling splashdown in the fountain.

The Hyatt also offered special "Regency Club" service, reserved for guests on the tenth floor of the hotel, who enjoyed the full-time attention of their own concierge in the private Regency Club lounge. Industry observers estimated that occupancy at both the Hyatt and the Ritz would reach 80–85 percent for 1979.

The Copley Plaza, located a few blocks from the Ritz in the Back Bay, had been built in 1912. According to Chekijian, "The Copley's physical plant is beautiful—as you approach from the outside, you know it's a luxury hotel." Like the Parker House, however, the Copley had suffered a long eclipse; during the 1940s it was bought by the Sheraton Corp. and renamed the Sheraton Plaza. The neighboring John Hancock Life Insurance Company bought the Copley in 1972, and in 1974, when the hotel regained

its former name, many rooms were lavishly redecorated with Chippendale chairs, bronze and marble chests, and ornate mirrors—what one local magazine called "the only true rococo grand-hotel-style chambers in Boston." But the same writer went on to say that some of the rooms, particularly those on the "inside" overlooking the hotel's maintenance plant, were "cramped and dingy." Occupancy was estimated at 75–80 percent for 1979.

The remaining large hotels in the city, according to Chekijian, were less attractive than the Parker House and its three serious competitors:

The Colonnade has an exceptional physical plant, built in 1971. It's not in a particularly convenient location, but President Ford stayed there when he visited Boston for the Bicentennial.

The Park Plaza was formerly the Statler Hilton, which fell on hard times and closed in November 1976. The building was renovated and reopened in February 1977. Its location is fairly convenient, but the neighborhood is somewhat unattractive. They only compete with us for the discount segments, where they do an exceptional job.

The Sheraton Boston is a typical large Sheraton. Everything about this hotel is middle-of-the-road: food and beverage, rooms, and its location on the far side of the Prudential center. The Sheraton attracts conventioneers and tour groups.

Howard Johnson's 57 has an excellent physical plant, built in 1972. The location is convenient but not very desirable—right on the edge of the adult entertainment district. Their restaurant is fairly good, and they have a movie house in the building. I think the Howard Johnson name and chain image negates the market position they're striving for.

Finally, there's the Holiday Inn. They have the highest occupancy rate in town because of their proximity to Massachusetts General Hospital. They have relatively spacious rooms and average, predictable Holiday Inn standards. In addition to visitors to the hospital, they get federal, city, and state government travelers, plus the people who always stay in a Holiday Inn.

Exhibit 7 summarizes key statistics for 20 hotels and motor inns in Boston and immediately adjacent suburbs.

Plans for New Construction

According to the Boston Redevelopment Authority, future business expansion would generate the need for almost 6,000 new rooms in Boston by 1985 (*Exhibit 5*) plus more than 4,000 additional rooms between 1985–90. However, some observers viewed these forecasts as optimistic. They pointed out that much of the new demand was projected to result from projects not yet approved—the construction of a second convention center and the expansion of existing convention facilities. Others pointed to the likelihood of a slowdown in demand resulting from the recession which economists had forecast for late 1979 or early 1980.

Developers and hotel chains alike had nevertheless become very interested in new hotel construction in Boston. By 1979, no fewer than 17 new hotels were in various stages of planning, although informed observers doubted that all proposed would actually be built (*Exhibit 6* shows the location of selected current and proposed hotels.) A plan to convert the liner *United States* to a hotel (known as *S.S. Boston*) and moor it next to Commonwealth Pier appeared particularly unlikely to materialize.

In the view of Bob McIntosh and his associates, the greatest threats to the Parker House would come from the proposed Marriott Hotel, the Meridien, the Inter-Continental Boston, and the hotel planned for Copley Place. The first three would all be located within a ten-minute walk of the Parker House. Architects' sketches of Marriott's Long Wharf Hotel showed a dramatically modern, low-rise design on a wharf jutting into Boston Harbor. It was rumored that construction on the 400-room property in the city's attractive new Waterfront area would begin in early 1980, and that the hotel would open in late 1981 or early 1982.

The shell of the elegant old Federal Reserve Bank building in the heart of the financial district was being converted into a new luxury hotel by Meridien Hotels of Paris, a subsidiary of Air France. Preliminary work had already begun. The 330-room hotel, to be called the Hotel Meridien, would be joined via a glass atrium to a new 40-story office tower. Construction was scheduled to begin in late 1979, with the opening expected in mid-1981. Plans called for the hotel to appeal primarily to the executive and luxury markets. The architect's design included large suites and guest rooms (some on two levels), ornate board rooms, a ballroom for banquets and conferences, and specialty retail shops on the ground floor.

Inter-Continental Hotels, a worldwide chain and wholly owned subsidiary of Pan American-World Airways, planned to build a 21-story, 500-room hotel, scheduled to open in late 1982, as a major element of Lafayette Place. This proposed new complex in Boston's reviving downtown retail area would include retail stores, a large circular public mall, and a parking garage for 1,300 cars. The hotel would contain a swimming pool, sun terrace, and health club as well as a large outdoor terrace for open-air receptions. Convention facilities, equipped with four simultaneous translation booths, could accommodate 1,000 people.

The proposed Copley Place complex, to be built over the Massachusetts Turnpike next to the Prudential Center, would be located near the Copley Plaza hotel on the fringe of the Back Bay, an area whose shops and art galleries already attracted many tourists and city residents. An 800-room luxury hotel was planned for Copley Place, in addition to enclosed parking for 1,500 cars; a two-level retail center; a five-story, mixed-income apartment building; and four connecting seven-story office buildings, each located on top of a two-level shopping mall. There was talk of the plans being revised to include a second hotel. The Copley Place project had generated considerable community opposition and had not yet been approved; the earliest completion date was seen as 1984.

The only other new hotel scheduled to open before 1985 was a 160-room tourist hotel near the waterfront; this was not considered major competition by Parker House management.

It was estimated that the average construction cost per room for each of the four new luxury hotels would range from $80,000 to $100,000. The pricing rule of thumb followed by the hotel industry in open-ing new properties was that the initial daily "rack rate" per room (i.e., the maximum published rate established by hotel management) should be set at one dollar for each thousand dollars of construction cost.

Contemplating the competitive challenge he would be facing in the next five years, Bob McIntosh summarized his position:

Unless we get a significant amount of corporate capital invested in substantial renovations for the Parker House, we'll be offering our guests fairly well-worn rooms that haven't been significantly redecorated since 1974. Faced with this or the chance to try out a brand-new luxury property, which do you think they're going to choose?

Singapore Airlines

Sandra Vandermerwe
Christopher H. Lovelock

As Robert Ang[1] left the marketing executives' meeting and walked through the open air gallery back to his office in Airline House, he remembered what J. Y. Pillay, Singapore Airlines' Chairman, had said four years earlier at the company's 40th anniversary celebrations in 1987. "At 40 the symptoms of middle age begin and that's when complacency sets in," he had warned. Ang thought to himself, "And now that we are 44, this risk is even greater if we don't do something to hold onto our customer-oriented image." The discussion at the meeting on this fine May morning had centered on the role of technology in achieving this goal.

Ang paused to watch a Boeing 747-400 coming in to land. Dubbed the "Megatop" because of its extended upper deck, the aircraft was the most recent addition to the company's ultra-modern fleet. Singapore Airlines' blue, white, and yellow colors shone brightly in the steamy midday heat.

As Ang entered the office complex that housed his marketing systems team, he imagined the passengers starting to disembark after a 12- to 13-hour nonstop trip from Europe. What sort of flight had they had? Had the long journey gone well, reinforcing Singapore Airlines' reputation as one of the world's best airlines? The cabin crew would now be saying goodbye, and the passengers would soon be welcomed into the spacious elegance of Terminal 2 at Changi Airport, one of the largest and most modern in the world.

Ang knew that the company's achievements were already considerable; it had become one of the world's 10 biggest international airlines. But now, on the threshold of a new decade, the question was: Could Singapore Airlines (SIA) continue to attract increasing numbers of international customers?

"We are leaders in service, in comfort and luxury. Our customers tell us they fall in love when they fly with us. Where do we go from here?" were some of the remarks voiced at the meeting. For Robert Ang, there was only one logical answer: They had to satisfy the needs of contemporary travelers, which meant being able to bring the sophisticated technology found in people's homes and offices into the air. "Very little attention has been given to adapting technology strategically for our business," he had

[1] Disguised name.

declared to his colleagues that morning. "For instance, home audio systems are fantastic. But in the air, they're terrible. We have to close this technology gap and provide modern customers with interesting and useful technology-based services."

Ang's views had been received with interest. His boss, the director of marketing planning, had closed the meeting by asking him to come up with some specific suggestions. "But," he had cautioned, "don't suggest anything that might conflict with the romance and superb personal service we're rightly famous for!"

BACKGROUND

"How did it all begin?" was a question that people encountering Singapore Airlines for the first time often asked. Many were surprised that a small island republic, measuring only 38km long by 22km wide (16 × 24 miles), and with a population of 2.7 million, could have one of the world's largest and most profitable airlines. Even more remarkable were the accolades bestowed by air travel organizations. In 1990, *Air Transport World* magazine named SIA "airline of the year"; *Conde Nast's Traveler* termed it the "world's best airline"; and *Business Traveler International* called SIA the "best international airline."

Republic of Singapore

Just north of the equator, with a command of the straits between Malaysia and Indonesia, Singapore was ideally located for both shipping and airline routes. Being at the intersection of East and West, it saw itself at the heart of trade and business between the two.

In the 26 years since its independence in 1965, the nation had made what most observers considered to be astonishing economic progress. Per capita national income had reached US$10,450, representing 37% of that of Switzerland, which Singaporean planners often cited as their economic model. It boasted not only one of the world's largest and most modern port facilities, but an airport, opened in 1981 and

expanded in 1990, of equal caliber. Other accomplishments included a state-of-the-art telecommunications system, well-engineered highways, and the new Mass Rapid Transit rail system. Heavy investments in education and a strong work ethic had created a well-trained and motivated workforce. By 1991, Singapore was one of the world's largest ship-building and ship-repairing centers, the third largest oil refining and distribution complex, and had also become an important banking and financial center.

Singapore had made a particular effort to attract high-technology firms, and many international companies had set up offices and plants on the island. Government planners saw technology as a driving force in the economy. As advances in telecommunications proceeded, and Singapore Telecom continued to push toward a fully digitalized system, planners spoke about creating an "intelligent island."

History of Singapore Airlines

Who would have believed that a country only one-quarter the size of Rhode Island, the smallest state in the US, would produce one of the most profitable airlines in the world? The story of Singapore Airlines officially started on May 1, 1947, when the first scheduled flight of Malaysian Airlines from Singapore landed in Penang. When both Malaysia and Singapore became independent in the mid-1960s, the name of the carrier was changed to Malaysia-Singapore Airlines. However it soon became obvious that the two nations had different priorities. Malaysia's main interest was having a flag carrier that would provide domestic and regional routes. But, being a small island, Singapore did not need domestic services; instead, its goal was to have long-distance international routes. It was agreed that the assets should be divided and two separate airlines created.

Singapore Airlines first flew under its own colors in October 1972. When it was announced that Malaysia and Singapore had agreed to establish two separate flag carriers, optimism was tempered by uncertainty and disbelief. Could an airline from such a small country compete in the international big league? Nevertheless, the 1970s seemed to be a good time for an airline to take off and succeed. Not only did the remarkable passenger growth of the 1960s—when traffic was doubling every five years—promise to continue, but ever increasing numbers of people worldwide were traveling to more places. In addition, exciting new high performance jets were being introduced.

Although Singapore Airlines was state owned, the government's role in policy making and day-to-day management was minimal; senior executives were told not to expect any subsidy or preferential treatment. What the government did do, however, was to offer foreign carriers the opportunity to operate out of Singapore, under the condition that SIA would receive similar rights, even if they were not exercised immediately. The new airline pushed relentlessly for growth and innovation. Three months before operations began, it signed a contract with Boeing for the delivery of two B747-200s, with an option on two more. It was the first airline in Southeast Asia to order jumbo jets.

Singapore Airlines also concentrated on marketing: The airline's name and its logo—a stylized yellow bird—decorating the aircraft's dark blue tail fin soon became well known on the routes it operated. The goal was to create a distinctly different airline that would be international but retain its Asian personality. Most importantly, top management insisted that it emphasize service to passengers who, they constantly reminded staff, were the unique reason for the airline's existence. In a world where one carrier resembled another, they realized that the cabin crew was the prime link between the passenger and the airline. The idea was to use the island's only real resource—the natural hospitality of its people—as a competitive advantage. In this way, it seemed certain that Singapore's national carrier would be remembered—and remembered favorably.

Research had shown that, when all other things were equal, passengers responded most to the appeal of high quality in-flight services. SIA was the first airline to put "snoozers" (fully reclining seats) in its aircraft. Since the company did not belong to IATA (International Air Transport Association), SIA's management went against the rules by serving free drinks, offering free movie headsets and other extras. The intent was to firmly establish an image of SIA in customers' minds as *the* airline for fine service.

The "Singapore Girl"—the personification of charm and friendliness—became a reality after painstaking recruiting, training and retraining. The best-looking and most helpful young women were selected as stewardesses. They were given a maximum of three contract terms of five years each, above average wages, and high status in the company. Better staff were given the possibility of promotion to senior jobs within SIA after the 15 year period. An extensive and distinctive advertising campaign promoted these stewardesses dressed in a striking uniform derived from the traditional sarong sebaya. It consisted of a multi-colored, ankle-length dress made from beautiful batik fabric designed by the Paris couturier Balmain. Male flight attendants were more conventionally dressed in light blue blazers and black trousers.

These young women became the symbol of the airline's mission to deliver high quality personalized service. Research showed that they had the most lasting impact on passengers. Travelers reported that their distinctive uniform and charm were, in reality, all that the advertising had promised, and that in-flight service was better than anything they had experienced in a long time.

Top management was equally concerned with services on the ground. In 1973 a subsidiary company, Singapore Airport Terminal Services (SATS), was formed to perform ground handling, catering, and related tasks. Later, it started offering its services on a contract basis to other carriers that had operations in Singapore. In 1985, SATS was restructured into a holding company with four subsidiaries—SATS Passenger Services, SATS Catering, SATS Cargo, and SATS Apron Services.

Singapore Airlines survived the two oil shocks of the 1970s and continued to grow, creating headlines with such innovations as supersonic Concorde service between London and Singapore, operated jointly with British Airways, featuring BA colors on one side of the aircraft and SIA colors on the other. It also expanded its route structure. Huge aircraft orders, including what was then the largest in civil aviation history, were made. Thanks to strong profits, the airline was able to invest in new equipment without incurring significant debt. These enormous purchases were not all incremental additions to the fleet, for the company resold used aircraft after only a few years. Because they had been so well maintained, the "old" aircraft found ready buyers at good prices in the second-hand market.

THE SITUATION IN 1991

As one industry observer remarked, "1990 was a year that most airlines would sooner forget!" Battered by recession, a hike in oil prices, high interest rates on heavy debt loads, and the tensions arising from the Iraqi invasion of Kuwait, most major airlines suffered heavy financial losses. The outbreak of hostilities in the Gulf intensified problems; fear of terrorist attacks sharply reduced passenger loads on most international routes. But, at a time when many other airlines were retrenching, Singapore Airlines actually increased its advertising budget.

SIA's consolidated financial results for the fiscal year ending March 31, 1991, showed only a slight decline in revenues, from S$5.09 billion to S$4.95 billion.[2] The number of passengers carried climbed from 6.8 million to 7.1 million, even though the load factor dropped from 78.3% to 75.1% as a result of a jump in fleet size. In 1990, SIA had the highest operating profit of any airline in the world: US$775 million. Apart from its marketing appeal, Singapore Airlines had another point in its favor—the higher margins obtained on airline services in Asia. The Asian carriers did not compete on price among themselves. They preferred non-price forms of competition such as better service, more destinations, more frequent schedules, and newer fleets. With the entry of American players into the region, however, price became a more important feature.

The airline's fleet of 29 Boeing 747s and 14 Airbus 310s was the youngest fleet of all international

carriers, with an average aircraft age of 4.75 years, compared to an industry average of around 10 years. The company had 36 new aircraft on order (of which 28 were the new B747-400s) and another 34 on option. Management was convinced that newer planes were not only more attractive to passengers and helped staff provide better service, but also offered other advantages, such as greater reliability and lower fuel consumption. (*Exhibit 1* compares Singapore Airlines' performance measures with those of other major international airlines.)

By 1991 Singapore Airlines was among the ten biggest airlines in the world, as measured in terms of international metric ton-kilometers of load carried. Its network linked 63 cities in 37 countries, and soon it would fulfill a long-held ambition to serve the East coast of the United States with transatlantic service from Frankfurt to New York. Singapore Changi Airport had become one of the world's largest and busiest terminals.

Government holdings had been reduced through stock sales to 54% of the company's assets. The airline had joined in a trilateral alliance with Swissair and the American carrier Delta Airlines to cooperate on customer servicing, interchangeable tour packages, through check-in, joint baggage handling, sharing of airport lounges, and joint promotions. It had also become a member of IATA in order to give the airline a voice in key industry forums, and greater access to their technical expertise and accredited sales agents. However, SIA did not want to participate in deliberations on tariff coordination where fare issues were discussed.

Despite the airline's achievements, there were some disquieting signs on the horizon. Competition was intensifying and service quality improving among a number of both Western and Asian airlines, including Hong Kong-based Cathay Pacific, Japan Airlines, a new strongly financed Taiwanese start-up called Eva Air, Thai International, and Malaysia Airlines. The latter two both featured stewardesses in eye-catching uniforms based on traditional costumes.

With rising living standards in Singapore came higher expectations among its more than 13,000 employees, of whom some 4,200 were cabin crew. The

---

[2] Typical exchange rates for the Singapore dollar (S$) in 1991 were: S$1.00 = US$0.60 = £0.33.

EXHIBIT I   KEY PERFORMANCE MEASURES 1990

1990 scheduled passengers carried (international)		1990 scheduled passenger-kilometers performed (international)		1990 operating profits of the top ten of these airlines	
Rank	**Numbers (in thousands)**	**Rank**	**Numbers (in millions)**	**Rank**	**US dollars (millions)**
1 British Airways	19,684	1 British Airways	62,834	1 Singapore Airlines	774
2 Lutfthansa	13,326	2 Japan Airlines	42,690	2 Cathay Pacific	468
3 Air France	12,417	3 Lufthansa	38,744	3 Japan Airlines	464
4 Pan American	10,096	4 Pan American	38,241	4 British Airways	345
5 Japan Airlines	8,354	5 United	35,334	5 SAS	264
6 American Airlines	8,343	6 Singapore Airlines	31,544	6 American Airlines	67.9
7 SAS	8,335	7 Air France	29,023	7 Lufthansa	0
8 Cathay Pacific	7,378	8 Qantas	27,687	8 KLM	(19.3)
9 Alitalia	7,105	9 KLM	26,382	9 Alitalia	(75.7)
10 Singapore Airlines	7,093	10 American Airlines	24,086	10 Air France	(286)

company was finding it increasingly difficult to attract younger people, motivate existing employees, and maintain its policy of employing the best staff for customer contact roles.

MAINTAINING THE CUSTOMER SERVICE PHILOSOPHY

Recognizing that the most exciting years were now over, top management continued to stress the importance of SIA's customer philosophy and service culture. The underlying principle that the customer came first was carried through at all levels of the organization. How customers were handled at each point of contact was considered of paramount importance. Company policy stated that if a trade-off had to be made, it should be made in favor of the customer. For example, contrary to the practice at other airlines, no customer was allowed to be downgraded for a Singapore Airlines senior executive who wanted a special seat.

Ground had recently been broken for a new US$50 million training center, designed to drill all employees in the fine art of serving customers. As reported in the *Straits Times,* Singapore's leading newspaper, everyone—from the floor sweeper to the deputy managing director—would receive this training. The un-

derlying philosophy was to enable staff to place themselves in the customer's position. A lot of the training time was thus experientially based. Key people were sent on special missions to see what other airlines were doing and how customers were handled. Special delay simulation games groomed staff on ways to cope with delay situations, one of the major complaints received from passengers.

One principle remained constant: Staff had to be as flexible as possible in their dealings with customers, even if it took more time and effort. Management constantly reiterated that customers could not be told what to do simply because it suited the company. Some passengers wanted to eat as soon as they boarded; others preferred to wait. Customers could not be pigeonholed; they often changed their minds. They might come on board intending to sleep and then decide to watch a movie after all. On long hauls, flexibility was especially important. Most passengers had individual habits that corresponded to their travel agendas, which could include sleeping at the beginning and working later, or vice versa.

Staff had learned that customers were happier when given a choice. Offering more meal variations automatically reduced the number of unhappy people. Menus, typically changed by other airlines no more than four times a year, were altered every week on SIA's high frequency flights. Information technology enabled the chefs to fine-tune menus and immediately withdraw any dishes that were poorly received. Although there were marginal costs associated with such tactics, management firmly believed that these efforts distinguished Singapore Airlines from its competitors. Staff was instructed to find other ways to save money. For instance, the chefs prepared meals only from ingredients in season. Crew members were briefed by the kitchen on how to prepare and serve anything new.

Complaints were encouraged, as they provided insight about problems. Once they were received, something could be done to rectify the situation; all complaints were tracked down and followed up. Travelers were invited to submit these complaints in writing. While some customers—typically Americans, Germans, and Australians—readily complied, others were less willing to do so in writing. These customers were specifically questioned in follow-up surveys.

A Service Productivity Index (SPI) was computed each quarter in order to assess service quality standards. Multilingual in-flight surveys were used to itemize customers' impressions on key issues; then this information was compiled along with data on punctuality, baggage mishandled/recovered per 1,000 passengers, and the ratio of complaints to compliments addressed to management.

As soon as a complaint relating directly to a specific in-flight experience was received, crew members could be temporarily taken out of the system and given training. Cabin crew members were released from their flight schedules three or four times a year to meet with training experts. Senior cabin crew members met every Monday morning for feedback and exchange sessions with service support personnel. One "ritual" practiced was to address the crew from the control center just before takeoff about topical issues, special promotions, and other issues relevant to services.

At the airport in Singapore, staff were encouraged to do everything possible to deal with legitimate customer problems. One story—now part of company folklore—was about a supervisor who found a tailor at midnight and paid a deposit from his own funds to have a suit made for a customer whose luggage had been lost so that the customer could attend an important meeting at noon the next day.

CUSTOMER PROFILE AND THE PRODUCT LINE

The product line was divided into three classes of travel—First, Raffles (business), and Economy. First Class accounted for 5% of passengers, Raffles Class for 10%, and Economy Class for 85%. About one million of the seven million seats sold annually were to Singaporeans. Revenues from non-Singaporeans were proportionately higher, since they tended to fly longer distances. Of the airline's passengers, 75% were from outside the country and 25% were from home base.

Flights varied in length—from less than one hour to over 13 hours for nonstop flights to Europe. Flights under four hours were all non-smoking, reflecting Singapore's strong national commitment to curtailing tobacco use. (*Exhibit 2* gives the airline's daily flights by number of hours and amount of overnight travel.)

EXHIBIT 2   DETAILS ON DURATION OF FLIGHTS

	Duration of flights		
	up to 3 hrs	4–8 hrs	9 hrs+
flights	60%	18%	22%
revenues	25%	25%	50%
mainly during day* / mainly during night	all	60% / 40%	25% / 75%

* Depending on whether it goes through midnight of the originating point.

On average, the load factor was somewhat higher in Economy Class (close to 80%) than in Raffles or First. Passengers who flew Raffles Class on a daytime flight might travel First Class on an overnight flight for the extra comfort.

Top management believed that the business passenger market held the future for the airline—both in numbers and yield. At the marketing executive meeting Robert Ang had just attended, everyone had concurred that technology was the key to improving service to this segment of the market. The expectations of these particular customers, the executives knew, were constantly rising and their needs had changed greatly since the previous decade. Research revealed that business travelers:

• Preferred to eat small amounts and less often
• Wanted more nutrition in their diet
• Tended to be impatient and resented having to wait
• Wanted to have the facilities found in airport lounges—such as showers and fax machines—also available in the sky
• Disliked wasting time on board and wanted to be occupied throughout the flight

At the start of the meeting, Robert Ang had pointed out that the only way for the company to genuinely cater to travelers' increasingly sophisticated needs was to use technology more strategically for enhancing the quality of service. It was not enough to simply pick easily replicated innovations on an *ad hoc* basis. He had declared:

Just going out and looking for technology-based solutions will give the market the impression that we are gimmicky and arbitrary in our approach. If we want to protect our competitive position, we've got to find ways to move faster than our competitors and create an enduring advantage for the company. There will be a million problems but, once we agree on the principle of "technology in the sky" as a competitive tool, we can solve the technical hassles. We have to use technology in the future as we used people in the past to serve customers. If we can match our high-tech services with our soft services, we will be irresistible to customers and will be distinguished from the rest.

Several technological innovations were already planned for introduction later that year. One was the installation of small TV screens at each First and Business Class seat, offering passengers video entertainment. Since other airlines were also doing this, ensuring variety would be pivotal. Another was satellite-linked air-to-ground telephone service which, unlike previously, allowed passengers to make calls even when the aircraft was above the ocean. Although these innovations were important, Ang felt it was not enough. He knew that there would be innumerable possibilities for adding value to the customers' total flying experience—but only if the know-how and technology could be applied correctly.

Almost 80,000 travelers were registered in the Priority Passenger Service (PPS) program. To become a member, a passenger had to fly at least 60,000 km (37,500 miles) a year in First or Raffles Class. Benefits included extra baggage allowance, automatic flight reconfirmation, priority wait listing, a complimentary magazine subscription, and discounts on car rentals, hotels, and shopping. Information about each PPS member—such as seat and meal preferences—was stored in a computer and could be automatically implemented when reservations were made. Ang considered this kind of service to be only the beginning; there was no end to what information technology could do to improve customer service. There was also no reason to confine the system to only 80,000 people simply because the company's technology capacity was limited.

ADVERTISING CAMPAIGNS

Around 2% of Singapore Airlines' gross income was devoted to advertising and promotion. All expenditures were carefully controlled by the head office, and strategic advertising decisions were all centralized. Tactical advertising that focused on specific routes, schedules, or promotions were handled locally, but were strictly monitored in Singapore to guarantee consistency.

The "Singapore Girl" theme had remained a key element in the company's advertising strategy since day one. Initially, the aim of this strategy was to impart a feeling of romance and luxury service, and so it was dominated by images of sarong-clad women against exotically romantic backdrops. The modem fleet campaign which followed featured aircraft exteriors or interiors with just a small cameo inset of a stewardess at one side.

The purpose of the fleet modernization campaign was to give another strong message to the market: that Singapore Airlines was a leader in aircraft technology. The object was to show that the "steel" did not overpower the "silk." The photographs gave the advertising a deliberately dream-like quality, a theme carried through in the 1990 Raffles campaign—SIA's first attempt to aim specifically at business class travelers.

Research revealed that two out of every three Europeans, Americans, and Australians preferred the romantic ads to the technical ones. These passengers were spellbound by the beauty of the stewardesses and impressed by their competence and caring. Japanese and other Asian clients, on the other hand, seemed to prefer the high-tech ads which denoted modernity, reliability, and new experiences. The Singapore Girl did not seem so exotic, unusual, or appealing to this group.

SALES AND DISTRIBUTION SYSTEM

Like most fleets, Singapore Airlines depended heavily on independent agents to sell its service. In 1973, the airline initiated its own computer reservation and check-in system, KRISCOM. By 1991 this had been replaced by Abacus, a computer reservation system which provided travel agents with an extended array of services including airline and hotel reservations, ground arrangements, and regional travel news. Originally created by Singapore Airlines and two other Asian carriers, Abacus was now owned and operated by SIA and nine other carriers, including three American firms. More than 100 carriers, 80 hotel chains, and many other travel services had signed up with Abacus to distribute their services through the system.

When reservations were made on Singapore Airlines by travel agents, the recorded preferences of Priority Passenger Service (PPS) travelers would automatically be retrieved from the computer. A wide variety of special meal options, reflecting travelers' many different health and religious needs, were offered. Special meal requests were forwarded to the catering department, which received a print-out of all such requests for each flight. The special meal request was linked to the seat allocated to the passenger. (*Exhibit 3* shows a simplified flowchart of the linkages between the different databases and the departure control system.)

TECHNOLOGY AND ON-THE-GROUND SERVICES

The Ground Service Department was responsible for the ground handling of passengers, baggage, cargo, and mail at all 63 airports in the Singapore Airlines network. At Changi, SATS were in charge, but at other airports the airline had to rely on subcontractors. Even though some Singapore Airlines employees were allocated to these stations, most staff members were host country nationals and frequently had a different way of thinking.

Since what people really wanted most was to get in and out of airports as quickly and easily as possible, Ang believed that interventions with staff should be kept to a minimum. Specific problems had to be dealt with and overcome:

It's easier to control the quality of service in the air than on the ground. Key decisions are made at the head office and implemented on board. Airports, on the other hand, are difficult to control. Technology is the key. The airports themselves are too crowded, with too few gates, too few counters, and long lines. While in-flight service staff typically *give* customers something—free headsets, free newspapers, free drinks, free meals, free movies—ground service staff *take*—tickets, excess baggage fees, or they say you can't have the seat you want. Thirty percent of all complaints relate to seat assignments, another 20% to aircraft delays. How these delays are handled has a big impact on customer opinion. Passengers become really unhappy when staff can't provide information, find them seats on alternative airlines, or obtain hotel rooms when they are delayed overnight. Lost baggage also accounts for about 20% of total complaints. With better technology and information, not only can we give the same kind of service on the ground as in the air, but we can minimize our risk by providing everyone around the world with a system we know works.

EXHIBIT 3   FLOWCHART OF DATA BASES

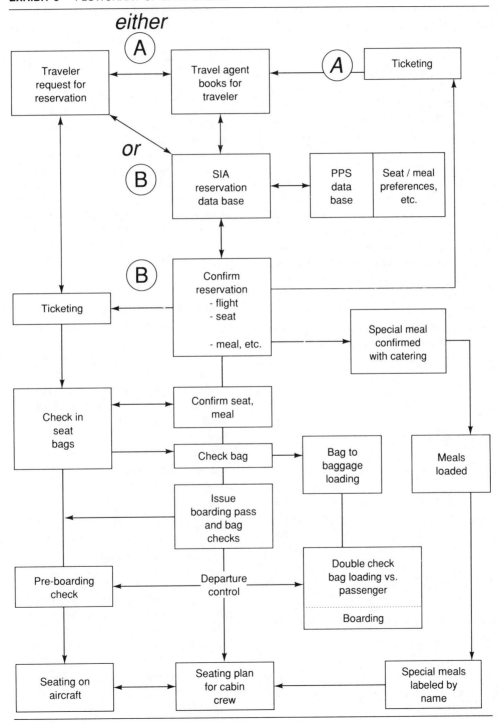

An Outstanding Service on the Ground (OSG) program had been started for all passengers and complemented the lounges, equipped with every possible luxury and convenience, instituted earlier for First and Business Class travelers. When Terminal 2 opened at Changi, a new Departure Control System (DCS90) was phased in. A key component was an improved simplified format for the screens used at check-in. It had become increasingly difficult to recruit and retain staff for check-in positions, and the complex software led to delays for passengers. A new user-friendly program, with menu-driven, on-screen commands was introduced, which simplified both the task and the training.

The benefits for passengers included a simplified and speedier check-in process, with boarding passes and baggage tags being automatically encoded and printed at the check-in. The boarding pass included seat allocation and gate information, and confirmed special requests, such as vegetarian meals. At the boarding gate, passengers would simply slip their boarding passes through a reader at the gate and the DCS90 software would verify check-in details against boarding passengers. An important security benefit was the automatic matching up of checked baggage with passengers going on board (refer to *Exhibit 3*).

A Telecar system was introduced to take baggage from one terminal to another within three minutes. It was then manually sorted and handled. If an urgent flight connection had to be made, this fact was communicated to the staff in advance so that baggage could be taken by trolley to the awaiting aircraft. Unlike the situation at most other airports, the Skytrain not only took passengers to and from terminals, but staff directed and accompanied passengers to flights with short connecting times, thus minimizing confusion and delays.

TECHNOLOGY AND IN-FLIGHT SERVICES

By realizing such innovations as video screens at each seat and better air-to-ground telecommunications, Ang wanted to transform the cabin into an "office and leisure center in the sky" which would enhance entertainment as well as business services. Surely almost anything could be possible in the future thanks to technology. But, what did customers value? What was feasible? What would distinguish Singapore Airlines from the competition? What were the real issues? At the meeting, he had told the others:

We have to be able to provide passengers with as much distraction—be it entertainment or professional—as possible during their flight. It's just the opposite from the situation on the ground. Customers must be able to do whatever they need to do throughout their time with us. And, the choice must be theirs, not ours. They shouldn't have to encounter any problems in dealing with our staff and should, in fact, be encouraged to interact with them as much as possible, since we're very good at that. If technology is used properly and creatively, we can personalize our services still more and make people feel that we really care. For instance, hand-held computers can tell on-board crews everything they need to know about each customer so that services can be customized.

After the meeting, Ang's boss, the director of marketing planning, commented on the suggestions Ang had made. Although the ideas were interesting, he said, there should be nothing to disturb other passengers, reduce valuable seating space, or adversely affect the company's high level of personal service. Ang, who had anticipated this reaction, responded by saying that the location of the technology on board would be the determining factor. He could think of several options: centering the technology at each passenger's seat; demarcating work and leisure centers at a given spot inside the aircraft; or, alternatively, using crew members to handle the bulk of passenger requests—for instance, sending faxes.

ANG SETS TO WORK

Back in his office, with a good feeling about the meeting that morning, Robert Ang thought about the three pillars which provided the quality experience the company insisted on for its customers: first, modern aircraft (where it was already well ahead); second, on-the-ground services (where much remained to be done, despite the accomplishments at Changi Airport). In particular, technology had to be devel-

EXHIBIT 4 FLOWCHARTING THE CUSTOMER EXPERIENCE

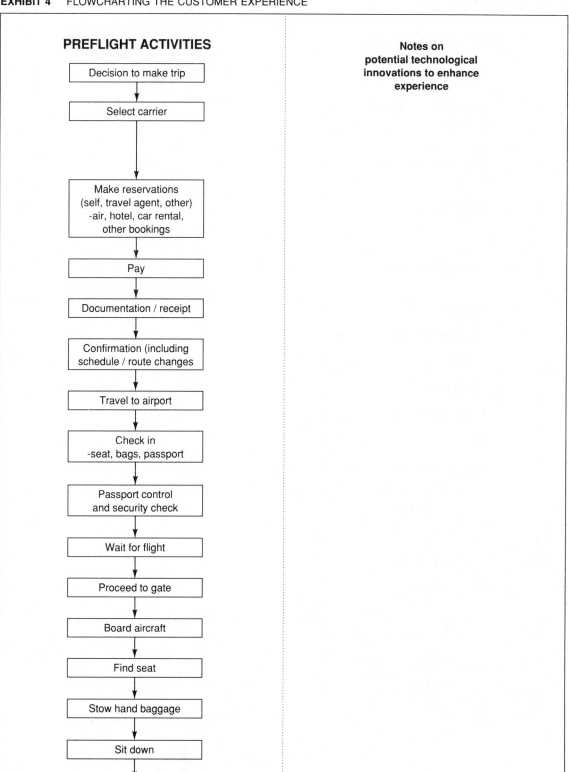

PREFLIGHT ACTIVITIES

Notes on potential technological innovations to enhance experience

- Decision to make trip
- Select carrier
- Make reservations (self, travel agent, other) -air, hotel, car rental, other bookings
- Pay
- Documentation / receipt
- Confirmation (including schedule / route changes
- Travel to airport
- Check in -seat, bags, passport
- Passport control and security check
- Wait for flight
- Proceed to gate
- Board aircraft
- Find seat
- Stow hand baggage
- Sit down

EXHIBIT 4   FLOWCHARTING THE CUSTOMER EXPERIENCE

INFLIGHT ACTIVITIES

Notes on potential technological innovations to enhance experience

Fasten seat belt

Safety demonstration and other mandatory announcements

Basics inflight amenities
- Audio / video system
- Seats
- Overnight kits
- Pillows, blankets
- Toilets

Informational announcements

Inflight diversions

- Newspapers, magazines

- News updates

- Games for kids / adults

- Food / beverages

- Movies

- Audio channels entertainment

- Audio / video for business and other purposes

- Medical help

- Assistance with work

- Physical exercise

Shopping

Pre-arrival connection / transfer activities

POSTFLIGHT ACTIVITIES

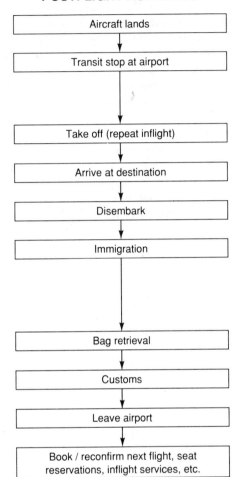

Notes on potential technological innovations to enhance experience

oped so that the company's worldwide network of sales and air staff, agents, and subcontractors could function in unison.

The third pillar was in-flight services. What technology-based services should be developed to improve the customers' experience in the air? Could an "office in the air" actually work? To what extent could more comfort and entertainment be provided, and how could the First and Business Class facilities be differentiated from those in Economy? Most importantly, how could all these ideas be consolidated and effected so that Singapore Airlines would be the technological leader in civil aviation?

Ang knew that the *how* questions needed a lot of thought before a formal presentation could be made to his boss. But, it was even more crucial to find a cohesive concept that would be appreciated and bought companywide. Perhaps it would be best to set out the various customer activities in a framework. He began to sketch out a rough flowchart showing the sequence of a typical journey. Before long, he had segmented the chart into three sections: preflight activities, flight activities, and postflight activities (refer to *Exhibit 4*). He began to fill in his ideas for using technology at each key point.

When he finally stopped for a coffee break, the sun had already begun to touch the horizon, creating a pale pink haze in the tropical sky. As he rose and stretched, he heard the soft hum of a plane above. "Must be the flight leaving for Frankfurt," he said aloud.

Loblaws

Gordon H. G. McDougall
Douglas Snetsinger

"It's been a year since we introduced green products at Loblaws and the decisions still are not getting any easier." In early July 1990, Scott Lindsay was reflecting upon his decision as to which, if any, of three possible products he would recommend for the G·R·E·E·N line: an energy-efficient light bulb, toilet tissue made from recycled paper, or a high-fiber cereal.

As Director of International Trade for Intersave Buying & Merchandising Services (a buying division for Loblaws), it was Scott's job to source and manage about 400 corporate brands (No Name, President's Choice, G·R·E·E·N)[1] for Loblaws in Canada. In four days Scott would have to make his recommendations to the buyers' meeting.

The "green line" for which Scott was sourcing products was a new concept for Loblaws and its customers. Launched in 1989 as part of the corporate President's Choice brands, green products had characteristics that were less hazardous to the environment and/or contributed to a more healthy lifestyle. At issue for Scott was deciding what was "green" and balancing the financial requirements of the company with the socially responsible initiative of the green line.

As well, his most pressing concern was his ability to convince the president, Dave Nichol, of the merits of his recommendations. Mr. Nichol was the driving force behind the corporate brands, and he maintained involvement and final authority on these important product decisions.

In preparation for the buyers' meeting, Scott had to have his written recommendations on Dave Nichol's desk that day. Dave Nichol required that recommendations include retail price and cost data, projected annual sales in units and dollars, as well as total gross margin expected. In addition to the expected results, best and worst case scenarios were also required. As well, primary reasons for and against the proposal needed to be given. Typically, the recommendations were made based on the Ontario market as it was the proving ground for new products.

The first product Scott was considering was a new energy-efficient light bulb, which had been success-

[1] No Name, President's Choice, and G·R·E·E·N are all trademarks, owned by Loblaw Companies Limited.

fully marketed in Germany. The bulb lasted at least ten times longer than a regular light bulb but was substantially more expensive. There was no question in Scott's mind that the energy-efficient bulb had strong "green" characteristics and would enhance Loblaws green image. However, a potential consumer price of $20 and low retail margins were a troubling combination. He knew that store managers, who were measured on sales volume and profits, would not be enthusiastic about a product that would not deliver sales or profits. These store managers controlled the individual products and brands that were carried in their stores.

The second new product was, in fact, not a new product at all. Loblaws had been selling a toilet tissue manufactured with 100% recycled material under its No Name corporate label. The existing product could be repackaged under the G·R·E·E·N label and sold beside the No Name line of products. The green packaging might alert consumers sensitive to the recycled feature, thereby generating greater volumes for the product. Further, Scott realized there was an opportunity to price the "green" toilet tissue at a higher price than the No Name, providing a higher profit margin.

The final product under consideration was a new corn flake product for the very "crowded" breakfast cereal category. The new cereal had an unusually high fiber content. The "body friendly" nature of the cereal was the basis for considering it for the green line. Its additional feature was that it could be sourced at a cost much lower than the national brands.

LOBLAW COMPANIES LIMITED

Loblaw Companies Limited is part of George Weston Ltd., a conglomerate of companies that operate in three basic areas: food processing, food distribution, and natural resources. George Weston is the sixth largest company in Canada with sales of $10.5 billion and net income of $988 million in 1989. The Loblaw Companies, an integrated group of food wholesaling and retailing companies, had total sales and net earnings in 1989 of $7,934 million and $70 million respectively (*Exhibit 1*).

At the wholesale level, divisions such as Kelly, Douglas & Company and Atlantic Wholesalers supplied over 1,280 corporate and franchise stores as well as over 12,300 independent retailers through its 54 company-owned warehouses. At the retail level, Loblaws operated both company-owned (corporate) stores including Loblaws, Zehrs, Superstore, and Real Canadian Superstore, and franchised operations including No Frills, Mr. Grocer, and Value Mart. Loblaws retail operations are spread across Canada, except in the province of Quebec, and in New Orleans and St. Louis in the United States. Eastern Canada generates approximately 50% of retail sales, western Canada approximately 33%, and the United States approximately 16% (*Exhibit 1*).

Two divisions within Loblaws co-ordinated the purchasing from outside suppliers for the corporate brands. Loblaw International Merchants under the direction of its president, Dave Nichol, was responsible for the development and merchandising of the corporate brand throughout the organization. These were approximately 3,000 corporate brands with about 200 new brands added each year. Intersave Buying and Merchandising Services was responsible for the procurement of goods from both foreign and domestic suppliers for the corporate brand program.

THE RETAIL FOOD INDUSTRY

Loblaws operated in the extremely competitive retail food business, an industry that was both highly concentrated and fragmented. Over 13,000 retail stores competed for the Canadian consumer's food dollar, yet 50% of the $41 billion sales in 1989 went through only 4% of the outlets—the supermarket chains—including Loblaws, Provigo, A&P, Oshawa, Safeway, and Steinberg. The approximately 4,800 convenience stores in Canada—Becker's, 7 Eleven, Mac's, and others—had sales of $2.3 billion. The over 8,000 independent retailers, ranging from small "mom and pop" corner stores to large independent supermarkets, generated sales of about $12.8 billion in 1989. The remaining industry sales, about $5.4 billion, were generated by specialty stores, such as bakeries and seafood stores ($3.2 billion) and a host

EXHIBIT 1
LOBLAWS—SELECTED FINANCIAL HIGHLIGHTS (1985–1989)

	1989	1988	1987	1986	1985
Operating results ($ millions)					
Sales	7,934	8,308	8,631	7,839	6,931
Trading profit*	291	258	290	249	225
Operating income	191	160	190	163	152
Net earnings	70	26	74	74	67
Return on sales (percent)					
Operating income	2.4	1.9	2.2	2.1	2.2
Earnings before income taxes	1.4	.8	1.5	1.5	1.7
Per common share ($)					
Net earnings	0.80	0.41	0.87	0.91	0.85
Earnings ratios (percent)					
Return on common equity	11.7	5.9	12.5	14.6	15.6
Return on capital employed	13.8	11.2	13.6	14.3	17.0
Regional sales ($ millions)					
Eastern Canada	3,988	3,705	3,602	3,070	2,781
Western Canada	2,650	2,340	2,087	2,028	1,887
United States	1,296	2,263	2,942	2,471	2,263
Total	7,934	8,308	8,631	7,839	6,931
Regional operating income ($ millions)					
Eastern Canada	90	76	106	74	72
Western Canada	67	56	47	56	45
United States	34	28	37	33	35
Total	191	160	190	163	152
Sales by segment ($ millions)					
Retail	5,025	4,921	4,777	4,430	3,940
Wholesale	2,909	3,387	3,854	3,409	2,991
Total	7,934	8,308	8,631	7,839	6,931

* Trading profit is defined as operating income before depreciation.
Source: Company Records.

of other types of stores, including drugstore retail outlets.

When adjusted for inflation, growth in the retail food industry was near zero for the past five years and forecasts for the early 1990s suggested a similar pattern. The low industry growth was due, in part, to little growth in the Canadian population and to increased expenditures by Canadians in fast-food and other restaurants. The intense competition within a mature industry meant that average net profit margins (pre-tax profits/sales) in the industry were low, averaging less than 2% in the past five years and only 1.5% in 1988. Consequently, the major chains were constantly examining new marketing and merchandising innovations as well as promotion incentives from manufacturers to build value for their customers and create store switching and preference.

The retail food business has seen a number of changes throughout the years including the following:

- While chain stores share of the market had been relatively stable, the sales per store had increased as some chains merged and closed stores during the past decade. For example, in early July 1990, Steinberg announced it was selling 69 Ontario stores (58 Miracle Food Marts and 11 Ultra Mart food and drug stores) to A&P. A&P already operated 194 stores in Ontario under the A&P and Dominion names.
- A variety of store formats had been introduced in response to changing consumer preferences, competitive pressures, and economic conditions. For example, "box" stores, warehouse stores, combination stores (selling both food and nonfood products), and superstores had been developed in the past fifteen years.
- Specialty stores, with their emphasis on quality and freshness, were increasing their market share.
- Generic (no-name) and store brands were increasing their share at the expense of national brands.
- Control in the industry had been shifting to the large chains, from the manufacturers. This trend was likely to continue as new sources of supply became available through free trade and as the chains reduced their emphasis on nationally branded products.

Six chains—Loblaws, Provigo, Oshawa, Steinberg, Safeway, and A&P—were the major competitors in the Canadian food business. In 1989, Loblaws was the largest of the six with total sales, wholesale and retail, of $7.9 billion, followed by Provigo ($7.4 billion), Oshawa ($4.9 billion), Steinberg ($4.5 billion), Safeway ($3.5 billion), and A&P ($2.2 billion).

While retail market share data was difficult to obtain because most of the chains operated both wholesale and retail divisions, industry sources estimated that Loblaws held the largest retail share in Canada at around 19%. Provigo held a 16% share, and it was estimated that the remaining chains held 10% or less of the market. Competition was regional in nature, with Provigo strong in Quebec, Safeway strong in western Canada, Loblaws and A&P with strengths in Ontario, and Sobey's (part of the Empire conglomerate) strong in the Maritimes.

The intense competition for market share was re-flected by industry experts, who, over the past year, made the following observations:

- Food retailers are locked in a cutthroat industry, scrambling to hold on to a shrinking market. The population is aging, leaving smaller appetites to whet.
- The grocery business is a treacherous one, characterized by low margins and dominated by giant companies. Niche players crowd the corners.
- The economic slowdown has hit supermarkets as consumers cut down on grocery spending. Consumers are buying more food on special and switching to cheaper foods.

LOBLAWS CORPORATE STRATEGY

Against this background of intense competition, changing consumer preferences, and changing economic conditions, Loblaws has been guided by a corporate strategy that had led to dramatic alterations in the way it does business. Loblaws envisioned the road to sustainable competitive advantage through innovative marketing, low costs, and a large network of suppliers. Traditionally, retailers in the food industry relied on price discounting to generate increased volume sales thereby increasing market share. Loblaws views this way of thinking as valid but narrow. Loblaws' umbrella strategy was to be the best low cost, high quality food distributor in the industry. This strategy led to four substantial changes at Loblaws: (1) the introduction of generics, (2) the development of the President's Choice corporate product line, (3) a broad-scale investment program, and (4) a new marketing strategy.

The Introduction of Generics

First sold in the United States in 1977, generics are unbranded, plainly packaged, less expensive versions of common products such as spaghetti, paper towels and canned peaches. Loblaws and a competing chain, Dominion, introduced generics in early 1978. Loblaws quickly became the leader in generic sales. In 15 months Loblaws expanded the line, called "No Name," from 16 to 120 products; by 1983, Loblaws carried over 500 generic products which accounted for about 10% of Loblaws' total sales. The generics appealed to price-sensitive consumers during an economic downturn in the Canadian economy.

Loblaws strategy with their generic line differed from competitors such as Dominion. Most food distributors positioned their generics as lower-priced products with lower quality than competing national brands. Loblaws produced a generic product that was of a higher quality. The quality of No Name products, coupled with lower prices, attractively packaged in an eye-catching yellow with heavy advertising against national brands led to the success of the line.

Development of the President's Choice Line

With the introduction of No Name, Loblaws recognized another unique marketing opportunity. Through internal market research in the early 1980s on the corporate brand philosophy, the company discovered that the target market for quality corporate products was the more affluent and educated consumer. It was found that this consumer did not require a national brand product to discern product quality and thus acceptability for purchase. It was at this time that Canada was also emerging from a recession. As consumer incomes rose, Loblaws saw an opportunity to meet the demands of this consumer. In 1984, President's Choice was introduced as a higher quality, high-value brand.

The President's Choice line was positioned directly against national brands. Loblaws plan was to develop consumer brand loyalty for this corporate line to such an extent that consumers would switch supermarkets to acquire President's Choice. An example of a very successful President's Choice product was the "Decadent" chocolate chip cookie. Based on product tests, Loblaws identified a lack of quality in the leading national brand chocolate chip cookie. The Decadent was made with a higher percentage (40%) of chocolate chips and real butter, and within a few months of its launch it was the best selling cookie in Ontario.

The increasing activity of Loblaws in developing corporate brands led to the establishment of the Weston Research Center, a product testing laboratory. The center was involved in the research and development of new products, quality control testing, and quality assurance programs. These activities were carried out on behalf of companies within the Weston and Loblaws group. By the late 1980s, the center had 100 employees and spent over $20 million each year to ensure product quality for corporate brands. Typically, a buyer for Loblaws would identify a possible product for inclusion in the corporate line. The buyer would then find a manufacturer to produce the product and the manufacturer would work with experts from the Weston Research Center to meet the required product quality standards. The product would then be launched as part of the President's Choice or No Name line.

The corporate line was well received by consumers. By 1989, approximately 2,200 No Name brands and 700 President's Choice brands made up 30% of Loblaw's total grocery sales. President's Choice and No Name brands earned an average 15% higher margin than the national brands. Approximately 200 new corporate brands were introduced annually with three-quarters of them being successful, as compared to a 10% success rate for national brands.

The Broad-Scale Investment Program

In 1984, Loblaws began a broad-scale investment program that, over the next five years, involved expenditures of approximately $1.8 billion on systems and market expansion through store developments. This included an information system to use store level scanner data to measure every product's sales. This made it possible to monitor the effectiveness of their merchandising strategy as sales, promotion, and pricing information could be examined weekly to determine individual product profitability and to support inventory management.

Market expansion was accomplished through substantial expenditures to upgrade existing stores, as well as to build new stores in strategic locations. To put this massive investment program in perspective, between 1985 and 1989, Loblaws opened 174 new stores, closed 130 stores, transferred 90 company-owned stores to franchise operations, and transferred 40 franchised stores to company-owned operations (*Exhibit 2*). Thirty-two of the new stores opened during this period were "superstores." Loblaws had identified superstores, also called combination stores or supercenters, as the "wave of the future" and the key to future success in the retailing industry. Superstores (typically over 130,000 square feet) were up to four times the size of conventional supermarkets. Approximately one-third of the space was devoted to nonfood items. For example, Real Canadian Superstore, which opened in Calgary in late 1988, was over 135,000 square feet, larger than two football fields, and stocked over 45,000 items.

Throughout the aggressive expansion program, Loblaws' management stressed they would maintain the company's financial objectives including: (1) to increase earnings per common share at an average of 15% per year over any five-year period, (2) to provide an average return on common shareholders' equity of 15% per year over any five-year period, and (3) to have less total debt than total equity in the business.

Through all this activity, the company was able to maintain a debt-equity ratio of 1:1 and shareholder returns averaging 12%. Although Loblaws did not meet its goals of a 15% average shareholder return and a 15% average annual increase in earnings per share over the 1984 to 1989 period that coincided with the repositioning and investment program, the results were still impressive compared to many firms in the industry.

The New Marketing Strategy

Dave Nichol, the president of Loblaws International Merchants, was the driving force behind the No

EXHIBIT 2   RETAIL OPERATIONS—SELECTED HIGHLIGHTS (1985–1989)

	1989		1988		1987		1986		1985	
	Stores	sq. ft. (millions)	Stores	sq. ft. (millions)	Stores	sq. ft. (millions)	Stores	sq. ft. (millions)	Stores	sq. ft. (millions)
Stores										
Beginning of year	311	10.6	361	11.3	380	10.8	363	9.2	381	9.2
Opened	55	1.2	21	1.2	20	1.2	60	2.4	18	0.6
Closed	(18)	(0.2)	(58)	(1.7)	(23)	(0.4)	46	(0.9)	26	(0.4)
Franchised:										
Transfer to:	(22)	(0.4)	(18)	(0.3)	(18)	(0.4)	13	(0.2)	19	(0.4)
Transfer from:	8	0.1	5	0.1	2	0.1	16	0.3	9	0.2
End of year	334	11.3	311	10.6	361	11.3	380	10.8	363	9.2
Average store size (in thousands)	33.9 sq. ft.		34.1 sq. ft.		31.4 sq. ft.		28.4 sq. ft.		25.3 sq. ft.	
Analysis by size										
>60,000 sq. ft.		40		33		26		18		10
40,000–60,000		48		44		47		46		33
20,000–39,999		148		154		176		179		171
10,000–19,999		64		68		93		112		129
<10,000 sq. ft.		34		12		19		25		20
Total		334		311		361		380		363
Sales										
Annual sales (in millions)		$5,025		$4,921		$4,777		$4,430		$3,940
Annual average sales per gross sq. ft.		$458		$440		$440		$457		$432

Name and President's Choice concepts. He travelled the world to identify new product opportunities for Loblaws. While market research was used to assist in the selection and launch of new products, it was Dave Nichol's innate sense of customer likes which underlay the selection—and success—of many of the corporate brands.

The communication campaign for the corporate brand was unique. From the beginning of the No Name launch, Dave Nichol was involved in advertising these products, often appearing in television campaigns to promote the No Name line. As a result, he became well known to many Canadian consumers. Nichol also introduced the *Insider's Report,* a multi-colored, comic-book size booklet that featured corporate brands and offered consumers shopping tips. Ten million copies of each issue were circulated four times a year as an insert with newspapers across Canada in areas where Loblaws or its affiliates had stores.

The main goals of the *Insider's Report* were to provide news of product availability and to highlight promotions. By consolidating advertising expenditures through the use of the *Insider's Report,* Loblaws spent considerably less on their advertising campaigns than did the national brands. The advertising-to-sales ratio for Loblaws brands was about 3%, less than half of that spent by many national brand manufacturers.

THE GREEN IDEA

The G·R·E·E·N line launch had its origins in one of Dave Nichol's buying trips to Germany in 1988, where he was struck by the number of grocery products that were being promoted as "environmentally friendly." He discovered that *The Green Consumer Guide,* a "how-to" book for consumers to become environmentally responsible, had become a best-seller in England. In late 1988, Loblaws began collecting information on Canadian attitudes about the environment. The results suggested that an increasing number of Canadians were concerned about environmental issues, and some expressed a willingness to pay extra to purchase environmentally safe products.

Further, many said they were willing to change supermarkets to acquire these products (*Exhibit 3*).

As well, increased attention was being drawn to Canada's environmental problems. The news media and environmental groups such as Greenpeace and

EXHIBIT 3
CONSUMER ATTITUDES ON ENVIRONMENT

1. National survey on issues.

   What is the most important issue facing Canada today?

Issues	1985	1986	1987	1988	1989
Environment	*	*	2	10	18
Goods and services tax	*	*	*	*	15
Inflation/economy	16	12	12	5	10
Deficit/government	6	10	10	6	10
National unity	*	*	*	*	7
Free trade	2	5	26	42	7
Abortion	*	*	*	*	6
Employment	45	39	20	10	6

   Source: Maclean's/Decima Research.
   *Not cited by a significant number of poll respondents.
   Note: Survey conducted in early January of each year.

2. National survey on willingness to pay for cleaner environment.

   Would you be willing to pay:
   50% more to clear garbage (67%)[1]
   10% more for groceries (66%)
   $1,000 more for a car (63%)
   5¢ a liter more for gas (63%)
   $250 more to clean sewage (58%)
   10% tax on energy (57%)

   Source: Angus Reid Group.
   [1]The numbers in brackets represent the percent of those surveyed who agreed with each statement.
   Note: Survey conducted in early 1989.

3. Loblaws customers surveys.

   How concerned are you about the environment? (%)
   Extremely (32), Quite (37), Somewhat (24), Not Very (5), Don't Care (2)

   How likely is it that you would purchase environmentally friendly products?
   Very (49), Somewhat (43), Not too (2), Not at all (4)

   How likely is it that you would switch supermarkets to purchase environmentally friendly products?
   Very (2), Somewhat (45), Not too (24), Not at all (10)

   Note: Survey conducted in early 1989.

Pollution Probe were providing Canadians with many disturbing facts. For example, Canadians use more energy per capita than any other nation in the world. Canadians also produce approximately 15 tonnes of carbon dioxide per person per year, the primary cause of the "greenhouse effect" (the warming of the world's atmosphere). On a per capita basis, Canadians are found to be one of the world's greatest contributors to acid rain, air and water pollution, and the degeneration of the ozone layer.

THE G·R·E·E·N LAUNCH

Armed with this supportive data, in late January 1989, Loblaws management decided to launch by July 1989 a line of 100 products that were either environmentally friendly or healthy for the body. These products would be added to the family of the corporate line and called G·R·E·E·N. Although the task was considered ambitious, the corporation believed it had the requisite size, strength, influence, network, imagination, and courage to be successful. Loblaws contacted a number of prominent environmental groups to assist in the choice of products. These groups were requested to make a "wish list" of environmentally safe products. Using this as a guide, Loblaws began to source the products for the G·R·E·E·N launch.

A few products, such as baking soda, simply required repackaging to advertise the already existing environmentally friendly qualities of the product. Intersave Buying and Merchandising Services were able to source some products through foreign suppliers, such as the Ecover line of household cleaning products, to be marketed under the G·R·E·E·N umbrella. All G·R·E·E·N products were rigorously tested as well as screened by environmental groups such as Pollution Probe and Friends of the Earth. This collaboration was developed to such an extent that a few of the products were endorsed by Pollution Probe.

The G·R·E·E·N product line, consisting of about 60 products, was launched on June 3, 1989. Initial G·R·E·E·N products included phosphate-free laundry detergent, low-acid coffee, pet foods, and biodegradable garbage bags (*Exhibit 4*). A holistic approach was taken in selecting these initial products; for example, the pet food products were included because they provided a more healthful blend of ingredients for cats and dogs. The G·R·E·E·N products were offered in a distinctively designed package with vivid green colouring. When the package design decisions were being made, it was learned that 20% of the Canadian population is functionally illiterate. Management felt that the distinct design would give these consumers a chance to readily identify these brands.

The G·R·E·E·N launch was supported with a $3 million television and print campaign. Consumers were informed of the new product line using the June 1989 issue of the *Insider's Report*. In an open letter to consumers, Mr. Nichol addressed Loblaws motivation for the G·R·E·E·N launch (*Exhibit 5*). Part of this motivation was also to offer consumers a choice which could, in the longer term, provide educational benefits for consumers on specific green issues. As well, by offering the choice, consumers could "vote at the cash register" and, in a sense, tell Loblaws what they were willing to buy and what green products they would accept.

The *Report* provided descriptive statements for many of the G·R·E·E·N products (*Exhibit 6*) and noted that Loblaws would continue to carry a broad range of products including national brands and President's Choice. The G·R·E·E·N line was to be typically priced below national brand products. The G·R·E·E·N introduction was not without its problems. Shortly after the launch, members of Pollution Probe rejected their previous endorsement of the G·R·E·E·N disposable diaper. These members felt that the group should not support a less than perfect product. The G·R·E·E·N diaper was more environmentally friendly than any other disposable brand. However, it was not, in Pollution Probe's opinion, environmentally pure. Further, it was felt that endorsing such products compromised the integrity and independence of the organization. This prompted the resignation of Colin Issac, the direction of Pollution Probe. The group subsequently discontinued its endorsement of the diaper, but continued its support of six other G·R·E·E·N products.

Controversy also arose around the introduction of

EXHIBIT 4
THE INITIAL G·R·E·E·N PRODUCTS

Food
Just Peanuts Peanut Butter
Smart Snack Popcorn
"The Virtuous" Soda Cracker
Cox's Orange Pippin Apple Juice
White Hull-less Popcorn
Reduced Acid Coffee
Boneless and Skinless Sardines
"Green" Natural Oat Bran
Naturally Flavoured Raisins: Lemon,
    Cherry, Strawberry
"Green" Turkey Frankfurters
100% Natural Rose Food
Norwegian Crackers
Turkey Whole Frozen
Gourmet Frozen Foods (low-fat)
"If the World Were PERFECT" Water

Cleaning/Detergent Products
All-Purpose Liquid Cleaner with Bitrex
"Green" Automatic Dishwasher
    Detergent
Ecover 100% Biodegradable Laundry
    Powder*
Ecover Dishwasher Detergent
Laundry Soil and Stain Remover with
    Bitrex
Drain Opener with Bitrex
Ecover Fabric Softener
Ecover 100% Biodegradable Toilet
    Cleaner
Ecover 100% Biodegradable Wool
    Wash
Ecover Floor Soap
"Green" 100% Phosphate Free
    Laundry Detergent

Pet Food
Low Ash Cat Food
Slim & Trim Cat Food
All Natural Dog Biscuits

Cooking Products
"The Virtuous" Canola Oil
"The Virtuous" Cooking Spray
Baking Soda

Paper-Based Products
Bathroom Tissue
"Green" Ultra Diapers
"Green" Foam Plates
Swedish 100% Chlorine-Free Coffee
    Filters
"Green" Baby Wipes
"Green" Maxi Pads

Oil-Based Products
Biodegradable Garbage Bags
Hi-Performance Motor Oil
Natural Fertilizer
Lawn and Garden Soil

Other Products
Green T-Shirt/Sweatshirt
Green Panda Stuffed Toy
Green Polar Bear Stuffed Toy
Cedar Balls

*The Ecover brands are a line of cleaning products made by Ecover of Belgium. These products are vegetable oil based and are rapidly biodegradable. Loblaws marketed these products under the G·R·E·E·N umbrella.

the G·R·E·E·N fertilizer. Greenpeace, a prominent environment group, rejected Loblaws' claims that the fertilizer had no toxic elements and therefore was environmentally pure. The group did not know that Loblaws had spent substantial funds to determine that the product was free of toxic chemicals.

Both incidents, although unfortunate, focused the attention of Canadians on the G·R·E·E·N product line. The media highlighted Loblaws as the only North American retailer to offer a line of environmentally friendly products. This publicity also prompted letters of encouragement from the public

who supported Loblaws' initiative. Surveys conducted four weeks after the line introduction revealed an 82% awareness of the G·R·E·E·N line with 27% of the consumers actually purchasing at least one of the G·R·E·E·N products. In Ontario alone, the G·R·E·E·N line doubled its projected sales and sold $5 million in June 1989.

THE FIRST YEAR OF GREEN

The launch of G·R·E·E·N was soon followed by a virtual avalanche of "environmentally friendly"

EXHIBIT 5   *THE INSIDER'S REPORT—OPEN LETTER*

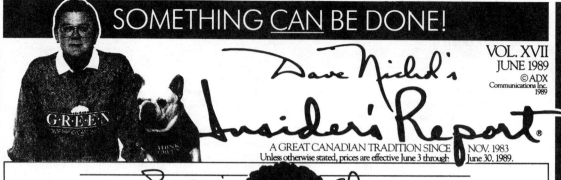

SOMETHING <u>CAN</u> BE DONE!

VOL. XVII
JUNE 1989
©ADX
Communications Inc.
1989

A GREAT CANADIAN TRADITION SINCE NOV. 1983
Unless otherwise stated, prices are effective June 3 through June 30, 1989.

President's Choice
G·R·E·E·N™

An Open Letter To Canadian Consumers about President's Choice G•R•E•E•N Products

Over the last year, while travelling the world looking for new products, I was astounded at the level of consumer interest in environmentally friendly products. For example, the best-selling book in England last year was an environmental handbook ranking retailers and their products.

Back in Canada, I noticed that every public opinion poll indicated that the environment was the number one concern of Canadian consumers — confirming what my mail had been telling me for at least a year.

Convinced that this concern was genuine, the Insider's Report team met with executives of many of Canada's leading environmental groups and asked them what products they would like to see us create that would in some way help to reduce pollution. Their guidance was the genesis of the G•R•E•E•N "Environment Friendly™" product program and in many cases we actually worked with these groups to develop specific products which they then felt confident in endorsing.

At the same time we also began development of "Body Friendly™" (low calorie, high fibre, low fat, low cholesterol, etc.) products under the G•R•E•E•N label. This Insider's Report highlights the first wave of our new President's Choice G•R•E•E•N product program.

Here are a few points of clarification about the program.

1. With few exceptions, President's Choice G•R•E•E•N products are priced at, or below the price of the national brand to which they are an alternative.
2. We do not intend to censor products that some may feel are "environmentally-unfriendly." We see our role as providing a choice so you may decide for yourself.
3. Protecting the environment is a young and therefore, imprecise science. As a result, not all groups agree on what the best products are to help control pollution. For example, some advise us to use paper pulp trays for all eggs while others say recyclable, ozone-friendly foam

trays made with pentane instead of chlorofluorocarbons (C.F.C.'s) are a better solution. We accept the fact that it is inevitable that not all environmental groups will agree with all of our President's Choice G•R•E•E•N products.
4. Some may accuse us of being "environmental opportunists." WE SEE OUR ROLE AS PROVIDING PRODUCTS THAT PEOPLE WANT. That's why we created No Name products when Canada's food inflation was running at 16%. That's why we created President's Choice products when a demand for superior-quality products arose. And that's why we've created G•R•E•E•N products when the overwhelming concern of Canadians is the environment.

We invite you to read about our new President's Choice G•R•E•E•N products in this Insider's Report and decide for yourself whether or not they fill a real need in our society.
5. A number of our G•R•E•E•N products are products that we've carried for years (such as baking soda). Putting them under the G•R•E•E•N label was in response to environmental groups who chided us by saying, "You have a number of products in your stores right now that could help fight pollution but you have to bring them to your customers' attention and then explain how to use them."

We acknowledge that we are not environmental experts and we readily admit that we do not have all the answers. However, we feel strongly that these products are a step in the long journey toward the solution of our enormous environmental problems. If G•R•E•E•N products do nothing more than help raise awareness of the need to address environmental issues NOW, and give Canadians hope that SOMETHING CAN BE DONE, then in the end, they will have made a positive contribution.

David Nichol, President
Loblaw International Merchants

Selected products also available at Mr. Grocer, valu-mart®, freshmart™ and Your Independent Grocer®.

PRINTED ON RECYCLED NEWSPRINT

178

SOMETHING CAN BE DONE!

Look For Pollution Probe's Endorsement On Every Package

THESE DIAPERS COULD SAVE 500,000,000 TREES A YEAR!!

The diapers you choose are very important because your baby will spend approximately 20,000 hours in them. I asked Pollution Probe if there was anything we could do to produce an Environment Friendly diaper. **"In the best of all worlds, everyone would use reusable cloth diapers,"** they said. I replied, **"But cloth diapers aren't always convenient." "In that case,"** Pollution Probe conceded, **"diapers made with non-chlorine-bleached fluff pulp are the next best thing!"**

In order to produce "whiter-than-white" diapers, most North American fluff pulp (that's the diaper padding) is bleached with chlorine-based chemicals. But at what cost to our environment?! Two years ago, scientists discovered that chlorine in the pulp-bleaching process combines with natural compounds in wood to form a startling variety of hazardous waste products, including environment-threatening furans and dioxins. ("TCDD," one of 75 dioxins known to exist, is the deadliest toxin ever synthesized by man!!)

Fortunately, it is no longer necessary to produce diapers using chlorine-bleached fluff pulp. The fluff pulp in our **NEW President's Choice G.R.E.E.N Ultra Diapers** is produced in Canada by one of the most technologically advanced mills in North America. The mill produces a very special type of pulp, called B.C.T.M.P. (Bleached Chemi-Thermal Mechanical Pulp), which is bleached with hydrogen peroxide instead of environment-threatening chlorine. Pollution Probe explained that the advantage of bleaching with hydrogen peroxide is that its primary waste products are OXYGEN AND WATER. THE ELIMINATION OF CHLORINE MEANS THAT ENVIRONMENT-THREATENING FURANS AND DIOXINS ARE LESS LIKELY TO BE CREATED IN THE PRODUCTION OF OUR FLUFF PULP. As a result, water pollution is kept to a minimum! Unlike the artificial whiter-than-white color of chlorine-bleached diapers, **the natural creamy color of the fluff pulp in our diapers is proof of their Environment Friendly manufacturing process!**

BUT THAT'S NOT ALL! **The special B.C.T.M.P. process gets double the number of diapers from a tree compared to conventional chlorine-bleached pulp production. THIS MEANS THAT IF EVERYONE IN THE WORLD USING DISPOSABLE DIAPERS SWITCHED TO DIAPERS MADE FROM B.C.T.M.P., NON-CHLORINE-BLEACHED FLUFF PULP, AS MANY AS 500,000,000 TREES WOULD BE SAVED ANNUALLY!** (According to the Financial Times of London, worldwide diaper manufacturing currently consumes 1 billion trees per year!)

Superior-quality President's Choice G.R.E.E.N Ultra Diapers FIT COMFORTABLY, HELP KEEP BABY DRY and PROTECT AGAINST DIAPER RASH. Until June 30, they're introductory-priced at just $9.99 for **44 MEDIUM** (12 to 24 lb), **32 LARGE** (over 22 lb) or **28 LARGE PLUS** (over 27 lb) diapers. Look for Pollution Probe's endorsement on every package.

P.S. WE'RE ALSO IN THE PROCESS OF PUTTING NON-CHLORINE-BLEACHED FLUFF PULP INTO OUR NO NAME ULTRA DIAPERS. Just $8.99 for a bag of 44 Medium, 32 Large or 28 Large Plus diapers. Ø Look for our new "Non-Chlorine-Bleached Fluff Pulp" sticker to identify those No Name diapers that have already been converted.

Like conventional disposable diapers, the main component in most baby wipes is chlorine-bleached pulp. **We searched the world to find a non-chlorine-bleached pulp product from which we could make quality baby wipes. At the last minute, we found a significantly more Environment Friendly, OXYGEN-BLEACHED** pulp in Sweden and flew it to Canada just in time for the break of our G.R.E.E.N Insider's Report! **NEW President's Choice G.R.E.E.N Baby Wipes with lanolin** (unscented, alcohol-free) are formulated for baby's delicate skin. **AND, FOR EXTRA SOFTNESS, THEY CONTAIN 33% NATURAL COTTON FIBRE!** Introductory-priced at just $3.99 for 84 sheets in a convenient "one-hand" dispenser (so that you can hold baby with the other!). Ø

NEW PRODUCTS FOR THE BAR-B-Q

BBQ REVOLUTION!

Chicken—Marinated & Ready For The Barbecue!!

WE'VE DONE THE WORK FOR YOU! Taking a cue from one of my favorite food purveyors, Marks & Spencer, which has revolutionized eating in England with refrigerated convenience foods such as marinated chicken, we decided to develop a FRESH, NEVER FROZEN, MARINATED CHICKEN that would be tasty and barbecue-ready.

Our NEW President's Choice Marinated Chicken Portions, in LEMON & HONEY MARINADE or BARBECUE MARINADE, mean NO MORE MESSY MIXING & NO MORE WAITING FOR CHICKEN TO MARINATE! Until June 30, they're introductory-priced at only $7.99 per 1.25 kg package (each pkg contains the parts of one whole roasting chicken). Ø

P.S. Here are two other great chicken entrees guaranteed to save you time: President's Choice **FRESH STUFFED CHICKEN BREAST WITH LEMON BUTTER AND CHIVES** and President's Choice **FRESH STUFFED CHICKEN BREAST WITH GARLIC BUTTER AND PARSLEY**—each priced at just $11/kg or $4.99/lb. Look for all products in the FRESH (not frozen) MEAT CASE. Ø

NOW SQUEEZABLE!

NEW! President's Choice Gourmet Barbecue Sauce now comes in a 1 L SQUEEZABLE bottle and is introductory-priced at only $2.99! We took it to Sylvia's, the best rib house in NYC (food writer Gael Greene calls them "the best ribs around"), where the chef ranked it tops in a blind-tasting of America's leading commercially available barbecue sauces! Her comments: "There's no comparison in taste—and I love the convenient SQUEEZE BOTTLE!" Also available —President's Choice Hickory-Smoked Gourmet Barbecue Sauce, 1 L SQUEEZABLE BOTTLE. Our special introductory price is just $2.99!!

P.S. PRESIDENT'S CHOICE TOMATO KETCHUP also comes in a 1 L SQUEEZABLE BOTTLE. Specially priced at just $1.99. Compare with Heinz, which costs up to $4.19 per 1 L squeezable bottle in many Toronto supers!

SUMMER...SUMMER...SUMMER...SUMMER...

BAR-B-Q ISSUE!!

Ø This symbol indicates that the product may not be available at No Frills, Zehrs, valu-mart, freshmart, Mr. Grocer and Your Independent Grocer.

products. Major consumer goods companies like Proctor & Gamble, Lever Brothers, and Colgate-Palmolive introduced Enviro-Paks, phosphate-free detergents, and biodegradable cleaning products. Competing supermarket chains had varied responses from launching their own "green" line (Miracle Mart introduced three "Green Circle" products, Oshawa Foods introduced about 10 "Greencare"products) to highlighting environmentally sensitive products in their stores (Safeway) to improving its internal practices through recycling and other activities (Provigo).

As well, companies from McDonald's to Labatt's positioned themselves in one way or another as environmentally responsible. These marketing activities created some consumer skepticism about whether some of these products were truly environmentally friendly. In addition, various companies had different ideas about what was environmentally friendly, which also created some consumer confusion. Part of the problem was that it was very difficult to determine what is and isn't environmentally safe. Serious environmentalists argued that to accurately assess the environmental impact of a product, it was necessary to conduct a "cradle-to-grave" analysis—a detailed review of the product, how it was manufactured, how it is used, and how it is disposed. Others argued that if a product was environmentally "better" than other brands (for example, a biodegradable disposable diaper versus a regular disposable diaper) then the consumer should be offered that choice.

It appeared that Loblaws' actions had an impact on corporations and consumers. For example, in a national survey of 1,500 Canadians conducted in November 1989, 56% of respondents answered "yes" to the question: "Over the past year, have environmental concerns influenced your purchase decisions?" Of those who answered yes, and were than asked "In what way?," it was found that 23% purchased environmentally friendly products, 21% avoided the purchase of hazardous products, 11% didn't purchase pesticides, and 7% boycotted certain products.

During the year, Loblaws continued to develop and promote the G·R·E·E·N product line. In the first year of G·R·E·E·N, Loblaws sold approximately $60

million worth of G·R·E·E·N products and "broke even" on the line.

THE DECISIONS

As Scott began to make his decisions on the three products, he reflected on the past year. He thought that $60 million in sales for the G·R·E·E·N line was reasonable, but he had hoped the line would do better. He remembered some of the products that just didn't fit in the line such as "green" sardines. "I don't think we sold 20 cans of that stuff." Scott and the other buyers at Intersave were very concerned when a product didn't sell. Individual store managers, who were held accountable for the sales and profits of their store, did not have to list (that is, stock in the store that he or she managed) any product, including any in the G·R·E·E·N line. If a store manager thought the product was unsuitable for the store, it wasn't listed. As well, if a buyer got a product listed and it didn't sell, his or her reputation with the store managers would suffer.

One thing that had changed was the product opportunities. When the G·R·E·E·N line was launched, Scott and the other buyers had to actively search to find products that could qualify as "green." Now it seemed that all kinds of suppliers were jumping on the "environmental bandwagon." However, the environmental advantages of many of these product proposals were difficult to verify. Some, despite good sales potential, could only be considered "pale green," a term used to describe products that had debatable or small positive impacts on the environment.

Light Bulb

The proposal by Osram, a well-known German manufacturer, was a true green product. The Osram light bulb was a compact fluorescent bulb that could replace the traditional incandescent light bulb in specific applications. The unique aspect of this product was that while fluorescent light technology was commonplace (these long-tube lights were common in office buildings), only recently had the product been modified to use it as a replacement for traditional light bulbs. The major benefits of fluorescent light bulbs were that they used considerable less energy than incandescent light bulbs (for example, a 9 watt fluorescent bulb could replace a 40 watt incandescent bulb and still provide the same lighting level, while using only 22.5% of the energy) and it lasted at least 10 times longer (an estimated 2,000 hours versus 200 hours for the incandescent bulb). To date the major application for compact fluorescents had been in apartment buildings in stairwells where lights remained on 24 hours a day. Apartment building owners purchased them because the bulbs lowered both energy costs and maintenance costs (less frequent replacement).

The compact fluorescent had limited applications in the home. Because of its unique shape it could not be used with a typical lampshade (*Exhibit 7*). The main application was likely to be in hallways where it was difficult to replace a burned-out bulb. Even in these situations, a new fixture (that is, an enclosure) might be required so that the compact fluorescent would fit.

The bulb's energy efficiency and long-lasting fea-

tures were well tested and had been sold for specialized industrial use for several years. The bulb was making satisfactory in-roads in Germany even though it was priced at the equivalent of $40 Canadian.

Loblaws sold a variety of 60 and 100 watt No Name and Phillips light bulbs in packages of four. In total the light bulb category generated over $1 million in gross margin for Loblaws in 1989 (*Exhibit 8*).

The initial Osram proposal was to sell the product to Loblaws at $19.00 per bulb. Even if the mark-up was set at 5%, Loblaw's retail price would be $19.99. Scott talked this over with a number of people at Loblaws and concluded that the price was too high to be accepted by Canadian consumers. At this time, Ontario Hydro entered the picture. Ontario Hydro was extremely concerned about its ability to meet the power demands of its customers in the next decade and was engaged in aggressive energy conservation programs. Ontario Hydro was prepared to offer $5 rebate for every light bulb that was sold in Ontario in the three months following the launch. Although it meant customers would have to request the rebate

EXHIBIT 7   THE OSRAM LIGHT BULB

EXHIBIT 8
LIGHT BULBS (1989)

	Average retail price[1] ($)	Average cost ($)	Annual sales ($000)	Total gross margin ($000)	Market share (%)
Loblaws					
60 Watt	2.25	1.25	470	209	18
60 Watt Soft	2.75	1.50	426	193	16
100 Watt	2.25	1.25	294	130	11
100 Watt Soft	2.75	1.50	279	127	11
Total Loblaws			1,468	659	56
Phillips					
60 Watt	2.40	1.50	367	138	14
60 Watt Soft	3.20	1.65	341	165	13
100 Watt	2.40	1.50	236	88	9
100 Watt Soft	3.20	1.65	210	102	8
Total Phillips			1,153	493	44
Total			2,621	1,152	100

[1]Based on four packs (that is, four light bulbs in a package). Total unit sales were 1,019,000 (four packs).

by mail it reduced the effective price of the bulb to the consumer to $14.99.

Scott felt that the combination of the rebate, a retail price at only half that paid by German consumers, and a strong environmental message had strong merchandising appeal that could be exploited in the launch of the bulb. Nevertheless, the sales potential was still unclear. Loblaw's annual sales in Ontario were nearly four million bulbs or $2.7 million. Because this product was unique and new, Scott had difficulty estimating its sales potential. His best guess was that Loblaws might sell anywhere from 10,000 to 50,000 Osram bulbs in one year. Scott thought that half the sales would come from regular customers and the other half from customers coming to Loblaws specifically to buy the bulb. Scott also felt that after three months, the price should be raised to $24.99 retail to generate a reasonable margin for Loblaws.

Scott thought that if half the volume were generated at the higher price, it would certainly be easier to maintain the support of the store managers. At the $24.99 price, the margin would be $5.99 per bulb.

Even considering the cannibalization issue, the margin on the higher priced Osram would be about four times higher than the margin for a four pack of regular bulbs. However, it would be necessary to calculate the contribution for the year to see what the net effect would be for the line. The shelf space required for these bulbs was minimal and could be handled by some minor changes to the layout of the existing bulbs.

BATHROOM TISSUE

The bathroom tissue category was a highly competitive, price-sensitive market. The category was one of the largest in the Loblaws lineup, generating over $31 million in retail sales in Ontario and $7 million in contribution (*Exhibit 9*). Bathroom tissue was more important to Loblaws than just a volume generator. It was one of the few product categories that would draw price-conscious buyers into the store. Loblaws listed 40 different sizes and colors from various manufacturers. There were six Loblaws brands in the category. Loblaws was aggressive at delisting any competitive or corporate brand that did not meet turnover or profitability goals. Manufacturers were just as aggressive at providing allowance and merchandising incentives to ensure satisfactory margins for Loblaws and to facilitate retail price reductions which in turn would enhance turnover and maintain volume goals. Two national brands—Royale and Cottonelle—held shares of 45% and 30% respectively.

For 1989, Loblaws' brands held 16% of the market with No Name White providing a total gross margin of over $1 million. Loblaws' No Name White was sourced for an average cost of $1.15 for a 4-roll package. These lower costs were largely based on the fact that the tissue was manufactured with totally recycled material. This product feature made it a candidate for G·R·E·E·N line consideration. The existing product could simply be repackaged with the distinctive G·R·E·E·N labeling and an emphasis placed on the recycled character of the product. No development or testing costs would be required, and art work and new labelling costs would be minimal.

Several decisions needed to be considered with respect to the repackaging of the No Name product. Should the new product replace the old or simply be added to an already crowded category? Should the price of the new product be set higher than that set for the old? Should the product be launched at all?

EXHIBIT 9
BATHROOM TISSUE (1989)

	Average retail price[1] ($)	Average cost ($)	Annual sales ($000)	Total gross margin ($000)	Market share (%)
Loblaws[2]					
President's Choice	2.50	1.95	1,542	339	5
No Name White	1.75	1.15	3,084	1,052	10
No Name Color	1.80	1.35	386	96	1
Loblaws Total			5,012	1,487	16
Royale					
White	1.85	1.55	10,795	1,751	34
Color	2.00	1.60	3,855	771	12
Royale Total			14,650	2,522	46
Cottonelle					
White	1.85	1.45	4,627	1,000	15
Color	1.95	1.50	4,627	1,068	15
Cottonelle Total			9,254	2,068	30
Other Brands					
Capri	1.50	0.90	945	378	3
April Soft	1.40	0.95	721	232	2
Jubilee	1.35	0.70	386	186	1
Dunet	2.45	1.60	405	140	1
White Swan	1.55	1.00	463	164	1
Other Brands Total			2,920	1,100	8
Total			31,836	7,177	100

[1]Statistics for the prices, costs and sales have been collapsed over the various sizes and reported in equivalent four-roll packs. Total unit sales were 17,125,000 (four-roll packs).
[2]Loblaws was offered in six different size and color combinations. Most major brands provided a similar variety of sizes and colors.

EXHIBIT 10
FAMILY CEREALS (1989)

	Average retail price[1] ($)	Average cost ($)	Annual sales ($000)	Total gross margin ($000)	Market share (%)
President's Choice					
Bran with Raisins	2.35	1.50	1,051	380	7.4
Honey Nut Cereal	3.00	1.40	324	173	2.3
Toasted Oats	3.00	1.45	221	114	1.5
Corn Flakes	1.75	1.20	193	60	1.4
Crispy Rice	3.20	1.50	263	139	1.8
Loblaws Total			2,052	866	14.3
Kellogg's					
Corn Flakes	2.30	1.80	1,436	312	10.1
Raisin Bran	2.75	2.00	1,236	324	8.7
Honey Nut Corn Flakes	3.95	2.70	460	141	3.2
Rice Krispies	3.95	2.52	899	315	6.3
Common Sense	4.40	2.70	433	167	3.0
Mini-Wheat	3.30	2.00	326	129	2.3
Variety Pack	5.90	3.90	309	105	2.2
Other Kellog's	3.41	2.26	258	87	1.8
Kellogg's Total			5,357	1,580	37.5
Nabisco					
Shreddies	2.35	1.70	2,725	754	19.1
Apple/Cinnamon	2.25	1.50	169	57	1.2
Raisin Wheat	3.30	2.10	139	50	1.0
Nabisco Total			3,033	861	21.2
General Mills					
Cheerios	3.80	2.60	1,171	370	8.2
Cheerios/Honey Nut	3.90	2.60	1,017	339	7.1
General Mills Total			2,188	709	15.3
Quaker					
Corn Bran	3.50	2.25	389	139	2.7
Life	3.15	2.10	358	119	2.5
Oat Bran	4.10	2.80	281	89	2.0
Muffets	2.65	1.60	92	36	0.6
Quaker Total			1,120	383	7.8
Others	2.40	1.45	573	227	4.0
Total			14,323	4,626	100.0

[1]Based on 500 gram size. Total unit sales were 4,950,000 (500 gram size).

Cereals are packaged in several different sizes. Some brands like Kellogg's Corn Flakes could have four different sizes (e.g. 350g, 425g, 675g, 800g) on the shelf at one time. To facilitate comparisons, all figures have been converted to a standard 500 g size and where brands had multiple sizes, the figures are reported as averages, weighted by the sales volume of the size.

If it is launched should it get prominence in the quarterly *Insider's Report?* Should it be positioned against some national brands? How much inventory should be ordered, and what was the expected profitability?

READY-TO-EAT CEREAL

Loblaws sold more than $14 million worth of family cereals (that is, cereals targeted at the "family" market) in Ontario in 1989 (*Exhibit 10*). Loblaws corporate brand share of the family cereal segment, at 14%, was lower than corporate objectives for this category. One of Scott Lindsay's goals was to increase Loblaws share for this category. The major obstacle was the dominance of the well-known national brands marketed by Kellogg's, Nabisco, General Mills, and Quaker Oats (*Exhibit 10*). The brand leaders, such as Kellogg's Corn Flakes, Nabisco Shreddies, and General Mills' Cheerios, were as familiar to shoppers as any other product or brand in a store. With decades of advertising and promotional support, these brands had become thoroughly entrenched in the minds and pantries of generations of Canadians.

The brand names of these market leaders provided the manufacturers with strong protection against competitors. However, the manufacturing process did not. The manufacturing processes were well known in the industry, and many firms could produce identical products at favorable costs. Loblaws had found several products from domestic sources that appeared to be as good if not better than the national brands. One such product was a corn flake product which had a very high fiber content. The new product would appeal to those customers who had been primed by the health claims of high fiber diets. In sensory tests it had proven to have an excellent taste and texture profile and was equal to or preferred in blind taste tests to some of the market leaders. Moreover, the product could be obtained for $1.40 per 500 g package.

The President's Choice brands were beginning to make in-roads in this market, and this new product could increase the share. However, it was not clear how to position the high-fiber corn flake product. Should it go in the regular President's Choice line as a line extension of the current corn flake product or should it be packaged as a G·R·E·E·N product? As a regular President's Choice product it would be positioned directly against Kellogg's as an all-round cereal with extra value. As a G·R·E·E·N product it would be positioned less against Kellogg's and much more towards a health/"good-for-you" claim. G·R·E·E·N positioning might also minimize any cannibalization of the President's Choice corn flakes. The lower sourcing costs provided some flexibility on pricing. It could be priced as low as $1.75, like the current President's Choice corn flakes, and still maintain good margins or it could be priced as high as Kellogg's Corn Flakes at $2.30 and generate superior margins.

Having reviewed the three proposals, Scott began the process of preparing his recommendations. "I'll start with the financial projections," thought Scott, "then consider the pros and cons of each proposal. Then it's decision time."

PART FOUR

Distribution Channels and Delivery Systems

Producers of goods and services often fail to think a lot about distribution channels, tending to take them as a given rather than as a marketing variable that needs to be planned and managed with the same care as product policy, pricing strategy, and communication efforts. No marketer should view the current distribution channel for its products as fixed, since better alternatives may be available. Distribution decisions should be taken with great care, since they may involve long-term commitments with intermediaries, raise important issues of control over marketplace activities, carry major financial implications, and affect the other elements of the marketing mix.

Distribution decisions are important to producers of both goods and services, but tend to be more complex for the former. Because goods are physical objects, their manufacturers need to find ways of transporting products from the factory to the customer. They also need to find ways of storing products safely during the period between manufacture and final sale. Should they choose to handle these tasks themselves or should they delegate them to one or more intermediaries, such as wholesalers and retailers?

Service firms, by contrast, usually create and deliver their services at local outlets—"factories in the field," as they have sometimes been called. Restaurants, hotels, hospitals, and universities, for example, all share this characteristic. Services which are heavily information based—such as financial services and the reservations component of airlines, hotels, and rental cars—may centralize some of their information-processing activities and then use electronic channels to transmit the desired information either to the customer or to an intermediary. (See *Exhibit 1* for commonly used distribution channel alternatives.)

Producers are not the only organizations that make distribution decisions.

187

EXHIBIT 1
SOME DISTRIBUTION CHANNEL ALTERNATIVES

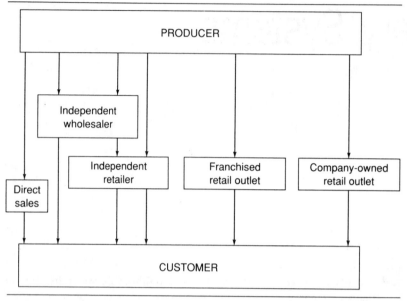

Intermediaries such as wholesalers and retailers are also marketing organizations with customers to consider. As service businesses operating in an often highly competitive environment, they too must worry about getting the right product to the customer at the right time and place.

A good starting point for distribution strategists is to consider the market segments the firm wishes to target. Other than looking for a good product, what specific benefits do customers in each segment seek from the buying process? Are they concerned about low price, easily accessible locations, convenient hours of service, an extensive choice of products under one roof, expert sales assistance? Insights into the needs of each target segment can serve as criteria for selecting the most appropriate channel, since channel intermediaries may vary widely in their ability to perform well on specific attributes.

When managers make distribution decisions, they need to think carefully about the different activities involved in getting the product to the customer. What are these different tasks for a particular type of product destined for a specific market segment? What are the relative costs of using an intermediary versus doing the work oneself (assuming that the latter is even feasible)? How much control does the marketer lose when certain tasks are delegated to any given intermediary? And what are the competitive implications of using one distribution and delivery strategy over another?

LOGISTICS MANAGEMENT

Logistics (also known as *physical distribution management*) is concerned with moving and storing goods on their way from the original point of manufacture to the customer.

Physical distribution tasks include transportation, order processing, warehousing, and inventory management. These tasks need to be managed collectively as a *system*, as opposed to focusing on each element separately. Computerization has made it easier for managers to analyze all the variables involved in taking such a systematic approach.

The criteria for selecting the most appropriate physical distribution system include (1) costs, (2) speed, (3) availability, and (4) physical protection.

In determining costs, management must examine the shipping costs associated with alternative transportation modes; the cost of using alternative storage and warehousing facilities; and additional expenses such as packaging, security, and insurance.

Speed often entails a trade-off against cost. For example, airfreight is faster but more expensive than the use of land or water-based transportation modes. On the other hand, some companies have found that by using airfreight they can do away with regional or local warehouses. New approaches to manufacturing, often characterized as just-in-time (JIT), may allow a firm to eliminate warehousing altogether.

Availability of the product when and where the customer needs it requires either fast, direct shipment from the factory or the use of intermediaries capable of supplying the product at times and in locations that meet the customers' needs.

Finally, there's the issue of protection. Nobody wants a damaged product or a perishable one that has "gone bad." The choice of packaging must be appropriate to the type of handling that the item will receive during transportation and storage. One reason some marketers like airfreight is that there is often less damage due to careless handling and deterioration due to prolonged storage than when other forms of transportation are used. Protection against pilferage, another important issue, may require a combination of tamperproof packaging and proper security during shipping and storage.

Distribution goals need to be concerned not only with directly measurable financial costs but also with the cost of lost sales resulting from being out of stock, delivering late, or generating customer ill will by delivering damaged goods that have to be replaced. As we will see below, marketers who choose not to distribute their products directly to final buyers can contract out most or all physical distribution decisions to intermediaries.

SELECTING CHANNELS FOR MANUFACTURED GOODS

Managers use the term *channels* to describe the ways in which products reach the ultimate consumer. Some manufactured goods are sold directly to their ultimate buyers. Others pass through one or more intermediary organizations on their way to the final buyers.

The most common distribution channel for consumer package goods and small consumer durables is:

Manufacturer → wholesaler → retailer → consumer

In the case of large consumer durables, such as automobiles, there is often no wholesaler in the channel, with cars being shipped directly from the domestic manufacturing plant to the retail showroom. With imported goods, however, an overseas factory may well ship to domestic distributors through an importer that performs certain wholesale roles.

Manufacturers of goods destined for industrial or institutional purchasers are more likely to minimize or eliminate the role of intermediaries. This strategy is most common when the product is custom-designed and built for the final buyer, when manufacturer and purchaser are geographically close, or when the product requires special expertise for installation and operator training which the manufacturer is best qualified to deliver. Large computers and specialized medical equipment are examples of goods for which direct distribution tends to be the norm. In most other instances, industrial goods pass through only one intermediary organization on their way to the ultimate consumer.

Some products, of course, are sold to both industrial and household buyers. In those instances, wholesalers may sell in bulk both to manufacturers who buy in large quantities (and require little in the way of customer service) and to retail stores which also buy in bulk but resell in small quantities.

Channels of distribution can accomplish several important functions for the marketer:

- Transfer ownership of the goods
- Physically move the goods from the manufacturer's facility to a retail location or even to the purchaser's home or place of business
- Store the product
- Grade or sort products (particularly important in the case of agricultural and other natural produce)
- Combine goods from several sources, like the components of a stereo system, to fill a buyer's needs
- Provide sales and promotional support for the product
- Accept orders from customers
- Grant credit to buyers
- Offer a variety of customer services, including information and advice, installation, and replacement or repair of items that malfunction while under warranty
- Relay market information to the manufacturer

The manufacturer needs to clarify not only which of these tasks is necessary for success in the marketplace but also which responsibilities are best assigned to which parties in a given situation.

DISTRIBUTION CHANNELS FOR SERVICES

Unlike manufactured goods, services do not need to be stored or physically transported. For this reason, service businesses are much more likely than manufacturers to create their own delivery systems. However, opportunities may exist for delegating certain tasks to intermediaries. Perhaps the most extensive form of delegation is in franchising, where the originator of the franchise concept—the franchiser—contracts with franchisees to create a tightly prescribed service and deliver it to customers.

In other instances, the service business still holds primary responsibility for creating the service but has the option of employing distributors for a fee or commission to deliver certain components of that service. For instance, banks can choose to deliver simple financial services through their own branches, through freestanding automated teller machines, or through point-of-sale machines or booths located in retail stores. Airlines and hotels manage their own core businesses—a fleet of aircraft or a chain of hotels—but they rely heavily on travel agents to provide information and promotional support, make reservations, and collect payment in advance from customers.

Sometimes service intermediaries will specialize in particular types of customers. For instance, some travel agents work only with business clients who make extensive use of airlines, hotels, and rental cars but have no need for the packaged vacation tours that are the bread and butter of the typical "retail" travel agent.

FINANCIAL IMPLICATIONS OF CHANNEL CHOICE

As was mentioned earlier, channel intermediaries can perform a wide variety of tasks for the producer of a good or service. However, performance of these tasks costs money.

In most instances, the intermediary is rewarded with a commission or margin that is proportional to the price of the product. Margins are usually expressed as a percentage of the final selling price. The size of the margin percentage is often preestablished within the industry, reflecting the costs and risks associated with handling particular categories of products. In situations where both wholesalers and retailers are involved in the channel, retailers usually receive a substantially higher margin, reflecting in part the higher costs associated with a retail location and with making numerous sales in small quantities.

A central issue for the marketing manager is whether he or she is getting good value from paying these wholesale and retain margins, which may collectively amount to more than half the recommended selling price for many consumer durables. Would it be cheaper to distribute directly to consumers and to have the firm incur the distribution costs? Alternatively, should the firm assume responsibility for certain distribution tasks and seek out distributors who will accept a smaller margin in return for doing less?

A thorough analysis of alternative channel strategies should begin with identification of all distribution tasks and their associated costs, if performed by the producer. At a minimum these tasks might include:

- Transportation
- Warehousing and other storage
- Maintenance of retail outlets
- Local promotions
- Provision of customer credit
- Handling customer service calls

Although some of these tasks, such as transportation, may represent variable costs that are incurred on a unit-by-unit basis, others—such as maintaining a warehouse or retail outlet—represent fixed costs which within certain limits are independent of the volume of sales. Distributors' margins, by contrast, are variable costs. So the financial desirability of performing one's own distribution functions versus using intermediaries will vary with the volume of sales.

In the case of consumer goods sold to mass markets, it is generally more cost effective for producers to use the services of distributors than to perform all the distribution tasks themselves. However, cost is not the only criterion. Marketers must also consider how much control they give up when they use one or more intermediaries in the distribution channel.

EFFICIENCY VERSUS CONTROL IN CHANNEL SYSTEMS

A marketing manager uses intermediaries because they increase the efficiency of the distribution system. As well, distributors offer specialized skills and knowledge, particularly of local market conditions, that most marketers lack and could not afford the time and expense of acquiring themselves.

However, the use of intermediaries reduces the company's control over a number of important functions. First is price. Although the marketer remains free to suggest the retail price and terms of sale, the retailer calls the shots. Second is retail display. Retailers will tend to emphasize those products that promise the greatest financial return, either directly or as loss leaders to draw customers into the store. Local advertising and promotion are other areas of potential conflict, as are the nature of the sales presentations given by the distributor's own sales force.

The marketing manager needs to consider how much power will be yielded to the distributors. At times, channels may be marked by conflict over which members will exercise the most power: the producer, who develops, produces, and markets the product; the wholesaler, who controls the interaction with retail outlets (including which outlets get to sell the product); or the retailer, who controls direct interactions with the ultimate buyer.

No matter who holds the most power in the channel, success in the marketplace requires that all parties be motivated to work jointly toward achieving sales of the product(s) in question. Distributors run their businesses to make a profit for their owners. Hence they will cooperate with their suppliers only to the extent that this arrangement advances their own enterprise. They are also customers of the producing organization and the marketing concept must be applied to them as well as to ultimate consumers. In evaluating alternative distributors, the marketing manager needs to ask how well a particular product, backed by specific financial terms and a marketing program, will fit the financial and operational goals of each potential intermediary.

LINKING DISTRIBUTION WITH MARKETING MIX STRATEGY

Distribution strategy must be consistent with product policy, pricing strategy, and marketing communication activities. Let's look briefly at each in turn.

Product Policy

When specific products are targeted at specific markets, competitive advantage is often a key consideration. This may take the form of a distinctive core product; but more likely, especially in mature product categories, product differentiation centers on augmentation through a variety of service-related features. The marketing manager needs to think carefully about who will be responsible for providing these augmenting features: the producer, the distributor, or the two acting jointly.

Among the product-related responsibilities to be assigned are:

• Information and consultation
• Installation (if any)
• Assembly (if needed)
• Receipt and replacement of defective merchandise
• Repairs and maintenance of spare parts inventory
• Other warranty-related activities

Pricing

Decisions about pricing concern both dollar figures and terms of sale:

1. Does the retailer take title to the product or sell only on a consignment basis? The latter approach is sometimes demanded by distributors dealing with a new product which is being marketed by a small firm with no proven track record. Consignment increases the risk to the producer and reduces it for the intermediary.
2. Will the producer agree to accept returns of unsold or damaged merchandise? Can this responsibility be delegated to others? A powerful manufac-

turer, dealing with weak distributors, may be able to enforce such a policy, thereby shifting risk to the intermediaries in the channel.

3. Can the producer set and enforce a recommended retail price, without resorting to illegal behavior? Alternatively, does the retailer have the sales volume and cost efficiencies to discount deeply without being given a more substantial margin?

4. Can the producer get the distributor to participate in promotional pricing programs, such as cents-off coupons for consumer packaged goods or special discounts? Can the retailer demand special terms from manufacturers competing for shelf space?

Advertising, Promotion, and Personal Selling

Distributors often play a crucial role in the marketing communication program. Some questions for the marketing manager to consider are:

1. Does the distributor rely on a push strategy (generated by the skill and persistence of its own sales force), or does it emphasize a pull strategy (relying on advertising and external promotions to pull prospective customers into the store)?

2. Will the distributor participate financially in cooperative advertising and promotional activities initiated by the producer?

3. Will retail distributors be willing to use point-of-purchase display materials developed by the producer at specific times as part of a national or regional marketing campaign?

EXCLUSIVITY

Producers sometimes seek to limit sale of a product to selected distributors. Possible reasons for such a choice include the desire to avoid head-to-head competition with competing products; avoidance of price competition between stores (especially between full-service department stores and self-service warehouse outlets); the desire to position the product in a way that is consistent with the image and service provided by a certain type of store or distributor; the need for a high level of familiarity with both the product and the producing firm; and demonstrated ability to provide aftersales service.

Although exclusive distribution offers important advantages, it takes time to select and nurture the most appropriate intermediaries. The latter may insist upon special terms and support. The downside of exclusivity is first that it limits geographic coverage (making it unsuitable for convenience products) and second that it may be difficult to enforce.

SUMMARY

Providing "the right product at the right place at the right time" is the primary goal of distribution management. Whether offering physical goods or services, marketers must manage a complex set of distribution tasks and relationships if this goal is to be achieved. Because of cost constraints, distribution strategies often represent a realistic compromise between keeping costs down and maintaining control over all elements of the marketing program.

A poor distribution strategy quickly leads to lost sales and ill will among both distributors and consumers. But a well-designed and properly implemented strategy for distribution and service delivery can yield important competitive advantages.

Granville Island Brewing Company

Shirley F. Taylor
John D. Claxton

In early 1986, Mitch Taylor, founder and president of Granville Island Brewing Company (GIBCO), sat contemplating the future of his company. GIBCO was the first cottage brewery in British Columbia. The brewery and an attached retail outlet were located on Vancouver's Granville Island and has been in operation for nearly two years. The brewery's primary product, Island Lager, appeared to be well accepted, with demand often exceeding supply. However, the cyclical nature of the beer market and changing competitive conditions were a continuing cause of concern.

Mr. Taylor's objective for GIBCO was to build a small capacity brewery producing an ultra premium quality beer and by focusing on Vancouver eventually capture 1% of the provincial beer market. Recent expansion of production capacity and distribution coverage were steps toward these objectives.

Copyright © 1988 by the Case Development Program, Faculty of Management, University of Manitoba. Support for the development of this case was provided by the Canadian Studies Program, Secretary of State, Ottawa; and the Management Excellence in Small Business Program, Department of Industry, Trade and Commerce, Ottawa. This case was prepared as the basis for class discussion rather than to illustrate either effective or ineffective handling of an administrative situation.

GIBCO's growth opportunities looked promising; however, Mr. Taylor's concerns included the following: (1) "cold beer stores," a new type of retail outlet, seemed both a threat to GIBCO's brewery store and an opportunity for broader distribution; (2) GIBCO's distribution in restaurants and bars was not expanding as quickly as planned; (3) Sunday beer sales were no longer exclusive to GIBCO's brewery store; (4) other cottage breweries were being licensed in the province; (5) product selection and space utilization in the brewery store needed review; (6) whether the product line should be expanded to include draft and light beers had to be examined; and (7) the idea of a "beer garden" added to the GIBCO brewery facility also required further study.

Mr. Taylor's major uncertainty was how to deal with these interrelated concerns and, in particular, how to set priorities for the GIBCO management team. His long-term goal was to open more cottage breweries in other parts of the country. However, it was clear that he first had to concentrate on making this one work.

BACKGROUND

In 1981, Mitch Taylor, a successful entrepreneur, began looking for a business opportunity that was recession proof. A local business that caught his attention was a "Brew-Pub" operating in Horseshoe Bay, a Vancouver suburb. The "Brew-Pub" had a license to brew its own natural beer and sell it on site. It appeared to be highly successful and led Mr. Taylor to investigate the possibility of a similar venture in the Vancouver area.

After considerable interest from and discussion with the B. C. Liquor Control and Licensing Board, he developed the idea of starting a small brewery that would produce a premium quality beer and sell it through its own retail store for in-house consumption. His early efforts centered on licensing arrangements, finding a location, and developing a product that would be successful. After nearly two years of negotiations with the provincial government, permission to develop and operate the brewery was obtained. The appendix at the end of this case provides a chronological history of GIBCO.

THE BREWERY LOCATION

Mr. Taylor had wanted a building with sufficient space to house both the brewery and the retail store, as well as being convenient to a large number of potential customers. The site selected was an old warehouse on Granville Island, an urban redevelopment area in the heart of Vancouver.

In 1973, the federal government initiated a project to convert the 38-acre Granville Island peninsula from industrial use to a retail-tourist area. By 1984, Granville Island was home to an indoor public market, as well as a number of tourist shops, restaurants and theaters. Surrounded by the newly developed and moderately affluent False Creek residential area and across the water from the downtown core, Granville Island attracted over 6 million visitors a year. Both tourists and local residents frequented the island. Approximately 65% of visitors were from the residential areas close to Granville Island. Tourists from outside the Vancouver area made up approximately 25% of its summertime traffic. A survey conducted on the island in the summer of 1985 revealed that 60% of the local visitors came to the island at least once a week in the summer and 46% at least once a

week in the winter. There were no government liquor outlets on the island, and the nearest was approximately 1.5 kilometers away. The location chosen for the brewery was just inside the entrance to the island, so that all vehicle and foot traffic had to pass the brewery upon entering Granville Island. Although technically an island, a short causeway linked the island to the mainland. Mr. Taylor considered it a perfect location for the new brewery.

THE PRODUCT AND PRODUCTION PROCESS

The product decisions centered on finding an approach to brewing a premium beer that would be of interest to the Vancouver market. Mr. Taylor hired a West German, Rainer Kallahne, who held a brew master's diploma from the University of Berlin. Mr. Kallahne directed all aspects of production, following the Bavarian Purity Law, which specified that beer must be made of hops, yeast and water and have no chemicals or preservatives. The distinctiveness of the beer was to be enhanced by a distinctive bottle. Instead of the traditional stubby brown bottle that characterized most of the domestic beers being sold in 1981, the Granville Island beer "Island Lager" was to be bottled in a tall-necked bottle, resembling the look of the imported, premium beers.

With the license, location and product decisions set, GIBCO started to take shape. By early 1984, the building had been renovated, and the equipment installed. The first production run began in the spring. Each production run involved one day of brewing, ten days of fermentation, forty-two days of aging, and two to three days for bottling. It took nine weeks from the start of production to having bottled beer on the shelves of the brewery store. Production capacity was determined by the size and number of aging tanks. At the time of Granville Island's first production run, there were fifteen sixty-hectoliter aging tanks.[1] This capacity allowed for the production of

---

[1] 1 hectoliter = 100 liters = 26.4 US gallons
1 dozen beer = 4.092 liters
1 barrel = approximately 28 dozen bottles

approximately 5,400 hectoliters per year of lager if the brewery produced at "full-tilt" throughout the entire year. However, since beer without preservatives has a shelf life of only 60 days, it was not possible to accumulate inventory during slow periods to prepare for the highly cyclical patterns that characterized beer sales. As a result, production had to be reduced during periods of low sales.

RETAILING REGULATIONS

Island Lager sales began in June 1984 through the Granville Island retail outlet. The retail outlet operated by special arrangement with the Liquor Control and Licensing Branch (LCLB) and the Liquor Distribution Branch (LDB) of the provincial government. Since government regulations dictated that all beer sold in the province be distributed through the Liquor Distribution Branch, the Granville Island Brewery store was required to act as a government liquor outlet. This meant that government regulations affected the pricing policy for the beer.

The brewery established a price at which they would sell their beer to the Liquor Distribution Branch. This price included all production costs and desired profit, as well as federal excise duty and federal taxes. The Distribution Branch then applied their markup (called a "malt levy") to this price, which was based on the alcoholic content of the beer. The 5% alcohol level in Island Lager resulted in a 50% markup. To this figure, the 7% provincial sales tax was added, resulting in a final price to the consumer. The LDB would allow only one price change per month, and prices were uniform across all retail outlets within the province. The prices set to the consumer for Island Lager in June 1984 were: $4.60 for a four-pack, $8.90 for an eight-pack and $12.50 for a twelve-pack. From these sales, the brewery would receive, after deducting the federal excise duty and taxes, $2.33 for four-packs, $4.60 for eight-packs, and $6.45 for twelve packs.

Although the pricing structure allowed for the desired profit to be set by the brewery, this profit was essentially determined by competitive forces. Granville Island Brewery established a retail price

and worked backwards from there to determine profit. The retail price was based on the positioning of Island Lager relative to its competitors. Since Mr. Taylor wanted Island Lager positioned as an ultra-premium product, it was priced as such—Island Lager's retail price was marginally below the price of imports and substantially above the price of domestic beers. In June, 1984, a six-pack of domestic beer ranged in price from $4.05 to $5, while imported beer ranged from $5.50 to $9.

VANCOUVER BEER MARKET

Three major breweries dominated the national beer market and together accounted for approximately 98% of the domestic beer sales in British Columbia. Mr. Taylor had hoped that Island Lager would compete directly with imported beer, which had risen to a 4.7% market share in the 1983–84 fiscal year (*Exhibit 1*). The recent upswing in import sales had not gone unnoticed as all three major breweries had taken action to produce their own versions of U.S. brands. For example, after Labatt introduced a Canadian version of Budweiser in March, 1981, Carling O'Keefe (in May, 1984) and Molson (in October, 1985) followed with U.S. brands brewed in Canada. Lager was the most popular type of beer consumed in the province, accounting for 98% of packaged beer sold; ale, porter and stout made up the remaining 2%. When Island Lager first entered the market in the

EXHIBIT 1

LITER BEER SALES IN B.C. FOR EACH FISCAL YEAR ENDING MARCH 31

Year	Domestic, 000s	Imported, 000s	Total, 000s
1980/81*	$182,853	$13,382	$196,235
1981/82	222,080	5,378	227,458
1982/83	225,235	6,807	232,042
1983/84	216,389	10,726	227,115
1984/85	221,458	9,806	231,264
1985/86	214,411	8,783	223,194

*A labor strike at B.C. breweries in 1980 resulted in increased sales of imported beer.

spring of 1984, total provincial beer sales exceeded 200 million liters a year, accounting for approximately 40% of total provincial alcohol dollar sales— 75% of total volume in liters (see *Exhibit 1*). It was estimated that the Metro Vancouver area accounted for approximately 68% of provincial beer sales.

GIBCO BUSINESS MISSION

While setting up Granville Island Brewery, Mr. Taylor spent many months on the product and location decisions, adjusting these decisions to government regulations, and evaluating market potential. The objectives that he used as guidelines were as shown in Exhibit 1.

1. To build a small capacity brewery and add incremental expansion as demand increased to a maximum of 25,000 barrels (approximately 700,000 dozen or 2,864,440 liters).
2. To realize gross margins of approximately 50%; control expenses and achieve a net operating income after tax of 15 to 20%.
3. To produce high quality ultra-premium products in bottles and kegs.
4. To service markets in the Greater Vancouver region only, where distribution and shelf life can be controlled.
5. To staff the operation with qualified and experienced employees who would eventually participate as shareholders.

GIBCO OPERATIONS JUNE 1984 TO DECEMBER 1985

Initial sales of Island Lager were promising, resulting in total sales through the brewery store of close to 40,000 dozen bottles in the first seven months of operation (*Exhibit 2*). The Granville Island Brewery became one of the tourist attractions on Granville Island, and line-ups for beer at the store were common. The inability to store the beer because of its limited shelf life resulted in stockouts during periods of heavy traffic. These stockouts were infrequent and never lasted more than one or two days. Yet, the stockouts served to enhance the image of Island Lager as a "hot item."

From the beginning beer sales were supplemented by sales of Granville Island Brewery souvenirs, such as beer mugs, sweaters, wine glasses, bottle openers, and various other items. Souvenir sales grossed close to $40,000 in the first seven months, with retail margins varying between 30 and 40%. Free tours of the brewery were also offered through the retail store. These tours, held at various times throughout the day, helped to establish the brewery as a tourist attraction, differentiating it from other government liquor stores. The brewery's store manager estimated that three quarters of those customers taking the tour were out-of-towners.

When Island Lager was first introduced to the public in June, 1984, it was sold through the brewery's own retail store, through some local restaurants and pubs, and later through cold beer stores.[2] Sales to these outlets, referred to by the brewery as licensees, were also channeled through the Liquor Distribution Branch, but the physical distribution of the lager to the licensees was handled by the brewery. By the end of 1984, Island Lager was sold in 60 local restaurants and pubs, resulting in total licensee sales of over 9,000 dozen bottles.

During 1985 Mr. Taylor implemented two major initiatives designed to (1) smooth sales patterns and (2) expand distribution to government liquor stores.

SMOOTHING SALES PATTERNS

While successful, Island Lager sales followed the traditional patterns for beer sales. Summer volume substantially surpassed winter volume, leaving summer sales to offset the high fixed overhead costs of running the brewery and maintaining its excess capacity in the winter months. In an attempt to utilize this excess production capacity and establish a more stable flow of revenue, plans for a "bock" beer were initiated in early 1985. Bock, a darker, heavier beer,

---

[2]In May, 1985, the provincial government announced that certain hotels and neighborhood pubs would be allowed to open Licensee Retail Stores on their premises for the sale of B.C. packaged beer, cider, wines and coolers. These are referred to as "cold beer stores."

EXHIBIT 2 MONTHLY SALES SUMMARY: JUNE 1984 TO DECEMBER 1985

								1984	
	Lager, dzs	Bock, dzs	Total store, dzs	LDB,* dzs	Licensee, dzs	Total, dzs	Souvenir	Wine	
June	4,989	0	4,989	0	424	5,413	$ 2,952	$	0
July	8,903	0	8,903	0	1,232	10,135	5,349		0
Aug	7,087	0	7,087	0	1,260	8,347	7,216		0
Sept	5,531	0	5,531	0	795	6,326	5,011		0
Oct	4,082	0	4,082	0	1,650	5,732	4,971		0
Nov	3,792	0	3,792	0	2,127	5,919	4,322		0
Dec	5,593	0	5,593	0	1,550	7,143	9,698		0
Total	39,977	0	39,977	0	9,038	49,015	$39,519	$	0

								1985	
Jan	3,336	0	3,336	0	1,636	4,972	$ 2,367	$	0
Feb	3,694	0	3,694	0	1,456	5,150	2,367		0
Mar	5,460	424	5,884	0	2,483	8,367	4,569		0
Apr	4,947	872	5,819	0	2,645	8,464	4,419		1,336
May	7,562	0	7,562	0	3,168	10,730	5,953		8,832
June	9,191	0	9,191	0	2,757	11,948	9,130		13,063
July	9,285	0	9,285	0	3,360	12,645	11,105		12,609
Aug	9,302	0	9,302	0	2,930	12,232	12,799		16,966
Sept	7,170	0	7,170	347	1,917	9,434	9,261		15,202
Oct	5,299	0	5,299	1,030	2,141	8,470	5,609		15,617
Nov	4,497	182	4,679	830	1,752	7,261	5,951		13,351
Dec	4,631	1,600	6,231	1,133	1,784	9,148	12,385		14,757
Total	74,374	3,078	77,452	3,340	28,029	108,821	$85,915		$111,733

*LDB refers to sales (in dozens of bottles) through government retail outlets.

goes through the same production process as lager but requires a longer aging time (11–12 weeks). One batch of 3,000 dozen bottles was planned for every March and November, with the first batch (at half the ultimate capacity) to be available in March 1985, in twelve-packs through the brewery store. Bock not only made use of facilities in slow lager periods, it also fit nicely into the Octoberfest and Easter celebration times, and both spring and fall batches sold out quickly.

In another attempt to establish a more stable flow of revenues, GIBCO obtained a license to sell wines through the brewery store. In April, 1985, Okanagan Estate wines (a collection of wines from one winery in British Columbia's Okanagan region) were sold in a self-serve fashion from shelves at the front of the store. Approximately 25 varieties were carried

on a 10% commission basis. The terms of the wine license had two important implications. First, the license stipulated that a cash system be maintained for wine sales that was separate from beer sales. This meant that customers had to wait in two lines when purchasing both wine and beer. Second, the wine license allowed the store to be open on Sunday. Normally, Sunday beer sales were not allowed in the Vancouver area (government liquor stores and pubs were closed on Sunday). However, the terms of the wine license designated Granville Island Brewery as an Estate Wine Store, and hence allowed for Sunday sales. Of the six Estate Wine Stores in the province, five were in the greater Vancouver area. These six establishments were the only stores in the province that were authorized to sell wine for off-site consumption on Sundays. Granville Island Brewing was the only one that also sold beer. Sunday openings proved to be a big asset for Granville Island Brewing, with more beer sold on Sunday than any other day of the week. For example, in July 1985, Sunday beer sales averaged 800 dozen bottles of Island Lager. This was more than three times the weekday average of 260 dozen bottles per day and more than twice the average 370 dozen bottles sold on Saturdays. Sunday sales were similarly higher for wine and souvenir sales.

EXPANDING TO GOVERNMENT LIQUOR STORES

With the brewery store successfully underway, Mr. Taylor looked for expanded distribution of Island Lager. In the summer of 1985, the brewery's sales manager, Turk Whitehead, began negotiations with the managers of several government liquor stores. Each liquor store had to be solicited individually, since the decision of whether to carry Island Lager was to be made by each store manager. In addition, all proposals to carry Island Lager had to be approved by the Liquor Distribution Board (LDB). Thus, upon acceptance of arrangements by a liquor store manager, an application in writing was presented to the LDB.

Solicitation of the liquor store accounts was handled primarily by Turk Whitehead, who as general manager and sales manager oversaw all sales activities. He had been with Granville Island Brewing since the fall of 1983, after 10 years with Carling O'Keefe Breweries. Although he held two management titles, his primary responsibility concerned the soliciting of liquor store accounts. There were 70 local liquor stores, and Mr. Taylor hoped to have Island Lager in all of these by 1987. While some of these accounts were actively sought by Mr. Whitehead, other placements resulted from initiatives taken by liquor store managers themselves. The first liquor store agreements were completed in September, 1985, and by the end of that year Island Lager was being sold through seven LDB outlets. Mr. Taylor decided to limit LDB store sales to the 8-pack. He considered the 8-pack more "marketable" in that it allowed customers to see the distinctive

Island Lager bottle, while the 12-pack was in an enclosed case. Over 5,000 8-packs were sold in the first four months that Island Lager was on liquor store shelves.

These sales were accompanied by minimal advertising support. Granville Island Brewing had relied primarily on word of mouth and any free publicity given by the media, such as a short spot on a news broadcast featuring "cottage breweries." Flyers advertising the brewery had been distributed throughout Granville Island and placed in racks at liquor stores. Paid advertising through the media had not been used. Mr. Taylor felt that since the brewery did not appear to be suffering from the lack of advertising, it was unnecessary to spend money on it until the brewery had built itself up.

RESULTS AS OF DECEMBER 1985

The combination of brewery sales, licensee sales, and sales through LDB outlets resulted in steady growth over the initial 19 months of GIBCO operations. As shown in *Exhibit 2*, July through December 1984 saw sales of 35,000 dozen bottles through the brewery store, 8,600 dozen through licensees, and $37,000 in souvenirs. During the same six months of 1985 the corresponding sales figures had grown to 42,000 dozen, 14,000 dozen and $57,000, plus 5,000 dozen through LDB outlets and $89,000 in wine sales. Based on this initial success, Taylor decided to expand the brewery's production capacity and look for further opportunities for growth.

DEVELOPMENTS IN 1986

The first five months of 1986 were a busy time for Mr. Taylor. He prepared a pro forma statement for GIBCO for the year based on certain assumptions that he hoped would become reality. As well, he took steps to improve distribution, added more capacity to the brewery, began producing a draft beer, added a new line of wines to his retail store, and contemplated changes in his retail operations. On top of this, Mr. Taylor was concerned about pending changes in the provincial legislation to the distribution and sale of liquor in the province. In late May he began reviewing these activities prior to making some funda-mental decisions about the future of the business.

GIBCO PROFITABILITY

Mr. Taylor prepared a pro forma statement that pro-jected total beer sales for the year of $1,614,131, store souvenir and commissions sales of $341,220, making for total gross sales of $1,955,351 (*Exhibit*

3). After deducting all costs, the projected net in-come for 1986 was $670,642. However, Mr. Taylor knew that the pro forma was based on the overriding assumption that everything would go well during the year. He was not sure it would happen as much depended on GIBCO sales during Expo '86, the world's fair to take place in Vancouver between April and October.

As well, the forecasted revenue from beer sales

EXHIBIT 3
GIBCO OPERATING STATEMENT ($000s) 1986

	First quarter actual	Second quarter budget	Third quarter budget	Fourth quarter budget	Total
Store Operations					
Beer sales and cost of goods					
Beer sales	90.6	201.6	270.2	138.0	700.4
Operating fee[1]	17.2	38.8	50.1	23.5	129.6
Total revenue	107.8	240.4	320.3	161.5	830.0
Cost of goods	47.8	94.4	121.2	62.0	325.4
Gross income	60.0	146.0	199.1	99.5	504.6
Wine sales and expenses					
Wine sales	22.9	59.8	89.7	84.1	256.5
Wine commissions[2]	3.4	9.0	13.5	12.6	38.5
Rental expense	0.6	1.6	2.4	2.2	6.8
Gross income	2.8	7.4	11.1	10.4	31.7
Souvenir sales and expenses					
Souvenir sales	18.6	43.0	73.0	38.0	172.6
Rental expense	0.0	2.2	3.7	1.9	7.8
Cost of goods	11.3	23.7	40.2	20.9	96.1
Gross income	7.3	17.1	29.1	15.2	68.7
Other income	0.2	0.1	0.2	0.1	0.5
Store administrative expenses					
Tours and hospitality	0.6	2.0	2.6	1.2	6.4
Sales promotion	0.7	1.5	1.5	1.5	5.2
Salaries and benefits	18.9	26.0	25.0	20.3	90.2
Store supplies	3.2	3.0	3.0	3.0	12.2
Credit card sales expense	0.7	1.3	1.7	0.9	4.6
Total expenses	24.1	33.8	33.8	26.9	118.6
Total store sales	132.1	304.4	432.9	260.1	1129.5
Net income[3]					
Beer	43.5	123.6	178.0	85.2	430.3
Wine	(1.3)	0.8	4.1	1.7	5.3
Souvenirs	4.0	12.4	23.5	11.3	51.2
Total store net income	46.2	136.8	205.6	98.2	486.8

EXHIBIT 3 (*Continued*)

	First quarter actual	Second quarter budget	Third quarter budget	Fourth quarter budget	Total
Off-Island Operations					
Liquor distribution branches (LDB) sales and expenses					
LDB sales	33.0	85.3	81.9	134.0	334.2
Cost of goods	17.0	39.0	35.8	58.8	150.6
Gross income	16.0	46.3	46.1	75.2	183.6
Car and salary expense	8.0	9.6	10.3	10.3	38.2
Delivery	2.1	3.0	3.0	2.9	11.0
Promotion	3.5	6.5	11.0	3.5	24.5
Net income	2.4	27.2	21.8	58.5	109.9
Licensee sales and expenses					
Licensee sales	39.4	82.0	97.4	162.8	381.6
Cold beer store sales	2.4	20.3	27.3	24.5	74.5
Total sales	41.8	102.3[1]	124.7	187.3	456.1
Cost of goods	22.9	49.7	58.0	87.3	217.9
Gross income	18.9	52.6	66.7	100.0	238.2
Commission expense	3.4	19.7	20.0	30.2	73.3
Delivery	2.8	3.8	4.9	4.3	15.8
Promotiion	3.5	6.5	11.0	3.5	24.5
Net income	9.2	22.6	30.8	62.0	124.6
Expo sales and expenses					
Expo sales	0.0	43.6	65.6	14.4	123.6
Cost of goods	0.0	21.2	30.5	6.7	58.4
Gross income	0.0	22.4	35.1	7.7	65.2
Advertising	0.0	4.7	7.0	1.5	13.2
Delivery	0.0	1.6	2.6	0.3	4.5
Net income	0.0	16.1	25.5	5.9	47.5
GIBCO total net income	57.8	202.7	283.7	224.6	768.8
Other company expenses					
Advertising	3.2	18.1	26.7	9.5	57.5
Car and salary	8.0	9.6	10.3	10.3	38.2
Travel	0.3	0.8	0.8	0.8	2.7
Total	11.5	28.5	37.8	20.6	98.4
Profit	46.3	174.2	245.9	204.0	670.4

[1]GIBCO received an operating fee from the Liquor Distribution Branch for running the beer store.
[2]GIBCO received a 15% commission on wine sales.
[3]Net income was calculated by allocating "Store Administrative Expenses" based on proportion of total sales.

was dependent on the distribution method; different sizes were carried by the various outlets, and similar sizes had higher margins. With federal duty and taxes subtracted, GIBCO revenue per dozen averaged $7.25 through the brewery store, $7.43 through LDB outlets, and $6.99 through licensees and Expo pavil-

ions. These figures were based on May 1986 retail prices of $5.25 per 4-pack, $10.20 for an 8-pack, and $14.50 for a 12-pack. These prices were about 30% above domestic beer prices, yet marginally below the prices of premium import beer.

In addition to revenue differences by outlet, there

were variations in marketing expenses. GIBCO paid $0.75 per dozen for sales to licensees by Mark Anthony representatives (see below), $0.75 per dozen to the Expo Corporation for sales through Expo pavilions, and delivery costs for all beer sold off the brewery site. On the other hand, beer sold through the brewery store received a commission from the Liquor Distribution Branch of 10% of the retail price. This commission was paid because of the licensing agreement designating the brewery store as a government liquor store.

DISTRIBUTION CHANGES

In the first four months of 1986, Turk Whitehead continued his efforts to have Island Lager stocked in local liquor stores. By the end of April, the number of local liquor stores carrying Island Lager had grown to 26. *Exhibit 4* lists these store accounts, the date GIBCO started supplying them, and the volume of Island Lager supplied to these outlets in April, 1986.

The number of licensee accounts had not grown as rapidly as the liquor store distribution, and Mr.

EXHIBIT 4   GREATER VANCOUVER GOVERNMENT LIQUOR STORE SALES

Store*	Date of first sales of Island Lager	Total fiscal 1986 store sales** ($ mil)	Estimated April 1986 sales of all brands of beer (dozens)	Sales in April 1986 (dozens)
GIBCO	June 1984	1.4		4,528
Lansdowne	Sept. 1985	7.1	26,700	100
39th & Cambie	Sept. 1985	12.6	42,200	260
Thurlow	Sept. 1985	7.0	20,300	80
Park Royal	Sept. 1985	8.9	22,700	90
Lougheed Mall	Sept. 1985	8.8	36,100	100
Whistler	Sept. 1985	3.0	12,200	60
Middlegate	Sept. 1985	10.2	44,300	80
Westwood	Feb. 1986	7.4	30,000	60
Tsawwassen	Feb. 1986	5.1	17,200	—
Kennedy Heights	Feb. 1986	11.0	48,500	60
North Burnaby	Feb. 1986	10.5	46,000	80
Westview	Feb. 1986	10.8	42,200	100
Seafair	Feb. 1986	6.9	26,100	60
White Rock	Feb. 1986	7.8	28,500	80
Guilford	Feb. 1986	7.7	31,500	80
Marpole	Feb. 1986	9.1	46,100	100
Kerrisdale	Feb. 1986	4.4	13,600	80
Kingsgate	Feb. 1986	7.7	34,700	64
Robson	Feb. 1986	8.9	32,800	240
Senlac	Feb. 1986	9.7	44,200	50
4th & Alma	Feb. 1986	8.5	33,200	270
Broadway & Maple	Feb. 1986	11.4	45,000	270
West Vancouver	Feb. 1986	8.0	23,800	140
New Westminster	Feb. 1986	8.3	36,500	100
Gibsons	Feb. 1986	2.9	11,900	60
AVERAGE (not including GIBCO)		8.2	32,900	107

*There were an additional 45 LDB outlets in Metro Vancouver that did not stock Granville Island Lager.
**The 1986 fiscal year ended March 31, 1986.

Taylor felt that changes were necessary. In March 1986, with only 200 of an estimated 800 potential licensee accounts in the Vancouver area stocking Island Lager, Mr. Taylor commissioned the Mark Anthony wine and spirit merchants to act as exclusive sales representatives for Island Lager. The Mark Anthony company had 10 representatives serving the Vancouver area. They carried approximately 150 products, none of which were beer. These reps were contracted to represent Island Lager to the licensees. Turk Whitehead would continue his contacts with the liquor stores.

ADDING CAPACITY

The distribution improvements and the preparation for Expo '86 led, in April 1986, to the addition of twelve 60-hectoliter aging tanks, almost doubling production capacity. As well, an additional 36 aging tanks were planned for the fall of 1986. With this increase in capacity, Mr. Taylor began production of a draft beer. British Columbia in contrast to other provinces was a strong draft beer market, averaging 20% of domestic beer sales. A new draft product would be sold through licensees, and by packaging it in a party keg, it could also be sold through the brewery store. However, Mr. Taylor had made commitments to supply both bottled and draft beer to Expo '86. Since the Expo demand for Island Lager was difficult to predict, it seemed best to delay the introduction of non-Expo draft until the fall.

As of May, production of draft beer was underway and shipments of both draft and bottled beer were being readied for Expo. If the Expo demand turned out to be less than expected, Mr. Taylor considered introducing draft kegs through the brewery store earlier than planned. Mr. Taylor thought that 10% of GIBCO's beer sales would consist of draft beer by the fourth quarter of 1986.

THE NEW LINE OF WINES

To increase sales revenue in the retail store, Mr. Taylor completed a deal with the Mark Anthony representatives to carry another line of estate wines,

Mission Hill, starting in May. Mission Hill offered a selection of over 70 wines, a selection deemed by the store manager to be much broader than the currently carried Okanagan Estate wines. In addition to Mission Hill wines, five kinds of cider and two kinds of wine coolers were to be carried. All of these products were currently offered in the government liquor stores and would be priced comparably in the brewery store. Mission Hill wines carried a commission of 15%, whereas Okanagan Estate wines carried only a 10% commission. However, Okanagan wines responded to the proposed introduction of Mission Hill wines by increasing their commission to 15%.

POSSIBLE CHANGES IN THE RETAIL OPERATIONS

Decisions regarding store operations were also concerning Mr. Taylor. How many Okanagan Estate wines to keep and how many Mission Hill wines to carry in the store had not been decided. The store had the capacity to carry between 60 and 70 types. However, if both wines were carried, a third cash till would be required. This requirement of the wine license was essentially the same as stipulated in the Okanagan Estate wine license—a separate cash system must be maintained for all types of wines carried. If both types of wines were carried, customers might have to wait in three line-ups to purchase all of their selections.

Plans for changes in the brewery store did not stop at product line decisions. The daily tours of the brewery conducted by the store's staff were also scheduled for revision. Mr. Taylor was considering an extended tour and tasting, and eventually the addition of a beer garden. The brewery had a mezzanine floor of approximately 4,700 square feet. This area could serve to enlarge the tour area allowing for bigger groups. Further development of this area would involve its conversion to a facility with a publike atmosphere where customers could purchase their beer for on-site consumption. It was estimated that this area could house a 200-seat beer garden. However, the beer garden concept was subject to the approval of the Liquor Control and Licensing

Branch. The decision of whether to staff the beer garden with brewery store employees or lease it out would have to be examined.

THE FUTURE

As Mr. Taylor reflected on the past two years he was pleased with GIBCO's initial progress and felt that future prospects looked very promising. His main concern was to set priorities that would help him to achieve the hoped-for growth. He believed in keeping his management team limited to a small number of people. As a result, the effective allocation of management energies was a key concern. It was clear to Mr. Taylor that growth priorities must be based on the relative profitability of his various options and on continual awareness of market trends that might affect future profitability.

With respect to market developments. Mr. Taylor noted several developments that could have a negative impact on his business. First, the uniqueness of Island Lager's tall-necked bottles was eliminated. By the end of 1985, all of the major breweries switched from the brown, stubby bottles to the tall-necked bottles for many of their domestic brands.

As a side issue, Mr. Taylor noted that all three major breweries had introduced and heavily promoted light beers in the past few years. Feedback from licensees indicated that consumer preference was shifting to light beer. This raised the question of introducing a light, low-alcohol beer.

Second, although it had only been a short period of time since the Mark Anthony group had been commissioned, the number of licensee accounts was increasing very slowly. Mr. Taylor wondered if his hopes for additional licensee accounts were too optimistic or if he might be going about it the wrong way.

Third, there were several recent developments that could adversely affect brewery store sales. Mr. Taylor was concerned that the increased availability of Island Lager in liquor stores would cut sales of Island Lager at the brewery store. Also, the Granville Island

Trust, the managing body for Granville Island, was considering plans to open an estate wine store in the Granville Island market. This outlet would provide direct local competition to the brewery store's wine sales and, being an estate wine store, would also be open for business on Sunday.

The brewery store's Sunday wine sales were not the only Sunday sales threatened. A more immediate problem existed with Sunday beer sales. The provincial government announced that during Expo pubs and bars could be open on Sundays. At these locations beer could be purchased for off-site consumption. Although the government stipulated that this would only be the case during Expo, public speculation was that these openings would continue past October. As well, the number of cold beer stores in the province had increased to seventeen. These outlets were similar to the brewery store in that they carried cold beer, a variety of B.C. wines, and souvenirs.

Fourth, the uniqueness of the Granville Island Brewery was also threatened. There were now four more cottage breweries in the province—two on the outskirts of Vancouver and two in the other regions of the province. However, none of these sold their products through government liquor stores.

As Mr. Taylor reviewed these market developments, he wondered what impact they would have on GIBCO profitability. He had hoped to capture 1% of the provincial beer market by 1987. Whether this goal was realistic was uncertain, but even if it were, questions as to how to proceed remained. Should he emphasize new products, such as draft or light beer? Should he put his efforts into sales through the brewery store, LDB outlets, or licensees? Further, he wondered what impact his distribution emphasis would have on other aspects of GIBCO, such as product line decisions. Mr. Taylor determined that he had five general options for growth (draft beer introduction, light beer introduction, focus on LDB sales, focus on licensee sales, or focus on store sales). He needed to set priorities that would ensure the future profitability and growth of Granville Island Brewing.

APPENDIX

Chronological History of GIBCO

Spring 1982	Negotiations with the Liquor Control and Licensing Branch of the provincial government begin.
Spring 1984	Licensing arrangements are complete. Granville Island Brewing Company begins production of Island Lager. Brewing capacity: 900 hectoliters.
June 1984	Granville Island Brewing retail store opens its doors to the public with sales of Island Lager (4, 8 and 12-packs) and GIBCO souvenirs. GIBCO begins sales of Island Lager through local licensees.
March 1985	GIBCO introduces Island Bock in 12-packs through the Brewery store.
April 1985	GIBCO starts selling Okanagan Estate wines through the Brewery store.
September 1985	Island Lager is first sold through government liquor stores (LDB).
March 1986	Mark Anthony wine and spirit merchants are engaged to act as sales representatives for Island Lager for sales to licensees.
April 1986	Production capacity to GIBCO is expanded. The addition of twelve 60-hectoliter tanks brings capacity to 1,620 hectoliters.
Fall 1986	Proposed capacity expansion to 3,750 hectoliters.

Jordan A/S

David H. Hover
Per V. Jenster
Kamran Kashani

Mr. Knut Leversby, managing director of Jordan A/S, took a good deal of pride in the certificate on his office wall in Oslo. In Norwegian, it proclaimed Jordan "Company of the Year 1986"—as judged by a broadly composed jury and the journal *Næringsrevyen*. The jury had stressed Jordan's ability to conquer market positions, especially in an international context. Four years later, in January 1990, Mr. Leversby remained proud of the award, but his internal compass guarded against pride turning into complacency. As Jordan's CEO, he knew better than anyone the strategic challenges that his company was facing. Jordan was a small company among multinational consumer goods giants like Unilever and Colgate Palmolive. And consumer goods was, more and more, a game that turned on volume, threatening to overwhelm smaller competitors.

Jordan had prospered by focusing its foreign strategy on "mechanical oral hygiene products"—mainly non-electric toothbrushes, but also dental floss and dental sticks (toothpicks). By combining high product quality with an innovative distribution strategy, Jordan had successfully defined and defended its niche to become the number 1 toothbrush maker in Europe, and number 4 in the world. But, Mr. Leversby was not sure that the tactics of the past would carry Jordan into the future. Increasingly, competition came from trade retailers and major multinationals, both of which had significantly greater resources than Jordan.

Jordan's retailers, mainly food-based mass retailers, were becoming increasingly concentrated to achieve economies of scale in purchasing and logistics. Larger scale also increased the bargaining power of retailers with suppliers on prices and trade terms. More and more, these trade terms included on-time delivery of increasingly smaller order lot sizes, as retailers implemented and refined just-in-time (JIT) systems.

Retail chains were also increasing their cross-border activity, often via acquisitions or strategic alliances, as they prepared for the "single European market"—the elimination of trade barriers between the 12 members of the European Community—due to be implemented in 1992. Consequently, they tended to favor pan-European brands for volume and ease of handling. Larger retailers could also contract production of "own label" products to compete with manufacturers' brands. In fact, about 13% of Jordan's sales came from contract production of these private labels. Mr. Leversby was concerned that Jordan's private label business might be cannibalizing name-brand sales and/or diluting the carefully built Jordan-brand image.

Concentration was also under way among European toiletries manufacturers, who performed contract distribution for Jordan. Mr. Leversby was especially concerned about the recent acquisitions of some of these distributors by multinational consumer goods companies. For example, in 1985 Procter & Gamble had acquired Richardson-Vicks, which distributed Jordan products in Italy and several other European countries. Quality distributors, like Richardson-Vicks, were difficult to replace.

COMPANY BACKGROUND

Jordan was founded by Wilhelm Jordan, a man familiar with hard times. Born in Copenhagen in 1809, he was the eldest of 11 children raised by his widowed mother. Leaving home at an early age, he apprenticed himself to one of the master combmakers of Hamburg. In 1837, Wilhelm Jordan moved to Christiania, Norway, with two fellow combmakers, starting a modest workshop destined to become the largest brush factory in Europe.

During the late nineteenth and early twentieth centuries, the Jordan company distinguished itself as a social pioneer. Despite frequent labor unrest in Norway, the Jordan factory never experienced a strike. In 1910, the company set up a pension fund wholly financed by profits. Considering the conditions of the time, Jordan was a good place to work, a fact reflected in the long-term employment and loyalty of its workers. Throughout Jordan's history, advancement from the shop floor was common; Per Lindbo, Knut Leversby's predecessor as managing director, began his career with Jordan as a 15-year-old on the production line. A Jordan publication issued in 1987 to commemorate 150 years of company

history referred to the internal "culture," strongly influenced by the founder's faith in the individual human being. For the employee with skill and the will to make the effort, the opportunity was there to accept the challenges, irrespective of formal education and qualifications.

Another continuous thread in Jordan's history was its commitment to product excellence. Brushmaking was a skilled worker's trade, and in 1989 Jordan still produced handcrafted "jewelry brushes" as nostalgia items. More importantly, the company continually invested in advanced technologies to maintain its competitive ability.

Jordan began producing toothbrushes in 1927 under the leadership of Hjalmar Jordan, grandson of the founder. By 1936, the company had captured half of the Norwegian market. In 1958, Jordan began to take a serious interest in exports, realizing that the oral hygiene field was largely underdeveloped. Jordan's subsequent success was evident. By 1988, foreign sales of dental products provided over 60% of Jordan's revenues. (Financial information on Jordan is shown in *Exhibit 1*, and an organization chart in *Exhibit 2*.) The company's sales for 1989 reached NKr330 million[1]; 44.6% of sales were made in Norway, 32.2% in the balance of Europe, and 10.0% in the rest of the world. The remaining 13.2% consisted of private label sales to other markets.

Management Challenges

In the early 1980s, Jordan suffered a period of reduced earnings. The success that Jordan achieved in increasing exports led to overemphasis on marketing and sales at the expense of financial performance. Steps were taken to re-emphasize the importance of financial results. Company-wide financial targets were set at 18% return on assets with 16% return on sales and were communicated directly to employees. In addition, efficiency measurements were established for the individual foremen to help them iden-

---

[1]Exchange rates had fluctuated widely in recent years. Approximate values for the Norwegian kroner were: NKr1.00 = FF0.88 = US$0.16 = £0.09.

EXHIBIT 1
SELECTED FINANCIAL RESULTS
(Millions of Norwegian kroner)

Income Statement

	1986	1987	1988
Operating revenues	265.0	307.0	321.0
Operating expenses:			
Depreciation		(14.0)	(15.6)
Other		(240.0)	(257.5)
Total operating expenses	(226.4)	(254.0)	(273.1)
Net operating revenues	38.6	53.0	47.9
Net financial income (cost)	(8.3)	(2.0)	1.2
Extraordinary items	1.3	(8.7)	2.2
Profit before allocations to funds and taxes	31.6	42.3	51.3
Allocations	(15.8)	(11.8)	(12.6)
Taxes	(7.4)	(15.4)	(21.2)
Net profit	8.4	15.1	17.5

Balance Sheet

Cash	31.9	55.2	81.5
Accounts receivable	42.8	35.8	52.9
Inventory	23.6	24.4	28.3
Total current assets	98.3	115.4	162.7
Long-term investments	10.8	12.9	14.2
Property, plant, and equipment	124.1	129.6	144.5
Total fixed assets	134.9	142.4	158.7
Total assets	233.2	257.9	321.4
Current liabilities	71.1	75.0	98.4
Long-term liabilities	61.1	57.0	66.2
Untaxed reserves	79.7	91.5	106.7
Minority interests	—	—	0.8
Shareholders' equity	21.3	34.4	49.3
Total liabilities and shareholders' equity	233.2	257.9	321.4
Return on assets	18.0	23.4	18.2
Cash ratio	14.6	20.2	28.0
Equity ratio	43.3	48.8	48.5

Source: Jordan.

tify their contribution to the overall profitability objectives of the company. Monthly reports and annual reviews for production looked at labor hours per unit, scrap rates, absentee rates, energy usage, and other measures of efficiency. Other reports for general distribution included weekly sales figures, profitability analysis, and accounts receivable.

The renewed emphasis on financial and efficiency measures made employees at all levels realize that the company was dependent on the successful interaction between production and marketing. This re-orientation of company values had a direct impact on performance. Sales more than doubled between 1979 and 1989, while employment stayed flat at 450 after falling from 700 between 1979 and 1982. The workforce reduction resulted from Jordan's policy to increase productivity through mechanization. The reduction was, however, achieved without major employee displacement. With government aid, older workers were retired and approximately 80 workers pensioned. Manufacturing efforts achieved productivity improvements at 6–8% per year.

Downsizing remained a priority in 1989. The personnel department spent a considerable amount of time helping people leave the company. New people, however, were hired occasionally as needed, particularly in marketing. Jordan had achieved the reputation of being a good company for international marketing. A few individuals took advantage of Jordan, staying with the company only long enough to learn its methods and techniques before leaving and joining another company. Internationally minded employees were in high demand in Norway.

THE COMPETITIVE ENVIRONMENT IN 1989

Jordan's products were marketed in more than 85 countries worldwide; 1.4 billion toothbrushes were bought in 1989. Market size and toothbrush replacement rates varied considerably among countries (refer to *Exhibit 3*). Japan was the largest consumer of toothbrushes both in total volume and on a per capita basis. Whereas Japanese consumers purchased an average of 3.2 toothbrushes per year, Irish consumers, for example, replaced their toothbrushes

EXHIBIT 2   ORGANIZATION CHART, JUNE 1989

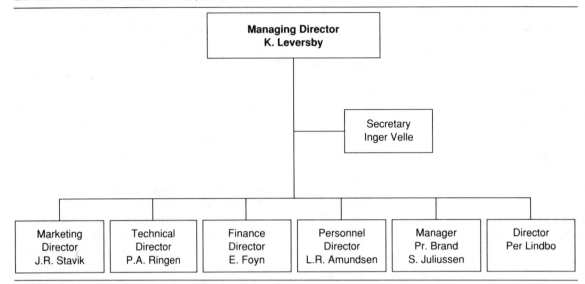

Source: Jordan.

about once every two years. (Jordan's market share in major markets is given in *Exhibit 4*. Information on major competitors is given in *Exhibit 5*. Key brands are listed in *Exhibit 6*.)

During the 1930s, Jordan had competed on quality, and its success had made Jordan-style quality an industry standard for toothbrushes. The company recognized that, as producing brushes was not a very difficult process, the battle of the future would not be about product development or production technology. As a result, Jordan shifted its focus toward product presentation and being responsive to end-user demands. Jordan concentrated its efforts on developing marketing techniques that reached the customer in the store, where most toothbrush purchase decisions were made. Through careful attention to point-of-sale promotions, packaging and product design, Jordan was able to establish and maintain a strong market presence.

In the increasingly competitive consumer product market, volume was a pre-condition for survival. Consequently, during the mid-1960s, Jordan considerably reduced its product lines (which included brushes, combs, toys, and wooden soles for foot-

wear). The slimmed-down product portfolio concentrated on products with volume-related potential. From that time onward, oral hygiene products became increasingly important to Jordan's success.

Jordan's cost structure was probably not typical for the industry, for two reasons. First, Norwegian labor costs were high. Hourly wages in Holland and Scotland, for example, were 70% and 30%, respectively, of the Norwegian rate. Manufacturing labor accounted for about 20% of the ex-factory sales price for toothbrushes. Second, as a small company with a niche strategy, Jordan did not have the financial or personnel resources for marketing and distribution that its large competitors had. Marketing expenses were generally allocated evenly between Jordan and the distributors in each country. Still, Jordan was limited in its ability to compete in some areas.

Jordan's experiences in the United Kingdom illustrated the problems Mr. Leversby expected to see develop in the rest of Europe. Although the UK had been one of Jordan's first export markets, the company's success there had been uneven. Despite repeated attempts, Jordan had been unable to secure ongoing distribution in several of the large retail

EXHIBIT 3
THE WORLD MARKET FOR TOOTHBRUSHES, 1985
(data unavailable for some countries)

Country	Total (millions)	Unit sales per capita
Japan	360.0	3.2
Australia	10.0	1.5
North America:		
US	300.0	1.4
Canada	25.0	1.1
Western Europe:		
*UK	53.0	0.9
*Italy	38.1	0.7
*France	36.0	0.7
*Spain	15.8	0.4
Sweden	15.0	1.8
*Netherlands	12.4	0.9
Switzerland	11.0	1.7
*Denmark	7.2	1.4
Norway	5.8	1.4
Finland	4.3	0.9
*Belgium	4.2	0.4
*Ireland	2.0	0.6
South America:		
Brazil	90.0	0.7
Colombia	21.0	0.7
Argentina	10.0	0.4
Venezuela	6.8	0.4
Chile	4.2	0.3

*Denotes member countries of the European Community (1990).
Source: EIU, trade sources.

EXHIBIT 4
JORDAN MARKET SHARE BY COUNTRY, 1987

Country	Market share (%)
Norway	90
Finland	70
*Netherlands	50
*Denmark	48
*Belgium	30
*Ireland	28
Sweden	20
Iceland	20
*Spain	16
Canada	15
*France	15
*Portugal	13
*Italy	3
Switzerland	4
*UK	4

*Denotes member countries of the European Community (1990).
Source: Jordan, company records.

chains. It was a perplexing problem. Retailers demanded that manufacturers support their products with advertising, which Jordan management felt was unnecessary given the impulsive nature of toothbrush purchases. In one case, a retailer wanted Jordan to spend £2 million on advertising, almost twice the company's annual budget for promotions in the UK. The 1988 toothbrush advertising budgets in the UK for several of Jordan's competitors were estimated as follows:

• £2 million for Johnson & Johnson's "Reach" brand
• £1.5 million for Gillette's "Oral B"
• £1 million for Unilever's "Mentadent P Professional"

Because Jordan would not meet their advertising demands, British retailers frequently placed Jordan products on lower shelves where the company's point-of-sales promotions were less effective. Under these conditions, sales could not meet expected levels, and so retailers would pull the line off the shelves entirely. Because of these difficulties, Jordan had only 4% of the UK market in 1987. (*Exhibit 7* shows a comparison of the leading brands and distributors in the UK.)

Some large retail chains increasingly demanded listing fees before they would stock a particular item.[2] For example, one large French chain required FF150 per store per variant for a similar product. The total listing fee for an initial introduction of 10 product variants in 1,200 stores would cost FF1,800,000. On the other hand, Jordan's relative scarcity of resources had led to the creative (and highly successful) use of marketing and distribution alliances, a key factor in the company's success.

By contractual agreement, most transactions between Jordan and its distributor and licensee partners

[2]Listing fees were a one-time fee, usually paid by the manufacturer or distributor at the time of new product introduction.

EXHIBIT 5

MAJOR COMPETITORS IN TOOTHBRUSHES, 1987

Selected financial and operating statistics ($ millions)

Company/ nationality	Sales Total	T/ brush	Net income	Return on assets (%)*	Employees
Lion Corp. (Japan)	2,451	20.3%	41	4.8	4,892
Gillette (US)	3,167	4.0%	230	19.5	30,100
Unilever (NL/UK)	31,279	0.002%	1,407	7.6	294,000
Johnson & Johnson (US)	8,012	.5%	833	19.2	78,200
Colgate-Palmolive (US)	5,648	1.6%	204	16.5	24,700
Anchor Brush Co. (US)	50	+50%	N/A	N/A	1,150
Jordan (N)	46	69.7%	2	23.4	475
Procter & Gamble	17,163	.01%	327	3.6	73,000

*Operating profit/total assets.
Source: Company records, *Advertising Age*, annual reports.

EXHIBIT 6

MAJOR COMPETING BRANDS OF TOOTHBRUSHES, 1987

Manufacture	Major toothbrush brands
Lion	Lion
Gillette	Oral-B, Dr. West
Unilever	Gibbs, Signal, Mentadent, Pepsodent, DX, FSP
Johnson & Johnson	Micron, Reach, Prevent, Tek, Alcance
Colgate-Palmolive	Colgate, Dentagard, Defend, Tonigencyl
Anchor	Various private labels
Jordan	Jordan, private labels
Procter & Gamble	Blendax
Addis	Wisdom

Source: Jordan, annual reports.

were denominated in Norwegian kroner. The few exceptions included transactions with affiliates in developing countries and in Holland, which used US dollars and Dutch guilders, respectively. The policy was a convenience. It was not Jordan's intention to push the foreign exchange risk onto its overseas partners. If its affiliates or distributors stopped making money because of exchange rate exposure (or any other reason), Jordan would soon lose them as partners. Jordan did not make currency denomination an issue in contract negotiations. Experience had shown that it was better to avoid involving the finance managers of the distributors, since "they would start to make all kinds of funny arrangements."

Retail Distribution

Toothbrush distribution varied from country to country. In France, for example, 83% of 1987 volume was accounted for by the grocery trade and 17% by pharmacists, while in the Netherlands the comparable figures (1986) were 62% and 38%, respectively. Overall, however, pharmacists were losing ground to food-based retailers.

A second significant industry trend was the increasing concentration of the European grocery trade. Hypermarkets were getting a growing market share along with organized retail groups, which pooled their members stores' purchases and supply. European supermarkets were more likely to be chain members, and retail outlets were generally getting larger, although there continued to be some variation amongst countries. The share of food turnover by the top 10 food buying organizations in West Germany

EXHIBIT 7
BRITISH TOOTHBRUSH MARKET, 1989

Brand	Jordan	Wisdom	Mentadent	Oral B	Reach
Distributor	Alberto Culver	Addid/ Wisdom	Elida Gibbs	Oral B (Gillette)	Johnson & Johnson
Number of salespeople	10	20	N/A	11	15
Market share	2.5%	26.3%	1.9%	22.4%	7%
Average consumer price	£0.99	£0.99	£1.19	£1.09	£0.99

Source: Jordan.

had reached 81%; in the UK, the figure was 66%; for France 62%, compared to only 36% in the US.

For the end-user, a larger sized retailer meant not only lower prices but a wider range of product choices. For the retailer, size meant more bargaining power with suppliers on prices, packaging, and other product characteristics, as well as payment terms, order lot sizes, and delivery times. The size of the new stores was a significant factor in managing distribution; one Euromarché hypermarket in France, for example, sold the same volume of toothbrushes as 260 Norwegian stores.

The retail price of toothbrushes also varied from country to country for a number of reasons, including distributor and retailer margins. For the product category, retailer margins across Europe averaged 35% of the final consumer price. Country differences, however, could be significant; margins in France were about 25% whereas UK retail margins reached 60% in some cases. Large retail chains and hypermarkets considered 30% the target margin in the product category. Wholesaler and distributor margins averaged 10–15%, although country differences could also be substantial. In Spain, distributor margins ranged as much as 20–25%, while margins in the UK averaged about 10%. Manufacturers' coverage of sales, marketing, and overhead expenses were approximately 30% of the final retail price.

Jordan management expected that after 1992, European integration would further concentrate the European retail distribution trade. As competition rose,

closures, acquisitions, and strategic alliances would accelerate. Carrefour, the leading French hypermarket chain, had already allied with Castorama, the leading French do-it-yourself chain, normalizing relations after a previous Carrefour takeover attempt. Cross-border activity was also increasing in retail distribution, in contrast to the previous tendency of retail multiples to operate entirely within their domestic markets.

Coinciding with retail concentration was the increasing sophistication of retailers in obtaining and using market information. Retailers were highly aware of consumer preferences, competitive products, and market opportunities. Processing this market information had been enhanced by point-of-sale scanner systems which evaluated product contribution per increment of shelf space. Armed with analytical data closely tied to their own bottom line, retailers were increasing their demands on suppliers' sales representatives for changes in packaging, pricing, and other product attributes. As retailers became more aware of the changing market, product and package life cycles were getting shorter. Also, retailers were increasingly using JIT, which reduced their inventories but put a heavier logistical burden on suppliers to deliver smaller orders with less lead time.

JORDAN'S EXPORT DEVELOPMENT

Jordan began to take a serious interest in exports in 1958 when the EFTA and EC were in their formative stages. According to Leversby, the primary motivation for developing exports was that "four million Norwegians did not consume enough toothbrushes to keep the company moving!" Jordan's initial exports, however, were vacuum cleaner brushes rather than toothbrushes. Choosing Great Britain as its first market because "they spoke the language," Jordan was disappointed with the results. The company realized that building a profitable business as a subcontractor was a difficult task.

The company, however, saw toothbrushes as an underdeveloped market, characterized by low usage rates and an increasing awareness of dental hygiene, with clear volume-related potential. With toothbrushes, Jordan could also take advantage of its dominant domestic market position to support developing overseas operations.

The strategy adopted by Per Lindbo, who was then managing director, and Mr. Leversby, was simple and inexpensive. Jordan asked distributors to cover product launch expenses in return for sharply discounted prices on toothbrushes. Because the toothbrushes were of good quality and supported by Jordan's marketing acumen, distributors found this offer attractive. It also allowed Jordan to enter new markets without substantial cash commitments.

Exports of toothbrushes were first made to Denmark, where Jordan entered into a distribution contract with the pharmaceutical company Astra. Denmark was chosen because of its physical proximity, cultural similarities, and the small size of the market. Later, owing to Danish import restrictions, a factory was established in Copenhagen. The Danish factory assembled parts supplied by the Oslo factory. Jordan continued to diversify its export markets by expanding the Astra partnership to include Astra-Wallco in Sweden and Finland. Jordan toothbrushes were introduced in the Netherlands in 1963, with 240,000 units sold in two and a half months. In 1964, Switzerland, Belgium, and France were added to the export map as Jordan became more confident in working with distributors and new markets.

A major boost to Jordan's initial export moves was a partnership with the large German consumer goods company, Blendax Werke, started in 1961.

A license contract allowed Blendax to produce and market Jordan-designed toothbrushes in West Germany under the Blend-A-Med name. This arrangement with Blendax was still operational in 1989, making Germany the only country in Europe where the Jordan brand name was not used. The relationship with Blendax was very important to Jordan in the competitive West German market. Mr. Leversby did not relish the idea of having to go it alone if something should happen to Blendax.

Export Strategy

Jordan's international strategy had a number of key elements. First, the company consciously and persistently pursued a niche policy, sticking to mechanical oral hygiene products. Shortly after Jordan went international, it selected one product only—toothbrushes—for export. Since then, the company had enlarged its foreign product line to include dental floss and dental sticks (interdental cleaners made from wood), but mechanical dental care remained Jordan's export business focus. The company's sales budget for 1989 estimated that 97% of dental product volume would be exported.

Jordan deliberately shunned the toothpaste market. Entering it would put Jordan into a larger and, therefore, more visible competitive arena, inhospitable to companies of Jordan's size. (About 80% of all oral hygiene sales were toothpaste.) Moreover, Jordan did not have either experience or any particular strength in this arena.

Second, international expansion was conducted step by step, one country at a time. Jordan's *modus operandi* involved getting to know the culture of a particular target country and making an assessment of the market. If conditions looked promising, the company would begin to search for a local distributor, possibly collaborating with a local advertising agency. This process could take between one and two years. Given the right "chemistry" with a distributor, marketing would begin, with Jordan being introduced as an international rather than a Norwegian brand.

Third, Jordan fielded its own sales force only in the Norwegian market. Foreign sales were entirely handled by local distributors. There were several reasons for this policy. Overseas sales forces would overstretch Jordan's resources. Moreover, with only a limited product range to offer retailers, Jordan had no real distribution strength. Finally, an independent sales force would challenge well-developed distributors on their own ground. Instead, as Mr. Leversby put it, "Company management traditionally viewed limited marketing resources as an advantage. We continued to think small by gradually building all new export markets through distributorships and working arrangements with established, successful firms." The development of local distributors as active partners was crucial to the success of this strategy.

Resources

Similarly, Jordan tried to conserve its resources by limiting its capital expenditures. In 1988, 30% of Jordan toothbrushes sold were produced by licensed subcontractors in eight different countries, including Venezuela, Thailand, and Syria. Relative to direct foreign investment, licensing was an efficient way for Jordan to avoid traffic barriers. Even the high perceived value of Jordan products did not allow the company to remain profitable when import duties were as high as 60–80%, as was the case in some countries.

Direct foreign investment was made only when market factors dictated it. Jordan opened a factory in Holland in 1988 as a manufacturing bridgehead within the EC, anticipating the abolition of intra-EC trade barriers scheduled for 1993. (Norway was not an EC member.) The Dutch plant was also used to separate private brand production from Jordan brand. Private brand production ran in small lots, requiring many changeovers. To optimize the volume-based manufacturing technologies available at the Norwegian plants, private label production was done almost entirely in Holland. The proximity of the Dutch plant to the major private label customers also facilitated integration with the JIT requirements of these companies. The decision to manufacture in the Netherlands was heavily influenced by the Dutch government's

offer to provide 35% of the plant cost. Other important factors included the sales volume available in the Dutch market as well as tax, culture, and language issues.

Despite Jordan's successes, the company had not been able to enter markets at will. In Great Britain the changing nature of the retail industry had disproportionately increased buyer power for the time being. High listing fees demanded by mass retailers exceeded the returns Jordan believed could be achieved. The situation in the US was different; in Mr. Leversby's words, it was "a big black hole." Despite the attractiveness of its size, the US market presented more risks than Jordan management was willing to undertake. Jordan, however, had not excluded the market and had actually begun working with an American company. In general, Jordan's managers believed that more attractive opportunities existed in countries with low toothbrush usage rates and limited penetration by competitors. Finance Director Erik Foyn emphasized, "We cannot succeed in all markets; we must be selective."

Private Label

Jordan management also faced the problem of how to balance the Jordan brand and private label parts of the company. Although the private label business provided only 13% of Jordan's sales, there was considerable debate about how this business fit into the company's future.

The private label business was organized as a separate company, Sanodnet, under the leadership of Mr. Juliussen, a member of the general management team. Toothbrush designs used for the private label were not the same as those used by the Jordan brand to distinguish the two. The private label business had a diverse customer base, including Colgate-Palmolive and Safeway, the American retail chain.

Jordan's management was acutely aware of the problems associated with having two similar competing brands in one company. Cannibalization of the carefully built branded sales by the private label products was one such problem. It was possible to have two Jordan products next to each other on shelves, one Jordan brand and the other Jordan designed and manufactured, but private label. For retailers and distributors, this could cause a conflict of interest between Jordan-made private label products with their name, and the Jordan brand. As one distributor commented, "I don't mind Jordan's private label business, but why do they have to be so good at it?"

International Management Issues

Control over the operations of licensees was also a major issue for Jordan. Because the company operated under the Jordan brand name throughout the world, it was felt that quality had to be uniform. Engineers were dispatched from Norway annually to inspect licensee plants, and product samples were sent to Oslo on an ongoing basis to ensure that standards were being met. Production volumes were controlled by supplying at least one part of the final product from Norway, usually the back of the package. Foreign accounts were relatively easy for Jordan to track, as there was usually only one distributor per country.

EXPANSION INTO GREECE

By the summer of 1988, Greece was one of the few European countries where the Jordan brand name was not known. Management felt that entering the Greek market was a logical step toward consolidating the company's position in Europe.

Preliminary market research, using readily available sources such as government statistics, trade journals, country reports, and Nielsen data, confirmed original suspicions that Greece was an attractive opportunity characterized by low usage rates and underdeveloped competition. More comprehensive research, including extensive discussions with various distributors, retailers, and consumers was carried out before securing a distributor. The interviews, besides giving Jordan management a firsthand account of local business practices, also allowed management to evaluate numerous potential in-country partners.

In Greece, as in many markets, it quickly became apparent that Jordan would have to work closely with the retail trade to create a new selling environment. Traditionally, Greek retailers kept toothbrushes behind the counter, forcing customers to ask for assistance, thus giving the store clerk a significant role in product selection. Jordan's competitive strategy relied on the impulsive nature of toothbrush purchases, which dictated that the products be readily visible to the customer.

To introduce the trade to Jordan's marketing concept, the company held two presentations for interested distributors. More than 250 representatives attended these meetings. The concept behind point-of-purchase displays was explained, samples were demonstrated, and results in similar countries were outlined.

After selecting a partner, Jordan made a successful launch in the Greek market. Jordan's first-year target was for 5% of the market. The company's first shipment (equal to 1.6% of total annual market sales volume) sold out in less than a month.

THE FUTURE

During 30 years of exporting, Jordan management had consistently relied on its knowledge of country markets and its ability to develop relations with experienced and qualified distributors. This had not always been easy. The changing European retail and economic environment implied that Jordan would face many more challenges in the future.

The consolidation of competitors in the industry, including the purchase of Jordan's local distributors by large multinationals, was straining the company's resources. The Jordan family, however, wanted to keep their company. Despite a number of attractive offers, the company was looked on as the family inheritance as well as a prestigious institution in Norway for well over 150 years. The greater financial and distribution power that would come from a merger would be beneficial, but "after 12 months the spirit would be gone," Mr. Leversby explained.

Despite the challenges facing his company, Mr. Leversby was optimistic about the future. "Fortunately, we have a long way to go."

Sullivan's Auto World

Christopher H. Lovelock

Viewed from Wilson Avenue, the dealership presented a festive sight. Strings of triangular pennants in red, white, and blue fluttered gaily in the late afternoon breeze. Rows of new model cars gleamed and winked in the sunlight. Geraniums graced the flowerbeds outside the showroom entrance. A huge rotating sign at the corner of Wilson Avenue and Route 23 sported the Ford logo and identified the business as Sullivan's Auto World. Banners below urged "Let's Make a Deal!"

Inside the handsome, high-ceilinged showroom, three of the new model Fords were on display—a dark-blue station wagon, a red convertible, and a white Thunderbird. Each car was polished to a high sheen. Two groups of customers were chatting with salespeople, and a middle-aged man sat in the driver's seat of the convertible, studying the controls.

Upstairs in the comfortably furnished general manager's office, Carol Sullivan-Diaz finished running another spreadsheet analysis on the computer. She felt tired and depressed. Her father, Walter Sullivan, had died four weeks earlier at the age of 56 of

a sudden heart attack. As executor of his estate, the bank had asked her to temporarily assume the position of general manager of the dealership. The only visible changes that she had made to her father's office were installing the computer and printer, but she had been very busy analyzing the current position of the business.

Sullivan-Diaz did not like the look of the numbers on the printout. Auto World's financial situation had been deteriorating for 18 months, and it had been running in the red for the first half of the current year. New car sales had declined, reflecting higher unemployment and a turndown in the regional economy. Margins had been squeezed by promotions and other efforts to move new cars off the lot. Industry forecasts of future sales were discouraging, and so were her own financial projections for Auto World's sales department. Service revenues, which were below average for a dealership of this size, had also declined, although the service department still made a small surplus.

Had she made a mistake last week, Carol wondered, in turning down Bill Froelich's offer to buy the business? It was true that the price offered had been substantially below the offer from Froelich that her father had rejected two years earlier, but the business had been more profitable then.

THE SULLIVAN FAMILY

Walter Sullivan had purchased a small Ford dealership in 1971, renamed it Sullivan Auto, and built it up to become one of the best known in the metro area. Six years back, he had borrowed heavily to purchase the current site at a major suburban intersection, in an area of town with many new housing developments.

There had been a dealership on the site, but the buildings were 30 years old. Sullivan had retained the service and repair bays, but torn down the showroom in front of them, and replaced it by an attractive modern facility. On moving to the new location, which was substantially larger than the old one, he had renamed his business Sullivan's Auto World.

Everybody had seemed to know Walt Sullivan. He had been a consummate showman and entrepreneur, appearing in his own radio and television commercials and active in community affairs. His approach to car sales had emphasized promotions, discounts, and deals in order to maintain volume. He was never happier than when making a sale.

Carol Sullivan-Diaz, aged 28, was the eldest of Walter and Carmen Sullivan's three daughters. After obtaining a bachelor's degree in economics, she had gone on to take an M.B.A. degree and had then embarked on a career in health care management. She was married to Dr. Roberto Diaz, a surgeon at St. Luke's Hospital. Her 20-year-old twin sisters, Gail and Joanne, who were college sophomores, lived with their mother.

As a college student, Sullivan-Diaz had worked part-time in her father's business on secretarial and bookkeeping tasks, and also as a service writer in the service department; so she was quite familiar with the operations of the dealership. At business school, she had decided on a career in health care management. After graduation, she had worked as an executive assistant to the president of St. Luke's, a large teaching hospital. Two years later, she joined Metropolitan Health Plan, a large health maintenance organi-

zation (HMO), as assistant director of marketing—a position she had now held for almost three years. Her responsibilities included attracting new members, complaint handling, market research, and member retention programs.

Carol's employer had given her a six-week leave of absence to put her father's affairs in order. She doubted that she could extend that leave much beyond the two weeks still remaining. Neither she nor other family members were interested in making a career of running the dealership. However, she was prepared to take time out from her health care career to work on a turnaround if that seemed a viable proposition. She had been successful in her present job and believed it would not be difficult to find another health management position in the future.

THE DEALERSHIP

Like other car dealerships, Sullivan's Auto World operated both sales and service departments, often referred to in the trade as "front end" and "back end," respectively. However, Auto World did not have a body shop for repairing damaged bodywork. Both new and used vehicles were sold, since a high proportion of new car and van purchases involved trading in the purchaser's existing vehicle. Auto World would also buy low-mileage used cars at auction for resale. Purchasers who decided that they could not afford a new car would often buy a "pre-owned" vehicle instead, while shoppers who came in looking for a used car could sometimes be persuaded to buy a new one.

The front end of the dealership employed a sales manager, seven salespeople, an office manager, and a secretary. One of the salespeople had given notice and would be leaving at the end of the following week. The service department, when fully staffed, consisted of a service manager, a parts supervisor, nine mechanics, and two service writers. The Sullivan twins often worked part-time as service writers, filling in at busy periods, when one of the other writers was sick or on vacation, or when—as currently—there was an unfilled vacancy. The job entailed scheduling appointments for repairs and maintenance, writing up each work order, calling customers with repair estimates, and assisting customers when they returned to pick up the cars and pay for the work that had been done.

Sullivan-Diaz knew from her own experience as a service writer that it could be a stressful job. Few people liked to be without their car, even for a day. When a car broke down or was having problems, the owner was often nervous about how long it would take to get it fixed and, if the warranty had expired, how much the labor and parts would cost. Customers were quite unforgiving when a problem was not fixed completely on the first attempt and they had to return their vehicle for further work.

Major mechanical failures were not usually difficult to repair, although the parts replacement costs might be expensive. It was often the "little" things like water leaks and wiring problems that were the hardest to diagnose and correct, and it might be necessary for the customer to return two or three times before such a problem was resolved. In these situations, parts and materials costs were relatively low, but labor costs mounted up quickly, being charged out at $40 an hour. Customers could often be quite abusive, yelling at service writers over the phone or arguing with service writers, mechanics, and the service manager in person.

Turnover in the service writer job was high, which was one reason why Carol—and more recently her sisters—had often been pressed into service by their father to "hold the fort," as he described it. More than once, she had seen an exasperated service writer snap back at a complaining customer or hang up on one who was being abusive over the telephone. Gail and Joanne were currently taking turns to cover the vacant position, but there were times when both of them had classes and the dealership had only one service writer on duty.

By national standards, Sullivan's Auto World was a medium-sized dealership, selling around 1,100 cars a year, equally divided between new and used vehicles. In the most recent year, its revenues totaled $23.1 million from new and used car sales and $2.51 million from service (including parts)—down from $26.5 million and $3.12 million, respectively, in the previous year. Although the unit value of car sales was high, the margins were quite low. The reverse was true for service. Industry guidelines suggested that the contribution margin (known as the departmental selling gross) from car sales should be about 5.5 percent of sales revenues, and from service, around 25 percent of revenues. In a typical dealership, 60 percent of the selling gross came from sales and 40 percent from service. The selling gross was then applied to fixed expenses, such as administrative salaries, rent or mortgage payments, and utilities.

For the most recent 12 months at Auto World, Sullivan-Diaz had determined that the selling gross figures were 4.6 percent and 24 percent, respectively, both of them lower than in the previous year and insufficient to cover the dealership's fixed expenses. Her father had made no mention of financial difficulties and she had been shocked to learn from the bank after his death that Auto World had been two months behind in mortgage payments on the property. Further analysis showed that accounts payable had also risen sharply in the previous six months. Fortunately, the dealership held a large insurance policy on Sullivan's life, and the proceeds from this had been more than sufficient to bring mortgage payments up to date and pay down all overdue accounts.

The opportunities for expanding new car sales did not appear promising, given the state of the economy. However, recent promotional incentives had reduced the inventory to manageable levels. From discussions with Larry Winters, Auto World's sales manager, Sullivan-Diaz had concluded that costs could be reduced by not replacing the departing sales rep, maintaining inventory at somewhat lower levels, and trying to make more efficient use of advertising and promotion. Although Winters did not have Walter Sullivan's exuberant personality, he had been Auto World's leading sales rep before being promoted, and had shown strong managerial capabilities in his current position.

As she reviewed the figures for the service department, Sullivan-Diaz wondered what potential might exist for improving its sales volume and selling gross. Her father had never been very interested in the parts and service business, seeing it simply as a necessary adjunct of the dealership. "Customers always seem to be miserable back there," he had once remarked to her. "But here in the front end, everybody's happy when someone buys a new car." The service facility was not easily visible from the main highway, being hidden behind the showroom. The building was old and greasy, although the equipment was modern and well maintained.

Customers were required to bring cars in for servicing before 8:30 A.M. After parking their cars, customers entered the service building by a side door and waited their turn to see the service writers, who occupied a cramped room with peeling paint and an interior window overlooking the service bays. Customers stood while work orders for their cars were written up by hand on large sheets. Ringing telephones frequently interrupted the process. Filing cabinets containing customer records and other documents lined the far wall of the room.

If the work were of a routine nature, such as an oil change or tune-up, customers were given an estimate immediately. For more complex jobs, they would be called with an estimate later in the morning once the car had been examined. Customers were required to pick up their cars by 6:00 P.M. on the day the work was completed. On several occasions, Carol had urged her father to computerize the service work order process, but he had never acted on her suggestions.

The service manger, Rick Obert, who was in his late forties, had held the position since Auto World had opened at its current location. The Sullivan family considered him to be technically skilled, and he managed the mechanics effectively. However, his manner with customers could be gruff and argumentative.

CUSTOMER SURVEY RESULTS

Another set of data that Sullivan-Diaz had studied carefully were the results of the customer satisfaction surveys that were mailed to the dealership monthly by a research firm retained by the Ford Motor Company.

Purchasers of all new Ford cars were sent a ques-

tionnaire by mail within 30 days of making the purchase and asked to use a five-point scale to rate their satisfaction with the dealership sales department, vehicle preparation, and the characteristics of the vehicle itself. The questionnaire asked how likely the purchaser would be to recommend the dealership, the salesperson, and the manufacturer to someone else. Other questions asked if the customers had been introduced to the dealer's service department and been given explanations on what to do if their cars needed service. Finally, there were some classification questions relating to customer demographics.

A second survey was sent to the new car purchasers nine months after they had bought their cars. This questionnaire began by asking about satisfaction with the vehicle and then asked customers if they had taken their vehicles to the selling dealer for service of any kind. If so, respondents were then asked to rate the service department on 14 different attributes—ranging from the attitudes of service personnel to the quality of the work performed—and then to rate their overall satisfaction with service from the dealer.

Customers were also asked about where they would go in the future for maintenance service, minor mechanical and electrical repairs, major repairs in those same categories, and bodywork. The options listed for service were selling dealer, another Ford dealer, "some other place," or "do-it-yourself." Finally, there were questions about overall satisfaction with the dealer sales department and the dealership in general, as well as the likelihood of their purchasing another Ford Motor Company product and buying it from the same dealership.

Dealers received monthly reports summarizing customer ratings of their dealership for the most recent month and for several previous months. To provide a comparison with how other Ford dealerships performed, the reports also included regional and national rating averages. After analysis, completed questionnaires were returned to the dealership; since these included each customer's name, a dealer could see which customers were satisfied and which were not.

In the 30-day survey of new purchasers, Auto World achieved better than average ratings on most dimensions. One finding which puzzled Carol was that almost 90 percent of respondents answered "yes" when asked if someone from Auto World had explained what to do if they needed service, but less than a third said that they had been introduced to someone in the service department. She resolved to ask Larry Winters about this discrepancy.

The nine-month survey findings disturbed her. Although vehicle ratings were in line with national averages, the overall level of satisfaction with service at Auto World was consistently low, placing it in the bottom 25 percent of all Ford dealerships.

The worst rating for service concerned promptness of writing up orders, convenience of scheduling work, convenience of service hours, and appearance of the service department. On length of time to complete the work, availability of needed parts, and quality of work done ("was it fixed right?"), Auto World's rating was close to the average. For interpersonal variables such as attitude of service department personnel, politeness, understanding of customer problems, and explanation of work performed, its ratings were relatively poor.

When Sullivan-Diaz reviewed the individual questionnaires, she found that there was a wide degree of variation between customers' responses on these interpersonal variables, ranging all the way across a five-point scale from "completely satisfied" to "very dissatisfied." Curious, she had gone to the service files and examined the records for several dozen customers who had recently completed the nine-month surveys. At least part of the ratings could be explained by which service writers the customer had dealt with. Those who had been served two or more times by her sisters, for instance, gave much better ratings than those who had dealt primarily with Jim Fiskell, the service writer who had recently quit.

Perhaps the most worrying responses were those relating to customers' likely use of Auto World's service department in the future. More than half indicated that they would use another Ford dealer or "some other place" for maintenance service (such as oil change, lube, or tune-up) or for minor mechanical and electrical repairs. About 30 percent would use another source for major repairs. The rating for overall satisfaction with the selling dealer after nine months was below average, and the customer's likelihood of purchasing from the same dealership again was a full point below that of buying another Ford product.

AN UNWELCOME DISTURBANCE

Sullivan-Diaz pushed aside the spreadsheets she had printed out and turned off the computer. It was time to go home for dinner. She saw the options for the dealership as basically twofold: either prepare the business for an early sale at what would amount to a distress price, or take a year or two to try to turn it around financially. In the latter instance, if the turnaround succeeded, the business could subsequently be sold at a higher price than it presently commanded, or the family could install a general manager to run the dealership for them.

Bill Froelich, owner of a Lincoln-Mercury dealership about two miles away, had offered to buy Auto World for a price that represented a fair valuation of the net assets, according to Auto World's accountants, plus $125,000 in goodwill. However, the rule of thumb when the auto industry was enjoying good times was that goodwill should be valued at $1,000 per vehicle sold each year.

As Carol left her office, she spotted the sales manager coming up the stairs leading from the showroom floor. "Larry," she said, "I've got a question for you."

"Fire away!" replied the sales manager.

"I've been looking at the customer satisfaction surveys. Why aren't our sales reps introducing new customers to the folks in the service department? It's supposedly part of our sales protocol, but it only seems to be happening about one-third of the time!"

Larry Winters shuffled his feet. "Well, Carol, basically I leave it to their discretion. We tell them about service, or course, but some of the guys on the floor feel a bit uncomfortable taking folks over to the service bays after they've been in here. It's quite a contrast, if you know what I mean."

Suddenly, the sound of shouting arose from the floor below. A man of about 40, wearing a windbreaker and jeans, was standing in the doorway yelling at one of the salespeople. The two managers could catch snatches of what he was saying, in between various obscenities: "...three visits...still not fixed right...service stinks...who's in charge here?" Everybody else in the showroom had stopped what they were doing and had turned to look at the newcomer.

Winters looked at his young employer and rolled his eyes. "If there was something your dad couldn't stand, it was guys like that, yelling and screaming in the showroom and asking for the boss. Walt would go hide out in his office! Don't worry, Tom'll take care of that fellow and get him out of here. What a jerk!"

"No," said Sullivan-Diaz, "I'll deal with him. One thing I learned when I worked at St. Luke's was that you don't let people yell about their problems in front of everybody else. You take them off somewhere, calm them down, and find out what's bugging them."

She stepped quickly down the stairs, wondering to herself, "What else have I learned in health care that I can apply to this business?"

BayBank Systems, Inc.

Christopher H. Lovelock

"WELCOME TO X-PRESS 24," read the screen. "WE ARE PLEASED TO SERVE YOU 24 HOURS A DAY, 7 DAYS A WEEK." It was a Friday afternoon in February 1990. All over Massachusetts, people were lining up at automated teller machines (ATMs) to make banking transactions. More than half were using one of the ubiquitous green and blue machines of the BayBank X-Press 24 network. At this busiest time of the week, over 900 X-Press 24 transactions were being made every minute.

"PLEASE INSERT YOUR CARD." Robert P. Shay put his BayBank card into the machine on the third floor of the BayBank Systems office building. "WELCOME. PLEASE ENTER YOUR PASSWORD." He punched in four digits and then touched the keys for Fastcash and Custom Cash in succession. Within seconds, Shay was collecting his usual customized withdrawal of $80. "PLEASE TAKE YOUR CARD AND RECEIPT. THANK YOU. PLEASE USE OUR BAYBANK X-PRESS 24 AGAIN

SOON." "That's one thing you can be sure of," he muttered to the machine. "But my real interest right now is finding other things for people to do with this card."

Shay walked back upstairs and strode into the conference room. The group of young men and women who had been working with him on the point-of-sale (POS) task force looked up expectantly. Shay, Vice President for Research and Development at BayBank Systems, Inc. (BBSI), had formed the task force to explore the possibility of using BayBank ATM cards to make debit purchases at POS in retail outlets. "Well folks," he said cheerfully, "It's decision time! Lindsey Lawrence [BBSI's president] told me this morning that she and Don Isaacs [the chairman] want a recommendation by next Thursday on whether or not to proceed with debit POS and, if so, which approach to adopt."

BANKING IN MASSACHUSETTS

Retail banking in Massachusetts was very competitive, especially in Greater Boston, which accounted for two-thirds of the state's 5.8 million population. As the commercial and financial center of New England, Boston had a large concentration of major financial institutions. Bank of Boston, Bank of New

England, BayBank, and Shawmut Bank dominated retail banking in Massachusetts. These four, plus Fleet/Norstar (headquartered in Rhode Island), were also the five largest banks in the six-state New England region (comprising Connecticut, Maine, Massachusetts, New Hampshire, Rhode Island, and Vermont) where interstate banking was already permitted. Observers predicted that national interstate banking would be permitted by the mid-90s.

Two large, regional ATM systems served New England. X-Press 24, owned by BayBanks, Inc., had 1,250 machines at 1,000 locations in Massachusetts and a few in Connecticut; Yankee 24, owned by a consortium that included Bank of Boston, Bank of New England, and Shawmut, had 3,700 machines in every New England state but New Hampshire. In Massachusetts, 50% of all checking account holders had ATM cards. But for BayBank customers the figure was a remarkable 96%. Some banks were also members of national and super-regional networks, such as Cirrus (30,000 ATMs in the US, Canada, and two other countries), NYCE (7200 ATMs), and Plus (31,000 ATMs). MAC, a Philadelphia-based super-regional was trying to expand into Massachusetts from New Hampshire.

After enjoying rapid growth during the 1980s, New England banks were entering the 1990s with some trepidation. Economic activity had turned down significantly, due to slowdowns in high tech and real estate in particular. But wages remained high, and it was still difficult for banks to hire and retain people with the skills needed for front-line positions in their urban branches.

Banks which had been aggressive lenders on real estate projects now found they had many non-performing loans. Most seriously affected was the Bank of New England (BNE). In January 1990, BNE stunned financial markets with the news that it had incurred an annual loss of $1.11 billion—one of the greatest losses ever recorded in American banking history. Each of the other large banks had sharply increased its loan loss provisions; Bank of Boston had also been forced to take write-downs on third-world debt. However, Fleet/Norstar was in strong financial shape and appeared eager to penetrate the Massachusetts market, perhaps by taking over BNE.

BayBanks, Inc.

BayBank Systems was a wholly owned subsidiary of BayBanks, Inc. ("BayBank"), a bank holding company. BayBank was the parent company of nine banks with a total of 217 branches in Massachusetts and seven in Connecticut. With total assets of some $10 billion, it ranked about sixtieth in size among all US banks. Within Massachusetts, BayBank's strong retail focus gave it a 30% market share of all retail accounts in the state.

Several of BayBank's subsidiaries traced their roots back to the mid-nineteenth century. In 1974, when William M. Crozier, Jr. was named chief executive officer, new customers were aware of the linkages between each subsidiary bank. Crozier pushed hard to create an overall unity and identity, adding the word "BayBank" to each subsidiary's name. Thus the Harvard Trust Company became BayBank Harvard Trust. A new logo and the distinctive green and blue color scheme adopted for all BayBank signage created the impression of a large bank operating across much of the state.

BayBank then moved to standardize the services offered so that they could be promoted by a common advertising campaign. The first step was a new single-statement banking product named "Something Better." Never before had a Massachusetts bank used television to promote a retail banking service. Customers using the product also received a "Something Better" cash card, allowing them to cash personal checks up to $100 a day at any BayBank office in eastern Massachusetts. This card, printed in green and blue on durable cardboard, was the same size as a credit card. BayBank's officers soon realized that "the more you can make your card do, and make the customer believe it does, the more essential you will be to the customer."

Electronic Banking at BayBank

The next task for the "Something Better" card—now made of plastic and bearing a magnetic stripe—came in 1977, when BayBank introduced its first ATMs. Customers could use these machines to make deposits, withdrawals and transfers between accounts, as well as to obtain account balances. To operate an

ATM, customers inserted their bank card into the machine and typed in their Personal Identification Number (PIN), a confidential password.

BayBank expanded its ATM network rapidly. In many parts of the US, people resisted using ATMs. BayBank, however, through advertising and employee support, did everything possible to make its customers comfortable with the machines. By 1979, the company was investing heavily in ATMs at a time when no competitors were doing so. In fact, the only other American bank making a major commitment to ATMs was Citibank in New York. Looking back, a BayBank officer observed:

ATMs were originally seen as a way of reducing costs by getting machines to replace human tellers. But we noticed that customers responded to the convenience of an easy-to-use, all-hours delivery system, and we saw ATMs as a way to differentiate BayBank from its competitors on a marketing basis. We also found that the people who started opening accounts with us were just the type of customers that banks like to get—they were younger, better educated, and had significant future earning potential.

To ensure reliability and reduce the risk of failure, BayBank invested millions of dollars in redundant systems. Hot-line phones were located in each ATM site, so that customers could always call a BayBank employee if they were having problems. One of the bywords at the bank was "There's nothing less convenient than a convenience that doesn't work."

The first ATMs were installed "through the wall" in bank branches, so that they could be used by customers outside on the street. Later, ATMs were installed inside the branches, in an area that could be sealed off from the main bank lobby after hours but was accessible from the street through a card-controlled door. BayBank then sought other locations for what it had named its X-Press 24 network, gaining exclusive rights to install its ATMs in terminals at Boston's Logan Airport. By 1981 BayBank had started placing ATMs in freestanding kiosks or in small storefronts, often far removed from the nearest branch. Bob Shay described the rationale:

The conventional wisdom is that remote ATMs are too expensive to justify. We view it differently. We have put

ATMs in locations where a branch might not be justified but where people still want the convenience. "Why not bring cash to the people?" we asked. We felt it would enhance customer convenience, of course, but with strong signage it also had another impact—the impression that BayBank was everywhere, because the signage was there on the kiosks. It was like having your own billboards in places where no billboards would ever be allowed and has greatly strengthened our regional image.

In 1984, BayBank teamed up with Bank of Boston to develop an in-store network of cash dispensing machines called Money Supply, which were located in rented space at supermarkets and other retail stores. Unlike X-Press 24, which was restricted to BayBank customers, use of Money Supply machines was open to other banks. The services offered by these machines were limited to cash withdrawals and information on balances. No deposits could be made. Previously, BayBank had begun franchising its X-Press 24 network to several small banks in Massachusetts and New Hampshire which paid a fee for the service.

Earlier, BayBank had joined with nine other banks across the US to found Cirrus, a national ATM network. Each bank enjoyed territorial exclusivity, so that access to Cirrus was denied to BayBank's competitors. Customers could use their bank cards to withdraw funds from any ATM in the network. In 1986, Cirrus was sold to MasterCard International, parent of the MasterCard credit card. The sale agreement allowed the new owner to open membership in Cirrus to all comers.

In late 1986, BayBank joined a second ATM network, the super-regional New York Cash Exchange (NYCE). This move gave its cardholders, who often traveled to New York for business or pleasure, better access to New York area financial institutions than Cirrus alone could do. Later, BayBank became an equity owner of NYCE. Meanwhile, its major competitors had joined together to create their own local ATM network, Yankee 24. Some of them also joined Cirrus or NYCE, thus enabling their customers to use X-Press 24 machines for cash withdrawals, balance information, and transfer of funds between accounts. Cirrus charged the account holder's bank a fee of $0.60 for each transaction, of which $0.50 went to the owner of the ATM terminal, while NYCE charged the amount holder's bank $0.54, of which $0.38 went to the ATM owner.

Around this time, management decided that the focal point of BayBank's advertising and positioning efforts should be the card itself, rather than the network. Research showed that people did not identify with the machines as such, but rather with the personalized card that enabled them to use the ATMs. However, "BayBank machine" seemed to have become a generic term to describe any ATM terminal in Massachusetts much like "Xerox" for photocopy, "Scotch" for adhesive tape, or "Kleenex" for paper tissues. The brand name on the green and blue card was changed from X-Press 24 to BayBank, and the BayBank name was given prominence over the X-Press 24 logo on all ATMs and kiosks.

By 1990, BayBank had a total of 760 ATMs in operation at 530 locations; 380 ATMs were in branches, and 380 in remote locations. The main branch of BayBank Harvard Trust—across the street from Harvard University—boasted 10 ATMs, each of which often recorded more than 25,000 transactions a month, making them among the busiest ATMs in the world.

BayBank now operated one of the country's largest regional ATM networks; it had also preempted most of the best sites in Massachusetts. In addition, the bank had 200 in-store machines, primarily in supermarkets. It had bought out Bank of Boston's share in Money Supply and renamed it Bay-Bank X-Press 24 CASH. This system was open to participants in X-Press 24, Yankee 24, Cirrus, and NYCE. BayBank customers paid a $0.50 fee to use X-Press 24 CASH, but no charges were imposed for using the regular X-Press 24 machines unless a customer's average monthly balance fell below a specified amount.

BAYBANK'S SYSTEMS, INC. (BBSI)

BayBank had originally established BBSI to manage data processing operations. As the ATM network expanded, BayBank's chairman, Mr. Crozier, charged the subsidiary with maintaining and marketing that network. BBSI was also responsible for ex-

ploring other ways in which BayBank could use electronic technology to enhance its productivity and add value to its services.

Few BBSI managers had followed a traditional banking career. Its chairman and CEO, Donald L. Isaacs (who was also executive vice president of the holding company), had joined BayBank in 1974 with an MS from the Sloan School of Management at MIT. His early career was spent as a staff assistant to Crozier, working on development of electronic funds transfer systems. He was named president of BBSI in 1981 and CEO three years later. Isaacs described BBSI as being at the "epicenter of the ATM world." More than ten million transactions a month were routed through BBSI's two separate computer centers, making it one of the largest ATM transaction processors in the United States.

BBSI's president, Lindsey C. Lawrence, a mathematician by training, had worked in both marketing and data processing. She had been the architect of the new branch automation system, and was now involved in systems technology and R&D. In her role as chief operating officer, she oversaw all BBSI operations. As BayBank's explosive growth in ATM installations and transactions began to slow (Refer to *Exhibit 1*)—from what Lawrence described as "100 miles per hour down to 55"—BBSI intensified its efforts to extend use of the bank's technological resources. Although management was monitoring Citibank's use of new touchscreen ATMs, which that bank had custom-designed, BayBank had no immediate plans to develop its own proprietary machines. Instead, it used Diebold ATMs, manufactured in Ohio.

Excluding land costs, a freestanding, two-unit kiosk cost about $35,000; buying and installing two full-service ATMs would add another $65,000. Annual operating and servicing costs for such a kiosk were around $30,000. Although 60% of the sites were equipped with just one machine, most kiosks or storefronts were designed so that a second machine could be added when monthly volume exceeded 17,000 transactions. Customers often made several transactions at an ATM; for instance, a deposit, a request for account balances, and a transfer of funds represented three transactions.

EXHIBIT 1
BAYBANK ATM TERMINALS AND TRANSACTIONS*

Year	Total ATMs in service (year-end)	Average monthly transactions (000s)	
		X-Press 24	X-Press 24 CASH**
1978	39	239	—
1979	78	524	—
1980	136	910	—
1981	235	1,490	—
1982	379	2,780	—
1983	490	3,990	—
1984	703	5,200	36
1985	843	5,830	213
1986	891	6,780	345
1987	977	8,010	529
1988	1,143	9,170	635
1989	1,249	9,000	720

*Totals include X-Press 24 ATMs operated under franchise agreements.
**Originally known as Money Supply.
Source: Company records.

Lawrence and Isaacs were particularly interested in developing informational or transactional products for which a fee could be charged. In 1988, BayBank introduced Account Update at its ATMs. This service offered a "mini-statement," printing out the numbers, dates and amounts of the last five checks received for payment, plus the three most recent card transactions and the latest deposit. This service, which cost $0.50, was debited automatically to the customer's checking account. Check Update, introduced in 1989, cost $0.15. Customers keyed in the number of a specific check to determine whether or not it had been received for payment. (*Exhibit 2* compares the services available to BayBank customers with those offered by banks participating in the Yankee 24 network.)

The two new products also became available by telephone in August 1989 through the bank's new Telephone Banking service. Customers with a touch-tone telephone could call a local phone number and follow computerized voice instructions to press specific keys, including their account number and password (PIN). Telephone banking offered several free services—account balances, fund transfers, and information on BayBank products and interest rates, as well as the fee-for-service Check Update and Account Update. By early 1990, the system was handling 150,000 calls a month.

ATMs in other parts of the country sometimes dispensed more than money. A bank in Portland, Oregon, used its machines to issue monthly bus and rail passes, printed on ATM receipt paper. Other uses for ATMs included selling discount movie tickets, postage stamps, retail gift certificates and grocery coupons. But Shay was concerned that adding such offerings, or even new banking services, might lead to unacceptable levels of queuing at ATMs. Further possibilities included greater use of telephone-based technology for enhanced transactions. With improvements in microchips and liquid crystal displays, BBSI expected that both desk and public telephones would soon be able to display information on small screens. Another direction lay in extending use of the Bay-Bank card.

THE SEARCH FOR NEW SERVICES

Responsibility for examining new applications for BayBank cards fell to Bob Shay in his role of vice president for research and development. Shay was

EXHIBIT 2   TYPES OF TRANSACTIONS AVAILABLE TO CARDHOLDER AT BAYBANK X-PRESS 24 AND YANKEE 24 ATMS

Transactions	BayBank cardholder at BayBank ATM	NYCE cardholder at BayBank ATM	Cirrus cardholder at BayBank ATM	Yankee 24 cardholder at Yankee 24 ATM*
Cash withdrawals	x	x	x	x
Fast Cash withdrawals**	x			
Custom Cash withdrawals**	x			
Deposits	x			
Deposits with cash back	x			
Account balances	x	x	x	x
Account transfers	x	x		x
Account update	x			
Check update	x			
Credit line cash advances	x			
Payments	x			

*at ATMs in Massachusetts.
**"Fast Cash" speeded the withdrawal process by saving the customer from having to enter the amount of the withdrawal. Instead four options were presented: $20, $50, and $100, and Custom Cash (a personalized amount pre-set by the customer and recorded in the X-Press 24 computer).
Source: Company records.

another of BBSI's "non-bankers." He held a PhD in British history from Columbia University and had briefly pursued an academic career. Seeing options in college teaching as limited, he had gone on to take an MBA at the Columbia Business School. After graduation, he joined a consulting firm where one of his assignments involved working on AT&T's early pilots of videotex technology. (Videotex allowed visual display of information transmitted over telephone lines or other communications media.) In 1982, BBSI hired Shay to head a task force to examine videotex possibilities, particularly ones related to home banking.

Home Banking

Home banking involved the delivery of banking services to consumers at the time and place of their choice, using personal computers linked to telephones. It offered such services as bill paying, account information, account transfers, budgeting, and record keeping. Potential applications included stock quotes, brokerage, and financial planning. A full service videotex offering also provided services rang-

ing from news and weather to sports and travel information, plus electronic mail, purchase of travel and entertainment tickets, and shopping.

Shay's task force evaluated several joint venture and franchising opportunities, as well as studying proprietary systems developed by Citibank and Chase Manhattan. At one point, BayBank unsuccessfully sought a pilot contract for Chemical Bank's "Pronto" home banking system. But after monitoring market acceptance of home banking and videotex offerings, including Shawmut Bank's poorly received "Arrive" service, the task force concluded that the technology would not win widespread retail acceptance until the mid-1990s.

Card Technology and Applications

Consumers' wallets were filled with a wide variety of cards. Some, such as driver's licenses and student IDs, simply offered visual proof of identification. Increasingly, though, cards were encoded with machine-readable information.

Some encoded cards were like pass keys, offering admission to restricted parking lots or other secured locations. Others served as financial tools. Prepayment cards, for instance, contained a magnetically stored cash value, which decreased each time the card was used to access a service. In Europe and Japan, such cards could be purchased in many locations, with values typically equivalent to $10 or $20. Used for a variety of purposes, they were a popular alternative to cash in public telephones. In the US, use of prepayment cards was limited mostly to rapid transit systems and photocopy machines.

The most common group of cards were credit, charge, and debit cards. Credit cards—such as Visa, MasterCard, Optima, Discover, and Eurocard—allowed the customer an extended time period to pay off the outstanding balance, but a substantial financial charge was levied on this balance after the monthly settlement date. By contrast, the charge cards issued by retailers, oil companies, and American Express did not always extend credit beyond the due date.

Debit cards provided no credit at all. Each transaction was deducted directly from the customer's account—just as a check would be—leading some people to describe debit cards as "plastic checks." Some users saw them as an alternative to carrying a checkbook or cash. Others, who worried about getting into debt, saw them as a way to pay by card without facing large, end-of-the-month bills. All ATM cards were debit cards, too, but confined to accessing ATM machines. Now the issue was how to extend their use to other types of transactions.

Credit, charge and debit cards had to be protected against fraudulent use. Security for bank cards involved use of a PIN (or password) chosen by the customer and revealed only to the bank's computer. Customers had to enter their PINs to access their accounts. Security for other cards was provided by checking a master file to ensure that the card was not stolen and that the account was good for the amount charged; vendors also compared the customer's signature on the sales slip with the one on the back of the card. Visa and MasterCard came in both credit and debit forms, and were issued through retail banks. BayBank offered Visa and MasterCard credit cards; they could also be used in ATMs to obtain cash advances, which were charged as a loan against the monthly credit card account.

In the US, all financial cards used a magnetic stripe to record and store information. *A magnetic stripe card* could store some 200 bytes of information (equivalent to roughly three lines of typescript). There was growing interest in "smart cards," which used microchip technology. These cards, the same size and shape as a traditional credit card, varied in sophistication.

Memory only smart cards were passive and could store 1–2 kilobytes (kb) of information. More advanced cards offered *memory plus intelligence* and could do limited processing. The embedded chip contained 2–16 kb—equivalent to as much as five pages—of EE-prom (electrically erasable—programmable read only memory) and an 8- to 16-bit processor. So-called *SuperSmart cards* added a two-line liquid crystal display (LCD) and a flat keypad. A smart card cost from $4 to $15, as compared with $0.15 or less for a traditional credit card. To handle smart cards, merchants would need to install new POS equipment. Card readers capable of handling both magnetic stripe and smart cards cost at least $800 each.

An alternative technology was *Optical Memory cards* which could contain almost 3Mb (1,500 pages) of WORM (write once read many [times]) memory. Although these cards only cost about $10 each, they had to be used with special laser-based reader-writer units—costing $3,000–$4,000 each. No financial service applications had yet been developed for these cards.

The French were the earliest to embrace smart card technology and had conducted over 300 test programs for a wide range of applications—including banking and an electronic yellow pages. These services involved as many as two million customers of the publicly owned telephone and postal authority, and were offered free of charge. The Japanese were also testing smart cards. In Canada, smart cards were being used by corporate customers of the Royal Bank of Canada to control access to cash management software at their own sites. In the US, however, there still were no commercial banking tests under way in the marketplace.

Visa planned to issue a SuperSmart card to its Platinum customers in 1993. Features might include a built-in calculator, world time clock, medical data, personal preferences in travel and accommodations, a transaction journal, and manually entered records and memos. In addition to using the card for credit purchases, the user might also be able to employ it for reserving airline seats, trading shares, checking personal bank records, and transferring funds.

The Toshiba-made Visa card could be used off line to conduct and authorize transactions; it stored a pre-programmed credit limit that was reduced by the appropriate amount each time a purchase was made. The user had to enter a PIN on the card's keypad (which would be internally validated), followed by the purchase amount. The card would then verify that the user was within his or her credit limit and display an approval code for the purchase amount, which the clerk would enter on a paper credit card slip in traditional fashion. If the purchase were for an amount greater than the existing balance, the card would display "OVER LIMIT." The user could check the card's credit limit and expiration date at any time. The balance could be updated by entering an amount, an expiration date, and a cryptographic code. If several attempts were made to enter an incorrect PIN or code, the card would "lock up" and only the issuer would be able to unlock it.

Lindsey Lawrence was enthusiastic about the potential of SuperSmart cards. She liked them from a systems standpoint because transactions could be approved and processed off line. Since they generated fewer demands on telecommunication links and central host computers, costs could be reduced.

POINT-OF-SALE DEBIT TRANSACTIONS

As Shay and his colleagues reviewed possible applications of the BayBank card, they looked at payment transactions at the retail point of sale (POS). What was the potential for transforming the card into a broad-based debit card? There were an estimated 258 million transactions a month in Massachusetts (refer to *Exhibit 3*); the payment method varied with transaction size (refer to *Exhibit 4*).

Cash was almost universally accepted, and was handled quickly and easily by both customers and cashiers. Disadvantages included risks of error and employee pilferage, plus the costs involved in obtaining, depositing, and storing it.

Checks had several shortcomings as a retail payment method, including slow handling by both customers and cashiers, as well substantial risk of fraud. When a check "bounced" because of insufficient funds in the account, it was the merchant's problem, not the bank's. The costs to merchants for processing checks were modest, but the cost incurred for verification or file maintenance were often significant. Only about 20% of all checks were written at POS—most of these at supermarkets. The cost to a bank of processing a check averaged about $0.02.

Credit cards were accepted at many locations,

EXHIBIT 3
POINT-OF-SALE PAYMENTS IN MASSACHUSETTS, BY MEDIUM

Payment medium	Cash	Check	Credit card	Other	Total
POS transactions/ month (mn)	226	18	12	2	258
Transactions/month per adult (units)	56.4	4.6	3.0	0.5	64.5
Average transaction value	$8.90	$72.68	$71.77	$20.00	$16.45
Median transaction value	$1.90	$28.00	$30.00	—	$2.40
POS spending/month per adult	$502	$331	$218	$10	$1,061

Source: Company records.

EXHIBIT 4 ESTIMATED DISTRIBUTION OF POS TRANSACTIONS IN MASSACHUSETTS

	Dollars spent per month (mn)				Transactions per month (mn)			
Value range	Cash	Checks	Credit cards	Total	Cash	Checks	Credit cards	Total
<$2	$109	$1	$0	$110	117.32	1.19	0.24	118.75
$2–4	$114	$3	$2	$119	38.36	1.00	0.67	40.03
$4–10	$187	$15	$10	$212	29.33	2.18	1.52	33.03
$10–20	$289	$50	$35	$374	20.31	3.37	2.43	26.11
$20–40	$327	$109	$73	$509	11.28	3.65	2.43	17.36
$40–100	$350	$215	$158	$723	5.64	3.37	2.43	11.44
$100–200	$356	$307	$215	$878	2.59	2.18	1.52	6.29
$200–400	$180	$264	$191	$635	0.64	0.91	0.67	2.22
>$400	$95	$361	$186	$642	0.14	0.38	0.24	0.76
Total	$2,007	$1,325	$870	$4,202	225.61	18.24	12.14	255.99

Source: Company records.

although food stores or small merchants were often unwilling or reluctant to take them; some stores required a $10–15 minimum purchase. Paying by credit card could be a slow and cumbersome process. The salesclerk or cashier had to phone for authorization, imprint the paper charge slip with details from the customer's card, write up purchase details, and have the customer sign. One copy of the slip was given to the customer, a second kept for the store, and a third sent to the bank for collection. New card-reading devices that were linked to telephone lines simplified the process, as the cashier simply had to pass the card through the reader and type in the purchase amount. The machine automatically called for authorization and, if approved, promptly printed out a receipt for the customers to sign. As long as transactions were authorized, there was little risk of fraud for the merchant, since the issuing bank was held responsible for extending credit (even on a stolen card). Merchants paid a fee expressed as a discount from the sales price of any transaction. This "merchant's discount" ranged from 1.2% for a large national retailer to as much as 5% for a boutique; the average was about 2.5%.

The Marketplace for Debit POS Transactions

Some observers felt that transactions under $10 were poor candidates for either credit or debit card use.

Merchants discouraged card use for small sums because of processing costs and the transaction time involved. Customers showed little interest in using their debit cards for small purchases, except for gasoline, where they and the retailers were both accustomed to card use. Shay believed that the potential for debit card use was limited above $100, on the grounds that purchasers would either need credit or prefer to gain the four to seven weeks' float available from using a credit card with a monthly billing cycle.

For the purpose of examining POS payments, Shay and his associates had divided merchants into three categories: high volume, high value added, and other. High volume merchants included supermarkets, convenience stores, fast food restaurants, and gas stations. They accounted for half of all transactions, but only 35% of dollars, spent at POS. The average transaction was $11.50 and margins were low. Both customers and stores sought to minimize transaction times. Except for gas stations, many high volume merchants preferred to avoid credit cards and, except for supermarkets, most avoided checks as well.

High value added merchants included department stores, specialty retailers, full-service restaurants, travel services, and personal service providers (such as hair salons). With an average sale of $30, they accounted for 55% of the money spent at point of sale and for 30% of transactions. Customer satisfaction and the opportunity to sell additional goods and services during a visit were important for success, since merchants enjoyed sizeable markups on most sales. Most accepted checks and credit cards; many offered their own charge card services, too.

Typical of the third category of merchants were the classic Mom and Pop stores and newsstands. They accounted for an estimated 20% of transactions but only 10% of POS dollars. The average transaction was about $8. Such merchants were usually reluctant to accept checks, and the few that offered sales on credit were likely to use non-credit card arrangements.

Alternative Methods of Implementing Debit POS

Direct debit at the point of sale (Debit POS) allowed customers to use debit cards for their purchases, with real-time authorization of the amount. Payment was automatically debited from the customer's bank account and credited to the merchant's account. All transactions had to be routed through a computer switch, typically operated by an intermediary organization, which went back and forth twice between the two banks to obtain authorization and then arrange settlement. There were three principal mechanisms for settling payments.

On-line Debit POS worked through an ATM network—either a super-regional network like NYCE or, potentially, a regional network such as X-Press 24 or Yankee 24. Customers could use their ATM cards to make purchases. To prevent fraud, customers were asked to enter their PINs on a keypad at the register before payment could be authorized. This on-line approach enabled transactions to be settled rapidly, with credits and debits being posted overnight to the relevant accounts. To offer this payment mechanism, merchants had to install terminals, purchasing them at $800 each or leasing them for $50 per month, including servicing. Each POS terminal had to be located beside a register. NYCE currently had only one chain of supermarkets participating in debit POS, located in upstate New York. So BayBank would have to lead the way in persuading New England merchants to accept NYCE or X-Press 24 POS debit.

Each debit card transaction involved two banks (the merchant's and the cardholder's), a switching organization, and a third-party processor. Sometimes, of course, both merchant and customer used the same bank. Merchants paid their own bank an average of $0.20 per transaction. In turn, that bank had to pay $0.04 to the switch, and $0.12 to a third-party processor. The cardholder's bank received no revenue unless it imposed a "hard charge" for each customer transaction. (Although some bank charges were waived when a customer's average balance exceeded a certain level, hard charges were imposed regardless of balance levels.) The customer's bank also had to pay $0.04 to the switch. In addition, there was an internal processing cost of $0.05 when a transaction was debited against a customer's account.

MasterDebit and Visa Debit used the switches of these two credit card networks. Debit cards were issued by the banks, which could expand the use of their customers' ATM cards by adding the relevant hologram, printed service mark, and a new numbering configuration. Customers had to be prequalified for a line of overdraft protection, known at BayBank as "reserve credit." Purchase authorization took place in real time, using the same procedures as for credit cards, including signature verification (no PINs were involved). But settlement and posting might take one to ten days to complete, depending in part on whether purchases were recorded electronically or on paper drafts. If the merchant already accepted credit cards, no new equipment was needed. The transaction cost ("discount") to merchants was similar to credit cards—averaging around 2% of sales price—but Shay thought that merchants might insist on a lower discount for debit cards if customers started using them widely instead of cash or checks. The discount was collected by the merchant's bank and shared with the bank issuing the card. The latter received an interchange fee averaging 1.3% of the transaction value, but incurred processing and settlement costs totaling about $0.15.

Proprietary Debit POS used cards issued by the merchant. The task force saw little potential for Bay-Bank in this approach. Customers needed a separate card for each merchant, as with department charge cards or supermarket check-cashing cards. Capital costs for the merchant were $125 or more per terminal. The cost per transaction for the merchant was about $0.25. One advantage of this system for merchants was that they could develop profiles of individual cardholders' buying habits and use them for research and marketing purposes. Shaw's, a local supermarket chain, was exploring proprietary debit cards.

Current Status of Debit POS

A number of on-line debit POS pilots and rollouts were already under way in North America, Europe, and Australia. The heaviest activity in the United States was in California (which accounted for 62% of all debit POS transactions in the country), as well as in Arizona and Texas. Interlink was one of the most active networks, providing switching for transactions based on ATM cards in Arizona, California, and Nevada. Some ten million customers—representing about 30% of the population of these three states—were eligible to use the service. Interlink boasted 12,500 terminals in 3,000 stores, including grocery stores, gas stations, convenience stores, and fast food restaurants. About five million transactions were recorded each month by 32 financial institutions. Two major banks reported that 19% of their cardholders had made debit POS transactions.

Lucky Stores, a California-based supermarket chain, was the largest merchant offering on-line debit POS. Lucky had installed a total of 3,000 terminals in 350 stores, advertised the service heavily, and promoted it at the checkout counters. It was recording two million debit POS transactions per month. To discourage banks from charging cardholders for such transactions, Lucky posted a list of banks which did and did not impose such charges.

In New England, on-line debit POS activity was limited. Any merchant accepting MasterCard or Visa would, of course, accept the debit versions of these cards. The only bank in the region offering Master-Debit was Fleet/Norstar. Mobil Oil was the only large merchant promoting use of debit POS. It had invested in a nationwide on-line system with terminals in all stations so as to get float faster on its own charge cards. Users of debit cards issued by other institutions

would be able to buy gas (petrol) at the cash discount rate, saving four cents per gallon (about one cent per liter) over the rate of credit card purchases. Many banks declined Mobil's invitation to participate, since the firm offered them no fee for processing transactions. Others found that building the necessary interface was too difficult. All systems, right back to the customer's statements, had to be changed. In Massachusetts, only BayBank was willing to build a link to the Mobil data center and create the software interface needed to allow its customers to use their ATM cards as debit cards at Mobil stations.

BayBank went on line with Mobil in May 1987 and promoted the service actively through statement inserts, dollar-off coupons, and posters at Mobil stations. The $65,000 cost was shared with Mobil. Monthly transactions rose to 61,911 in June 1988 (refer to *Exhibit 5*). In July, BayBank imposed a hard charge of $0.15 charge per transaction. Transactions then fell sharply, stabilizing at around just under 40,000 a month by a total of 15,000 BayBank ATM cardholders.

DEVELOPING A DEBIT POS PLAN FOR BAYBANK

As Shay reviewed the information that the task force had collected on debit POS, it was clear to him that BayBank faced a wide array of options. The ideal scenario would be one that allowed BayBank to develop a distinctive advantage for its cardholders that was not available to customers of other banks.

An on-line debit POS system switched through X-Press 24 would achieve that purpose, whereas one switched through NYCE would open participation to many of BayBank's competitors. An important issue, regardless of who performed the switching, was to market the concept of on-line debit POS to merchants, so they would be willing to make needed investments in terminals and staff training. It was not clear who would take responsibility for the necessary marketing effort, which could cost $750,000 or more in Massachusetts alone. Systems development costs for BayBank were estimated at $800,000 for the X-Press 24 option and at $600,000 for the Cirrus or NYCE option. Start-up time would be 8–12 months.

EXHIBIT 5 BAYBANK POS TRANSACTIONS THROUGH MOBIL OIL CO., 1987–89

Month	Monthly transactions		
	1987	1988	1989
January	—	40,521	37,451
February	—	38,604	35,696
March	—	41,285	39,068
April	—	42,062	38,301
May	8,924	46,997	41,439
June	18,645	61,911	40,595
July	30,250	55,388*	38,721
August	40,874	52,244	38,036
September	57,783	41,774	36,756
October	52,764	41,748	38,975
November	41,259	38,949	36,888
December	41,138	39,575	38,367

*A charge of $0.15 per transaction was imposed in mid-July 1988 (debited directly from the customer's account).
Source: Company records.

With the MasterDebit/Visa Debit option, it would not be necessary for merchants who already accepted MasterCard and Visa credit cards to make any upfront investment. If BayBank decided to opt for this alternative, Shay favored MasterDebit. It would be relatively simple to add a hologram to the front of the BayBank ATM card. Upfront development costs for this option would be $500,000.

The task force members debated what proportion of ATM cardholders in Massachusetts might use their cards to make debit POS purchases. They also wondered what percentage of present cash, check, and credit card transactions could be converted to debit card purchases. One important determinant would doubtless be the pricing policy that BayBank adopted.

BayBank already had one of the most aggressive fee structures for electronic funds transfers (EFT) in New England. It could employ the same approach for POS debits as for checks and ATM transactions. Customers whose average monthly balance fell below a predefined minimum (typically $1,500) paid 35 cents for each check or ATM withdrawal. Histori-

cally, about one-seventh of all transactions incurred such a charge. As with Mobil debit purchases, however, a supplementary hard charge could be imposed on each POS debit transaction by any BayBank customer. Whichever approach was selected, significant planning and expense was involved when debit card capability was added to ATM cards.

If the bank selected the on-line debit POS route, all 750,000 BayBank ATM cardholders would be eligible to use this service. But a vigorous promotional effort, costing an estimated $250,000, would be needed to encourage BayBank customers to make debit card purchases on a regular basis. Since any competing bank could join NYCE, choosing that option would be unlikely to attract new customers to BayBank; indeed Shay believed that BayBank customers would probably account for only half of all debit POS transactions if NYCE were the switch. If X-Press 24 were used as the switch, the outcome might be very different.

If the MasterDebit option were selected, about 50% of BayBank ATM cardholders could be prequalified because of existing credit relationships with the bank. These customers could be targeted by direct mail at a cost of $0.75 each. Many other BayBank account holders could be qualified on application. One opportunity to reach them would be when ATM cards were reissued every two years. The debit card option could also be promoted to non-customers as one more reason to open an account with BayBank.

Shay estimated the cost of credit screening at $250,000 and account opening at $50,000 during the first two years. A large-scale promotional campaign, using television and newspapers to attract new customers to a BayBank debit card, would cost an estimated $1,975,000 over two years.

At the Task Force Meeting

Bob Shay looked around at his team and declared:

Our task this afternoon is to review the numbers that John and Terry have prepared for us on the proportion of all unit and dollar transactions at POS that debit cards might be expected to capture in Massachusetts for the on-line and MasterDebit options. On Tuesday morning, we'll meet again to finalize our recommendations. Don Isaacs and Lindsey Lawrence have scheduled a meeting with Bill Crozier a week from today, and that's when the final decision will be made.

A key issue is whether this is the right time to act, with the New England economy in a downturn and our profits squeezed. If we recommend a "go" decision on one of these options, will that constrain future directions that BayBank might take as a result of new technological developments, the advent of national interstate banking, evolving trends in retailing, or changes in customer needs and preferences? And what opportunities might we miss if we don't act now?

So there's lots to think about. Right now, Terry and John, let's hear your opinions on POS debit's prospects for penetrating the retail transactions market.

Thompson Respiration Products, Inc.

James E. Nelson
William R. Woolridge

Victor Higgins, executive vice president for Thompson Respiration Products, Inc. (TRP), sat thinking at his desk late on Friday in April 1986. "We're making progress," he said to himself. "Getting Metro to sign finally gets us into the Chicago Market. . .and with a good dealer at that." *Metro*, of course, was Metropolitan Medical Products, a large Chicago retailer of medical equipment and supplies for home use. "Now, if we could just do the same in Minneapolis and Atlanta," he continued.

However, getting at least one dealer in each of these cities to sign a TRP Dealer Agreement seemed remote right now. One reason was the sizeable groundwork required—Higgins simply lacked the time to review operations at the well over 100 dealers currently operating in the two cities. Another was TRP's lack of dealer-oriented sales information that went beyond the technical specification sheet for each product and the company's price list. Still another concerned two conditions in the Dealer Agreement itself—prospective dealers sometimes balked at agreeing to sell no products manufactured by TRP's competitors and differed with TRP in interpretations of the "best efforts" clause. (The clause required the dealer to maintain adequate inventories of TRP products, contact four prospective new customers or physicians or respiration therapists per month, respond promptly to sales inquiries, and represent TRP at appropriate conventions where it exhibited.)

"Still," Higgins concluded, "we signed Metro in spite of these reasons, and 21 others across the country. That's about all anyone could expect—after all, we've only been trying to develop a dealer network for a year or so."

THE PORTABLE RESPIRATOR INDUSTRY

The portable respirator industry began in the early 1950s when polio-stricken patients who lacked control of muscles necessary for breathing began to leave treatment centers. They returned home with hospital-style iron lungs or fiberglass chest shells, both being large chambers that regularly introduced a vacuum about the patient's chest. The vacuum caused the chest to expand and, thus, the lungs to fill with air.

However, both devices confined patients to a prone or semiprone position in a bed.

By the late 1950s, TRP had developed a portable turbine blower powered by an electric motor and battery. When connected to a mouthpiece via plastic tubing, the blower would inflate a patient's lungs on demand. Patients could now leave their beds for several hours at a time and realize limited mobility in a wheelchair. By the early 1970s, TRP had developed a line of more sophisticated turbine respirators in terms of monitoring and capability for adjustment to individual patient needs.

At about the same time, applications began to shift from polio patients to victims of other diseases or of spinal cord injuries, the latter group existing primarily as a result of automobile accidents. Better emergency medical service, quicker evacuation to spinal cord injury centers, and more proficient treatment meant that people who formerly would have died now lived and went on to lead meaningful lives. Because of patients' frequently younger ages, they strongly desired wheelchair mobility. Respiration therapists obliged by recommending a Thompson respirator for home use or, if unaware of Thompson, recommending a Puritan-Bennett or other machine.

Instead of a turbine, Puritan-Bennett machines used a bellows design to force air into the patient's lungs. The machines were widely used in hospitals but seemed poorly suited for home use. For one thing, Puritan-Bennett machines used a compressor pump or pressurized air to drive the bellows, much more cumbersome than Thompson's electric motor. Puritan-Bennett machines also cost approximately 50 percent more than a comparable Thompson unit and were relatively large and immobile. On the other hand, Puritan-Bennett machines were viewed by physicians and respiration therapists as industry standards.

By the late 1970s, TRP had developed a piston and cylinder design (similar in principle to the bellows) and placed it on the market. The product lacked the sophistication of the Puritan-Bennett machines but was reliable, portable, and much simpler to adjust and operate. It also maintained TRP's traditional cost advantage. Another firm, Life Products, began its

operations in 1981 by producing a similar design. A third competitor, Lifecare Services, had begun operations somewhat earlier.

Puritan-Bennett

Puritan-Bennett was a large, growing, and financially sound manufacturer of respiration equipment for medical and aviation applications. Its headquarters were located in Kansas City, Missouri. However, the firm staffed over 40 sales, service, and warehouse operations in the United States, Canada, United Kingdom, and France. Sales for 1985 exceeded $100 million, while employment was just over 2,000 people. Sales for its Medical Equipment Group (respirators, related equipment, and accessories, service, and parts) likely exceeded $40 million for 1985; however, Higgins could obtain data only for the period 1981–1984 (see *Exhibit 1*). Puritan-Bennett usually sold its respirators through a system of independent, durable medical equipment dealers. However, its sales offices did sell directly to identified "house accounts" and often competed with dealers by selling slower-moving products to all accounts. According to industry sources, Puritan-Bennett sales were slightly more than three-fourths of all respirator sales to hospitals in 1985.

However, these same sources expected Puritan-Bennett's share to diminish during the late 1980s because of the aggressive marketing efforts of three other manufacturers of hospital-style respirators: Bear Medical Systems, Inc.; J. H. Emerson; and Siemens-Elema. The latter firm was expected to grow the most rapidly, despite its quite recent entry into the U.S. market (its headquarters were in Sweden) and a list price of over $16,000 for its basic model.

Life Products

Life Products directly competed with TRP for the portable respirator market. Life Products had begun operations in 1981 when David Smith, a TRP employee, left to start his own business. Smith had located his plant in Boulder, Colorado, less than a mile from TRP headquarters.

EXHIBIT 1
PURITAN-BENNETT MEDICAL EQUIPMENT GROUP SALES

	1981	1982	1983	1984
Domestic sales				
Model MA-1				
Units	1,460	875	600	500
Amount, $ millions	8.5	4.9	3.5	3.1
Model MA-2				
Units	—	935	900	1,100
Amount, $ millions	—	6.0	6.1	7.8
Foreign sales				
Units	250	300	500	565
Amount, $ millions	1.5	1.8	3.1	3.6
IPPB equipment, $ millions	6.0	6.5	6.7	7.0
Parts, service, accessories, $ millions	10.0	11.7	13.1	13.5
Overhaul, $ millions	2.0	3.0	2.5	2.5
Total, $ millions	28.0	34.0	35.0	37.5

Source: The Wall Street Transcript.

He began almost immediately to set up a dealer network and by early 1986 had secured over 40 independent dealers located in large metropolitan areas. Smith had made a strong effort to sign only large, well-managed durable medical equipment dealers. Dealer representatives were required to complete Life Product's service training school, held each month in Boulder. Life Products sold its products to dealers (in contrast to TRP, which both sold and rented products to consumers and to dealers). Dealers received a 20 to 25 percent discount off suggested retail price on most products.

As of April 1986, Life Products offered two respirator models (the LP3 and LP4) and a limited number of accessories (such as mouthpieces and plastic tubing) to its dealers. Suggested retail prices for the two respirator models were approximately $3,900 and $4,800. Suggested rental rates were approximately $400 and $500 per month. Life Products also allowed Lifecare Services to manufacture a respirator similar to the LP3 under license.

At the end of 1985, Smith was quite pleased with his firm's performance. During Life Products' brief history, it had passed TRP in sales and now ceased to see the firm as a serious threat, at least according to one company executive:

We really aren't in competition with Thompson. They're after the stagnant market and we're after a growing market. We see new applications and ultimately the hospital market as our niche. I doubt if Thompson will even be around in a few years. As for Lifecare, their prices are much lower than ours but you don't get the service. With them you get the basic product, but nothing else. With us, you get a complete medical care service. That's the big difference.

Lifecare Services, Inc.

In contrast to the preceding firms, Lifecare Services, Inc. earned much less of its revenues from medical equipment manufacturing and much more from medical equipment distributing. The firm primarily resold products purchased from other manufacturers, operating out of its headquarters in Boulder as well as from its 16 field offices (*Exhibit 2*). All offices were stocked with backup parts and an inventory of respirators. All were staffed with trained technicians under Lifecare's employ.

Lifecare did manufacture a few accessories not readily available from other manufacturers. These items complemented the purchased products and, in the company's words, served to "give the customer a complete respiratory service." Under a licensing

EXHIBIT 2
LIFECARE SERVICES, INC., FIELD OFFICES

Augusta, Ga.	Houston, Tex.
Baltimore, Md.	Los Angeles, Calif.
Boston, Mass.	New York, N.Y.
Chicago, Ill.	Oakland, Calif.
Cleveland, Ohio	Omaha, Nebr.
Denver, Colo.	Phoenix, Ariz.
Detroit, Mich.	Seattle, Wash.
Grand Rapids, Mich.*	St. Paul, Minn.

*Suboffice.
Source: Trade literature.

agreement between Lifecare and Life Products, the firm manufactured a respirator similar to the LP3 and marketed it under the Lifecare name. The unit rented for approximately $175 per month. While Lifecare continued to service the few remaining Thompson units it still had in the field, it no longer carried the Thompson line.

Lifecare rented rather than sold its equipment. The firm maintained that this gave patients more flexibility in the event of recovery or death and lowered patients' monthly costs.

THOMPSON RESPIRATION PRODUCTS, INC.

TRP currently employed 13 people, 9 in production and 4 in management. It conducted operations in a modern, attractive building (leased) in an industrial park. The building contained about 6,000 square feet of space, split 75/25 for production/management purposes. Production operations were essentially job shop in nature; skilled technicians assembled each unit by hand on workbenches, making frequent quality control tests and subsequent adjustments. Production lots usually ranged from 10 to 75 units per model and probably averaged around 40. Normal production capacity was about 600 units per year.

Product Line

TRP currently sold seven respirator models plus a large number of accessories. All respirator models were portable but differed considerably in terms of

style, design, performance specifications, and attendant features (see *Exhibit 3*). Four models were styled as metal boxes with an impressive array of knobs, dials, indicator lights, and switches. Three were styled as less imposing, "overnighter" suitcases with less prominently displayed controls and indicators. (*Exhibit 4* is a photograph of the M3000, as illustrative of the metal box design.)

Four of the models were designed as *pressure machines*, using a turbine pump that provided a constant, usually positive, pressure. Patients were provided intermittent access to this pressure as breaths per minute. However, one model, the MV Multivent, could provide either a constant positive or a constant negative pressure (i.e., a vacuum, necessary to operate chest shells, iron lungs, and body wraps). No other portable respirator on the market could produce a negative pressure. Three of the models were designed as *volume machines*, using a piston pump that produced intermittent, constant volumes of pressurized air as breaths per minute. Actual volumes were prescribed by each patient's physician based on lung capacity. Pressures depended on the breathing method used (mouthpiece, trach, chest shell, and others) and on the patient's activity level. Breaths per minute also depended on the patient's activity level.

Models came with several features. The newest was an assist feature (currently available on the Minilung M25 but soon to be offered also on the M3000) that allowed the patient alone to "command" additional breaths without having someone change the dialed breath rate. The sigh feature gave patients a sigh, either automatically or on demand. Depending on the model, up to six alarms were available to indicate a patient's call, unacceptable low pressure, unacceptable high pressure, low battery voltage, power failure, failure to cycle, and the need to replace motor brushes. All models but the MV Multivent also offered automatic switchover from alternating current to either an internal or an external battery (or both) in the event of a power failure. Batteries provided for 18 to 40 hours of operation, depending on usage.

Higgins felt that TRP's respirators were superior to those of Life Products. Most TRP models allowed

EXHIBIT 3 TRP RESPIRATORS

Model*	Style	Design	Volume, cc	Pressure, cm H₂O
M3000	Metal box	Volume	300–3,000	+ 10 to +65
MV Multivent	Metal box	Pressure (positive or negative)	n.a.	− 70 to +80
Minilung M15	Suitcase	Volume	200–1,500	+ 5 to +65
Minilung M25 Assist (also available without the assist feature)	Suitcase	Volume	600–2,500	+ 5 to +65
Bantam GS	Suitcase	Pressure (positive)	n.a.	+ 15 to +45
Compact CS	Metal box	Pressure (positive)	n.a.	+ 15 to +45
Compact C	Metal box	Pressure (positive)	n.a.	+ 15 to +45

Model	Breaths per minute	Weight, lbs.	Size, ft.³	Features
M3000	6 to 30	39	0.85	Sigh, four alarms, automatic switchover from AC to battery
MV Multivent	8 to 24	41	1.05	Positive or negative pressure, four alarms, AC only
Minilung M15	8 to 22	24	0.70	Three alarms, automatic switchover from AC to battery
Minilung M25 Assist (also available without the assist feature)	5 to 20	24	0.70	Assist, sigh, three alarms, automatic switchover from AC to battery
Bantam GS	6 to 24	19	0.75	Sigh, six alarms, automatic switchover from AC to battery
Compact CS	8 to 24	25	0.72	Sigh, six alarms, automatic switchover from AC to battery
Compact C	6 to 24	19	0.50	Sigh, four alarms, automatic switchover from AC to battery

*Five other models considered obsolete by TRP could be supplied if necessary.
Note: n.a. = not applicable.
Source: Company sales specification sheets.

pressure monitoring in the airway itself rather than in the machine, providing more accurate measurement. TRP's suitcase-style models often were strongly preferred by patients, especially the polio patients who had known no others. TRP's volume models offered easier volume adjustments, and all TRP models offered more alarms. On the other hand, he knew that TRP had recently experienced some product reliability problems of an irritating—not life threatening—nature. Further, he knew that Life Products had beaten TRP to the market with the assist feature (the idea for which had come from a Puritan-Bennett machine).

TRP's line of accessories was more extensive than that of Life Products. TRP offered the following for separate sale: alarms, call switches, battery cables, chest shells, mouthpieces, plastic tubing, pneumobelts, bladders (equipment for still another breathing method that utilized intermittent pressure on a patient's diaphragm), and other items. Lifecare Services offered many similar items.

Distribution

Shortly after joining TRP, Higgins had decided to switch from selling and renting products directly to patients to selling and renting products to dealers. While it meant lower margins, less control, and more

EXHIBIT 4
THE M3000 MINILUNG

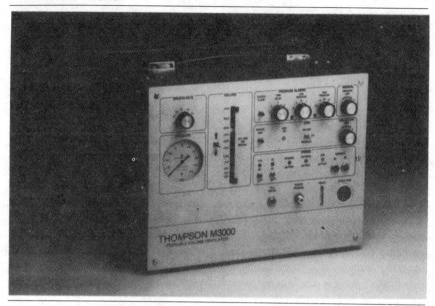

infrequent communication with patients, the change had several advantages. It allowed TRP to shift inventory from the factory to the dealer, generating cash more quickly. It provided for local representation in market areas, allowing patients greater feelings of security and TRP more aggressive sales efforts. It shifted burdensome paperwork (required by insurance companies and state and federal agencies to effect payment) from TRP to the dealer. It also reduced other TRP administrative activities in accounting, customer relations, and sales.

TRP derived about half of its 1985 revenue of $3 million directly from patients and about half from the dealer network. By April 1986, the firm had 21 dealers (see *Exhibit 5*) with 3 accounting for over 60 percent of TRP dealer revenues. Two of the three serviced TRP products as did two of the smaller dealers; the rest preferred to let the factory take care of repairs. TRP conducted occasional training sessions for dealer repair personnel, but distances were great and turnover in the position high, making such sessions costly. Most dealers required air shipment of respirators, in quantities of one or two units.

Price

TRP maintained a comprehensive price list for its entire product line. (*Exhibit 6* reproduces part of the current list.) Each respirator model carried both a suggested retail selling price and a suggested retail rental rate. (TRP also applied these rates when it dealt directly with patients.) The list also presented two net purchase prices for each model along with

EXHIBIT 5
TRP DEALER LOCATIONS

Bakersfield, Calif.	Salt Lake City, Utah
Baltimore, Md.	San Diego, Calif.
Birmingham, Ala.	San Francisco, Calif.
Chicago, Ill.	Seattle, Wash.
Cleveland, Ohio	Springfield, Ohio
Fort Wayne, Ind.	Tampa, Fla.
Greenville, N.C.	Tucson, Ariz.
Indianapolis, Ind.	Washington, D.C.
Newark, N.J.	
Oklahoma City, Okla.	Montreal, Canada
Pittsburgh, Pa.	Toronto, Canada

Source: Company records.

EXHIBIT 6   CURRENT TRP RESPIRATOR PRICE LIST

	Suggested retail			Dealer price	
Model	Rent/month	Price	Dealer rent/month	1–2	3 or more
M3000	$380	$6,000	$290	$4,500	$4,185
MV Multivent	270	4,300	210	3,225	3,000
Minilung M15	250	3,950	190	2,960	2,750
Minilung M25	250	3,950	190	2,960	2,750
Bantam GS	230	3,600	175	2,700	2,510
Compact CS	230	3,600	175	2,700	2,510
Compact C	200	3,150	155	2,360	2,195

Source: Company sales specification sheets.

an alternative rental rate that TRP charged to dealers. About 40 percent of the 300 respirator units TRP shipped to dealers in 1985 went out on a rental basis. The comparable figure for the 165 units sent directly to consumers was 90 percent. Net purchase prices allowed an approximate 7 percent discount for orders of three of more units of each model. Higgins had initiated this policy early last year with the aim of encouraging dealers to order in larger quantities. To date one dealer had taken advantage of this discount.

Current policy called for TRP to earn a gross margin of approximately 35 percent on the dealer price for one to two units. All prices included shipping charges by United Parcel Service (UPS); purchasers requesting more expensive transportation service paid the difference between actual costs incurred and the UPS charge. Terms were net 30 days with a 1.5 percent service charge added to past due accounts.

CONSUMERS

Two types of patients used respirators, depending on whether the need followed from disease or from injury. Diseases such as polio, sleep apnea, chronic obstructive pulmonary disease, and muscular dystrophy annually left about 1,900 victims unable to breathe without a respirator. Injury to the spinal cord above the fifth vertebra caused a similar result for about 300 people per year. Except for polio, incidences of the diseases and injury were growing at

about 3 percent per year. Most patients kept one respirator at bedside and another mounted on a wheelchair. However, Higgins did know of one individual who kept eight Bantam B models (provided by a local polio foundation, now defunct) in his closet. Except for polio patients, life expectancies were about five years. Higgins estimated the total number of patients using a home respirator in 1981 at:

Polio	3,300
Other diseases	6,500
Spinal cord injury	1,000

Almost all patients were under a physician's care as well as that of a more immediate nurse or attendant (frequently a relative). About 95 percent paid for their equipment through insurance benefits or foundation monies. About 90 percent rented their equipment. Almost all patients and their nurses or attendants had received instruction in equipment operation from respiration therapists employed by medical centers or by dealers of durable medical equipment.

The majority of patients were poor. Virtually none were gainfully employed and all had seen their savings and other assets diminished to varying degrees by treatment costs. Some had experienced a divorce. Slightly more patients were male than female. About 75 percent lived in their homes with the rest split between hospitals, nursing homes, and other institutions.

Apart from patients, Higgins thought that hospitals might be considered a logical new market for

EXHIBIT 7

REGIONAL SPINAL CORD INJURY CENTERS

Birmingham, Ala.	Houston, Tex.
Boston, Mass.	Miami, Fla.
Chicago, Ill.	New York, N.Y.
Columbia, Mo.	Philadelphia, Pa.
Downey, Calif.	Phoenix, Ariz.
Englewood, Colo.	San Jose, Calif.
Fishersville, Va.	Seattle, Wash.

TRP to enter. Many of the larger and some of the smaller general hospitals might be convinced to purchase one portable respiratory (like the M3000) for emergency and other use with injury patients. Such a machine would be much cheaper to purchase than a large Puritan-Bennett and would allow easier patient trips to testing areas, X-ray, surgery, and the like. Even easier to convince should be the fourteen regional spinal cord injury centers located across the country (*Exhibit 7*). Other medical centers that specialized in treatment of pulmonary diseases should also be prime targets. Somewhat less promising but more numerous would be public and private schools that trained physicians and respiration therapists. Higgins estimated the numbers of these institutions at:

General hospitals (100 beds or more)	3,800
General hospitals (fewer than 100 beds)	3,200
Spinal cord injury centers	14
Pulmonary disease treatment centers	100
Medical schools	180
Respiration therapy schools	250

DEALERS

Dealers supplying home care medical products (as distinct from dealers supplying hospitals and medical centers) showed a great deal of diversity. Some were little more than small areas in local drugstores that rented canes, walkers, and wheelchairs in addition to selling supplies like surgical stockings and colostomy bags. Others carried nearly everything needed for home nursing care—renting everything from

canes to hospital beds and selling supplies from bed pads to bottled oxygen. Still others specialized in products and supplies for only certain types of patients.

In this latter category, Higgins had identified dealers of oxygen and oxygen-related equipment as the best fit among existing dealers. These dealers serviced victims of emphysema, bronchitis, asthma, and other respiratory ailments, a growing market that Higgins estimated was about 10 times greater than for respirators. A typical dealer had begun perhaps 10 years ago selling bottled oxygen (obtained from a welding supply wholesaler) and renting rather crude metering equipment to patients at home under the care of a registered nurse. The same dealer today now rented and serviced oxygen concentrators (a recently developed device that extracted oxygen from the air), liquid oxygen equipment and liquid oxygen, and much more sophisticated oxygen equipment and oxygen to patients cared for by themselves or by relatives.

Most dealers maintained a fleet of radio-dispatched trucks to deliver products to their customers. Better dealers promised 24-hour service and kept delivery personnel and a respiration therapist on call 24 hours a day. Dealers usually employed several respiration therapists who would set up equipment, instruct patients and attendants on equipment operation, and provide routine and emergency service. Dealers often expected the therapists to function as a sales force. The therapists would call on physicians and other respiration therapists at hospitals and medical centers, on discharge planners at hospitals, and on organizations such as muscular dystrophy associations, spinal cord injury associations, and visiting nurse associations.

Dealers usually bought their inventories of durable equipment and supplies directly from manufacturers. They usually received a 20 to 25 percent discount off suggested list prices to consumers and hospitals. Only in rare instances might dealers instead lease equipment from a manufacturer. Dealers aimed for a payback of one year or less, meaning that most products began to contribute to profit and overhead after 12 months of rental. Most products lasted physically for upwards of 10 years but technologically for only 5 to 6: every dealer's warehouse contained idle but perfectly suitable equipment that had been superseded by models demanded by patients, their physicians, or their attendants.

Most dealers were independently owned and operated, with annual sales ranging between $5 million and $10 million. However, a number had recently been acquired by one of several parent organizations that were regional or national in scope. Such claims usually consisted of from 10 to 30 retail operations located in separate market areas. However, the largest, Abbey Medical, had begun operations in 1924 and now consisted of over 70 local dealers. Higgins estimated 1985 sales for the chain (which was itself acquired by American Hospital Supply Corporation in April 1981) at over $60 million. In general, chains maintained a low corporate visibility and provided their dealers with working capital, employee benefit programs, operating advice, and some centralized purchasing. Higgins thought that chain organizations might grow more rapidly over the next 10 years.

THE ISSUES

Higgins looked at his watch. It was 5:30 and really time to leave. "Still," he thought, "I should jot down what I see to be the immediate issues before I go—that way I won't be tempted to think about them over the weekend." He took a pen and wrote the following:

1. Should TRP continue to rent respirators to dealers?
2. Should TRP protect each dealer's territory (and how big should a territory be)?
3. Should TRP require dealers not to stock competing equipment?
4. How many dealers should TRP eventually have? Where?
5. What sales information should be assembled in order to attract high-quality dealers?
6. What should be done about the "best efforts" clause?

As he reread the list, Higgins considered that there probably were still other short-term-oriented questions he might have missed. Monday would be soon enough to consider them all.

Until then, he was free to think about broader, more strategic issues. Some reflections on the nature of the target market, a statement of marketing objectives, and TRP's possible entry into the hospital market would occupy the weekend. Decisions on these topics would form a substantial part of TRP's strategic marketing plan, a document Higgins hoped to have for the beginning of the next fiscal year in July. "At least I can rule out one option," Higgins thought as he put on his coat. That was an idea to use independent sales representatives to sell TRP products on commission: a recently completed two-month search for an organization had come up empty. "Like my stomach," he thought, as he went out the door.

PART FIVE

Advertising and Promotion

Communication, which includes advertising, promotion, and personal selling, is the most visible or audible of marketing activities. Through communications, the marketer is able to inform existing or prospective customers about the product and its features, its price, and where to buy it and other distribution details; to create (where appropriate) persuasive arguments for using the service or buying the goods; and to remind people of the product. In this note, we will first discuss some broad issues concerning marketing communication, and then focus on advertising and promotion. In Part 6, a subsequent note will address issues relating to personal selling and sales force management.

THE COMMUNICATION PROCESS

Communication involves sending a message through one or more media to a receiver in order to generate a response. The messages sent, however, may not reach the target audience; either they may miss some people altogether or get lost in the general clutter or "noise" of everyday life. Even if a message reaches a specific individual, it may not be understood as intended or remembered long enough to result in the response desired by the sender. Of course, consumers, their interest whetted by need or curiosity, may be actively seeking information. While this curiosity increases the chance of their receiving communications on the topic of interest, it does not guarantee it.

Criteria for Effective Communication

What factors determine whether a marketing communication will be effective in stimulating an individual to behave in ways desired by the marketer?

First, a communication strategist must understand the day-to-day behavior of the target audience, so that messages can be delivered in places and at times likely to result in exposure. For mass-media advertising, this requires an understanding of the media habits of the target audience—the specific newspapers and magazines that they read; the times at which they are likely to watch television and listen to the radio, together with the types of broadcast programs they are most likely to turn to; and the routes and transportation modes that they use for traveling to work and on shopping or recreational trips. A sales representative needs to schedule calls for times at which prospects are likely to be willing to listen to a presentation.

Second, the placement, scheduling, format, and content of the communication must be designed in such a way that it stands out among competing stimuli, thereby gaining the target audience's attention. Success in this area involves skill in copy writing, design, and production. A visual ad that looks different (or an audio ad that sounds different) from other advertisements in the selected medium is one way of achieving this goal.

Next, the message must be stated in terms that the target audience will understand. The symbols used in communication are many; they include verbal language, body language, color, shape, music, and other sounds. But for communication to be effective, both communicator and audience must place similar interpretations on these symbols. Effective salespeople tailor their presentations to the characteristics of the prospect.

It is also very important that the communication be remembered by the receiver long enough to have the desired result. Essentially, the message must be designed to strike some responsive chord in the target audience. Good copy writing, like effective personal selling, requires an understanding of the needs, wants, concerns, and even fears of the audience.

THE COMMUNICATION MIX

The term *communication mix* is sometimes used to describe the array of communication tools available to marketers. Just as marketers need to combine the elements of the marketing mix (including communication) to produce a marketing program, they also need to select the most appropriate ingredients for the constituent communication program. The elements of the communication mix fall into four broad categories:

1. Personal selling
2. Advertising
3. Public relations/publicity
4. Promotional activities

Personal selling involves representatives of the marketer engaging directly in two-way communications with customers, either in person or via electronic media. In contrast, the latter three elements are all forms of one-way impersonal communications—from the marketer to the customers.

Personal Communication

Communication between individuals has a powerful advantage over mass-media communication in that the message usually goes directly from sender to recipient. A second major advantage is that personal communications are usually reciprocal, with the recipient being able to ask the sender (salesperson, retail clerk, or telephone operator) for clarification or additional information. A sender can adapt the content and presentation of the message to the characteristics of the recipient, and to that individual's needs and concerns as revealed during the interaction.

Different communication channels may be relatively more effective in moving consumers from one stage of the purchase decision process to another. At the beginning of the process, the use of mass media is likely to be the most cost-effective channel for stimulating awareness and providing background knowledge. As consumers move toward evaluation and purchase, however, they may actively seek out two-way personal communications that will enable them to ask specific questions that will help them make their final decisions.

Impersonal Communication

Although personal communication provides a powerful channel for messages, it is also costly and time-consuming. Much information can be delivered far more cheaply through impersonal sources, particularly when the objective is to generate initial awareness. Broadcast and print are the principal impersonal communication channels available to marketers.

Television is a powerful communication medium because it combines both audio and visual images. On the other hand, the high cost of producing quality commercials puts television outside the price range of many smaller or regional firms. Radio messages are less expensive than television messages, but radio messages leave more to the listener's imagination, because no visual images can be shown. Radio, however, can often reach people at times and in locations where television sets are unlikely to be found—for instance, while they are driving cars or at the beach.

A key characteristic of both television and radio is that broadcast messages are fleeting; they cannot be retained for later reference. Radio advertising is often used for short reminder advertising to encourage people to take action after previous messages, perhaps in other media, have built up awareness and knowledge of the product.

The print medium may be more effective than broadcasting for transmitting messages containing a great deal of information. Newspaper and magazine ads may be clipped for future reference; direct mail not only provides a message in tangible form but also offers the advantage that the content of the message can be personalized to meet the particular situation of the recipient. Like personal communications, a printed message is sometimes used to close the sale—typically, through the use of an order coupon in the body of the ad or an order form and postage paid envelope in a direct-mail communication.

Promotional ingenuity knows few bounds. A wide variety of promotional activities are available to the marketer. Coupons, premiums, contests, and price-packs (cents-off deals, two-for-one offers, etc.) are some of the short-term incentives offered to consumers to stimulate purchase of a product. These promotions all focus on the buying act itself, and not on such prior steps as building awareness of a brand. Even more targeted are point-of-purchase displays and in-store demonstrations which call the shopper's attention to the brand being promoted. In addition to consumer promotions, marketers also use trade promotion to gain wholesaler and retailer cooperation for their marketing programs. Trade promotions include buying-allowances (discounts on each unit of the product bought during a specified time period), free goods (for example, one case free for every twelve cases ordered), and display allowances (payments for devoting store space to, and setting up, retail displays). While all elements of a marketing communication plan need to be integrated, this is particularly true for promotional activities. If used indiscriminately, promotion can detract from a product's positioning strategy. Used wisely, it helps to support a longer term marketing strategy and also to deal with immediate problems that arise when sales goals are not being met.

MAKING COMMUNICATION DECISIONS

Situation Analysis

The starting point for making communication decisions as shown in *Exhibit I* is a situation analysis. This analysis should include an appraisal of:

- The organization's strengths, weaknesses, and objectives
- Product characteristics, pricing, and distribution systems
- Market segment characteristics and behavior
- Strategy and marketing activities of competitors and their anticipated responses to new initiatives
- Nature of suppliers and intermediaries and their own marketing strategy
- Possible constraints on future use of specific communication elements

Marketing Objectives

Based on the situation analysis, marketing opportunities and problems can be identified. Marketing objectives can then be set for the organization as a whole and for specific products (or product lines).

EXHIBIT 1   MARKETING COMMUNICATION DECISIONS

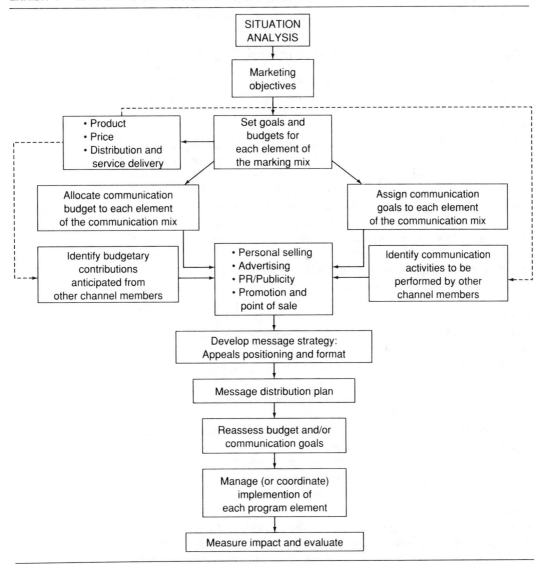

The objectives for individual products should relate to a specific time frame and may include:

- A positioning statement identifying the market segments at which the product is to be targeted and its distinctive features relative to competing alternatives
- Sales goals in terms of volume and revenues during the period
- Market share goals at specific points in time, with careful delineation of the market boundaries within which these shares will be computed

- Intermediate measures of performance, such as increased awareness, knowledge, preference, and intention to buy among target customers

Goals and Budgets for Communication Mix Elements

From establishment of overall marketing goals, managers must move to establish specific goals and strategies for each element of the communication mix, with tentative budgets being allocated for the substrategy associated with each element.

In any given campaign, each communication element should be assigned a specific role to play in achieving overall objectives. Communication goals may refer to the states of mind that a prospective customer may go through or the actions that a person may take in response to advertising, a sales presentation, or another communication activity. Often different elements in the communication mix are assigned different goals, such as moving a customer from unawareness to awareness of a product, from awareness to interest, from interest to brand preference, and from preference to purchase.

Setting the communication budget—both overall and for each element of the communication mix—is a difficult decision. Many companies appear to budget for the next year based on what they spent in the previous year. Some do this just by extrapolating the dollar level from the previous year, and others relate expenditures to sales, usage, or some other activity. This approach assumes, of course, that previous budgeting decisions were correct and also that there have been no significant changes in the marketplace.

A related budgeting philosophy is to spend whatever can be afforded. This assumes, at the extreme, that advertising and sales are unrelated and the value of advertising cannot be shown.

Another approach is to base expenditures on what competitors are doing. Paying attention to competition is important, and such information can play an important role in budget setting. But this approach of "competitive parity" ignores the differing goals, media efficiencies, and market segments of competitors. Moreover, this method implicitly assumes that competitors are spending optimally.

A frequently used approach is the "objective-and-task" method in which sub-objectives are established for the communication program (and its constituent elements) and a budget is set and allocated in terms of the tasks deemed necessary to achieve the assigned objectives. This is a sound approach when based on a detailed situation analysis, good understanding of the response of communication targets (e.g., awareness, knowledge, attitude) to different advertising levels, and careful evaluation of the worth of achieving different goals.

How can a marketing manager coordinate such varied communication activities as advertising copy writing, management of sales territories, and liaison with media outlets for publicity purposes? The answer lies in taking decisions across the entire communication mix in four key areas.

1. Communication goals
2. Message appeals positioning
3. Message format
4. Message-distribution plan

The balancing of goals, positioning, format, and distribution must reflect the current situation and available budget and may need to be changed over time in light of the product's performance in the market place as well as competitive responses and initiatives.

Message Appeals Positioning

Message strategy consists of two parts: what to say (*appeals positioning*) and how to say it (*format*). A campaign's appeals positioning, sometimes called the *copy platform* or *message idea,* should be based on the notion that each audience segment will be motivated by specific appeals or product features. The statement of appeals positioning or copy platform provides the framework or "blueprint" on which specific copy messages are built.

Message Format

Given a goal and a copy platform, what form should the message take? Should the advertising be humorous, use testimonials, include a demonstration, create fantasy, or evoke concern? What types of salespeople are needed and what should be included in their presentations to customers? Should the publicity release include pictures or not? Is there a role for a short-term sales promotion to dramatize some feature of the product?

Development of a message format is a creative process; many managers look for professional advice to help in copy execution. Suppliers of creative marketing services—such as advertising agencies, public-relations firms, and promotional specialists—can be retained to design and implement the necessary steps.

Message Distribution Plan

Once messages have been developed, the task is to decide how they should be sent. Advertising agencies are often well placed to undertake sophisticated analyses of media alternatives in order to allocate the budget in the most effective way, and they typically work with management to develop a media plan.

The objective of the media plan is to reach the desired target audience most effectively within a limited budget. Generally, a mix of media vehicles is required because achievement of communication goals usually requires that a message (or set of messages) be seen more than once and because only rarely can one medium reach all members of a segment.

SUMMARY

Communication decisions should be taken across the full array of communication mix elements instead of being compartmentalized, element by element. This poses a need for an integrated approach to advertising, personal selling, public relations, and promotional activities, instead of treating these as unrelated tools that are independent of one another. *Interdependence* and *synergy* should be the watchwords of communication planning. In particular, marketers should note the use of different elements to move the target audience through a sequence of stages—becoming aware of a problem, learning about a solution to that problem, and actually doing something to help resolve it.

A systematic approach to communication planning should begin with a situation analysis and proceed through the definition of marketing objectives, the establishment of size of a total communication budget, and the selection of a tentative budget mix for each element. Subsequent steps involve clear definition of goals for each communication element, determination of message appeals and positioning, selection of message format, and choice of message-distribution plan. Mass-media advertising has the advantage of low cost per impression, but to be successful it must make its way through a great clutter of competing messages. Personal selling is expensive, but it has the advantage of allowing direct two-way contact between the salesperson and the customer or prospect.

Vancouver Public Aquarium

Grant N. Poeter
Charles B. Weinberg

Richard Knight, Public Relations Director for the Vancouver Public Aquarium, reread the memo he had just received from Elizabeth Dewey, the aquarium's Educational Programs Co-ordinator. Ms. Dewey had proposed that, starting the following fall, the Vancouver Aquarium restrict weekday admissions to only school tours during the hours from 10:00 a.m. to 3:00 p.m. and exclude the general public during those hours.

During the 1986/1987 school year, the Vancouver Public Aquarium (VPA) offered five formal educational programs for students from kindergarten to grade 12. Further, the aquarium's trained guides (docents) gave children guided tours which included various performances offered to the general public. Though these tours were successful, there was evidence that both individual visitors and the schools felt that the aquarium could be better utilizing their facilities. For instance, some members of the general paying public found it irritating to browse through the galleries with "all the screaming kids around." Also, the teachers felt that the feeding performances, one of the highlights of the aquarium, could be geared more to the predominantly younger weekday market.

Because the school market was important to the aquarium and weekday attendance by the general paying public was low, Mr. Knight felt that he must examine the proposal fully before giving Ms. Dewey a response.

BACKGROUND

The VPA opened its doors on June 3, 1956, in Vancouver's Stanley Park, a popular recreational area adjacent to downtown Vancouver. Accessible by bus or car, the park was centrally located within the Greater Vancouver Regional District (GVRD), an association of Vancouver and its surrounding communities (Burnaby, North Vancouver, Richmond, West Vancouver, and others). Most of the GVRD's population of 1.3 million people lived within ten miles of Stanley Park.

The aquarium's facilities had undergone numerous renovations in the 30 years following its opening. In 1967, the B.C. Telephone Pool was constructed to hold dolphins, but the aquarium acquired a killer whale (orca) instead. It quickly became evident that the pool was unsuitable for such a large mammal, and so in 1972, the killer whale pool was opened. In conjunction with these outdoor "gallery" changes, the aquarium continued to improve its indoor exhibits. Perhaps the most significant indoor change was the addition of the Amazon Gallery, which recreated the environment of an Amazon River valley. Opened in 1983 by Queen Elizabeth II, the Amazon Gallery, with its 2,200 specimens, was the only indoor exhibit of its kind in the world. Funds for it were donated by government, VPA members, and private donations. In May 1986, the Max Bell Marine Mammal Centre was opened, incorporating the first Killer Whale Habitat in the world. Designed and constructed to house only killer whales, this exhibit set what many experts viewed as the world standard in both exhibit philosophy and animal husbandry.

With Expo '86, Vancouver's 100th birthday, and the aquarium's 30th birthday, 1986 was a record year for attendance with 876,825 visitors (*Exhibit 1*).

Increasing attendance beyond that level was a challenge that faced Mr. Knight.

Current Offerings

In 1987, the aquarium housed some 7,100 specimens (669 species) of marine and aquatic life. Its sea otter breeding program was most successful and had helped to preserve this once endangered species; since 1983, five pups had been born at the aquarium. The aquarium saw itself on the leading edge of both marine research and display of mammals and Northern Pacific marine species.

The main product offered to visitors by the aquarium was the opportunity to see its collection of aquatic life. Related species were housed in "galleries," usually by geographic region. In addition, the

EXHIBIT 1   ANNUAL ATTENDANCE, 1982–1986

Attendance	1982	1983	1984	1985	1986
Paid					
Adults	216,161	257,400	237,312	248,742	329,334
Youths and senior citizens	76,123	84,276	70,713	79,285	—
Groups	43,465	45,665	46,605	34,983	55,280
Education programs	10,580	6,226	8,983	14,638	—
Family rate	166,696	181,107	166,736	120,409	196,481
Children and seniors	—	—	—	—	86,186
Youths	—	—	—	—	22,784
	513,025	574,674	530,349	498,057	690,065
Other attendance					
Members	54,783	91,891	73,604	66,963	73,148
Other	70,399	89,003	99,614	87,162	113,612
Total	638,207	755,568	703,567	652,182	876,825
Single admission, per person					
Adults	$ 4.25	$ 4.50	$ 4.50	$ 5.00	$ 5.25
Senior citizens	$ 2.00	$ 2.25	$ 2.25	$ 2.50	$ 2.75
Youths (5–18 yrs.)	$ 2.00	$ 2.25	$ 2.25	—	—
Youths (12–18 yrs.)	—	—	—	$ 3.75	—
Youths	—	—	—	—	$ 4.00
Children	—	—	—	$ 2.50	$ 2.75
Group admission					
Family	$10.00	$11.00	$11.00	$13.00	$13.25
Adults, 10–34 persons	$ 3.00	$ 3.25	$ 3.25	—	—
35 or more	$ 2.50	$ 2.75	$ 2.75	—	—
Adults, 10 or more	—	—	—	$ 3.75	$ 4.00
Youths, 10 or more	$ 1.25	$ 1.50	$ 1.50	$ 2.00	$ 2.25

aquarium offered whale shows, films, tours, and special showings (such as "Fishes of China"), all included in the admission price. There were no restaurants or food services on the aquarium's grounds, although a number of food stands were located nearby in Stanley Park.

The aquarium also offered several secondary products. It had rented its facilities for social functions; companies could have staff parties, meetings, and dinner/dances in the various galleries; for children, birthday parties, complete with cake, were available. The aquarium also offered special lectures and school programs on aquatic life. Members could take advantage of whale watching tours, beach walks, and special previews. These programs had been very successful.

The aquarium also ran a retail operation, the Clam Shell Gift Shop, which sold aquarium-related books, animal prints, nature calendars, and numerous aquarium souvenirs.

MISSION

The VPA stated its mission as follows:

The Vancouver Aquarium is dedicated to the preservation and enhancement of aquatic life through education, recreation, and research. It is a private, non-profit society, and is completely self-supporting.

This mission statement was the driving force behind the aquarium. Every program had to fit into one of the three categories in the statement; all staff were required to follow its guidelines. As expressed by VPA staff and literature, the aquarium's main business was to educate the public about aquatic life. The aquarium accomplished this through such activities as demonstrations and interpretive programs. In particular, the VPA offered numerous programs—such as lectures, tours, and beach walks—to educate school children, teens, and adults.

MARKETS

During the past two years, the aquarium's average weekday attendance in winter had been 550 patrons per day (see *Exhibit 2*). Weekends were busier, with

Saturdays averaging 1,300 patrons and Sundays averaging 2,100. Mr. Knight felt that Saturday's attendance could be higher, possibly reaching Sunday's levels.

During this summer, there was still a difference between weekdays and weekends but general attendance levels were higher. In fact, the weekday levels were more than double those of the winter months.

The aquarium had at least six significant markets: schools, members, general admissions, donors, volunteers, and scientists. Mr. Knight felt that the first five markets would be affected by any decision relating to school tour admissions.

Members

By the end of 1986, the Vancouver Public Aquarium Association had 39,360 members, based on the sale of 15,077 memberships (up from 11,850 in 1985) to individuals, couples, and families. Members accounted for 73,148 of the aquarium's total attendance of 876,825.

Diverse programs were offered to this group, which ranged from special educational programs to free admission to the aquarium; educational programs included whale watching in Johnstone Strait, previews of special displays, Galiano Island beach walks, and behind-the-scenes tours. Members received a 10% discount on gift shop purchases and an informative newsletter, called the *Sea Pen,* about once a month.

Mr. Knight realized that the membership was vital to the aquarium's finances and philosophy. He wondered how the members would react to not being allowed to use "their" aquarium on demand.

General Admissions

According to the 1986 Annual Report, the general admissions category accounted for 61% of revenues (see *Exhibit 3*). A recent survey of summer visitors found that 97% of those surveyed felt they had received good value for their entertainment dollar. The aquarium offered various programs to educate and entertain this public. For example, there were feeding shows, interpretive talks, films and volunteers to an-

EXHIBIT 2 VANCOUVER PUBLIC AQUARIUM AVERAGE DAILY ATTENDANCE FOR 1985 AND 1986

1985

	Monday	Tuesday	Wednesday	Thursday	Friday	Saturday	Sunday	Holidays	Total/ month
January	436	493	400	391	434	1,399	2,157	1,036	26,147
February	725	545	395	376	949	1,301	2,622	0	26,644
March	832	712	707	818	1,042	2,139	2,866	1,293	44,267
April	928	812	746	858	888	1,944	2,508	2,420	54,335
May	1,458	1,041	1,085	1,214	1,283	2,144	3,081	3,105	50,452
June	1,883	2,157	1,646	1,882	2,155	2,365	3,189	0	66,664
July	4,361	3,314	3,822	3,694	3,357	3,858	4,181	4,052	119,047
August	3,731	3,801	4,221	3,477	3,268	4,161	4,992	5,436	123,214
September	957	1,121	1,081	968	1,489	2,287	3,265	3,883	49,136
October	957	678	578	419	957	1,764	1,694	1,687	28,271
November	405	274	498	378	347	925	1,961	2,831	21,916
December	340	341	359	249	254	532	1,475	1,482	29,263
Winter av.*	616	507	491	439	664	1,343	2,129	1,388	29,418
Total av.	1,418	1,274	1,296	1,227	1,369	2,068	2,833	2,269	53,280

1986

	Monday	Tuesday	Wednesday	Thursday	Friday	Saturday	Sunday	Holidays	Total/ month
January	447	401	350	311	535	1,426	2,289	1,452	28,341
February	475	401	585	494	750	1,027	1,675	0	21,622
March	687	523	553	709	758	1,798	2,596	2,633	41,076
April	672	641	684	635	586	1,261	1,741	2,162	34,483
May	1,614	1,997	2,613	2,080	1,928	3,244	3,366	4,746	79,204
June	3,396	3,825	3,711	3,662	3,496	4,409	4,763	0	117,200
July	6,342	5,615	5,819	5,173	5,715	6,472	6,950	4,609	182,367
August	6,238	5,810	6,142	5,290	4,944	5,450	6,622	7,550	180,315
September	2,152	1,966	2,361	2,711	2,231	3,417	4,304	5,209	82,848
October	688	978	1,041	869	1,202	2,005	2,813	2,740	43,540
November	406	442	535	327	555	1,029	1,277	1,840	22,021
December	434	443	341	382	307	523	1,216	1,832	29,402
Winter av.*	523	531	568	515	685	1,301	1,978	1,750	31,000
Total av.	1,963	1,920	2,061	1,887	1,917	2,672	3,301	2,898	71,868

*January, February, March, October, November, December.

swer exhibit enquiries. In addition, the aquarium was open for extended hours during the summer.

The VPA's primary market was the Greater Vancouver Regional District. This area accounted for 28% of summer admissions and for 65% of off-season visitors (see *Appendix*). A second market was the province of British Columbia, outside Greater Vancouver.

Other areas served included the Pacific Northwest of the United States to the south and the province of Alberta to the east. Though no programs were designed for these markets, visitors from these areas did patronize the aquarium during the summer months.

During the summer months, visitor parking, although free, could be a problem. Unfortunately, the

EXHIBIT 3 ANNUAL FINANCIAL REPORTS FOR VANCOUVER PUBLIC AQUARIUM, 1982–1986
(in 000s)

	1982		1983		1984		1985		1986*	
	$	%	$	%	$	%	$	%	$	%
Revenue										
Admissions	$1,612	70%	$1,989	70%	$1,855	71%	$1,937	69%	$2,786	61%
Gross margin/store	268	12	303	11	308	12	313	11	894	20
Membership fees	198	9	300	10	278	11	288	10	409	9
Deferred income transfer	101	4	100	4	—	—	—	—	—	—
Donations and grants	84	4	84	3	83	3	148	5	226	5
General operating revenue	44	2	69	2	74	3	134	5	232	5
	$2,308	100%	$2,844	100%	$2,599	100%	$2,820	100%	$4,548	100%
Expenditure										
Specimen care and display	$ 670	29%	$ 868	31%	$ 790	30%	$ 563	20%	$ 941	25%
Engineering and operations	597	26	714	26	668	25	751	27	—	—
Administration	359	15	414	15	392	15	673	24	—	—
Attendance and membership	353	15	398	14	414	15	385	14	—	—
Education and research	344	15	404	14	425	16	407	15	—	—
Life support/building operations	—	—	—	—	—	—	—	—	875	23
Administration and services	—	—	—	—	—	—	—	—	652	17
Store and admissions	—	—	—	—	—	—	—	—	513	14
Education and visitor services	—	—	—	—	—	—	—	—	339	9
Promotion	—	—	—	—	—	—	—	—	229	6
Member services	—	—	—	—	—	—	—	—	130	3
Scientific studies	—	—	—	—	—	—	—	—	109	3
	$2,323	$100%	$2,798	100%	$2,698	100%	$2,779	100%	$3,789	100%

*In 1986, the VPA implemented a new accounting system with redefined accounts.

VPA could do little to alleviate this problem because adjacent land in Stanley Park could not be appropriated for extra parking.

Donors

The donor market was seen as very important for the aquarium. Without donor support, many of the aquarium's capital projects could not have been completed. For instance, some 17,000 individuals, 130 corporations, 4 foundations, and the federal government contributed more than $4.3 million to build the Max Bell Marine Mammal Centre. The aquarium recognized donors in various ways, including plaques, exhibit names (like the H. R. MacMillan Tropical Gallery), and publication of donors' names in VPA publications.

Volunteers

The 180 VPA volunteers, made up of Aquarium Association members and their families, volunteered 13,000 hours to the aquarium in 1986. They supervised educational tours, served as docents for school tours, and worked in the Clam Shell Gift Shop. Management believed that the main attractions for volunteers were their sense of pride in the aquarium and genuine concern for its success.

Schools

Over 7,500 students took part in the following VPA educational programs in the most recent year:

Water Wonders	Kindergarten, grades 1 and 2
Secrets of Survival	Grades 3 and 4
Mysterious Marine Mammals	Grades 5, 6, 7
Spineless Wonders (a laboratory program)	Grades 5, 6, 7
B.C.'s Marine Invertebrates (a laboratory program)	Grades 11 and 12
Royaume Aquatique	French-speaking groups
Traveling Teacher	Outreach program—an aquarium teacher visiting schools

In addition to these formal programs, tours of the aquarium, films, and interpretive workshops were offered to school groups. To accommodate French Immersion classes, the aquarium offered French-language tours. There was also a "traveling teacher," employed by the aquarium, who toured the province teaching students in out-of-town schools about aquatic life and the work being done by the aquarium.

To make teachers aware of the aquarium's programs, each school in the Vancouver area received a descriptive brochure at the beginning of the school year. During the third week of September, the VPA offered an "Open House for Educators" that gave teachers the opportunity to participate in workshops, preview the programs offered, and pick up various resource materials. Afterwards, teachers could book their classes into the programs and tours.

These programs were very popular. Usually most available spaces for the formal programs were filled by the second week in October. During the school year, the aquarium averaged five school tours per day. At present, the aquarium could handle no more than six tours in a day. Though school groups were given special group rates and a volunteer was provided to guide the tours, no other special accommodations were offered by the aquarium.

Ms. Dewey's memo offered one possible response to the popularity of these programs. Her memo read, in part, as follows:

During the recent professional development programs, held by my department, many teachers expressed some disappointment in their inability to book their students into the aquarium's programs ... With such a demand for these programs, an increase in service to the children of Vancouver will be beneficial to both parties. First, if the aquarium were to offer more programs, the aquarium would increase exposure and also help revenues. Second, the children would be more aware of the work done by the aquarium and may become active aquarium members in the future.

To accomplish this increase in school programs, we would need to set aside certain hours for the use by students. Since most school tours are conducted in the mornings and early afternoons, we propose that these tours be run between the hours of 10 a.m. and 3 p.m. During these hours only children and their supervisors would be able to view the galleries ... This would at least double our current capacity for handling school tours. If such a program were adopted, the feedings and interpretive segments could be targeted to a younger population. Though it would be more work at the beginning, I feel that such a program could be very successful.

Ms. Dewey's proposal would require the VPA to alter its presentations (such as the killer whale feedings) to better suit a school-age audience and to restrict the VPA's galleries to school children until 3 p.m. on weekdays. Closing the galleries to the general public on school days would have two effects on the VPA's operation. First, the "conflict" between the general public and school tours would be eliminated; the public would not be fighting the crowds of school children. However, the frustrations of aquarium members and the general admission market might shift from annoyance with the school children to anger at not being allowed admission at all. Secondly, the Clam Shell Gift Shop's hours of operation could be reduced; the shop would not need to be open during the hours of school tours. Currently, the aquarium used two full-time salaried employees and one part-time staff member, in addition to volunteers, to handle admissions and run the gift shop during weekdays. If the proposal were adopted, the aquarium's staffing needs could be reduced by at least one paid position during the school tour periods.

Mr. Knight sat down to do a preliminary study to see if the proposal was economically feasible. During the winter months, an average of 550 people per day visited the aquarium on weekdays. Of these 550, roughly 70% were "General Admission" (385 persons). A "typical" weekday group consisted of two adults ($5.50 each) and one child ($3). Mr. Knight felt that for the school proposal to be implemented, revenues from the school programs would have to be increased to cover at least part of the $1,700 loss of general admissions revenues. Of course, some proportion of the weekday visitors would come another time. There was also the possibility of opening the aquarium to general admission after 3 p.m., but currently few winter visitors came at that time.

School admissions were priced at $2.50 per student and the average school group's size was 34 students. Mr. Knight wondered if the aquarium, particularly the volunteer guides, could handle a significant increase in school tours. If not, could the aquarium attract new volunteer docents? He was relatively confident that the aquarium would not have to hire more paid staff.

PRICING AND PROMOTIONS

VPA's prices were to be increased by an average of 10% on April 1, 1987 (see *Exhibit 4*). Adult admission would then cost $5.50, a price that included both the killer whale and beluga whale shows, tours, seal feedings, films, and entrance to all galleries.

Pricing policy was ultimately determined by the Vancouver Public Aquarium Association membership through its Board of Governors. Though the board had the final say, most pricing changes were initiated by VPA staff. The pricing policy was cost-oriented. The aquarium budgeted its expenditures for the coming year and then set ticket prices, membership fees, etc., to balance these expenses. Discounting practices were usually reserved for the aquarium's membership and groups of ten people or more.

The aquarium had two short-term promotional pricing programs. Both were offered in December

EXHIBIT 4

THE VANCOUVER PUBLIC AQUARIUM'S PRICE LIST (as of April 1, 1987)

General admission	Price	Membership fee	Price
Individuals			
Adult	$ 5.50	Adult	$20.00
Youth or senior	4.25	Special*	15.00
Child	3.00	Couple†	30.00
Family	14.00	Family	35.00
Group (10 +)			
Adult	4.25		
Child	2.50		
School	2.50		

*This group included students, out-of-province residents, and seniors.

†A senior couple could purchase a membership for $15.00.

Source: Vancouver Public Aquarium's Annual Report.

and were marketed as the aquarium's gift to the city. During the first week in December, general admission was free. In 1986, 6,906 people took advantage of this opportunity. There were occasional other free days. For example, on March 9, 1987, the aquarium had a free day to thank Vancouver for its general support of the Tropical Fish Gallery restocking. An astounding 12,000 people visited the aquarium.

The second promotion was the Christmas train program, which the aquarium participated in for the first time in 1986. In conjunction with Vancouver's Stanley Park Zoo, the aquarium had special nightly openings during one week of the Christmas holiday period. Patrons purchased a train ticket, entitling them to ride on a specially decorated miniature train. The train ride ran through a portion of Stanley Park as a tourist and family attraction. For most of the year, the train was run only during daylight hours. After the ride, the VPA offered admission to the aquarium and special performances of killer whale shows at a reduced price. The program helped increase awareness of the aquarium, but rain during four of the five nights kept attendance down to only 860 people.

Communication

The aquarium's communication objective was to increase awareness of VPA programs. The membership was kept informed through special direct mail communication and regular quarterly editions of *Sea Pen* magazine. The local, non-member segments were exposed to PSA advertisements on both radio and television. In addition, newspaper advertising was used to promote special events/exhibits. Aquarium brochures were available at Tourist Information Centres, Grayline Tour Booths, and at the Vancouver Travel Infocentre. During the summer months, billboard advertising was used.

Advertising budgets were set in December for the following year, with few changes in the mix from year to year. (See *Exhibit 5*.)

Relations with the media were very good—so good that sometimes things got a little hectic. Along with regular coverage of aquarium events by local news media, major promotions generated wider coverage. The opening of the new Killer Whale Habitat, the appearance of the killer whales in the Vancouver Bach Choir/Vancouver Symphony Orchestra's "In Celebration of Whales" concert, the birth of two sea otters, and the major "Fishes of China" display all received national coverage in 1986. When an act of vandalism wiped out almost the entire tropical marine collection in late 1986, media around the world picked up the story. In addition to news coverage, TV programs like "Midday," "Sesame Street," and "The Nature of Things" featured segments on the Vancouver Public Aquarium. "Danger Bay," the CBC/Disney series, was filmed at the aquarium for a third season in 1986, continuing the adventures of Grant Roberts and his family.

The aquarium had recently started to track its visitors and ask how they found out about the aquarium. For instance, in a summer 1986 survey, 24% of people surveyed stated that they had seen an aquarium brochure. However, 54% stated that they hadn't seen any advertising. With a 1987 budget of $120,000, Mr. Knight wondered how he could be more effective in increasing awareness.

Operating Hours

The aquarium had three distinct sets of operating hours. During the summer, the aquarium was open

EXHIBIT 5 FISCAL BUDGET 1986: PUBLIC RELATIONS/ADVERTISING

	Jan.	Feb.	March	April	May	June	July	August	Sept.	Oct.	Nov.	Dec.	Total
Radio			600		700	700	500	500	300	300	500	500	4,600
Television				1,500									1,500
Newspapers			500		500	200	500		500	300		500	3,000
"Thank-you"*					5,000								5,000
Magazines	18,860	1,670	170	580	7,580	1,980	1,910	860	580	720	670	1,220	36,800
Brochures		3,000	20,000										23,000
Brochure distribution	325	325	325	325	729	729	729	729	379	379	325	325	5,624
Photography		1,000	1,000	1,000	1,000	1,000							5,000
Passes		250			250			250			250		1,000
Billboards						6,300	6,300	6,300					18,900
Clam Shell†		200			400		400		400		400		1,800
Schedules				5,000									5,000
Contingency	1,000	1,000	1,000	1,000	1,000	1,000	1,000	1,000	1,000	1,000	1,000		11,000
Total month	20,185	7,445	23,595	9,405	17,159	11,909	11,339	9,639	3,159	2,699	3,145	2,545	122,224

 * "Thank-you" was budgeted as a full-page advertisement to thank contributors for their support in building the Max Bell Marine Mammal Centre.

 †Point-of-purchase display materials to be used in the Clam Shell gift shop.

from 9:00 a.m. to 9:00 p.m., seven days per week. VPA managers felt that the extended summer hours increased attendance and also took advantage of the longer daylight hours. However, a 1982 study found that only 28% of visitors were aware of the extended summer hours. During the spring and fall, the aquarium was open from 10:00 a.m. to 6:00 p.m. Management felt that the public would not patronize the aquarium during winter evenings, so for winter months, the hours were further reduced to 10:00 a.m. to 5:00 p.m. To increase revenues, the aquarium offered evening and restricted daytime rentals of the facilities from September to May. The typical fee ranged from $100 for a luncheon meeting using a small room in the aquarium to $1,700 for use of the entire facility during an evening. (Food was provided by outside caterers.) In 1986, the VPA received more than $200,000 in rental revenue.

Though the aquarium had used these opening hours in the past, Mr. Knight had heard of other non-profit groups who had altered their hours to "fit" the working public. In essence, these institutions would not be open in the mornings or early afternoons but would keep their facilities open during the evening to accommodate the working public.

Weekend hours could be kept the same or extended into the evening. This might allow the aquarium to keep its present weekend customers, and if the public knew that the aquarium was open until the same hour every night, awareness of the later hours would increase. If management were to set the same operating hours for the whole year, much of the confusion caused by the changing hours might be alleviated.

THE DECISION

At February's board meeting, various alternatives for more effective use of aquarium facilities had been raised. Board approval would be required prior to implementation of any recommendation to change opening hours significantly. Also, all programs had to be compatible with the aquarium's mission statement. Though the VPA had been successful in the past, Mr. Knight felt that a new approach to marketing could improve usage of the aquarium.

He recognized that Ms. Dewey's proposal had merits and that the survey results might help the aquarium better target its winter markets.

As Mr. Knight drove home, he wondered, "Can I solve these problems?" Specifically, he needed to answer these questions:

1. How could the $120,000 promotional budget be better spent?
2. How could the aquarium boost its attendance on weekdays and on Saturday?
3. Should Elizabeth Dewey's school proposal be implemented? If so, what communications would have to be done to minimize the risks associated with it and maximize the benefits? If not, how should the issues Ms. Dewey raised be addressed?

APPENDIX

SELECTED RESULTS FROM JANUARY, 1987, QUESTIONNAIRE*

Question	Response	No. Surveyed	
		Weekday	**Weekend**
1. Are you a resident of the Greater Vancouver Regional District?	Yes	71	60
	No	51	20
2. Are you currently a member of the Vancouver Aquarium?	Yes	26	34
	No	96	46
3. Is this your first visit to the Aquarium?	Yes	47	23
	No	75	57
4. Was your last visit to the Aquarium within the last two years?	Yes	23	46
	No	52	11
5. On average, how much time did you spend on this visit?	Less than ½ hour	0	0
	½–1 hour	44	30
	1–3 hours	72	50
	Over 3 hours	6	0
6. Are you alone or are you visiting with others?	Alone	9	4
	Others	113	76
7. How did you first learn about the Aquarium?	Friend/relative	29	15
	TV	9	0
	Radio	2	0
	Tourist magazine	2	0
	Brochure	8	4
	Newspaper	0	1
	Magazine article	2	0
	Billboard	0	0
	"Discovered"	14	0
	"Just knew"	40	40
	Other	16	10
8. Do you feel that you have received your entertainment dollar value at the Aquarium?	Yes	122	78
	No	0	2
9. Sex:	Male	85	47
	Female	37	33
10. What is your age group?	18–25	22	4
	26–30	34	18
	31–35	14	18
	36–40	22	14
	41–50	10	10
	51–60	12	8
	Over 61	8	8

*Total respondents: Weekdays: 122; weekends: 80.

Source: Based on a survey conducted during two weeks in January 1987. Interviewers were stationed near the exit and asked visitors, as they were leaving, to answer a brief questionnaire.

Montecito State College

Christopher H. Lovelock

"We need to take a hard look at how we're going to promote our extension programs and courses next year." Dr. Rosemary Shannon, Dean of Extension Studies at Montecito State College, was meeting in March 1992 with her assistant, Harry Fourman, to discuss plans for advertising and other communications for the 1992–93 school year.

BACKGROUND

Montecito State College (MSC) was located in Montecito, a suburb of the large western city of Sherman. The City of Sherman had a population of 755,000, while the metro area had a population of 1.8 million. On average, there were 2.6 persons per household.

The college, one of several in the Jefferson State College System, was comprised of the undergraduate day division, the graduate school, and the Division of Extension Studies.

MSC enrolled a total of 6,200 students in the day

division, 2,950 in extension studies, and 1,100 in the graduate school. Its undergraduate courses emphasized a variety of technical and business-related subjects, education, and the liberal arts. The graduate school offered MA, MS, and M.Ed. degrees in a number of fields, and had a good regional reputation for its programs in education, management, hotel administration, and psychology.

EXTENSION STUDIES

The Division of Extension Studies was responsible for a wide range of undergraduate and graduate courses offered during the late afternoon, weekday evenings, and Saturday morning hours, as well as for day and evening courses during two intensive summer sessions. Although these offerings were directed primarily at people holding jobs or having other responsibilities that made it difficult to attend on a full-time basis during the day, about 15 percent of the enrollees in extension courses were full-time undergraduates.

In addition, the division also sponsored a range of continuing education (CE) programs—short, noncredit workshops, courses, and seminars. Certificates were awarded upon satisfactory completion of selected courses. The structure and format of these ranged from one- to two-day workshops and seminars, to courses of five two-hour sessions given at weekly intervals, to twelve three-hour sessions offered twice weekly over a six-week period.

The tuition for degree courses in the Extension Division was $75.00 per credit hour for state residents and $125.00 for nonresidents and foreign students; auditors (noncredit) paid $50.00. Tuition fees were set by the Regents of the Jefferson State College System and had to be approved by the State Legislature. These fees were the same for all seven colleges in the system. Although degree courses ranged in length from 2 to 5 credits, the great majority carried 3 credits. After excluding cancellations, a total of 185 extension degree courses were offered at MSC. Fees for the continuing education programs ranged from $75–300—depending on the nature and length of the offering—and were at the discretion of the dean, subject to the approval of the president of the College.

The division had substantial autonomy with the College. It was required to be self-supporting, but was not assessed for many institutional costs, such as classroom space. Courses were taught by both full-time and adjunct faculty who, in most instances, were paid a fixed stipend per course. Part-time faculty were paid a flat rate of $2,500 to $3,200 per semester for a 3-credit course, depending on rank. Typically, courses met once a week for 2½ hours, although a few had two 75-minute classes each week.

The College brochure listed 109 different extension sources for credit, many of them offered in both semesters. But, with a few exceptions, courses were automatically cancelled if student registrations failed to reach a pre-defined minimum. Some 900 of the students in Extension Studies in 1991–92 were participants in continuing education programs. (This figure excluded participants in one- and two-day seminars or company-sponsored programs.) The balance of 2,050 accounted for a total of some 5,200 course registrations during fall and spring semesters. Not all students were enrolled both semesters.

Dr. Shannon, a tenured associate professor of political science, was appointed dean of extension stud-ies in July 1991 and had essentially inherited her predecessor's strategy for the current school year (including the two summer sessions). She expressed the view that MSC needed to devote greater commitment to its extension program, whose quality she regarded as uneven.

SATELLITE CAMPUSES

In addition to the permanent campus in Montecito, where all-day undergraduate and graduate courses were offered, MSC also operated four "satellite" campuses in the evenings for its degree courses. These consisted of high school facilities, made available to MSC free of charge, in Sherman City, and the suburban towns of North Sherman, San Lucas, and Puget. Course registration in these four satellite campuses accounted for 20 percent of the total; enrollments per course were lower than at the main Montecito campus and there was a much higher rate of course cancellations. *Exhibit 1* summarizes enrollments in extension studies at MSC over the past five years, while *Exhibit 2* shows the geographic breakdown of students' home locations.

Continuing education programs were generally held at the Montecito campus, although a few had been held at one or other of the satellites. Periodically, CE courses would be commissioned from MSC by a large employer or other organization. In this case the employer's offices or a nearby hotel would be used.

MSC had operated a satellite campus in Sherman City ever since 1962, when the main campus had relocated from there to Montecito. For many years, this had been the only satellite operation, but from 1979 onwards the College began to experiment with different locations, some of which had subsequently been closed due to lack of success in attracting students. Past experience had shown that satellite campuses tended to draw from a much smaller radius than did the main campus. In selecting specific facilities, the division now looked for easily accessible sites situated near major highways. Availability of adequate parking was essential, while access to public transportation services was a strong plus.

EXHIBIT 1

COURSE REGISTRATIONS IN DIVISION OF EXTENSION STUDIES,
MONTECITO STATE COLLEGE, 1987–92

Campus	1987–88	1988–89	1989–90	1990–91	1991–92
Montecito	3,775	3,829	4,006	4,218	4,163
Sherman City	615	603	545	421	481
North Sherman	—	110	213	246	232
Weston	68	96	—	—	—
Puget	—	—	—	113	98
Arvin	118	—	—	—	—
San Lucas	—	165	198	214	209
Total academic course registrations*	4,576	4,803	4,962	5,312	5,203
Total continuing education enrollments**	628	714	773	820	903

*About 80 percent of these registrants sought academic credit; the balance enrolled as auditors.
**Not broken out separately by campus since almost all continuing education courses were held at MSC's main campus in Montecito.
Source: Division of Extension Studies, Montecito State College.

EXHIBIT 2

HOME LOCATIONS OF EXTENSION REGISTRANTS AT
MONTECITO STATE COLLEGE, 1991–92*

Location**	Students Enrolled for Credit in Extension Courses	Participants in Continuing Education Seminars
City of Sherman	29%	17%
Balance of Sherman County	7	8
North Sherman	9	11
Balance of Orezona County	30	23
Santa Rosa County	9	22
Wendell County	14	16
Other	2	3

*This included students taking courses at the satellite campuses.
**See Exhibit 3.
Source: Division of Extension Studies, Montecito State College.

After careful appraisal of the performance of the different satellite campuses in fall semester 1991 Dean Shannon had decided to close the existing Puget campus and to look for a new location in northwest Sherman County. She believed she had identified a promising site in Pine Creek.

One of the objectives of the satellite campuses was to attract students who might begin their studies at a satellite and then later go on to complete their degrees by taking more advanced courses at Montecito. However, few appeared to be doing this. On the other hand, students who lived near a satellite would sometimes travel all the way into Montecito to take courses there which were available at the satellite. Dean Shannon was not entirely sure why this happened (but surmised that it might reflect the greater use of part-time, adjunct faculty at the satellites). She noted that this practice indirectly led to cancellation of courses at satellites, because course registrations there had often been only one or two students short of the minimum (typically 15 students).

COMPETITION

Dean Shannon described the market for evening credit courses in the Greater Sherman area as "highly competitive," with strong competition coming from the University of Sherman and Wallace College (both private institutions), Sherman State College, Lakeview Junior College, and Valley Junior College. Additional competition came from the University of Jefferson and two county-financed community colleges in the metropolitan area. The dean did not consider the two proprietary schools in Sherman City to be direct competitors, since they were oriented primarily towards vocational education in fields such as computer programming and dental hygiene.[1]

Like Montecito State, a growing number of both public and private institutions operated satellite campuses in the suburbs and in outlying towns. Typically, the facilities used were local high schools whose classrooms were available for evening use. *Exhibit 3* shows the location of all main and satellite campuses in the Greater Sherman area.

Tuition at private institutions was sometimes twice as high per credit hour as MSC's. Wallace College, which emphasized business and the social sciences, had been very aggressive in promoting its offerings, making extensive use of radio and newspaper advertising. Although enrollments had risen steadily at their main campus in Santa Rosa, Dean Shannon had heard that their three satellite campuses were not doing especially well.

The two proprietary schools, one owned by a major industrial conglomerate, advertised widely on TV. The *Sherman Monitor* had recently published an exposé of one of these schools, charging that its advertising deliberately misled prospective students. It was rumored that the state attorney general's office would soon undertake an investigation.

COMMUNICATIONS

The principal approaches used to promote the Extension Division had been to undertake advertising in the *Monitor* and selected suburban papers, and to publish a catalog. Some 20,000 copies of the catalog were prepared and printed each summer at a total cost of $18,500. About 4,000 were mailed out to a variety of organizations and agencies, including public libraries and company personnel departments. Others were sent out in response to requests or dis-

tributed at various locations on campus. The unit cost of printing an extra copy was 27.7 cents, and bulk rate mailing costs were 11.1 cents per copy. The catalog was printed in black and white on medium quality stock.

For its advertising, the division had traditionally used the *Sherman Monitor* and selected local newspapers. Although some competitors took full-page newspaper advertisements, and used these to list each and every course offered, MSC's strategy had been to take smaller format advertisements (between one-eighth and one-fourth of a page) which promoted the Montecito State name, listed the locations of the main campus and the various satellite campuses, highlighted the fields in which extension courses were offered, and provided a clip-out coupon and a telephone number which could be used to obtain further information.

In early December 1990, the Extension Division had joined forces with other divisions of the College to develop a four-page newsprint brochure, mailed to 100,000 homes in Montecito and surrounding towns. This included a listing of all spring semester extension courses. The total costs of this mailing (of which Extension Studies paid one-third), were $6,600 for production and printing, plus $9,700 for preparation and mailing. A certain amount of radio advertising had been used by the division of extension studies; 1991-92 costs amounted to about $8,500. However, Dean Shannon expressed doubts about the value of radio advertising. Few registrants could be traced to radio advertising in a recent survey (*Exhibit 4*), nor was radio often mentioned when telephone enquirers were asked by extension staff how they had learned of Montecito State.

In February 1992, the division had conducted a mail survey of evening degree students registered in the fall who did not graduate at the end of that semester and had not reregistered in January for the spring semester. Among other things, this asked respondents their primary source of learning about the courses they took. Of the 638 questionnaires mailed, 206 had been completed and returned. Selected responses are shown in *Exhibit 4*. Friends and relatives were given as the primary source of information

---

[1]Proprietary schools are run as profit-making businesses offering vocationally oriented courses. Typically, they do not offer courses for academic credit (although certificates are awarded on completion of a course) and are not accredited.

EXHIBIT 3

MAP OF GREATER SHERMAN AREA SHOWING CITIES IN WHICH ACADEMIC EXTENSION COURSES WERE OFFERED

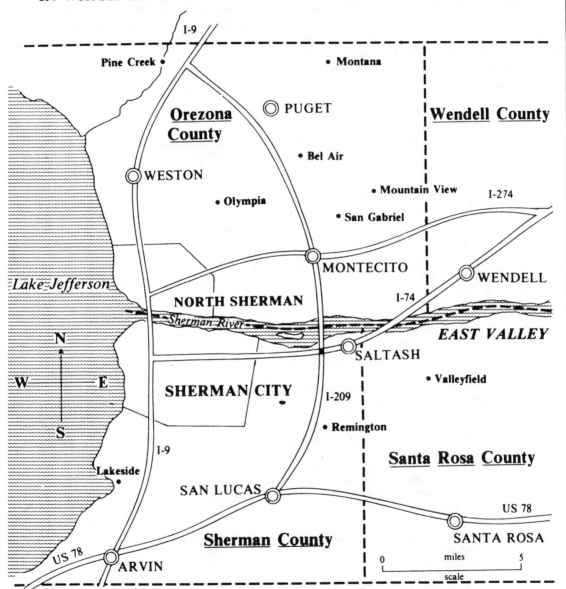

NOTE: The Greater Sherman Metropolitan Area includes all Sherman and Orezona Counties, plus SW Wendell County and NW Santa Rosa County. There are over 40 separate towns and municipalities in the Metro area (which is heavily urbanized), but only selected town names are shown on the map, which also shows the major freeways serving the Metro area. The largest suburban centers outside Sherman City and North Sherman are marked with a double circle.

about courses, followed by professional referrals, *Monitor* advertising, and advertisements in local suburban newspapers.

In addition to being listed in the catalog, most of the 70 continuing education courses offered at MSC were also promoted by direct mail. The division had developed or purchased several mailing lists, enabling it to target brochures promoting specific courses or seminars at groups likely to be interested in the programs in question. These lists included:

members of professional organizations (e.g., accountants, lawyers); employers (divided into several categories, according to size, location, and activities or product of the organization); school superintendents, chambers of commerce, public libraries throughout the state, and past participants.

Mailings were running at the level of 200,000 a year. The unit cost of producing and printing a brochure ranged from two cents to twelve cents, depending on length and format, paper stock, and use

EXHIBIT 4

RESPONSES TO MAIL SURVEY OF FALL 1991 EXTENSION DIVISION STUDENTS AT MONTECITO STATE (ALL CAMPUSES) WHO DID NOT RE-REGISTER IN SPRING 1992

Total Number of Courses for Which You Registered in Fall 1991
One	126
Two	45
Three	3
Four	2

Your Primary Purpose in Registering Last Semester
Degree credit	105
Professional advancement	44
Desire for knowledge	21
General interest	15
Self-improvement	11
Meet new people	5

Your Primary Source of Learning About the Course(s)
A friend or relative	45
Employer/employment agency or education/training office	20
Advertisement in *Sherman Monitor*	16
Advertisement in local suburban newspaper	16
A student enrolled in the program	11
Receipt of unsolicited pamphlet, bulletin, brochure	10
Solicited pamphlet	10
Instructor/counselor at another institution	8
Official pamphlet, bulletin, brochure seen at work	7
Advertisements/information on radio/television	7
Close to home	5
Other	9

Did All the Courses You Took Last Fall Measure Up to the Description in College Material Received By You?*
1 Completely	96
2 Reasonably so	57
3 To some degree	17
4 Not at all	12

Did You Feel that All the Courses You Took Last Fall Were Effectively Taught?†
1 Very Effective	84
2 Fairly Effective	43

EXHIBIT 4 *(continued)*

3 Average	25
4 Rather Ineffective	12
5 Very Ineffective	10

Principal Reason for Not Attending Spring 1992

Job responsibilities conflicted	36
Financial difficulties	30
Moved too far to travel	21
Program required more time than am prepared to invest right now	17
Couldn't find any course of interest	14
Family problems or conflicts	13
Health problems (mine or in family)	12
Veterans benefits discontinued	9
Wanted more advanced courses	8
Completed all degree requirements	5
Did not fit schedule	5
Course not offered	4
Other	20

Planning to Register Again in Evening Division?

Next summer	24
Next fall	44
No—attending a private institution	8
No—attending another public institution	19
No—planning to attend a private institution	9
No—planning to attend another public institution	13
No	21
Uncertain	38

Your Sex

Male	97
Female	109

Your Present Age

17–19	4
20–24	51
25–29	48
30–34	36
35–39	22
40–44	10
45–49	6
50–54	5
55 or over	2

Highest Level of Educational Achievement

Master's degree or higher	13
Bachelor's degree	48
More than 2 years of college	35
Associate degree	25
Some college but less than 2 years	56
High school graduate/equivalency	9

*4-point scale.
†5-point scale.
Note: Survey was conducted February 1992. 206 completed questionnaires were received, giving a response rate of 32%. Selected questions only are listed below and non-responses are not shown.
Source: Division of Extension Studies, Montecito State College.

of color in printing. Bulk mailing costs were 11.1 cents per unit. No mass media advertising had been used to promote continuing education (CE) courses, although press releases promoting specific courses were sometimes picked up by the newsletters and other periodicals published by state and local professional associates. CE mailing expenditures were currently budgeted at $30,000.

Several changes were planned for the coming year. Dean Shannon had assigned primary responsibility for advertising decisions to her assistant, Harry Fourman, and had also placed him in charge of the satellite campus program. Fourman, who held an MBA from the University of Jefferson, combined his appointment as assistant dean of Extension Studies with a half-time appointment as instructor in management at MSC. As a start, Fourman had compiled some information on the nature of the extension programs offered at MSC and each of its competitors (*Exhibit 5*).

Advertising and Publicity at MSC

The responsibility for advertising and publicity at Montecito State was in the hands of Roberta Jensen, director of public information. The public information office served every department on campus, including alumni activities. It handled all news items for the College and developed publicity to promote major events. Jensen headed up a group of four people, including a publications editor and a news bureau coordinator. Her own background included a degree in communications, work for the *Chicago Tribune* and a Sherman advertising agency, and three years as assistant director of public relations for a major hospital in Sherman. She had joined MSC the previous fall.

Total expenditures on publications at MSC amounted to $170,000 a year. The Division of Extension Studies accounted for about 30 percent of this. Although large pieces, such as catalogs and the annual report, were sent to outside printers, Jensen noted that more work was being done in-house than before, with small flyers being designed, pasted up, and typeset on campus. The public information office

did not know the total costs incurred by the College for mailing of publications, since mailings were handled on a departmental or division basis. Certain items were bulk-mailed by third class mail, and the College also had two second class mailing permits enabling it, as a nonprofit organization, to mail items such as catalogs more cheaply but supposedly faster. However, various constraints and restrictions had to be observed to qualify for this reduced rate.

MSC did not use a public relations agency for publicity and news releases, preferring to handle such activities in-house. For media advertising, though, the College used a local advertising agency. The total advertising budget was relatively small compared to that of some of the private junior colleges and proprietary schools in the area. Including both media purchases and production costs, MSC's advertising expenditures for the coming year were projected to total just over $153,000. The Division of Extension Studies accounted for over 50 percent of this total.

Rather than working on a commission basis with the advertising agency (whereby the latter's remuneration came from a 15 percent commission received from the media with whom the advertising was placed), MSC had put the agency on a retainer of $2,200 per month and had arranged for it to rebate the commissions directly to the college. This retainer covered consulting services and development of media campaigns, including design of copy and artwork. The advantage of the retainer from the agency's standpoint was that it provided a guaranteed income which would not be affected by fluctuations in the college advertising expenditures. From MSC's standpoint, it meant that there was no incentive for the agency to recommend additional advertising outlays with a view to boosting its commission income.

In an effort to maximize exposure for Montecito State, the public information office used public service announcements (PSAs) on radio and television to promote college events and programs, as well as seeking newspaper listings in the "Calendar" sections. However, Jensen felt that the media were generally reluctant to accept PSAs to promote academic courses. Commenting on the different media in the Greater Sherman area, she observed:

Institution	Type	Main Campus Location	1991–92 Satellite Campus Locations	Extension Course Registrations 1991–92	Fee per Credit Unit	Academic Calendar	1992 Fall Classes Begin	Principal Communications Efforts
Montecito State C.	Public 4-Year Some Grad Programs	Montecito	North Sherman, Puget, San Lucas, Sherman City	5,312	$75	Semester (finishes before Xmas)	Sept. 22	Direct mail, Sherman Monitor, Local newspapers, Radio (some)
Arvin Comm. C.	Public 2-Year	Arvin	—	2,102	$60	Quarter	Oct. 2	Direct mail, Local newspapers
Lakeview Jr. C.	Private 2-Year	Weston	Bel Air, Puget, Olympia, North Sherman	5,100	$135	Semester (finishes before Xmas)	Sept. 9	Sherman Monitor, Local newspapers, OCT buses, Radio
Orezona Comm. C.	Public 2-Year	Mountain View	Montana	2,311	$60	Quarter	Oct. 2	Local newspapers, Radio
St. Anne's C.	Private 4-Year	Bel Air	—	484	$145	Semester (finishes after Xmas)	Sept. 22	Local newspapers (?)
Sherman State C.	Public 4-Year	Sherman City	—	2,950	$75	Semester (finishes before Xmas)	Sept. 22	Sherman Monitor
U. of Jefferson	Public 4-Year Many Grad Programs	Lakeside	Arvin, Sherman City, Remington	6,442	$95	Quarter	Sept. 15	Direct mail, Sherman Monitor, Local newspapers, Radio
U. of Sherman	Private 4-Year Many Grad Programs	Sherman City	North Sherman, Olympia, Puget, Valleyfield, Weston	7,106	$125	Quarter	Sept. 29	Direct mail, Sherman Monitor, Local newspapers, Radio, television, buses
Valley Jr. C.	Private 2-Year	Saltash	Mountain View, Remington, San Gabriel, San Lucas	6,421	$120	Semester	Sept. 16	Radio, Sherman Monitor, Television, Billboards, San Lucas Post
Wallace College	Private 4-Year Some Masters Programs	Santa Rosa	Saltash, San Lucas, Wendell	500	$160	Semester (finishes before Xmas)	Sept. 15	Direct mail, Radio, Sherman Monitor, San Lucas Post
Wendell College	Private 4-Year	Wendell	—	1,244	$150	4-1-4	Sept. 9	Local newspapers

Sherman has one major, metropolitan daily paper, the *Sherman Monitor*. There used to be both morning and evening editions, but now it's only published mornings. Frankly, it's not one of the great newspapers of America, but it is quite widely read, and gives us an opportunity to hit a wide variety of people.

We have a half-dozen varying quality suburban dailies, and a terrific number of weekly papers, both independent and chain. Most of the suburban dailies are published in the evening. Some households subscribe to both the *Monitor* and a suburban daily. The further you get from Sherman City, the more likely people are to buy a local daily rather than the *Monitor*.

The problem with advertising in suburban papers is that the costs really mount up—collectively, they nickel and dime you to death. The advertising agencies all tell me that the *Monitor* is more effective, though sometimes I have my doubts. But the agencies tell you to use those suburban papers for publicity. They'll nearly always run your news stories, since they need "filler." The *Monitor* doesn't.

We've not purchased television time at all. We wouldn't settle for anything less than first-rate commercials. Just to produce two different 30-second television spots and two different 10-second spots could run anywhere from fifteen to twenty-five thousand dollars. The cost of running the ads would be relatively inexpensive by contrast, depending on what station and time slot you use. My question is whether any return we might generate would justify the cost.

We've used radio for extension studies, but always in conjunction with other media, such as newspapers, and direct mail. The theory behind this is that one medium reinforces another. We tend to use radio towards the end of a campaign—for instance during the last two weeks of a six-week campaign. We believe that it provides a good reminder, a final "push" to make your prospects act. Our extension students are mostly employed, working people, so we often go after "drive time," which is expensive.[2] There are a large number of different radio stations in this area and most of them tailor their programs to fairly specific market segments.

We haven't been able to trace many enquiries to those radio ads. However, advertising agencies will tell you that people don't always remember accurately where they

learned about a specific product. We've surveyed people on where they first heard about our programs, and often they'll list a newspaper in which we *didn't* advertise!

Two things we haven't used are car cards on the buses and billboards. I have noticed that Lakeview advertises quite heavily on the buses—their ads have little brochures you can tear off and mail in for further information. Nobody around here except the proprietary schools and Valley Junior seems to use billboards, although I know colleges in other cities do.

Developing a Communications Program

In early March, the extension studies staff was evaluating alternative communications strategies for the coming academic year. Although the start of the fall semester was still over six months away, a long lead time was required. Meetings were also being held with the director of public information, Roberta Jensen, and would be held later with MSC's advertising agency.

At their first meeting together, Roberta Jensen told Harry Fourman:

One of the things MSC hasn't done as well as it might is to figure out the effectiveness of different advertising approaches. I suspect that habit and intuition have played a significant role in making advertising decisions. Candidly, it looks as though the advertising agency has played a very passive role in media selection in recent years.

Harry Fourman looked thoughtful. "The trouble," he said, "is that we don't have one single funnel through which all our responses flow." He paused, then continued:

We do know that the phone starts to ring as soon as advertising begins. We've also found that while we get good response rates from return of newspaper coupons and self-mailer cards asking for information, the ultimate registration rates resulting from these enquiries have been relatively low.

The division's budget in 1991–92 for promoting degree and continuing education programs offered during the fall and spring semesters had been set at $151,000 (the budget for the summer sessions was set separately). Expenditures were broken down as follows:

---

[2] "Drive time" is time during the morning and evening commute periods when large numbers of people are listening to the radio in their cars as they drive to or from work.

Printing of catalogs, brochures, etc.	$35,400
Postage costs	27,000
Radio advertising	8,500
Labor (mailroom, labeling, etc.)	11,900
Newspaper advertising:	
Sherman Monitor	57,300
Selected suburban dailies	11,600
Advertising production costs	4,900
Total budget	$156,600

Despite rising costs, the vice president–finance had indicated that this budget figure would have to remain unchanged next year.[3] The question was how

---

[3]Although bulk rate mailing costs were expected to remain at 11.1 cents per unit for the coming year, it was estimated that printing and production costs in 1992–93 would be 5 percent higher than currently and that labor costs at MSC would be 5 percent higher. The newspapers and radio advertising costs shown in *Exhibits 6* and *7* were about 4 percent above the rates paid by MSC in 1991–92.

to allocate these expenditures among the different alternative media. Of particular interest to the dean and assistant dean of Extension Studies was the relative emphasis that should be given to promoting the satellite campuses and the many continuing education programs. To help him in analyzing the situation, Harry Fourman had compiled a table highlighting the home locations of extension students (*Exhibit 2*). At his request, Roberta Jensen had provided some basic cost data on advertising in Sherman area newspapers (*Exhibit 6*), and also sent him a short memo concerning advertising costs for radio, television, billboard, and transit advertising (*Exhibit 7*).

Enrollment figures had dropped slightly for extension courses over the past year, but risen for continuing education (CE) programs. The goal that Shannon and Fourman had agreed on for 1992–93 was to increase CE enrollments from 900 to 1,000 and to increase the number of extension course registrations from 5,200 to 5,500.

EXHIBIT 6   SAMPLE ADVERTISING RATES FOR NEWSPAPERS CIRCULATING IN GREATER SHERMAN AREA

Newspaper	Rate per line[1]	Lines per page[2]	Total circulation (thousands of copies)
Major Dailies			
Wall Street Journal,			
(western edition)	13.25	1,776	2,000[3]
Sherman Monitor	9.25	2,400	511
Suburban Local Dailies[4]			
Arvin Independent	0.65	2,400	9
East Valley Star Advocate	0.85	2,400	40
Montecito Sun	1.34	2,400	55
Pine Creek Enquirer	0.50	2,352	11
San Lucas Post	1.55	2,464	73
Weston Journal	0.51	2,352	14
Suburban/Local Weeklies[5]	0.46–0.94		

[1]The agate line is the basic advertising cost unit for newspapers. (There are 14 agate lines per column inch in classified advertising.) Rates tend to vary according to location in the paper and discounts may be given for large format ads or multiple insertions. For the purposes of case analysis, please work from these line rates and assume no discounts.
[2]This provides some sense of the format and size of the paper's pages. The *Sherman Monitor* page format of 2,400 lines represents approximately $13\frac{1}{2}'' \times 21''$ (284 sq. ins.) of space within the printed margins. In making rough calculations for case analysis, take 12 lines as equivalent to $1'' \times 1''$ of display advertising space.
[3]Estimated circulation in Sherman Metro area: 69,000.
[4]Most of these suburban dailies also circulated in adjoining towns and cities.
[5]Thirty-one of the towns and cities within or near Greater Sherman had their own local weekly newspaper.
Source: Newspaper Rates and Data, *Standard Rate and Data Service, Inc.*

EXHIBIT 7 MONTECITO STATE COLLEGE MEMO ON RADIO, TELEVISION, BILLBOARD, AND TRANSIT ADVERTISING COSTS

March 3, 1992

TO: Harry Fourman
FROM: Roberta Jensen

It's easier said than done to give you "representative" advertising rates for radio and television stations in the Greater Sherman area, since these rates are subject to so many variations, but I'll try to give you some feel at least for the numbers involved.

Television

There are five commercial television stations which can be received in the Sherman metro area. Four have their transmitters in or near Sherman City, while the fifth broadcasts from Wendell and its signal can be picked up in most parts of the metro area, but the quality of reception varies. These stations are:

KZBA-TV	Channel 3	CBS affiliate
KCCL-TV	Channel 4	NBC affiliate
KFFO-TV	Channel 8	ABC affiliate
KSSM-TV	Channel 12	NBC (Wendell)
KIRM-TV	Channel 23	Independent

Rates for each of these stations vary substantially by time of day and nature of program, reflecting both type and size of audience reached. The table below should give you some feel for the ranges of rates charged for different stations at different times of day. All rates are for a single 30-second spot, based upon the purchase of 10–12 such spots. Exact times for running the spots cannot be specified but are at the discretion of the station. Smaller purchases would cost more on a per-unit basis.

		Times			
TV Channel	Early AM	Local Daytime	Evening Prime Time	Late Evening	Late Night
3, 4, 8	$135–255	$340–850	$2,200–5,400	$595–1,000	$170–420
12	85–200	255–360	1,200–2,550	500–750	110–150
23	70–120	85–250	510–1,000	255–425	70–120

Radio

We certainly have a lot of radio stations in the metro area. There are 15 AM stations and 9 FMs. Some of these, such as KQFD and KRPC-FM, are National Public Radio affiliates, and accept no advertising. Below, I've listed some sample advertising rates for a 30-second radio spot (assuming, again, a purchase of 10–12 such spots). I've confined the list to AM stations—FMs are usually cheaper, but tend to reach a smaller audience; among other things, not that many people have FM car radios, and FM transmissions—being UHF and usually lower power—tend to reach a smaller geographic area than AM.

EXHIBIT 7 (*continued*)

Station	Programming	Principal Target Audience	Times			
			Drive Time (AM)	Drive Time (PM)	Mid-day/ Evening	Late Night
KEFJ	Music, easy listening	Adults 35–49	$ 75	$ 55	$50	$45
KHHD	Talk, sports, news, music	Adults 18–65	200	160	85–135	85
KMPC	Top 40s, rock	Teens, adults 18–35	70	50	37	20
KROQ	Rock, etc.	Teens, young adults	190	125	90–210	75–110
KJIM	Talk shows, popular music for adults	Adults 35 +	190	145	100–170	50
KHRP	Classical music	Adults 18 +	100	95	90	85
KCSB*	Black oriented	Black adults	50	42	37	*
KMNC	Continuous news and information, traffic reports	Adults 18–49	320	220	95–195	50–95
KCHX	Spanish language (talk and music)	Spanish-speaking adults 18 +	55	42	42	25

*Goes off air at sundown.

Outdoor Advertising

It's a bit easier to give an answer on billboards. (I'm assuming you are not interested in the fancy painted variety, just the type you stick paper on.) Billboard rentals vary somewhat according to location and whether or not they're illuminated. A typical cost in the Sherman area would be $530 per month. To this, you've got to add design and production costs of 15–40 percent, plus the cost of putting them up. At a very rough guess, I'd say that a three-month campaign involving ten billboards would cost you a total of about $19,500; for one month, the cost would be around $9,200.

Transit Advertising

As you probably know, there are two transit districts in the metropolitan area—the Sherman Santa Rosa Transit Authority, which operates south of the river, the Orezona County Transit which serves all Orezona County and has commuter services into Sherman City. The SSRTA has 500 buses and a daily ridership of 22,000 passengers; OCT has 300 buses and 100,000 riders. OCT is generally regarded as the better run of the two. Most of their buses are fairly new, they attract a lot of commuters, and there's relatively little vandalism (I know all this because my husband Jack takes OCT to work every day!). Both sell 11″ × 28″ car cards for interior display in the vehicles. They usually charge $20 per card per month and you've got to specify at the outset how many months you want; I should be able to get us a 25 percent discount because we're a public operation. Each transit district has a minimum placement of 50 cards, and you have to take pot-luck on which routes they appear on. But they won't put in more than one car card per bus unless you request it. To print up a three-color card averages $7.30 per card on a print run of 200 cards. After that, the incremental cost is about $2.45 per card.

A NEW DEVELOPMENT

As Fourman sat working at the desk in his rather cramped little office with the door ajar, he heard his name called. It was Dean Shannon. "Hi, Rosemary!" he said. "What's up?"

Shannon pulled over a chair and sat down.

I just got out of a meeting with the president. He agreed to increase our communications budget for next year when he heard that we had signed up Pine Creek High for our new satellite campus. He lives up that way himself and agrees with me that the north county area has real growth potential. The problem with our Puget campus was that access was difficult, whereas Pine Creek is just two blocks from a freeway exit and also has very good bus service.

But he's not happy with MSC's satellite program and told me that next year may be our last chance. Unless we can get course registrations up to a total of 1,200 at the four satellites, he says he'll be forced to consider eliminating them, except the Sherman one, which he has to keep for political reasons.

Fourman leaned forward, anxiously. "So how much money is he willing to let us have next year?"

One hundred sixty-five thousand, but it's not exactly carte blanche. On the one hand, he said that we should try to be innovative, that he thinks the division has been in a rut as far as its communications are concerned. Then in the next breath he said that he feels our advertising should be "dignified"—whatever *that* may mean—and shouldn't make us look like one of those proprietary schools. He also had to overrule Harvey Stimson, the VP–Finance, who was furious about our increased budget—he feels advertising is a waste of money.

She pulled a face, then continued:

The main thing is, he wants to go over the division's marketing plan for fall and spring semesters with us personally next month. He says it is high time he educated himself as to what marketing is all about!

Castle Coffee Company, I

William F. Massy
David B. Montgomery
Charles B. Weinberg

In May of 1982, Adrian Van Tassle, Advertising Manager for the Castle Coffee Company, tugged at his red mustache and contemplated the latest market share report. This was not one of his happier moments. "I've got to do something to turn this darned market around," he exclaimed, "before it's too late for Castle—and me. But I can't afford another mistake like last year. . . . "

Indeed, William Castle (the president and a major stockholder of the Castle Company) had exhibited a similar reaction when told that Castle Coffee's share of the market was dropping back toward 5.4%—where it had been one year previously. He had remarked rather pointedly to Van Tassle that if market share and profitability were not improved during the next fiscal year "some rather drastic actions" might need to be taken.

Adrian Van Tassle had been hired nearly two years ago by James Anthoney, Vice President of Marketing for Castle. Prior to that time he had

worked for companies in Montreal and Toronto and had gained a reputation as a highly effective advertising executive. Now, he was engaged in trying to reverse a long-term downward trend in the market position of Castle Coffee.

CASTLE'S MARKET POSITION

Castle Coffee was an old, established company in the coffee business, with headquarters in Squirrel Hill, Pennsylvania. Its market area included the East Coast and Southern regions of the United States, and a fairly large portion of the Midwest. The company had at one time enjoyed as much as 15 percent of the market in these areas. These were often referred to as the "good old days," when the brand was strong and growing and the company was able to sponsor such popular radio programs as "The Castle Comedy Hour" and "Castle Capers."

The company's troubles began when television replaced radio as the primary broadcast medium. Although Castle Coffee was an early television advertiser, the company experienced increasing competitive difficulty as TV production and time costs increased over time. Further problems presented themselves as several other old-line companies were absorbed by major marketers. For example, Folgers Coffee was bought by Procter and Gamble and Butter Nut by Coca Cola. These giants joined General Foods Corporation (Maxwell House, Sanka, and Yuban brands of coffee) among the ranks of Castle's most formidable competitors. Finally, the advent of freeze-dry and the increasing popularity of instant coffee put additional pressure on the company, which had no entry in these product classes.

The downward trend in share continued during the 1970's; the company had held 12 percent of the market at the beginning of the decade but only about 5½ percent at the end. Share had held fairly stable for the last few years. This was attributed to a "hard-core" group of loyal buyers plus an active (and expensive) program of consumer promotions and price-off deals to the trade. Anthoney, Vice President of Marketing, believed that the erosion of share had been halted just in time. A little more slippage, he said, and Castle would begin to lose its distribution. This would have been the beginning of the end for this venerable company.

OPERATION BREAKOUT

When William Castle succeeded his father as president four years ago, his main objective was to halt the decline in market position and, if possible, to effect a turnaround. While he seemed to have achieved success in reaching the first objective, both he and Anthoney agreed that the same strategy, i.e., intensive consumer and trade promotion, would not succeed in winning back any appreciable proportion of the lost market share.

Both executives believed that it would be necessary to increase consumer awareness of the Castle brand and develop more favorable attitudes about it if market position were to be improved. This could only be done through advertising. Since the company produced a quality product (it was noticeably richer and more aromatic than many competing coffees), it appeared that a strategy of increasing advertising weight might stand some chance of success. A search for an advertising manager was initiated, which culminated in the hiring of Adrian Van Tassle.

After a period of familiarizing himself with the Castle Company and the coffee market and advertising scene in the United States, Van Tassle began developing a plan to revitalize Castle's advertising program. First, he "released" the company's current advertising agency and requested proposals from a number of others interested in obtaining the account. While it was generally understood that the amount of advertising would increase somewhat, the heaviest emphasis was on the kind of appeal and copy execution to be used. Both the company and the various agencies agreed that nearly all the advertising weight should go into spot television. Network sponsorship was difficult because of the regional character of Castle's markets, and no other medium could match TV's impact for a product like coffee. (There is a great deal of newspaper advertising for coffee, but this is usually placed by retailers under an advertising allowance arrangement with the manufacturer. Castle Coffee included such expenditures in its promotional budget rather than as an advertising expense.)

The team from Ardvar Associates, Inc., won the competition with an advertising program built around the theme, "Only a Castle is fit for a king or a queen." The new agency recommended that a 30 percent increase in the quarterly advertising budget be approved, in order to give the new program a fair trial. After considerable negotiation with Castle and Anthoney, and further discussion with the agency, Van Tassle decided to compromise on a 20 percent increase. The new campaign was to start in the autumn of 1981, which was the second quarter of the company's 1982 fiscal year (the fiscal year started July 1). It was dubbed "Operation Breakout."

PERFORMANCE DURING CURRENT YEAR

Castle had been advertising at an average rate of $2.0 million per quarter for the last several years. Given current levels of promotional expenditures, this was regarded as sufficient to maintain market share at about its current level of 5.4 percent. Castle's annual expenditures of $8 million represented somewhat more than 5.4 percent of industry advertising, though exact figures about competitors' expenditures on ground coffee were difficult to obtain. This relation was regarded as normal, since private brands accounted for a significant fraction of the market and these received little or no advertising. Neither Van Tassle nor Anthoney anticipated that competitive expenditures would change much during the next few years regardless of any increase in Castle's advertising.

Advertising of ground coffee followed a regular seasonal pattern, which approximated the seasonal variation of industry sales. The relevant figures are presented in *Exhibit 1*. Total ground coffee sales in Castle's market area averaged 22 million cases per quarter and were expected to remain at that level for several years. Each case contained 12 pounds of coffee in one-, two-, or three-pound containers. Consumption in winter was about 15 percent above the yearly average, while in summer the volume was down by 15 percent.

Advertising expenditures by both Castle Coffee and the industry in general followed the same basic pattern, except that the seasonal variation was between 80 percent and 120 percent—somewhat greater than the variation in sales. The "maintenance" level of expenditures on advertising, shown in *Exhibit 1*, was what Castle believed it had to spend to maintain its "normal" 5.4 percent share of the market in each quarter. Van Tassle had wondered whether this was the right seasonal advertising pattern for Castle, given its small percentage of the market, but decided to stay with it. Therefore, the 20 percent planned increase in quarterly advertising rates was simply added to the "sustaining" amount for each

quarter, beginning in the second quarter of the year, as shown in *Exhibit 1*.

In speaking with Castle and Anthoney about the proposed changes in the advertising program, Van Tassle had indicated that he expected to increase market share to 6 percent or perhaps a little more. This sounded pretty good to Castle, especially after he had consulted with the company's controller. *Exhibit 2* presents the controller's memorandum on the advertising budget increase. While a fraction of a share point might seem like a small gain, each additional share point was worth nearly $4 million in annual gross contribution (before advertising) to the company.

Van Tassle had, of course, indicated that the hoped-for 6 percent share was not a "sure thing" and in any case, that it might take more than one quarter before the full effects of the new advertising program would be felt.

The new advertising campaign broke as scheduled on October 1, the first day of the second quarter of the fiscal year. Adrian Van Tassle was somewhat disappointed in the commercials prepared by the Ardvar agency and a little apprehensive about the early reports from the field. The bi-monthly store audit report of market share for September–October showed only a fractional increase in share over the 5.4 percent of the previous period. Nevertheless, Van Tassle thought that, given a little time, things would work out and that the campaign would eventually reach its objective.

The November–December market share report was received in mid-January. It showed Castle's

EXHIBIT 1 INDUSTRY SALES AND CASTLE'S ADVERTISING BUDGET

Quarter	Industry Cases*	Sales Index	Maintenance advertising		Planned advertising	
			Dollars*	Index	Dollars*	% Increase
1 Summer	18.7	0.85	1.6	0.80	1.60	0%
2 Autumn	22.0	1.00	2.0	1.00	2.40	20%
3 Winter	25.3	1.15	2.4	1.20	2.88	20%
4 Spring	22.0	1.00	2.0	1.00	2.40	20%
Average	22.0	1.00	2.0	1.00	2.32	16%

*In millions.

EXHIBIT 2
AUGUST MEMO

August 1, 1981

CONFIDENTIAL

Memo to: W. Castle, President
From: I. Gure, Controller
Subject: Proposed 20 Percent Increase in Advertising

I think that Adrian's proposal to increase advertising by 20 percent (from a quarterly rate of $2.0 million to one of $2.4 million) is a good idea. He predicts that a market share of 6.0 percent will be achieved compared to our current 5.4 percent. I can't comment about the feasibility of this assumption: that's Adrian's business and I presume he knows what he's doing. I can tell you, however, that such a result would be highly profitable.

As you know, the wholesale price of coffee has been running about $17.20 per twelve-pound case. Deducting our average retail advertising and promotional allowance of $1.60 per case, and our variable costs of production and distribution of $11.10 per case, leaves an average gross contribution to fixed costs and profit of $4.50 per case. Figuring a total market of about 22 million cases per quarter and a share change of from 0.054 to 0.060 (a 0.006 increase), we would have the following increase in gross contribution:

$$\text{Change in gross contribution} = \$4.50 \times 22 \text{ million} \times .006 = \$0.60 \text{ million}$$

Subtracting the change in advertising expense due to the new program and then dividing by this same quantity gives what can be called the advertising payout rate:

$$\begin{aligned}\frac{\text{Advertising}}{\text{payout rate}} &= \frac{\text{change in gross contribution}}{\text{change in advertising expense}} \\ &= \frac{\$0.20 \text{ million}}{\$0.40 \text{ million}} = .50\end{aligned}$$

That is, we can expect to make $.50 in net contribution for each extra dollar spent on advertising. You can see that as long as this quantity is greater than zero (at which point the extra gross contribution just pays for the extra advertising), increasing our advertising is a good deal.

I think Adrian has a good thing going here, and my recommendation is to go ahead. Incidentally, the extra funds we should generate in net contribution (after advertising expense is deducted) should help to relieve the cash flow bind which I mentioned last week.

---

share of the market to be 5.6 percent. On January 21, 1982, Van Tassle received a copy of the memorandum in *Exhibit 3*.

On Monday, January 24, Anthoney telephoned Van Tassle to say that the president wanted an immediate review of the new advertising program. Later that week, after several rounds of discussion in which Van Tassle was unable to convince Castle and Anthoney that the program would be successful, it was decided to return to fiscal 1981 advertising levels. The television spot contracts were renegotiated and by the middle of February advertising had been cut back substantially toward the $2.4 million per quarter rate that had previously been normal for the winter

EXHIBIT 3
JANUARY MEMO

January 20, 1982

Memo to: W. Castle, President
From: I. Gure, Controller
Subject: Failure of Advertising Program

I am most alarmed at our failure to achieve the market share target projected by Mr. A. Van Tassle. The 0.2 point increase in market share achieved in November–December is not sufficient to return the cost of the increased advertising. Ignoring the month of October, which obviously represents a start-up period, a 0.2 point increase in share generates only $200,000 in extra gross contribution on a quarterly basis. This must be compared to the $400,000 we have expended in extra advertising. The advertising payout rate is thus only −0.50: much less than the breakeven point.

I know Mr. Van Tassle expects share to increase again next quarter, but he has not been able to say by how much. The new program projects an advertising expenditure increase of nearly half a million dollars over last year's winter quarter level. I don't see how we can continue to make these expenditures without a better prospect of return on our investment.

season. The advertising agency complained that the efficiency of their media "buy" suffered significantly during February and March, due to the abrupt reduction in advertising expenditure. However, they were unable to say by how much. The spring 1982 spending rates were set at the normal level of $2.0 million. Market share for January–February turned out to be slightly under 5.7 percent, while that for March–April was about 5.5 percent.

PLANNING FOR FISCAL 1983

So, in mid-May of 1982, Adrian Van Tassle was faced with the problem of what to recommend as the advertising budget for the four quarters of fiscal 1983. He was already very late in dealing with this assignment, since additional media buys would have to be made soon if any substantial increase in advertising weight were to be implemented during the coming summer quarter. Alternatively, fast action would be needed to reduce advertising expenditures below their tentatively budgeted "normal" level of $1.6 million.

During the past month, Van Tassle had spent considerable time reviewing the difficulties of fiscal 1982. He had remained convinced that a 20 percent increase in advertising should produce somewhere around a 6 percent market share level. He based this partly on "hunch" and partly on a number of studies that had been performed by academic and business market researchers with whom he was acquainted.

One such study which he believed was particularly applicable to Castle Coffee's situation indicated that the "advertising elasticity of demand" was equal to about ½. He recalled that the definition of this measure when applied to market share was:

Advertising elasticity of demand
$$= \frac{\text{percent change in market share}}{\text{percent change in advertising}}$$

One researcher, whose judgment Van Tassle trusted, assured him that it was valid to think of "percent changes" as being deviations from "normal levels" (also called maintenance levels) of advertising and market share. However, any given value of advertising elasticity would be valid only for moderate deviations about the norm. That is, the value of ½ he had noted earlier would not necessarily apply to (say) plus or minus 50 percent changes in advertising.

Van Tassle noted that his estimate of share change (6.0 − 5.4 = 0.6 percentage points) represented about an 11 percent increase over the normal share level of 5.4 points. Since this was to be achieved with a 20 percent increase in advertising, it represented an advertising elasticity of 11%/20% = 0.55. While this was higher than the 0.5 found in the study, he had believed that his advertising appeals and copy would be a bit better than average. He recognized that his ads may not actually have been as great as expected, but noted that, "even an elasticity of 0.5 would produce 5.94 percent of the market—within striking distance of 6 percent. Of course, the study itself might be applicable to Castle Coffee's market situation to a greater or lesser degree."

One lesson which he had learned from his unfortunate experience the last year was the danger inherent in presenting too optimistic a picture to top management. On the other hand, a "conservative" estimate might not have been sufficient to obtain approval for the program in the first place. Besides, he really did believe that the effect of advertising on share was greater than implied by performance in this past autumn. This judgment should be a part of management's information set when they evaluated his proposal. Alternatively, if they had good reason for doubting his judgment he wanted to know about it—after all, Castle and Anthoney had been in the coffee business a lot longer than he had and were pretty savvy guys.

Perhaps the problem lay in his assessment of the speed with which the new program would take hold. He had felt it "would take a little time," but had not tried to pin it down further ("That's pretty hard, after all"). Nothing very precise about this had been communicated to management. Could he blame the controller for adopting the time horizon he did?

As a final complicating factor, Van Tassle had just received a report from Ardvar Associates about the "quality" of the advertising copy and appeals used the previous autumn and winter. Contrary to expectations these ads rated only about 0.90 on a scale which rated an "average ad" at 1.0. These tests were based on the so-called "theater technique," in which the various spots were inserted into a filmed "entertainment" program and shown to a sample of consumers brought together in a theater. The effect of an ad was tested by a questionnaire designed to measure brand purchasing behavior. Fortunately, the ads currently being shown rated about 1.0 on the same scale. A new series of ads scheduled for showing during the autumn, winter, and spring of 1983 appeared to be much better. Theater testing could not be undertaken until production was completed during the summer, but "experts" in the agency were convinced that they would rate at least as high as 1.15. Van Tassle was impressed with these ads himself, but recalled that such predictions tended to be far from perfect. In the meantime, a budget request for all four quarters of fiscal 1983 had to be submitted to management within the next week.

Colgate-Palmolive: Cleopatra

Sandra Vandermerwe
J. Carter Powis

The Canadian launch extravaganza in February 1986 began with cocktails served by hostesses dressed like Cleopatra, the queen of ancient Egypt. Then followed a gala dinner with a dramatic multimedia presentation of the new brand, ending with the award-winning commercial and these words:

Today the memory comes alive,
a new shape rises up, a new texture,
a new standard of beauty care
worthy of the name it bears,
Today the memory frozen in ancient stones comes
alive . . . Cleopatra.

Each of the retailer guests had received an exclusive golden three-dimensional pyramid invitation to the launch, and expectations were high. They were sick of the discounted brands, all basically the same, and were looking for something different and exciting. Finally, the new soap Cleopatra was revealed to the audience of nearly 1,000, a huge turnout by Canadian standards, and their response was overwhelmingly positive.

So enthusiastic were they, that by the end of the evening the Colgate-Palmolive salespeople had received orders for 2,000 cases. Bill Graham, the Divisional VP Marketing for Canada, and Steve Boyd, Group Product Manager, agreed that the night had been a grand success and that Cleopatra's future looked very rosy.

THE FRENCH EXPERIENCE WITH CLEOPATRA

Cleopatra soap was first introduced in France in November 1984. By May of the following year the brand had reached an amazing market share of 10%, despite its 23% price premium compared to other brands. In fact, Colgate-Palmolive's biggest problem was keeping up with demand. By the end of 1985, market share shot up to 15%. Cleopatra had actually become the number one brand in France.

The success in France received a great deal of publicity within the organization. Encouraged by the experience, the "Global Marketing Group" situated in New York set out to find other markets for the product. They reasoned that if it had worked so well in France, it should do likewise elsewhere in the world.

Canada, especially French-speaking Quebec, seemed like an obvious choice to them. At the annual update meeting in New York, this group strongly recommended to the Canadian management that a test be done in Canada to see if Cleopatra was a proposition for them.

THE REACTION OF THE CANADIAN SUBSIDIARIES TO CLEOPATRA

The idea of a market test for Cleopatra was greeted with mixed feelings by the Canadians. Some managers, such as Assistant Product Manager Stan House, were enthusiastic, especially because they knew that Steve Boyd, Group Product Manager for Canada, was convinced it would work. In Steve's opinion, Canada could show the people in New York that the same formula would do as well or even better than in France.

Other managers, like Ken Johnson, were more skeptical. They resented having a brand thrust on them. Ken believed that what Canada really needed was a strong "national" brand, and he doubted that Cleopatra could ever be that.

Nonetheless, a decision was taken to proceed and test the market. One fundamental question that had to be answered: Was there reasonable certainty that Cleopatra would be accepted by consumers in Quebec?

Two types of research were done, both conducted in Toronto, to try to answer the question. The first was among a "super group" of articulate professional women, specially chosen and brought together for the event. They were introduced to the product, its price and advertising, and then were asked to openly discuss their likes and dislikes. On balance, the results were positive; they seemed to like the soap and the concept.

The second research study used more typical consumers; they were exposed to the proposed advertising for Cleopatra and then asked whether they would buy it. Fifty percent said they would. They were also given a bar of soap to try at home and were phoned a week later for their reactions. Sixty-four percent of the group who used the soap said they would buy Cleopatra as soon as it was available on the shelves.

The research confirmed the feelings of Steve Boyd and most of the marketing team in Toronto that Cleopatra could indeed be a winner. Immediately, plans were made for an early launch the following year.

The Canadian marketing team was determined not to allow Cleopatra to go to war with all the other brands. They felt something had to be done to reverse the negative profit trends that had been brewing in the industry for some time. This was the ideal opportunity. They would position Cleopatra as the premium quality, premium priced soap and differentiate it from all the others. They wanted to avoid having a price war at all costs.

SOME BACKGROUND ON COLGATE-PALMOLIVE CANADA

Colgate-Palmolive, a multinational consumer packaged goods corporation operating in 58 countries, marketed a variety of personal care and household products worldwide. With annual sales of $5.7 billion, many of its brands were global leaders. For example, Colgate toothpaste was number 1, and Palmolive soap was number 2 in the world in their respective markets.

The Canadian subsidiary opened its doors in 1912 and since then had grown into a $250 million-a-year corporation. Together with two competitors, Procter & Gamble and Lever, both $1 billion subsidiaries of their parent companies, they dominated the aggressive and innovative personal care and household market sectors in Canada.

Colgate-Palmolive Canada manufactured and marketed a wide range of personal care and household products inside Canada and also supplied brands to the United States and Puerto Rico. The major products marketed in Canada were:

Personal Care Products	Household Products
Colgate Toothpaste	Palmolive Liquid
Colgate Toothbrushes	Palmolive Automatic
Colgate Mouth Rinse	ABC Detergent
Halo Shampoo	Arctic Power Detergent
Irish Spring Soap	Fab Detergent
Palmolive Soap	Baggies Food Wrap
Cashmere Bouquet	Ajax Cleanser
Cleopatra Soap	Ajax All-Purpose Liquid

The Colgate-Palmolive head office and factory were both located in a building in Toronto. Sales offices were in each of the six major regions across Canada, namely the Maritimes, Quebec, Ontario, the Prairies, Alberta, and British Columbia.

Marketing was organized at the head office under a product management system, whereby each person was responsible for a brand or group of brands, reporting to a group product manager who in turn was responsible to the VP marketing (refer to *Exhibit 1*). The brand managers made decisions on all aspects of marketing planning and execution, from market research to consumer and trade promotion. The product managers made sure that their brands received the needed resources from the head office.

THE STATE OF THE CANADIAN SOAP MARKET

In 1986, the soap market in Canada was worth $105 million to manufacturers. This revenue figure was projected to grow by 4–5% in the years ahead. This market was probably one of the most competitive in which Colgate-Palmolive competed, a fact that even average consumers could see, with the ongoing battle for their attention each time they turned on a television set or opened a magazine.

The competition would continue at the store level, where limited shelf space was at a premium. Because of the intense competition, retailers were all-powerful. They literally could pick and choose with whom to do business. Inside the store, a brand's fate was in their hands; they decided what to promote, which prices to cut, and the allocation of shelf spots.

There were some good reasons why competition was so fierce:

1. Volume growth in the market had slowed and coincided with the growth of the Canadian population (1.0%–1.5% annually). No further rapid expansion was expected.
2. There were many new brands and new variants of existing brands, whose only method of survival was to steal share from other products in the market.
3. There was increased competition from no-name and private label products.
4. Technological advances were slowing and relaunches were increasingly "cosmetic" in nature (new color, new fragrance, etc.).

EXHIBIT 1 MARKETING DEPARTMENT STRUCTURE

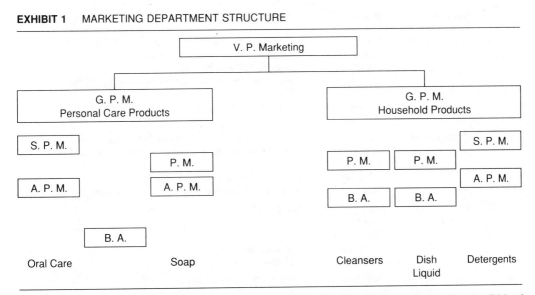

Note: V. P. Marketing reports to the General Manager of Colgate-Palmolive Canada who, in turn, reports to the divisional V. P. of the Colgate-Palmolive Company, based in New York. (G.P.M. = Group Product Manager, S.P.M. = Senior Product Manager, P.M. = Product Manager, A.P.M. = Assistant Product Manager, B.A. = Brand Assistant)

5. Consumers had a group of "acceptable" brands that they were willing to purchase (usually 3 or 4 in number). Buying decisions within this group were based on price. There were 15 mainstream brands, along with 20–25 minor ones, fighting to become one of these "acceptable" choices.

6. Trends toward larger bundle packs had developed (more than one bar of soap packaged and sold as a unit), which reduced the number of purchases each consumer made during the year. For example, in the skin care segment, twinpacks (2 bars sold together) were becoming the norm, whereas the refreshment segment was dominated by 3- and 4-packs, and the utility segment by 4-, 5- and 6-packs.

7. Competition was based on price, as there were no real competitive advantages or meaningful differences among most brands, and because of increased pressure from the retail trade to meet competitive deals and prices.

8. Liquid soaps had entered the market and held an 8% share. Based on current consumer reaction, the maximum share was not expected to grow beyond 10% in the future.

For most consumers, "a soap is a soap is a soap" with few perceivable differences among brands. Bombarded by advertising in every conceivable type of media, consumers mainly bought the "acceptable brands" on price. Therefore, becoming and staying an "acceptable brand" was where the ongoing competitive battle among the various brands took place.

The market was divided into three distinct groups: the skin care segment, the refreshment segment, and the utility segment (refer to *Exhibit 2*). The skin care market was the largest of the three markets, which were split as follows:

	1985	1986	1987
Skin care	37.3%	38.4%	38.8%
Refreshment	34.9%	33.4%	32.3%
Utility (price)	27.8%	28.2%	28.9%

EXHIBIT 2
MARKET SEGMENTS AND BRAND ADVERTISING CLAIMS 1986

Segment	Brand	Advertising copy claim
Skin Care	Dove	For softer, smoother skin, try Dove for 7 days
	Camay	Skin care as individual as you are
	Caress	The body bar with bath oil
	Cleopatra	New soap: rich as a cream, sensual as a perfume
	Aloe &	
	Lanolin	Good for skin because it has natural ingredients
	Palmolive	Not advertised
Refreshment	Zest	Zest leaves you feeling cleaner than soap
	Coast	Coast picks you up and pulls you through the day
	Irish	
	Spring	Fresh fragrance, double deodorancy
	Dial	You will feel clean and refreshed all day long
Utility	Jergens	Not advertised
(price)	Woodbury	Not advertised
	Cashmere	
	Bouquet	Not advertised
	Lux	Not advertised
—	Ivory[1]	Ivory is 99 $^{44}/_{100}$ pure soap

[1]Ivory competes with different creative executions in each of the three segments.
Source: Colgate-Palmolive Canada.

(Details of market share for each of the three large companies and their competitors are shown in *Exhibit 3*.)

Although there were at least 15 mainstream brands, only 4 had managed to create a really distinctive niche.

In the skin care segment, *Dove* had been advertised for years as the facial soap. It had a loyal customer base, mainly because of its unique formulation and moisturizing capabilities. Low on additives and scent, it was seen as the "Cadillac" of this segment and priced accordingly.

Ivory was an "institution" in the Canadian soap market, with its 100-year heritage and ever-powerful "I use it because my mother used it" pure soap positioning. The market leader, it successfully competed in all three markets.

Irish Spring, made especially for men, did well in the male market as a refreshment soap, although females used it as well. Its strong scent and high lathering capability was associated with cleaning strength by consumers.

Zest was also positioned in the refreshment segment. Seen as the "family brand that gets you cleaner

EXHIBIT 3

CLEOPATRA SOAP CATEGORY MARKET SHARES[1]

Quebec	1985	1986	1987 YTD[2]
Colgate-Palmolive:			
Irish Spring	6.2	6.0	6.5
Palmolive	3.7	3.6	6.4
Cashmere Bouquet	3.3	3.4	2.8
Cleopatra	0	0.9	1.1
Total	13.2	13.9	16.8
Lever:			
Lux	4.3	6.0	8.3
Dove	7.1	9.6	10.8
Caress	1.5	1.7	2.9
Other	3.9	2.7	1.2
Total	16.8	20.0	23.2
Procter & Gamble:			
Ivory	28.2	24.9	22.9
Zest	4.9	6.1	4.7
Coast	5.6	5.5	6.4
Camay	6.4	5.3	2.6
Other	0.1	0.1	0.1
Total	45.2	41.9	36.7
Jergens:			
Aloe & Lanolin	2.4	3.2	2.6
Woodbury	0.3	0.8	1.4
Jergens	5.4	5.4	5.4
Total	8.1	9.4	9.4
Canada packers:			
Dial	2.4	2.4	3.2
Other	0.1	0	0
Total	2.5	2.4	3.2
Other Manufacturers	14.2	12.4	10.7

[1]Market share is calculated on an equivalent case basis.
[2]Year end is the October/November share period. Therefore 1987 YTD (year-to-date) is made up of 2 bimonthly share periods–December/January and February/March.
Source: Colgate-Palmolive Canada.

than soap," it was low in additives and perfume. It especially appealed to people in "hard water" areas of the country. Its detergent formulation allowed it to make special claims against other brands, such as "it rinses clean and doesn't leave a soapy film."

THE QUEBEC MARKET

Quebec is Canada's second largest province in population and largest in geographical size. The 6.7 million people (or 26% of Canada's total population) are clustered throughout the southern portion of this immense region, which is 2½ times the size of France.

Unlike the other 9 provinces, which have British ancestry, most of Quebec's population came originally from France. In fact, over 80% of the 2.3 million households in Quebec list French as their mother tongue. Needless to say, with this unique culture, marketing strategies sometimes differ from those used in the rest of the country.

Quebec accounts for 28% of Canadian soap market volume and is, therefore, slightly overdeveloped in proportion to the country's total population. The major brands and their positions in the Quebec market are similar to those throughout the rest of Canada. The exceptions are Zest, which does poorly because Quebec is mainly a soft water market, and Lux, which has done extremely well due to its strong European image.

THE CANADIAN CLEOPATRA MARKETING STRATEGY

Cleopatra looked like an excellent prospect for Canada. Not only was it a premium quality product in all respects, but it complemented Colgate-Palmolive's Canadian product line and had a past history of success. If launched, the product line would include: Irish Spring, well positioned and strongly niched in the refreshment segment; Cashmere Bouquet, performing well in the utility segment; Palmolive Soap, positioned as the all-family skin care bar; and Cleopatra, the premium quality skin care brand worthy of competing with the segment leader, Dove.

After considering these facts as well as the positive research results from the two analyses, the decision was taken to launch Cleopatra as the "premium quality, premium priced beauty soap." However, the marketing team decided that it would not be financially feasible to launch Cleopatra like any other soap, where ultimately its success would be determined by its ability to compete on price.

Although they knew the risks, they wanted to avoid having to rely on retailers and being forced to offer large trade allowances and discounts. Rather, they wanted the demand to come directly from the consumers, by generating their interest in Cleopatra through strong media and consumer promotions.

This approach was very different from the industry norm, where manufacturers traditionally had to pay large sums of money to retailers just to get the product listed in their "accounts order books." Then, they would have to pay even more in discounts and allowances to have a showing in the retailer's weekly advertising fliers. Having decided to forgo these payments, it was critical for Colgate-Palmolive to make the best ever media and consumer promotion schedule for the launch.

The objective set by the company was ambitious: a 4.5% market share for 1986; 100% distribution of the product with retail accounts; maximum shelf presence, defined as the same number of facings as the current segment leader, Dove; proper shelf positioning, which meant being next to Dove; and, finally, maintaining Cleopatra's premium pricing strategy.

To make the strategy work, especially since targets were based on an 11-month first year, they knew they had to get both consumers and salespeople enthusiastic about the brand. Therefore, it was essential to generate excitement from day one. Their promotion had to be very powerful. In fact, it had to be so good that consumers would demand the brand and force retailers to keep it.

That meant the emphasis would be on advertising. Television was chosen as the most obvious way to focus resources and create an impact and instant awareness among the target group, women between the ages of 18 and 49. The campaign, which the marketing team wanted to be "an event," began the first week in May.

The budget was set to make Cleopatra the number one spender in the entire soap market. The objective was clear to all: ensure that Cleopatra got the most "share of voice" in its category in Quebec, which amounted to 15%. In other words, for every 100 minutes of advertising for soaps, 15 minutes would go to Cleopatra.

The Quebec TV commercial (shown in *Exhibit 4*) was the same as the one used in France with one or two minor and hardly noticeable modifications. This commercial had been one of the most memorable parts of the French marketing strategy. Shot in Rome on a very elaborate set, the feedback from consumer research in France had been particularly positive, and it had won a number of excellence awards.

Equally important in the marketing strategy was sales promotion, always popular with the average Canadian consumer. Since the team's research had established that 64% of the market would buy Cleopatra after trying it at home, the first and foremost aim was to be sure that people tried it.

Thus the promotion campaign, scheduled to run from May to October, centered around being tried. "Free Bar Coupons," given to 250,00 households in Quebec, could be exchanged for a free bar of soap at the nearest store. All stores were fully informed.

There was also the "Cleopatra Gold Collection and Sweepstakes Promotion," which offered consumers a wide range of popular and fashionable costume jewelry at very reasonable prices. For example, one could send away for a necklace and earrings that cost only $12.99. Consumers who bought the jewelry received forms and automatically were entered into the grand prize draw, a chance to win a Cleopatra-style 14-carat gold necklace worth $3,500. Research among current brands on the market showed that mail-in offers and sweepstakes were very successful with consumers, and management had high hopes that this promotion would stimulate interest in the brand. The promotion began in August and ended with the draw in early January 1987.

Since Cleopatra had been positioned as the premium quality brand in soap, no discounts were offered. Single cartons were packed 48 to a case, at a price of $41.71. Cleopatra's pricing strategy was to be higher than Dove, historically the most expensive brand. (Comparative prices are shown in *Exhibit 5*.)

The product itself had been developed in France, with no changes made for the Canadian market. As it turned out, Cleopatra was the finest quality soap made by the company in Canada. Its unique formulation contained the best ingredients, including the equivalent of 15% beauty cream, which delivered a rich, creamy lather and was noticeably soft on the skin.

The perfume, blended in France, was said "to produce an unforgettable fragrance." The soap was also carved into a special shape to make it different, easy to hold and to use. The Cleopatra logo was stamped on the ivory-colored bar, another differentiating feature, intended to convey quality, luxury, and prestige. The size of the bar was slightly bigger than the French product, to conform with the other brands.

Each bar of soap came in its own gold-colored laminated carton, a difference from France where it was wrapped in paper. The laminated material was unique as it not only reflected light, which made it stand out against the other brands on the shelves, but it also prevented the perfume from escaping.

THE RESULTS OF THE CANADIAN LAUNCH

Due to the launch, sales had started off with a bang. On that evening alone, 67% of the first month's objectives were achieved. But from then on, the brand started missing its targets.

Steve Boyd had warned his team not to expect an instant miracle. After all, the Quebec soap market was one of the most competitive, and it took time to establish a brand. As the retail trade had been so positive at the launch, he felt sure that things would eventually pick up.

However, the results continued to be discouraging well into the first year. Cleopatra simply was not selling and could not seem to reach the explosive growth that everyone was anticipating and expecting to be "just around the corner."

EXHIBIT 4 CLEOPATRA SOAP TELEVISION COMMERCIAL

SON NOM EST LIE A UN SECRET
DE BEAUTE
CREME ET PARFUM.

ONCTUEUX COMME UNE CREME,

CLEOPATRA UN SAVON CREME
ET PARFUM.
UN SECRET DE BEAUTE.

CLEOPATRA,FEMME ETERNELLE
DETENTRICE DE TOUS LES
SECRETS.

CLEOPATRA UN SAVON

CLEOPATRA, UN SAVON QUI
POURRAIT BIEN CHANGER
LA FACE DU MONDE.

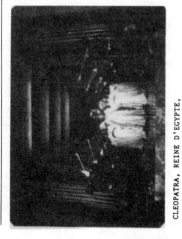

CLEOPATRA, REINE D'EGYPTE,

SENSUEL COMME UN PARFUM.

292

EXHIBIT 5
PRICE AND TRADE DISCOUNT STRUCTURE

	Cleopatra	Dove
Case size[1]	48 × 140 g	48 × 140 g
Case price	$41.71	$39.72
Unit cost	$ 0.87	$ 0.83
Regular selling price	$ 1.29	$ 1.19
Off-invoice allowance	—	$ 3.00
Deal unit cost	—	$ 0.77
Feature price	—	$ 0.99

[1]Dove is also available in a Twinpack (24 × 2 × 140g case size).
Note: The average manufacturer's price for Cleopatra was 87 cents per single bar, compared to an average manufacturer's price of 31 cents per single bar for all toilet soaps.

After 13 weeks, the advertising commercial had created an awareness of 63%, the highest in the skin care segment. At that time Camay was 49%, Dove 24%, and Aloe and Lanolin 13%. By the end of 1986, Cleopatra had achieved its share of voice target, i.e., the number one position in Quebec.

By the end of the promotion period, the Free Bar Coupon had been distributed to households throughout Quebec, and 21% of the coupons had been redeemed. The sweepstakes, however, had been disappointing; only 1,500 people had entered by the December deadline.

Market share reached only 0.9%, peaking in October/November at 1.8%, compared to the 4.5% goal. Sales, which were expected to reach $3,775,000 were only $755,000. Instead of a $389,000 positive contribution to sales, contribution was a negative $442,000. (The performance figures for 1986 and the first three months in 1987 are shown in *Exhibit 6*.)

The financial losses of 1986 and the first part of 1987 are given in *Exhibit 7*. Distribution also fell short of expectations, and presence and shelf positioning gradually deteriorated (refer to *Exhibit 8*). However, the sales force did manage to restrict any discounting of the brand.

Over the first year, some small-scale research had been done in store to determine consumer reaction, but nothing else had taken place. By·January 1987 it was clear that some serious market research was needed, and a full-blown tracking study was commissioned.

Two panels were chosen from Quebec:

• A random sample of 204 consumers
• An oversample of 99 Cleopatra "triers"

Over 90 questions were asked in order to learn the key information needed: "brand awareness," "usage," "brand ratings," "likes and dislikes," "advertising recall," and "trial information" (refer to *Exhibits 9–14*).

EXHIBIT 6   PERFORMANCE-TO-DATE

	1986											1987		
Quebec	Feb.	Mar.	Apr.	May	June	July	Aug.	Sep.	Oct.	Nov.	Dec.	Jan.	Feb.	Mar.
Shipments (cases):														
Forecast (000s)	3.0	5.0	5.0	15.0	15.0	6.0	5.0	10.0	7.0	9.0	10.5	8.0	7.5	7.5
Actual (000s)	3.6	3.0	0.4	2.5	2.1	1.3	0.6	0.9	1.3	0.7	1.7	1.9	0.9	1.2
% achieved	120	60	8	17	14	22	12	9	19	8	16	24	12	16
Market share[1]	0.1		0.7		1.1		1.7		1.8		1.1		1.1	
Distribution[2]	44		51		65		68		69		69		72	
Out-of-stocks[3]	4		3		5		2		3		1		4	

[1]Market share is calculated on an equivalent case basis (i.e. all brands' case packs are made equivalent based on weight, and market share is then calculated as a percentage of this base).
[2]Percentage of accounts in Quebec where the brand is listed.
[3]Percentage of accounts in Quebec where, at the time of audit, the brand was sold out.
Source: Colgate-Palmolive Canada.

EXHIBIT 7
PROFIT & LOSS STATEMENT (000's)

		Actual 1986	1st quarter 1987
Sales	$	755	167
Margin[1]	$	477	108
	%	63.2	64.8
Trade[2]	$	53	12
	%	7.0	7.2
Consumer[3]	$	401	34
	%	53.1	20.3
Media[4]	$	465	94
	%	61.6	56.3
Total expenditures	$	919	140
	%	121.7	83.8
Contribution[5]	$	(442)	(32)
	%	(58.5)	(19.2)

[1]Includes direct product costs, freight/warehousing, etc.
[2]Includes all expenditures directed to the retail trade.
[3]Includes all consumer promotion expenditures.
[4]Includes costs of developing a commercial plus air-time.
[5]Contribution toward allocated overheads and operating profit.
Source: Colgate-Palmolive Canada.

THE DILEMMA

Group Product Manager Steve Boyd fumbled with his papers as he listened to Bill Graham, Divisional Vice President for Marketing Canada, say, "I can't understand it. It was a star performer in France. The French loved it, and Quebec is, after all, part of the French culture. Why has the brand flopped so badly?"

Steve was deep in thought. For Cleopatra to succeed as a major brand in Quebec and perhaps also in all of Canada, as the "Global Marketing Group" had first suggested, he knew he had to react quickly to rectify the situation. But how?

The research results on Cleopatra lay on the table. Product Manager Ken Johnson and Assistant Product Manager Stan House had been over the research with him to try to solve the Cleopatra riddle. But they could not agree about what should be done.

Ken wanted to scrap the brand. He said that Cleopatra was just plain wrong for Canada and should never have been launched there in the first place. There was no point letting more good money chase a loser.

Stan was adamant that what the brand needed was time. He accused Ken of being shortsighted and impatient. It was, he felt, totally unrealistic to expect

EXHIBIT 8
CLEOPATRA SOAP: SHELF POSITION

	Liquid Soaps					
Top shelf	Ivory			Irish Spring		Lux
	Jergens	Caress		Dove		Aloe & Lanolin
	Generic	Dial		Zest	Coast	Palmolive
Bottom shelf	Others	Cashmere Bouquet		Woodbury	Cleo-patra	Generic

Typical 12-foot soap section: 1st quarter 1987

Source: Colgate-Palmolive Canada.

EXHIBIT 9
CONSUMER RESEARCH ON BRANDS (QUEBEC)

Quebec	Brands (total random sample)[1]				
	Aloe & Lanolin	Camay	Cleopatra	Dove	Palmolive
Brand awareness[2] (%)	54.4	98.5	73.5	99.5	96.1
Brand in home[3] (%)	3.5	15.2	6.9	23.9	7.4
Ever tried[4] (%)	12.3	86.3	14.2	83.5	65.2
Brand used[5]:					
All of the time (%)	1.5	8.3	2.9	12.3	3.9
Most of the time (%)	0.5	3.9	1.5	5.4	3.9
Occasionally (%)	7.4	47.6	8.8	46.6	36.3
Stopped using (%)	2.9	26.5	1.0	19.2	21.1

[1] Total random sample—204 respondents.
[2] Question: Have you ever heard of ———?
[3] Question: What brands do you have in your home now?
[4] Question: Have you ever tried ———?
[5] Question: Do you use ———? If yes, would you say you use it all of the time, most of the time, or occasionally? If no, did you use ——— at some time in the past?
Source: Tracking Study, Colgate-Palmolive Canada.

a new brand to succeed overnight, and Cleopatra had only been on the market a little over a year. With a sizeable investment and some patience, he believed they could recreate momentum and achieve a target of 4.5% market share.

The "Global Marketing Group" in New York felt strongly that there was nothing wrong with the brand, but that implementation had been poor. They proposed rethinking the basic strategy; they suggested that perhaps Cleopatra should not be positioned as a skin care product at all, competing head on with Dove. A smaller niche might be more sensible.

Steve Boyd knew that he had three options:

1. Admit defeat and discontinue the brand.
2. Continue the strategy with minor modifications, if necessary, and try to get a 4.5% market share by giving it more time and support.
3. Alter the strategy or even the product itself.

He could not help feeling that he should try to find a way to make Cleopatra work. Giving up would be such a shame. Yet, with retailers already literally pulling the brand off the shelves, did he really have a choice?

EXHIBIT 10   CONSUMER RESEARCH ON PERCEIVED BRAND ATTRIBUTES (QUEBEC)

Brands Best For . . .[1]

Number of respondents citing each brand as . . .[3]

Brand	Being good value for money		Being mild and gentle		Having a rich, creamy lather		Having a pleasant fragrance		Moisturizing your skin		Suitable for the whole family		Leaving skin soft and smooth	
	Total sample[2]	Cleo triers[3]	Total sample	Cleo triers	Total sample	Cleo triers	Total sample	Cleo triers	Total sample	Cleo triers	Total sample	Cleo triers	Total sample	Cleo triers
Aloe & Lanolin	11	2	31	9	8	0	13	0	27	2	13	1	19	1
Camay	40	11	31	7	50	9	53	13	28	7	32	10	41	10
Cleopatra	10	30	8	33	27	51	21	53	15	31	6	23	20	49
Dove	26	13	53	29	63	31	51	16	39	20	49	21	68	24
Palmolive	36	18	20	5	12	5	19	9	9	3	43	19	19	4
All	26	10	5	5	19	2	29	5	9	4	6	5	5	8
None	22	7	28	8	8	0	6	2	38	19	25	12	15	2
Don't know	33	8	28	3	17	1	12	1	46	13	30	8	17	1

[1]Question: Which of these 5 brands _____, _____, or _____ is best for "Being good value for the money" (for example).
[2]Total random sample = 204 respondents.
[3]Cleopatra trier sample (people who have tried Cleopatra in the last 6 months) = 99 respondents.
Note: the 2 sets of data are from seperate panels (i.e. the 99 Cleopatra triers are not included in the total random sample of 204 respondents).
Source: Tracking Study, Colgate-Palmolive Canada.

EXHIBIT 11
CONSUMER RESEARCH: LIKES/DISLIKES OF CLEOPATRA[1]

Likes	% of triers[2]
The smell/good/nice/pleasant/perfume	29
Makes a lot of suds/foam/suds well	26
Mild perfume/light	22
Miscellaneous	21
Softens skin/soft for skin/leaves skin smooth	20
It's mild/good for skin/the mildness	19
The smell/perfume lasts/leaves nice smell on skin	12
It's creamy/creamier	11
The fresh smell/refreshing	10
It's soft/as silk/like satin/like milk	7

Dislikes[3]	
Price too high	20
Too strong a smell/contains too much perfume/harsh	17
Too harsh a soap/not mild enough	12
It melts too fast	10
The smell/the smell left on skin	7
Irritates the skin/burns skin/too much perfume	6
Dries the skin	5
Miscellaneous	5
Doesn't suds enough/not enough foam	3
Doesn't moisturize skin	3

[1]Question: Given that you have tried Cleopatra, what are your likes and/or dislikes of the brand?
[2]Cleopatra Trier Sample (people who have tried Cleopatra in the last 6 months) = 99 respondents
[3]42 respondents had no dislikes.
Note: Only the 10 most frequent responses are shown here. Also, for many French Canadians, the level of perfume is perceived to vary directly with the cleaning strength and harshness of the product.
Source: Tracking Study, Colgate-Palmolive Canada.

EXHIBIT 12
CONSUMER RESEARCH: USAGE[1]

	% of respondents
Do You Plan On Buying Cleopatra Again?	
Regularly	27
Occasionally	66
No intention to buy again	7
Do You Use Cleopatra Every Day?[2]	
Yes	41
No	59
What Part Of The Body Do You Use Cleopatra On?	
Face only	3
Body only	76
Face and body	21
Who Uses Cleopatra In Your Household?	
Yourself only	65
Others	35
How Often Do You Use Cleopatra?	
Regularly	33
Occasionally	67

[1]Questions asked of those who have tried Cleopatra in the last 6 months (Cleopatra Trier Sample = 99 respondents).
[2]Showers outnumber baths 4 to 1 in the province of Quebec.
Source: Tracking Study, Colgate-Palmolive Canada.

EXHIBIT 13
CONSUMER RESEARCH: ADVERTISING

	% of respondents[2]
Main Point Recall[1]	
It's a beauty soap/soap for women	22
It's perfumed/contains perfume	18
It's mild/a mild soap/mild as milk	16
Contains cream/milk/oils	15
Cleopatra/beauty linked together	14
Cleopatra/Egyptians linked together	14
It suds well/lots of lather	10
Fresh smell/it's refreshing	8
Smells good/nice	5
Makes skin soft/smoother skin	5
Reaction To Cleopatra After Seeing Advertising[3]	
Positive	41
Negative	13
No reaction	46
Intention To Try Cleopatra After Seeing Advertising[4]	
Yes	37
No	63

[1]Question: Do you recall Cleopatra advertising? If yes, what were the main points of the ad? *Note:* Only the top 10 responses are shown here.
[2]Number of respondents out of the total random sample who recalled Cleopatra advertising = 128.
[3]Question: What is your reaction to Cleopatra?
[4]Question: Do you intend to try Cleopatra?
Note: Questions 3 and 4 were asked of those in the total random sample who had seen the advertising but who had not tried Cleopatra at the time of the study.
Source: Tracking Study, Colgate-Palmolive Canada.

EXHIBIT 14
CONSUMER RESEARCH: TRIAL

	% of respondents
Why Haven't You Tried Cleopatra?[1]	
Not available where I shop	29
Haven't needed any soap	21
Too expensive	19
Happy with my present brand	19
Has too much perfume in it	16
I don't think about it	10
Miscellaneous	9
Waiting to get a coupon	6
It's new	4
Don't know	4

Note: Only the top 10 responses are shown here.
[1]Question: Why haven't you tried Cleopatra Soap? (Asked of those who have seen the advertising and had originally intended to try the brand.)
Source: Tracking Study, Colgate-Palmolive.

E. I. Du Pont de Nemours & Co., Inc.

Jonathan Guiliano
Cornelius A. deKluyver

David T. Blake, marketing director for the Spun-bonded Division in the Textile Fibers Department of Du Pont, reviewed the 1984 marketing plan as he thought about the 1985 plan, which was due in a few weeks. The overall strategy for Sontara fiber in the surgical gown and drape market and for Tyvek fiber in the construction industry had already been formulated; now he wondered whether the budget proposals on his desk fit the strategies.

COMPANY BACKGROUND

Du Pont, with 1983 sales of $35.4 billion, ranked seventh in the Fortune 500 list of companies. Comprising 90 major businesses and operating in more than 50 countries, Du Pont organized its more than 1,700 products in eight industry segments: biomedical products; coal; petroleum exploration and production; industrial and consumer products; polymers; agricultural and industrial chemicals; petroleum re-

fining, marketing and transportation; and fibers (see *Exhibit 1*).

The fibers segment (1983 sales: $4.8 billion) marketed the world's most extensive offering of man-made fibers, including fiber products for apparel, carpets, tire and aircraft component reinforcement, road support, packaging, protecting clothing, and medical apparel. The company sold the fiber products to textile and other manufacturers that processed them into consumer goods. Four groups made up this segment of the business: apparel fibers, carpet fibers, industrial fibers, and spunbonded products.

THE SPUNBONDED PRODUCTS DIVISION

The Spunbonded Division (1983 sales: ca. $500 million) produced and marketed four products:

REEMAY®—spunbonded polyester
TYPAR®—spunbonded polypropylene
TYVEK®—spunbonded olefin
SONTARA®—spunlaced fabrics

Manufacturing the first three of these generally involved a continuous process of spinning, bonding, and finishing, as diagrammed in *Exhibit 2;* the process to make Sontara involved fiber entanglement and related steps.

Reemay,® a polyester, was a lightweight, hygienically safe, heat-resistant fiber that was used as apparel interliner, coverstock (e.g., to cover diapers), and agricultural crop cover. Typar® was a strong, stable, low-cost polypropylene used as a primary carpet backing, as a geotextile (to provide drainage under

EXHIBIT 1
INDUSTRY SEGMENTS: E. I. DU PONT DE NEMOURS & CO., INC.

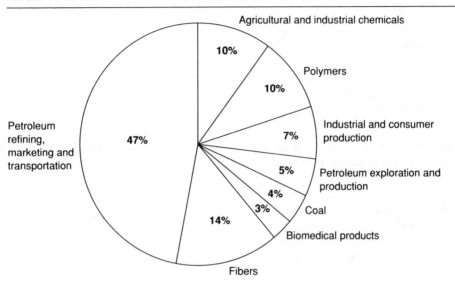

Industry Segment	1983 Sales (billions)	Products
• Petroleum refining, marketing and transportation	16.8	gasoline, jet fuel, diesel fuel, heating oil, fuel oil, asphalt, petroleum coke, natural gas liquids
• Fibers	4.8	man-made fibers
• Agricultural and industrial chemicals	3.5	fungicides, herbicides, insecticides, pigments, organic chemicals, fluoro-chemicals, petroleum additives, mineral acids
• Polymer products	3.4	plastic resins, elastomers, films
• Industrial and consumer products	2.5	photographic products, electronic products, analytical instruments, explosives, nonstick coatings, sporting firearms and ammunition
• Petroleum exploration and production	1.9	crude oil, natural gas
• Coal	1.4	steam coal, metallurgic coal
• Biomedical products	1.1	clinical instruments, biomedical instruments, prescription pharmaceuticals, radio pharmaceuticals

EXHIBIT 2
SPUNBONDED PRODUCT MANUFACTURE

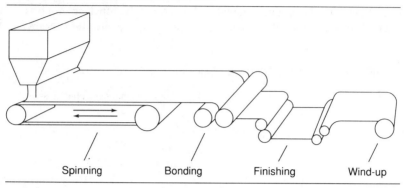

Spinning   Bonding   Finishing   Wind-up

roads), and in furniture as a replacement for burlap. Tyvek,® a strong and opaque olefin with a protective barrier, was used for envelopes, disposable apparel, sterile packaging, bookcovers, tags and labels, and "housewrap" (material to provide a barrier against air infiltration). Sontara® structures were noted for softness, absorbency, and comfort, and were used in curtains, bedspreads, and surgical gowns and drapes.

The Spunbonded Division was managed by a division director. Reporting to him were a technical director, a manufacturing director, and a marketing director, David T. Blake. Reporting to Mr. Blake were a number of marketing managers responsible for various end-user markets for the division's products; each marketing manager was assisted by several marketing and technical representatives. Throughout the Spunbonded Division, managers used a communications network through personal computers, on which they also ran their own software for analysis and control. The Spunbonded Division was one of the first divisions to use computer networking at Du Pont.

Marketing managers submitted annual budget proposals to the marketing director, who reviewed and usually approved them. If Mr. Blake thought a proposal was unreasonable, he asked the marketing manager to modify it and then combined the various proposals into an overall marketing plan for consideration by the division director.

SONTARA SPUNLACED PRODUCTS

Sontara, introduced in 1975, was a sheet structure of entangled fibers. It looked and felt like a conventional textile, and was made from 100 percent polyester, or a blend of polyester and rayon, or from a wood pulp/polyester blend. This last was used primarily for disposable surgical gowns and drapes in hospital operating rooms; the gowns were worn by operating personnel and the drapes were used for patient apparel and to cover objects. Sontara accounted for about 17 percent of all division sales in 1983.

THE SURGICAL GOWN AND DRAPE MARKET

The U.S. market for surgical gowns and drapes in 1983 was approximately 637 million square yards, and its annual growth rate was about 2 percent. The market was divided into two parts: reusable fabric, or cotton; and disposable fabrics, such as Sontara. The benefits of cotton, such as comfort, absorbency, and in the short term, cost, were increasingly becoming outweighed by the advantages of disposables—principally, convenience and infection-barrier qualities. Market share for disposables was 55 percent in 1983 with a forecast annual growth rate of 8 percent for the next few years (see *Exhibit 3* for market trends). It was thought unlikely that more than 90 percent of the market would ever switch to dispos-

EXHIBIT 3

U.S. SURGICAL GOWN AND DRAPE MARKET TRENDS

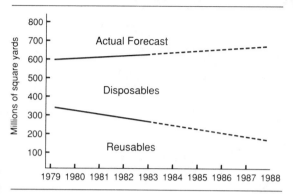

fabrics, Boundary and Signature, made them into gowns and drapes, and sold them to hospitals.

Among companies selling gowns and drapes to hospitals, AHS held a dominant position, with J&J and P&G a strong second and third. Among disposable materials used for the gowns and drapes, Sontara barely trailed the two K-C products combined, as shown in *Exhibit 5*. Du Pont's Tyvek also held a 1 percent share of all gown and drape fabric sales. *Exhibits 6* and *7* provide additional information on the U.S. surgical and drape market.

Competition, which had already eroded gown-maker profit margins, was widely expected to grow more intense. Du Pont's main competitors were K-C, P&G, and J&J's Chicopee Division. K-C (1983 total sales: $3.3 billion), though steadily losing market share, had begun to consolidate its position as a fully integrated supplier to the medical apparel market; it had recently added production capacity and expanded its sales force. K-C's Regard continued to lose share to Sontara at AHS; of course, because K-C also supplied hospitals with gowns and drapes made of its Spunguard, AHS both bought from K-C and competed against it. P&G (1983 sales: $12.5 billion) had entered the market several years ago as a vertically integrated supplier and touched off protracted price competition. To strengthen its position, P&G had reorganized its highly visible medical apparel sales force, a few years previously. Like P&G, J&J (1983 sales: $6.0 billion) recently had invested heavily in research and development. Production costs at Chicopee were now high, but because

ables. Fabric manufacturers, or fabric suppliers, in the disposables market, made the fabric and sold it to firms that made the gowns and drapes and sold them to hospitals. Unlike Du Pont, several companies were both fabric manufacturers and gown and drape makers and suppliers, as shown in *Exhibit 4*. Du Pont sold Sontara to Johnson & Johnson (J&J) and to American Hospital Supply (AHS). J&J also manufactured a fabric, Chicopee, or Fabric 450, which it made into gowns and drapes and sold to hospitals. AHS sold gowns and drapes of both Sontara and Regard, a Kimberly-Clark (K-C) product. Besides Regard, K-C, the first company in the disposables market, also manufactured Spunguard, a fabric which K-C made into gowns and drapes and sold to hospitals. Procter & Gamble (P&G) manufactured two

EXHIBIT 4

RELATIONSHIPS AMONG COMPANIES IN THE U.S. SURGICAL GOWN AND DRAPE MARKET

Fabrics and Manufacturers	Gown & Drape Makers and Hospital Suppliers
Chicopee (Johnson & Johnson)	Johnson & Johnson
Sontara (DuPont)	American Hospital Supply
Regard (Kimberly-Clark)	
Spungard (Kimberly-Clark)	Kimberly-Clark
Boundary (Procter & Gamble)	
Signature (Procter & Gamble)	Procter & Gamble
Assure I (Dexter)	
Assure III (Dexter)	AHS and others

EXHIBIT 5
A: MARKET SHARES OF COMPANIES SELLING DIRECTLY TO HOSPITALS

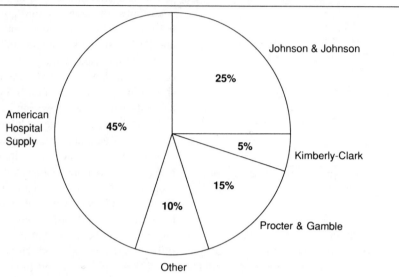

B: MARKET SHARES OF MATERIALS USED BY HOSPITALS

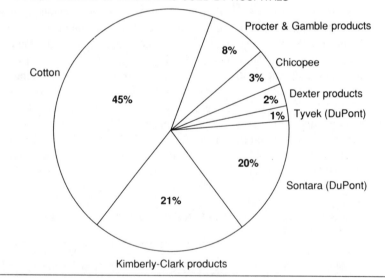

of J&J's large volume, it was expected that the company would move quickly down the experience curve and costs would drop. J&J's Chicopee was much softer than Sontara, but was therefore also more difficult to process. J&J often sold gowns and drapes made of Sontara and later substituted Chicopee, which was relatively simple to do because neither J&J nor AHS used the Sontara name on their products.

In addition to these complex company rivalries

EXHIBIT 6
U.S. SURGICAL GOWN AND DRAPE MARKET

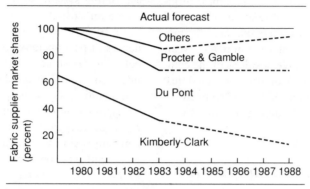

EXHIBIT 7
U.S. SURGICAL GOWN AND DRAPE MARKET

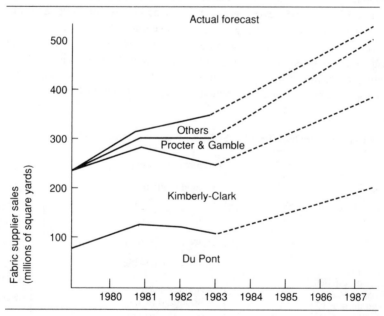

and relationships, there were still others of possible significance. K-C, for example, also competed against Sontara in the home furnishings, furniture, and bedding market, and against Tyvek in the industrial apparel market. Although a competitor of Du Pont, P&G was also a customer; P&G used Du Pont's spunbonded fabric Reemay as a coverstock for disposable diapers. And although the Spunbonded Products Division was engaged in sales of Sontara only to hospital suppliers and not in sales of Sontara apparel to hospitals, Du Pont did have sales forces that sold other Du Pont products directly to hospitals.

Cost, "barrier," and "flexural rigidity" were the three most important qualities used to compare surgical gowns and drapes. "Barrier" referred to how well the fabric protected against infection, and "flexural rigidity" defined the material's comfort and wear. *Exhibit 8* diagrams the relative positions of the competing fabrics in terms of each of these three qualities; the fabrics most directly comparable and competitive with Sontara were P&G's Boundary and J&J's Chicopee.

STRATEGY AND TACTICS FOR SONTARA

The future of Sontara involved several problems. First, because of increasing price competition, R&D was needed to lower unit production costs. Second, end-user brand awareness for Sontara was relatively low, primarily because J&J and AHS never identified the Sontara name. Third, hospitals, under government pressure to reduce costs, were becoming more price sensitive, and purchase decisions were increasingly made by administrators rather than by operating room nurses who used the gowns and understood

Sontara's value. Fourth, every hospital had its own accounting system, so it was difficult to prove the long-term cost-effectiveness of Sontara products. Fifth, because hospitals would rarely admit to incidences of post-operative infection, it was also difficult to demonstrate Sontara's ability to reduce such infections. Sixth, disposables threatened to become commodities as more hospitals switched from cotton to disposable products. Finally, Du Pont faced potentially severe capacity limitations, which impeded the company's ability to compete aggressively.

Despite these problems, the market offered opportunities as the preference for disposable fabric increased, as professional groups, such as the Association of Operating Room Nurses (AORN), made statements favoring disposables as more clinical proof of Sontara's efficacy became available, and as new uses for Sontara, such as for scrub suits, developed.

In view of these circumstances, Du Pont's two principal strategic objectives for Sontara were (1) to at least maintain market share over the next two years, without further price erosion, until the capacity

EXHIBIT 8 KEY FABRIC PROPERTIES OF SURGICAL GOWNS AND DRAPES

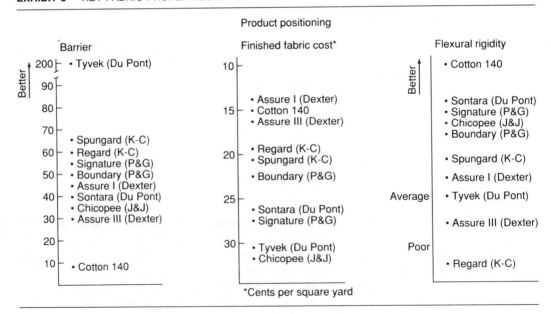

Product positioning

*Cents per square yard

problems had been resolved, and (2) to convince garment makers that Du Pont could support them in promoting Sontara to end-users and would remain a strong force in the disposable fabric business. At the same time, the company planned to continue R&D to lower production costs as a hedge against further price reductions and to restore profit margins.

To implement this strategy, the 1984 budget for Sontara had consisted of $450,000 for the sales force and $92,000 for advertising and promotion. Advertising and promotion were principally targeted toward operating room nurses, who traditionally decided what garments and drapes to buy. About $50,000 of this amount was spent on repeating the "Scrubby the Surgical Bear" campaign at the next annual AORN conference. Nurses had to listen to a 10-minute presentation about Sontara by a mind reader to receive a small teddy bear dressed in Sontara surgical garb and enclosed in a Tyvek sterile package. Scrubby had become a favorite at the conferences, and many nurses would stop by "Bear Mountain" to hear Scrubby's message:

Hi!

I'm Scrubby the Surgical Bear! I'm wearing soft, single-use surgical garments made with SONTARA spunlaced fabric from Du Pont. SONTARA keeps me cool and comfortable, and helps prevent infections in my patients.

Notice that my package has a tough lid of TYVEK spunbonded olefin from Du Pont. Sterile packing of TYVEK gives me superior protection. It keeps out water and bacteria, resists punctures and tears, peels open cleanly and has proven shelf life.

Take good care of me, just as SONTARA and TYVEK take good care of you and your patients in the O.R.!

Love,
Scrubby

The costs of the bears was $20,000. Brochures depicting Scrubby were $10,000. Du Pont also sent direct mail material (shown in *Exhibit 9*) to AORN nurses at a cost of $7,000, and ran advertisements (shown in *Exhibit 10*), at a cost of $5,000, in the AORN Journal (circulation 50,000) to give away big Scrubbies (*Exhibit 10*). Du Pont estimated that over the past two years, this program had put Sontara in touch with 25 percent of the 55,000 operating room nurses in the U.S.

The sales force allocation for Sontara was an estimate. It assumed that the marketing division assigned the equivalent of four and one half people to the gown and drape market, and that each person represented about $100,000 in total cost. Tentative plans for 1985 called for the same sales force expenditure and an increase of 25 percent for each item in the advertising and promotion budget.

EXHIBIT 9
THE DU PONT BEAR LAIR

Sample of mailer sent out to 6,000 preregistered O.R. nurses prior to the 1984 A.O.R.N. Congress in Atlanta.
Mailer tied together the "bear theme," also made it easier for nurses to find Du Pont booth among the hundreds they could visit, and promoted the annual Du Pont Vacation Sweepstakes (which helps pull traffic to the booth).

Make Tracks
for the DuPont Bear Mountain
• Scrubby the Surgical Bear
• The Amazing Zellman, Psychic Perceptionist
• The Du Pont 1984 AORN Vacation Sweepstakes

THE
DU PONT
BEAR
LAIR

EXHIBIT 10
WIN YOUR OWN "SCRUBBY THE BEAR"

Just answer these easy questions about SONTARA® spunlaced fabric for single-use O.R. gowns and drapes.

You may be one of 75 lucky O.R. nurses who'll win a 3-foot high "Scrubby the Surgical Bear" dressed in cap, mask, and gown of SONTARA.* SONTARA is the *soft* gown and drape fabric . . . the one with over 10 years' proven O.R. experience. And made only by Du Pont, a leader in health-care product research.

You're always a winner if you ask for SONTARA by name . . . from such leading O.R. gown and drape manufacturers as American Converters, Surgikos, Kendall, and Mars.

Now . . . answer the questions, and qualify to win a giant "Scrubby" bear. Use either this form or a reasonable facsimile.

	Yes	No
• SONTARA is the most cloth-like, single-use O.R. fabric.	☐	☐
• SONTARA is remarkably strong, light, and comfortable.	☐	☐
• SONTARA is a proven barrier material.	☐	☐
• SONTARA lints less than reinforced paper or cotton.	☐	☐
• SONTARA fabric is available in gowns and drapes from leading manufacturers.	☐	☐

Winners will be selected at random from all entries received before March 1, 1984. You must be an O.R. nurse to win. Send your completed entry form to:

"Scrubby" Contest, Du Pont Company, Room X40201, Wilmington, DE 19898

Name_____ Title_____
Hospital_____ Address_____
City, State, Zip_____

*Du Pont registered trademark. Du Pont makes SONTARA® spunlaced fabric, not gowns and drapes.

TYVEK

Tyvek spunbonded olefin was a sheet of extremely fine, high-density polyethylene fibers. It was a high-strength, high-barrier, low-weight structure, resistant to tearing, puncturing, shrinking, and rotting. One of the many uses for Tyvek was as "housewrap," an air infiltration barrier for homes, introduced in 1981. U.S. sales for Tyvek housewrap in 1983 were $2.8 million, or 800,000 pounds, while international sales were $0.8 million, or 400,000 pounds. Total Tyvek sales in 1983 were in excess of $100 million.

Tyvek housewrap was stapled to the sheathing of a home under construction before siding was put up. An average house required 16 pounds of Tyvek; the cost of Tyvek to the home builder averaged less than $200, including labor, for a conventional wood frame house. In a National Association of Home Builders study, Tyvek was reported to reduce heating costs by an average of 30 percent and air conditioning expenses by approximately 10 percent. The Tyvek wrap covered cracks and seams, thereby enhancing or protecting the effectiveness of a home's insulation.

THE MARKET FOR HOUSEWRAP

Housewrap sales were directly related to new housing starts. As interest rates declined in 1983, starts for one-family houses soared to 0.9 million, and Tyvek housewrap sales exceeded forecasts by 60 percent. The 1984 forecast for new one-family homes was 1.0 million. It was estimated that Tyvek housewrap sales in the U.S. would reach 2.3 million pounds in 1984 (see *Exhibit 11*).

Tyvek's only direct competitor as a housewrap

EXHIBIT 11
SALES OF TYVEK HOUSEWRAP

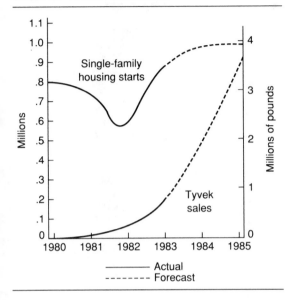

─── Actual
------- Forecast

was 15-pound felt, or tar paper, which was thick, heavy, and difficult to install because it tore easily. Although tar paper's price was about one-third less, Tyvek cost less overall because of labor savings during installation.

Because of the size of the market, and despite numerous patents on Tyvek, Du Pont expected competition for housewrap to increase significantly in the near future. Among potential competitors were Boise Cascade (1983 sales: $3.5 billion), Certain-Teed (1983 sales: $1.0 billion), Georgia-Pacific (1983 sales: $6.5 billion), and Kimberly-Clark (1983 sales: $3.3 billion).

Du Pont sold Tyvek to 42 leading building supply distributors with 83 warehouses throughout the U.S. These distributors, carefully selected by Du Pont, sold to dealers, who in turn sold to home builders. In some areas, the distributor's sales force called directly on home builders.

Builders were the key buying influence for housewrap. Secondary influences included architects, government agencies, city and state building code officials, and energy conservation specialists at

public utilities. Home buyers, increasingly energy-conscious, were also becoming more important.

STRATEGY AND TACTICS FOR TYVEK

Du Pont's principal objective for Tyvek was to achieve maximum market penetration in the shortest possible time. The 1985 strategy for Tyvek, therefore, was to continue to gain visibility, to strengthen the distributor network, and to promote the product as effectively as possible.

The 1984 budget for Tyvek housewrap consisted of $250,000 for the sales force and as listed in *Exhibit 12,* $475,000 for advertising and promotion. Ads, such as the one shown in *Exhibit 13,* were placed in trade and professional magazines to reach home builders and architects. Sales aids were developed for distributors, dealers, and home builders; and a direct mail campaign was mounted to buyers of blueprints for house designs from certain companies. (See *Exhibit 14* for a Tyvek direct-mail piece.) In addition, the division had initiated co-op advertising with distributors, and made information about research findings on Tyvek's ability to conserve energy available to various publications through press releases. Finally, the budget covered trade shows, such as Du Pont's exhibit at the National Association of Home Builders' annual convention. Tentative budget plans for 1985 kept the sales force expenditure at the current level and increased advertising and promotion by 50 percent, with allocations similar to those of the 1984 plan.

THE 1984 BUDGET REVIEW

In considering how the 1985 budget proposals fit his strategies for Sontara and Tyvek, Mr. Blake had several questions. How would each product's push and pull emphasis change in 1985? How did the marketing mix affect push and pull, and how did the elements of the mix interact? What results would the various elements cause at different expenditure levels? He wondered how competitors' marketing strategies affected Sontara. He also thought about buyer behavior: How well would each product do in

EXHIBIT 12
TYVEK 1984 ADVERTISING AND PROMOTION BUDGET

Advertising	
Builder magazine, 8X	$ 55,000
Professional Builder, 8X	53,000
Multi-Housing World, 8X	28,000
Progressive Architecture, 8X	16,000
Sweet's 1985	8,000
Test publications	5,000
Preparation	12,000
Du Pont magazine	1,000
Total	$178,000
Sales Aids	
Builder Support:	
Model home display	$ 3,000
Homebuyer sell sheet	2,000
'Wise Builder' certificate	4,000
Mailing to *Home Planners* and *Home Magazine* plan buyers	10,000
Retailer Support:	
Literature	50,000
Co-op support	110,000
Co-op merchandising	1,000
Distributor Support:	
Distributor sales meeting	9,000
Distributor handbook	2,000
Sweet's brochure	8,000
LaBelle presentation	7,000
Masthead mailings	6,000
NAHB exhibit	20,000
Multi-Housing World exhibit	20,000
Regional shows	12,000
Manufactured-home support	12,000
Inquiry handling	1,000
Postage/freight	1,000
Store room	1,500
List maintenance	500
Total	$280,000
Product Information	
Press release production	$ 8,000
Press release distribution	3,000
Cost Saving release	4,000
Photography	2,000
Total	$ 17,000
Total advertising and promotion 1984	$475,000

a use test at the current price? Of the total value that buyers of Sontara and Tyvek received, how much of that value was built into the product and how much was added by marketing? Which mix elements contributed the most value? To find answers to these questions, he talked with the Sontara and Tyvek marketing managers.

John Murray, marketing manager for Sontara in the surgical gown and drape market, described the emphasis behind the 1984 budget as push rather than

EXHIBIT 13

TYVEK HOUSEWRAP

New test proves TYVEK Housewrap cuts heating costs 29%. And that sells homes.

Give yourself a competitive edge and a faster sale by offering homebuyers the extra value ot TYVEK Housewrap.

The NAHB Research Foundation determined that there is a 29% reduction in heating costs in a home wrapped with TYVEK*. Placed over sheathing, TYVEK seals cracks and seams and significantly reduces interior air exchange rate.

It also keeps air out of the wall cavity, preserving insulation R-value and reducing heat loss through walls. And because it passes moisture vapor, it won't cause in-wall condensation.

It costs under $200 to wrap an average-size house. That includes labor. Two workers can put up 1,800 square feet in less than two hours with just a knife and staple gun.

TYVEK helps homes sell faster, and Du Pont helps you get the word out with free literature and model display.

Order TYVEK Housewrap—made only by Du Pont—from your building supply dealer. And for free test data literature and the name of your nearest distributor, call (302) 999-5088. Or write Du Pont Company, Room G-39982, Wilmington, DE 19898.

---

*Before-and-after test on a conventionally constructed 2-by-4 wood-frame home with R-11 insulation in walls. Your savings may be more or less depending on climate and construction.

TYVEK Housewrap is a Du Pont trademark for its air infiltration barrier.

---

pull. He estimated that 75 percent of the current effort was push and that the percentage should go unchanged until he had something with which to launch a cost-effective pull campaign. For example, Sontara was under clinical study for the next two or three years, after which he could put the findings in professional journal ads and in direct mail to doctors, nurses, hospital administrators, and others. With this type of campaign, the push/pull percentage could approach 50/50.

Mr. Murray believed that it was misleading to identify specific budget items in the 1984 advertising and promotion budget as mix elements. It was more accurate, he said, to think of the overall budget as one third advertising activity and two thirds trade support. He said that the difference between the two was that the intent of advertising was to create a favorable image for the product, and the intent of trade support was to assist indirectly the sales effort of Du Pont customers. Because all budget items were part advertising and part trade support, it was more useful to look at the total budget rather than at each item. The $92,000 advertising and promotion expenditure in 1984, he said, was in effect $31,000 for

advertising and $61,000 for trade support. He thought that the same proportion was appropriate for the 1985 proposal of $115,000: $40,000 for advertising, and $75,000 for trade support. So, with $450,000 for the sales force, the three general mix elements were sales force, advertising, and trade support.

As he looked at the market, however, Mr. Murray found that these three elements did not fully capture the marketing activity of both Du Pont and its competitors. He believed that the sales force actually involved two functions: to maintain the current sales effort, and to do missionary sales. He said that he could make the same distinction concerning trade support, and that he could divide advertising between advertising to intermediate-users (i.e., gown and drape makers) and to end-users (i.e., hospitals). The 1985 proposal, he said, thus involved six mix elements: $450,000 in sales force/maintenance, $0 in sales force/missionary, $75,000 in trade support/maintenance, $0 in trade support/missionary, $10,000 in advertising/intermediate-users, and $30,000 in advertising/end-users.

Mr. Murray believed that the effective level of competitors' marketing spending was $900,000 sales

EXHIBIT 14
TYVEK HOUSEWRAP

Energy-saving air infiltration barrier.

A simple, inexpensive way to improve energy efficiency and make your homes more appealing.

Cold air infiltration consumes up to 40% of home heat. At the same time, cold air passing through insulation significantly reduces R-value. Housewrap of TYVEK spun-bonded olefin seals cracks and seams in sheathing and at plates and sills. It keeps cold air out of insulation, so insulation delivers its full R-value. And it keeps cold air out of the house and warm air in.

TYVEK reduces heat loss.

Tests on an NAHB research home showed a 29% reduction in heating costs after applying TYVEK. That's the kind of energy-savings home buyers are looking for. And it costs very little to add to your homes.

TYVEK won't cause condensation build-up.

It's a durable sheet of high-density polyethylene fibers. It's not a film or paper. It allows moisture vapor to pass through (94 perm), so there's no danger of in-wall condensation. It's lightweight, tear-resistant and will never rot or shrink.

TYVEK is easy to install.

Start at one corner and roll over the entire wall, wrapping around corners and over doors and windows. One man rolls, the other follows, applying staples or roofing nails.

When house is wrapped, go back and x-out windows and doors, pulling TYVEK in over window frame.

TYVEK comes in two sizes: 3 ft. wide rolls covering 999 sq. ft. and 9 ft. rolls covering 1755 sq. ft. One 9 ft. roll covers an average-size house and weighs only sixteen pounds.

Two men can do a typical house in less than two hours, so labor cost is minimal.

Find out from your building dealer how little it costs to add this important energy-saving feature to your homes.

force/maintenance, $100,000 sales force/missionary, $150,000 trade support/maintenance, $75,000 trade support/missionary, $25,000 advertising/intermediate-users, and $100,000 advertising/end-users.

The effectiveness of the marketing mix elements was interrelated. Examined individually, spending on sales force/maintenance, trade support/maintenance, and advertising/intermediate-users exhibited decreasing (concave) returns to scale. The market share response curve for the other elements was S-shaped: little effect of low spending, with first increasing and then decreasing returns to scale as spending increased.

The weighted-average price for Sontara was $.26 per square yard, and the variable cost was $.12. Sontara's relatively high price did not discourage purchases, he thought; for example, he said, in a use test, roughly 30 percent of the respondents said they would buy Sontara on the next occasion.

Mr. Murray described the effect of budget changes on sales in terms of three scenarios: (1) sales expected with the proposed budget, (2) the effect on sales of raising one mix element to its maximum reasonable expenditure level while holding the others constant at the proposed level, and (3) the impact of reducing one mix element to zero while holding the others at their proposed spending level.

With the current proposal of $565,000, he estimated that 1985 sales could reach 210 million square yards. This represented 32 percent of the total market or 50 percent of the smaller disposable market. If sales force/maintenance expenditures were to be raised from the proposed level of $450,000 to a maximum reasonable expenditure level of $550,000 while holding other spending to what had been proposed, Mr. Murray thought market share could reach 33 percent of the total market. Similarly, if the other mix elements were increased to their maximum reasonable levels while holding the remaining expenditures at their proposed levels, he thought market share increases would be likely as well, although not as dramatically. Specifically, if $200,000 were to be spent on sales force/missionary instead of the proposed $0, he thought market share would increase to 33 percent; if trade support/maintenance would be increased to $100,000, a 33 percent market share would result; if $100,000 would be spent on trade support/missionary, market share would be 33 percent; if advertising to intermediate users were to be increased to $50,000, the net effect would be a 1 percent increase in market share; while an increase in advertising to end-users to $300,000 would also result in a 1 percent share gain.

Reductions in spending were thought to have the opposite effect. Reducing sales force/maintenance expenditures to zero while holding other spending at the proposed level was thought to reduce share to 22 percent of the total market during the next 12 months. Similarly, reductions to zero spending for sales force/missionary expenditures, trade support/maintenance, support/missionary, advertising to intermediaries, and advertising to end-users were thought to reduce expected market share to 32, 27, 32, 31, and 28 percent respectively.

As a validity check on the above estimates, Mr. Murray described what he thought would happen if all mix elements were to be raised simultaneously to their maximum reasonable expenditure levels, or if all support were to be withdrawn from the product. With maximum effort he thought a 39 percent share could be realized, although he was not sure how viable such an aggressive strategy would be for the long run. If all support were to be withdrawn, he estimated that market share would drop to 22 percent in the next 12 months before declining further.

Glenn White, marketing manager for Tyvek housewrap, said his marketing emphasis was mostly push, but increasingly pull. The push/pull percentage was 95/5 in 1984, he believed, and would become 65/35 in 1985, and 50/50 in 1986.

Mr. White categorized his marketing plan in terms of seven mix elements: sales force, advertising/end-users, advertising/intermediate-users, press releases, builder support, retailer support, and distributor support. He believed that interactive effects could occur among the mix elements, though he did not know what they were or how to account for them. For advertising/end-users, he believed that the effectiveness of additional expenditures followed an S-shaped curve, and that for the other elements the curve was concave.

The current price for Tyvek housewrap was $3.60 per pound, and the variable cost was about $1.50. In a use test, Mr. White estimated that between 20 percent and 25 percent would purchase the housewrap on the next occasion.

Mr. White, like Mr. Murray, described the effects of budget changes on Tyvek sales in terms of a number of scenarios: (1) sales expected from the baseline proposal, (2) the effects of item-by-item budget increases, and (3) the effects of item-by-item reductions as well as what would happen if all budget elements were increased to their maximum reasonable expenditure levels or if all support for the product would be withdrawn.

Specifically, Mr. White thought the proposed budget of $250,000 for the sales force, $0 for advertising to end-users, $230,000 for advertising to intermediaries, $25,000 for press releases, $35,000 for builder support, $225,000 for retailer support, and $195,000 for distributor support would result in sales of 3.6 million pounds, which translates into a 23 percent market share.

Raising the budget on an item-by-item basis was thought to have the following effects: sales force expenditures to $800,000, a 4 percent share increase; advertising to end-users of $1,100,000—a pull campaign—an 8 percent share increase; more advertising to intermediaries (to $460,000), an additional 2 share points; increased builder support (to $100,000) or retailer support (to $325,000), a 1 percent share gain; additional funds for press coverage (to $50,000), 1 percent share increase; and finally, additional distributor support (to $300,000), a 1 percent share increase. In similar fashion, reduction of the above mix elements to zero was thought to reduce market share for sales force expenditures to 20 percent, for advertising to end-users to 23 percent, for advertising to intermediaries to 20 percent, for press releases to 21 percent, for builder support to 22 percent, for retail support to 17 percent and for distributor support to 19 percent.

In judging the overall effects of budget adjustments, Mr. White thought that if all elements were increased to their maximum reasonable expenditure limits, market share could reach 33 percent. On the other hand, if all support was withdrawn, a likely market share of 13 percent would result.

CONCLUSION

As he listened to the various arguments and estimates, Mr. Blake wondered about their consistency and what their implications would be for the 1985 budget. Should the Sontara and Tyvek budget proposals be revised? If so, how?

PART SIX

Personal Selling and Account Management

Account management is, in many ways, similar to advertising management. Both are forms of communication and must address the fundamental question of "who says what to whom." Both advertising and sales-force managers need to be concerned with designing messages, with choosing communications targets, and with working within the budget constraints and communication goals of a marketing plan. The fundamental difference is that personal selling involves people—who must be recruited and trained—to deliver the message and to interact directly with customers or prospects.

The big advantage of personal selling as a communication or promotional tool is that it involves person-to-person contact with a potential user. This allows the sales representative to tailor the message to fit a particular customer's concerns and interests. During a sales call—which may take place in person or by phone—communication flows in both directions, allowing the salesperson to respond to immediate feedback from the customer. Questions and objections can be met and answered, and alternative approaches can be tried when the initial ones do not seem to be working. Sales representatives can also communicate a large amount of complex information in one or a series of sales calls. Visual aids and working models can also be used. By calling on the same client repeatedly, the salesperson can educate the client over time about the particular advantages of the product or company. Regular contact over an extended period is particularly important when offering a product that can be tailored to the needs of an individual consumer. When the customer is a regular purchaser of the company's products, personal contact can be used to deepen and strengthen that loyalty, as well as to deal with any operational problems and concerns that may arise from time to time.

FACE-TO-FACE VERSUS TELEPHONE CONTACT

The major advantages of personal over impersonal communication are often offset by the major disadvantages of cost. Heavy monetary costs are incurred to pay, manage, and provide support for a sales force. In many selling situations of a technical nature, average costs exceeding $100 per call are quite common.

In an attempt to increase sales force productivity, many organizations are turning to the use of the telephone as a sales management channel. Not all products and services require face-to-face contact between salespeople and their customers. Instead of traveling to visit their accounts, telephone account managers maintain contact by phone. Aided by computer databases that maintain an updated file of account activity, as well as relevant background information on the account and details of customer needs and concerns, a telephone-based salesperson can provide a high level of service to existing accounts in addition to proactively seeking new selling opportunities.

This approach reduces wasteful travel time, to say nothing of achieving substantial savings on travel costs. On those occasions where face-to-face contact is deemed essential—for instance, to demonstrate new equipment—customers can be brought to a company demonstration center. Technical personnel can be sent to visit the company's premises and, if necessary, the account manager can accompany them. But in any event, by making the majority of contacts by phone, firms can often achieve significant productivity improvements.

Telephone selling is increasingly common in retail business activity, too. In some instances, "telesales" personnel prospect aggressively for new customers, cold calling prospects from a list. Stockbroking, insurance, and publications are often sold this way. In other instances, the salesperson's role is more reactive, waiting for the customer to call. To a growing extent, telephone ordering is replacing mail order for many products. In such instances, however, the salesperson (like many retail store personnel) is often little more than an order taker with only limited ability to provide advice and consultation.

ORGANIZATION

A major organizational decision is whether the sales force should be organized on a geographic, product, or market basis or some combination of these. Among companies whose salespeople travel over wide areas to visit accounts, geography almost always becomes a basis for organization at some level. One problem that arises is how to coordinate local geographic efforts with the nationwide concerns of major customers.

A related organizational concern is the number of levels of sales management to use and the number of individuals who report to each type of manager—what is called the *span of control*. Lowering the number of sales representatives reporting to a manager allows for closer supervision, but also increases the proportion of the personal selling budget spent on nonselling tasks. Also, too narrow a span of control can lead to overcontrol and reduce salesperson initiative and motivation. On the other hand, personal selling activities need to be monitored carefully to keep them on target.

Once the basic sales organization has been determined, decisions must be made about how the sales force should be deployed. The issues include the assignment of accounts to sales representatives—the territory-design problem—and allocation of sales-force time to accounts, product lines, and activities such as opening new accounts versus servicing existing ones. Proper territorial design is a persistent problem for sales management. The needs of sales representatives—particularly senior ones who often have strong preferences and long-term ties to certain accounts—must be balanced against the requirements of the marketing plan and current market forces.

RECRUITING, SELECTION, AND TRAINING

Clearly defining the role that personal selling is to play in the marketing program and the specific tasks that salespeople will be assigned can suggest the types of individuals needed, likely sources for recruitment, and appropriate selection criteria. Corporate resources, sales-force size, and job requirements often determine whether the company should try to hire experienced or inexperienced people.

Almost all firms must do some training. For newly hired, inexperienced salespeople, training should cover selling skills, a detailed understanding of customers and their needs, and extensive knowledge of the company's products and its policies and procedures in general. Besides an initial program of familiarization, experienced sales personnel may benefit from more intensive training to improve their selling skills, inform them about new products and policies, or prepare them for more responsible positions within the sales organization.

REWARDS AND INCENTIVES

Rewards and incentives include both financial and nonfinancial elements. Rewards can be subdivided into two main categories, intrinsic and extrinsic. The former include such intangibles as feelings of competence, completion, and self-worth. Managers are paying increasing attention to the importance of intrinsic rewards. This can be done by defining jobs and responsibilities carefully, providing feedback, and, more generally, trying to understand a salesperson's view of his or her job and role in the company.

Extrinsic rewards—tangible external elements controlled by the company—include financial and other benefits. Compensation systems should be designed to encourage the types of behavior desired by the firm. Guaranteed salaries, commissions, and bonuses should be combined in appropriate proportions. There is growing concern by sales managers about too much reliance on commissions, since these may cause sales representatives to focus on the short term and not pay sufficient attention to building long-term account relationships. Company recognition, such as distinguished-service awards for successful salespeople, can often be an important motivator. The design of the compensation system plays an important role in attracting and retaining qualified people for the sales force.

EVALUATION AND CONTROL

Procedures are needed so that sales executives can monitor the performance of individuals and sales groups against certain standards. Information on how actual performance relates to targets can then be fed back to the involved parties so that any necessary corrective action can be taken. The standards may take the form of measures of input (such as the number of sales calls to be made, the number of new accounts to be contacted, and the level of a salesperson's knowledge) or measures of output (such as dollar sales achieved as compared with sales quotas for different products, market segments, etc.). Performance against some of these standards can be measured quite objectively, while performance against others must often rely on the subjective judgment of the field sales manager. A good evaluation and control system provides both the field sales manager and the salesperson with an opportunity to identify areas of strength and weakness and to develop programs to correct any deficiencies that are identified.

SUMMARY

Because personal selling involves two-way communication between the marketing organization and its customers, it is a potentially more powerful medium of communication than impersonal, one-way channels such as advertising and public relations. The salesperson has an opportunity not only to tailor the message to the individual customer, but also to learn about customers' needs and concerns.

However, personal selling tends to be a relatively expensive communication medium. Marketers need to be clear about the role that personal selling is to play in the broader communication mix and to use lower-cost channels, including the telephone instead of face-to-face contact, when these approaches may be more cost effective.

Personal selling activities often have more impact when planned in conjunction with advertising, publicity, and promotional campaigns, since the latter may help to build awareness and knowledge of the product in advance of the salesperson's interactions with the customer (which may be initiated by either party). Once a relationship has been established, the challenge is to manage the account effectively over time. Good record keeping and an appropriate level of contact through a designated account manager help to create and maintain account relationships that are rewarding to both parties. For many products, telephone account management offers a desirable alternative to face-to-face contact.

Effective sales management requires selection of appropriate structures for assigning accounts (and prospects) and coordinating selling efforts by the sales force. Among the other key issues to be addressed by sales managers are recruitment and selection, training, choice of appropriate reward and incentive programs, evaluation of sales personnel against defined criteria, and exercise of appropriate controls.

Mediquip S.A.

Kamran Kashani

On December 18, Kurt Thaldorf, a sales engineer for the German sales subsidiary of Mediquip, S.A., was informed by Lohmann University Hospital in Stuttgart that it had decided to place an order with Sigma, a Dutch competitor, for a computer tomography (CT) scanner. The hospital's decision came as disappointing news to Thaldorf, who had worked for nearly eight months on the account. The order, if obtained, would have meant a sale of DM 2,370,000 for the sales engineer.[1] He was convinced that Mediquip's CT scanner was technologically superior to Sigma's and, overall, a better product.

Thaldorf began a review of his call reports in order to better understand the factors that had led to Lohmann University Hospital's decision. He wanted to apply the lessons from this experience to future sales situations.

BACKGROUND

At the time, the CT scanner was a relatively recent product in the field of diagnostic imaging. This med-

ical device, used for diagnostic purposes, allowed examination of cross sections of the human body through display of images. CT scanners combined sophisticated X-ray equipment with a computer to collect the necessary data and translate them into visual images.

When computer tomography was first introduced in the late 1960s, radiologists had hailed it as a major technological breakthrough. Commenting on the advantages of CT scanners, a product specialist with Mediquip said, "The end product looks very much like an X-ray image. The only difference is that with scanners you can see sections of the body that were never seen before on a screen—like the pancreas. A radiologist, for example, can diagnose cancer of the pancreas in less than two weeks after it develops. This was not possible before CT scanners."

Mediquip was a subsidiary of Technologie Universelle, a French conglomerate. The company's product line included, in addition to CT scanners, X-ray, ultrasonic and nuclear diagnostic equipment. Mediquip enjoyed a worldwide reputation for ad-

[1]For the purposes of this case, use the following exchange rates for the Deutschmark (DM): DM 1.00 = SF 0.85, $0.60, Ecu 0.50, £0.35.

vanced technology and competent after-sales service.

"Our competitors are mostly from other European countries," commented Mediquip's Sales Director for Europe. "In some markets they have been there longer than we have, and they know the decision makers better than we do. But we are learning fast." Sigma, the subsidiary of a diversified Dutch company under the same name, was the company's most serious competitor. Other major contenders in the CT scanner market were FNC, Eldora, Magna, and Piper.

Mediquip's executives estimated the European market for CT scanners to be around 200 units per year. They pointed out that prices ranged from DM1.5 to DM3.0 million per unit. The company's CT scanner sold in the upper end of the price range. "Our equipment is at least two years ahead of our most advanced competition," explained a sales executive. "And our price reflects this technological superiority."

Mediquip's sales organization in Europe included eight country sales subsidiaries each headed by a managing director. Within each country, sales engineers reported to regional sales managers who, in turn, reported to the managing director. Product specialists provided technical support to the sales force in each country.

BUYERS OF CT SCANNERS

A sales executive at Mediquip described the buyers of CT scanners as follows:

Most of our sales are to what we call the public sector, health agencies that are either government-owned or belong to non-profit support organizations such as universities and philanthropic institutions. They are the sort of buyers that buy through formal tenders and have to budget their purchases at least one year in advance. Once the budget is allocated, it must then be spent before the end of the year. Only a minor share of our CT scanner sales goes to the private sector, profit-oriented organizations such as private hospitals or private radiologists.

Of the two markets, the public sector is much more complex. Typically, there are at least four groups that get involved in the purchase decision: radiologists, physicists, administrators, and people from the supporting agency—usually the ones who approve the budget for purchasing a CT scanner.

Radiologists are the ones who use the equipment. They are doctors whose diagnostic services are sought by other doctors in the hospital or clinic. Patients remember their doctors, but not the radiologists. They never receive flowers from the patients! A CT scanner could really enhance their professional image among their colleagues.

Physicists are the scientists in residence. They write the technical specifications which competing CT scanners must meet; they should know the state of the art in X-ray technology. Their primary concern is the patient's safety.

The administrators are, well, administrators. They have the financial responsibility for their organizations. They are concerned with the cost of CT scanners, but also with what revenues they can generate. The administrators are extremely wary of purchasing an expensive technological toy that will become obsolete in a few years.

The people from the supporting agency are usually not directly involved with decisions as to which product to purchase. But, since they must approve the expenditures, they do play an indirect role. Their influence is mostly felt by the administrators.

The interplay among the four groups, as you can imagine, is rather complex. The power of each group in relationship to the others varies from organization to organization. The administrator, for example, is the top decision maker in certain hospitals. In others, he is only a buyer. One of the key tasks of our sales engineers is to define for each potential account the relative power of the players. Only then can they set priorities and formulate selling strategies.

The European sales organization at Mediquip had recently started using a series of forms designed to help sales engineers in their account analysis and strategy formulation. (A sample of the forms, called Account Management Analysis, is reproduced in *Exhibit 1*.)

LOHMANN UNIVERSITY HOSPITAL

Lohmann University Hospital (LUH) was a large general hospital serving Stuttgart, a city of one million residents. The hospital was part of the university's medical school. The university was a leading teaching center and enjoyed an excellent reputation. LUH's radiology department had a wide range of X-ray equipment from a number of European manufacturers, including Sigma and FNC. The radiology department had five staff members, headed by a senior and nationally known radiologist, Professor Steinborn.

Thaldorf's Sales Activities

From the records he had kept of his sales calls, Thaldorf reviewed the events for the period between May 5, when he learned of LUH's interest in purchasing a CT scanner and December 18, when he was informed that Mediquip had lost the order.

May 5

Office received a call from a Professor Steinborn from Lohmann University Hospital regarding a CT scanner. I was assigned to make the call on the professor. Looked through our files to find out if we had sold anything to the hospital before. We had not. Made an appointment to see the professor on May 9.

May 9

Called on Professor Steinborn, who informed me of a recent decision by university directors to set aside funds next year for the purchase of the hospital's first CT scanner. The professor wanted to know what we had to offer. Described the general features of our CT system. Gave him some brochures. Asked a few questions which led me to believe other companies had come to see him before I did. Told me to check with Dr. Rufer, the hospital's physicist, regarding the specs. Made an appointment to see him again ten days later. Called on Dr. Rufer, who was not there. His secretary gave me a lengthy document on the scanner specs.

May 10

Read the specs last night. Looked like they had been copied straight from somebody's technical manual. Showed them to our Product Specialist, who confirmed my own hunch that our system met and exceeded the specs. Made an appointment to see Dr. Rufer next week.

May 15

Called on Dr. Rufer. Told him about our system's features and the fact that we met all the specs set down on the document. He did not seem particularly impressed. Left him with technical documents about our system.

May 19

Called on Professor Steinborn. He had read the material I had left with him. Seemed rather pleased with the features. Asked about our upgrading scheme. Told him we would undertake to upgrade the system as new features became available. Explained that Mediquip, unlike other systems, can be made to accommodate the latest technology, with no risk of obsolescence for a long time. This impressed him. Also answered his questions regarding image manipulation, image processing speed, and our service capability. Just before I left, he inquired about our price. Told him I would have an informative quote for him at our next meeting. Made an appointment to see him on June 23 after he returned from his vacation. Told me to get in touch with Carl Hartmann, the hospital's general director, in the interim.

June 1

Called on Hartmann. It was difficult to get an appointment with him. Told him about our interest in supplying his hospital with our CT scanner, which met all the specs as defined by Dr. Rufer. Also informed him of our excellent service capability. He wanted to know which other hospitals in the country had purchased our system. Told him I would provide him with a list of buyers within a few days. He asked about the price. Gave him an informative quote of DM2,850,000—a price my boss and I had determined after my visit to Professor Steinborn. He shook his head saying, "Other scanners are cheaper by a wide margin." I explained that our price reflected the

EXHIBIT 1   MEDIQUIP, S.A. ACCOUNT MANAGEMENT ANALYSIS FORM

Key Account: _____

ACCOUNT MANAGEMENT ANALYSIS

The enclosed forms are designed to facilitate your management of:

1. A key sales account

2. The *Mediquip* resources that can be applied to this key account

Completing the enclosed forms, you will:

• Identify installed equipment, and planned or potential new equipment
• Analyze purchase decision process and influence patterns, including:
— Identify and prioritize all major sources of influence
— Project probable sequence of events and timing of decision process
— Assess position/interest of each major influence source
— Identify major competition and probable strategies
— Identify needed information/support

• Establish an account development strategy, including:
— Select key contacts
— Establish strategy and tactics for each key contact, identify appropriate *Mediquip* personnel
— Assess plans for the most effective use of local team and headquarters resources

KEY ACCOUNT DATA

☐ Original (Date: _____)   Account No.: _____   Type of Institute: _____

☐ Revision (Date: _____)   Sales Specialist: _____   Bed Size: _____

                               Country/Region/District: _____   Telephone: _____

1. CUSTOMER (HOSPITAL, CLINIC, PRIVATE INSTITUTE)

Name: _____

Street Address: _____

City, State: _____

2. DECISION MAKERS — IMPORTANT CONTACTS

INDIVIDUALS	NAME	SPECIALTY	REMARKS
Medical Staff			
Administration			
Local Government			
State Government			

This exhibit presents a condensed version of the forms.

EXHIBIT 1 (*continued*)

3. INSTALLED EQUIPMENT

TYPE	DESCRIPTION	SUPPLIED BY	INSTALLATION DATE	YEAR TO REPLACE	VALUE OF POTENTIAL ORDER
X-ray Nuclear Ultrasound RTP CT					

4. PLANNED NEW EQUIPMENT

TYPE	QUOTE NO.	DATE	% CHANCE	EST. ORDER DATE 1980	EST. ORDER DATE 1981	EST. DELIVERY 1980	EST. DELIVERY 1981	QUOTED PRICE

5. COMPETITION

COMPANY/PRODUCT	STRATEGY/ TACTICS	% CHANCE	STRENGTH	WEAKNESS

6. SALES PLAN   Product: _____ Quote No: _____   Quoted Price: _____

KEY ISSUES	*Mediquip's* PLAN	SUPPORT NEEDED FROM:	DATE OF FOLLOW-UP REMARKS

7. ACTIONS — IN SUPPORT OF PLAN

SPECIFIC ACTION	RESPONSIBILITY	DUE DATES ORIGINAL	DUE DATES REVISED	DUE DATES COMPLETED	RESULTS/REMARKS

8. ORDER STATUS REPORT

REVISION DATE	ACCOUNT NAME AND\LOCATION	ISSUES/COMPETITIVE STRATEGY	ACTIONS/ STRATEGY	RESPON- SIBILITY	% CHANCE	EXPECTED ORDER TIMING	WIN/LOSE

fact that the latest technology was already built into our scanner. Also mentioned that the price differential was an investment that could pay for itself several times over through faster speed of operation. He was noncommittal. Before leaving his office, he instructed me not to talk to anybody else about the price. Asked him specifically if that included Professor Steinborn. He said it did. Left him with a lot of material about our system.

June 3

Went to Hartmann's office with a list of three hospitals similar in size to LUH that had installed our system. He was out. Left it with his secretary, who recognized me. Learned from her that at least two other firms, Sigma and FNC, were competing for the order. She also volunteered the information that "prices are so different, Mr. Hartmann is confused." She added that the final decision will be made by a committee made up of Hartmann, Professor Steinborn and one other person whom she could not recall.

June 20

Called on Dr. Rufer. Asked him if he had read the material about our system. He had, but did not have much to say. I repeated some of the key operational advantages our product enjoyed over those produced by others, including Sigma and FNC. Left him some more technical documents.

On the way out, stopped by Hartmann's office. His secretary told me that we had received favorable comments from the hospitals using our system.

June 23

Professor Steinborn was flabbergasted to hear that I could not discuss our price with him. Told him about the hospital administration's instructions to that effect. He could not believe this, especially when Sigma had already given him their quote of DM2,100,000. When he calmed down, he wanted to know if we were going to be at least competitive with the others. Told him our system was more ad-

vanced than Sigma's. Promised him we would do our best to come up with an attractive offer. Then we talked about his vacation and sailing experience in the Aegean Sea. He said he loved the Greek food.

July 15

Called to see if Hartmann had returned from his vacation. He had. While checking his calendar, his secretary told me that our system seemed to be the "radiologists' choice," but that Hartmann had not yet made up his mind.

July 30

Visited Hartmann accompanied by the regional manager. Hartmann seemed to have a fixation about the price. He said, "All the companies claim they have the latest technology." So he could not understand why our offer was "so much above the rest." He concluded that only a "very attractive price" could tip the balance in our favor. After repeating the operational advantages our system enjoyed over others, including those produced by Sigma and FNC, my boss indicated that we were willing to lower our price to DM 2,610,000 if the equipment was ordered before the end of the current year. Hartmann said he would consider the offer and seek "objective" expert opinion. He also said a decision would be made before Christmas.

August 14

Called on Professor Steinborn, who was too busy to see me for more than ten minutes. He wanted to know if we had lowered our price since the last meeting with him. I said we had. He shook his head and said with a laugh, "Maybe that was not your best offer." He then wanted to know how fast we could make deliveries. Told him within six months. He did not say anything.

September 2

The regional manager and I discussed the desirability of inviting one or more people from the LUH to visit the Mediquip headquarter operations near Paris. The three-day trip would give the participants a chance to see the scope of the facilities and become better acquainted with CT scanner applications. This idea was finally rejected as inappropriate.

September 3

Dropped in to see Hartmann. He was busy but had time to ask for a formal "final offer" from us by October 1. On the way out, his secretary told me there had been "a lot of heated discussions" about which scanner seemed best suited for the hospital. She would not say more.

September 25

The question of price was raised in a meeting with the regional manager and the managing director. I had recommended a sizeable cut in our price to win the order. The regional manager seemed to agree with me, but the managing director was reluctant. His concern was that too big a drop in price looked "unhealthy." They finally agreed to a final offer of DM 2,370,000.

Made an appointment to see Hartmann later that week.

September 29

Took our offer of DM 2,370,00 in a sealed envelope to Hartmann. He did not open it, but he said he hoped the scanner question would soon be resolved to the "satisfaction of all concerned." Asked him how the decision was going to be made. He evaded the question but said he would notify us as soon as a decision was reached. Left his office feeling that our price had a good chance of being accepted.

October 20

Called on Professor Steinborn. He had nothing to tell me except that "the CT scanner is the last thing I want to talk about." Felt he was unhappy with the way things were going.

Tried to make an appointment with Hartmann in November, but he was too busy.

November 5

Called on Hartmann, who told me that a decision would probably not be reached before next month. He indicated that our price was "within the range," but that all the competing systems were being evaluated to see which seemed most appropriate for the hospital. He repeated that he would call us when a decision was reached.

December 18

Received a brief letter from Hartmann thanking Mediquip for participating in the bid for the CT scanner, along with the announcement that LUH had decided to place the order with Sigma.

BT: Telephone Account Management

Martin Bless
Christopher H. Lovelock

"So what would you do in my place, Michael?" asked the regional sales manager.

Michael Tarte-Booth, sales development manager at BT (formerly British Telecom) listened over a pub lunch as his colleague, John Lambert, described the situation. It concerned a small business customer whose telecommunication needs were handled by BT's telephone account management (TAM) program. Tarte-Booth was very familiar with TAM, having been involved with the program from its early days.

The customer in question had grown in size, and with the addition of a sixth line, now qualified for personal contact with an account executive. But, when informed of what BT viewed as an upgrade in account handling service, the customer demurred, asking to remain with TAM. Said Lambert:

They wrote us a letter—I've got it here in my briefcase. It was polite but very firm. They don't want to shift from TAM. But now the field sales people are raising hell, claiming these folks as their own. This situation challenges the whole basis of our account management structure for different sizes of business customer.

BRITISH TELECOMMUNICATIONS

The United Kingdom (UK) was the first European country to depart from the traditional PTT (post, telegraph, telephone) model under which postal and telecommunications services were administered by the same government agency. After being transformed from a government department into a public corporation in 1969, the postal and telecommunications businesses were split apart in 1981. Post Office Telephones became British Telecom. Under the conservative government of prime minister Margaret Thatcher, numerous public corporations such as British Airways and British Gas were privatized. Soon the government announced its intention to privatize BT and sell up to 51% of the corporation to the public. In November 1984, more than two million people, including 222,000 BT employees, applied for the one billion shares available. A total of £3.9 billion was raised.[1]

As the sole licensing authority for telecommunication operators, the government took the view that competition and choice between operators would be beneficial to customers. In 1984 it awarded a licence

---

[1]The value of the pound sterling (£) varied widely against other currencies during the 1980s. Typical exchange rates in 1991 were: £1.00 = US$1.70 = SF2.50. A second sale of government shares in BT took place in 1991.

to provide domestic services to Mercury Communications, owned by Cable & Wireless (a recently privatized operator of international telecommunication services).

The government provided breathing space to BT and Mercury by making clear its intention not to license any further fixed network operators for seven years. Separate licences were awarded to four operators of mobile telecommunication services, including BT and Mercury. To ensure that BT did not abuse its initial virtual monopoly position of fixed network services, an Office of Telecommunications (Oftel) was established to protect the interest of customers. Oftel was widely empowered to oversee and regulate the business conduct and pricing policies of both BT and Mercury. Among other things, it prohibited access by BT marketing personnel to information on customer billing records.

Privatization and the introduction of domestic competition forced a refocusing of BT's activities. Between 1984 and 1991, the company went through two major reorganizations. The second, termed Project Sovereign, was one of the most ambitious attempts to date by a British company to reform its organization, management, and culture. These reforms were meant to prepare BT for three challenges. First, the industry's traditional structure—national monopoly operators supplied by national manufacturers—was breaking down throughout the world. Regulatory barriers to international competition were expected to crumble, gradually in some countries, faster in the UK. Second, as companies internationalized, they might prefer to deal with a single telecommunications company worldwide. Providers of telecommunications services would have to tailor their products less to neatly defined geographic markets and more to groups of customers, who could be located globally. And third, more intense international competition and the growing costs of the technology race would lead to concentration of the industry. One manager commented:

Many people welcomed the changes because of the greater freedom they offered us to respond to evolving market needs and to take advantage of new technologies. But, an equally large group continued to think and act like civil servants, as though we were still a government department. A third group were fence sitters who took a "wait and see" attitude, but were willing to be converted.

During the 1980s, telecommunications had made tremendous technological strides. For many corporate users, data communications became as important as voice communications. The use of fax machines and electronic mail exploded. BT invested heavily in modernization, unconstrained by the public sector borrowing requirements that the government had imposed before privatization. Coaxial copper cables were replaced by fiber optic cables which offered much greater capacity and better signal quality. New electronic exchanges with digital switches not only operated faster and more accurately but also enabled BT to offer a host of extra services such as automatic call forwarding.

In April 1991, the company changed its trading name from British Telecom to BT and adopted a new motto "Putting customers first." The new organization was structured around three customer-centered divisions: Business Communications, Personal Communications, and Special Businesses (including mobile and operator services). Each would deal directly with customers for sales and services, while being supported by other divisions that either managed BT's products and services, operated a worldwide networking capability, or provided development and procurement services. The 31 districts were abolished and only five regions remained of the original geographical structure.

Current Situation

With 1990–91 revenues of £13.15 billion, BT was Britain's second largest company (after British Petroleum plc). Reflecting the growth in both domestic and international markets, plus significant cost-cutting efforts, BT's pre-tax operating profit in fiscal 1991 rose to £3.08 billion.

BT operated a technologically advanced network, boasting the highest proportion of optical fiber in its system of any major telecommunications operator. The long-distance digital network was complete, while more than three quarters of all customers in the UK were connected to modern electronic exchanges (a few percentage points behind France, which had the highest share of digitalized exchanges of any major country). Further modernization continued at a rapid pace. Britain and Spain remained the only European nations to have privatized their telecommunication services, but a number of others were expected to follow in 1992–93. BT had also invested heavily in international ventures.

Domestically, BT retained a 94% market share. However, Mercury had adopted a strategy of penetrating the business market, starting with the largest customers—which might have thousands of lines. It was not uncommon for big customers to split their telecommunications business between BT and Mercury. At the consumer level, Mercury's presence was minimal except for pay telephones in busy locations—such as city centers and airports (*Exhibit 1* shows the breakdown of the market by type of subscriber and number of lines.)

Since Mercury had built its network from nothing, it could offer customers state-of-the-art technology and had pioneered a number of service innovations, which BT was seeking to match. But, Mercury's network was still geographically limited, being focused on connecting London to Britain's business

centers. Broader penetration required connecting customers to its network via BT's local lines, which often still used conventional technology. Mercury planned to spend £500 million annually during the three years 1992–1994 to extend its network and boost its share of the domestic market. It already had 15% of the UK's international traffic and a greater share of private networks. The American telecommunications giant, AT&T (described as the 800 pound gorilla of the industry), was rumored to be eager to invest in Mercury's future.

Additional network competition was expected to come from British Rail Telecom and from a joint venture between US Sprint and British Waterways (which planned to lay cable along the bottom of its canal network). Local competition was seen as coming from cable television operators, many of whom were affiliated with American regional phone companies, and from operators of mobile (cellular) services.

CREATING A PILOT TELEMARKETING OPERATION

"You are the most difficult people in the world to buy from!" was how a customer described BT to

EXHIBIT 1

BT'S EXCHANGE CONNECTIONS IN SERVICE BY TYPE OF SUBSCRIBER, 1980–1990 UNITED KINGDOM

Year (at March 31)	Total exchange connection (000s)	Residential subscription (000s)	Business subscribers (000s)
1980	17,353	13,937	3,416
1981	18,174	14,671	3,503
1982	18,727	15,159	3,568
1983	19,186	15,546	3,640
1984	19,812	16,044	3,768
1985	20,528	16,596	3,932
1986	21,261	17,120	4,141
1987	21,908	17,549	4,359
1988	22,857	18,145	4,712
1989	23,946	18,737	5,209
1990	25,013	19,281	5,732

Source: British Telecom.

Anna Thomson soon after she joined the marketing department of the newly created Thameswey district in 1985. Her colleagues quickly came to recognize Thomson's energy, drive, and enthusiasm for seeking out innovative approaches. Although recruited as network marketing manager, her responsibilities were soon extended to marketing BT's products and services, and she became district marketing operations manager.

Thomson's prior experience had been in the electricity industry, marketing network usage. In her new position, she demonstrated the value of selling customer premises equipment (CPE) as a means of generating network revenues rather than as an end in itself. She adopted an integrated approach to marketing both networks and CPE as complementary products. Thomson remarked that "inevitably the selling of the one would lead to the selling of the other." She emphasized that network sales were far more profitable than CPE sales, but traditionally BT had found it difficult to sell the more intangible product.

While analyzing customer relationships at BT, Thomson singled out small business customers, as a neglected market.

The crux of the whole thing is that effective use of modern telecommunications products and services can make a real difference to the development of any small business today. Use of mobile communication tools, the choice of the right fax machine, installation of a switch than can grow easily and cost effectively to cover extra lines, the use of toll-free numbers and a wide range of datacoms services—all these things help a small business to be flexible as it reorganizes to meet its own customers' changing needs.

The right telecom choices at the right time can enable a small business to offer new services (like out-of-hours customer service with call redirect), cut operating costs, and steal a march on their competitors. But, small business owners don't have time to research this all alone and so either miss opportunities altogether or make the wrong choices.

In her view, BT had not devoted enough time and energy to building the type of relationship that created loyalty. The only contact BT generally had with these customers was when they called with a problem or a bill was sent out. Typically, BT sales staff were only talking to small business customers once every three to five years, except when the customer initiated contact. Thomson warned that if nothing changed, BT was liable to lose these customers to competition.

Further analysis revealed that some 750,000 inquiries from customers of all types had not been followed up the previous year. The existing sales process, which was almost entirely focused upon reactive responses to inbound customer calls, was obviously not working. Large accounts (served by field-based account managers) and those that screamed for attention were catered to at the cost of ignoring a huge market of smaller accounts. What was needed, argued Thomson, were telephone-based reps (representatives) to look after smaller business accounts.

Recognizing that the most sophisticated applications of telemarketing strategy were to be found in the USA, Thomson convinced headquarters to retain a leading American consultant, Rudy Oetting, to advise on conducting a pilot test in the Thameswey district. This district extended west and south of London, beyond Heathrow airport, along the M3 and M4 motorway corridors. It contained many vibrant business communities, including a significant number of small high-technology firms. The consultant recommended that BT recruit and train telephone-based sales representatives to sell proactively into exactly that market.

Telephone Account Management

A variety of terms were used to describe the use of the telephone as a marketing tool. *Telesales* was often used to describe use of the telephone by salespeople as a communication channel through which prospects could be contacted and a single sales transaction consummated. *Telemarketing* was a broader umbrella term for all types of marketing-related telephone usage. *Telephone account management* was defined as proactive contact through the telephone channel to customers who required a continuing personal relationship—but not necessarily face-to-face contact—with skilled sales representatives who could function as communication consultants to small businesses.

Rudy Oetting described such people as bright, aggressive account managers who had been trained to listen carefully to customer needs and ask structured, probing questions about each business and its communication activities. The goal was to build a data base of information on each customer which would enable managers to farm a territory systematically without ever leaving the office. In some cases, Oetting declared, they would work jointly with field sales; sometimes they called the shots for the field force, and in other instances, they were the *only* sales force.

Thomson recognized the potential of such an approach for BT, using its own channel—the telephone—to contact the company's small business customers. She did not accept the traditional view that British business culture would not respond positively to telephone sales contact, being confident it would work well providing the process was oriented toward uncovering and meeting customer needs. But, she saw that the approach would have to be non-threatening and employ well-trained representatives who operated on a much higher level than conventional sales support or customer service personnel. As the concept took shape, Thomson coined the term *telemanaging,* which she defined as:

Managing the customer primarily through the medium of the telephone, using all the sales, marketing systems, and management disciplines of account management.

THE TAM CONCEPT

The term *TAM* came to be used at BT as an acronym for both telephone account management and a telephone account manager. The latter would be a carefully selected salesperson trained to handle a wide portfolio of products and services, working with up to 1,000 assigned accounts entirely by telephone. TAMs would be trained to develop specific objectives for each call. During the call, they were expected to update their knowledge of the customer's situation and needs, check whether any problems needed solving, advise on products and services, take orders, and plan a specific date for the next call. The basic goals would be to ensure that the accounts

continued buying from BT rather than the competition, and to develop accounts by selling additional products and services. Said Thomson:

The job of TAMs is to understand the business objectives and organization of their customers and to help their customers make the right investment decisions at the right time—so that we *and* they become increasingly successful. It's a partnership based on trust, which has to be earned through proven good advice over time. BT believes that this is the way you become a customer's preferred supplier. The basic goal is to continually build and refresh knowledge of the account base, and be the first to address or even anticipate communications needs. This is true relationship marketing but effected within a volume market because the TAM goes through this process a thousandfold. We use our own core product—the telephone—to do the job, because it allows us to manage and market efficiently to hundreds of thousands of customers. You could say we practice what we preach!

Each TAM would endeavor to develop a relationship based on trust. The customer call would remain the focal point throughout the contact cycle. Whether an order was taken or not, the TAM would establish when the next call was to take place and put it on the calendar. All the information collected would be fed into each customer's electronic file.

Thomson emphasized that the value of an account to BT was much more than just line rental charges and fees for network usage. The company also sold a wide range of telecommunications equipment (ranging from individual handsets to private branch exchanges), installation and maintenance, and an array of value-added services (refer to *Exhibit 2* for examples).

When face-to-face contact with the customer was needed, the field sales staff would work together with the TAM. The ultimate responsibility for managing an account, however, would remain with the TAM. Thomson saw teamwork as an essential part of the process. One TAM later described the relationship as follows:

It works on the basis of whoever can close the sale, should close the sale. This means that we have to work as a team; you cannot have a "them and us syndrome." If the TAM is in contact with a customer who wants somebody to pay a visit, the field representative can go out with a better

EXHIBIT 2
SAMPLE VOICE AND DATA SERVICES OFFERED BY BT, 1992

Voice services

CityDirect provides direct connections between London and the USA offering call facilities such as abbreviated dialing and security safeguards.

SpeechLines is a service for intra-company speech connection.

LinkLine is an automatic freefone service which allows business to offer their customers a free inquiry and ordering facility.

CallStream is a service for information providers who sell stored voice or data information via the normal telephone line.

Network services offers call facilities such as call diversion, call barring, call waiting, last number redial, abbreviated dialing, and conference call.

Voicecom International provides a 24-hour network of voice mailboxes to send, receive, or forward messages from any telephone in the world.

Data services

Datel is a data transmission service available internationally to over 100 countries.

KeyLine provides analog private circuits for data transmission using modems.

Leaseline offers analog circuits that enable subscribers to transport voice, facsimile, data, and telegraph messages nationally and internationally.

KiloStream and MegaStream provide digital, private circuits between centers at high operating speeds.

PSS is a nationwide public data network using packet switching techniques.

MultiStream enhances access to the public network at local call rates for the business community.

Data Direct is a high-speed public data service to the USA and Japan.

Prestel is BT's public Videotex service.

SatSteam is a satellite service for business communication with Norh America and Europe.

Telecom Gold is an electronic mail service with over 250,000 mailboxes in 17 countries.

Integrated Services Digital Network (ISDN) allows customers to transmit voice, data, text, or image information at high speeds and assured quality without dedicated private circuits.

understanding. And if, after the visit, it's clear that the sales representative cannot sign the customer up there and then, he or she will pass the case back to the TAM to monitor it. The principle is that if I achieve, we both achieve.

Michael Tarte-Booth

To assist her in implementing the TAM concept, Thomson hired Michael Tarte-Booth, a man with experience in telemarketing on both sides of the Atlantic. Thomson later insisted that, although the vision was hers, nothing would have happened in the field without her colleague's determination to get it right, day after day. His original career had nothing to do with telecommunications. As he observed, "How I fell into telephone marketing is pure chance."

After obtaining his undergraduate degree from a British university, Tarte-Booth obtained a master's degree in geography from the University of Minnesota. Then he went to work in Minneapolis for the American Heart Association, a major nonprofit organization. They needed someone with demographic expertise to analyze census data and pinpoint those geographic locations (down to specific street blocks) where their best potential lay for recruiting volunteer fund-raisers. Tarte-Booth also inherited responsibility for the association's telemarketing operation. He developed the use of the telephone as a primary contact for volunteer recruitment or direct solicitation of donations. One objective was to ensure that the volunteer callers should use their precious phone hours wisely by contacting only the better prospects. The potential power of this marriage between database marketing and the phone as a delivery channel was demonstrated when revenues increased by over 60% during the first year and 90% in the second.

On returning to Britain, Tarte-Booth was hired by a manufacturer of business systems to set up its telemarketing operation. The company was running a large direct field salesforce, but had neglected its customer base for paper-based products, and had disposed of its customer records for this market. The firm's telephone contact strategy was limited to proactive cold calls by sales representatives to new prospects. Thereafter, the channel strategy was simply inbound, waiting for customers to come back by phone or mail with repeat orders. Tarte-Booth's job was to set up a team that would revitalize the business:

The goal was to re-create the database by acquisition and integration of lists from numerous different sources so that we knew, after telephone contact, who the customers were and who the prospects were. Our initial objective was to derive sales principally through referrals out to the salesforce. But, we had to start out by qualifying our prospects and calling all the names on our list. The response was impressive.

Other groups within the sales organization recognized the value of this activity. Within two years, the company was also targeting other vertical markets in the hospitality, leisure and car retail and after-sales industries. Said Tarte-Booth:

The program diversified into new markets and more sophisticated applications. We had truly graduated to an account management operation with a primary focus on repeat purchase. Historically, customers had made repeat purchases roughly once every three years, now they were making them every three months! The whole thing about account management is getting to know and anticipate customers' needs by amalgamating the power of the database, the information you glean from customers, and the immediacy of contact by telephone. We found that customers liked the cloak of invisibility provided by the telephone contact. It gives them greater perceived control. Ultimately, they can drop the neutron bomb and hang up.

Inauguration of the TAM Pilot

After three months' preparation, the new pilot program was inaugurated in November 1986. Almost immediately, BT found that customers demanded a continuing dialogue focused on an understanding of their needs, as opposed to a tactical contact aiming to sell them "the flavor of the month." Customers were also motivated by continuity of contact, wanting to deal with a specific person on a regular basis. They would spend up to 20 minutes disclosing information about their business and needs; but having invested that amount of time, they expected the relationship to be perpetuated.

Thomson's primary mission was to tackle the strategic and political issues related to getting TAM accepted within BT and to develop an overall "integrated channel strategy" to show how all the sales, service and marketing channels (including TAM) should interrelate for BT's objectives to be met. The success of the pilot attracted growing attention. Over the course of the first year, Thameswey achieved a tenfold increase in account coverage and a threefold increase in customer purchasing levels among the pilot customers. These results were achieved at a lower ratio of cost-to-sales revenues than could have been obtained with face-to-face contact. It also left the field sales force with more time to talk to larger customers, and enabled them to achieve the high level of consultancy needed in that sector. Tarte-Booth observed:

The project succeeded strategically because of senior management sponsorship and the interest that Anna generated in the program. It was driven through centrally and had very high visibility within the organization.

NATIONAL IMPLEMENTATION

Anna Thomson and Michael Tarte-Booth kept in sight the ultimate aim of national implementation. Achieving that goal required careful documentation of the whole process. Other districts would have to be convinced rather than coerced to adopt TAM. In 1987, Thomson left the district to become national telemarketing manager. She saw her role as selling the concept of telemarketing to senior BT managers. Monthly steering committee meetings were held to discuss the progress of the pilot and make tactical changes. Progress reports, detailing success in achieving evolutionary benchmarks, were widely circulated. As Tarte-Booth recalled, Thomson did not try to convince the corporation that TAM was the "greatest thing since sliced bread." Instead, he pointed out:

We allowed it to prove itself and concentrated on keeping colleagues around the country advised of progress through workshops and seminars. As a result, other districts came of their own accord to inquire about possible implementation. As soon as a district showed serious interest, we followed up with more information in order to gain a commitment. With district autonomy and the fact that TAM was to be implemented on a voluntary basis, the soft sales approach was critical.

In early 1988, Tarte-Booth was appointed national implementation manager. He found that districts whose customer base was dispersed over a wide territory were quick to recognize TAM's value. During 1988, six districts established teams to focus on the small business market. A central development program was created to train the trainers, build the necessary support structure, and develop the database software for TAM. That program provided implementation expertise through a "franchise" package which demanded adherence to the proven methods established in the pilot in exchange for implementation assistance.

By early 1989, districts fell into three distinct categories. In the vanguard were six districts that had already established teams. The second group, described as "the soft underbelly of resistance," was interested but wanted to wait until TAM had proved itself elsewhere. Some sales managers were reluctant to embrace TAM, which was perceived as threatening, since it involved a reappraisal of their approach to customers and a reorganization of field sales responsibilities. Strong resistance came from a third group of districts, principally in London and the South East. This hard core was located in the region that not only had the highest customer density but also faced the greatest competitive threat.

Following the Project Sovereign reorganization, the districts were abolished and field sales territories expanded, thus increasing field reps' travel times. (*Exhibit 3* shows the reorganized sales structure, in which first Thomson and later Tarte-Booth held the position of manager of sales development, operating at the same level as the five regional sales managers.)

Training

Tarte-Booth emphasized that "the TAM program is not about creaming the market. It's about building loyalty and defending against future competition." Given the complexity of the task demanded of a TAM, considerable effort was placed on recruiting the right people. The initial interview with candidates was conducted by telephone, followed by written tests and face-to-face interviews, and concluding with psychometric profiling of each candidate prior to final selection. Recruitment was followed by intensive training. BT built three special training schools to develop a consistent approach to customer care.

Training covered attitudes, as well as skills, ranging from how not to sound like a robot when using a call guide (recommended dialogue) to how to gather and enter relevant information about customers. Training also included hands-on experience with the equipment that TAMs would be selling. Over a 12-month period, a future TAM would follow five training modules interlinked with live frontline

EXHIBIT 3 ORGANIZATION CHART

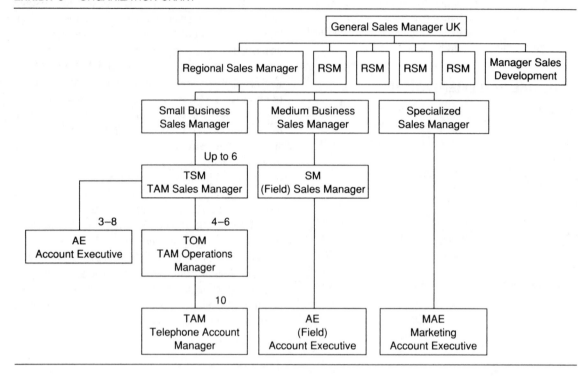

experience at his or her home base. The five modules collectively lasted for 13 weeks. Said Tarte-Booth:

The training program is designed to be holistic and so embraces the skills, the techniques, the methods, the tools, and the product knowledge integral to the future TAM's job. Their understanding is tested by rigorous role-playing and coaching sessions. The entire account team is trained together, so all members emerge with a clear understanding of how their jobs interrelate. Before returning to their home units, each team converts theory into practice by making live customer calls from the training centre.

FUTURE PLANS

By early 1992, BT operated 25 TAM call centers around the UK. Total staffing, including TAMs, TOMs (TAM operations managers) and support personnel, exceeded 450 persons. The annual cost of a TAM was around £41,000, of which 50% was salary

(in comparison, field account managers cost £40,000–£60,000 a year, of which about 65% was salary). Anna Thomson had been promoted to a new position, where her task was to develop a global customer service strategy for BT as the company began to expand into a worldwide organization. In this context, TAM was just one part of the jigsaw.

With TAM catering for small business accounts having two to five lines each, Tarte-Booth now turned his attention to other categories of business. His objective was to apply comprehensive account management to the entire customer base, integrating field and phone account management to address the needs of any type of customer. He saw BT's accounts as grouped into slices across a pyramid, with national accounts at the apex and single-line customers at the base. (*Exhibit 4* documents the number of accounts in each group and representative average annual revenues per account.)

In three regions, BT was piloting TAM for me-

EXHIBIT 4   PROFILE OF THE ACCOUNT MANAGEMENT PYRAMID AT BT

Group	No. of accounts	No of lines per account	Representative account data		
			Annual revenue per line (range)	Annual revenue from sales or rental of customer premises equipment	Annual revenue from value added network (range)
National accounts	300	100+	£1000–3000	£100,000	£200,000–500,000,000
Key regional accounts	3,000	15+	1000–2000	3,000	25,000—200,000
Medium business accounts	200,000	6–15	900–1500	500	5,400–22,500
Small business accounts	650,000	2–5	600–900	200	1,200–4,500
Very small business accounts	800,000	1	200–600	100	400

dium-sized business customers with 6 to 15 lines. Since these customers required an expanded portfolio of products and services, the new program was more complex than the small business TAM. Bigger customers tended to have a more sophisticated approach to decision making. This process had to be reflected in the call guides, the systems, and the training. Tarte-Booth described the new program as follows:

It's an evolution of TAM and premised on the same channel structure. As such, it shares much of the methodology established for the small business program, but has evolved to fit the needs of a new market segment.

Further up the pyramid were the key regional accounts, those with more than 15 lines. These customers would continue to be managed on a face-to-face basis through a field sales force channel. Account managers and specialist executives were in the field to support them, backed by proactive and reactive telephone support. At the top of the pyramid were national accounts—large and lucrative customers with sophisticated communications needs, often international in nature.

Very small business (VSB) customers with a single line, such as the consultant who worked from home or the small retail establishment, remained an untapped market. BT had experimentally incorporated the top 10% of this group in TAM but quickly learned that the use of TAMs was not a cost-effective

proposition. The cost of TAMs was viewed by some as prohibitively expensive for VSB customers. Tarte-Booth contended that "it's inappropriate to think of TAM in purely cost substitution terms, since BT's objectives are market coverage resulting in account protection and development."

His proposed solution was to test the use of direct mail, designed to generate inbound calls to a VSB account management team. Catalogs of telephone equipment and services useful to very small businesses would be mailed to large numbers of prospects. The goal would be to stimulate the purchase of upgraded telephone products and services. As these single-line customers grew and acquired second lines, they could migrate up the account management pyramid.

Looking ahead, Tarte-Booth envisaged the desirability of creating a more flexible account management structure:

Developing and implementing account management structures is a fundamentally different task from sales force management, and the two may well conflict. They also require different skills. What we need is a range of account management options based on different channel configurations. TAM is just one channel within the sales structure at BT. We need a totally integrated and flexible structure for customers, in which their changing needs and preferences will be consistently catered for, whether their need for products and services grows, stabilizes, or shrinks.

THE CASE OF GREEN & MEAKIN LTD.

Green & Meakin Ltd. was a manufacturer of aircraft parts. When the TAM program was first initiated, the firm had three lines and was assigned to Helen Dewhurst, who had exclusive responsibility for this account. As their TAM, she kept in touch with the company on a regular basis and followed through on all its requests, be it for a single socket, a new piece of telecommunications equipment, or an additional line. Feedback from the two partners who owned the firm was very positive. They were pleased, they said, with the prompt and efficient way in which Dewhurst handled their business needs. Their experiences with BT prior to the introduction of TAM had been far from satisfactory: hours had been wasted chasing up requests passed from one person who didn't know or couldn't help to another who often proved to be no better.

As the company grew, so did Green & Meakin's use of telecommunication services. One December day, a sixth line was installed. Unknown to the firm, this additional line automatically set in motion the upgrading process. Dewhurst compiled a file on the company which was handed up to the new team. She then contacted Green & Meakin to inform the company that in the future it would be handled by a field account executive, reflecting the growing size and importance of the Green & Meakin account. But, the partners were unhappy. One of them called Dewhurst to state that the firm liked the service she had provided and did not view reassigning their account to a new account group as a useful move. Dewhurst responded that, unfortunately, this was company policy, but added that she was sure they would receive excellent service in the future. When the senior partner still expressed dissatisfaction with the proposed move, she suggested that he call her supervisor, the TAM operations manager. Meeting a similar response from this individual and in turn from

her superior, the TAM sales manager, the senior partner wrote to John Lambert, the regional sales manager, to complain.

The Letter

"Ah, here it is!" exclaimed Lambert, pulling a sheet of paper from his briefcase. "Read it for yourself, Michael."

Michael Tarte-Booth unfolded the letter and quickly read it through. It was firm, and to the point (refer to *Exhibit 5*). "This is dated ten days ago," he said. "What's happened in the meantime, John?"

"Well, I simply made copies and sent one each with a covering memo to the relevant TAM operations manager and the sales manager, and told them to sort it out. Neither could agree on a course of action because both claimed Green & Meakin as their own. So they passed the buck back up to their superiors."

"And then?" queried Tarte-Booth.

"Same problem!" responded Lambert, gloomily. "Neither of those two folks could agree, either. So yesterday it landed neatly back on my desk like a boomerang. What do you suggest I do?"

The waitress came, cleared away their plates, and brought them coffee, which gave Tarte-Booth a moment's breathing space to think. "This could well happen again in the future," he said finally, sipping his coffee. "We can't spend all our time deciding when to make exceptions to the rules. I've been working on a plan to restructure the whole account management function at BT. Let me get back with a draft proposal to you in a few days, and I'll tell you then what I think we should do about Green & Meakin, too."

Tarte-Booth swallowed the rest of his coffee, put down the cup, and stood up. "Be in touch with you on Tuesday, John. Thanks for lunch. You did say you were paying, didn't you?"

EXHIBIT 5
LETTER TO BT FROM GREEN & MEAKIN, LTD.

Green & Meakin, Ltd
582 Thamesview Centre
Reading, Berkshire

Mr John Lambert   7 January 1992
Regional Sales Manager
BT Southwest Region

Dear Mr Lambert,

I am writing to you to express my concern over a proposed change in our account coverage status with BT. For the past four years, we have received excellent service through our telephone account manager, Helen Dewhurst. Recently, she informed us that, due to our acquisition of a sixth line, we were scheduled to be "upgraded" in the New Year to a field-based account manager who would make personal visits to us at our offices.

My partner, Jim Meakin, and I phoned Helen (using the new speakerphone we recently acquired from BT) to tell her that we were very happy with the service she provided and did not wish to change to a new account manager. But she told us that the decision was company policy and not hers to change.

Subsequently, I called her superior, Ms Anderson, and got a similar response. Next, the field sales manager called to introduce himself and the account manager who would be taking over from Helen. Jim took the call and said we didn't want to change, but we got the same story about "company policy." We had a similar response when we called the small business manager and the medium business sales manager, respectively. They don't seem to get the point that we are happy being served by Helen over the telephone.

So now I'm writing to you and appealing to your common sense rather than to company rulebooks. I know it's your internal policy to reassign customers when they reach a certain size (and we're flattered that you now consider us a "medium-sized company"). But the fact is, we don't need someone to keep coming out to visit us all the time, unless it's to install new equipment or undertake maintenance—which is a technician's job in any case. We feel strongly we're better off remaining with Helen.

We thank you for your consideration and look forward to your response.

Yours sincerely,

W. F. F. Green

/s/ W. F. F. GREEN, Partner

First National Bank

Christopher H. Lovelock

"I'm concerned about Karen," said Margaret Costanzo to David Reeves. The two bank officers were seated in Costanzo's office at the First National Bank's branch in Federal Square.

Ms. Costanzo was a vice president of the bank and manager of the Federal Square branch, the third largest in First National's 92-branch network. She was having an employee appraisal meeting with Mr. Reeves, customer service director at the branch. Reeves was responsible for the Customer Service Department, which coordinated the activities of the customer service representatives (CSRs, formerly known as tellers) and the customer assistance representatives (CARs, formerly known as new accounts assistants).

Costanzo and Reeves were discussing Karen Mitchell, a 24-year-old customer service rep, who had applied for the soon-to-be-vacant position of head CSR. Mitchell had been with the bank since graduating from junior college with an associate in arts degree three and a half years earlier. She had applied for the position of what had then been called head teller a year earlier, but the job had gone to a candidate with more seniority. Now that individual

was leaving—his wife had been transferred to a new job in another city—the position was once again open. Two other candidates had applied for the job.

Both Costanzo and Reeves were agreed that, against all criteria used in the past, Karen Mitchell would have been the obvious choice for head teller. She was both fast and accurate in her work, presented a smart and professional appearance, and was well liked by customers and her fellow CSRs.

However, the nature of the teller's job had been significantly revised nine months earlier to add a stronger marketing component (*Exhibit 1* shows the previous job description for teller; *Exhibit 2* shows the new job description for customer service representative.) CSRs were now expected to offer polite suggestions that customers use automatic teller machines for simple transactions. They were also required to stimulate customer interest in the broadening array of financial services offered by the bank. "The problem with Karen," as Reeves put it, "is that she simply refuses to sell."

THE NEW FOCUS ON CUSTOMER SERVICE AT THE FIRST

Although it was the largest bank in the state, the "First" had historically focused on corporate business

EXHIBIT 1 FIRST NATIONAL BANK: POSITION DESCRIPTION FOR TELLER
(Effective September 1982)

Function: Provides customer services by receiving, paying out, and keeping accurate records of all monies involved in paying and receiving transactions. Promotes the bank's services.

Responsibilities:

1. Serves customers:
   - Accepts deposits, verifies cash and endorsements, and gives customers their receipts.
   - Cashes checks within the limits assigned or refers customers to supervisor for authorization.
   - Accepts savings deposits and withdrawals, verifies signatures, and posts interest and balances as necessary.
   - Accepts loan, credit card, utility, and other payments.
   - Issues money orders, cashier's checks, traveler's checks, and foreign currency and issues or redeems U.S. savings bonds.
   - Reconciles customer statements and confers with bookkeeping personnel regarding discrepancies in balances or other problems.
   - Issues credit card advances.
2. Prepares individual daily settlement of teller cash and proof transactions.
3. Prepares branch daily journal and general ledger.
4. Promotes the bank's services:
   - Cross-sells other bank services appropriate to customer's needs.
   - Answers inquiries regarding bank matters.
   - Directs customers to other departments for specialized services.
5. Assists with other branch duties:
   - Receipts night and mail deposits.
   - Reconciles ATM transactions.
   - Provides safe deposit services.
   - Performs secretarial duties.

---

and its share of the retail consumer banking business had declined in the face of aggressive competition from other financial institutions. Three years earlier, the Board of Directors had appointed a new CEO and given him the mandate of developing a stronger consumer orientation at the retail level. The goal was to seize the initiative in marketing the ever-increasing array of financial services now available to retail customers. The new CEO's strategy, after putting in place a new management team, was to begin by ordering an expansion and speed-up of the First's investment in electronic delivery systems. The bank had tripled the number of automatic teller machines in its branches during the past 18 months, and was engaged in an active branch renovation program. One year ago, the First had also joined a regional ATM network, which boasted freestanding 24-hour booths at shopping centers, airports, and other high-traffic locations.

These actions seemed to be bearing fruit. In the most recent six months, the First had seen a significant increase in the number of new accounts opened, as compared to the same period of the previous year. And quarterly data released by the Federal Reserve Bank showed that the First was steadily increasing its share of new deposits in the state.

CUSTOMER SERVICE ISSUES

New financial products had been introduced at a rapid rate. But the bank found that existing platform staff—known as new accounts assistants—were ill equipped to sell these services because of lack of product knowledge and inadequate training in selling skills. Recalled Ms. Costanzo,

The problem was that they were so used to waiting for a customer to approach them with a specific request, such as a mortgage or car loan, that it was hard to get them to take

EXHIBIT 2 FIRST NATIONAL BANK: POSITION DESCRIPTION FOR CUSTOMER SERVICE REPRESENTATIVE
(Effective February 1988)

Function: Provides customers with the highest quality services, with special emphasis on recognizing customer needs and cross-selling appropriate bank services. Plays an active role in developing and maintaining good customer relations.

Responsibilities:

1. Presents and communicates the best possible customer service.
   - Greets all customers with a courteous, friendly attitude.
   - Provides fast, accurate, friendly service.
   - Uses customer's name *whenever* possible.
2. Sells bank services and maintains customer relations.
   - Cross-sells retail services by identifying and referring valid prospects to the customer assistance representative or customer service director. When time permits (no oher customers waiting in line), should actively cross-sell retail services.
   - Develops new business by acquainting noncustomers with bank services and existing customers with additional services that they are not currently using.
3. Provides a prompt and efficient operation on a professional level.
   - Receives cash and/or checks for checking accounts, savings accounts, taxes withheld, loan payments, MasterCard/Visa, mortgage payments, Christmas clubs, money orders, traveler's checks, cashier's checks, premium promotions.
   - Verifies amount of cash and/or checks received, being alert for counterfeit or fraudulent items.
   - Accepts deposits and withdrawals, verifying signatures where required by policy.
   - Cashes checks in accordance with bank policy. Identifies payees; verifies signatures; checks dates and endorsements; compares written dollar and figure amounts; ensures that numbers are included on all counter checks, deposit slips and savings withdrawal and deposit slips; watches for stop payments and holds funds per bank policy.
   - Where applicable, pays credit card cash advances and savings withdrawals. Accepts credit merchant deposits. Receives payment for collection items, safe deposit rentals, and other miscellaneous items. Confers with head CSR or customer service director on nonroutine situations.
   - Sells traveler's checks, money orders, and cashier's checks and may redeem coupons and sell or redeem foreign currency.
   - Handles sale and redemption of U.S. savings bonds.
   - Sells monthly transit passes.
   - Ensures timely batching and preparation of work for transmittal to proof department.
   - Prepares coin and currency orders as necessary.
   - Services, maintains, and settles automatic teller machines as required.
   - Ensures only minimum cash exposure necessary for efficient operation is kept in cash drawer; removes excess cash immediately to secured location. Ensures maximum control over cash drawers and other valuables on hand throughout daily operation.
   - Prepares accurate and timely daily settlement of work.
   - Performs bookkeeping and operational functions as assigned by customer service director.

a more positive approach that involved actively probing for customer needs. Their whole job seemed to revolve around filling out forms.

As the automation program proceeded, the mix of activities performed by the tellers started to change. A growing number of customers began to use automatic teller machines for cash withdrawals and deposits, as well as for requesting account balances. The ATMs at the Federal Square branch had the highest utilization of any of the First's branches, reflecting the large number of students and young

professionals served at that location. Costanzo noted that customers who were older or less well-educated seemed to prefer being served by "a real person, rather than a machine."

A year earlier, the head office had selected three branches, including Federal Square, as test sites for a new customer service program. The Federal Square branch was in a busy urban location, about one mile from the central business district and three blocks from the campus of the state university. The branch was surrounded by retail stores and close to commercial and professional offices. The other two branches were among the bank's larger suburban offices and were located in a shopping center and next to a big hospital, respectively. As part of the branch renovation program, each of these three branches had previously been remodeled to include no fewer than four ATMs (Federal Square had five), a customer service desk near the entrance, and two electronic information terminals that customers could activate to obtain information on a variety of bank services. The teller stations were redesigned to provide two levels of service: an express station for simple deposits and for cashing of approved checks, and regular stations for the full array of services provided by tellers. The number of stations open at a given time was varied to reflect the volume of anticipated business. Finally, the platform area in each branch was reconstructed to create what the architect described as "a friendly, yet professional, appearance."

HUMAN RESOURCES

With the new environment came new training programs for the staff of these three branches and new job descriptions and job titles: customer assistance representatives (for the platform staff), customer service representatives (for the tellers), and customer service director (instead of assistant branch manager). The head teller position was renamed head CSR. Position descriptions for all these jobs are reproduced in *Exhibits 2* through *5*. The training programs for each group included sessions designed to develop improved knowledge of both new and existing retail products. (CARs received more extensive training in this area than did CSRs.) The CARs also attended a 15-hour course, offered in three separate sessions, on basic selling skills. This program covered key steps in the sales process, including building a relationship, exploring customer needs, determining a solution, and overcoming objections. The sales training program for CSRs, by contrast, consisted of just two 2-hour sessions designed to develop skills in recognizing and probing customer needs, presenting product features and benefits, overcoming objections, and referring customers to CARs.

All staff members in customer service positions participated in sessions designed to improve their communication skills and professional image: clothing and personal grooming and interactions with cus-

---

EXHIBIT 3   FIRST NATIONAL BANK: POSITION DESCRIPTION FOR HEAD CUSTOMER
SERVICE REPRESENTATIVE
(Effective February 1988)

Function: Supervises the customer service representatives in the designated branch office, ensuring efficient operations and the highest quality service to customers. Plays an active role in developing and maintaining good customer relations. Assists other branch personnel on request.

Responsibilities:

1. Supervises the CSRs in the branch.
   - Allocates work, coordinates work flow, reviews and revises work procedures.
   - Ensures teller area is adequately and efficiently staffed with well-trained, qualified personnel.
   - Assists CSRs with more complex transactions.
   - Resolves routine personnel problems, referring more complex situations to the customer service director.
   - Participates in decisions concerning performance appraisal, promotions, wage changes, transfers, and terminations of subordinate CSR staff.

2. Assumes responsibility for CSRs' money.
   - Buys and sells money in the vault, ensuring adequacy of branch currency and coin supply.
   - Ensures that CSRs and cash sheets are in balance.
   - Maintains necessary records, including daily branch journal and general ledger.

3. Accepts deposits and withdrawals by business customers at commercial window.

4. Operates teller window to provide customer services (see Responsibilities for Customer Service Representative).

EXHIBIT 4 FIRST NATIONAL BANK: POSITION DESCRIPTION FOR CUSTOMER ASSISTANCE REPRESENTATIVE (Effective February 1988)

Function: Provides services and guidance to customers/prospects seeking banking relationships or related information. Promotes and sells needed products and responds to special requests by existing customers.

Responsibilities:

1. Provides prompt, efficient, and friendly service to all customers and prospective customers.
   - Describes and sells bank services to customers/prospects who approach them directly or via referral from customer service reps or other bank personnel.
   - Answers customers' questions regarding bank services, hours, etc.
2. Identifies and responds to customers' needs.
   - Promotes and sells retail services and identifies any existing cross-sell opportunities.
   - Opens new accounts for individuals, businesses, and private organizations.
   - Prepares temporary checks and deposit slips for new checking/NOW accounts.
   - Sells checks and deposit slips.
   - Interviews and takes applications for and pays out on installment/charge card accounts and other credit-related products.
   - Certifies checks.
   - Handles stop payment requests.
   - Responds to telephone mail inquiries from customers or bank personnel.
   - Receives notification of name or address changes and takes necessary action.
   - Takes action on notification of lost passbooks, credit cards, ATM cards, collateral, and all other lost or stolen valuables.
   - Demonstrates automatic teller machines to customers and assists with problems.
   - Coordinates closing of accounts and ascertains reasons.
3. Sells and services all retail products.
   - Advises customers and processes their applications for all products covered in CAR training programs and updates.
   - Initiates referrals to the appropriate department when a trust or corporate business need is identified.

---

tomers were all discussed. Said the trainer, "Remember, people's money is too important to entrust to someone who doesn't look and act the part!" CARs were instructed to rise from their seats and shake hands with customers. Both CARs and CSRs were given exercises designed to improve their listening skills and their powers of observation. All employees working where they could be seen by customers were ordered to refrain from smoking, drinking soda, and chewing gum on the job.

Although First National management anticipated that most of the increased emphasis on selling would fall to the CARs, they also foresaw a limited selling role for the customer reps, who would be expected to mention various products and facilities offered by the bank as they served customers at the teller window.

For instance, if a customer happened to mention a vacation, the CSR was supposed to mention traveler's checks; if the customer complained about bounced checks, the CSR should suggest speaking to a CAR about opening a personal line of credit that would provide an automatic overdraft protection; or if the customer mentioned investments, the CSR should refer him or her to a CAR who could provide information on money market accounts, certificates of deposit, or the First's discount brokerage service. All CSRs were supplied with their own business cards. When making a referral, they were expected to write the customer's name and the product of interest on the back of a card, give it to the customer, and send that individual to the customer assistance desks.

In an effort to motivate CSRs at the three test branches to sell specific financial products, the bank experimented with various incentive programs. The

EXHIBIT 5   FIRST NATIONAL BANK: POSITION DESCRIPTION FOR CUSTOMER SERVICE DIRECTOR
(Effective February 1988)

Function: Supervises customer service representatives, customer assistance representatives, and other staff as assigned to provide the most effective and profitable retail banking delivery system in the local marketplace. Supervises sales efforts and provides feedback to management concerning response to products and services by current and prospective banking customers. Communicates goals and results to those supervised and ensures operational standards are met in order to achieve outstanding customer service.

Responsibilities:

1. Supervises effective delivery of retail products.
   - Selects, trains, and manages the customer service representatives and customer assistance representatives.
   - Assigns duties and work schedules.
   - Completes performance reviews.

2. Personally, and through those supervised, renders the highest level of professional and efficient customer service available in the local marketplace.
   - Provides high level of service while implementing most efficient and customer-sensitive staffing schedules.
   - Supervises all on-the-job programs within office.
   - Ensures that outstanding customer service standards are achieved.
   - Directs remedial programs for CSRs and CARs as necessary.

3. Develops retail sales effectiveness to the degree necessary to achieve market share objectives.
   - Ensures that all CSRs and CARs possess comprehensive product knowledge.
   - Directs coordinated cross-sell program within office at all times.
   - Reports staff training needs to branch manager and/or regional training director.

4. Maintains operational adherence to standards.
   - Oversees preparation of daily and monthly operational and sales reports.
   - Estimates, approves, and coordinates branch cash needs in advance.
   - Oversees ATM processing function.
   - Handles or consults with CSRs/CARs on more complex transactions.
   - Ensures clean and businesslike appearance of the branch facility.

5. Informs branch manager of customer response to products.
   - Reports customer complaints and types of sales resistance encountered.
   - Describes and summarizes reasons for account closings.

6. Communicates effectively the goals and results of the bank to those under supervision.
   - Reduces office goals into format which translates to goals for each CSR or CAR.
   - Reports sales and cross-sell results to all CSRs and CARs.
   - Conducts sales- and service-oriented staff meetings with CSRs/CARs on a regular basis.
   - Attends all scheduled customer service management meetings organized by regional office.

---

first involved cash bonuses for referrals to CARs that resulted in sale of specific products. During a one-month period, CSRs were offered a $50 bonus for each referral leading to a customer's opening a personal line of credit account; the CARs received a $20 bonus for each account they opened, regardless of whether or not it came as a referral or simply a walk-in. Eight such bonuses were paid to CSRs at Federal Square, with three each going to just two of the seven full-time CSRs, Jean Warshawski and Bruce

Greenfield. Karen Mitchell was not among the recipients. However, this program was not renewed, since it was felt that there were other, more cost-effective means of marketing this product. In addition, Mr. Reeves, the customer service director, had reason to believe that Bruce Greenfield had colluded with one of the CARs, his girlfriend, to claim referrals which he had not, in fact, made. Another test branch reported similar suspicions of two of its CSRs.

A second promotion followed and was based upon

allocating credits to the CSRs for successful referrals. The value of the credit varied according to the nature of the product—for instance, a cash machine card was worth 500 credits—and accumulated credits could be exchanged for merchandise gifts. This program was deemed ineffective and discontinued after three months. The basic problem seemed to be that the value of the gifts was too low in relation to the amount of effort required.

Other problems with these promotional schemes included lack of product knowledge on the part of the CSRs and time pressures when many customers were waiting in line to be served.

The bank had next turned to an approach which, in David Reeves' words, "used the stick rather than the carrot." All CSRs had traditionally been evaluated half-yearly on a variety of criteria, including accuracy, speed, quality of interactions with customers, punctuality of arrival for work, job attitudes, cooperation with other employees, and professional image. The evaluation process assigned a number of points to each criterion, with accuracy and speed being the most heavily weighted. In addition to appraisals by the customer service director and the branch manager, with input from the head CSR, the First had recently instituted a program of anonymous visits by what was popularly known as the "mystery client." Each CSR was visited at least once a quarter by a professional evaluator posing as a customer. This individual's appraisal of the CSR's appearance, performance, and attitude was included in the overall evaluation. The number of points scored by each CSR had a direct impact on merit pay raises and on selection for promotion to the head CSR position or to platform jobs.

To encourage improved product knowledge and "consultative selling" by CSRs, the evaluation process was revised to include points assigned for each individual's success in sales referrals. Under the new evaluation scheme, the maximum number of points assignable for effectiveness in making sales—directly or through referrals to CARs—amounted to 30 percent of the potential total score. Although CSR-initiated sales had risen significantly in the most recent half-year, Reeves sensed that morale had dropped among this group, in contrast to the CARs,

whose enthusiasm and commitment had risen significantly. He had also noticed an increase in CSR errors. One CSR had quit, complaining about too much pressure.

Karen Mitchell

Under the old scoring system, Karen Mitchell had been the highest scoring teller/CSR for four consecutive half-years. But after two half-years under the new system, her ranking had dropped to fourth out of the seven full-time tellers. The top-ranking CSR, Mary Bell, had been with the First for sixteen years, but had declined repeated invitations to apply for a head teller position, saying that she was happy where she was, earning at the top of the CSR scale, and did not want "the extra worry and responsibility." Mitchell ranked first on all but one of the operationally related criteria (interactions with customers, where she ranked second), but sixth on selling effectiveness (*Exhibit 6*).

Costanzo and Reeves had spoken to Mitchell about her performance and expressed disappointment. Mitchell had told them, respectfully but firmly, that she saw the most important aspect of her job as giving customers fast, accurate, and courteous service.

I did try this selling thing [she told the two bank officers] but it just seemed to annoy people. Some said they were in a hurry and couldn't talk now, others looked at me as if I were slightly crazy to bring up the subject of a different bank service than the one they were currently transacting. And then, when you got the odd person who seemed interested, you could hear the other customers in the line grumbling about the slow service.

Really, the last straw was when I noticed on the computer that this woman had several thousand in her savings account so I suggested to her, just as the trainer had told us, that she could earn more interest if she opened a money market account. Well, she told me it was none of my business what she did with her money, and stomped off. Don't get me wrong, I love being able to help customers, and if they ask for my advice, I'll gladly tell them about what the bank has to offer.

Selecting a New Head CSR

Two weeks after this meeting, it was announced that the head CSR was leaving. The job entailed some

EXHIBIT 6 FIRST NATIONAL BANK: SUMMARY OF PERFORMANCE EVALUATION SCORES FOR CUSTOMER SERVICE REPRESENTATIVES AT FEDERAL SQUARE BRANCH FOR TWO HALF-YEAR PERIODS

CSR name[1]	Length of full-time bank service	Operational criteria[2] (max: 70 points)		Selling effectiveness[3] (max: 30 points)		Total score	
		1st half	2nd half	1st half	2nd half	1st half	2nd half
Mary Bell	16 years, 10 mos	65	64	16	20	81	84
Richard Dubois	2 years, 3 mos	63	61	15	19	78	80
Bruce Greenfield	1 year, 0 mos	48	42	20	26	68	68
Karen Mitchell	3 years, 7 mos	67	67	13	12	80	79
Sharon Ronsky	1 year, 4 mos	53	55	8	9	61	64
Naomi Rubin	7 mos	—	50	—	22	—	72
Jean Warshawski	2 years, 1 mo	57	55	21	28	79	83

[1]Full-time CSRs only (part-time CSRs were evaluated separately).
[2]Totals based on sum of ratings against various criteria, including accuracy, work production, attendance and punctuality, personal appearance, organization of work, initiative, cooperation with others, problem-solving ability, and quality of interaction with customers.
[3]Points awarded for both direct sales by CSR (e.g., traveler's checks) and referral selling by CSR to CAR (e.g., ATM card, cerificates of deposit, personal line of credit).

supervision of the work of the other CSRs (including allocation of work assignments and scheduling of part-time CSRs at busy periods or during employee vacations), consultation on—and, where possible, resolution of—any problems occurring at the teller stations, and handling of large cash deposits and withdrawals by local retailers (see position description in *Exhibit 3*). When not engaged on such tasks, the head CSR was expected to operate a regular teller window.

The pay scale for a head CSR ranged from $7.00 to $12.00 per hour, depending on qualifications, seniority, and branch size, as compared to a range of $5.40 to $9.00 per hour for CSRs. The pay scale for CARs ranged from $6.20 to $10.50. Full-time employees (who were not unionized) worked a 40-hour week, including some evenings until 6:00 p.m. and certain Saturday mornings. Ms. Costanzo indicated that the pay scales were typical for banks in the Midwest, although the average CSR at the First was better qualified than those at smaller banks and therefore higher on the scale. Karen Mitchell was currently earning $7.80 per hour, reflecting her associate's degree, three-and-a-half years' experience, and significant past merit increases. If promoted to

head CSR, she would qualify for an initial rate of $9.50 an hour.

When applications for the positions closed, Mitchell was one of three candidates. The other two candidates were Jean Warshawski, 42, another CSR at Federal Square branch; and Curtis Richter, 24, the head CSR at one of First National Bank's smaller suburban branches, who was seeking more responsibility.

Warshawski was married with two sons in high school. She had started working as a part-time teller at Federal Square three years previously, switching to full-time work a year later in order, as she said, to put away some money for her boys' college education. Warshawski was a cheerful woman with a jolly laugh. She had a wonderful memory for people's names and Reeves had often seen her greeting customers on the street or in a restaurant during the lunch hour. Reviewing her evaluations over the past three years, Reeves noted that she had initially performed poorly on accuracy and at one point, while still a part-timer, had been put on probation because of frequent inaccuracies in the balance in her cash drawer at the end of the day. Although Reeves considered her much improved on this score, he still saw room for improvement. The customer service director had also had occasion to reprimand her for tardiness during the past year. Warshawski attributed this to health problems with her elder son who, she said, was now responding to treatment.

Both Reeves and Costanzo had observed Warshawski at work and agreed that her interactions with customers were exceptionally good, although she tended to be overly chatty and was not as fast as Karen Mitchell. She seemed to have a natural ability to size up customers and to decide which ones were good prospects for a quick sales pitch on a specific financial product. Although slightly untidy in her personal appearance, she was very well organized in her work and was quick to help her fellow CSRs, especially new hires. She was currently earning $7.20 per hour as a CSR and would qualify for a rate of $9.10 as head CSR. In the most recent six months, Warshawski had ranked ahead of Mitchell as a result of being very successful in consultative selling (*Exhibit 6*).

Richter, the third candidate, was not working in one of the three test branches, so had not been exposed to the consultative selling program and its corresponding evaluation scheme. However, he had received excellent evaluations for his work in the First's small Longmeadow branch, where he had been employed for three years. A move to Federal Square would increase his earnings from $8.20 to $9.10 per hour. Reeves and Costanzo had interviewed Richter and considered him intelligent and personable. He had joined the bank after dropping out of college midway through his junior year, but

had recently started taking evening courses in order to complete his degree. The Longmeadow branch was located in an older part of town, where commercial and retail activity were rather stagnant. The branch had not yet been renovated and had no ATMs, although there was an ATM accessible to First National customers one block away. Richter supervised three CSRs and reported directly to the branch manager, who spoke very highly of him. Since there were no CARs in this branch, Richter and another experienced CSR took turns to handle new accounts and loan or mortgage applications.

Costanzo and Reeves were troubled by the decision that faced them. Prior to the bank's shift in focus, Mitchell would have been the natural choice for the head CSR job which, in turn, could be a stepping stone to further promotions, including customer assistance representative, customer service director, and, eventually, manager of a small branch or a management position in the head office. Mitchell had told her superiors that she was interested in making a career in banking and that she was eager to take on further responsibilities.

Compounding the problem was the fact that the three branches testing the new customer service program had just completed a full year of the test. Costanzo knew that sales and profits were up significantly at all three branches, relative to the bank's performance as a whole. She anticipated that top management would want to extend the program systemwide after making any modifications that seemed desirable.

Crestlight Paper Company

Kenneth Simmonds

The speed of David Farrel's management changes had surprised everyone. Aged 33, Farrel was the first of the firm's graduate M.B.A. recruits to reach the divisional general management level. He always seemed quiet and reserved, but interested in and understanding of others' viewpoints, and his promotion from Assistant Manager in the Forms division to General Manager of the Education division had been a popular one. Three weeks after he took over from the retiring general manager, however, the Education division had a new personnel manager, a replacement for the accountant and two entirely new posts advertised for product managers. Now Farrel was calmly asking Andrew Smythe to take over as Divisional Sales Manager. "Wesley McFarlane expressed his interest in early retirement," said Farrel, "and we agreed that there would be little purpose in a drawn-out handover period. He will formally retire from Crestlight at the end of March, but hand over the reins of the sales force to you as from Friday week, 24th February. Unfortunately, I shall be away at the

Group Conference all next week, but we can go over the situation in detail as soon as I am back—let's say the afternoon of Monday, 27th February."

Farrel's approach was so unexpected and his manner so direct, that in five minutes Smythe found he had accepted the promotion, agreed to clean up his outstanding commitments at Group Head Office within two days and to spend the next week, Wesley McFarlane's last, learning all he could from Wesley. As he walked back to his office, Andrew was elated with his new appointment; but he had a strange feeling of his future vanishing into a vacuum. Farrel had somehow stopped him, asking about where he, Farrel, wished to head the Education division and had avoided any discussion at all about Wesley McFarlane's sales achievements. Had Wesley been good, bad or indifferent? Whatever the answer, this was the sort of opportunity Andrew had been waiting for. In fact, it was beyond his immediate expectations. He had believed his image in Crestlight to be that of a future "comer" who would be given a year or two to prove himself in some assistant sales management post before he would be offered a senior divisional appointment. Farrell had certainly picked Andrew up and put him on the escalator.

ANDREW SMYTHE

Andrew Smythe had joined Crestlight eighteen months ago, on completing his Master of Business Administration degree at Manchester Business School. He had been based at the Group Head Office as assistant to the Group Marketing Director and given a succession of non-repetitive problems to sort out—mainly concerned with matching supply and forecasts for Crestlight lines. Off and on over the past six months he had also participated as a member of a team sorting out a new group acquisition. But at 28 he was becoming restless in a staff position. He felt that he should get into some operating post. Operations seemed the only way to the top at Crestlight. At Business School he had positioned himself as a finance specialist, but then became disillusioned with capital asset pricing theory and rather low finance grades and, anyway, marketing had seemed from outside the function of the future in Crestlight. From within, he was not so sure. He had come to regard the Marketing Director as little more than the Group's senior sales person, with the added concern for investigating major foreign orders and new agency possibilities.

Prior to his two years at Business School, Andrew had been a sales management trainee with a branded food company. There, too, the position had been a misnomer—probably titled to attract graduates. The post had amounted to two and a half years as a field representative, calling on supermarket buyers and store managers and arranging special promotions. He supposed it was good experience, but he had not really enjoyed the job and he could see that his Bachelor's degree in Economics from Nottingham was not going to move him along in any way at all—he needed an M.B.A. for that.

Andrew shared a flat in London with two other Business School graduates and led an active social life. He still played rugby, turning out for a team in Esher on Sundays, and for the last two years he had taken winter skiing holidays. He had no plans for marriage and the idea of settling into a suburban house in Croydon, as one of his friends had done, did not appeal to him, although he had toyed with the idea of buying a house in order to build up some equity.

CRESTLIGHT EDUCATION DIVISION

Crestlight had grown from a small beginning in the late 1940s, based on a license from the U.S. to manufacture and distribute throughout the U.K. a coated paper used in industrial drawing offices. Over the years the firm had added a whole range of photographic and reproduction papers and supplies, together with a line of equipment for reproduction of large size drawings. Then in 1964 Crestlight had moved onto the acquisition trail and added a specialty paper merchant and a major form printing house. A divisional organization pattern had emerged almost without planning. There were now five principal divisions—Equipment, Supplies, Paper, Education and Forms—and four non-integrated subsidiaries.

The Education division had been formed in 1970 to give specialist attention to the increasing demand from the education sector for special paper and reproduction supplies and equipment. Nine years later the division carried a range of 1,000 items and sold directly to Local Education Authorities (LEA's), Central Supplies Departments (which usually supplied several authorities), universities, polytechnics and some large schools. Several education wholesalers were also supplied. Some of these carried a much broader line of education supplies than Crestlight—including, for example, scientific apparatus—and had very active sales forces calling on similar direct customers.

Profit margins differed from order to order. The standard gross margin for direct supply to Local Education Authorities and individual establishments was 40 percent of total sales value, while on sales to wholesalers and central purchasing stores the average margin was only 26 percent.

LEARNING FROM WESLEY McFARLANE

Wesley McFarlane was friendly and relaxed when Andrew moved in with him the following Monday.

Tall and well-dressed, he reminded Andrew of a trained athlete as he seemed to flow around the office without effort. Although he was only 52, he seemed to have welcomed the early retirement and gave no hint at all that he felt he had been moved out. Andrew rather gauchely tried to sound him out about the internal politics behind the move by asking him whether he minded moving at this stage in his career. Wesley came back without any hesitation, "Should have done it years ago. Sales management will never get you anywhere against the engineers and account-ants, and a safe middle-of-the-road salary is a living death in Britain today." He then went on to outline to Andrew his plans for a partnership with his brother in a caravan[1] sales agency south of London. Now that his three children were safely through school and launched on their own careers, he could turn his sales skills to his own advantage without family demands requiring him to draw too much out of the business at the wrong times. Wesley was so convinc-ing with the detail of his own plans that he spent an hour explaining to Andrew the "ins" and "outs" of the caravan business. Andrew couldn't help but feel it more fascinating than selling school supplies.

Wesley finally brought Andrew back to earth by starting on a comprehensive survey of the Education division sales force. As Wesley talked, Andrew took his own brief notes and asked for photocopies of the annual sales figures and sales force and territory details that Wesley showed him. *Exhibit 1* shows the divisional sales figures and *Exhibits 2* to 6 the terri-tory and sales force details and performance. *Exhibit 7* sets out the notes on individual salesmen as Wesley pictured them—but, as Wesley said, Andrew would get a better picture by meeting them himself. He had, accordingly, arranged the next sales meeting for Wednesday, so that he could introduce the sales force to Andrew before he formally took over.

The remainder of Monday vanished rapidly as Wesley outlined his overall sales philosophy to Andrew:

---

[1]"Caravan" is the British term for trailer.

EXHIBIT 1

CRESTLIGHT PAPER COMPANY: EDUCATION DIVISION MARKET AND SALES BY PRODUCT (£000s)

	Market estimates		Sales	
	1978	1977	1978	1977
Special paper	3,600	3,050	696	560
Reproduction supplies	2,200	1,850	401	311
Reproduction equipment	1,300	1,100	363	311
Total	7,100	6,000	1,460	1,208

Last year's sales of one and a half million were just above a 20 percent increase over 1977. Most of this represented price increases rather than volume and by my guess market penetration has gone up slightly from 19.5 percent. When I say "guess" I am basing this on my estimates of market size for the three product lines. These have been asked for each year for the annual plans and what I do is to identify all the competitors and place a sales figure against each. One or other of the salesmen is bound to have heard some-thing about a competitor's sales levels, and I do some questioning around outside as well, and check the competi-tor's annual reports and published estimates of educational purchasing. There are too many customers to build a figure up from their estimated annual order potential and industry figures don't coincide with our narrow line definitions.

They are all good men. There is not a bad egg among the nine and they work willingly if you don't push them too hard. Of course there are differences in sales perfor-mance, but these occur in all sales teams. Besides, you have to bear in mind the travel times some of them need to reach quite small accounts as well as the amount of work that has been done in the past to build up our accounts in a territory.

These same factors have to be taken into account in territory sizes. I think we have them about right now. As you can see from the territory variation in numbers of secondary and higher level pupils, the range between small-est and largest is only a factor of two—which is, in fact, very small. But each salesman has plenty of potential to uncover, no matter what his territory size.

The basic salaries can't be adjusted very much. You have to keep the basic high enough to attract new reps,

EXHIBIT 2
MAP OF SALES TERRITORIES

EXHIBIT 3 SALES TERRITORY DETAILS

Territory	Salesman	Area (000s sq km)	Secondary and higher-level pupils 1978 (millions)	Estimated potential accounts	Home base
Greater London	Halbert	1.6	1.60	570	Twickenham
South East	Jennings	25.6	2.27	1,060	Bromley
South West & Wales	Bindon	44.6	1.55	934	Cardiff
Midlands East	Vereker	28.2	1.18	653	Leicester
West Midlands	Prince	13.0	1.24	566	Solihull
North West	Anderson	7.3	1.65	699	Liverpool
Humberside	Randall	15.4	1.16	531	Bradford
North	Thompson	15.4	.83	423	Newcastle
Scotland	Campbell	78.8	1.32	529	Glasgow
Total		229.9	12.80	5,965	

EXHIBIT 4 SALES FORCE DETAILS

Salesman	Age	Year joined Crestlight	Educational qualifications	Previous experience
Halbert, Russell	54	1965	—	Textile salesman (10 years) Accounts clerk (7 years)
Jennings, Frederick	42	1973	Higher National Certificate	Post Office Teleprinter salesman (4 years) Equipment maintenance (16 years)
Bindon, Harold V.	33	1971	B.A. (Geography)	Joined as sales trainee
Vereker, John	29	1975	—	Head storeman (3 years) Dispatch clerk (3 years)
Prince, Alan	57	1976	—	Salesman, etc. (35 years)
Anderson, Graham	37	1969	B. Tech.	Production scheduling (5 years)
Randall, John	48	1951	—	Joined as clerk in original Crestlight unit Appointed salesman 1964
Thompson, Herbert	33	1975	B.Sc. (Metallurgy)	Wallpaper sales rep (4 years) Research technician (2 years)
Campbell, Ian	43	1971	B.A. (English)	Teacher (12 years)

EXHIBIT 5   SALES FORCE PERFORMANCE

	1978				1977			
	Sales (£000s)	Accounts sold	Gross margin (£000s)	Calls made	Sales (£000s)	Accounts sold	Gross margin (£000s)	Calls made
Halbert	258	239	75	1,230	217	279	69	1,260
Jennings	239	509	79	1,168	198	539	69	1,194
Bindon	156	476	59	1,051	129	503	48	1,018
Vereker	112	353	41	1,409	98	356	36	1,290
Prince	154	413	55	1,196	123	382	43	1,185
Anderson	112	398	39	1,450	97	412	34	1,410
Randall	142	202	50	1,171	125	198	42	1,293
Thompson	123	364	47	1,220	101	323	39	1,163
Campbell	143	317	53	1,135	123	326	46	1,088
	£1,439		£498		£1,211		£426	

who might not make much commission for a while, and yet not so high that they have an easy time. Actually, I had been thinking about raising the commission rates. I think the carrot works a lot better than any pseudoanalytical target that tries to push from behind. Commission rates are only 1½ percent and if we raised them a further 1 percent instead of a salary increase this year, I think we would get five times as much back in gross margin.

Expenses are pretty much under control; I get the daily call reports and I know who they are entertaining and where they are traveling. Harold Bindon spends more time away from home than any of the others and his entertainment goes up as a result, but if life were too dreary we would have problems with that territory.

Tuesday rushed quickly past as Wesley and Andrew waded through the files for each of the product groups in the Crestlight Education range. Eighty per cent of the sales came from internal production in the other divisions but the remaining twenty per cent included a very long list of products. In some of the cases, Wesley had been required as part of the agency agreement to provide detailed reports on the sales efforts and results.

THE SALES MEETING

The Wednesday meeting got underway in the conference room with a great deal of joking and laughter.

As Andrew came in, Wesley was called away to the telephone, but the salesmen knew all about the management change and introduced themselves in ones and twos before drifting towards the table with coffee cups in hand. Wesley took the seat at the head of the long table and Andrew drew up a chair towards the other end between John Randall and Ian Campbell.

Andrew could feel that Wesley was genuinely well liked and respected. He admired the way Wesley led the group smoothly through the agenda, starting with a discussion of the January sales figures and the effects that anticipation of a change in political party had had on educational spending. One foreign manufacturer of educational forms had been threatening to withdraw his line from Crestlight and this provoked a comparison of current buyers with those who had rejected the line. Wesley also had a spate of announcements concerning new items and replacements in the line. Under "Other Business" a long discussion boiled up around order procedure problems that had stemmed from some abstruse ruling in the Department of Education.

As the meeting was drawing to a close, John Randall stood up and on behalf of the salesmen made a short farewell speech thanking Wesley for his years of leadership. Wesley acknowledged the round of

EXHIBIT 6
REMUNERATION AND EXPENSES, 1978 EDUCATION DIVISION
SALES FORCE (£)

Name	Salary 12/31/78	Commissions 1978	Total remuneration	Expenses 1978
Halbert	5,800	3,870	9,670	1,980
Jennings	4,800	3,585	8,385	2,810
Bindon	4,200	2,340	6,540	5,010
Vereker	3,800	1,680	5,480	3,820
Prince	4,900	2,310	7,210	2,600
Anderson	5,100	1,680	6,780	1,940
Randall	5,200	2,130	7,330	3,400
Thompson	4,000	1,845	5,845	3,200
Campbell	5,000	2,145	7,145	3,300
	42,800	21,585	64,385	28,060

EXHIBIT 7   WESLEY MACFARLANE'S COMMENTS ON SALESMEN

Russell Halbert	Our star salesman. Very experienced. Knows central area. Reacts well to new ideas and well liked by customers. Has a smooth, competent air about him.
Frederick Jennings	Very sound man, systematic and conscientious and well dressed. Moved across from equipment side, so knows the technical aspects. Had some marital problems last year but apparently straightened them out.
Harold Bindon	Very large area but really gets round it. Presents himself well. Sales coming along nicely. Could go a long way in the company.
John Vereker	Sales not really very high. Young man with a lot to learn. Probably as a young man-about-town is taking time off for other things.
Alan Prince	Grandad of the team. An old sales lag. Joined only 3 years ago. Will not readily adopt new approaches, but you cannot teach an old dog new tricks. Will not be around for more than five years. No really formal education, so unlikely to make general impact on buyers in the education area. Nevertheless, doing quite acceptably.
Graham Anderson	Has a degree, but very disappointing sales results. Technically competent and extremely conscientious in covering his territory. A good worker and a rather engaging personality.
John Randall	Bright and attractive personality. Good salesman type. Always thinking up new ideas. A bit of a troublemaker. Fairly lazy and sales below what they might be. A good pep talk should move him along.
Herbert Thompson	Only been with us a few years, but keen to perform. Will take time to develop the polish of the true salesman, but the material is there. Needs guidance from sales manager about sales technique.
Ian Campbell	Very solid and unexciting. Always quiet at sales meetings. Suspect he will never make an outstanding salesman. Knows the Scottish educational buying scene very well. A chess player at competition level as a hobby.

applause, thanked them warmly, and then everybody headed for the "Three Feathers," where Wesley had booked a table for lunch.

The lunch went on rather a long time with numerous rounds of drinks and a series of wild sales stories directed at Wesley. John Randall and John Vereker were the most vociferous. Randall elaborated at great length about a female purchasing officer from a Local Education Authority who had him take her out until 3 a.m. every night for a week before placing an order for a gross of protractors—while Vereker seemed the authority on landladies' daughters. At one point,

Andrew ventured a story about clam digging that had been told with much hilarity at the Rugby Club. It went reasonably well, but was quickly lost in the stream of wisecracks and competing comments.

Finally, about 2:30 p.m., Wesley looked at his watch and the group began to break up. Andrew and Wesley were separated by the salesmen as they said their farewells. What struck Andrew as strange was that although each salesman used his own words, their message was the same: "If I can be of any help in showing you the ropes, don't hesitate to ask."

PART SEVEN

Pricing

hrough pricing, management attempts to recover the costs of the separate elements in the marketing mix—the product itself, associated advertising and personal selling expenses, and the various services provided to consumers by the channels of distribution—as well as to generate *profits* and the funds necessary to operate the company.

Price is a very visible part of the marketing mix—easily observed by both customers and competitors. Establishing an appropriate pricing strategy is thus a critical part of any marketing plan. The foundations underlying pricing strategy are like a tripod, with the three legs representing (1) the costs incurred by the marketer, (2) the prices charged by competitors, and (3) the value of the product to prospective purchasers.

From a consumer viewpoint, the price of a product is the amount of money paid or to be paid for the benefits offered by the "bundle" of attributes represented by the product and its supporting services. Changes in the nature of this bundle may increase or reduce not only the marketer's costs but also the product's perceived value and thereby the price that consumers are willing to pay.

It is important to recognize that consumers may view a product according to its perceived and not actual value. A product may be of very high quality but customers may consider it as being "cheap," possibly because of a low price or a poorly designed package. Conversely, consumers may regard an expensive, well-packaged product as being of high quality when in fact it is of poor quality. Repeat sales of such a product, however, may be limited.

Pricing policy should consequently be seen as only one of several interdependent elements in the marketing mix. Economic theorists have historically tended to overemphasize the role of price as a determinant of demand, at

357

the expense of such nonprice variables as product attributes, communication activities, and distribution. In addition, the economic concept of pricing generally emphasizes the level of price charged, overlooking such important marketing considerations as how prices are paid by consumers. "Can I charge it?" or "What terms can you give me?" may be equally or more important in some purchase decisions than the basic "How much is it?"

An organization's pricing objectives are normally derived from its overall marketing strategy and may change over time in response to changing conditions, both in the marketplace and in the firm's own resources. A trade-off often has to be made between short-run profits and market share targets which may reduce profits in the short run but enhance them in the long run.

Pricing strategies must take into account not only the response of the ultimate consumer or industrial buyer but also the needs and characteristics of intermediaries in the channels of distribution. Sufficient margins must be offered at each level of distribution to make it financially attractive for the distributor to carry the goods or to represent the service organization in question.

Finally, pricing policies may reflect a communication objective. Many firms cultivate a "value-for-money" image. For example, "Cheap-O" laundry detergent (with its advertising line, "I can't see a difference—Can you see a difference?") positions itself as being equivalent in quality to higher priced brands. Taking this policy a step further, some firms may offer one or more "loss leaders"—perhaps on just a temporary basis—to attract attention to the entire product line. At the other end of the spectrum are situations in which the marketer seeks to enhance the quality image of the product by deliberately charging a relatively high price.

SETTING PRICES

Assuming that the company has identified its target markets, the first step in setting prices is to establish the company's objectives for each target market. What segments does the company want to compete in and what goals has it set for each segment? In some segments, for example, the company may be determined to become the market share leader and to keep out new market entrants. In other segments, the company may be content with its current position and seek to maximize the cash flow generated from that market. Each of these goals requires a different marketing plan and marketing mix.

The next step is to determine the role of price within the marketing mix. If for example, the firm has decided on a plan placing great emphasis on service by the retailer, then the pricing policy needs to allow for sufficient retailer margins. If, on the other hand, the plan is to become the dominant supplier for high-volume customers, then prices must be set low enough to meet that goal. Within this framework, the company must then determine its pricing strategies and policies. Factors influencing these decisions are discussed in the next section.

Pricing involves a number of tactical decisions. Particularly for consumer products, these include such elements as when to run promotions, whether to price at or below critical pricing points (for example $0.99 versus $1.00), and whether to develop price lines. (For example, including a high-price model in a line might make the medium-price model seem more reasonably priced.) Other factors include how to communicate prices, what types of discounts to provide, and, for retailers, whether to use credit cards and allow payment over time. These tactical issues are quite important; neglect of them can make otherwise sound pricing policy ineffective.

FACTORS INFLUENCING PRICING STRATEGIES AND POLICIES

Apart from marketing goals, a number of other factors also influence the determination of pricing strategies and policies. Key elements are the cost structure of the firm, the price elasticity of both primary (overall market) and selective (secondary or brand-level) demand, and the competitive structure of the industry in which the product is competing. Other important considerations include product characteristics, the interrelationship among the products in the company's product line, the availability of supply relative to demand, and government regulations. *Exhibit 1* summarizes factors to consider when reaching a pricing decision.

Cost Structure

Several aspects of an organization's cost structure need to be considered:

- The level of variable costs per unit and extent to which these are likely to form a high proportion of selling price
- The level of fixed costs
- The potential for economies of scale
- The possibility of changing cost structures over time
- The firm's costs relative to those of its competitors

When a company has high fixed costs and relatively low costs per unit of sale, such as with a computer service bureau or airline, the incremental cost of accommodating new customers or sales is comparatively low in relation to the prices charged. Under such circumstances, earnings may rise sharply if sales increase. Alternatively, for some businesses the reverse may be true; fixed costs may be comparatively low and variable costs per unit very high. Clothing products and certain foodstuffs are examples of products which may require substantial material or labor cost, or both. In these cases, since competition tends to force prices down, unit contribution is often low and even a substantial increase in sales volume by itself may not improve earnings dramatically. However, even here, the potential for economies of scale presents

EXHIBIT 1
A SUMMARY OF INPUTS TO PRICING DECISIONS

1. Target objectives and plan
2. Cost—both variable and fixed—associated with the product
3. Availability of funds to finance new products, competitive battles, and long-term plans
4. Total capacity available
5. Alternative products offered by the company
6. Extent and nature of competition
7. Pricing policies of competitors
8. Potential market size for a specific product offering, reflecting:
   - Type of offering
   - Location
   - Scheduling
9. Price elasticity of potential customers, reflecting:
   - Different market segments
   - Variations in product characteristics
   - Value of product (and product variations) to customers
10. Additional costs (beyond purchase price) incurred by patrons or consumers
11. Purchasing behavior of potential customers:
    How far in advance is purchase/use decision made?
12. Preferred payment/reservation procedures
    - Payment made directly to originating organization versus payment through retail intermediary
    - Cash versus check or credit card
13. Reactions of distribution channels to pricing policies
14. Changes in the external environment that may affect:
    - Customer's ability or willingness to pay
    - Nature of competition
    - Size of market (and segments within that market)
    - Company's costs and financial situation
    - Ability of organization to determine preferred pricing policies without third-party "interference"
15. Legal and regulatory considerations

opportunities for some organizations, since manufacturing, marketing, or administrative efforts toward efficiency may result in reduced costs per unit as the scale of operations increases. This situation provides an opportunity to enhance both profits and unit market share. In some industries, such as electronics, increasing cost savings over time, due to technological and other advances, have an important influence on both short- and long-term pricing strategies.

Price Elasticity of Demand

A key factor influencing pricing decisions for any product is the sensitivity of demand to changes in selling prices. If demand rises sharply when prices are lowered (or falls when they are increased), then demand is said to be highly *elastic*. Conversely, if demand is little affected by price changes, it is said to be *inelastic*.

The price sensitivity of demand for a particular product category reflects the importance of the product for consumers, the income level of present consumers, the existence of substitute products, the extent to which potential exists for increasing consumption (i.e., whether demand is close to saturation), and whether or not demand for the product is dependent on sales of another product (such as in the link between jet engine and aircraft sales). Price elasticity may vary sharply between market segments. For instance, business travelers are likely to be less sensitive to a change in hotel prices than are tourists, since the former may have little choice but to travel and, in any case, their employers will be paying the bills.

The price sensitivity for a given product category is not necessarily the same as that for an individual brand within that category. For example, if the price of Brand A's soap is raised, people may switch to another brand, decreasing Brand A's sales. However, if the prices of all brands of soap are raised, the sales of all brands may decline, but Brand A's sales will decline less than if it was the only company to raise prices. The less that individual brands are differentiated in consumers' eyes, the more difficult it is for a marketer to charge premium prices without losing substantial market share. Conversely, a small price cut by one organization may lead to destructive price competition unless one of the firms in the industry is able to act as a price leader and stabilize prices.

Competitive Structure of the Industry

The number of firms in an industry often has a direct effect on pricing policy. When many competitors are selling an undifferentiated product—such as agricultural produce—individual marketers have little discretionary power to influence the prices at which they sell. In the absence of government regulation or a cartel, price is set by free-market conditions and the marketer has little option but to accept it. Marketing boards for commodities such as eggs, chickens, and milk are one approach that has been used in a number of agricultural industries to limit price competition.

At the other extreme are marketers who face no direct competition for a much needed product like electricity service. In theory, these monopolists have complete discretionary power to establish their own selling prices. However, in practice, government regulatory bodies, such as state public utilities commissions, often monitor rate structures.

In oligopolistic situations, where there are relatively few competitors, such as long-distance telephone service in the United States, one or two of the principal firms may act as price leaders. Other firms are often content to follow their lead, settling for a stable market share in return for an acceptable margin of profits. Although the industry leaders have some discretionary influence over selling prices in such situations, they risk losing this role if their own prices stray too far from those dictated by underlying supply and demand forces in the industry.

In addition to evaluating the nature and extent of existing competition, the marketing manager must also evaluate the possibility of new companies entering the market. If barriers to entry are high—because of the need for substantial capital investments or access to scarce resources or expertise, or both—then the prospect of new entrants may be remote. However, high prices and high earnings within an industry may attract new competitors who are prepared to make the necessary investment for entry now in order to earn profits in the long run. Recognizing this, many firms in oligopolistic industries adopt low, "keep-out" prices, preferring lower earnings in the short run to more competitors.

Typically, a firm attempts to escape from the constraints that the industry structure imposes on general pricing policy by differentiating other elements of the marketing mix. An analysis of competitive offerings, distribution channels, advertising and promotion options, and consumer needs (by segment) can provide insights into the realistic and operational feasibilities of such differentiation.

A further consideration is the level of the company's costs relative to those of the competition. A low-cost situation makes it possible to choose among such alternatives as:

- Enjoying extra profits
- Allocating more resources to marketing activities, including research and development, in an effort to build sales and satisfy consumers better
- Initiating an aggressive, low-price strategy

A firm with relatively high costs lacks this flexibility and will probably seek to avoid a low-price strategy which will put it at a financial disadvantage relative to competitors.

The most extreme example of competitive pricing concerns markets in which firms compete on the basis of bids, such as in the case of government procurement and the supply of certain industrial goods and services. While nonprice factors such as service, reliability, and product features can sometimes influence the outcome, the contract usually goes to the firm offering the lowest price for a product that meets the customer's specifications. For the marketer, cost and competition are the key factors in preparing a bid. If the company bids too low, it may not cover its costs; as the price increases, the chances of a competitor underbidding the company increase. Of course, the company does not know what its competitors will bid, so the company must trade off its chances of winning at a given price against the profit it would earn if it did win, in order to calculate its expected profit at different prices and to set its bid. Analysis of competitors is thus quite important in setting the appropriate bid price.

PRICING POLICIES FOR NEW PRODUCTS

In establishing the price for a new product, managers should recognize that the characteristics of the product itself play a central role. If it is merely a "me-too" item, not strongly differentiated from competitive offerings, then the level of existing prices may prove the crucial determinant. However, greater price discretion may be available to the marketer of a distinctively different product which has no close substitutes and is likely to be imitated in the short term.

Other inputs to the pricing decision include an analysis of the market, prospective consumer segments, existing or potential competitors, and the needs of intermediaries in the distribution channel. Management must estimate potential demand in each major segment and the speed with which it will develop. Demand may be sensitive to changes in both price and the level of marketing effort. Sometimes a new product may be test-marketed at different prices in matched cities in order to obtain a better feel for the product's price sensitivity. An evaluation of competitive activity, if any, should provide details of the competitors' price range and the terms they offer to intermediaries. It may also help the marketer evaluate the possibility of price retaliation by firms that are marketing products likely to be displaced by the newcomer.

Communication and distribution decisions likewise have implications for pricing. The larger the communication budget, the higher fixed costs will be; further, the margin requirements of different distribution channels may influence the factory selling price and/or the recommended retail selling price.

By reviewing all these factors and undertaking a sensitivity analysis of the economic implications of alternative strategies, the marketing manager may be able to resolve the question of whether to adopt a "skim" or "penetration" policy.

Skimming is usually limited to distinctively different products. It involves setting a high initial price which skims the cream of demand at the outset, yielding high profits during the period before competition enters the market and prices start to fall. (High initial prices are sometimes also employed as a means of restricting demand at a time when product supply is limited.)

Market penetration is the opposite approach. It involves use of a low price to stimulate market growth and enable the firm to gain a dominant position; the goal is to preempt competition and ensure long-run profitability.

As the product matures and competitive activity increases, periodic evaluations are necessary to ensure that the pricing policy is realistic in the light of market conditions and the objectives of the firm.

SUMMARY

When establishing pricing policies, marketing managers must be aware of the costs to be recovered, the prices charged by competitors for broadly similar products, and the value of the product to prospective purchasers. In a strict economic sense, the price set must yield a sufficient contribution so that, at the anticipated volume of sales, it will cover fixed costs and yield a satisfactory profit. Setting a price, however, is more complex than just simply choosing a dollar amount to charge for a particular good or service. All pricing decisions must be made within the context of a marketing plan, which includes a clear specification of the objectives for each of the company's selected target markets and the linkage of pricing to other elements of the marketing mix.

Cascade Foods

Charles B. Weinberg

Sylvia Boaz, product manager for the newly formed fruit drinks division of Cascade Foods,[1] was addressing her product management team in early March 1984.

We've now completed the last of the test market experiments for the new line of fruit drinks in aseptic packages or "paper bottles," as many people call them. Although this packaging system is new to our market, it's been well accepted in Europe for a number of years and has gained market share rapidly in several U.S. cities. We've all agreed that the test market results are favorable for launching the product, but we can't make a final recommendation to top management until we settle on a pricing strategy. We might like to charge a premium for these fruit drinks but not if it'll damage sales too severely or open up the market for competition. It's ironic: here's a drink that tastes better than fruit drinks in cans, but is actually cheaper to package and ship in aseptic cartons. Do we price on cost or on value?

With these comments, Boaz began a meeting with Harold Mann, market research manager for Cascade Foods; Carol Gomez, her product assistant; and Scott Green, an experienced marketing consultant who had

worked for Cascade Foods a number of times in the past. Cascade had been considering entering the fruit drink market for a number of years, but had not been able to find a profitable niche in the market. The advent of aseptic packaging methods in which a container was made of laminated paperboard appeared to offer the opportunity that Cascade had been waiting for.

COMPANY BACKGROUND

Cascade Foods was founded in 1959 by Benjamin Adam, the son of the controlling owner of Adam Food Stores, a leading supermarket chain in the midwest. Benjamin Adam, a college graduate and World War II veteran, had worked in various executive positions, becoming president of Adam Food Stores in 1952. In 1958, the Adam supermarkets were sold to an expanding national company that wanted to establish a strong presence in the midwest. Although asked to remain as chief executive of the parent company's midwest division, Benjamin Adam resigned shortly after the takeover. He wanted neither to move from his home city nor to work as an employee in a large company.

Benjamin Adam began Cascade Foods as a regional marketer of branded packaged goods to supermarkets and other food stores. While many product categories—such as cereals, cake mixes, detergents, and toothpastes—were dominated by a few large companies that competed nationally, other product categories—such as many dairy products, baked goods, and several varieties of fruit juices—did not have nationally dominant brands. This situation is commonly observed by people who move from one region of the country to another and cannot find their favorite brands available. In the early 1980's, for example, Mott's Apple Juice, a leading brand on the East Coast, and Tree Top, a leader in the West, were generally not available in each other's main markets.

Based on his years in the supermarket business, Benjamin Adam believed that there was considerable opportunity for a good regional marketer in many product categories. Some of the companies that sold to Adam Food Stores were professionally managed, but others maintained their position mainly due to a lack of effective competition.

Cascade Foods soon prospered. Its first products were baked goods (breads, rolls, cakes, etc.) and paper products (paper towels, napkins, toilet tissue, paper plates, etc.), but it soon developed a wider range of products. Different brand names were used in different product categories. Adam's strategy was to concentrate on the marketing of branded supermarket products and to use contract packers to manufacture the products sold by Cascade. Cascade presently used more than two dozen contract packers and monitored them under very tight quality control standards.

Cascade used brand advertising, primarily on regional television and in newspapers, to establish strong brand images for its products. Coupled with an efficient distribution system, the company had earned a favorable reputation with the supermarket chains and food stores in the area. Although Cascade had experienced some costly failures, such as its brand of packaged cookies and its line of tomato sauces, more than 60 percent of its product introductions were still in the market. Two product lines had been bought by a national food manufacturer who desired to use the brand name and positioning strategy to launch nationwide brands. Similar strategies

had been used by a number of national companies; Duncan Hines cake mixes and Charmin toilet paper were two examples of small regional companies bought by Proctor & Gamble and developed into leading national brands.

At present, Cascade Foods marketed only one beverage product, apple juice. That product had been marginally successful with an approximately 7 percent market share in Cascade's region over the past five years. Although the total volume of apple juice sold had grown in recent years, Cascade's market share had remained flat. About a year ago, a representative of Brik Pak Inc., the major supplier of aseptic packages ("paper bottles") in North America, had demonstrated the advantages of its packaging system to Cascade for its apple juice. Cascade management, however, had quickly recognized the opportunity that being first in the region's fruit drink market to use this system presented to Cascade.

Aseptic Packaging

Aseptic packaging was a dramatically different process for packaging milk, wine, fruit juices and drinks, and other liquid and semi-liquid products. Tetra-Pak, a family owned Swedish company with almost $1.5 billion in sales in 1983, was the inventor of this packaging system and the dominant supplier of aseptic packages worldwide. In Western Europe, almost 50 percent of all milk was sold in Tetra-Pak containers which allowed milk to be kept unrefrigerated for up to five months without loss of nutritional value or flavor. Not only did this provide a benefit for customers, but there were important savings in not having to use refrigerated shipment and storage. Up to 60 percent of a typical supermarket's energy bill was for refrigeration.

Although the refrigeration savings and longer shelf life were of limited application in the fruit juice and fruit drink industries, aseptic paper cartons cost less than bottles and cans. One liter aseptic boxes were estimated to cost only about 30 percent as much as bottles and 50 percent of the cost of cans. Although the filling process for aseptic containers was more complicated (both the container and contents needed to be sterilized), one research firm estimated that the cost of filling juice concentrate in 8 ounce Brik Pak boxes was 18 percent less than that for bottles or metal cans. Similar savings prevailed for larger sizes.

Cost savings were just one of the advantages for fruit drinks of the compact Brik Pak container, Tetra-Pak's most popular shape, which came in two main sizes—a 250 milliliter box (8.4 oz.), with a drinking straw attached, for the convenience market and a 1 liter container. (Other sizes were available and in 1984 Tetra-Pak was working on advancements such as a resealable half-gallon package for milk.) Aseptic packaging required only flash sterilization during packing, rather than the longer heating process for canned and bottled goods (juice was usually pasteurized after bottling). Consequently, for fruit juices and drinks, the flavors were reported to be truer than in cans and bottles. On the other hand, some people felt that the sterilization process for milk gave it a slightly "cooked" flavor. The rectangular shape of the Brik-Pak (whose shape fit its name quite well) allowed it to be easily stacked. Twelve Brik-Paks in the one liter size took only about two-thirds as much supermarket display space as twelve one-liter bottles. However, Brik-Paks lacked the rigidity necessary for packaging carbonated beverages.

The convenience in use factor was particularly critical for the quarter-liter Brik Pak carton that measured approximately 2½" wide × 4" tall × 1½" deep. It appeared to be just the right size for lunch boxes and snacks and was being sold in specially designed vending machines in some markets. According to a senior executive of Ocean Spray Cranberries Inc., the first company to feature aseptic packaged drinks (such as Cranapple) nationally, "The kinds of products we offer suddenly become portable." One company reported a 20 percent increase in fruit drink sales due to aseptic packaging and classified these volume gains as almost completely incremental. Some soft drink bottlers had begun selling aseptic packages of fruit drinks and stocking them next to soda in supermarkets.

Brik Pak Inc., the U.S. subsidiary of Tetra-Pak, built a manufacturing plant near Dallas, Texas, that produced nearly 1 billion aseptic packages in 1983.

In addition, there were several other U.S. companies either producing or planning to produce aseptic packages in the near future. After a review by Scott Green of the aseptic packaging industry, Cascade had decided to use Brik Pak cartons for its proposed entry into the fruit drink market. Cascade, in fact, would not do the manufacturing itself but would buy the finished product from a contract packer who would prepare the product according to Cascade's specifications. Cascade had successfully used this contract packer for several other product lines and had been extremely pleased with the quality and service provided by this firm.

FRUIT DRINK MARKET

Background

Fruit drink sales in Cascade's market area had grown 80 percent in the past five years (see *Exhibit 1*). Fruit drinks were only one type of beverage refreshment.

EXHIBIT 1
FRUIT DRINK SALES IN CASCADE MARKET AREA

	Quarter	000s of cases*
1979	1	428
	2	415
	3	452
	4	413
1980	1	456
	2	463
	3	532
	4	479
1981	1	502
	2	543
	3	627
	4	568
1982	1	715
	2	699
	3	732
	4	701
1983	1	768
	2	750
	3	791
	4	731

*1 case = 12 litres of fruit drinks.

The most immediate competitors were fruit juices (which had a higher fruit content than fruit drinks) and powdered fruit drink mixes, to which a consumer added water and sometimes sugar. Other competitors included carbonated beverages, plain and flavored milks, and plain water. Few brands competed in more than one of these markets, although some companies had brands in more than one market.

The fruit drink market was very competitive with a number of national and regional brands available; market share data are reported in *Exhibit 2*. Among the familiar brand names in the category were Hawaiian Punch and Hi-C. Despite its competitive intensity, the market seemed to hold high potential profitability. At current prices, a national brand was estimated to have a gross contribution margin of $3.00 per case (before advertising, promotion, and other marketing costs).

Although the brands differed in number of flavors offered and competed, at times, by introducing new flavors, three flavors accounted for the bulk of sales. These were an apple drink, a grape drink, and a mixed fruit drink. The fruits combined in the mixed fruit drink differed from brand to brand, and some consumers showed a strong preference for the taste of a particular brand's mixed fruit drink. Often, the mixed fruit drink was the company's main focus in advertising and the basis on which the brand had been launched. The apple, grape, and other drink flavors often had been introduced to provide variety and to satisfy the taste preferences of consumers.

The national brands were heavily advertised. Although Carl Gomez, the product manager's assistant, could not obtain estimates of advertising and promotion levels on a regional basis, he was able to obtain estimates of expenditures for one national brand for three recent years:

	Cases sold (000's)	Advertising (000's)	Promotion (000's)
1980	970	$ 950	$680
1981	1,300	1,340	870
1982	1,560	1,500	950

EXHIBIT 2
MARKET SHARE DATA FOR FRUIT DRINKS
(ALL SIZES AND FLAVORS), BASED ON VOLUME
IN CASCADE'S MARKET AREA

	1980	1981	1982
Brand A	26%	26%	25%
Brand B	12	13	13
Brand C	12	9	7
Brand D	1	5	10
Store brands and private labels	21	24	26
Other brands	28	23	29

About 25 percent of the market was accounted for by store brands. These brands competed primarily on price; 1 liter of a store brand fruit drink would typically sell for about $.20 less than a nationally advertised brand retailing at $1.29. Store brands were more successful in the grape and apple flavors than in mixed fruit flavors.

Entry into the Market

Sylvia Boaz had led a new product team that had investigated the possibility of using aseptic packaging systems as a vehicle for entry into the fruit drink market. Although some products, such as the Ocean Spray Cranberry drinks, were already sold in Cascade's market, as yet there was only limited availability of fruit drinks in aseptic packages. By moving quickly, Boaz had estimated that Cascade would develop the first major brand in its area to use the Brik Pak system. The major consumer benefits to be featured were the flavor of the product and the convenience of the package. Senior management approval had been given to carry the project through the test market stage and Boaz was appointed product manager in charge of the product.

Cascade had tentatively decided on an initial three flavor (mixed fruit, grape, and apple) line in 250 milliliter and 1 liter Brik Pak cartons. In consultation with its contract packer, Cascade had developed the fruit drinks. Harold Mann, the market research manager, had conducted a number of taste tests for the new product and found that the Cascade drinks were favored, on average, by about 65 percent of respondents in paired comparison taste tests in which subjects did not know the brand name of the product they were drinking. This was considered to be a very strong score.

The marketing plan for the first year called for an aggressive advertising and promotion budget of $500,000 for advertising and $350,000 for consumer and trade promotion. (Generally, Cascade budgeted about 50 percent more funds to a new brand introduction than would be required to maintain an established brand at the same volume of sales.) Sales force costs were estimated at $225,000; distribution costs were included in the production costs and not charged against the contribution. The only other charge against the contribution margin was the $250,000 budget for the new product management team, which included the salaries of Boaz and Gomez, costs for market research and consultants, and similar expenses that were incurred by Boaz and her group. At Cascade, entries into new product categories were not expected to break even until the second or third year of marketing.

Pricing Decisions

Sylvia Boaz and her team had recognized that pricing was one of the most critical decisions that had to be made. If Cascade priced on a par with other branded versions of fruit drinks (equivalent to $1.29 per liter and $.40 per 250 milliliter carton), the cost savings from aseptic packaging would allow a gross contribution margin of $4.00 per case, $1.00 per case greater than that presently estimated to be earned by the leading advertised brands. Assuming the introductory advertising and promotion policy described above, market research tests conducted under the supervision of Harold Mann and Scott Green had estimated a market share of 10 percent of the fruit drink market at the end of the first year. Cascade had developed a relatively sophisticated market research, simulation, and test market system to forecast the

sales of new products. In the past, that system had estimated the share of market obtained by the new entrant at the end of one year within 1.5 percent of the actual share 80 percent of the time. In other words, Cascade believed there was an 80 percent probability that Cascade fruit drinks would have market share between 8.5 percent and 11.5 percent at the end of one year with the planned introductory campaign.

Parity pricing was not the only alternative. Gomez had argued strongly that Cascade should charge a premium price for the product. Cascade's real strength, he suggested, was its ability to market branded products in its regional area. Here was a product with superior flavor and convenience, so the customer should be willing to pay more for it. Gomez had claimed:

If it cost more to manufacture than canned drinks, we would charge a higher price without question. Why shouldn't Cascade take the extra profit for itself? Furthermore, a premium price will help convey to consumers the superiority of the product. With a strong advertising campaign, we can position ourselves at the top of the market. If we set the price as the first entrants, others will price at our level. There's very little price variation among major brands at present.

Scott Green had questioned that approach.

High prices only provide an umbrella for competition to enter the market. Besides, why would consumers pay more? A high price could really depress sales. The package itself is novel enough, without imposing a price barrier as well for consumers. Pricing below current prices for canned drinks might even provide an incentive for initial trial, but Cascade shouldn't have to do that in the long run.

The product management group recognized that the pricing decision was too important to be left to guesses. Market research data might help narrow down some of the issues. Harold Mann, the market research manager, had over time built Cascade management's appreciation of both the value and limits of market research. While market research could not eliminate all uncertainty, it could often reduce some of it.

Two years ago, Cascade had run an experiment for its apple juice brand on the effect of short-term price promotions on sales. This study is summarized in the Appendix. It clearly showed that price reductions had a significant impact on sales, especially when combined with special supermarket displays.

However, the apple juice test, while helpful, was not directly relevant to the fruit drink market. Here Cascade was concerned with a permanent price for a new product. As a result, Boaz asked Mann to use the test market not only to assess the likely success of the product and its expected first year market share, as reported earlier, but also to test the effect of different prices on sales of fruit drinks. As a group, the product management team helped design an experiment. Three price levels were tested:

Low	$1.19/liter; $.35/250 mL
Regular	$1.29/liter; $.40/250 mL
High	$1.39/liter; $.45/250 mL

A change in the retail price of $.10/liter and $.05/250 milliliter was equivalent to a change of $.90 in Cascade's contribution per case, given the mix of sizes likely to be sold.

In addition, there was considerable discussion as to the effect of advertising on price sensitivity. Some believed that higher levels of advertising decreased price sensitivity by establishing a strong brand image. Others, however, felt that higher advertising expenditures expanded the potential market for the brand as compared to lower advertising expenditures, but that the additional potential consumers were more price sensitive. Hence, they argued for a strategy of high advertising and low prices. Recognizing the importance of this factor, Cascade designed the test market to test two levels of introductory advertising:

| Normal | annual rate of $500,000 |
| High | annual rate of $1,000,000 |

These six different price and advertising (3 price times 2 ad budget) levels were tested in 24 supermarkets in four cities. Two cities received high advertising levels and two cities received low advertising levels. Because price could be set individually by store, high, regular, and low prices were tested in

two stores in each of the four cities used. Sales in units (normalized for store volume) were recorded bimonthly for each size and flavor for the four months that the test ran. However, there were no major differences in sales among flavors and sizes, so the data were summarized more compactly as shown in *Exhibit 3*. These data showed a clear effect of price and advertising on sales, but did not fully resolve the issue of the price and advertising levels to use.

A week after receiving these data, Boaz convened a meeting of the product management group. She had asked both Gomez and Green independently to

EXHIBIT 3
PRICE AND ADVERTISING EXPERIMENT

Sales in units for months 1 & 2	Sales in units for months 3 & 4	Price	Advertising
331	280	L	N
394	256	L	N
329	279	L	N
403	217	L	N
662	430	L	H
478	357	L	H
552	337	L	H
665	474	L	H
253	247	R	N
289	190	R	N
276	270	R	N
335	203	R	N
351	224	R	H
535	394	R	H
409	203	R	H
424	305	R	H
252	220	H	N
293	151	H	N
255	181	H	N
210	156	H	N
221	148	H	H
321	254	H	H
310	172	H	H
312	249	H	H

Note: Sales in each store were adjusted for the overall volume of fruit drinks sold in each supermarket. The prices tested were *Low* ($1.19, $.35), *Regular* ($1.29, $.40), and *High* ($1.39), $.45); the advertising budgets tested were *Normal* ($500,000) and *High* ($1,000,000). See the text for a description of the experiment.

prepare recommendations on a pricing strategy for Cascade fruit drinks in aseptic packages. The purpose of the meeting was to hear both presentations and to resolve the issue of the right pricing strategy to use. Following that, Boaz would need to prepare a report for senior management with a recommendation on whether or not to enter the fruit drink market and, if so, with what marketing plan and goals.

Apple Juice Experiment

In conjunction with one supermarket chain, Cascade had conducted an extensive test of the impact of price promotions and display space on sales of its Cascade brand of apple juice. In brief, Cascade tested three price levels—its regular price level of $1.59 per quart of apple juice and prices of 10 cents off and 20 cents off—and two display conditions, regular shelf space and a special end-of-aisle

display. Thus there were six different conditions (3 price levels times 2 display levels). The experiment was conducted in six stores over a twelve week time period. In weeks 2, 4, 6, 8, 10, 12 each store was randomly assigned one of the six treatments and over the six experimental weeks, each store received each combination of price and display once. In the alternative weeks, price and display space were set at their normal levels. The impact on units sold was as follows:

	Normal display	End-aisle display
Regular price	100	131
10 cents off	124	143
20 cents off	136	157

where 100 represents the level of sales at the regular price and with the normal display. In the week immediately following an experimental treatment, sales of apple juice declined about 10 percent in all cases except for the combination 20 cents off and end-of-aisle display where sales in the week following the experiment declined almost 20 percent. After the experiment ended Cascade apple juice sales returned to their normal levels.

Southwest Airlines

Christopher H. Lovelock

Braniff's " 'Get Acquainted Sale': Half Price To Houston's Hobby Airport" trumpeted the headlines of the full-page advertisement in the February 1, 1973, edition of the *Dallas Morning News.*

M. Lamar Muse, president of Southwest Airlines, held up the advertisement for members of the airline's management team and advertising agency executives to see, commenting as he did so: "OK, at least we now know what Braniff's response to our San Antonio promotion will be. They are hitting us hard in our only really profitable market. Every decision they have made to date has been the wrong decision, so how can we turn this one to our advantage?"

SOUTHWEST AND ITS COMPETITION

Southwest Airlines Co. had been organized as a Texas corporation in March 1967 with the objective of providing improved quality air service between

the cities of Dallas/Fort Worth, Houston, and San Antonio. These cities, each 190 to 250 miles apart, formed a triangular route in eastern Texas. Southwest had been certified as an intrastate carrier on these routes by the Texas Aeronautics Commission in February 1968, but lawsuits by Braniff International Airways and Texas International Airlines (TI) had delayed the initiation of service by Southwest until June 1971.

The Dallas-Houston market, the largest of the three, was dominated by Braniff, which carried some 75% of the local traffic on that route during the first half of 1971 (see *Exhibit 1*). A major international carrier with an all-jet fleet of 74 aircraft, Braniff reported systemwide revenues in 1970 of $325.6 million and carried 5.8 million passengers. Southwest's other principal competitor, Texas International, served the southern and southwestern United States and Mexico. In 1970, TI had a fleet of 45 aircraft, carried 2.2 million passengers, and generated $77.8 million in total revenues.

There was considerable public discontent with the quality of service provided by these two carriers on intrastate routes within Texas—a fact that Southwest hoped to exploit. Among other things, their local flights typically represented segments of longer, in-

EXHIBIT 1 SOUTHWEST AIRLINES AND COMPETITORS: AVERAGE DAILY LOCAL PASSENGERS CARRIED IN EACH DIRECTION, DALLAS–HOUSTON MARKET

	Braniff[a]		Texas International[a]		Southwest		Passengers in total local market[b,c]
	Passengers[b]	Market share (%)	Passengers[b]	Market share (%)	Passengers[b]	Market share (%)	
1967	416	86.1	67	13.9	—	—	483
1968	381	70.2	162	29.8	—	—	543
1969	427	75.4	139	24.6	—	—	566
1970							
1st half	449	79.0	119	21.0	—	—	568
2nd half	380	76.0	120	24.0	—	—	500
Year	414	77.5	120	22.5	—	—	534
1971							
1st half	402	74.7	126	23.4	10	1.9	538
2nd half	338	50.7	120	18.0	209	31.3	667
Year	370	61.4	123	20.4	110	18.2	603
1972							
January	341	48.3	105	14.9	260	36.8	706
February	343	47.6	100	13.9	277	38.5	720
March	357	47.5	100	13.3	295	39.2	752
April	367	48.3	97	12.8	296	38.9	760
May	362	48.5	84	11.3	300	40.2	746
June	362	46.8	81	10.5	330	42.7	773
1st half	356	48.0	93	12.5	293	39.5	742
July	332	48.1	74	10.7	284	41.2	690
August	432	53.7	56	6.9	317	39.4	805
September	422	54.9	55	7.2	291	37.9	768
October	443	53.1	56	6.7	335	40.2	834
November	439	50.6	55	6.3	374	43.1	868
December	396	52.1	56	7.4	308	40.5	760
2nd half	411	52.1	59	7.5	318	40.4	788
Year	384	50.1	77	10.0	306	39.9	767
1973							
January[d]	443	51.5	62	7.3	354	41.2	859

[a]These figures were calculated by Muse from passenger data that Braniff and TI were required to supply to the Civil Aeronautics Board. He multiplied the original figures by a correction factor to eliminate interline traffic and arrive at net totals for local traffic.

[b]Average number of local passengers carried in each direction each day. The numbers should be doubled to yield the total number of passenger trips between the two cities.

[c]Excludes figures for another carrier that had about 1% of the local market in 1969 and 1970.

[d]Projected figures from terminal counts by Southwest personnel.

Source: Company records.

terstate flights, and it was often hard for local passengers to get seats.

After carefully assessing costs, Southwest settled on a $20 fare for each route. This compared with existing Braniff and TI coach fares of $27 from Dallas to Houston and $28 from Dallas to San Antonio. Management hoped that Southwest could anticipate an initial price advantage, although Braniff and TI would probably reduce their own fares promptly.

Southwest executives had calculated that an average of 39 passengers per flight would be required to break even. They considered this level of business (and better) a reasonable expectation in light of the market's estimated potential for growth and the frequency of flights that Southwest planned to offer. Nevertheless, they predicted a period of deficit operations before this break-even point was reached.

OPERATING EXPERIENCE

Southwest inaugurated scheduled revenue service with a blaze of publicity on June 18, 1971. The airline offered all coach-class flights and introduced a number of innovations and attractions, including new Boeing 737 twin-jet aircraft, fast ticketing, glamorous hostesses, and inexpensive, exotically named drinks.

Despite extensive promotion, initial results were hardly spectacular. Between June 18 and June 30, 1971, Southwest had an average of 13.1 passengers per flight on its Dallas–Houston service and 12.9 passengers on the Dallas–San Antonio route; passenger loads during July showed only marginal improvement (see *Exhibit 2*). Both competitors had met Southwest's lower fares immediately, as well as improving the frequency and quality of their services on the two routes served by the new airline, and heavily promoting these changes.

Management concluded that it was essential to improve schedule frequencies to compete more effec-

EXHIBIT 2 MONTHLY FLIGHTS AND PASSENGER COUNTS ON EACH ROUTE BY TYPE OF FARE, PASSENGERS IN 000s

	Dallas–Houston				Dallas–San Antonio			
	Full fare		Discount		Full fare		Discount	
	Passengers	Flights	Passengers	Flights	Passengers	Flights	Passengers	Flights
1971								
June[a]	3.6	273	—	—	1.9	148	—	—
July	10.3	642	—	—	5.2	346	—	—
August	11.3	672	—	—	4.8	354	—	—
September	11.7	612	—	—	4.8	327	—	—
October	14.6	764	—	—	6.5	382	—	—
November	14.0	651	0.1	3	4.2	240	—	—
December	14.5	682	0.2	5	4.0	165	—	—
Total	80.0	4,296	0.3	8	31.4	1,962	—	—
1972								
January	16.0	630	0.2	4	2.8	141	—	—
February	15.9	636	0.2	4	2.8	142	—	—
March	17.9	664	0.4	5	3.9	204	0.3	5
April	17.4	601	0.3	4	4.3	185	0.3	4
May	17.1	554	1.5	30	3.5	177	0.7	21
June	16.5	474	3.3	47	3.8	170	1.4	31
July	13.6	447	4.0	47	3.3	162	1.8	31
August	15.7	496	4.0	50	3.2	177	1.8	31
September	13.7	436	3.8	53	3.1	154	1.6	30
October	16.0	474	4.8	71	3.4	173	1.8	27
November	15.1	403	7.4	104	2.4	122	4.2	77
December	12.8	377	6.3	91	2.4	117	3.9	69
Total	187.7	6,192	36.2	510	38.9	1,924	17.8	326
1973								
January[b]	15.1	404	6.8	101	1.4	75	6.3	122

[a]Part month only.
[b]Estimated figures.
Source: Company records.

tively with Braniff and TI. This became possible with the delivery of the company's fourth Boeing 737 in late September 1971, and on October 1 hourly service was introduced between Dallas and Houston, and flights every two hours between Dallas and San Antonio.

Surveys of Southwest passengers departing from Houston showed that a substantial percentage would prefer service from the William P. Hobby Airport, 12 miles southwest of downtown Houston, rather than from the new Houston Intercontinental Airport, 26 miles north of the city. Accordingly, arrangements were completed in mid-November for 7 of South-

west's 14 round-trip flights between Dallas and Houston to be transferred to Hobby Airport (thus reopening this old airport to scheduled commercial passenger traffic). Additional schedule revisions included elimination of the extremely unprofitable Saturday operation on all routes.

These actions contributed to an increase in transportation revenues in the final quarter of 1971 over those achieved in the third quarter, but Southwest's operating losses in the third quarter fell only slightly, from $1,001,000 to $921,000 (see *Exhibit 3*). At year's end 1971, Southwest's accumulated deficit stood at $3.75 million (see *Exhibit 4*).

EXHIBIT 2 (*continued*)

| | San Antonio–Houston | | | | | |
| | Full fare | | Discount | | Grand Totals | |
	Passengers	Flights	Passengers	Flights	Passengers	Flights
1971						
June[a]	—	—	—	—	5.5	424
July	—	—	—	—	15.5	988
August	—	—	—	—	16.1	1,026
September	—	—	—	—	16.4	939
October	—	—	—	—	21.0	1,146
November	0.9	72	—	—	19.1	966
December	1.7	134	—	—	20.4	986
Total	2.6	206	—	—	114.0	6,475
1972						
January	2.0	128	—	—	20.9	903
February	2.1	134	—	—	20.9	916
March	2.8	146	—	—	25.4	1,024
April	2.3	130	—	—	24.7	924
May	2.5	138	—	—	25.3	1,020
June	2.6	140	—	—	27.6	862
July	2.1	131	—	—	24.7	818
August	2.4	146	—	—	27.0	900
September	2.2	127	—	—	24.4	800
October	2.5	139	—	—	28.5	884
November	2.3	123	0.5	16	32.0	845
December	2.0	110	0.5	16	27.8	780
Total	27.8	1,592	1.0	32	309.2	10,676
1973						
January[b]	2.4	120	0.5	16	32.5	838

[a]Part month only.
[b]Estimated figures.
Source: Company records.

EXHIBIT 3   QUARTERLY INCOME STATEMENTS, $000s

	1971		1972			
	Q3	Q4	Q1	Q2	Q3	Q4
Transportation revenues[a]	$ 887	$ 1,138	$1,273	$1,401	$1,493	$1,745
Operating expenses						
Operations and maintenance	1,211	1,280	1,192	1,145	1,153	1,156
Marketing and general administration	371	368	334	366	313	351
Depreciation and amortization	311	411	333	334	335	335
Total	1,893	2,059	1,859	1,845	1,801	1,842
Operating profit (loss)	(1,006)	(921)	(586)	(444)	(308)	(97)
Net interest revenues (costs)	(245)	(253)	(218)	(220)	(194)	(204)
Net income (loss) before extraordinary items	(1,260)	(1,174)	(804)	(664)	(502)	(301)
Extraordinary items	(571)[b]	(469)[b]	—	533[c]	—	—
Net income (loss)	$(1,831)	$(1,643)	$ (804)	$ (131)	$ (502)	$ (301)

[a] Includes both passenger and freight business. Freight sales represents 2% of revenues in 1972.
[b] Write-off of preoperating costs.
[c] Capital gain on sale of one aircraft.
Source: Company records.

Although the majority of ticket sales were made over the counter at airport terminals, sales were also made through travel agents and to corporate accounts. Travel agents received a 7% commission on credit card sales and 10% on cash sales. Corporate accounts—companies whose personnel made regular use of Southwest Airlines—received no discount but benefited from the convenience of having their own supply of ticket stock (which they issued themselves) and of receiving a single monthly billing.

Between October 1971 and April 1972, average passenger loads systemwide increased from 18.4 passengers per flight to 26.7 passengers. However, this was still substantially below the number necessary to cover total costs per trip flown, some components of which had been tending to rise (see *Exhibits 3* and *5*). It had become evident that the volume of traffic during the late morning and early afternoon could not realistically support flights at hourly intervals. It was also clear that most Houston passengers preferred Hobby Airport to Houston Intercontinental, and the decision was made to abandon the latter airport altogether.

On May 14, 1972, Southwest reduced the total number of daily flights between Dallas and Houston from 29 to 22. Eleven daily flights continued to be offered on the Dallas–San Antonio route and six between San Antonio and Houston–Hobby. (Braniff quickly retaliated by introducing service from Dallas to Hobby and promoting it extensively.) The new schedule allowed the company to dispose of its fourth Boeing 737. Southwest had no trouble finding a ready buyer for this aircraft and made a profit of $533,000 on the resale.

CHANGES IN PRICING STRATEGY

June 1972 saw Southwest Airlines celebrating its first birthday. This provided an opportunity for more of the publicity stunts for which the airline was already becoming renowned. Posters were hung inside the aircraft and in the waiting lounges, the aircraft cabins were decorated, and there was an on-board party every day for a week. This activity, promoted by newspaper advertising, generated considerable publicity for the airline and, in management's view, rein-

EXHIBIT 4 BALANCE SHEET AT DECEMBER 31, 1972, 1971, AND 1970

	1972	1971	1970
	Assets		
Current assets			
Cash	$ 133,839	$ 231,530	$ 183
Certificates of deposit	1,250,000	2,850,000	—
Accounts receivable			
Trade	397,664	300,545	—
Interest	14,691	35,013	—
Other	67,086	32,569	100
Total accounts receivable	479,441	368,127	100
Less allowance for doubtful accounts	86,363	30,283	—
	393,078	337,844	100
Inventories of parts and supplies at cost	154,121	171,665	—
Prepaid insurance and other	75,625	156,494	31
Total current assets	$ 2,006,663	$ 3,747,533	$ 314
Property and equipment, at cost			
Boeing 737-200 jet aircraft	12,409,772	16,263,250	—
Support flight equipment	2,423,480	2,378,581	—
Ground equipment	346,377	313,072	9,249
	15,179,629	18,954,903	9,249
Less accumulated depreciation and overhaul allowance	2,521,646	1,096,177	—
	12,657,983	17,858,726	9,249
Deferred certification costs less amortization	371,095	477,122	530,136
Total assets	$15,035,741	$22,083,381	$539,699
	Liabilities and Stockholders' Equity		
Current liabilities			
Notes payable to banks (secured)	$ 950,000	—	—
Accounts payable	124,890	$ 355,539	$ 30,819
Accrued salaries and wages	55,293	54,713	79,000
Other accrued liabilities	136,437	301,244	—
Long-term debt due within one year	1,226,457	1,500,000	—
Total current liabilities	2,493,077	2,211,496	109,819
Long-term debt due after one year			
7% convertible promissory notes	—	1,250,000	—
Conditional purchase agreements— Boeing Financial Corporation (1½% over prime rate)	11,942,056	18,053,645	—
	11,942,056	18,053,645	—
Less amounts due within one year	1,226,457	1,500,000	—
	10,715,599	16,553,645	—
Stockholders' equity			
Common stock, $1.00 par value, 2,000,000 shares authorized, 1,108,758 issued (1,058,758 at 12/31/71)	1,108,758	1,058,758	372,404
Capital in excess of par value	6,062,105	6,012,105	57,476
Deficit	(5,343,798)	(3,752,623)	—
	1,827,065	3,318,240	429,880
Total liabilities and stockholders' equity	$15,035,741	$22,083,381	$539,699

Note: Notes to financial statement are not shown here.
Source: Southwest Airlines Co. annual reports, 1971, 1972.

EXHIBIT 5   INCREMENTAL COSTS PER FLIGHT AND PER PASSENGER, 1971–1972[a]

Category	Last Half 1971	First Half 1972	Last Half 1972
Incremental costs per flight			
Crew pay	$ 46.62	$ 50.61	$ 56.82
Crew expenses and overnight	5.28	4.24	4.93
Fuel	93.50	93.35	94.91
Airport landing fees	10.44	12.87	12.37
Aircraft maintenance	69.98	69.51	75.19
	$225.82	$230.58	$244.22
Variable costs per passenger			
Passenger-handling personnel	$ 1.09	$ 0.88	$ 0.80
Reservation costs[b]	0.92	0.11	0.10
Ramp, provisioning, and baggage handling[c]	0.98	0.40	0.29
Baggage claims and interrupted trip expenses	0.01	0.01	0.01
Passenger beverage and supplies	0.25	0.13	0.43
Traffic commissions and bad debts	0.61	0.62	0.74
Passenger liability and insurance[d]	0.90	0.38	0.43
	$ 4.76[e]	$ 2.53	$ 2.80

[a] Includes all costs treated as variable by Southwest management for the purposes of planning and analysis.
[b] Initially, Southwest contracted out its reservation service to American Airlines; after October 1, 1972, SWA's own employees handled this task.
[c] Initially contracted on a minimum cost-per-flight basis, subsequently SWA used its own employees on a phased schedule as facilities permitted.
[d] During the last half of 1971, SWA paid a minimum total premium for passenger liability insurance due to the low number of passenger carried.
[e] Comment by management: "The high figures for costs per passenger during the last half of 1971 represent the effect of minimum staffing with very few passengers. The minimum staffing effect declines substantially in later periods and begins to represent a true variable."
Source: Company records.

forced Southwest's image as the plucky, friendly little underdog that had survived an entire year against powerful, entrenched competition.

At this point Southwest management decided it was time to take a hard look at the fare structure and its relationship to costs and revenues. For some months, Southwest had been experimenting with a $10 fare on Friday evening flights after 9:00 P.M. In May this reduced fare was extended to post-9:00 P.M. flights on a daily basis. The result was sharply higher load factors on these discount flights relative to the average achieved on full-fare flights (see *Exhibit 2*). But management soon concluded that the airline could no longer afford a $20 fare on daytime flights. New tariffs were therefore filed with the Texas Aeronautics Commission, effective July 9, 1972. These raised Southwest's basic one-way fare from $20 to $26; established a round-trip fare of $50; and offered

a $225 Commuter Club Card, entitling the purchaser to unlimited transportation on all routes for 30 days.

The key consideration was how the competition would react. "For a few days," admitted the vice president of marketing, "we were really sweating." Braniff's initial response was to devote an additional aircraft to its Dallas–Hobby Airport flights on July 11, thus permitting on-the-hour service most of the business day. However, on July 17, Texas International increased its fares to the same level as Southwest's; then on July 21 Braniff met all aspects of the fare and on-board service changes, also adding a $10 Sundowner flight to Hobby at 7:30 P.M. As a result of Braniff's increased service and the higher fares, Southwest's patronage fell 2% between the second and third quarters, but transportation revenues increased.

During September new advertising was launched,

based on the slogan "Remember What It Was Like Before Southwest Airlines?" which the agency saw as a war cry to rally consumers. The principal media used in this campaign were billboards and television. TV commercials cited the advantages of flying Southwest, notably its dependable schedules.

At the end of October, another major change was made in pricing strategies. The $10 discount fares, which had never been advertised, were replaced by half-fare flights ($13 one way, $25 round trip) on the two major routes each weekday night after 8 P.M. Saturday flights were reintroduced and all weekend flights were offered at half fare. An intensive three-week advertising campaign accompanied these new schedules and price changes, using one-minute radio commercials on country and western, Top 40, and similar stations[1] (see *Exhibit 6*). The response was immediate, and November 1972 traffic levels were 12% higher than those in October—historically the best month of the year in Southwest's commuter markets.

In the new year, management turned its attention to its largest single remaining problem. The company was making money on its Dallas–Houston flights,

---

[1]A Top 40 station is one that specializes in playing popular rock music recordings.

EXHIBIT 6   SAMPLE RADIO COMMERCIAL FOR HALF-FARE, OFF-PEAK FLIGHTS, FALL 1972

Number:	98-23-2 **Length:** 60 seconds (Dallas version) **Date:** 10/13/72
Music:	*Fanfare*
Announcer:	Southwest Airlines introduces the Half-Fare Frivolity Flights.
Hostess:	Now you can afford to fly for the fun of it.
Sound effects:	*Laughter of one person building from under, with music.*
Announcer:	Now you can take any Southwest Airlines flights any weeknight at eight o'clock and all flights on Saturday or Sunday for half fare. Just $13 or $25 round trip.
Sound effects:	*Laughter, music out. Street sounds under.*
Man:	You mean I can visit my uncle in Houston for only $13?
Announcer:	Right.
Man:	That's weird. My uncle lives in St. Louis.
Music:	*Mexican fiesta sound.*
Chicano:	Take your wife or lover on a Southwest Airlines Half-Fare Frivolity Flight to San Antonio this weekend. Float down the river while lovely senoritas strum their enchiladas and sing the beautiful, traditional guacamoles.
Sound effects:	*Rocket blasting off.*
Announcer:	Take a Southwest Airlines Half-Fare Frivolity Flight to Houston and watch the astronauts mow their lawns.
Sound effects:	*Football crowd noises.*
Announcer:	Take a Southwest Airlines Frivolity Flight to Dallas and watch the Cowboys hurt themselves.
Sound effects:	*Others out. Rinky-tink music up.*
Hostess:	Half-Fare Frivolity Flights, every weeknight at eight o'clock and *all* weekend flights. Only $13. Almost as cheap as the bus. Cheaper than your own car. So relax with me, and stop driving yourself.
Announcer:	Southwest Airlines' Half-Fare Frivolity Flights.
Hostess:	Fly for the fun of it.

Source: Company records.

but was still incurring substantial losses in the Dallas–San Antonio market. Southwest offered only 8 flights a day on this route, versus 34 by its major competitor (see *Exhibit 7*), and in January was averaging a mere 17 passengers on each full-fare flight. The Dallas–San Antonio market had not grown as rapidly as had Dallas–Houston, and Southwest held a smaller market share (see *Exhibit 8*).

Management concluded that unless a dramatic improvement in patronage was quickly achieved on this route, it would have to be abandoned. Management decided to make one last attempt to obtain the needed increase and on January 22, 1973, announced a "60-

Day Half-Price Sale" on *all* Southwest Airlines flights between Dallas and San Antonio. This sale was promoted by TV and radio advertising. If successful, it was Lamar Muse's intention to make this reduced fare permanent, but he felt that by announcing it as a limited period offer, he would stimulate consumer interest even more effectively while also reducing the likelihood of competitive response. (*Exhibit 9* shows a sample radio script.)

The impact of these half-price fares was even faster and more dramatic than the results of the evening and weekend half-price fares introduced the previous fall. By the end of the first week, average

EXHIBIT 7   ANALYSIS OF WEEKLY FLIGHT SCHEDULES BY SOUTHWEST AND COMPETING CARRIERS, JANUARY 1973

	Dallas–Houston[a]						Houston[a]–Dallas						Total no. flights (both directions)	
	Weekdays		Sat.		Sun.		Weekdays		Sat.		Sun.			
						Total						Total	Full Fare	Discount
	I	H	I	H	I	H	I	H	I	H	I	H		
Braniff	80	35	8	5	12	7	147	70	45	9	7	12	7	150	297	—
Texas International	45	—	6	—	9	—	60	49	—	6	—	10	—	65	125	—
Southwest	—	55	—	2	—	5	62	—	55	—	3	—	4	62	100	24
Total	125	90	14	7	21	12	269	119	100	15	10	22	11	277		

	Dallas–San Antonio				San Antonio–Dallas					
	Weekdays	Sat.	Sun.	Total	Weekdays	Sat.	Sun.	Total		
Braniff	85	16	15	116	85	14	17	116	232	—
Texas International	10	1	2	13	5	1	1	7	20	—
American	10	2	2	14	10	2	2	14	38	—
Southwest	20	1	3	24	20	2	2	24	30	18
Total	125	20	22	167	120	19	22	161		

	San Antonio–Houston[b]				Houston[b]–San Antonio					
	Weekdays	Sat.	Sun.	Total	Weekdays	Sat.	Sun.	Total		
Braniff	5	—	1	6	10	2	1	13	19	—
Texas International	10	2	2	14	15	3	3	21	35	—
American	5	1	1	7	5	1	1	7	14 [c]	—
Continental	45	9	9	63	45	9	9	63	126 [c]	—
Eastern	20	4	4	28	20	4	4	28	56 [c]	—
Southwest	15	1	1	17	15	1	1	17	30	4
Total	100	17	18	135	110	20	19	149		

[a] I = flights to/from Houston Intercontinental; H = Houston Hobby.
[b] Southwest flights on this route used Houston Hobby Airport; all other airlines used Houston Intercontinental.
[c] Some flights offered thrift or night fares with savings of $3 to $5 over regular fare.
Source: Data generated from schedules published in *World Airline Guide*, North American edition, January 1973.

EXHIBIT 8   ESTIMATED MARKET SIZE, DALLAS-HOUSTON AND DALLAS-SAN ANTONIO ROUTES[a]

	Local passengers carried annually (both directions)			
	1969	**1970**	**1971**	**1972**
Dallas–Houston				
Braniff	268,630	265,910	246,170	300,780
Texas International	91,690	70,950	69,790	51,010
Other	4,390	4,790	1,830	1,910
Southwest	—	—	80,187	223,581
	364,710	341,650	397,977	577,281
Dallas–San Antonio				
Braniff	144,010	124,690	135,660	177,020
Texas International	10,400	15,040	5,290	1,800
American	4,100	4,120	3,600	2,580
Other	520	560	380	330
Southwest	—	—	31,302	56,653
	159,030	144,410	176,232	238,383

[a] These estimates were made by Southwest Airlines' economic consultant in New York.
Source: Company records.

EXHIBIT 9   SAMPLE RADIO ADVERTISING FOR HALF-FARE SAN ANTONIO FLIGHTS, JANUARY 1973

Number: **118-23-2**   **Length:** 60 seconds (Dallas version)   **Date:** 12/21/72

Woman: Harold, this is your mother in San Antonio talking to you from the radio, Harold. I want you to know that Southwest Airlines is having a half-price sale, Harold. For 60 days you can fly between San Antonio and Dallas for half price. Only $13, Harold. I expect to see a lot of you for those 60 days. Are you listening, Harold? Harold! [*station wind*] I'm talking to you!

Music: *Light, happy.*

Hostess: Southwest Airlines half-fare flights. Every flight between San Antonio and Dallas every day. Only $13.

Sound effects: *Street noises.*

Irate male voice: Hey! You people fly Southwest Airlines during this half-price sale, you're gonna have a lonely bus driver on your conscience. Take the bus. It only costs a little more, but it's four hours longer! You'll have a lot more time with me, won't you? [*fade*] Well, won't you?

Sound effects: *Street noises.*

Man: There is a cheaper way than Southwest Airlines. Put on roller skates, tie yourself to a trailer truck. . . .

Music: *Light, happy.*

Hostesses: Fly Southwest Airlines. Half price between Dallas and San Antonio on every flight every day. Why pay more?

Voice: Half price? Can they do that?

Second voice: They did it!

Source: Company records.

EXHIBIT 10

BRANIFF NEWSPAPER ADVERTISING FOR DALLAS-HOBBY HALF-PRICE SALE, DALLAS NEWSPAPERS, FEBRUARY 1973

Braniff's 'Get Acquainted Sale'

Half-price to Houston's Hobby Airport.

$13 Coach $17 First Class

To Hobby			Back to Dallas-Fort Worth		
Leave		Arrive	Leave		Arrive
7:30 a.m.	Non-stop	8:20 a.m.	8:00 a.m. (Ex Sun)	Non-stop	8:50 a.m.
9:30 a.m.	Non-stop	10:20 a.m.	9:00 a.m. (Ex Sun)	Non-stop	9:50 a.m.
11:30 a.m.	Non-stop	12:20 p.m.	11:00 a.m	Non-stop	11:50 a.m.
2:30 p.m.	Non-stop	3:20 p.m.	1:00 p.m	Non-stop	1:50 p.m.
3:30 p.m. (Ex Sat)	Non-stop	4:20 p.m.	4:00 p.m.	Non-stop	4:50 p.m.
5:30 p.m.	Non-stop	6:20 p.m.	5:00 p.m. (Ex Sat)	Non-stop	5:50 p.m.
6:30 p.m. (Ex Sat)	Non-stop	7:20 p.m.	7:00 p.m. (Ex Sat)	Non-stop	7:50 p.m.
			9:00 p.m.	Non-stop	9:50 p.m.

Sale lasts 'til April 1

From now until April 1, all Braniff International flights to Houston's Hobby Airport are priced to go. Half price to be exact. 50% off.

A one-way ticket in coach is $13.00 Round-trip is an even better bargain at $25.00. And in first class, $17.00 one-way, $34.00 round-trip.

We believe we have the best service to Hobby Airport. But not enough people know about it. So, we're offering you a chance to sample our big 727 Wide-Body jets to Houston's Hobby at half the regular price. We call it our "Get Acquainted Sale"

Half price and a reserved seat too. Call Braniff International at 357-9511 in Dallas; 335-5811 in Fort Worth.

You'll like flying Braniff Style.

BRANIFF

U.S. MAINLAND HAWAII MEXICO SOUTH AMERICA

loads on Southwest's Dallas–San Antonio service had risen to 48 passengers per flight and continued to rise sharply at the beginning of the following week.

On Thursday, February 1, however, Braniff employed full-page newspaper advertisements to announce a half-price "Get Acquainted Sale" between Dallas and Hobby on all flights, lasting until April 1 (see *Exhibit 10*). However, fares on Braniff's flights between Dallas and Houston Intercontinental remained at the existing levels.

Lamar Muse immediately called an urgent management meeting to decide what action Southwest should take in response to Braniff's move.

Columbia Plastics Division of Fraser Industries Inc.

Charles B. Weinberg

Alice Howell, president of the Columbia Plastics Division of Fraser Industries, Inc., leaned forward at her desk in her bright, sunlit office and said, "In brief, our two options are either to price at a level that just covers our costs or we face losing market leadership to those upstart Canadians at Vancouver Light. Are there no other options?" Thomas Chu, Columbia's marketing manager, and Sam Carney, the production manager, had no immediate reply.

Columbia Plastics, based in Seattle, Washington, had been the area's leading manufacturer of plastic molded skylights for use in houses and offices for almost fifteen years. However, two years earlier Vancouver Light, whose main plant was located in Vancouver, British Columbia, Canada, 150 miles to the north of Seattle, had opened a sales office in the city and sought to gain business by pricing aggressively. Vancouver Light began by offering skylights at 20 percent below Columbia's price for large orders. Now Vancouver Light had just announced a further price cut of 10 percent.

COMPANY BACKGROUND

The primary business of Fraser Industries, which had recently celebrated the fiftieth anniversary of its existence, was the supply of metal and plastic fabricated parts for its well known Seattle neighbor, Boeing Aircraft. Until the 1970s Boeing had accounted for more than 80 percent of Fraser's volume, but Fraser then decided to diversify in order to protect itself against the boom and bust cycle which seemed to characterize the aircraft industry. Even now, Boeing still accounted for nearly half of Fraser's $50 million[1] in annual sales.

Columbia Plastics had been established to apply Fraser's plastic molding skills in the construction industry. Its first products, which still accounted for nearly 30 percent of its sales, included plastic garage doors, plastic gutters, and plastic covers for outdoor lights, all of which had proved to be popular among Seattle home builders. About 15 years ago, Columbia began production of what was to be its most successful product, skylights for homes and offices. Sky-

---

[1]All prices and costs are in U.S. dollars.

lights now accounted for 70 percent of Columbia's sales.

THE SKYLIGHT MARKET

Although skylights varied greatly in size, a typical one measured $3' \times 3'$ and would be installed in the ceiling of a kitchen, bathroom, or living room. It was made primarily of molded plastic with an aluminum frame. Skylights were usually installed by home builders, upon initial construction of a home or by professional contractors as part of a remodeling job. Because of the need to cut through the roof to install a skylight and to then seal the joint between the roof and skylight so that water would not leak through, only the most talented of "do-it-yourselfers" would tackle this job on their own. At present 70 percent of the market was in home and office buildings, 25 percent in professional remodeling, and 5 percent in the do-it-yourself market.

Skylights were very popular. Homeowners found the natural light they brought to a room to be quite attractive and perceived skylights to be energy conserving. Although opinion was divided on whether the heat loss from a skylight was more than the light gained, the general perception was very favorable. Homebuilders found that featuring a skylight in a kitchen or other room would be an important plus in attracting buyers and often included at least one skylight as a standard feature in a home. Condominium builders had also found that their customers liked the openness that a skylight seemed to provide. Skylights were also a popular feature of the second homes that many people owned on Washington lakes or in ski areas throughout the Northwest.

In Columbia Plastics' primary market area of Washington, Oregon, Idaho, and Montana, sales of skylights had leveled off in recent years at about 45,000 units per year. Although Columbia would occasionally sell a large order to California home builders, such sales were made only to fill slack in the plant and, after including the cost of transportation, were only break-even propositions at best.

Four homebuilders accounted for half the sales of skylights in the Pacific Northwest. Another five

bought an average of 1,000 each, and the remaining sales were split among more than 100 independent builders and remodelers. Some repackaged the product under their own brand name; many purchased only a few dozen or less.

Columbia would ship directly only to builders who ordered at least 500 units per year, although it would subdivide the orders into sections of one gross (144) for shipping. Most builders and remodelers bought their skylights from building supply dealers, hardware stores, and lumber yards. Columbia sold and shipped directly to these dealers, who typically marked up the product by 50 percent. Columbia's average factory price was $200 when Vancouver Light first entered the market.

Columbia maintained a sales force of three persons for making contact with builders, remodelers, and retail outlets. The sales force was responsible for Columbia's complete line of products which generally went through the same channels of distribution. The cost of maintaining the sales force, including necessary selling support and travel expense, was $90,000 annually.

Until the advent of Vancouver Light, there had been no significant local competition for Columbia. Several California manufacturers had small shares of the market, but Columbia had held a 70 percent market share until two years ago.

Vancouver Light's Entry

Vancouver Light was founded in the early 1980s by Jennifer McLaren, an engineer, and Carl Garner, an architect, and several of their business associates, in order to manufacture skylights. They believed that there was a growing demand for skylights, but there was no ready source of supply available in western Canada. Their assessment proved correct and their business was successful. The signing of a Free Trade Agreement between Canada and the US had apparently stimulated Vancouver Light's interest in the Seattle market.

Two years ago the Canadian company had announced the opening of a sales office in Seattle. McLaren came to this office two days a week and devoted her attention to selling skylights only to the large volume builders. Vancouver Light announced a price 20 percent below Columbia's with a minimum order of 1,000 units to be shipped all at one time. It quickly gained all the business of one large builder, True Homes, a Canadian owned company. In the previous year that builder had ordered 6,000 skylights from Columbia.

A year later, one of Columbia's sales representatives was told by the purchasing manager of Chieftain Homes, a Northwest builder who had installed 7,000 skylights the previous year, that Chieftain would switch to Vancouver Light for most of its skylights unless Columbia was prepared to match Vancouver's price. Columbia then matched that price for orders above 2,000 units, guessing that smaller customers would value highly the local service that Columbia could provide. Chieftain then ordered 40 percent of its needs from Vancouver Light. Two smaller builders had since switched to Vancouver Light as well. Before Vancouver's latest price cut had been reported, Thomas Chu, Columbia's marketing manager, projected that Vancouver Light would sell about 11,000 units this year, compared to the 24,000 that Columbia was now selling. About 14,000 units that Columbia sold were priced at the discount level of $160 per unit. Columbia's volume represented a decline of 1,000 units per year in each of the last two years, following the initial loss of the True Homes account. The California manufacturers, who mainly sold to retail chains and builders with home offices in California, had seen their sales decline to 10,000 units.

Columbia had asked its lawyers to investigate whether Vancouver Light's sales could be halted on charges of export dumping, i.e., selling below cost in a foreign market, but a quick investigation revealed that Vancouver Light's specialized production facility provided a 25 percent savings on variable cost, although a third of that was lost due to the additional costs involved in importing and transporting the skylights across the border.

THE IMMEDIATE CRISIS

Alice Howell and her two colleagues had reviewed the situation carefully. Sam Carney, the production manager, had presented the cost accounting data which showed a total unit cost of $135 for Columbia's most popular skylight. Vancouver Light, he said, was selling a closely similar model at $144. The cost of $135 included $15 in manufacturing overheads, directly attributable to skylights, but not the cost of the sales force nor the salaries, benefits, and overheads associated with the three executives in the room. General overheads, including the sales force and executives, amounted to $390,000 per year at present for Columbia as a whole.

Thomas Chu was becoming quite heated about Vancouver Light by this time. "Let's cut the price a further 10 percent to $130 and drive those Canadians right out of the market! That Jennifer McLaren started with those big builders and now she's after the whole market. We'll show her what competition really is!"

But Carney was shocked: "You mean we'll drive her and us out of business at the same time! We'll both lose money on every unit we sell. What has that sales force of yours, Thomas, been doing all these years if not building customer loyalty for our product?"

"We may lose most of our sales to the big builders," cut in Howell, "but surely most customers wouldn't be willing to rely on shipments from Canada. Maybe we should let Vancouver Light have the customers who want to buy on the basis of price. We can then make a tidy profit from customers who value service, need immediate supply, and have dealt with our company for years."

Jacobs Suchard: Nabob Summit

John R. Oldland

"I'm running the most successful new brand that Nabob has introduced in the last twenty-five years, and now you're telling me my sales are too high," Bruce McKay, Summit's product manager complained. "I feel like the proverbial Canadian grain farmer; the more I sell the less I make."

"That's right. Summit's not making enough money, and you've until year end to solve the problem," John Bell, Nabob's general manager, told the upset product manager, and, as Mr. Bell left the room, he delivered a parting comment, "And don't destroy the brand while you're solving that problem!"

Despondently Mr. McKay looked at the packages and documents that cluttered his office. His eye was caught by the bright blue Summit Decaffeinated package, the line extension that had just been successfully introduced. Beside it was the March/April, 1987, A.C. Nielsen report which had arrived that morning. It was open at the section revealing performance in the critical Metro Toronto market. The Summit share had shot upwards and was now close to 8%. The other document that caught his attention

was the latest cost analysis and profitability statement. It confirmed his worst fears. The profitability per case of Nabob Tradition was 30% greater than that of Summit. Every Tradition user who switched to Summit cost the company money.

THE NABOB STORY

Although Nabob had been making food products for 70 years, nothing in its history was as momentous as the purchase of the company in 1976 by Jacobs Suchard of Zurich, Switzerland. Nabob, which made over 150 products, had been owned by Weston, the larger grocery retailer and bread manufacturer. After Jacobs purchased it, Nabob either stopped manufacturing many small brands that had been private labels for Super Valu, a Weston company, or sold those with a solid franchise to other companies. By 1984 the product line had been reduced to only two businesses, ground coffee and tea. Tea was only sold in Alberta and British Columbia. Nabob ground coffee was sold nationally but with very little penetration in Quebec. The size of the Canadian ground coffee market was 78 million pounds and, at an average retail price per pound of $3.50, the dollar value of the market was $275 million.

Jacobs brought to Nabob a singlemindedness of purpose, enthusiasm for the products it sold, and a marketing entrepreneurial zeal with which to take on far larger competitors. This was Jacobs's first entrance into North America, and the company had no intention of remaining content with its dominant position in the Western Canada ground coffee market. Klaus Jacobs, the parent company's chairman, explained one of his management philosophies—"To set high expectations and performance standards for everyone in everything we do"—by saying, "We want to be not just as good as our competitors but better. We have to be, in order to equalize their greater size and scale. If they are the Goliaths, we have to be the David." Nabob was Jacob's window on the North American market.

In 1978 Nabob entered the Ontario market with its Tradition brand of roast coffee. The coffee was packaged in a unique vacuum package, quite different from the soft paper bag packaging that then dominated the Eastern Canadian market.

Nabob test marketed Tradition in Peterborough and Kingston and then rolled out the brand to the rest of Ontario with heavy promotional support and extensive advertising. Memorable advertising copy had the Nabob spokesman compare the difference between Nabob's hard packaging and the competitor's soft paper bags while delivering the message. "Nabob comes in a hard vacuum pack, not in a soft paper bag that lets in stale air. Nabob's fresh flavor and aroma can't get out until you release it. Want a fresher better tasting cup of coffee? Start with a fresher better tasting coffee. Nabob." The introductory "Microphone" commercial is provided in *Exhibit 1*.

The major competitor was Maxwell House, from General Foods, with a 15.5% share of the market in 1978 (see *Exhibit 2*). Ground coffee was considered by many to be a commodity business with pricing as the dominant marketing factor. Maxwell House was also able to rely on the halo effect from heavy advertising behind its instant coffee brand.

By 1982 Nabob had reached an Ontario market share of 22.5%, just below the 24.4% share of Maxwell House, while keeping its 30% market share in Western Canada. During 1982 Nabob introduced a better tasting Tradition as a result of new high-yield roasting technology, and in 1983 Tradition Decaffeinated was added to the line, giving further impetus to brand growth.

By 1983 Maxwell House had moved to vacuum packaging and was supporting the brand with heavy advertising, featuring the company's long-term spokesman, Ricardo Montalban. In Ontario, Maxwell House remained the best known brand and had been able to build its market share in the face of Nabob's dramatic growth in this market. Maxwell House Decaffeinated was added in 1982, just months before the Nabob Decaffeinated launch. General Foods also marketed three other ground coffee brands—Sanka, Brim, and Chase and Sanborn.

Nabob, drawing from its European experience, believed that the Canadian roast coffee market, although seemingly a commodity business, could be segmented. "Our objective," said John Bell, "is to segment the roast coffee market as much as we can." Nabob set about testing two premium roast coffees. The first was Signature, a fine blend of arabica coffees featuring high quality beans from Kenya, test marketed in Alberta. The name, package graphics and advertising signalled a luxury positioning, reflecting the quality of the coffee. The brand failed to meet its targets. Consumers were accustomed to the taste of their regular brands, often found the premium taste too bitter, and were unwilling to pay the premium price.

The second brand was Select Discoveries, a family of four flavors, Mocha Java, French Bistro, Columbian Classic and Swiss Chocolate Café. They were sold in 200-gram tins (rather than 369-gram vacuum packaging) and were introduced in Ontario in 1983. A small market developed for this specialty product, but there did not appear to be the same desire for premium quality coffees as in Europe.

Maxwell House, in anticipation of an expansion of Nabob Signature from the Alberta test market into Ontario, had launched a premium brand of its own, Maxwell House Gold, sold in a one-pound tin. This brand achieved around a 1% share of the market, making it more difficult for Nabob to introduce another premium brand.

EXHIBIT 1   THE MICROPHONE COMMERCIAL

NABOB

Nabob Foods Limited
Tradition Roast Coffee
60 Second Television Commercial
"Microphone"

MAN: Inside these ordinary, old-fashioned, soft paper bags ...

... is ground coffee. You can smell the coffee inside, on the outside.

Stale air keeps getting in, flavour and aroma keep getting out. That's bad. Now for the good news.

Inside this extraordinary...

...hard (knock, knock) foil vacuum pack is a truly superior blend of ground coffee, Nabob. Western Canada's leading fresh ground coffee.

You can't smell a thing. Stale air can't get in, so Nabob's famous flavour and aroma can't get out.

But listen ...

WHOOSH.

Smell that ... that's fresh aroma.

Now I ask you, which one do you think makes a better, fresher cup of coffee?

You're absolutely right.

SCALI, McCABE, SLOVES LTD.

Source: Scali, McCabe, Sloves Ltd.

389

EXHIBIT 2 ROAST COFFEE SHARES IN EQUIVALENT POUNDS (NATIONAL), %

	1978	1979	1980	1981	1982	1983	1984	1985
Nabob								
Tradition	13.4	17.3	21.8	21.3	22.9	24.9	23.5	21.4
Tradition Decaffeinated						2.0	2.4	2.7
Other Nabob	1.0	0.6	0.2	0.1	0.9	0.4	0.5	0.4
Total Nabob	14.4	17.9	22.0	21.4	23.8	27.3	26.4	24.5
Maxwell House								
Regular	15.5	16.5	16.9	17.2	17.0	18.7	19.0	19.0
Decaffeinated				0.1	0.9	1.3	1.3	1.3
Gold						0.9	1.2	0.9
Total Maxwell House*	15.5	16.5	16.9	17.3	17.9	20.9	21.5	21.2
Sanka*			1.1	1.2	1.7	1.8	1.9	1.6
MJB	3.8	4.4	4.5	5.5	5.2	5.5	5.0	5.2
Chase & Sanborn*	8.3	8.5	8.3	9.6	8.7	5.9	4.6	4.6
Melitta	4.4	4.5	4.4	4.7	4.4	4.4	5.2	4.6
Brooke Bond	5.3	4.5	4.0	3.9	2.6	1.9	2.0	2.4
Hills Bros.			2.0	4.2	3.5	3.1	3.1	2.9
Private Label	39.4	33.9	30.9	26.3	26.6	24.1	26.2	28.5
All other	8.9	9.8	5.9	5.9	5.5	5.2	4.1	4.5
Total	100.0	100.0	100.0	100.0	100.0	100.0	100.0	100.0

*Brands marketed by General Foods.
Note: 1 pound = 453.6 grams.
Source: A.C. Nielsen National Food Index.

THE DEVELOPMENT OF SUMMIT

It was at this stage that John Bell, then vice-president of marketing and sales, Roger Barnes, the market research manager and Bruce McKay, the product manager, met to evaluate new product opportunities. The concept that seemed to offer the greatest promise was coffee that used 100% Colombian beans.

This was not an original idea. General Foods had introduced a premium Colombian coffee, Yuban, in the early seventies that had a lackluster career in the market, peaking at only a 2% share and discontinued in 1978. It still survived as a strong premium brand in parts of the American market. To match the Yuban launch in Canada, Nabob rushed its own premium Colombian brand to market, Boban (Nabob spelled backwards). Needless to say this brand name creativity was not appreciated by consumers and the brand was quickly withdrawn from the market. Even Safeway entered this market with its own premium Colombian coffee, but it, too, was discontinued in a short time.

Nabob decided to launch a separate brand but one still clearly within its stable of brands. In a study that probed the strength of the Colombian beans proposition, it was found that 65% of a national sample believed that Colombian coffee was the best tasting in the world, and that 93% recognized Colombia as a coffee-producing country. This high level of awareness had been developed by the National Federation of Colombian Coffee Growers, which had been spending more than $1.5 million annually on television and print advertising in Canada.

Summit, prepared with 100% Colombian beans, was launched in October 1985. Each aspect of the marketing mix had been carefully developed.

Name and Packaging

Summit, as a name, had many advantages. It was short, not used by other manufacturers, and carried the connotation of high quality. Also, the best beans were grown on the high mountainsides in subtropical countries, and there was an appreciation of this through previous advertising. Consideration was given to calling the brand Nabob Colombian. However, this use of a generic name would have inhibited the development of a distinct brand image and could have been easily matched by the competition. The packaging had to be clearly positioned within the Nabob family. The pack retained the key Nabob logo elements and was red (distinct from the green for Tradition and brown for Tradition Decaffeinated) in order to reinforce Summit's tropical mountain imagery and stand out strongly on the shelf.

Advertising

Creative copy themes were developed to communicate to coffee drinkers that Colombian coffees were known for their rich and distinctive taste and that new Nabob Summit was the best tasting Colombian coffee. The advertising was to have the same tone consumers had come to associate with Nabob advertising—confident, demanding and assertive.

Summit's copy strategy was clearly stated on the package: "Like all great tasting Nabob coffees, Nabob Summit must meet our strict standards for flavour and aroma. That means we don't just pick 100% pure Colombian coffee beans. We go further by choosing only the few that pass Nabob's test. Only then will you find the rich, distinctive flavour that makes Colombian coffees both legendary and good enough for Nabob."

To provide continuity, Nabob once again turned to Mike Reynolds, spokesman for the Nabob brand since its 1978 introduction in Ontario. The "Sword" commercial (*Exhibit 3*) was tested, using the Day-after-Recall technique to measure memorability of the advertising and its ability to communicate the copy strategy. Two hundred women between the ages of 18 and 64 were contacted by telephone the day

after the commercial was aired in major centers across Canada. The commercial was remembered as well as the average thirty-second commercial (see following).

	Norm for 30-Second Commercials
Unprompted recall of ad	20%
Prompted recall	60%

There was concern that the visual device of the sword dominated the commercial and obscured the message that this was a new brand named Summit and that it was made exclusively from Colombian beans. The idea that Nabob used only the best beans in their coffee, a communication objective in all Nabob advertising, was the strongest message recalled in the commercial.

Pricing and Promotion

Summit trade pricing was at parity with Tradition in spite of the fact that Colombian beans were a more expensive blend than regular Tradition. Retail pricing would be slightly above Tradition because retailers would take a higher margin. It was also hoped that Summit could benefit from the leverage of the popular Tradition brand to generate strong retail advertising, merchandising and price feature support for the new brand.

A fifty-five cent direct mail coupon was sent to three million households in Canada in February/March 1986 to initiate trial buying. Total costs including printing, handling, and redemption expenses were expected to amount to $250,000.

Ground coffee was sold extensively on promotion. Summit was to be promoted simultaneously with Tradition so that the new brand could benefit from the merchandising leverage that the larger brand offered. Approximately thirty cents per unit would be offered to the trade, and this was expected to generate trade support and feature pricing at least one week every month.

If, for example, the regular list price to the retailer

EXHIBIT 3   THE SWORD COMMERCIAL

NABOB

CLIENT: NABOB
PRODUCT: Summit
TITLE: "Sword"
LENGTH: 30 sec. T.V.

MIKE: This... is 100%
Colombian coffee, famous
for its legendary flavour.

And this is also 100%
Colombian. New Nabob
Summit.

They're both 100% Colombian,
so they both taste the same,
right?

Wrong.

Some of these Colombian
coffee beans simply don't
measure up...

to Nabob's standards
for flavour and aroma.

Ah, but the ones that
do make all the difference
in Nabob Summit.

A taste we'd call,

a cut above.

392

was $3.19 for a 369-gram package, an off-invoice reduction of 20 cents a unit would be offered on an almost continuous basis to produce a net regular price of $2.99. A fluctuating merchandising allowance would also be offered on a regular basis and could be paid to those retailers who would feature price the brand. The usual merchandising allowance was 10 cents a unit, bringing the cost to the retailer down to $2.89. The feature retail price target would be $2.99. The merchandising allowance might change as the regular list price changed to achieve this feature price. Since ground coffee was often a loss leader for retailers, this slim retail margin was acceptable. In addition, other allowance promotions might be run in specific regions and would be used to pay for the retail advertising that supported coffee promotions. Lastly there was a cooperative allowance of 3% off the regular list price. This allowance, based on volume, was accumulated and available to retailers who supported the brand with promotional activity.

Media

The media plan called for 1,800 gross rating points (GRPs) of television advertising in the major television markets in Ontario and Western Canada. The advertising ran in two flights. The introductory flight lasted 12 weeks starting in mid-December. The second, sustaining flight, at a lower weight level of 60 GRPs a week, ran for a further ten weeks in the fall of 1986 (see *Exhibit 4*).

Nabob, in allocating its media dollars, took into consideration the sales per capita of the regular coffee market by region, its own share of market provincially and the cost of purchasing air time in each city area (see *Exhibit 5*). Summit advertising, scheduled to begin in January, was brought forward to December as distribution had grown faster than was anticipated. To maximize Summit awareness, GRP levels were raised to 150 GRPs in mid-January. In March Summit advertising was replaced by Tradition Decaffeinated advertising.

As well, the National Federation of Colombian Coffee Growers was prepared to subsidize Nabob Summit advertising, up to $0.162 per pound. To earn the maximum subsidy, Nabob had to spend $0.23 per pound and, if it did, it would receive a rebate from the National Federation of $0.162 per pound.

Summit's First Year

The Summit launch must be viewed in the context of worldwide coffee commodity prices. The 1985 Brazilian coffee harvest had been a disaster and had a dramatic effect on coffee futures. Between August, 1985, and February, 1986, the commodity price of roast coffee rose by 70%. Commodity prices peaked at $3.20 per pound. Consumer prices were to some extent cushioned from this volatile market. The large companies stopped buying at the higher prices. Also, manufacturers squeezed margins as prices rose, hoping to increase them once the prices started to fall.

EXHIBIT 4   SUMMIT MEDIA SCHEDULE (GRPs PER WEEK)

	1985 December			January				1986 February				March
	16	23	30	6	13	20	27	3	10	17	24	3
All markets— numbers of GRPs* per week	←——— 60 ———→			←——— 150 ———→					←——— 100 ———→			

*GRP (gross rating point). A rating point is the percentage of the viewing households tuned in to a television market. If 10% of the potential audience sees the commercial, it has a rating of 10. GRPs are the totals of the ratings for commercials shown during a given period.

EXHIBIT 5   NABOB—1986 MEDIA PLANNING INDEX

Market	CPM*	MDI†	CPM index‡	MDI/CPM index	1985 weekly GRP levels§
Ottawa E	11.30	100	134	75	50
Barrie	8.50	100	101	99	50
Sudbury	9.60	100	115	87	50
Kingston	11.40	100	136	74	50
Peterborough	9.05	100	107	93	50
Sault Ste. Marie	9.30	100	110	91	50
Kitchener	7.75	100	92	109	60
London	6.50	100	78	128	50
Toronto	7.00	100	84	119	60
Thunder Bay	13.30	180	159	63	50
Winnipeg	6.50	180	78	230	100
Regina	8.00	180	95	189	60
Brandon	12.35	180	147	122	—
Swift Current	18.50	180	221	81	—
Prince Albert	12.50	180	149	121	—
Yorkton	7.60	180	91	198	90
Saskatoon	7.50	180	89	202	70
Lloydminster	6.40	180	76	236	90
Medicine Hat	6.60	179	198	90	—
Red Deer	8.85	179	106	169	80
Edmonton	10.30	179	123	145	70
Calgary	10.50	179	125	143	60
Vancouver	6.45	175	77	227	100
Okanagan	12.50	175	149	117	50
Prince George	17.20	175	205	85	—
Dawson Creek	25.70	175	307	57	—
Weighted average	8.38				

*CPM is the cost per thousand messages delivered against a target group in a television market over a fifty-two week period. The target group is women 18+.

†MDI is the market development index for ground coffee, with the Ontario index 100. It reflects the much higher development (sales per capita) of ground coffee in Western Canada. The main reason for this is the lower consumption of instant coffee in the West.

‡CPM index is the cost per thousand divided by the weighted average.

§A rating point is a percent of the viewing households tuned in to a television market. If 10% of the potential audience sees the commercial, it has a rating of 10. GRPs are the totals of the ratings for commercials shown during a given period.

As a result, the retail price of coffee increased from $3 to just over $4 per pound during the first six months of Summit's launch. This spiralling cost of coffee was of grave concern to Nabob, as it could have adversely affected early trial of Summit. Retailers had stocked up with coffee just prior to the Summit launch in anticipation of higher prices. In an escalating price market consumers could also be expected to either reduce their purchases or stock up on their regular brand before prices rose. *Exhibit 6*

provides information for Summit pricing through 1986.

These pricing concerns proved to be illusory. The signals of success were almost immediate. The retail trade was quick to appreciate the value offered by the product and decided to give shelf space to the brand immediately. The trade saw that Nabob was going to market the brand aggressively. As well, ground coffee was a very visible product in that it was heavily promoted, the pricing was extremely

EXHIBIT 6 SUMMIT AVERAGE RETAIL PRICE (369-GRAM UNITS) IN 1986

	Jan.	Feb.	Mar.	Apr.	May	June	July	Aug.	Sept.	Oct.	Nov.	Dec.	Total
Tradition	$ 3.08	3.37	3.65	3.91	3.86	3.97	3.87	3.64	3.50	3.67	3.75	3.59	3.59
Summit	$ 3.05	3.52	3.54	4.05	4.12	4.15	4.07	3.74	3.48	3.60	3.89	3.48	3.69
Difference vs. Tradition	$ −0.03	+0.15	−0.11	+0.14	+0.26	+0.18	+0.20	+0.10	−0.02	−0.07	+0.13	+0.11	+0.10

competitive, and many retailers used it as a loss leader.

The parity pricing strategy and accompanying trade support plant proved important in determining the product's rapid success and overcoming "price increase" fears. In its first full Nielsen audit, Summit exceeded 50% distribution in all areas where it was marketed, reaching a high of 89% distribution in Alberta. The trade, in turn, supported the product, and a 2% national share was achieved in the first audit. This share was the minimum level at which the trade would begin to give the brand ongoing support. By comparison, the best share ever reached by Signature was 1.9%. In Alberta and British Columbia, market shares of 3.4% and 4%, respectively, were reached. This was achieved before advertising and coupon support had a chance to make an impact. Despite price increases, the trade aggressively priced Summit, averaging only a $0.10/pack premium for the year. In addition, the brand was co-op advertised (featured in weekly supermarket advertisements) and displayed. Summit's share of weighted co-op averaged 10%, an excellent result for a new product.[1]

---

[1]Co-op advertising is retail advertising, in which the cost is shared by the retailer and the national advertiser. Weighted co-op is the percentage of times that a brand, like Summit, was featured in a given time period compared to all coffee brands that were featured.

By the end of the year, Summit had exceeded all the marketing objectives set out for it (*Exhibits 7* to *9* provide further details of Year 1 performance).

	Objective, %	Actual, %
Year 1 share	2.7	3.3
Distribution where marketed	80	82
Trial of coffee-buying households	12	12
Repeat purchase	35	42

In early May 1986 an awareness, attitude, and usage survey was conducted in Vancouver, Calgary and Toronto. Nabob contacted by telephone 130 principal grocery shoppers (the individual in the household primarily responsible for grocery shopping), in each of the three cities, who were 18 years and over and who had purchased ground coffee in the last month. At that stage, awareness and trial were still relatively low. Results were more favorable in Calgary than either Vancouver or Toronto (see below).

Overall perceptions of Summit were favorable among those who were aware of the brand and prepared to comment. Summit was seen as a "top-of-the-line," "richer," "better" coffee. Summit advertising was reinforcing the consistent message of Nabob

	Unaided awareness		Summit total— unaided & aided awareness, %	Summit purchase, %
	Total Nabob, %	Summit, %		
Vancouver	65	4	35	9
Calgary	72	13	48	15
Toronto	62	4	25	6

EXHIBIT 7 GROUND COFFEE SHARES

	1985 total	1986 Dec./Jan.	Feb./Mar.	Apr./May	June/July	Aug./Sept.	Oct./Nov.	Total	1987 Dec./Jan.
Nabob									
Tradition (369 gram)	21.4	19.5	17.0	19.0	18.8	20.7	17.7	18.8	15.9
Tradition (200 gram)	—	—	—	—	0.1	1.4	1.7	0.6	1.7
Tradition Decaffeinated	2.7	2.3	2.5	2.6	2.6	2.6	2.7	2.6	2.6
Summit	—	2.0	3.0	3.7	3.1	4.2	4.0	3.3	3.9
Summit Decaffeinated	—	—	—	—	—	—	—	—	0.2
Other Nabob	0.4	—	—	—	—	—	—	—	—
Total Nabob	24.5	23.8	22.5	25.3	24.5	28.9	26.1	25.3	24.3
Maxwell House									
Regular	19.0	18.3	16.1	17.4	19.3	17.7	17.5	17.7	18.5
Decaffeinated	1.3	1.1	1.4	1.4	1.4	1.3	1.4	1.3	1.3
Gold	0.9	1.0	1.0	1.7	2.0	1.6	1.7	1.5	2.2
Total Maxwell House	21.2	20.4	18.5	20.5	22.7	20.6	20.6	20.5	22.0

Source: A. C. Nielsen Food Index.

advertising—that Nabob used only the best beans in its coffee.

In the competitive Toronto market where Maxwell House and Nabob Tradition were close rivals, Nabob had after nine years achieved a very strong image. Nabob conducted periodic attitude and image studies which measured consumer perceptions of Nabob and Maxwell House on a number of attributes. In the past, Maxwell House had a strong reputation in the market, based, in part, on the fact that Maxwell House marketed both ground and instant coffee and heavily advertised both product categories. While Maxwell House was still considered the best selling brand, over the years Nabob had steadily improved its reputation on all taste and quality attributes to the extent that the Maxwell House image advantage had now been eliminated.

Competitor reaction was swift. General Foods reformulated and repackaged its Maxwell House Gold brand. The brand moved from packaging in tins to vacuum packaging and was offered in two varieties, Colombia and Arabica. The pricing strategy was changed from premium to parity with Summit. Maxwell House Gold share increased from 1% in December/January, 1986, to 2.2% in December/January,

1987. MJB, an important brand in Western Canada, introduced MJB Colombian, and several generics also introduced Colombian varieties.

THE IMPACT OF THE PRICING DECISION

Success can be your worst enemy. Nabob had planted the seeds for continued growth for 1987. Research conducted on a decaffeinated Colombian product had yielded favorable results. Accordingly Summit Decaffeinated had been introduced in late 1986 to capitalize on the momentum of the brand.

An aggressive marketing plan had been approved to enhance the Summit brand. For example, spending on advertising at $0.17 U.S. per pound on Summit in 1987 would generate advertising support for the brand almost equivalent to that of the main brand, Tradition.

If Nabob continued to fuel the marketing fires behind Summit, the brand would continue to grow. Unfortunately, much of that growth would probably be at the expense of the more profitable Tradition brand. The cost premium for an all-Colombian blend of beans was 10%. However the cost gap could widen depending on fluctuating commodity markets, and

EXHIBIT 8 SUMMIT FACT SHEET

	1986						1987	1986
	Dec./Jan.	Feb./Mar.	Apr./May	June/July	Aug./Sept.	Oct./Nov.	Dec./Jan.	total
Market Shares*								
National	2.0	3.0	3.7	3.1	4.2	4.0	3.9	3.3
Ontario	1.6	3.8	4.7	3.5	5.5	5.3	4.8	4.0
Manitoba/Saskatchewan	1.6	1.8	2.5	3.2	3.1	2.7	3.4	2.4
Alberta	3.4	4.6	5.7	4.7	5.2	6.3	5.3	5.0
B.C.	4.0	4.1	3.7	3.4	4.7	3.9	4.9	4.0
Distribution†								
National	44	51	54	54	55	55	55	
Ontario	54	70	75	77	77	78	78	
Manitoba/Saskatchewan	58	68	77	69	69	74	70	
Alberta	89	91	99	88	89	81	82	
B.C.	78	83	85	82	83	86	89	
Share of weighted co-op‡								
Tradition								
National	24	17	16	21	21	18	16	20
Ontario	31	28	20	22	26	21	15	25
Manitoba/Saskatchewan	47	15	37	33	40	22	34	27
Alberta	38	25	23	31	31	29	22	29
B.C.	18	16	26	23	21	17	19	20
Summit								
National	6	10	11	10	11	9	10	10
Ontario	7	17	14	11	16	18	14	15
Manitoba/Saskatchewan	14	14	13	19	10	5	13	12
Alberta	11	10	18	12	15	12	13	20
B.C.	7	9	13	15	11	6	14	11

*In equivalent pounds.
†In stores accounting for x% of the business.
‡% of stores providing retail advertising support.
Source: A. C. Nielsen National Food Index.

quite possibly a premium of up to 20% might have to be paid. The Tradition user who switched to Summit might be a satisfied customer but, at the same time, a less profitable one for Nabob. The company, in developing its own projections, had forecasted that a third of Summit volume would be cannibalized from Tradition. The latest figures, particularly from the Toronto market, showed a cannibalization rate in excess of 50%. In 1986 the Summit share was 3.3%, but corporate share had edged ahead only 2%.

Nabob case prices (each case contained 12 369-gram packages) varied depending on order quantity, as the following shows:

Case order quantity	Price
25–99	$39.81
100–199	39.05
200–399	38.66
400 case plus	38.28

EXHIBIT 9 SUMMIT COFFEE—CUMULATIVE TRIAL AND REPEAT PURCHASE FREQUENCY, 1986

	Jan.	Feb.	Mar.	Apr.	May	June	July	Aug.	Sept.	Oct.	Nov.	Dec.
Monthly households buying	1.8%	1.8	1.9	1.6	2.1	1.7	1.0	2.1	2.2	1.5	1.7	2.0
New	100.0	85.5	68.4	54.1	55.3	48.4	63.4	44.6	52.6	33.5	32.7	37.3
Repeat	0	14.5	31.6	45.9	44.7	51.6	36.6	55.4	47.4	66.5	67.3	62.7
Cumulative households buying	1.8	3.4	4.7	5.6	6.7	7.6	8.2	9.2	10.3	10.8	11.4	12.1
Households buying once	94.9	83.1	76.4	69.3	67.2	64.9	65.7	60.5	60.6	58.9	58.0	58.1
Repeating once	5.1	14.0	17.2	21.5	18.5	20.4	19.4	22.8	22.1	22.2	22.4	21.0
Repeating twice	—	2.9	4.9	5.4	9.0	7.9	8.2	9.5	8.7	9.4	8.7	7.3
Repeating 3 times	—	—	1.5	2.6	4.3	2.8	2.2	2.8	4.3	4.4	3.2	5.9
Repeating 4 times	—	—	—	1.2	.0	2.2	2.1	.6	.6	1.2	3.9	1.8
More than 4 times	—	—	—	—	1.0	1.8	2.4	3.8	3.7	3.9	3.8	5.9

Source: Consumer Panel of Canada.

The relative cost and profit ratios on Summit and Tradition were as follows:

	Tradition, %	Summit, %
Gross sales	100	100
Gross profit	50	42
Marketing cost	30	25
Administrative and other	10	10
Profits before tax	10	7

In May 1987 General Foods reintroduced all its decaffeinated ground coffees in smaller 300-gram packages at parity with their regular coffees. Apart from the obvious absolute reduction in price, the big advantage to General Foods was that regular and decaffeinated coffees could now be jointly promoted.

A further complication was the fact that the Federation of Colombian Coffee Growers was starting to put pressure on Nabob to raise the price of Summit. While they found Canadian results satisfactory, they believed that parity pricing was inconsistent with the premium image they were trying to create worldwide. In every previous instance when the Federation had supported and endorsed a Colombian coffee, they had been able to achieve premium pricing.

Mr. McKay felt extremely uncomfortable about the current predicament. He had gained enormous satisfaction from the brand's success and knew it had more potential. Summit Decaffeinated was a superb new coffee. The small retail price differential with Tradition was narrowing as the trade support of the brand was increasing. New copy had been developed that he felt was stronger than the introductory "Sword" commercial. Was it right to put the brakes on the brand before its full potential was realized? Was Nabob over the long haul right to muzzle a brand that was in fact a superior coffee to its leading brand? What would be the repercussions to his own career if he placed the brand's profitability in front of the brand's volume? With these thoughts in mind, he began to decide the future strategy for Summit.

PART EIGHT

Marketing Research

S ound marketing decisions require accurate, timely information about markets, competitors, and consumer behavior. Marketing research, which is one form of marketing information, is primarily concerned with special-purpose research projects, although the same techniques may be used repeatedly on the same or different classes of problems. Managers utilize marketing research to increase the likelihood of making more informed, and hence usually better, decisions. Every marketing research project should begin with a clear understanding of the organization's specific information needs. Given the uncertain, dynamic, and competitive nature of the marketing environment, no manager can hope to gain perfect understanding of the organization's market. Rather, the goal of marketing research is to reduce uncertainty to tolerable levels at a reasonable cost.

STEPS IN THE MARKETING RESEARCH PROCESS

Marketing research is properly viewed as a sequence of steps which can be termed the *research process*. A summary of the research process is presented in *Exhibit 1*. When beginning a study, managers are often tempted to go straight to the instrument design and data collection stages, without thinking through the prior steps. This is a serious mistake, and often leads to market research reports which are not useful because the wrong questions are asked or the data collected turn out to be unreliable and inaccurate.

399

EXHIBIT 1   THE MARKET RESEARCH PROCESS

1. Defining the purpose of the research—Why is information to be gathered?
2. Statement of research objectives—What information is needed?
3. Review of existing data—What is already known?
4. Value analysis—Is the research worth the cost?
5. Research design
   a. Exploratory
   b. Descriptive
   c. Causal
6. Methods of primary data collection
   a. Communication
   b. Observation
7. Research tactics—sampling procedures and instrument design
   a. Target population
   b. Sample selection
   c. Sample size
   d. Instrument design
   e. Pretesting
8. Field operations—data collection
9. Data analysis
10. Completion of the project
    a. Interpretation of data
    b. Recommendations
    c. Final report

Defining the Purpose of the Research

The primary questions to be asked before beginning any marketing research project are "Why is this information needed?" and "What will the implications of this research be?" Only if the findings can influence management decisions should the research be carried out.

The reasons for conducting marketing research can be categorized by examining the process of decision making. A useful three-stage model is

- Recognizing and defining problems
- Generating and selecting alternative courses of action
- Monitoring performance.

The first stage of any decision is recognition that a problem exists. Often, the initial signals that managers receive are only vague indications or symptoms of a problem—but once the problem is detected, marketing research can be very useful in defining and understanding it.

Following problem recognition, marketing research can help managers better understand the problem or opportunity as well as help search for and evaluate alternative courses of action. Much of the work done in this area is characterized by formal research procedures. Indeed, the careful gathering of descriptive data and the evaluation of specific alternatives through questionnaire and observational studies is probably the area in which the most money is spent. Market surveys and test marketing are both examples of such studies.

Once a marketing plan is implemented, progress should be measured against the original purpose through performance monitoring. The information gathered should help ascertain not only whether the program is meeting its goals, but also *why* it is succeeding or failing. Performance monitoring may indicate a need for changes in a specific plan or its execution; moreover, it enables managers to learn from their mistakes and successes and to redirect the business accordingly.

Statement of Research Objectives

After establishing that the research will serve a useful purpose, the next step is to state explicitly the research objectives: What specific information is needed? In other words, this stage involves going from the general to the particular.

Information requirements should be stated in writing. These requirements can then be reviewed to see if they are specific enough to provide guidance to the researchers, set forth the issues to be investigated, and include all the relevant questions to be asked. Some managers determine their information requirements by stating their beliefs about the market as a set of hypotheses. For example, a brand manager might wish to test the hypothesis that increasing the advertising budget by 25 percent will expand sales by at least 20 percent. It's often helpful to prepare samples of possible outputs and see what issues the sample report raises. Are other data needed before the results can be used? For example, is it enough to know that an ad budget should be increased, or must the media be specified as well?

Review of Existing Data

Before gathering new data, researchers should investigate the possibility of using data that already exist. Markets researchers divide information into two classes, primary data and secondary data. *Primary* data are new information collected specifically for the research project being undertaken; *secondary* data, in contrast, have previously been collected separately for other purposes. An organization's own internal record-keeping system, the observations of staff, easily accessible published data, reports from the trade, and other kinds of information can often be readily assembled to give a good deal of valuable information. Federal and state governments gather and publish voluminous amounts of statistical data; government agencies also publish studies on a wide range of topics. A good general rule to follow is not to gather primary data until it becomes clear that no satisfactory secondary data are available. Even then, it's best to start with secondary data and restrict primary data collection to topics that remain unresolved.

In addition to internally generated accounting and transaction data, many companies use their sales force, distributors, and other employees or associates as important sources of market and competitive information. A formalized system of collecting and retrieving such data, along with adequate incentives for the sales force, is necessary to make the process useful.

Many trade associations and marketing service firms gather information about various markets and make it available to companies at a fee. Trade associations, for instance, typically report on market trends, industry sales, and government actions in documents that are restricted to their members. Market research firms offer many syndicated services. One such service compiles data collected from a panel of more than 5,000 households, who keep a weekly diary in which they record purchases (e.g., brand, price, quantity) of many items. A company selling toothpaste, for example, can then buy information on such factors as toothpaste buyers' brand loyalty, socioeconomic characteristics, and purchase frequency. Directories describing proprietary sources of marketing information may be found in many business libraries.

Value Analysis

Management's next task is to ask whether the research is worth doing in terms of the value of the information obtained for decision making. Not all information is worth the monetary and time costs associated with its collection. No research project should be implemented unless management is committed to using the findings as an input to decision making. Before carrying out a research project, a manager should be satisfied that its findings will be useful in reducing the likelihood either that a bad (and costly) mistake will be made or that a marketing program will lack the fine tuning necessary to achieve its full financial potential. By relating the cost of the research to the estimated incremental value of improved decision making, a manager can then determine whether the proposed study represents a worthwhile investment.

A second consideration in value analysis is timeliness. Because of market dynamics and competitive pressures, marketing decisions often must be made quickly. Partial information that can be obtained next week may be worth more than detailed information that will be available next quarter. Similarly, a more expensive research project may be justifiable if it can deliver the required data more quickly.

Research Design

A research design guides the collection and analysis of data. Although each study has its own specific purpose, it is useful to classify marketing research into three broad groupings:

- Exploratory studies
- Descriptive studies
- Experiments and other causal studies

Exploratory studies are most often used in the problem discovery and definition phases of decision making. They are more informal and less rigidly controlled than standardized questionnaire interviews, and include such methods as reviews of related literature, interviews with experts, in-depth interviews of small samples of typical consumers, and detailed case histories.

Managers should not overgeneralize from the results of exploratory research. Caution is necessary since the results are not based on a representative sample of the population and cannot be projected to the entire market. The semistructured nature of the research, the role of the interviewer in directing the responses, and the subjectiveness of the answers do not usually allow for unambiguous interpretation of the results. Qualitative research should be used to gain insights into the consumer perspective and suggest hypotheses for further testing and alternatives to pursue.

Descriptive studies are used to:

- Portray the attitudes, behavior, and other characteristics of persons, groups, or organizations
- Determine the extent of association among two or more variables and to draw inferences about these relationships
- Make predictions about the future and/or the results of different management actions

In general, descriptive studies can be subdivided between cross-sectional and longitudinal studies. Cross-sectional studies examine the population of interest at one point in time. For example, one appliance company carried out a survey to determine whether such characteristics as income, number and age of children, and wife's employment status was associated with owning microwave ovens and other kitchen appliances. By contrast, a longitudinal or panel study investigates a fixed sample of people who are measured at a number of points in time. While cross-sectional or aggregate data describe total consumption, a panel allows researchers to monitor an individual's behavior over time, such as a customer's brand loyalty.

Experiments provide the best means for establishing a causal relationship. In an experiment, various levels of the causal factor—the treatment—are assigned on a statistically random basis to subjects. Then differences in response between those receiving the different treatments and those receiving no treatment—the controls—are measured and analyzed to see if there is evidence of a causal relationship.

The goal of *test marketing,* one form of experiment, is to determine how consumers react to a new product under market conditions. Test markets can be used to estimate the likely sales of a new product in order to help decide whether to launch the product nationally. Another use of test marketing is to evaluate several marketing plans. For instance, a company uncertain as to whether to use a standard or high promotion budget may test these alternatives in different cities. Test markets also help a company to study wholesaler and retailer response to its marketing program and to observe consumer purchasing patterns and foresee possible problems that could occur when the product is bought and used under normal buying conditions.

Competitive reactions to a test market, however, are somewhat problematic. A competitor who makes no reaction to a test market may later compete actively, perhaps with an imitative product. Other competitors may react aggressively to disrupt a test market in order to lower the value of information gained and to discourage a company from implementing its new product plans. Despite test marketing's costs and difficulties, test markets are usually helpful in increasing a good product's likelihood of success and avoiding major failures.

Methods of Primary Data Collection

The two major methods of data collection are (oral and written) communication and observation. Observation involves the recording of behavior or the identification of readily observable personal characteristics such as age and sex. In some cases subjects may not even be aware that they are being observed. Other characteristics such as a person's awareness and attitudes can only be obtained by asking. Also it is usually cheaper and faster to ask people about their behavior through interviews or questionnaires than it is to observe it.

One advantage of observation is that it does not depend on the ability or willingness of the respondent to provide data. Some people may seek to hide from interviewers the fact that they buy cheaper, generic brands; others may try to overclaim their thriftiness. Observation describes actual behavior.

Research Tactics

In choosing the subjects for a study, it is important to distinguish between the population or universe, the sampling frame, the sample, and the respondents. The *target population* is the group we wish to study. For example, if a bank is planning a financial services program for people over 65, then that is the target population.

The *sampling frame* specifies the members of the target population to be surveyed. It is not always easy to identify. For the bank's program, the sampling frame might be a list of all those who receive Social Security payments. However, the frame may not be a perfect representation of the population, since not everyone who is over 65 receives Social Security payments, yet some younger, disabled workers do receive payments. A sampling frame is needed whenever a researcher wishes to conduct a survey of people who are preselected by name. If an interviewer is sent to a shopping center to question every fifth person who enters, then a list of preselected names is not needed.

In *probability samples,* every person in the frame has a known chance of being selected; the actual choices will be made probabilistically. (A random sample is one kind of probability sample in which each person has an equal chance of being selected.) The great advantage of probability sampling is that this known chance of selection allows the researcher to make a statistical estimate of the size of the sampling error, and thereby determine how far the findings might differ from those that would be obtained by studying the entire population.

In *nonprobability samples,* the interviewer has more discretion in selecting respondents. Convenience samples are composed of subjects who volunteer or who are readily available to the researcher, such as people walking through a shopping center, church groups, or students in class. Quotas may be established to ensure that respondents reflect a mix of prespecified characteristics, such as being equally split between men and women.

One danger associated with giving interviewers control over the choice of respondents is that they will tend to choose those individuals who are easiest to interview—people who look friendly or live in convenient locations, e.g., apartment houses in "good" neighborhoods. Such respondents may not be representative of the population as a whole, even though they may share some of that population's readily measurable characteristics.

In practice, researchers use nonprobability designs quite frequently. They are the logical choice for informal exploratory research and can save time and money in other studies. Also such samples may provide better control of error due to factors other than sampling.

Sample Size   "How large should the sample be?" is one of the most frequently asked and seemingly simple questions raised in planning research studies. The answer depends on the purpose of the research, the sampling design used, the characteristics being studied and their variation within the population, the precision desired from the estimate, the desired level of confidence in the accuracy of the estimate, the cost of the study, and the time available. Mathematical formulas can be used to help determine the optimal sample size.

In general, precision increases with the square of the sample size, so doubling precision requires multiplying the sample size by four. Other factors, such as the nature of the analysis to be performed on the data, can be very important in setting sample size. Too small a sample in segmentation studies, for example, may make it impossible to conduct meaningful analyses of cross-tabulated data.

Response Rate   People fail to respond to surveys for two reasons—either they are not reached by the researchers (not-at-homes in interviews, wrong address in mail surveys) or they refuse to participate. Mail questionnaires typically achieve response rates in the 10 to 50 percent range; personal and telephone interviews (with three or four callbacks) reach 50 to 80 percent of subjects. High response rates are needed to limit nonresponse bias because responders and nonresponders generally differ. Those who do not answer morning telephone calls, for instance, may be employed outside the home, in contrast to homemakers, who are easier to reach. The researcher needs to determine how significant these differences are and to make adjustments where appropriate.

Large sample sizes do not in themselves compensate for biases resulting from low response rates. Often, greater validity is achieved by increasing the response rate than by increasing the number of people sampled. Special incentives, prior mailings, a well-written, well-designed questionnaire, a combination of interview methods, and intensive follow-up efforts can lead to higher response rates.

Methods of Administration   Telephone and personal interviews and mail questionnaires are the three major ways of collecting information, although various combinations of these methods can be used. While mail is usually the cheapest of the three, the cost of data collection and analysis per completed mail questionnaire usually exceeds $5.00. Telephone can be two or four times as expensive, and personal interviews even more so. In addition to lower cost, *mail questionnaires* offer the advantage of uniformity of administration, since the interviewers themselves may add variation to personal and telephone surveys. In mail questionnaires respondents may also have greater confidence in their anonymity (when it is promised) than they feel when being interviewed. On the other hand, mail questionnaires usually cannot be used to probe the subject in great depth. Moreover, considerable time must be allotted for the mailing and return of questionnaires.

Although *personal interviews* are costly, they provide the researcher with considerable flexibility and control. Samples of the product can be shown. An interview is particularly appropriate for revealing information about complex, emotional subjects and for probing the sentiments that underlie expressed opinions.

Telephone interviews are less expensive than personal interviews and quicker to complete. Political candidates, for instance, often use telephone interviews to monitor voters' changing opinions before an election. Telephone interviews combine many of the advantages of the mail and personal methods. Of course, telephone interviews cannot use graphic materials and cannot be as rich in content or as long as personal interviews.

Content and Wording of the Questions   In designing a questionnaire, each individual question needs to be carefully constructed in order to obtain accurate data. For example, in wording questions, clear, simple words should be used and leading or biased questions avoided. Answers to socially sensitive or personally embarrassing questions are potentially unreliable and particular care must be taken in asking for such information and the ordering of questions. Additionally, it's important to consider whether the respondent knows the answer or can get the requested information without too much time and effort. While unnecessary questions should be avoided, the researcher should make sure that all needed information is obtained.

Pretesting   The researcher should never expect that the first draft of a questionnaire will be usable. After completion, it must be reexamined as a whole and revised. Even then the design is far from complete; the key test of a questionnaire is how it performs in practice. Two types of pretesting are required. The first is conducted through personal interviews with a convenience sample to identify major errors. More critical is a pretest that simulates the actual administration of the questionnaire. Those who design a questionnaire are much closer to a topic than the respondents will be, and the pretest identifies problems that arise because of these vast differences in perception. Additionally, the researcher should attempt to tabulate the data from the pretest to see if, in fact, the analyses that were planned can be carried out. In brief, pretesting is a *must*.

Field Operations

Field operations include those parts of the research process during which the data are collected and coded. Since a number of professional market research firms specialize in these tasks, most organizations contract out all or part of the fieldwork. As with all such tasks, management must ensure that it has an effective way to monitor the quality and performance of data collection and coding. Otherwise errors can occur. In one study of theater attendance, 35 percent of the nonsubscribers were falsely classified as new subscribers because the analysts interpreted no reply to a question as equivalent to a check by the number zero, an answer which represented a new subscriber.

Data Analysis

Data analysis often involves complex, sophisticated techniques. The manager should not reject a specific technique just because it is complex, since it may contribute new insights to understanding a market. On the other hand, not all useful analysis techniques are necessarily complicated.

Although data analysis is one of the last steps in the market research process, its impact appears much earlier. For example, the type of analysis to be done often influences the content and form of the questions. It is often a good idea to create dummy versions of the tables that are expected to appear in the final report and to make sure that the questions included (and their format) lend themselves to the kind of analysis required to complete those tables.

Interpretation of Data, Recommendations, and Report Writing

Depending upon their skills, interest, and organizational policies, researchers and managers may share a good deal of the writing and interpretation, or none at all. Two cautions are in order. First, the interpretations of the data should be based on an analysis of what the survey actually discovered, not on what managers and researchers hoped would be found. Second, the report should be written clearly and concisely so that the newly discovered information and insights are communicated to the relevant decision makers. Graphic presentations of data are often more easily understood by decision makers than tables.

SUMMARY

Successful market research requires a disciplined approach to problem specification and data collection and analysis; it is not simply a matter of asking questions. Many market research projects fail to influence decision making because of weaknesses in planning, execution, analysis, and presentation. Both managers and researchers are more likely to obtain findings that will be useful for decision making if they follow a systematic approach to doing market research; clarity of thinking pays handsome dividends and everyone would do well to remember the old saying "a problem well defined is half solved."

Lausanne Tourist Office and Convention Bureau

Kimberly A. Bechler
Christopher H. Lovelock
Dominique Turpin

Pierre Schwitzguebel, director of the Lausanne Tourist Office and Convention Bureau, called the meeting of the management committee to order. "How can we prove that we mean business?" the director asked. "We need hard data in order to convince the cantonal government of the magnitude of tourism's economic impact on Lausanne and then to win their financial support. Our visitor statistics have been flat for several years. We need assistance if we're to pick up speed in this very competitive field."

With the anticipated passage of legislation that would grant financial aid to tourism in the mountain communities of the Canton of Vaud (providing a financial aid package that would be funded 40% by the Swiss federal government, 40% by the canton and 20% by the individual communities), there was no time like the present for action. This legislation would mean that a budget of SF 200 million[1] would go toward supporting tourism in the mountain regions to the north and east of Lake Geneva.

"We've got to show them that tourism in Vaud means a lot more than just visits to the mountain villages," agreed the tourist office's assistant director, Claude Petitpierre, gesturing at the sailboats on Lake Geneva outside the window. "Why, the cities of Lausanne, Montreux, and Vevey alone together account for more than 40% of all tourism in the canton! But just lobbying for money won't do any good. I agree with you, we've got to come up with some solid documentation. We also need better information on why people come to Lausanne and what they think of their experience as a visitor here. That could help us know how we should tailor our services and shape our promotional strategy."

SWITZERLAND: THE "CROSSROADS OF EUROPE"

From the time the Romans crossed the Alps on their way north, the major land route connecting northern and southern Europe had been through Switzerland. A key route for east-west European travel had also

[1] The exchange rate for the Swiss franc in 1991 was approximately SF 1.00 = US$0.70 = £0.40.

409

passed through Switzerland between Lakes Constance and Geneva. In more recent years, the country had become connected with cities all over the world via two intercontinental airports—at Zurich and Geneva. Someone had jokingly defined Europe as "anywhere within two hours of Geneva Airport."

At the beginning of the 1990s, the Swiss Confederation spanned 41,000 km^2 (16,000 miles^2) and included 6.8 million inhabitants, of whom one-sixth were foreigners. In both area and population, the country was roughly the same size as Massachusetts and New Hampshire combined (two states in the US). About one-quarter of Switzerland's land area consisted of lakes, glaciers, or high mountains, some of which reached altitudes of over 4,000 meters (13,000 feet). One of the best known was the Matterhorn, 4,478 meters high, dominating the skyline above Zermatt, 169 km (105 miles) southeast of Lausanne.

Switzerland had four official national languages: German, French, Italian, and Romansh. Although German was the native language of 65% of all Swiss residents, people at all levels of society spoke one of a variety of local dialects collectively known as *Schwytzertüusch*. Eighteen percent of the population were native French speakers, while Italian was the mother tongue of 10% of Swiss residents (more than half were immigrants or migrant workers). One percent (located in southeastern Switzerland) spoke Romansh, a Romance language said to be closest to the Latin spoken by ordinary people in Roman days.

Government

The Confederation comprised 26 cantons and half-cantons. The Swiss parliament sat in Bern, the national capital. The federal government was responsible for foreign affairs, national defense, customs, communications, and monetary controls. Other state functions were the responsibility of the cantons—for example, education, road construction and maintenance, health and police—and were often delegated to the communes (towns and villages).

The Canton of Vaud (officially known as l'Etat de Vaud) was in the western, French-speaking part

of Switzerland, often referred to as Suisse Romande. Lausanne was its capital (refer to *Exhibit 1B*). With 571,973 inhabitants (1989), Vaud was the most populous canton in Suisse Romande, and ranked as one of the largest and fastest growing in the Confederation. However, like many parts of Switzerland, it was currently facing both recession and inflation.

TOURISM

The World Tourism Organization estimated that during 1990, there were 390 million tourists worldwide. Tourism provided employment in a wide range of activities with jobs in hotels, restaurants, tourist offices, travel agencies, transport operations, and recreational establishments. The revenues generated worldwide were estimated at $194 billion. Industry predictions showed tourism growing at an annual rate of 4% through the year 2000.

The lack of a precise definition of just what constituted a "tourist" made collection of data difficult. Popular definitions included an individual on vacation, a business traveler, a convention participant, a person staying in a hotel, someone attempting to change housing accommodations, a foreign student, a foreigner receiving medical treatment on an outpatient basis, an individual visiting family or friends for a short time period, and someone taking a day trip.

According to the World Tourism Organization, the expenses of the classical tourist (traveling for either vacation or business) could be separated into the following six categories: lodging (34%), food and drink (25%), shopping (15%), recreation (8%), local transportation (5%), and miscellaneous (13%).

Swiss Tourism

It was popularly held that the tourist industry started in Switzerland. The first modern tourists, the British, began to come "on holiday" in the nineteenth century, followed by other Europeans and North Americans. Switzerland soon became known as a "nation of hotelkeepers," by 1991 hosting more than 20 million visitors annually

EXHIBIT 1
(A) SWITZERLAND'S LOCATION IN EUROPE

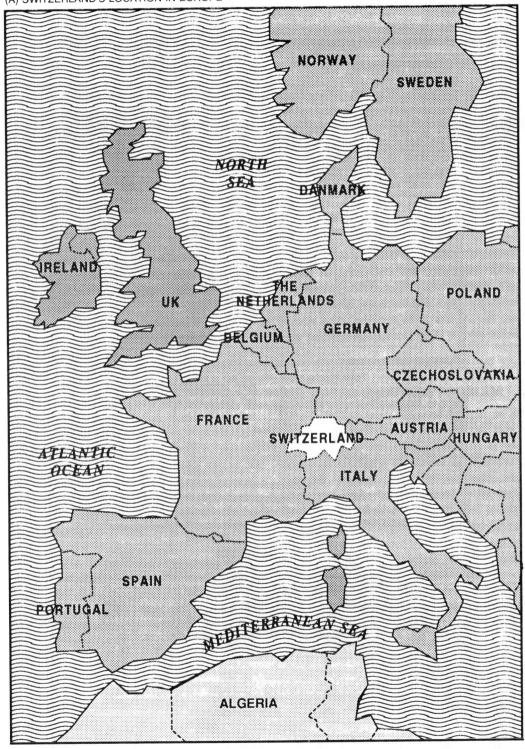

EXHIBIT 1 (CONT.)
(B) SWITZERLAND AND THE CANTON OF VAUD

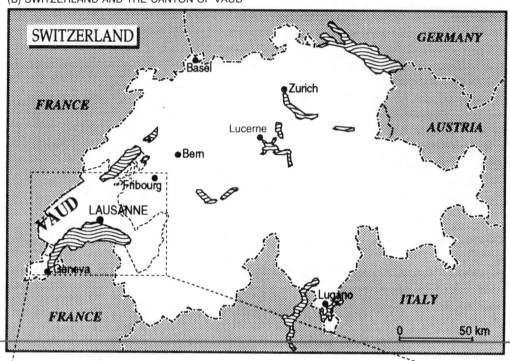

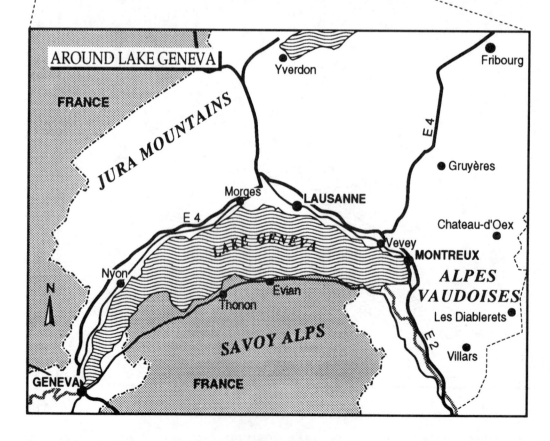

Tourism ranked third among Switzerland's export industries, after machinery and components, and chemicals, and well ahead of the textile and watch-making industries. In 1988, international tourism brought in SF 10.4 billion. Providing 350,000 jobs, Swiss tourism contributed 6% of GNP. However, tourism received little financial support and had no "lobby" at the federal level. In recent years, industry observers felt that Switzerland was not taking adequate steps to renew its image as a country dedicated to tourism.

The Swiss "tourism structure" consisted of the Swiss National Office of Tourism with 24 offices worldwide, regional tourist offices (one per canton), as well as local tourist offices. The Swiss National Office, which promoted Switzerland abroad as a tourist destination, was funded 60% by the Confederation and 40% by partners such as Swissair and the Swiss Federal Railways. Budgetary cuts had already forced the closing of the office in Sydney, Australia, and other cutbacks in offices and promotional expenditures were expected. At the local level, tourism officials—such as Lausanne's Mr. Petitpierre—were quite worried about this trend, especially since neighboring Austria was aggressively promoting its own similar offering of lakes, mountains, and picturesque alpine villages.

THE CITY OF LAUSANNE

Lausanne was located on the shores of Lake Geneva (known in French as Lac Léman), the largest freshwater lake in western Europe. The lake was 80 km (50 miles) long and some 13 km across at its widest point. Some described its shape as like a croissant, others more romantically, as like a leaping fish with its tail still in the water. Most of its southern shore was in France, and across the lake from Lausanne stood Evian-les-Bains, famous for its baths and bottled water.

Lausanne, situated 60 km (38 miles) east of Geneva, had a stunning location, built on the side of a steep hill which rose up from the lakeshore. The 30 km stretch of coastline from Lausanne to Montreux, with its combination of manicured flower gardens

and terraced vineyards, picturesque villages, harbors and pleasure boats, villas and luxury hotels, was often known as the Swiss Riviera. On a clear day, one could see not only the Savoy Alps across the lake to the south, but east to the upper Rhone Valley and the 3,000 meter (10,000 ft) peaks of the Alpes Vaudoises, and then west to the Jura mountains. Lausanne's elevation ranged from 372 m above sea level at the harbor in Ouchy to 930 m at the top of Mt. Jorat. The lake exercised a moderating influence on the local climate; winters were mild and summer temperatures rarely rose much above 30°C (86°F).

The early history of Lausanne dated back to Roman times when Lousonna became the crossroads and staging post on the main lines of communication leading from Italy via the St. Bernard Pass to Gaul (modern France), and from the Mediterranean to the Rhine via the Rhône valley.

Remnants of Lausanne's early beginnings provided reminders of its legendary past. The thirteenth century Gothic cathedral overlooking the city was an important pilgrim destination until it became Protestant during the Reformation, at which time the Calvinists stripped out most of its interior decoration. And in Lausanne's center was the Tour de l'Ale, an old watchtower which was the only surviving remains of the ramparts which used to surround the city. In 1803, when the Canton of Vaud was carved out of the Canton of Bern, Lausanne became the new canton's capital. During the late eighteenth and early nineteenth centuries, Lausanne welcomed many historic personalities, including Voltaire, Byron, Napoleon, Goethe, and Rousseau.

By 1991, with 127,000 inhabitants (250,000 including the surrounding communities), Lausanne was the second largest French-speaking city after Geneva and the fifth largest city in Switzerland.

The city was well known for its institutions of higher education—such as the University of Lausanne, the Swiss Federal Institute of Technology of Lausanne (EPFL), the Lausanne Hotel School (EHL), and the International Institute for Management Development (IMD)—as well as for its many private schools and language institutes. The region boasted many highly regarded hospitals and medical clinics. Lausanne was the headquarters of the International Olympic Committee, and also hosted the main European offices of such multinational companies as Philip Morris, W. R. Grace, and Tetra Pak. The international headquarters of Nestlé was located in the neighboring town of Vevey.

The city provided inhabitants and visitors with a variety of cultural offerings. Performing arts included the Béjart Ballet, the Vidy Theatre, the Lausanne Municipal Theatre and Opera House, the Orchestre de la Suisse Romande, and the Lausanne Chamber Orchestra. Museums included the Cantonal Museum of Archaeology and History, the Decorative Arts Museum, the Cantonal Museum of Fine Arts, the Cathedral Museum, the Musée de l'Elysée (photography museum), the Fondation de l'Hermitage (art museum), the Natural History Museum, and the Vidy Roman Museum. One especially unusual collection was at the Musé de l'Art Brut (museum of crude art), where works by non-traditional artists such as recluses, eccentrics, prisoners, and inmates of lunatic asylums could be seen. Other distinctive attractions included the Olympic Museum, the Pipe and Tobacco Museum, and the Swiss Film Archives. These offerings were further enhanced by Lausanne's Botanical Garden, the Vivarium, and the Servion Zoo.

Tourism

Tourism was often considered to be Lausanne's main economic activity. Unlike the towns of Montreux, Interlaken, and Zermatt, Lausanne was not a world renowned tourist center. Rather, the city was known for the diversity of its "tourist offer," also serving as a starting point for scenic excursions into the Lavaux vineyards, the surrounding countryside, and nearby mountains or for steamer trips on the lake. Tourism was estimated to generate SF 350 million per year for the Lausanne area.

Lausanne depended on five travel segments: vacation stays by individuals or groups; business travel, including seminars, conventions, incentive travel, trade fairs, and exhibitions; travel related to teaching or learning; medically related tourism; and event-related tourism such as the Eurovision Song Contest

or sports championships such as the European Figure Skating Championship.

Nuitées hôtelières (overnight hotel stays) were the unit of measure used to evaluate tourism trends. Since reaching a peak of 1.1 million in 1970, overnight stays in the Lausanne area had fallen significantly during the following decade, stabilizing during the 1980s at around 850,000 per year (refer to *Exhibit 2*). This unit of measure considered a night spent in a luxury hotel the same as one in a local campground. But the relative "economic impact" was in no way comparable. "We have always wanted to have a system that would enable us to better evaluate the eco-

EXHIBIT 2
HOTEL OVERNIGHT STAYS 1966–1990:
LAUSANNE VS. ALL SWITZERLAND*

Year	Lausanne (thousands)	All Switzerland (thousands)
1966	891	28,400
1967	947	28,800
1968	991	29,100
1969	1,048	30,300
1970	1,101	32,300
1971	1,037	33,100
1972	1,005	33,700
1973	987	33,300
1974	890	31,700
1975	802	30,800
1976	745	29,600
1977	795	33,100
1978	705	32,100
1979	733	29,300
1980	778	33,000
1981	856	34,300
1982	850	32,800
1983	836	32,600
1984	872	33,000
1985	893	33,300
1986	790	32,800
1987	817	32,800
1988	788	32,400
1989	867	34,100
1990	866	34,600

*Excludes permanent guests.
Source: Lausanne Tourist Office.

nomic impact of tourism," commented Mr. Petit-pierre. At present, statistics were mostly descriptive, showing the breakdown of hotel stays by month or by nationality (refer to *Exhibits 3 and 4*). No attempt had ever been made to examine spending patterns or to obtain information about one-day visitors who were merely passing through the area, perhaps en-route to or from somewhere else in Switzerland or neighboring France.

The Tourist Office promoted accommodations in small one-star hotels as well as those at the four- and five-star level. "In order to reach the client looking for a one-star hotel as well as those who prefer the Beau-Rivage, you must promote the qualities of each class of accommodations," commented the assistant director.

Accommodations

Lausanne had a wide range of lodging establishments catering to meet a variety of needs (refer to *Exhibit 5*). They included deluxe hotels like the Beau-Rivage Palace and the Lausanne Palace; medium-priced and upper-bracket hotels such as the Hotel Aulac, the Château d'Ouchy, the Hôtel la Résidence, and the Royal Savoy; and then several "budget" to medium-priced hotels, including the Hôtel d'Angleterre (where Lord Byron stayed in 1820) and the Hôtel AlaGare. In total, Lausanne had 5,103 beds with an average bed occupancy in 1990 of 46%[2] (for a comparison with other Swiss cities and resorts, refer to *Exhibit 6*). Collectively, Lausanne's hotels were believed to be less profitable than hotels in most other parts of Switzerland.

A few distinctive hotels, like the Beau Rivage, were destinations in their own right. But others, like the Hôtel AlaGare, near the railway station, either had to be sold along with the rest of Lausanne's "tourist offer" or had a loyal clientele composed of tour group operators and business travelers. Lausanne also had a youth hostel (180 beds), a camping site by the lake at Vidy (450 tent sites), furnished

---

[2] One person staying in a room with two beds would represent a bed occupancy of 50%. Switzerland did not collect room occupancy statistics.

EXHIBIT 3
LAUSANNE OVERNIGHT STAYS BY MONTH
(in thousands)

	1990			1981–1990 ten-year distribution (%)
	Swiss	**Foreigners**	**Total**	
January	18	30	48	5.6
February	19	29	48	5.7
March	23	42	65	6.6
April	21	46	67	7.9
May	22	56	78	9.5
June	22	63	85	10.3
July	18	71	89	10.1
August	19	75	95	11.2
September	24	67	91	10.8
October	26	58	84	9.7
November	21	38	59	6.9
December	24	33	57	5.7
Total	258	607	866	100.0

Note: Row and column totals may not add because of rounding.
Source: Lausanne Tourist Office and Convention Bureau, Annual Report 1990.

EXHIBIT 4   LAUSANNE OVERNIGHT STAYS BY COUNTRY OF ORIGIN
(in thousands)

Country	1981	1985	1988	1989	1990	Analysis of 1990 data	
						% of total	Average no. of nights per visitor
France	95	87	87	92	94	10.8	2.0
USA	87	135	66	88	79	9.1	2.1
Germany	85	55	62	64	74	8.6	2.2
Italy	53	46	51	54	57	6.5	1.9
UK and Ireland	46	46	43	53	53	6.2	2.4
Spain	19	19	19	24	30	3.4	1.9
Japan	9	12	19	23	25	2.9	1.5
Greece	11	12	11	15	16	1.8	2.7
Netherlands	20	13	13	17	16	1.8	2.9
Belgium	22	14	15	16	15	1.8	2.4
Other countries	153	174	134	144	148	17.2	3.2
Total foreign visitors	600	613	520	590	607	70.1	2.3
Swiss visitors	256	280	269	277	258	29.9	2.6
Grand total	856	893	788	867	866	100.0	2.4
Percentage change over previous year							
Lausanne	+ 10.1	+ 2.4	− 3.6	+ 10.0	− 0.1		
All Switzerland	+ 4.0	+ 1.1	− 1.3	+ 5.6	+ 1.4		

Note: Column totals may not add because of rounding.
Source: Lausanne Tourist Office and Convention Bureau.

rooms (41 beds), apartments, homes and studios (510 beds), special student hostels, and hostels for union members (350 beds). In the hills above the city, there were two campgrounds in Vers-chez-les-Blanc. This wide variety of accommodations reflected Lausanne's strategy of catering to all economic levels from all over the world.

In 1990, the total number of overnight stays in Lausanne had dropped 0.1% over 1989, as compared to a gain of 1.4% for the whole of Switzerland (refer to *Exhibit 4*).

Restaurants

The attractiveness of Lausanne's "tourist offer" extended to its restaurant offerings, with cuisine rang-

ing from high gourmet to traditional Swiss, and from classical family fare to fast food.

One of Europe's most renowned restaurants, Girardet, located on the outskirts of Lausanne, was on every serious gourmet's gastronomic tour of Europe. Located in the modest 1929 Crissier town hall, Girardet's nouvelle cuisine included such specialties as ragoût of fresh quail with vegetables, baby veal in lemon sauce, and hot duck liver in a vinaigrette sauce. Fixed-price menus started from SF 150 ($105) and dinner reservations often needed to be made at least three months in advance.

Local culinary specialties included cheese fondue, *raclette,* Vinzel fritters, and cabbage or liver sausage. Fish was popular too; fresh lake fish included *omble chevalier* (char) and trout; fillet of perch was a local favorite. Restaurants featuring Italian, Greek, Chinese, or Indian food were also well represented.

Convention Facilities

Many conferences and trade fairs were held in Lausanne. One of the largest events, held each September, was the Comptoir Suisse, which provided a good picture of the dynamism and diversity of the Swiss economy, from agriculture to high technology.

Lausanne's prime facility for conventions (congresses/conferences) was the Palais de Beaulieu. However, there were also convention facilities at academic institutions and at several of Lausanne's hotels (refer to *Exhibit 7*). Among the events held recently at the Palais de Beaulieu, 9.5% included 1,000–2,000 participants, 4.5% had 2,000–3,000, and 3% attracted 3,000–7,000.

In 1991, the convention/congress schedule was to include the International Conference on Conventional and Nuclear District Heating, the Culinary Institute of America, the Swiss Society of Fertility and Sterility with the Swiss Society of Family Planning, the Swiss Society of Tropical Medicine and Parasitology, and the Kiwanis International Europe Twenty-fourth Annual Convention. Attracting visitors for all hotel categories, conventions also provided the clientele for restaurants, public transport, boat cruises on Lake Geneva, excursion-related services, and admissions to museums and cultural events.

Transportation

Lausanne had an excellent local public transportation network for a city of its size, operated by Transports Lausannois (TL). A dense network of electric trolley buses and diesel buses funneled through the center of the town, connecting to two metros (one a cog railway running down to the lakeside at Ouchy), the LEB light rail line operating north of the city, and various stations served by main line and regional CFF (Swiss Federal Railways) trains. A ride on the TL system cost one franc for up to three stops and two francs for longer distances, but visitors could save money by buying multiple-ride tickets and system passes.

Lausanne's central railway station was one of the busiest intercity railway junctions in Europe. Connected to all the big European rail networks, Lausanne was 3.4 hours from Paris by TGV (French high-speed trains) with four services daily, 3.2 hours from Milan, and 5.2 hours from Frankfurt. There were frequent intercity and direct trains between the big Swiss urban centers: Geneva, Bern, Basel, Zurich, and St. Gallen, as well as connections to towns and villages across the country. Located on the Autoroute du Léman (a limited-access motorway), the city was also easily accessible by road.

Lausanne had no passenger airport of its own, so it was served by Geneva's Cointrin intercontinental airport, only 50 minutes away by highway or train (the airport station was underneath the terminal). Lausanne had a small airfield at La Blécherette, where private aircraft could land and small air taxis could be chartered.

The harbor at Ouchy provided Lausanne with access by water during the warmer months to all the cities on the lakeshore: east to Vevey, where Charlie Chaplin's long residency was commemorated by a statue on the waterfront; to Montreux to attend one of its many festivals; or to the Château de Chillon, a superbly renovated medieval castle in the lake which was made famous by Lord Byron's poem "The Prisoner of Chillon." Passengers might find themselves riding a beautifully renovated 80-year-old paddle steamer or a modern motor vessel. Boat trips were also available west to Morges, Nyon, and Geneva or south across the lake to Evian, Thonon, and Yvoire in France. The Lausanne-Evian/Thonon service operated all year long. Marinas at Ouchy and nearby Vidy were equipped with a total of 1,522 berths for sailing and pleasure boats.

THE LAUSANNE TOURIST OFFICE AND CONVENTION BUREAU

The Office du Tourisme et des Congrès was founded in 1887. Although its services had evolved over time, its mission had remained unchanged: to welcome

EXHIBIT 5 PROFILE OF LAUSANNE AREA HOTELS

Hotels in Lausanne	Date of construction	No. of stars	Double room price	No. of beds	Meeting room(s)	Private garden/ terrace	Within 500 m of Lake Geneva	Within 1,000 m of Lausanne railway station
Hôtel du Marché		*	SF90–120	35	Y	Y		
Hôtel d'Angleterre	1820	**	120–160	55			Y	
Hôtel de la Forêt	1960s	**	120–150	30				
Hôtel Régina	1957–58	**/*	130	55				Y
Hôtel AlaGare	1967	***	140–210	92	Y			Y
Hôtel Aulac	1906	***	150–200	150	Y		Y	
Hôtel le Beau-Lieu	1989	***	140–210	115	Y			
Hôtel Bellerive	1960s	***	140–200	60		Y	Y	
Hôtel du Boulevard	1895	***	140–210	46	Y	Y		
Hôtel City	1946	***	150–210	110	Y			Y
Hôtel Crystal	1960s	***	140–210	80				Y
Hôtel Elite	1937	***	140–210	57				Y
Hôtel Jan	1957–58	***	150–220	110	Y	Y		Y
Hôtel de l'Ours								
Hôtel Rex	1960s	**/***	130	46				Y
Hôtel des Voyageurs	c. 1910	***	140–210	52	Y			
Hôtel Agora	1973	****	170–250	180	Y			Y
Hôtel Alpha	1915	****	170–250	240	Y			Y
Hôtel Carlton[2]	c. 1910	****	196–266	80	Y			
Le Château d'Ouchy	1893	****	180–250	85	Y	Y	Y	
Hôtel Continental	1964	****	170–1250	180	Y	Y	Y	Y
Hôtel Mirabeau	1904–12	****	180–250	100	Y	Y		Y
Hôtel Moevenpick-Radisson	1988	****	215–260	470	Y	Y	Y	
Hôtel de la Navigation	1954	****	190–240	50	Y		Y	
Hôtel de la Paix	1904/1950	****	220–300	210	Y		Y	
Hôtel la Résidence[1]	1960s	****	220–300	95	Y	Y	Y	
Royal Savoy[1]	c. 1910	****	235–295	170	Y	Y		Y
Hôtel Victoria	1904	****	180–250	100	Y	Y		
Beau-Rivage Palace[123]	1861/1912	****	310–440	320	Y	Y	Y	
Lausanne Palace[23]	1915	****	270–400	270	Y			Y

Hotels on Outskirts of Lausanne	Date of construction	No. of stars	Double room price	No. of beds	Meeting room(s)	Private garden/ terrace	Distance to Lake Geneva	Distance to a local train station
Hôtel Beau-Site	1899	***	SF130–160	22	Y			(6.5 km to Lausanne)
Hôtel de Belmont						Y		1 km
Hôtel Bellevue		***	130–160	45	Y	Y	2 km	(15 km to Lausanne)
Hôtel Cécil[1]		***			Y	Y		
Hôtel du Château	1875							
Hôtel Les Chevreuils		***	140–180	61	Y	Y	8 km	(6.5 km to Lausanne)
Hôtel à la Chotte		***	140–160	28		Y		(7 km to Lausanne)
Hôtel du Commerce		****	220–300	26	Y	Y		6 km
Hôtel le Débarcadère								
Hôtel la Fleur-de-Lys		***						(9 km to Lausanne)
Hôtel du Galion		**						
Hôtel Ibis		***	140–160	230	Y	Y		
Hôtel Intereurope		***	140–180	140	Y	Y	130 m	100 m (10 km to Lausanne)
Novotel Bussigny[3]			180	200	Y	Y	4 km	6 km
Hôtel l'Oasis		***						
Hôtel Pré Fleuri[1]		**	150–190	40		Y	600 m	6 km
Hôtel Près-Lac		--	110–130	70			100 m	4 km
Hôtel du Raisin		***	180–220	12	Y			500 m
Auberge de Rivaz		*	100–120	25	Y	Y	100 m	50 m
Motel des Fleurs		**	110	50	Y	Y	15 km	13 km
Motel Vert-Bois[2]	1960s	***	100–150	62	Y	Y	8 km	(8 km to Lausanne)

[1] Swimming pool
[2] Tennis.
[3] Sauna/fitness.
Y = yes
Sources: Lausanne Tourist Office and Convention Bureau. Lausanne—Palace History and Chronicles, 75 Years (Lausanne: Presses Centrales Lausanne SA, 1991), pp. 147–175; various guides

EXHIBIT 6
AVAILABLE HOTEL BEDS IN SWITZERLAND

	No. of available beds, 1990
All Switzerland	222,624
Canton of Vaud	19,313
Principal tourist-oriented cities*	
Basel	4,581
Bern	3,219
Geneva	14,826
Lausanne	5,103
Lucerne	5,408
Lugano	7,949
Montreux	3,457
Zurich	15,310

*Figures are for metropolitan areas.
Source: Lausanne Tourist Office and Convention Bureau.

EXHIBIT 7
LAUSANNE CONFERENCE ROOM CAPACITY

Facility	Largest room (no. of persons)		Total capacity (no. of persons)
Palais de Beaulieu	8,000		12,000
Ecole Polytechnique	520	(Lausanne)	650
Fédérale de Lausanne (EPFL)	500	(Ecublens)	1,500
Université de Lausanne	450	(Palais de Rumine)	450
	300	(Dorigny)	1,500
Hôpital Cantonal Universitaire Vaudois (CHUV)	400		1,000
Hôtel Beau-Rivage Palace	400		1,000
Hôtel Lausanne-Palace	400		850
Hôtel Moevenpick-Radisson	340		750
Hôtel de la Paix	200		350
Hôtel Royal-Savoy	100		250

Source: Lausanne Tourist Office and Convention Bureau.

visitors and to promote Lausanne as a tourist center. Currently, the Lausanne Tourist Office's main goal was to achieve one million overnight stays a year, up from 865,762 in 1990.

Structure and Organization

The Lausanne Tourist Office was a private association, receiving 27% of its SF 4.9 million budget from the city of Lausanne and another 18% from hotel room taxes. The rest of the budget came primarily from other "partners" such as hotel and restaurant owners who were directly affected by tourism and conventions.

A member of the Association of Les Six Villes Suisses—grouping Lausanne with Geneva, Zurich, Bern, Basel, and St. Gallen—the tourist office collaborated with these towns to explore common tourist and development issues. But each town was responsible for promoting its own "tourist offer." The tourist office did work with Montreux/Vevey (a strong competitor for business and incentive travel as well as for conventions) to develop general promotional campaigns, "for greater effectiveness and more affordable results," commented Mr. Petitpierre.

In 1987, a new main office and visitor information center opened in Ouchy. This site, on the lake and close to seven hotels, the steamer terminal, and the Ouchy Metro station, was in one of Lausanne's most popular tourist areas. The tourist office employed 40 full-time workers and 30 freelance hostesses who provided reception and information services on an as needed basis. A second, smaller information center was located two kilometers away at the main railway station.

The activities of the tourist office were directly supervised by the director and a seven-member management committee, which included the Mayor of Lausanne and representatives from the society of hotel managers, the society of café and restaurant managers, local businesses, the banking and legal communities, and the Palais de Beaulieu.

Responsibility for day-to-day activities was divided among five departments: Management and Administration oversaw the general management of the office; Information Services managed the two visitor information centers; Publications and Public Relations ensured a liaison with the local press and produced the different office publications; Marketing was responsible for performing market studies and organizing promotion in Switzerland and abroad (an example of recent advertising to promote corporate incentive visits to Lausanne is shown in *Exhibit 8*) and Reception-Groups-Conferences organized conventions, group stays, and incentive trips.

The Information Services department was spread between the tourist office's two visitor centers. At these two locations, the tourist office's employees, each speaking a minimum of three languages (French, German, and English) provided visitors with information every day of the year (except Christmas) from 08:00 to 19:00 hours, with office hours extending until 21:00 in the summer.

Each visitor center had its own information service "mission." The smaller office at the station was a one-person operation and focused on Lausanne-related information, providing schedules for the bus, trolley, and metro system, youth hostel information, and maps. Having a broadly defined "tourist" service, the main visitor center provided information not only on the Greater Lausanne area, but also on Switzerland's other major tourist areas. Additionally, this office had an on-line "Billetel" computer system for ticket sales and reservations, and provided tours of Lausanne as well as summer excursions to the local Lavaux vineyards.

At the main office, multiple copies of some 3,500 different publications (collectively weighing four tons) were stored in an enormous electrically operated filing cabinet which rotated through two floors of the building. 100,000 guidebooks of Lausanne and 80,000 local maps were distributed annually.

Reception and information services at the main office were provided by up to seven people during Lausanne's "high season" in the summer, when the office received an average of 250 telephone calls, 140 visitors, and 20 letters or telefaxes a day. "We believe in answering written requests as quickly as possible," commented Mr. Marko Jankovic, Manager of Information Services. "But we keep them brief to

EXHIBIT 8   EXAMPLE OF INCENTIVE ADVERTISING

Lausanne

A town that is bound to delight your clients !

A really exceptional setting on the shores of Lake Geneva, with the Savoy Alps forming a magnificent backdrop.

1 hr 30 min by plane from London or 1 hr from Paris (3 hr 40 min by TGV). Geneva Intercontinental Airport only 37 1/2 miles away (35 minutes by car or 42 minutes by direct train service).

A host of monuments and sights richly steeped in history: an old city clustering round the 13th century Cathedral.

Shows, exhibitions, shopping, lake cruises, and excursions in the programme of every stay in Lausanne !

At your disposal for the organisation of any special arrangements for your groups or incentive tours. All facilities for meetings and conventions:

Lausanne Tourist Office and Convention Bureau
2, avenue de Rhodanie - P.O. Box 248 CH-1000 Lausanne 6, Tel. (21) 617 73 21, Tx 454 833, Fax (21) 26 86 47

avoid sending everyone two kilograms of material." During the rest of the year, there were three people providing these services, with at least one person available during the office's open hours.

THE CASE FOR NEW RESEARCH

After more than two hours of discussion, the management committee had agreed that the idea of tourism as an economic sector was not easily perceived, since tourism functioned as the coordinating "hub" of a myriad of services. But, committee members were determined to find ways of quantifying—for both the cantonal government and local residents—the significant contribution that tourism made to Lausanne's economy.

At this point in the discussion, Mr. Petitpierre had the floor:

If we look at cities like Nice, Cannes, Paris, Birmingham, The Hague, Amsterdam, and Hamburg, it's incredible the financial means they have to promote their cities and their convention centers. At this level, we are absolutely not competitive for the moment. The only way we're going to get the necessary funds is to document the contribution that tourism, in all its forms, makes to the local economy. The statistics we have at present are insufficient. We also need new and more detailed information about our visitors to help us develop strategies for attracting them and then serving them better once they get to Lausanne. And that will require one or more specially commissioned studies.

The director of the tourist office looked around the table. There were murmurs of agreement from other members of the management committee and heads were nodding. As if to emphasize the point, a long blast came from the hooter of one of the lake steamers a few hundred meters away as it prepared to leave for Evian.

"It sounds as though both the local economy and this committee are in agreement with you, Claude," said the director with a smile. "Why don't you review the possibilities for us and outline a plan of action for some new research?"

MacTec Control AB

James E. Nelson

"The choices themselves seem simple enough," thought Georg Carlsson in January 1989. "We enter the U.S. market in Pennsylvania and New York, we forget about the U.S. for the time being, or we do some more marketing research." The difficult part was the decision.

Georg was president of MacTec Control AB, a Swedish firm located in Kristianstad. Georg had begun MacTec in 1980 along with his wife, Jessie. MacTec had grown rapidly and now boasted of some 30 employees and annual revenues of about $2.8 million. Since 1985, MacTec had been partly owned by The Perstorp Corporation, whose headquarters were located nearby. Perstorp was a large manufacturer of chemicals and chemical products, with operations in eighteen countries and annual revenues of

about $600 million. Perstorp had provided MacTec with capital and managerial advice, as well as chemical analysis technology.

MACTEC'S AQUALEX SYSTEM

MacTec's product line centered about its Aqualex System, a design of computer hardware and software for the monitoring and control of pressurized water flows. Most often these water flows consisted of either potable water or sewage effluent as these liquids were stored, moved, or treated by municipal water departments.

The System employed MacTec's MPDII microcomputer (see *Exhibit 1*) installed at individual pumping stations where liquids are stored and moved. Often these stations were located quite far apart, linking geographically dispersed water users (households, businesses, etc.) to water and sewer systems. The microcomputer performed a number of important functions. It controlled the starts, stops, and alarms of up to four pumps, monitored levels and available capacities of storage reservoirs, checked pump capacities and power consumptions, and recorded pump flows. It could even measure amounts

EXHIBIT 1   MPDII CONTROLS AND MONITORS PUMPING STATIONS

MPDII which controls and monitors the pumping stations

An MPDII microcomputer is installed at a pumping station and then works as an independent, intelligent computer. When required, it can go on line with the central computer and report its readings there.

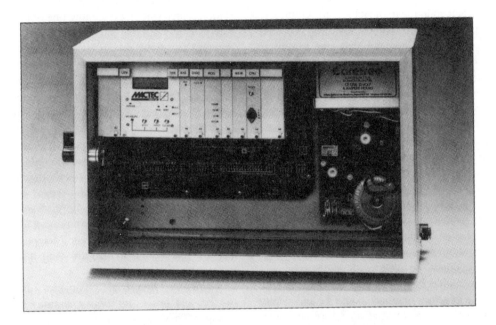

Here are some of the functions of the MPDII

— It governs the starts, stops and alarms of up to four pumps, controlled by an integrated, piezo-resistive pressure-level sensor.

— It checks the sump level.

— It checks pump capacity and changes therein.

— It activates an alarm when readings reach preset deviation limits.

— It registers precipitation and activates an alarm in case of the heavy rain.

— It constantly monitors pump power consumption and activates an alarm in case of unacceptable deviation.

— It registers current pump flow by means of advanced calculations of inflow and outfeed from the sump.

— It can register accumulated time for overflow.

— It switches to forward or reverse action, even by remote command.

— It stores locally the last nine alarm instances with time indications.

— These may be read directly on an LCD display.

— It can be remotely programmed from the central computer.

An MPDII does a great job, day after day, year after year.

of rainfall entering reservoirs and adjust pump operations or activate an alarm as needed. Each microcomputer could also be easily connected to a main computer to allow remote control of pumping stations and produce a variety of charts and graphs useful in evaluating pump performance and scheduling needed maintenance.

The Aqualex System provided a monitoring function that human operators could not match in terms of sophistication, immediacy, and cost. The System permitted each individual substation to: control its own pumping operations; collect, analyze, and store data; forecast trends; transmit data and alarms to a central computer; and receive remote commands. Alarms could also be transmitted directly to a pocket-sized receiver carried by one or more operators on call. A supervisor could continually monitor pumping operations in a large system entirely via a computer terminal at a central location and send commands to individual pumps, thereby saving costly service calls and time. The System also reduced the possibility of overflows that could produce disastrous flooding of nearby communities.

MacTec personnel would work with water and sewage engineers to design and install the desired Aqualex System. Personnel would also train engineers and operators to work with the System and would be available 24 hours a day for consultation. If needed, a MacTec engineer could be physically present to assist engineers and operators whenever major problems arose. MacTec also offered its clients the option of purchasing a complete service contract whereby MacTec personnel would provide periodic testing and maintenance of installed systems.

An Aqualex System could be configured a number of ways. In its most basic form, the System would be little more than a small "black box" that monitored two or three lift station activities and, when necessary, transmitted an alarm to one or more remote receivers. An intermediate system would monitor additional activities, send data to a central computer via telephone lines, and receive remote commands. An advanced system would provide the same monitoring capabilities but add forecasting features, maintenance management, auxiliary power back-up, and

data transmission and reception via radio. Prices to customers for the three configurations at present were about $1,200, $2,400, and $4,200.

AQUALEX CUSTOMERS

Aqualex customers could be divided into two groups—governmental units and industrial companies. The typical application in the first group was a sewage treatment plant having some 4 to 12 pumping stations, each station containing one or more pumps. Pumps would operate intermittently and—unless an Aqualex or similar system were in place—be monitored by one or more operators who would visit each station once or perhaps twice each day for about a half hour. Operators would take reservoir measurements, record running times of pumps, and sometimes perform limited maintenance and repairs. The sewage plant and stations typically were located in flat or rolling terrain, where gravity could not be used in lieu of pumping. If any monitoring equipment were present at all, it typically would consist of a crude, on-site alarm that would activate whenever fluid levels rose or fell beyond a present level. Sometimes the alarm would activate a telephone dialing function that alerted an operator some distance from the station.

Numerous industrial companies also stored, moved, and processed large quantities of water or sewage. These applications usually differed little from those in governmental plants except for their smaller size. On the other hand, there were a considerably larger number of industrial companies having pumping stations and so, Georg thought, the two markets often offered about identical market potentials in many countries.

The two markets desired essentially the same products, although industrial applications often used smaller, simpler equipment. Both markets wanted their monitoring equipment to be accurate and reliable, the two dominant concerns. Equipment should also be easy to use, economical to operate, and require little regular service or maintenance. Purchase price often was not a major consideration—as long as the price was in some appropriate range, customers seemed more interested in actual product performance than in initial outlays.

Georg thought that worldwide demand for the Aqualex System and competing products would continue to be strong for at least the next ten years. While some of this demand represented construction of new pumping stations, many applications were replacements of crude monitoring and alarm systems at existing sites. These existing systems depended greatly on regular visits by operators, visits that often continued even after new equipment was installed. Most such trips were probably not necessary. However, many managers found it difficult to dismiss or reassign monitoring personnel that were no longer needed; many were also quite cautious and conservative, desiring some human monitoring of the new equipment "just in case." Once replacements of existing systems were complete, market growth would be limited to new construction and, of course, replacements of more sophisticated systems.

Most customers (as well as noncustomers) considered the Aqualex System to be the best on the market. Those knowledgeable in the industry felt that competing products seldom matched Aqualex's reliability and accuracy. Experts also believed that many competing products lacked the sophistication and flexibility present in Aqualex's design. Beyond these product features, customers also appreciated MacTec's knowledge about water and sanitation engineering. Competing firms often lacked this expertise, offering their products somewhat as a sideline and considering the market too small for an intensive marketing effort.

The market was clearly not too small for MacTec. While Georg had no hard data on market potential for western Europe, he thought that annual demand here could be as much as $9 million. About 40% of this came from new construction while the rest represented demand from replacing existing systems. Industry sales in the latter category could be increased by more aggressive marketing efforts on the part of MacTec and its competitors. Eastern European economies represented additional, new potential. However, the water and sewer industries in these countries seemed less interested than their Western

counterparts in high technology equipment to monitor pumping operations. Additionally, business was often more difficult to conduct in these countries. In contrast, the U.S. market looked very attractive.

MACTEC STRATEGY

MacTec currently marketed its Aqualex System primarily to sewage treatment plants in Scandinavia and other countries in northern and central Europe. The company's strategy could be described as providing technologically superior equipment to monitor pumping operations at these plants. The strategy stressed frequent contacts with customers and potential customers to design, supply, and service the Aqualex System. The strategy also stressed superior knowledge of water and sanitation engineering along with up-to-date electronics and computer technology. The result was a line of highly specialized sensors, computers, and methods for process controls in water treatment plants.

This was the essence of MacTec's strategy, having a special competence that no firm in the world could easily match. MacTec also prided itself on its being a young, creative company, without an entrenched bureaucracy. Company employees generally worked with enthusiasm and dedication; they talked with each other, regularly, openly, and with a great deal of give and take. More importantly, customers—as well as technology—seemed to drive all areas in the company.

MacTec's strategy in its European markets seemed to be fairly well decided. That is, Georg thought that a continuation of present strategies and tactics should continue to produce good results. However, an aspect that would likely change would be to locate a branch office having both sales and manufacturing activities somewhere in the European Community (EC), most likely the Netherlands. The plan was to have such an office in operation well before 1992, when the 12 countries in the EC (Belgium, Denmark, France, Greece, Ireland, Italy, Luxembourg, the Netherlands, Portugal, Spain, United Kingdom, Germany) would mutually eliminate national barriers to the flow of capital, goods, and services. Having a

MacTec office located in the EC would greatly simplify sales to these member countries. Moreover, MacTec's presence should also avoid problems with any protective barriers the EC itself might raise to limit or discourage market access by outsiders.

Beyond establishing this branch office, Georg was considering a major strategic decision to enter the U.S. market. His two recent visits to the U.S. had led him to conclude that the market represented potential beyond that for western Europe and that the U.S. seemed perfect for expansion. Industry experts in the U.S. agreed with Georg that the Aqualex System outperformed anything used in the U.S. market. Experts thought that many water and sewage engineers would welcome MacTec's products and knowledge. Moreover, Georg thought that U.S. transportation systems and payment arrangements would present few problems. The System would be imported under U.S. Tariff Regulation 71249 and pay a duty of 4.9%.

Entry would most likely be in the form of a sales and service office located in Philadelphia. The Pennsylvania and New York state markets seemed representative of the U.S. and appeared to offer a good test of the Aqualex System. The two states together probably represented about 18% of total U.S. market potential for the System. The office would require an investment of some $200,000 for inventory and other balance sheet items. Annual fixed costs would total upwards of $250,000 for salaries and other operating expenses—Georg thought that the office would employ only a general manager, two sales technicians, and a secretary for at least the first year or two. Each Aqualex System sold in the U.S. would be priced to provide a contribution of about 30%. Georg wanted a 35% annual return before taxes on any MacTec investment, to begin no later than the second year. At issue was whether Georg could realistically expect to achieve this goal in the U.S.

MARKETING RESEARCH

To this end, Georg had commissioned the Browning Group in Philadelphia to conduct some limited marketing research with selected personnel in the water and sewage industries in the city and surrounding areas. The research had two purposes: to obtain a sense of market needs and market reactions to MacTec's products and to calculate a rough estimate of market potential in Pennsylvania and New York. Results were intended to help Georg interpret his earlier conversations with industry experts and perhaps allow a decision on market entry.

The research design itself employed two phases of data collection. The first consisted of five one-hour interviews with water and sewage engineers employed by local city and municipal governments. For each interview, an experienced Browning Group interviewer scheduled an appointment with the engineer and then visited his office, armed with a set of questions and a tape recorder. Questions included:

1. What procedures do you use to monitor your pumping stations?
2. Is your current monitoring system effective? Costly?
3. What are the costs of a monitoring malfunction?
4. What features would you like to see in a monitoring system?
5. Who decides on the selection of a monitoring system?
6. What is your reaction to the Aqualex System?

Interviewers were careful to listen closely to the engineers' responses and to probe for additional detail and clarification.

Tapes of the personal interviews were transcribed and then analyzed by the project manager at Browning. The report noted that these results were interesting in that they described typical industry practices and viewpoints. A partial summary from the report appears below:

The picture that emerges is one of fairly sophisticated personnel making decisions about monitoring equipment that is relatively simple in design. Still, some engineers would appear distrustful of this equipment because they persist in sending operators to pumping stations on a daily basis. The distrust may be justified because potential costs of a malfunction were identified as expensive repairs and cleanups, fines of $10,000 per day of violation, lawsuits, harassment by the Health Department, and public embarrassment. The five engineers identified themselves as key individuals in the decision to purchase new equipment. Without exception, they considered MacTec features innovative, highly desirable, and worth the price.

The summary noted also that the primary use of the interview results was to construct a questionnaire that could be administered over the telephone.

The questionnaire was used in the second phase of data collection, as part of a telephone survey that had contacted 65 utility managers, water and sewage engineers, and pumping station operators in Philadelphia and surrounding areas. All respondents were employed by governmental units. Each interview took about 10 minutes to complete, covering topics identified in questions 1, 2, and 4 above. The Browning Group's research report stated that most interviews found respondents to be quite cooperative, although 15 people refused to participate at all.

The telephone interviews had produced results that could be considered more representative of the market because of the larger sample size. The report had organized these results about the topics of monitoring procedures, system effectiveness and costs, and features desired in a monitoring system:

All monitoring systems under the responsibility of the 50 respondents were considered to require manual checking. The frequency of operator visits to pumping stations ranged from monthly to twice daily, depending on flow rates, pumping station history, proximity of nearby communities, monitoring equipment in operation, and other factors. Even the most sophisticated automatic systems were checked because respondents "just don't trust the machine." Each operator was responsible for some 10 to 20 stations.

Despite the perceived need for double-checking, all respondents considered their current monitoring system to be quite effective. Not one reported a serious pumping malfunction in the past three years that had escaped detection. However, this reliability came at considerable cost—the annual wages and other expenses associated with each monitoring operator averaged about $40,000.

Respondents were about evenly divided between those wishing a simple alarm system and those desiring a sophisticated, versatile microprocessor. Managers and engineers in the former category often said that the only feature they really needed was an emergency signal such as a siren, horn, or light. Sometimes they would add a telephone dialer that would be automatically activated at the same time as the signal. Most agreed that a price of around $2000 would be reasonable for such a system. The latter category of individuals contained engineers desiring many of the Aqualex System's features, once they knew such equipment was available. A price of $4000 per system seemed acceptable. Some of these respondents were quite knowledgeable about computers and computer programming while others were not. Only four respondents voiced any strong concerns about the cost to purchase and install more sophisticated monitoring equipment. Everyone demanded that the equipment be reliable and accurate.

Georg found the report quite helpful. Much of the information, of course, simply confirmed his own view of the U.S. market. However, it was good to have this knowledge from an independent, objective organization. In addition, to learn that the market consisted of two, apparently equally sized segments of simple and sophisticated applications was quite worthwhile. In particular, knowledge of system prices considered acceptable by each segment would make the entry decision easier. Meeting these prices would not be a major problem.

A most important section of the report contained an estimate of market potential for Pennsylvania and New York. The estimate was based on an analysis of discharge permits on file in governmental offices in the two states. These permits were required before any city, municipality, water or sewage district, or industrial company could release sewage or other contaminated water to another system or to a lake or river. Each permit showed the number of pumping stations in operation. Based on a 10% sample of permits, the report had estimated that governmental units in Pennsylvania and New York contained approximately 3000 and 5000 pumping stations for waste water, respectively. Industrial companies in the two states were estimated to add some 3000 and 9000 more pumping stations, respectively. The total number of pumping stations in the two states—20,000—seemed to be growing at about 2% per year.

Finally, a brief section of the report dealt with the study's limitations. Georg agreed that sample was quite small, that it contained no utility managers or engineers from New York, and that it probably concentrated too heavily on individuals in larger urban areas. In addition, the research told him nothing about competitors and their marketing strategies and tactics. Nor did he learn anything about any state regulations for monitoring equipment, if indeed any existed. However, these shortcomings came as no surprise, representing a consequence of the research design proposed to Georg by the Browning Group some six weeks ago, before the study began.

THE DECISION

Georg's decision seemed a difficult one. The most risky option was to enter the U.S. market as soon as possible; the most conservative was to stay in Europe. In between was the option of conducting some additional marketing research.

Discussion with the Browning Group had identified the objectives of this research as to rectify limitations of the first study as well as to provide more accurate estimates of market potential. (The estimates of the numbers of pumping stations in Pennsylvania and New York were accurate to around plus or minus 20%.) This research was estimated to cost $40,000 and take another three months to complete.

Hinesbury Mills, I

Christopher H. Lovelock
Gerald J. Eskin

Marjorie Halstein, group product manager at Hines-bury Mills, Inc., a leading foods manufacturer, was concerned over competitive developments which posed a potentially severe threat to her brand's share of the United States cake mix market. Hinesbury was one of three major brands in this market; it also faced competition from several minor brands and private label brands.

Until recently, all brands had been selling essen-tially the same product line of regular cake mixes in which shortening cake predominated. Each brand offered a basic core of staple flavors, such as choco-late, yellow and white cakes, to which were added a variety of minor flavors which changed periodically. The strategy of the three major brands was essentially one of flavor proliferation; minor and private label brands offered less choice, competing primarily on the basis of price. Six months earlier, Hinesbury Mills (HM) had introduced a new line of premium cake mixes, containing superior quality ingredients which included real butter. However, before the company

had time to evaluate the impact of the new line on the market and conduct any meaningful market re-search, its two major competitors both introduced new cake mixes. The new entrants looked as though they might also offer the higher quality appeal of HM's new premium line, achieved in their case through requiring purchasers to add their own butter.

THE CAKE MIX MARKET

Consumers had three major sources of cake avail-able: (a) ready-make cakes purchased from bakeries or supermarkets, (b) entirely home-made cakes, (c) cakes prepared at home from manufactured mixes. Total cake consumption per capita had remained fairly constant over the years, with cake mixes ac-counting for about one-third of all cakes consumed. Three main types of cake mix products were avail-able: regular two-layer size, loaf or one-layer size, and angel/chiffon type.

The product category of immediate concern to Hinesbury executives was the two-layer which, with an annual market of some thirty million 12-pack cases, accounted for the major portion of the total cake-mix market. Although experiencing a modest annual growth rate, the long-term outlook for the two-layer cake mix market suggested that the product might be reaching the mature stage in its life cycle. Halstein knew that the per capita consumption of this type was declining gradually in the face of increasing competition for the consumer's dollar from other prepared desserts.

Hinesbury's Market Strategy

Hinesbury Mills had pioneered the development of modern cake mixes. Over the years, the company had faced strong competition from Allied Foods Corporation and Concorn Kitchens, Inc. and, to a lesser extent, from a number of regional and private label brands—generally referred to as "price brands" since this formed the main basis of their competitive strategy. The other two major brands (Allied and Concorn) focused their marketing efforts on a strategy of heavy and consistent promotion aimed at building up distinctive images of themselves in consumers' minds. Allied Foods emphasized the moistness characteristic of cakes made with its mix, while Concorn's advertising concentrated on the flavor quality of its product. Hinesbury's response to these competitive attitudes was to adopt a strategy of proliferating its product line by offering an even wider range of flavors and by building markets through widespread use of deals.[1] By combining a continuous program of product improvement with new flavor introductions and heavy promotional expenditures, HM had been able to maintain its position as the market leader.

Eventually, however, Hinesbury began to find itself faced with a disturbing loss of market share and weakened distribution. The company fought back with strategic actions that included curtailing the proliferation of flavors, intensively pushing sales, and making heavy promotional expenditures with an em-

phasis on price deals. Most important of all, in the view of HM executives, was the introduction of a premium line of high quality cake mixes with superior ingredients including real butter and a guaranteed shelf life of 24 months. This was a technological breakthrough and was designed to appeal to an identified consumer need, capitalizing on the large section of the existing market whom research had shown to want a moister, higher quality cake. It was also the first product innovation to disturb the existing structure of the market.

Although it retailed at a recommended price of $1.19, as against a recommended 79 cents for the standard mix, initial acceptance of the premium line appeared very favorable and the decision was soon made to expand distribution nationwide. Like all cake mixes, heavy emphasis was placed on price deals. However, it was anticipated that six months would be needed to build up the product and obtain conclusive data on its impact on both regular cake mix sales and HM's overall market share.

Competitive Actions

To the dismay of Halstein and other Hinesbury executives, their premium line had only been in national distribution seven weeks when both major competitors countered with strategic moves that posed a severe threat to Hinesbury's own strategy. Virtually identical product lines were launched within a few days of each other by Concorn (into a midwestern test market) and by Allied Foods (which immediately went national). Their entries were both regularly priced (recommended retail price of 79¢) cake mixes in two flavors called Butter Chocolate and Butter Yellow. Unlike the standard mix, which contained an inexpensive shortening, or Hinesbury's premium mix with its butter content, these new products contained no shortening at all. Instead, they called for consumers to add their own butter to a "specially prepared formula," thus allegedly producing the same end product for which Hinesbury was asking consumers to pay an extra 40 cents. In practice, there were certain distinguishable differences between the

---

[1] Deals are cut-price offers to consumers, such as "5 cents off," "three for the price of two," etc. Dealing is widely practiced in the packaged foods industry as well as in certain product areas of the drug and cosmetics industries, notably when there are several large brands competing with essentially similar products.

premium and add-butter end products. Premium mix cakes, while perceived by many as being of higher quality and more moist than the standard mix versions, still retained the latter's light and fluffy consistency. The add-butter cakes, by contrast, tended to have somewhat denser and closer-grained texture, more akin to brownies or cupcakes. Again, it was believed that many consumers regarded the add-butter end product as of higher quality than standard mix cake.

Halstein assumed that if the initial move with chocolate and yellow flavors was successful, the two competitors would subsequently introduce add-butter versions to other flavors. Moreover, Halstein noted three significant strengths to the competition's approach. First, ingredient costs to the manufacturer were reduced in that no shortening need be placed in the mix; since the add-butter product sold at the same price as the standard mix, this meant higher unit profits. Second, the new products possessed a similar appeal to Hinesbury's premium line—that of the higher quality resulting from inclusion of butter as an ingredient—but with the further characteristic of allowing each consumer to add butter to the prepared mix and thus "individualize" the cake. On the other hand, of course, this method lacked the convenience inherent in a complete mix. Third, it seemed likely that many consumers would not see the addition of butter, which they already had in the home, as an incremental cost. If the cost of butter were added to the price of the competitive mix, this would bring the total cost of the cake up to the same level as Hinesbury's premium offering, but it seemed probable that in many cases the consumer would still see the cost of the cake as 79 cents.

HINESBURY MILLS DEBATES ITS RESPONSE

HM was now offering two lines of cake mix (standard and premium) while its two major competitors were offering standard and add-butter lines. No information existed on how market share might break down among these three lines and among the different

brands once the situation stabilized. The principal question for Halstein was how the introduction of the new add-butter line by the competition would affect its own brand standing; but there were other problems too. Would the add-butter line appeal to the same consumers as HM's premium line? Should Hinesbury Mills also offer an add-butter product? To what extent would consumers be willing to pay a higher pack price for a better quality, convenience product? In essence HM could pursue a myriad of possible alternatives in terms of the flavor, texture, quality, price, and convenience of the mix itself. Beyond that, a wide variety of marketing strategies might be employed. Halstein felt it was imperative to respond quickly to the competitive threat, but wondered how to obtain quickly sufficient information to permit an early strategic decision. At that point, nobody really had any firm information at all on the current state of the market.

Following an all-day conference with other marketing executives, Halstein took three immediate actions. First, she told the Research and Development department to begin developing an add-butter line in case it was subsequently decided to offer such a product on the market under the Hinesbury Mills label. Second, she contracted with the A.C. Nielsen Company to monitor the performance of both the Allied Foods and Concorn Kitchens add-butter lines in the market. Last, she and her colleagues decided to undertake development of a computer model of the cake market. They believed that by actually simulating, in a computer-based model, the decision process that various types of consumers made in buying a cake, they could develop an understanding of the purchase process and how decisions were arrived at under different circumstances. This might then permit predictions of the market performance of standard, premium, and add-butter lines. The simulation approach had the added advantages of being much faster and cheaper than actual market testing of different product formulations under differing marketing strategies, as well as keeping HM actions secret from the competition.

Halstein assigned the marketing research department the task of building the simulation model. After some discussion, it was agreed that they should begin by developing an explicit but fair representation of the consumer decision process involved in the purchase of a cake mix. At the same time, it was decided to identify clearly some of the principal needs that a consumer might have concerning cakes. To help them in this task, the director of marketing research proposed to draw on transcripts of some interviews with consumers on their cake-buying and cake-making habits. These interviews had been conducted recently for the company by a well-known research firm. Some extracts from the interviews are shown in *Exhibit 1*.

EXHIBIT 1 RESEARCH COMPANY'S REPORT ON CONSUMERS' CAKE-BUYING AND -MAKING HABITS

Extracts from Interviews Conducted with Consumers

1 "Yes, I use quite a lot of cake mixes. You know how it is with three young boys—they like to have something sweet at dinnertime, so I often quickly whip up a cake for them. My husband likes them too, but I won't let him have too much if it's one of those rich, heavy ones: he's really got to watch his weight these days (laughs). . . . I guess I bake about one cake a week, sometimes two. Generally I get Concorn's. I think their flavors are nicer than the other brands, and the quality's good, too. But usually I'll look first to see if any of the main brands have got any special offers. My husband's been on short-time at the plant for nearly three months now, so I have to watch the pennies. Can't afford to be too extravagant. Cake's quite a good buy really."

2 "No, I don't buy cake mixes that often—usually it's just for some special occasion and when I do I like to get the best, and then take a bit of time and trouble over it. You know, even with a good brand like Hinesbury or Concorn you've got to be prepared to put in a few ingredients of your own. I've got a special recipe I use adding sour cream—makes a delicious cake, you know, rich and moist."

3 "I bake a lot of cakes. We often have them with the evening meal. Most times we prefer to have a light spongy cake which I serve with ice cream. For special occasions though, I'll make an extra fancy one and decorate it real nicely. I enjoy doing my own cooking, but with a full-time job I just can't give it the time that I'd like to. So I want something that's quick and fairly foolproof."

4 "I've got two kids—and they're always demanding sweet things, so I try to have some sort of cake around most of the time. Mostly, I just put it on the table at dinnertime and let them have as much as they want. Don't care for it much after a meat dish myself, but sometimes I'll make myself a snack during the day and have a sandwich and some cake with a glass of milk when the kids are off at school and I can't be bothered to cook myself lunch. . . . No, I really don't worry about the brand, can't say I can tell the difference myself, especially when there's a frosting on top. They're all good enough. I just look to see if any brand has a few cents off, same as I do with detergent."

5 "I'm pretty choosy about the brands I buy—the quality does vary. Allied Foods makes the best lemon I think, but I don't like their chocolate so well—Hinesbury is much the nicest there. . . . One thing, though, I like to put in a few extra touches of my own—makes me feel it's my cake and not just some home economist's. That way I feel I can still take some of the credit for the way it turns out. I've still got all of my mother's old cookbooks and sometimes I get ideas out of these, particularly if I want to make a really rich cake for some special occasion."

6 "Yeah, I guess we occasionally have cake with the evening meal. They're pretty quick and easy to make and my nine-year-old likes putting on the topping. Usually I pick up two or three packages of mix at the market whenever I notice there's a good deal on. Quality? No I don't think there's really much difference between the main brands, though I guess some of the others mightn't be too hot. I tried a private label once because it was cheaper, but it was pretty bad. Came out all heavy and tasteless. So now I stick with brands like Concorn, Hinesbury and Allied. Better to be safe than sorry, I guess."

7 "I reckon the only time we have cake is just three or four times a year when it's someone's birthday or something. I'm not much of a cook, but if you stick with one of the quality brands and get a flavor you know people like, it's pretty hard to go wrong if you just follow the instructions. Mind you, there was the time I forgot to set the timer . . . ." (laughs)

EXHIBIT 1 (*continued*)

8 "My husband says I spend more on gas driving around the different markets than I save on discounts and special offers. But I get a real charge out of looking for bargains. If I see something like Concorn cake mix with a really good offer on it, I just can't resist it. D'you know, last week I bought six packets of some new flavors they were bringing out—they were offering ten cents off a pack. I guess we'll all be eating cake now every day for the next three weeks."

9 "I like to make a rich fudge cake as a treat for my grandchildren when they visit me, but personally I prefer something lighter and not so sweet to have with coffee around mid-morning."

10 "There are four of us sharing this apartment, see, and we take turns doing the cooking. It's really neat the way it works out—we each do a week at a time. I can never get over how good the two boys are at it. I'm the only one who makes cake though—it's a fun thing to do and I like experimenting with different types of cake and adding little touches of my own. . . ."

11 ". . . I like a cake with a nice fluffy consistency. Not one of those heavy ones you get in some flavors . . . ."

12 "Generally, I make a cake about once a month. My husband has a sweet tooth and likes cake at dinner sometimes or for a quick bite when we get home from afternoon classes. I like a fairly moist consistency, not too sickly sweet with lots of flavor and a pretty appearance. I guess they're all fairly easy to make. Usually, I get Hinesbury, except I watch out for specials—I'd buy any major brand on special. Some of the really cheapo ones haven't much taste. Too dry, too."

13 "We often have cake for dinner. Personally, I prefer buying the frozen kind—the ready-made ones. They taste nicer and they're much easier. My daughters'll bake a cake from a mix recipe sometimes. I really don't know why, because they always seem to manage to have them crumble all over. So if I'm buying a mix, I just look for something cheap."

14 "The two things I look for in a good cake are taste and consistency. I don't like eating something that looks like a bathroom sponge, but want a cake I can get my teeth into."

Ethical Dilemmas in Marketing Research

Charles B. Weinberg

Marketing managers and marketing researchers are frequently confronted by ethical problems and dilemmas. Gathering, analyzing, and presenting information all are procedures that raise important ethical questions in which the manager's need to know and understand the market in order to develop effective marketing programs must be balanced against an individual's right to privacy. The interpretation and use of data can also raise ethical questions.

The following scenarios present a set of ethical dilemmas that might arise in marketing research. Your assignment is to decide what action to take in each instance. You should be prepared to justify your decision. Bear in mind that there are no uniquely right answers; reasonable people may choose different courses of action.

1. As market research director of a pharmaceutical company, you are given the suggestion by the executive director that physicians be telephoned by company interviewers under the name of a fictitious market research agency. The purpose of the survey is to help assess the perceived quality of the company's products, and it is felt that the suggested procedure will result in more objective responses.

   What action would you take?

2. Your company is supervising a study of restaurants conducted for an agency of the federal government. The data, which have already been collected, include specific buying information and prices paid. Respondent organizations have been promised confidentiality. Agency officials demand that all responses be identified by business name. Their rationale is that they plan to repeat the study and wish to limit sampling error by returning to the same procedures. Open bidding requires that the government maintain control of the sample.

   What action would you take?

3. You are the market research director in a manufacturing company. The project director requests permission to use ultraviolet ink in precoding questionnaires on a mail survey. She points out that the accompanying letter refers to a confidential survey, but she needs to be able to identify respondents to permit adequate cross-tabulation of the data and to save on postage costs if a second mailing is required.

   What action would you take?

436

4. You are employed by a marketing research firm and have conducted an attitude study for a client. Your data indicate that the product is not being marketed properly. This finding is ill-received by the client's product management team. They request that you omit that data from your formal report—which you know will be widely distributed—on the grounds that the verbal presentation was adequate for their needs.

   What do you do?

5. You are a project director on a study funded by a somewhat unpopular federal policing agency. The study is on marijuana use among young people in a community and its relationship, if any, to crime. You will be using a structured questionnaire to gather data for the agency on marijuana use and criminal activities. You believe that if you reveal the name of the funding agency and/or the actual purposes of the study to respondents, you will seriously reduce response rates and thereby increase nonresponse bias.

   What information would you disclose to respondents?

6. You are a student in a marketing research course. The professor assigns a project where each student is required to conduct personal interviews with executives of high technology companies concerning their future plans. The professor has stated that all the information is confidential and will only be used in the research course. However, two days after the professor has assigned the project, you overhear him talking to a colleague where he mentions that this research project will be sold to a major technology firm in the industry.

   What action would you take?

7. You are employed by a market research company. A clothing manufacturer has retained your firm to conduct a study for them. The manufacturer wants you to know something about how women choose clothing, such as blouses and sweaters. The manufacturer wants to conduct group interviews, supplemented by a session which would be devoted to observing the women trying on clothing, in order to discover which types of garments are chosen first, how thoroughly they touch and examine the clothing, and whether they look for and read a label or price tag. The client suggests that the observations be performed unobtrusively by female observers at a local department store, via a one-way mirror. One of your associates argues that this would constitute an invasion of privacy.

   What action would you take?

8. You are a study director for a research company undertaking a project for a regular client of your company. A study you are working on is about to go into the field when the questionnaire you sent to the client for final approval comes back drastically modified. The client has rewritten it, introducing leading questions and biased scales. An accompanying letter indicates that the questionnaire must be sent out as revised. You do not believe that valid information can be gathered using the revised instrument.

   What action would you take?

9. A well-respected public figure is going to face trial on a charge of failing to report his part ownership of certain regulated companies while serving in government. The defense lawyers have asked you, as a market research specialist, to do a research study to determine the characteristics of people most likely to sympathize with the defendant and hence to vote for the acquittal. The defense lawyers have read newspaper accounts of how this approach has been used in a number of instances.

   What action would you take?

10. You are the market research director for a large chemical company. Recent research indicates that many customers of your company are misusing one of its principal products. There is no danger resulting from this misuse, though the customers are wasting money by using too much of the product at one time. You are shown the new advertising campaign by the advertising agency. The ads not only ignore this problem of misuse, but actually seem to encourage it.

    What action would you take?

PART NINE

Strategic Market Planning

Managers often don't devote enough attention to strategic market planning because they are too busy reacting to immediate market situations. This can lead to a long-term decline of the company's established market position and an inadequate development of profitable new opportunities.

At the highest level of the organization, strategic planning involves defining the corporate mission or purpose, setting objectives, and formulating strategy. However, a number of layers of strategy are necessary in a large company, each layer being progressively more detailed, to provide operational guidance for the next level of subordinate managers. At each level (business unit, product line, market, brand) the strategy must be coordinated with those above and below. Critical to the success of a strategy is the marketing plan, which summarizes the strategy and its development as well as lays the framework for its implementation.

Strategic market planning integrates all elements of marketing. Consequently, this section serves not only to introduce new material but also to review many of the concepts discussed throughout this book.

Marketing's concern ranges from the overall design of strategy to the implementation of a myriad of programs. Even superb execution cannot save a misdirected strategy; only good execution can transform a sound strategy from plans on paper to reality. Marketing success depends on all elements of a plan working together to accomplish the organization's goals.

THE STRATEGIC PLANNING PROCESS

Mission

Fundamental to a firm's overall strategy is a definition of its mission or purpose, a basic statement of what the organization seeks to do in the long term, and the rationale for its existence. A company's mission is determined by answering such simple questions as "What business are we in?" "Who are our customers?" and "What value do we provide to our customers?" Profit making, often said to be every firm's goal, is not so much the purpose of a company, but the outcome that results from the successful fulfillment of the company's mission.

Probably the most important test for a good mission is that it is both externally and internally oriented. Many organizations define themselves solely in product or technological terms, not in market terms. They suffer from "marketing myopia." For instance, many metal can manufacturers ran into difficulties because they defined themselves in just that way—not as being in the packaging business. They therefore did not take advantage of innovations in materials to meet changes in customer needs. Of course, in using a market definition, an organization must be careful not to move too far away from its resources and abilities—defining a metal can manufacturer as being in the packaging business does not necessarily mean that the company should be supplying paper bags to supermarkets.

Objectives and Goals

Once defined, the purpose should be translated into a set of goals or objectives that indicate the specific accomplishments to be attained in fulfilling that purpose. Objectives, which should be based on a realistic assessment of what can be done, can have varying time horizons, degrees of interrelatedness, and levels of priority. However, too many goals for a manager result in an effort that is not well focused. The manager becomes the proverbial "Jack of all trades, master of none." Without a few major, specific, measurable objectives, strategy becomes merely a statement of good intentions. Efficient achievement of objectives within the available resources is the key criterion of strategic choice.

Strategy

If the objectives specify *what* is to be accomplished, the strategy specifies *how*. Strategic decisions include both where to commit resources and how to use the resources, once committed.

There are a number of analytic tools available that can help management formulate strategy. A *product-market growth matrix* (see *Exhibit 1*) categorizes opportunities for growth in terms of the business's current products (or technologies) and markets. A growth oriented company can then look for expansion through *market penetration* (increased usage of current products by current market segments), *product development* (adding new products that appeal to current markets), *market development* (offering existing products to new markets), or *diversification* (growth strategies encompassing both new markets and new products). In addition, some growth opportunities arise from forward integration (for example, by buying out wholesalers or retailers) or from

EXHIBIT 1
PRODUCT-MARKET GROWTH MATRIX

Growth through backward integration
(supplier systems)

	Current products	New products
Current markets	Market penetration	Product development
New markets	Market development	Diversification

Growth through forward integration
(distribution systems)

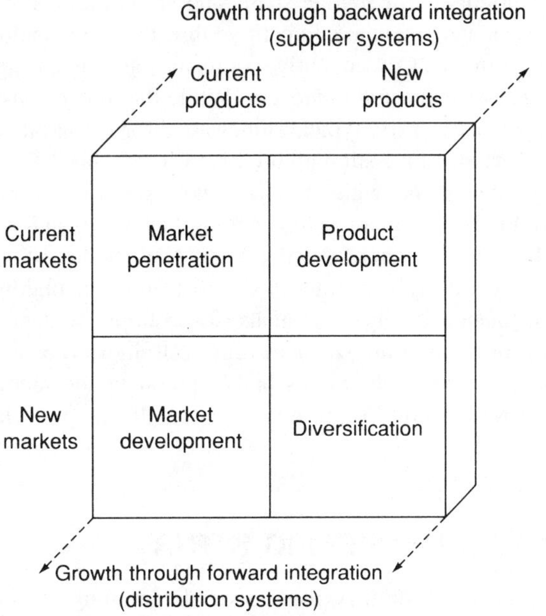

backward integration (for example, by taking over suppliers, as some depart-ment stores have done with clothing manufacturers). When considering any growth strategy, even one based on diversification, management should look for attractive opportunities that use at least some of the firm's strengths and have some link to current activities. The product-market growth matrix helps a firm to identify which opportunities rely primarily on its strengths in market-ing and which on its strengths in technology or other areas. Further analysis can then be done to determine the specific abilities required to compete successfully in the attractive growth opportunities that were identified.

Portfolio management can also be a useful aid to making strategic resource allocation decisions. In *portfolio analysis,* a division or strategic business unit is usually evaluated along two dimensions: the overall attractiveness of the market and the unit's competitive strength in the market. Portfolio analysis helps in highlighting critical strategic issues and in deciding whether to invest, maintain, or withdraw resources from a unit.

One popular approach to portfolio management, the *growth/share matrix,* uses growth to represent market attractiveness and share to represent competi-tive strength. While these two dimensions have the advantage of concreteness and are readily quantifiable, provided that relevant markets can be properly defined and future growth rates can be well estimated, the dimensions of growth and share may not be sufficiently comprehensive for decision making. For example, current market share may not be a good indicator of a company's ability to increase its future market share, and growth leaves untouched such factors as present and potential competitive threats and technological, regulatory, and social trends. Consequently, companies are increasingly turning to the use of *multifactor portfolio matrices.* While the dimensions underlying a firm's portfolio matrix vary, typical dimensions for (1) attractiveness of the market and (2) competitive strength are given in *Exhibit 2.*

Portfolio models are not without their weaknesses. They do not allow a full consideration of the interrelationships among businesses and concentrate on current products versus future development. Nevertheless, they provide an overview of a company's various businesses and can highlight areas for resource investment and help to set goals (for example, to generate money in the short term or to build market share) for each division or unit. Combined with a manager's knowledge of his or her products and markets, portfolio models can provide useful insight into resource allocation decisions.

COMPETITIVE MARKETING STRATEGY

Competitive marketing strategy focuses on determining the critical factors necessary for success in the chosen markets and determining the means by which to compete. Once the critical success factors are identified, management must objectively evaluate its company's strengths and weaknesses in meeting those requirements as compared to those of present and potential competitors. True strength is usually based on accumulated experience and consistent success; occasional flashes of brilliance are rarely dependable in the long run.

Strategies can be broadly summarized as being the overall *low cost producer* and/or establishing a *differential competitive position* (through product or other forms of differentiation, and market segment specialization, or both). However, the next questions to ask are, "How is cost leadership to be attained?" and "What are the bases for a differentiation or segmentation strategy?" These in turn lead to a long list of alternatives. Ultimately, strategy formulation is a creative process; no analyst can really claim to offer a complete list of strategy types.

The proposed strategies must be evaluated on such criteria as:

- Direct financial analysis
- Ability to meet the objectives set
- External and internal consistency
- Degree of risk undertaken and robustness of the strategy in the light of market and environmental uncertainty

One reason strategic choice is difficult is that seldom does one alternative uniformly exceed the others on all criteria.

EXHIBIT 2
MULTIFACTOR PORTFOLIO MATRIX WITH TYPICAL DIMENSIONS

ATTRACTIVENESS OF MARKET

		High	Medium	Low
COMPETITIVE STRENGTH	High	I	I	M
	Medium	I	M	W
	Low	M	W	W

I = Invest or build commitment
M = Maintain or hold position
W = Withdraw resources

Dimensions of a Multifactor Portfolio Matrix

Attractiveness of the market
1. What is the industry sales growth rate?
2. How large is the market?
3. Are industry sales susceptible to cyclical, seasonal, or other fluctuations?
4. What is the competitive stucture of the industry?
5. What is the profitability of the industry?
6. Does extensive government regulation constrain actions or pose uncertainties?
7. How powerful are suppliers?
8. How powerful are buyers?
9. What is the industry's technological status?
10. What environmental, social, etc., trends have an impact on the industry?

Competitive strength
1. How strong is our market share? What is our competitive position?
2. What trends are there in market share?
3. How are we perceived by customers?
4. Are our distributors well established and supportive?
5. Do we have reliable suppliers?
6. Does our cost structure enable us to compete profitably?
7. Are our production facilities modern and efficient?
8. Do we have the technology required for innovation and product development?
9. Do we have the managerial skills needed to compete?
10. What environmental, social, etc., factors have an impact on our firm and its marketing position?

DEVELOPING A MARKETING PLAN

The marketing plan is a systematic way of structuring an analysis of a market, an organization's position in that market, and a program for future marketing activities. The elements of a plan are interrelated, so that its development may involve cycling through its components several times before satisfactory results are achieved. The following discussion briefly highlights selected portions of the marketing plan format suggested in *Exhibit 3*. In addition to providing an integrated format for marketing decision making, the discussion of the marketing plan provides a means to review topics discussed earlier in the book.

Situation Analysis

The situation analysis examines the relevant external and internal environments. The situation analysis includes a historical summary, an evaluation of previous marketing efforts, an analysis of the present situation, and an assessment of future trends.

Identifying and assessing threats and opportunities is the purpose of a situation analysis. A forecast of year-end position, which assumes that present conditions will continue, can be constructed based on the situation analysis. This momentum forecast is then compared with the desired year-end position, and with the gaps between the forecast and the desired position identified.

Marketing Strategy

As discussed earlier, strategy specifies the means by which the marketing goals are to be achieved. It is the core of the marketing plan.

Positioning is a fundamental statement of what the organization and its products represent to chosen market segments. In brief, the first step in positioning is defining the target segments. Next is setting the organization's competitive stance, which is the degree to which its products will be similar or different in each of the target segments. Depending on the segment and the competition, the most profitable competitive stance can vary considerably. The final step in positioning is to establish the usage incentive—that is, the primary benefits to be offered to current and potential users in each segment. The positioning strategy is vital not only for reaching consumers; it also provides a focus for management efforts and ultimately channels the efforts of the entire marketing organization.

The *marketing mix* is a convenient way of summarizing a set of activities that support the marketing goals of the organization. Given the target market and competitive stance, the manager must ensure that the products offered will serve customer needs, the price is appropriate, the products are distributed so that consumers in the target segments can easily purchase them, and communication with the target segment is efficient and effective.

Because the marketing mix activities are the most visible, many people think that that's all there is to marketing. In fact, some people think advertising

EXHIBIT 3
MARKETING PLAN FORMAT—EXECUTIVE SUMMARY

Situation analysis (Where are we now?)
  External
    Environment (political, regulatory, economic, social, technical, and other relevant areas)
    Consumers and markets
    Employees
    Suppliers and distributors
    Competition
  Internal
    Objectives
    Strengths and weaknesses
  Problems and opportunities
    Momentum forecast
    Gap identification
Marketing program goals (Where do we want to go?)
Marketing strategies (How are we going to get there?)
  Positioning
    Target segments
    Competitive stance
    Usage incentive
  Marketing mix
    Product
    Price
    Distribution
    Marketing communication: advertising, personal selling, promotion, etc.
  Contingency strategies
Marketing budget (How much do we need and where should we allocate it?)
  Resources (money, people, time)
  Amount and allocation
Marketing action plan (What do we need to do?)
  Detailed breakdown of activities required
  Responsibility by name
  Activity schedule in milestone format
  Tangible and intangible results expected from each activity
Monitoring system (Are we performing?)

is synonymous with marketing. On the contrary, advertising is only one of several communication activities, which are themselves only one element in the marketing mix, and the marketing mix is only one part of marketing.

A marketing plan should include *contingency strategies*. Since it is difficult to predict the future precisely, the manager should anticipate and be prepared for major surprises. Having well thought out, timely contingency strategies can provide a competitive advantage especially in a crisis situation.

Marketing Budget

For each element in the plan, the resources required to operate at different levels and the results at these different levels should be determined and evaluated. Trade-offs must often be made and interrelationships among marketing elements need to be considered.

Marketing Action Plan

The marketing action plan is a detailed breakdown of the activities necessary to achieve each of the goals. Planning without implementation is worth little; much effort in planning is wasted because of inadequate execution, as we discuss more fully in the next section.

Monitoring Systems

The marketing plan and its action implications serve as the basis for a firm's monitoring system. Significant deviations from the marketing plan and unanticipated events may require management to make adjustments to the original plan or substitute a contingency strategy.

PLANNING FOR QUALITY

There's growing recognition that product quality is a key determinant of an organization's success in the marketplace. To the extent that products succeed or fail in the market, based upon customer-based evaluation criteria, quality must reflect customer needs, preferences, and perceptions. An often used definition of quality is "consistently meeting customers' expectations." Since quality requires attention to detail, research and planning are needed to ensure that quality objectives are met and maintained.

Whether one is marketing goods or services, the perception of quality applies to all aspects of a firm's interactions with its customers, including activities undertaken by designated intermediaries such as retailers and authorized service agencies. Customers may base their perception of quality upon many elements of the augmented product, not just the core product.

Research into quality has identified eight dimensions that are useful as a framework for both analysis and strategic planning.[1]

- *Performance* relates to the primary operating characteristics of the product. For a car or airline service, these might be speed, safety, and comfort.
- *Features* can be described as the "bells and whistles" of products. The distinction between these and performance elements has to do with both their centrality to the product's function and their salience to the user—which may vary on a segment by segment basis.
- *Reliability* reflects the probability that a service or manufactured product will malfunction or fail within a specified period of time (or number of uses).

[1]David A. Garvin, *Managing Quality.* New York. The Free Press, 1988.

- *Conformance* is concerned with the product's ability to meet specifications. It goes beyond reliability to include physical dimensions such as color and taste and technical elements such as ease of operation. Relevant service elements include consistency in the attitudes and behavior of service personnel, the speed with which services are executed, and so forth.
- *Durability* is a measure of how long a product continues to provide value to the customer before it wears out physically, becomes technically obsolete, or passes out of fashion. Durability can also be applied to certain services in terms of how long the benefits of the service last.
- *Serviceability* concerns the speed, competence, courtesy, and ease of access associated with supplementary service elements such as placing orders and reservations, obtaining repairs, receiving consultation or advice, and getting problems resolved.
- *Aesthetics* is a highly subjective dimension of quality, and concerns the product's appeal to any or all of the user's five senses. Examples of visual aesthetics include the appearance of physical products and their packaging, the architecture and furnishings of a service facility, and the clothing worn by service employees. Quietness or pleasant sounds, feel, taste, and smell are also important for evaluating many goods and services.
- *Perceived quality* represents associations such as the reputation of the producer (and perhaps that of the intermediary as well) and the brand name. Advertising can generate positive images that create or reinforce perceptions of quality. A high price may also signal higher quality.

These quality dimensions provide a useful checklist when developing a strategic marketing plan. Every element of the marketing mix must be examined for its ability to contribute to quality. Consistency across the elements of the mix is essential, since each quality dimension should reinforce the others.

Market research will be needed up front to determine customer needs, wants, and expectations. Insights from this research must then be translated into product specifications for all facets of the augmented product, including elements such as packaging, distribution systems, and both presale and aftersale services. Execution must conform to these specifications so that the product performs in accordance with the customer's expectations. To ensure that these expectations are realistic, advertising and personal selling must avoid the trap of overstating product performance, features, or serviceability. Finally, planners must identify distributors and other intermediaries capable of providing the level of service required by customers for this product at the recommended price.

SUMMARY

Strategy at all levels of the organization is the means of guiding management action and resource allocation. It is rooted in a clearly articulated mission and a well-defined set of objectives. For long-run profitability, planning is needed to help the organization overcome the vagaries of the immediate environment and do more than just react to competitive initiatives. A well-conceived, creative marketing plan that recognizes the capabilities and limitations of the organization and environmental threats and opportunities is a critical tool for successful marketing management.

Often organizations seem not to be marketing-oriented at all. Sometimes, this is an illusion—the marketers and the production people just aren't speaking the same language. In this case, the marketing manager has to communicate in terms that are meaningful—and not threatening—to other areas in the firm. Sometimes, however, the organization just is not marketing-oriented. The marketer's task in this case is to market marketing to his or her colleagues.

Air BP: Aviation Service Centers

Christopher H. Lovelock

Graham Evans finished reading the last memo, returned it to the file, and shook his head. "How did we get ourselves into this pickle?" he asked himself. Based not far from London's Heathrow Airport, Evans was the newly appointed strategic planning manager for Air BP—the aviation fuel operations of British Petroleum. He had just spent several hours reading through a series of memos dating back five years to June 1986, when Air BP had taken its first steps toward developing a chain of company-owned business aviation service centers around the world. The tone of the memos, originally enthusiastic and optimistic, had become steadily more cautious over the years as both progress and setbacks were recorded.

Aviation service centers, commonly known in the industry by the American term of FBOs (fixed-base operations), were airport-based fueling, maintenance, and terminal service facilities for corporate aircraft, although not all FBOs provided all services. One BP executive had described FBOs as "truckstops for executive jets." In the mid-1980s, the outlook for

continued increases in the demand for jet fuel for such aircraft had seemed encouraging. However, competition from other oil companies was stiff; jet fuel itself was a commodity. BP wanted to defend market share and increase its margins. Investing in FBOs that provided added-value services had seemed an attractive strategy.

Pursuing this strategy, Air BP had made significant investments on three continents, creating FBOs at Cleveland and Atlanta in the USA, at Melbourne (Australia), at Cologne (Germany), and at two of Britain's major airports, London-Heathrow and London-Stansted. Other locations under review in Europe included Paris-Le Bourget, Rome, and Budapest. But by June 1991 the mixed results achieved to date had led the CEO of Air BP to request a thorough review. "Should we continue our global strategy of spending $80 million to purchase FBOs in various parts of the world or come up with a different approach?" he had asked Evans.[1] "I find myself wonder-

---

---

[1] Currency exchange rates varied widely between 1986–91; for instance, the value of the US dollar against the British pound ranged from US$ = £0.51 to £0.70. For simplicity, financial data will be reported first in the currency in which they were originally stated, and then converted to US dollars at the following exchange rates: US$1.00 = £0.57 = Aus$1.33 = DM1.77.

449

ing whether there may be other, better ways to achieve our goals!"

CORPORATE AVIATION

Air traffic comprised commercial, general, and military aviation. Commercial traffic involved scheduled passenger airlines, airfreight, and certain charter operations. General aviation, by contrast, consisted of privately owned aircraft flying for business or recreational purposes, together with small charters and air taxi operations.

The most important segment of the general aviation fleet consisted of aircraft owned by corporations (or wealthy individuals) and used for business travel. By 1991, there were almost 6,900 jets and some 8,000 turboprops in corporate service around the world. Two-thirds of corporate aircraft were based in the United States; other key regions included Europe and South America. There seemed to be little relationship between national wealth and executive jet ownership on a country-by-country basis, with Japan having a surprisingly small number (refer to *Exhibit 1*).

EXHIBIT 1   CORPORATE AIRCRAFT IN USE AROUND THE WORLD, 1991

	Jets	Turbo-props	Total		Jets	Turbo-props	Total
Africa				Europe			
Libya	7	14	21	Austria	39	31	60
Morocco	9	13	22	Belgium	13	19	32
Nigeria	25	19	44	Denmark	20	33	53
South Africa	59	129	188	Finland	13	15	28
All other	72	117	189	France	179	292	471
Total	172	292	464	Germany	91	182	273
Asia				Italy	181	75	256
India	3	31	34	Netherlands	18	23	41
Indonesia	16	26	42	Norway	9	22	31
Iran	9	20	29	Spain	38	43	81
Japan	18	56	74	Sweden	31	56	87
Philippines	9	48	57	Switzerland	87	52	139
Saudi Arabia	76	9	85	United Kingdom	188	112	278
All other	105	42	147	Yugoslavia	15	7	22
Total	236	232	488	All other	45	26	71
Australia and Oceania				Total	945	978	1,923
Australia	84	148	232	North America and Caribbean			
All other	7	18	25	Bermuda	20	2	22
Total	91	166	257	Canada	182	334	516
Central and South America				Mexico	286	175	461
Argentina	24	76	100	United States	4,591	5,052	9,643
Brazil	225	230	455	All other	17	23	40
Colombia	8	188	196	Total	5,096	5,586	10,682
Peru	9	19	28	World total	6,882	8,035	14,917
Venezuela	52	187	239				
All other	16	52	68				
Total	334	752	1,086				

Note: Figures are shown for individual countries only when total corporate aircraft in use amount to 20 or more.
Source: Reorganized from information in *Flight International*, May 29–June 4, 1991, p. 54.

For much of the 1980s, the number of corporate aircraft had grown at an annual rate of around 3%. Growth was higher outside the United States, which had become a fairly mature market. Worldwide, corporate aircraft consumed over 5 million tonnes (1.65 billion US gallons) of jet fuel each year.[2]

Executive jets were expensive to own and operate. Purchase prices ranged from $2 million for a Learjet which could fly six people up to 3,000 km (1,900 miles) to $24 million for a 19-seat Gulfstream IV capable of flying Chicago to Paris nonstop. But few aircraft were capable of transoceanic flight. Turboprops were slower than jets and often had less range, but were also cheaper. Companies needing more seat capacity sometimes purchased used airliners, which they refitted to suit their needs.

A small executive jet had a fuel capacity of some 3,000 to 4,000 liters—double that of a twin-engined turboprop. By contrast, a Gulfstream IV could load over 16,000 liters of jet fuel. But even this volume paled by comparison to the fuel needs of a Boeing 747-400, which might load 140,000 liters for the 13-hour flight from Singapore to London.

The major rationale for purchasing a corporate aircraft was travel time savings over commercial airline services. Another key advantage was flexibility. Executives were freed from the constraints of airline schedules, did not have to change flights at intermediate airports, and could land at small airfields not served by passenger airlines. Other perceived benefits included security and secrecy.

The average jet flew only about 400 hours a year. Shareholders often criticized these aircraft as unjustified perks for top management. Still, more corporations were making seats available to any employee whose need to get somewhere quickly was important to the firm, provided that the journey could not be completed more efficiently by other means. Pilots of

corporate aircraft were responsible for more than just flying—economic pressures to cut costs meant that they had to be good business managers, too, and seek operating economies without compromising safety.

AIRCRAFT SERVICING NEEDS

Corporate aircraft destinations ranged from major international airports—where there was a trend to restrict small corporate aircraft—to unpaved airfields in remote locations. Rugged turboprops, such as the Twin Otter, could land on short, rough runways that would be unsuitable for executive jets. General aviation airports received no commercial airlines—their focus was on corporate transports (including chartered air taxis) and recreational flying. At commercial airports, corporate aircraft were usually directed to areas reserved for general aviation.

When flying away from home, the pilot would call ahead to arrange ground services. Speed was of the essence for busy corporate executives; to save time they sometimes even held business meetings in a private lounge at the airport before departing on the next stage of their journey. While waiting, the aircraft might need refueling and cleaning, and to be kept in a secure location. Occasionally, diagnostic tests or emergency maintenance was required, but most aircraft maintenance was undertaken on a scheduled, preventive basis at the home base. Food and beverages might be requested for the upcoming flight. Pilots—who often complained that they spent more time waiting at airports than actually flying—might want a quiet space to plan the next flight segment or attend to management issues. Access to a fax machine, telephones, weather forecasts, and air traffic control briefings was also important.

At small airfields, a pilot might find just a handling agent who could arrange for fueling and find independent suppliers for other services. But at airports where several aircraft had their home base, there was often a fixed-based operation (FBO) with a small terminal and hangar offering storage, maintenance, avionics (aviation electronics), and other services. Some American airports were served by several FBOs, and the pilot would select on the basis of the

---

[2]Both jets and turboprops consumed jet fuel (kerosine). Piston-engined aircraft used avgas, a high-octane leaded petrol (gasoline). Jet fuel was sold in liters or US gallons (usg), but ex-refinery prices tended to be quoted worldwide in US dollars per tonne. Conversion: 1 usg = 0.8 imperial gallons = 3.78 liters; 1 (metric) tonne = 1,250 liters.

range and level of services offered, the quality of facilities, and which oil company credit cards were accepted. Price cutting was not generally used as a competitive tool by FBOs. However, the European and American markets took very different approaches to pricing fuel and other services.

FBOs in Europe

Europe had some 200 commercial airports and 200 general aviation fields accessible to corporate jets. In total, there were about 120 FBOs (often referred to as aviation service centers), of which only 12 ran large full-service operations. About 30 FBOs were Air BP branded. Some competition came from handling agents who could coordinate delivery of various services that they did not actually provide themselves. Commercial airlines sometimes offered handling services for corporate aircraft, as well as use of terminal lounges and other facilities for passengers and crew.

Once an oil company had acquired the right to sell fuel at an airport served by commercial airlines, it could sell directly to any type of customer. However, at small airfields, a single FBO or fueling service generally enjoyed a monopoly. European retail margins on fuel sales to corporate aircraft were the equivalent of $0.15 per US gallon (as compared with $0.02 for airline fuel sales). FBOs in Europe billed pilots on an itemized basis for hangaring, cleaning, local transportation, use of office facilities, and other services.

FBOs in the United States

There were over 1,200 airports in the US accessible to corporate jets (plus many smaller airfields). And the nation accounted for more than 90% of the world's FBOs. Over 3,300 FBOs sold fuel (another 400 sold no fuel but provided other aviation-related activities). Some busy general aviation airports boasted three or four FBOs. However, price cutting had not traditionally been used as a competitive weapon.

The great majority of fuel-selling FBOs were individual businesses—often family owned—and many were said to be undercapitalized. Most FBOs, in fact, provided nothing but fueling services. Their physical facilities might be limited to a small office, plus underground storage tanks and a couple of fuel tankers. Annual revenues for a small American FBO ranged from $100,000 to $1,000,000. Only about 500 FBOs had revenues over $1 million, usually achieved by combining fuel sales with maintenance and other services. Of these, only 100 were large, full-service operations offering sophisticated maintenance and avionics services and achieving annual turnovers above $5 million.

Some 150 FBOs were part of a chain. During the second half of the 1980s, interest in purchasing FBOs by corporate buyers who wished to form chains had led to sharp increases in selling prices. By 1991, the principal chains were Page Avjet with 20 FBOs, Butler with 19, and AMR-Combs (a subsidiary of American Airlines) with 10.

About 2,200 FBOs were branded with the name and colors of a major oil company (refer to *Exhibit 2*). Other FBOs sold regional brands or were unbranded, purchasing from third-party resellers who bought jet fuel on the spot market. Oil companies provided various services, including credit cards and promotional support designed to enhance brand loyalty for their dealers. Most fuel contracts ran for one year at a time, and were normally renewed automatically. But a lower fuel price or the offer of extra services might encourage an FBO to change brands and switch to a different supplier. Fuel prices varied from one airport to another.

At most airports, FBOs were licensed only to sell to general aviation aircraft. But some operators augmented their income by acting as subcontractors to oil companies and refueling commercial aircraft with fuel drawn from oil company tanks. For this service, FBOs negotiated a fee ranging from $0.01 to $0.05 per gallon. When oil companies sold directly to commercial airlines, they obtained a margin of as little as $0.005 per gallon; when they sold at wholesale to FBOs their margin was typically $0.05–$0.10. American FBOs provided many services free of charge, including use of their parking aprons, hang-

EXHIBIT 2
NUMBER OF BRANDED FBOs CONTRACTED WITH
SPECIFIC OIL COMPANIES IN THE UNITED STATES,
1985 vs. 1990

Brand	1985	1990
Phillips	800	825
Exxon	400	340
Chevron	350	360
Texaco	300	315
Air BP (and predecessor brands)[1]	300	260
Shell[2]	275	50
Mobil[2]	125	45
Pride/Avfuel	50	155
Triton	—	200
Other brands	200	175
Unbranded	700	590
Total FBOs selling fuel in USA	3,500	3,315

[1]In 1985 Air BP sold primarily through predecessor brands such as Sohio, Gulf, and Boron; By 1990, most had been rebranded as Air BP.

[2]Shell and Mobil had made a strategic decision to withdraw from branded FBO outlets and were selling their franchises to minor brands such as Pride/Avfuel and Triton.

ars, and terminal facilities. Larger FBOs went to great lengths to appeal to pilots, offering such extras as aircraft cleaning, weather briefings, and use of conference rooms and showers free of charge in the hope of obtaining their fuel business. The FBO added a margin of $0.80 to $1.00 per gallon (plus relevant taxes) to the wholesale price to cover the cost of all these other services. Separate charges were made for maintenance work, catering, and long-distance phone calls or faxes.

BRITISH PETROLEUM COMPANY

BP was the third largest oil company in the world (after Royal Dutch Shell and Exxon), conducting business in 70 countries on six continents. On a 1990 turnover of £33 billion ($58 billion), BP achieved pretax profits of £2.8 billion. It had four businesses: exploration, oil, chemicals, and nutrition. BP Exploration was responsible for upstream activities, including oil and gas production. About one-third of its oil came from the North Sea and 55% from the US, chiefly Alaska.

With a turnover of over £20 billion, BP Oil was responsible for activities in the downstream oil sector. It operated five refineries in Europe, five in the US, two in Australia, and one in Singapore, plus a large shipping fleet. BP sold branded oil products and services in over 50 countries. The brand was strongly represented in Europe, Australasia, parts of Africa and Southeast Asia. In the United States, where BP had purchased the Standard Oil Company of Ohio (the legendary company founded by John D. Rockefeller) and renamed it BP America in 1987, building awareness of the new brand name was a major objective. However, the company had almost no presence in Canada.

Key markets for fuel and lubricants included road vehicles, ships, and aircraft. BP boasted almost 20,000 retail service stations worldwide, of which 38% were located in the US, 45% in Europe, and 10% in Australia/Asia. Some were company owned; others were operated by independent franchisees. The goal was to focus on large, strategically sited stations offering 24-hour self-service fuel plus an array of other motorist services, including (at some sites) a car wash and a convenience store. All stations were being "reimaged" to feature a new design treatment using BP green with yellow lettering. In 1990 the company had begun rebranding its US stations from Sohio and Gulf (and other names) to feature the distinctive BP shield.

To better serve the road freight industry, BP Oil was developing a network of company-owned BP Truckstops. These offered fast refueling, full maintenance and repair services, a shop, and facilities where drivers could eat, relax, and shower. There were video games and TV, a self-service laundry, telephones, and fax. Since fuel was priced competitively to encourage drivers to stop, profitability was very dependent on achieving good sales of other services. BP had opened 14 purpose-built truckstops in Europe and would soon have 10 in Australia. It operated 43 company-owned sites in the US under the name Truckstops of America. More were planned.

As a division of BP Oil, Air BP supplied fuel and services to some 400 airline customers at over 600 locations worldwide, as well as to corporate aircraft and to individuals who flew small aircraft for pleasure. Air BP's annual turnover was around £1.4 billion ($2.5 billion) and it sold some 13 billion liters (3.5 billion usg) of aviation fuel worldwide. Over 95% of this total was jet fuel.

Aviation fuel was first shipped from BP's refineries to its own terminals, where two distribution alternatives presented themselves. One was for Air BP to transport the fuel to its own airport-based tank farms, from where the company could transport it to aircraft parking bays and pump it directly "into plane." A variant of this strategy was to subcontract the actual into-plane activity to independent intermediaries (such as FBO operators) who would draw fuel as needed from the Air BP tank farm. A second alternative was to sell the fuel wholesale to FBOs and other airport-based dealers, who then stored it in their own underground tanks for resale under the Air BP brand name to retail customers. Any refined fuel not sold through BP's own outlets was sold unbranded to traders (jobbers) at currently prevailing prices. Competition came from many other oil companies, notably Exxon (Esso in some countries), Shell, Mobil, Texaco/Caltex, Chevron (in the US), and Total (especially in Europe).

Air BP and the FBO Industry

Traditionally, large oil companies had not been especially interested in selling fuel to general aviation customers. An Air BP executive explained why:

During the 1970s, the aviation business was growing so quickly—particularly international aviation—that we thought we'd have our arms full just selling to the major airlines. And we'd organized our assets around this business. At a time when everyone was going from 707s to 747s, everything kept getting bigger.

The small customer on an airfield was a nuisance. There was no schedule. We didn't know when they were coming in or when they were leaving. Our operations were geared around the schedules of international airlines. Our contracts said we had to meet them on time and turn them around in, say, 45 minutes. Our whole staffing and equipment were designed to meet that requirement. Small customers were simply served as and when we had the availability. At an

airport like Heathrow, where small aircraft were based at the far side of the field, it could be four to five hours before we got a tanker over there. General aviation represented about 10% of all aircraft movements there and less than ½% of fuel sales.

Evolution of a European FBO Strategy

Following the recession of 1980–81, airlines became desperate to get fuel prices down. Finding its margins squeezed, Air BP started to look more closely at small customers who were paying substantially higher prices for the same fuel. Around 1983, Field Aviation Ltd., owner of the Executive Jet Centre, the large FBO at Heathrow, started to complain about the slow fueling service provided by BP and other oil companies. An Air BP executive recalled his company's response:

We said to Field's, "If you could deliver all your customers to us, we would be willing to base a vehicle over at your facilities." Our interest was sharpened by concern that a competitor, Total, might be about to make similar overtures. Fortunately, Field's agreed to work with us and so we developed a relationship. Not only was the margin attractive, but now we had the volume to justify dedicating a vehicle to their operation.

By the mid-1980s, the general aviation market in the United Kingdom accounted for only 7% of Air BP's British sales but close to a third of its profits. In mid-1986, Air BP and Field's (which was a subsidiary of a large holding company) agreed to form a 50-50 joint venture called Field Aviation Enterprises Ltd. (FAEL) to develop an international chain of FBOs. BP would supply experience in fueling and in international operations and Field's would contribute its operational experience and personnel. The flagship of the new chain would be Field's Executive Jet Centre, described as one of the best FBOs in Europe. Air BP agreed to pay £1 million ($1.7 million) for its 50% share in FAEL, projecting an internal rate of return of 16.9% on its investment.

The Executive Jet Centre (EJC) was close to Heathrow's new Terminal 4 complex. It comprised offices, a reception area and lounges, a large modern hangar, and a start-of-the-art maintenance facility.

FAEL rented these facilities, constructed in 1983 at a cost of £4.5 million ($7.5 million). The EJC had 24 "resident" aircraft—mostly large and medium-sized jets—whose owners paid a fixed annual fee that covered hangaring, a certain level of maintenance, and various other services. Fuel was not included. Pilots of visiting aircraft paid for services as they were consumed. The EJC's main competition came from British Airways, which offered handling services and terminal facilities for corporate aircraft, passengers, and crew.

Heathrow was vulnerable to a possible future ban on corporate aircraft as commercial airline traffic continued to build. The government had already designated Stansted, north of London, as the capital's long-term general aviation airport, so FAEL decided to develop a second FBO at Stansted, where Air BP already had a fueling operation. In August 1987, it purchased an existing FBO at this airport; Air BP's 50% investment amounted to £500,000 ($850,000).

FAEL wanted to create a chain of five FBOs to serve Europe and the Middle East. After reviewing corporate air travel patterns, Air BP planners identified several key sites for investigation, including Paris, Brussels, Geneva, Milan, and Madrid. But further study revealed that Jet Aviation, which operated 10 FBOs in Europe and the US, had a dominant position at both the Geneva and Zurich airports, which eliminated Switzerland. The idea of developing an FBO at Abu Dhabi in the Persian Gulf was dropped when research showed that most corporate jet owners from that region liked to have their aircraft serviced on their frequent visits to Europe.

Then Germany was suggested. Air BP already had a large contract with the German national carrier, Lufthansa. It had also developed contracts to supply fuel to a number of general aviation airports. Among the larger airports where BP had a fueling service was Cologne (Köln), which also served Bonn. Learning that the entrepreneur who ran the FBO at Cologne was looking for a buyer and that Total had expressed interest, BP decided that it had to protect its fuel sales there and so made an offer. A price was agreed and for an investment of DM 2.9 million ($1.6 million), FAEL took over the Cologne FBO in early 1988.

Much of the business at Cologne involved service to visiting aircraft. There was no resident corporate fleet. Most corporate jets in Germany were based in the big industrial cities like Frankfurt and Dusseldorf. But the FBO's new managing director soon came up with a promising opportunity. UPS (United Parcel Service), the large American package delivery firm, was busy expanding its international services and was seeking both a base and a contractor to run a European airfreight operation on its behalf. Negotiations were initiated, went well, and FAEL-Cologne obtained not just a resident fleet but the challenge of running a small freight airline as well.

Activities in the United States

Through its purchase of Standard Oil (Sohio), BP could trace its involvement in FBO activities back to 1955, when Sohio obtained an operating lease at the Cleveland Hopkins Airport, built an FBO, and leased it to an independent dealer. In 1971, the dealer experienced financial problems and Sohio decided to run this FBO with its own employees. The facilities were leased from the airport, so Sohio's investment was mainly in vehicles. This model of an oil company owning an FBO was unique at that time and it enjoyed substantial sales from refueling commercial aircraft. Sohio decided to focus on this "into-plane" business, which provided a margin of $0.05–$0.15 per gallon. It discouraged maintenance and eventually decertified the mechanics, and eliminated high-service activities for executive jets. The other FBOs at Hopkins chose to concentrate on the general aviation business and did not aggressively pursue the commercial into-plane business.

The Cleveland operation proved very profitable, consistently earning half a million dollars a year. A number of BP executives became familiar with the Hopkins FBO, since Cleveland was the headquarters city for Standard Oil and its successor, BP America. In 1987, James E. Timmons, whose previous assignment had included management of the Hopkins facility, was transferred to Texas as manager of general aviation at Air BP's head office in Houston.

At this time, one of Air BP's largest west coast customers was Chuckair, a profitable, family-owned business. It operated FBOs at two mid-sized California airports, both widely used by executive jets. At the busy San Felipe airport, Chuckair enjoyed a monopoly as the only FBO on the field.[3] Its general aviation fuel sales at San Felipe totaled $6 million a year; other activities, including maintenance, a restaurant, and various ground services, yielded a further $4.2 million. When the owner's son took over the business, he proposed that Chuckair and Air BP form a joint venture to operate two new FBOs; one involved building a new facility at an airfield in Nevada, the other a chance to buy an existing FBO at a big airport in Arizona.

Attracted by the opportunity to share in the large retail margins, BP agreed in June 1987 to a 50–50 joint venture and to put in its share of the investment, estimated at $2 million. Plans for development of the two new FBOs went ahead, but soon Chuckair confessed that it was having trouble coming up with its full share of the money: the banks questioned its ability to meet principal repayments and interest out of projected income. When Chuckair fell heavily behind in payments to BP for fuel purchases, Air BP decided to sell out its share, dissolve the partnership, and avoid future joint ventures in the U.S. But it remained interested in operating new FBOs.

CREATING A GLOBAL STRATEGY

With interest in FBO acquisitions building on both sides of the Atlantic, the suggestion was made that Air BP should be thinking globally. Based upon the experience of FAEL-Heathrow and knowledge of the finances of selected American FBOs, such as Chuckair's operation in San Felipe, the business development group in London drew up a proposal for presentation to Air BP's Executive Committee. This called for a total investment over five years of $80 million to develop fifteen new sites: $50 million would be allocated to the US, and another $30 million for four in Europe and two in Australia, where BP had a very strong presence. The base case financial

analysis projected an internal rate of return of 18%. In November 1988, the plan was approved, and $13 million allocated for capital expenditures in 1989.

From a worldwide perspective, Air BP's strategy was to establish an international network of FBOs with a strong image of quality fuel and service. Specific goals were to secure BP's market position at existing locations, to expand into high-volume/high-growth locations, and to erect entry barriers. But there were also different emphases on different continents. In the US, the priority was to gain access to the large retail margins available, instead of just selling at wholesale. In Europe and Australia, it was to secure Air BP's retail market share at current retail margins.

In its search to add value through better service, Air BP developed enhanced information systems to help FBOs receive faster payment on credit card sales. But the company recognized that this innovation would be relatively easy for competitors to copy. Looking to the future, Air BP hoped to develop systems to help corporate pilots improve flight planning and cost management.

Expansion in the United States

Since the American market for FBOs was close to saturation, Air BP saw little opportunity to build a new FBO chain from scratch in the United States. So the Houston office set to work looking at possible acquisitions. Jim Timmons and his staff identified several key selection criteria.

Critical success factors for an FBO were that it should be conveniently located on the airfield, with a site lease of at least 15 years, have annual retail fuel sales of more than 1 million gallons, and good facilities. To avoid excessive competition, BP would not invest at airports with more than three FBOs. Timmons categorized FBO activities into three types: (1) mostly fuel with very limited maintenance services; (2) a full-service FBO deriving 25–50% of its revenues from maintenance and avionics; and (3) FBOs where maintenance and avionics accounted for over 50% of the revenues. The intent was to purchase a mix of all three types with an emphasis on Type 1.

The company came close to purchasing an FBO

---

[3]Chuckair and San Felipe are both disguised names.

at John Wayne Airport in Orange County, south of Los Angeles. The business included a charter airline, thus guaranteeing sufficient maintenance business. But Air BP had to withdraw when it could not get around the federal regulation that prohibited a non-American company from owning more than 25% of an American-certified charter operation.

Then Timmons found a very attractive new FBO for sale at the Peachtree-DeKalb airport (PDK) in Atlanta. It was one of three FBOs at this site. PDK served as an official reliever airport to attract general aviation customers away from Atlanta's Hartsfield International Airport. The facility comprised a recently built two-story terminal with 12,000 square feet (1,150 m²) of floor space offering lounges, conference rooms, office space, flight planning, weather service, and a canteen. Its most distinctive feature was a huge exterior canopy with room below for two executive jets to park out of the sun or rain. Other elements included an executive hangar and well-equipped maintenance and avionics departments capable of a wide variety of projects.

BP made an offer, hoping for quick agreement, but because of legal and financial problems faced by the seller, the deal (for $5.2 million) was not struck until April 1990. Timmons believed that the delay had hurt business, because some customers had lost confidence in the future of this operation and taken their business to other FBOs. He retained the highly regarded staff, rebranded the facility from Texaco to Air BP, and began an aggressive promotional effort, emphasizing the quality of both the physical facility and its services (refer to *Exhibit 3*).

The Atlanta FBO had won much favorable publicity for Air BP in the US, including awards from *Aviation International News* and *Professional Pilot* magazines for superior performance as evaluated by corporate pilots. A much repeated story told of a corporation that switched its business to Air BP after its chairman, soaked to the skin while running from his jet to a competing FBO in a downpour, had angrily told his captain to park under the Air BP canopy on future occasions. But despite significant marketing activities and effective cost control, the facility made a small loss during 1990.

In contrast, the Cleveland FBO continued to be profitable, netting $400,000 a year, primarily from commercial into-plane fueling. Almost two-thirds of Air BP's business came from a refueling contract with Continental Airlines, which used Cleveland as one of its hubs.

Entry into Australia

Although a much smaller market than either the US or Europe, Australia was seen as having significant potential. The distance between cities was considerable, business activity was expanding, and the number of aircraft was growing.

The nation had 54 airports capable of receiving executive jets. The 40 FBOs were somewhat smaller than their European counterparts, but 20 of them were Air BP branded. Only 5 FBOs were large, full-service operations, although a sixth was under construction in Melbourne.

The wholesale margin taken by oil companies on sales to FBOs was $0.04 per gallon, reflecting high transportation costs in this vast country. Oil companies obtained a $0.02 margin on sales to commercial airlines, while FBOs enjoyed a retail margin of $0.15 on jet fuel sales to corporate aircraft.

An FBO opportunity was soon identified at Melbourne's main airport, Tullamarine. Thirteen executive jets were based in Melbourne, most of them at the old municipal airport, which was threatened with closure.

Elders IXL, a major brewing corporation, had just acquired a Boeing 737, bringing its fleet of corporate aircraft to three. In partnership with the Australia New Zealand Bank (ANZ), which based an aircraft of its own at Melbourne, Elders was building the Melbourne Jet Base (MJB). When finished, this large and beautifully equipped facility would contain three executive suites—one each for Elders and ANZ, plus a third for an undetermined future client of the MJB. There would also be a dedicated customs facility, rental office space—notoriously short at Tullamarine—for airport suppliers, and an executive hangar and maintenance facility. Air BP was invited to take

EXHIBIT 3 ADVERTISING FOR PEACHTREE–DEKALB FBO IN ATLANTA

Picture Perfect.

Even a thousand words can't describe our dramatic airside canopy. It keeps dry things dry and cool things cool. Like passengers and planes. And unless you've experienced

Air BP Atlanta, words aren't enough. And neither are pictures. Twenty-four hours a day, we're at your service. Get the picture?

Line Service
- 8,000 square foot convenience canopy
- UVair Facility at PDK
- BP Jet Fuel pre-blended with additive
- BP 100LL
- Crew cars
- Courtesy van

Maintenance
- Authorized Learjet Service Station
- Turbine airframes, Including: Learjet Citation King Air
- GE CJ-610 Garrett TFE-731 P&W JT 15 D P&W PT 6

Avionics
- State-of-the-art avionics shop
- Full Capability for: Design, Engineering, Installation, Retrofit and Repair
- Dealer/ distributor for all major manufacturers

Facilities
- Luxurious Passenger Lounges
- Pilot lounge with 'Snooze Room'
- BP Jet Fuel pre-blended with additive
- On site Hertz rental cars
- Executive conference room with full a/v

AIR BP ATLANTA

PDK• DeKalb Peachtree Airport
One Corsair Drive • Atlanta, Ga 30341
(404) 452-0010 • Fax (404) 457-1775
UNICOM 122.95 • ARINC 128.97

an equity share of up to 30% in return for the fuel rights.

Examining the market, Air BP saw opportunities to service the VIP fleet of the Royal Australian Air Force and perhaps to build a pipeline to distribute fuel to a new maintenance base that Qantas (Australia's international airline) planned to build nearby. In 1989, BP agreed to take 10% of the equity with the balance split between Elders and ANZ. After construction of fuel tanks and related facilities, BP's investment totaled A$3.3 million (US $2.5 million).

But a serious blow struck the jet base, even before completion. Discontented with Elders' financial performance, the board dismissed its chief executive. His successor promptly instituted major cost-cutting moves, including elimination of the corporate fleet. ANZ had to take on Elders' share in the MJB. By September 1990, BP's accumulated losses amounted to A$1.5 million (US$1.2 million).

Activities in Europe

Air BP continued to look for new FBOs on the Continent while trying to make its existing ones profitable. Heathrow made a profit, yet Stansted barely broke even, and Cologne was losing money. The view was that Stansted would turn the corner once a resident fleet was attracted, which would justify construction of a hangar and maintenance facilities and in turn attract more business.

The Cologne FBO was having trouble running UPS's freight airline. Margins were squeezed as UPS sought to reduce its costs and as the aircraft lessor pushed for higher leasing fees. Losses in 1990 amounted to DM1.4 million ($790,000). The managing director kept predicting profits but the losses continued. Finally, he was replaced by a new man hired from Deutsche Bank. In early 1991, a task force reviewed the operations. Identifying the major problem as the UPS airline, it suggested that consideration be given to scaling down or eliminating this side of the business. Other options were seen as selling the FBO, winding it up, or continuing to subsidize operations in the hope of future improvements.

REASSESSMENT

By mid-1991, many industrialized countries remained stuck in recession. Sales and utilization of corporate aircraft had slowed or declined in many parts of the world as companies tightened their belts. The margins on FBO fuel sales in the US were under pressure owing to increased price competition in a soft market.

Meanwhile, BP had redefined its strategic goals to emphasize secure placement of company-produced aviation fuels under the Air BP brand. The company wanted to sell all the fuel it refined under its own brand name, capturing as much margin as possible, rather than selling surplus fuel to traders who would then resell it through another distribution channel. Future investments, declared the CEO of Air BP, would be evaluated with reference to the sales volume secured relative to the amount invested. At the same time, renewed emphasis was to be placed on achieving "quality service and customer responsiveness second to none."

Other developments concerned individual FBOs. BP had decided to move its own corporate fleet of three aircraft from another field in southern England to the more conveniently located Stansted. This would provide FAEL-Stansted with the resident fleet it needed to justify leasing hangar space and adding additional services. In Cologne, the German managing director had found a prospective buyer for the facility if the company wanted to sell that FBO. Meantime, Melbourne's situation had stabilized and there was a prospect of new resident aircraft moving to MJB.

In the US, sentiment was moving away from acquisition of company-owned FBOs toward increasing the number of Air BP branded FBOs that were owned and operated by other parties. Jim Timmons told the London office that recent federal legislation had created some interesting opportunities:

The Environmental Protection Act focused on underground storage tanks as a potential source of contamination. The new law says that tanks over a certain age must be upgraded or removed and replaced by new ones. This could be very expensive for FBOs. Most have several tanks for jet fuel and avgas. Upgrading and adding leak detection devices will cost a few thousand, but replacing a whole system could run more than $100,000.

Fuel trucks, too, are getting more expensive because of new environmental requirements. One 2,000-gallon truck today costs maybe $70,000, a 5,000-gallon [19,000-liter] model will run you $100,000 to $125,000. It's getting to the point where FBOs are facing a real capital crunch.

Timmons urged that Air BP offer loans at competitive rates to help FBOs upgrade their fuel farms (storage facilities), in return for a fuel supply contract covering the 5–7 year duration of the loan. Exxon and Phillips already had very limited programs of this nature. Timmons felt that it would be unwise for BP to share ownership of a dealer's fuel farm, since that would increase the company's exposure to legal liability in the event of a spill or accident. He also suggested that BP expand its truck-leasing operation to offer dealers the chance to lease new fuel trucks on a monthly basis—a service already available from Exxon, Phillips, and Texaco. The bottom line, declared Timmons, was that Air BP could use its capital to secure fuel sales far more effectively in this way than by spending millions to buy a single FBO.

In Europe, there was still interest in buying more FBOs. A handsome new facility at Paris-Le Bourget (a location coveted by Air BP, since it was at the center of European business aviation) was nearing completion. The project even included a hotel. The developer had gone bankrupt and prospective buyers were being courted.

New opportunities were opening up in Central Europe. Berlin was seen as an increasingly important destination for executive jets, but no one could forecast which of Berlin's airports would be designated for general aviation. In Hungary, the Budapest airport already received five corporate jets a day. The recently privatized airport authority had awarded general aviation fuel rights to Air BP, but Field's and BP thought the authority might be prepared to contract out many other services, too, as part of a general upgrading and repositioning of the airport. Further west, Rome, Milan, and Madrid remained under consideration.

Evaluation

Evans reviewed his notes again. He had prepared a summary of the situation at each of Air BP's six existing FBOs (refer to *Exhibit 4*). Taking a clean pad, he wrote "NOW WHAT?" and then jotted down some questions:

- Goals and priorities—the same worldwide or vary by continent?
- Investment criteria: volume versus margins—or can we have both?
- What do we mean by "service" and "quality"? How do they add value?
- Hold, expand, or sell our own FBO network? What
- percentage share?
- How to build up the number of Air BP branded dealers in the States?
- Strategies for Europe, Australia, rest of world?
- Lessons from experience to date? For Air BP? BP in general?
- Actions: what to do and when?

EXHIBIT 4 AIR BP FBO STRATEGY REVIEW

	Air BP equity	Year acquired	Air BP investment (US$000)	Assessed pretax ROI	Fuel volume (usg million)	Net fuel margin[1] (US cent/usg)	Air BP income[2] (US$000)	Notes
USA								
Cleveland	100%	1972	n/a	n/a	85.0	0.47	400	Dividend on JV equity.
Atlanta	100	1990	6,300[3]	9.0%	0.95	0.93	9	
Europe								
Heathrow	50	1986	1,750	34.0	2.7	n/a	114	Commission from fueling.
Stansted	50	1987	850	−6.8	0.7	n/a	0	Commission from fueling.
Cologne	51	1988	650	−56.0	1.2	n/a	0	Commission from fueling.
Australia								
Melbourne	10	1990	2,500	−0.4	2.3	7.00	161	Investment excludes fuel farm.

[1]Net fuel margin is margin direct to Air BP from fuel sales. This excludes any wholesale margin (which Air BP would earn irrespective of whether or not it owned the FBO).
[2]Air BP income is net income directly received by Air BP from its investment and excludes any wholesale fuel margin.
[3]Includes $1.1 million in working capital injected by Air BP.

O & E Farm Supply

Thomas F. Funk
E. Gimpel
O. Guindo

On a cool, rainy day in November 1986, Len Dow, manager of O & E Farm Supply, was sitting in his office looking over the past season's records. He felt he had brought the fertilizer outlet a long way since he purchased it in February of 1985. Volume, which had declined to 7,000 tons in 1984 due to poor management, increased to 8,400 tons in 1985, and to 10,000 tons in 1986 (see *Exhibit 1*). Total sales for 1986 reached $2,400,000. Profit margins, which were also lower in 1984, had returned to their normal 6% level in 1986 due to Mr. Dow's good managerial abilities. In spite of all this, he was not completely satisfied; he wanted to increase the volume and profitability of the outlet, but was not sure what direction he should take.

THE COMPANY

O & E Farm Supply was located in Goodland, a town centrally located in a major corn- and potato-producing area of Ontario. O & E does most of its business within a five-mile radius of Goodland (60%); however, it did have some sales and distribu-

EXHIBIT 1
O & E FERTILIZER SALES

Year	Tons of liquid and dry fertilizers	Tons of micronutrients
1982	11,000	—
1983	11,000	—
1984	7,000	—
1985	8,400	10
1986	10,000	100

tion extending 20 miles from its plant (35%), and a very small wholesale market over 100 miles away in northern Ontario (5%). At the time, O & E was involved only in the sale of fertilizers and related services. Dry bulk blends and bagged blends made up the majority of O & E's fertilizer volume (9,000 tons) with 28% liquid nitrogen making up a much smaller portion (1,000 tons). Potato and vegetable farmers purchased almost 60% of O & E's production, corn and cereal farmers accounted for 33%, and sod farmers purchased the remaining 7% (see *Exhibit 2*).

O & E sold a custom application service for bulk

EXHIBIT 2
O & E FERTILIZER SALES BY FARM TYPE, 1986

Farm Type	Percentages of dry fertilizer sales	Percentages of acres served
Potato and vegetable	60	35
Corn and cereals	33	60
Sod	7	5

fertilizers and rented application equipment to farmers who wished to apply their own fertilizer. Current equipment consisted of two dry fertilizer spreader trucks, two feeder delivery trucks to refill spreader trucks on the farms, and three four-ton tractor-pulled spreaders which were rented out to customers who spread fertilizer themselves. Since Mr. Dow purchased the organization he had cut the full-time staff from seven to five including himself. One of his newest employees was a young agricultural university graduate who spent most of his time in a sales capacity calling on present and potential customers in the area. He also spent some of his time making farm calls.

Of O & E's 85 local customers in 1986, five were merchant dealers who resold to farmers. These five dealers accounted for 2,000 tons of O & E's business and ranged in volume from 100 to 1,000 tons each. For the most part these dealers were located on the fringes of O & E's 20-mile trading area. Of the remaining 80 local customers, Mr. Dow's records showed that 70 were within five miles of the Goodland plant and ten were at a greater distance. Almost all of these customers purchased more than 50 tons of fertilizer a year from O & E.

O & E sold 10 tons of micronutrients in 1985 and over 100 tons in 1986. Micronutrients were basic elements that a plant requires in relatively small amounts, compared to the larger amounts of nitrogen, phosphorus, and potassium found in most regular, blended fertilizers. Micronutrients had been proven by university and industry research in the United States to improve the quality and yield of crops. Commercial trials carried out in Ontario had indicated similar positive results.

THE MARKET AND COMPETITION

The total market for fertilizers in O & E's trading area had been remarkably stable at approximately 50,000 tons for the past several years. This was not expected to change significantly in the future although some shifts in types used were possible. Within five miles of Goodland there were four major fertilizer outlets competing with O & E for approximately 25,000 tons of fertilizer business, and within 20 miles there were an additional three fertilizer outlets competing for the remaining 25,000 tons. Mr. Dow estimated that there were approximately 550 farmers within a five-mile radius of Goodland.

Although the market for fertilizer was very competitive, Mr. Dow felt that he had been able to better his competition by offering excellent service, remaining open extended hours, offering advice and timely delivery to his customers, and knowing how to deal with the large farmer. He had quickly come to realize that farmers placed service ahead of price when deciding where to buy fertilizer as long as the price was close to that of competitive outlets. He felt that by offering a superior service, he had nurtured a high level of dealer loyalty in his customers which resulted in a lower turnover relative to his competition.

GROWTH OPPORTUNITIES

Although the business had been doing well, Mr. Dow realized that growth was essential to future success. He had therefore been giving this matter considerable thought the past couple of months. So far, he was able to identify several avenues of growth, and now his aim was to evaluate each and arrive at some plan for 1987 and beyond.

Liquid Nitrogen

Mr. Dow had been toying with the idea of getting into 28% liquid nitrogen in a bigger way. He estimated that the total current market in his 20-mile trading area was 4,000 tons, of which he sold 1,000 to three corn farmers. This type of fertilizer was of interest mainly to the larger corn farmer because it could be mixed with herbicides for combined application and because of its ease of handling. Although its price per ton was less than the price per ton for dry fertilizers, it was comparable in terms of price per unit of actual nitrogen. This was because it was usually less concentrated than other forms of nitrogen such as dry urea, which contained 45% nitrogen compared to the 28% concentration in the liquid form. The product was very corrosive, which meant that the farmer must also purchase a stainless steel sprayer costing about $2,000 if he were to use 28% liquid nitrogen. This relatively high initial capital outlay restricted use to fairly larger farmers. Of the 400 corn farmers in his trading area, approximately 200 had sufficient acreage to be possible 28% liquid nitrogen users, and Mr. Dow estimated that about 20 farmers were using 28% liquid nitrogen in 1986. Price was the major purchase criterion since the product was a commodity and little service was involved. Most of the volume of 28% liquid nitrogen was sold in December for delivery in the spring. Prices and margins for O & E's fertilizers are provided in *Exhibit 3*. O & E's current holding capacity was 10,000 gallons or 50 tons. If output was increased, additional storage and nurse tanks would have to be purchased,

as well as another pumping system. A pumping system was priced at $4,000, storage tanks were $0.15 per gallon, and a 1,400 gallon nurse tank was $1,000. Mr. Dow felt one additional pumping system, one more 10,000 gallon storage tank, and two more nurse tanks should allow a large increase in sales. No matter what Mr. Dow decided to do, he wanted to stay ahead of his competition by at least two years. Because he felt 28% liquid nitrogen could be a big thing in the future, he was excited about this possibility. He had seen a new type of potato planter which required only liquid fertilizer. If this type of planter became popular, the potential for liquid fertilizer would increase dramatically. Despite these positive feelings about this market, he was concerned about a number of things, including the relatively low liquid nitrogen margins and the slow growth of this market in the past. He also wondered whether he should offer a weed and feed service in which O & E would apply liquid fertilizer and herbicides for the farmer all in one operation. He was not really sure of the demand for this service or what was involved in operating a weed service. There was no one currently offering such a service in his area.

Micronutrients

Another opportunity facing Mr. Dow was to try to expand micronutrient sales in a major way. At the present time, O & E was a dealer for the Taylor Chemical Company, which produced and sold a complete line of micronutrients. Included in their line

EXHIBIT 3
FERTILIZER PRICES AND MARGINS

	Dry fertilizers		28% liquid nitrogen				Micronutrients	
			Winter		Spring			
	$/ton	%	$/ton	%	$/ton	%	$/ton	%
Average selling price	248	100	138	100	170	100	700	100
Cost of sales	203	82	131	95	136	80	595	85
Gross margin	45	18	7	5	34	20	105	15
Estimated fixed costs	$260,000		$20,000				$5,000	

were manganese, zinc, iron, copper, molybdenum, boron, calcium, and sulfur. These materials were sold separately or in various combinations designed to treat specific crops. An example of the latter was the company's vegetable mix, which contained magnesium, sulfur, copper, iron, manganese, and zinc in fixed proportions. The individual materials and mixes were sold in two ways: in a dry form for mixing by the dealer with other fertilizer products, and in liquid form for spray application by the farmer on the foliage of the growing crop. Although foliar (that is, leaf) application was more bother for the farmer and may have resulted in some leaf burning, some farmers preferred it because they could postpone micronutrient application until visible signs of deficiencies occurred. Also, there was some research which indicated that micronutrients could be most effective if absorbed through the leaves at the peak growth period of the plant. Despite the apparent advantages of foliar application, Mr. Dow had not sold any micronutrients in this form during the first two years in this business. If properly applied, he felt liquid micronutrients offered the most value to his customers, yet he noticed a great deal of reluctance and skepticism on the part of even the most progressive farmers in his area to try this product form.

Sales of the dry, mixed micronutrients had grown considerably over the past year and it appeared that the products offered real value to customers. One of Mr. Dow's customers applied micronutrients to half of a large potato field and treated the other half as he normally did. The treated field yielded 327 hundredweight, whereas the untreated portion only yielded 304 hundredweight. This 23 hundredweight gain resulted in a $111.55 higher revenue per acre when computed at the $4.84 per hundredweight price to the farmer. Unfortunately, the University of Guelph, which farmers looked to for technical information, was not promoting or even recommending the use of micronutrients. Their soil testing service, which analyzed soil samples for most Ontario farmers and made fertilizer use recommendations, didn't even include an analysis for micronutrients. The competition did not want to get involved in this business unless there was a very high demand and they started to lose their other fertilizer business. Of the 100 tons sold in 1986, 75 went to six large potato farmers representing 3,500 acres, 10 tons went to vegetable farmers, and 15 tons went to corn farmers (see *Exhibit 4*).

Mr. Dow had been receiving excellent service and advice from the company distributing the micronutrients. He felt that the use of micronutrients was becoming accepted by the farmers using them, and that sales should rise in the future. He chuckled to himself as he recalled the day two very large potato farmers who were brothers were sitting in his office and the subject of micronutrients came up. One of the brothers, Jack, asked the Taylor sales rep if he thought they should be using micronutrients. The sales rep related all of the advantages of using micronutrients to them, whereupon Jack turned to his brother and asked, "Well, what do you think?" Peter replied, "Yes, I think we should be using them." With that, Mr. Dow landed a micronutrients order worth several thousand dollars.

Mr. Dow was convinced that micronutrients had potential in his area. His major concern was how he could convince farmers to spend an additional $10 to $15 per acre on a product for which there was no objective basis for determining need.

EXHIBIT 4
MICRONUTRIENT SALES BY CROP, 1986

Crop	Tons sold	Acres	Application rate	Cost/acre
Potatoes	75	3,500	50 pounds per acre	$15.90
Corn	15	1,300	25 pounds per acre	$ 8.00
Vegetables	10	400	50 pounds per acre	$15.90

Northern Ontario

Mr. Dow was also considering expanding sales in northern Ontario. He had three dealers selling bagged fertilizer for him in Sault Ste. Marie, New Liskeard, and Kenora. O & E's volume was approximately 500 tons of bagged fertilizer only—several co-op outlets had most of the market in this area. Prices were very competitive and there appeared to be strong dealer loyalty to the co-ops. There were many small farms in the region with 75 to 100 acres of workable land per farm. The crop types in the area were mixed grain, barley, hay, and a few hundred acres of potatoes near Sudbury. On the average, farmers in northern Ontario who used fertilizer purchased 2 to 3 tons of bagged fertilizer per year and did their purchasing in the winter months. Because the retail price of fertilizer in northern Ontario was similar to that around Goodland, the margin to O & E was reduced by about $17 a ton, the sum of the $12 dealer commission and the $5 freight cost. The lower margin was offset to some extent by lower personal selling costs, since dealers were used. Although the growing season was only two to three weeks behind that of Goodland, because most sales in the area occurred in the winter months, O & E's ability to service the Goodland area in the spring was not affected. One reservation about dealing with the distant northern Ontario market was that credit could be a problem, particularly because the cost of collection could run very high due to the distance involved. On the more positive side Mr. Dow was quite optimistic about the long-run potential growth of this market. He felt that there was an ultimate total industry potential in this market of 50,000 to 60,000 tons of dry fertilizer, of which perhaps 10 to 20% had been developed at the present time.

Agricultural Chemicals

So far, O & E's product line consisted only of fertilizers. However, Mr. Dow observed that all of his competitors carried insecticides, herbicides, and fungicides as well, and he wondered if he should be getting into this business too. He had always believed that concentrating on one line was the way to go.

Agricultural chemicals were very competitively priced, leaving small margins in the neighborhood of 5 to 10% for the dealer. He felt that farmers in his trading area bought fertilizer and chemicals each on their own merits. For example, if a dealer had a great price on fertilizer, this would not mean that farmers also would buy their chemicals from the same dealer unless, of course, they were also the lowest price. At any rate, he sized up his customers as not wanting to buy everything from one dealer, so he was satisfied to receive all of their fertilizer business and to leave the other lines to the other dealers. The set-up costs for carrying chemicals would be approximately $20,000 for an additional warehouse. No other direct costs would be attributable to the chemical line, but he knew that servicing the line would take valuable time away from servicing and selling the fertilizer line, which could possibly result in lower sales and profits. He estimated that the average farmer in his trading area spent $3,000 to $5,000 per year on agricultural chemicals.

Dry Fertilizers

An alternative Mr. Dow thought particularly attractive was to expand dry fertilizer sales in his local trading area. Although he had a substantial share of this market already, he felt he could pick up more through aggressive pricing and continued good service. He was especially interested in this alternative because, no matter what he did, he knew his present plant, which was over 20 years old, would have to be upgraded. As part of his plant improvement program, he planned to set up a new mixing system that would be adaptable to adding micronutrients without any downtime. This mixer could be purchased in two sizes: the smaller size was similar to his present system with a maximum capacity of 15,000 tons and cost $100,000, while the larger size had an annual capacity of 20,000 tons and cost $160,000. Because of this opportunity to increase his capacity, he wondered if he shouldn't just try to sell more dry fertilizer to both his current customers and possibly some new ones in his local trading area. To do this, he was thinking of adding another person to his staff who would act as a second salesperson to develop and offer a comprehensive crop management service to interested farmers. He was also considering the possibility of developing a local advertising program aimed at developing more awareness and interest among farmers outside his immediate five-mile concentrated area. The total cost of the new sales specialist would be about $35,000 per year, and the local advertising would cost about $10,000 per year.

THE DECISION

Mr. Dow knew he would have to make a decision soon if he were to make some changes for 1987. Although he had identified what he thought were several good opportunities for future growth, he knew he could not pursue all of them right away, and, therefore, he would have to establish some priorities. To help in this assessment, he recently wrote away to the University of Guelph and received a publication entitled "Farmer Purchasing and use of Fertilizers in Ontario." (The Appendix provides a summary of the study.) With this new information, plus his own analysis of the situation, he began planning for 1987 and beyond. He knew that economic conditions in 1987 were not expected to be good. This made the necessity of coming up with a successful plan all the more important to him.

APPENDIX
RESULTS OF FERTILIZER MARKETING RESEARCH STUDY

1. Only 7% of total crop acreage in southern Ontario is not fertilized at the present time. This acreage is almost entirely in soybeans, pasture, and forages.
2. The average fertilizer application rate for southern Ontario farmers is 384 pounds per acre. Most farmers use soil test recommendations from the University of Guelph to determine the application rate. There is some tendency for farmers to apply more fertilizer than recommended by their soil tests.
3. The major types of fertilizer used by southern Ontario farmers are dry bulk blends and liquid nitrogen. Of less importance are dry bagged fertilizers, anhydrous ammonia, and liquid mixes (N-P-K). Liquid nitrogen fertilizers are almost exclusively used by very large farmers.

4. Most farmers find the quality and availability of fertilizers very good.
5. In southern Ontario as a whole, a relatively small percentage of farmers purchase a large percentage of the fertilizer products sold. The breakdown is as follows:

	% of farmers	% of purchases
Under 25 tons	30	10
26–50 tons	35	25
51–100 tons	20	20
Over 100 tons	15	45

6. Over 70% of all dry fertilizers are sold to farmers in April and May. This figure is somewhat lower (50%) for liquid nitrogen.
7. Thirty percent of Ontario farmers use dealer custom application services, while 75% apply the fertilizer themselves using rented dealer application equipment. There is some preference by larger farmers for custom application services.
8. In the course of a year, farmers discuss their fertilizer program with a number of parties to get information and advice on various aspects of fertilizer use and dealer selection. The influence groups most widely consulted are the local fertilizer dealer, other farmers, and family members. In addition to these influence groups, fertilizer company representatives, agricultural extension officials, and university scientists are consulted by some farmers. Proportionately more larger farmers visit company representatives and university scientists than smaller farmers.
9. Farmers also obtain fertilizer information from soil test results, various government publications, company-sponsored farmer meetings, dealer demonstration plots, and company and dealer displays at farm shows and fairs.
10. Over 60% of all farmers contact more than one fertilizer dealer before making a purchase. Larger farmers have a tendency to contact more dealers than smaller farmers.
11. Over 50% of all farmers reported receiving an on-farm call by a fertilizer dealer in the last year. Larger farmers reported receiving more dealer calls than smaller farmers.
12. In addition to fertilizers, southern Ontario farmers purchase, on the average, more than three other products from their fertilizer supplier. Of these, the most common are herbicides, insecticides, general farm supplies, and seeds. Large farmers are more likely to purchase herbicides and insecticides from their fertilizer supplier than are small farmers.
13. Six dealer services were identified as essential to all but a very small proportion of farmers: application equip-

ment, which is available when needed and in good repair; custom application services; custom fertilizer blending fertilizer information through a well-informed staff, brochures, newsletters, and farmer meetings; soil testing; and demonstrations.

14. Other dealer services which were reported as being important to smaller groups of farmers were: crop management assistance, help in securing expert assistance with problems, and custom herbicide application.

15. Dealer location, price, and availability of product when needed are the major factors farmers consider when selecting a fertilizer dealer. In general, dealer location and availability of product when needed are more important to smaller farmers, while price is more important to larger farmers.

16. Over 45% of all farmers purchase fertilizer from their nearest dealer. On the average, farmers purchase from dealers located less than five miles from their farms.

17. Thirty percent of all farmers purchase from more than one dealer. Larger farmers have a greater tendency to spread their purchases over more dealers than do small farmers.

18. Analysis of dealer switching showed that one-third of the farmers made no dealer changes in the past five years, one-third made only one change, and the remaining one-third made two or more changes. Those farmers making several dealer changes are the larger, younger farmers.

Water Conservation in Palo Alto

Peter T. Hutchison
Don E. Parkinson
Charles B. Weinberg

Mr. Alan Jay, Chief Engineer of the Department of Water, Sewage and Gas (DWSG) in Palo Alto, California, did not know how to react to the first rain in weeks in drought-stricken California. It was the beginning of March 1977 and close to the end of what was normally considered the "wet" season in the region.

He wondered whether a few days of rain would result in a decrease in water conservation efforts. One thing the Chief Engineer knew for certain was that he could not continue to rely on the effect of the strong and extensive newspaper stories that had announced the launching of the initial water conservation campaign in January with headlines such as "Save Water or Else . . . Area Warned" and "Water Cut Target 10 Percent."

THE DROUGHT

For the second year in a row, Northern California had experienced record drought conditions, with rainfall

less than 50 percent of normal and reservoir levels at record lows.

In the early months of the year, *Time, Newsweek,* and many other national magazines had reported extensively on the drought. The television networks had brought films and reports on the drought to Eastern viewers suffering from record cold and snow falls. People generally smiled at solutions such as the use of pipelines to send Eastern snow west and at slogans like "Save Water—Shower with a Friend," while trivia buffs prospered with such gems as "The toilet accounts for 40 percent of all indoor household water usage (up to seven gallons a flush)." However, the lack of rain had serious consequences for both the nation and the West.

Because 85 percent of the water used in California was consumed by farmers supplying 40 percent of the country's fresh vegetables and fruits, the reduced water supply was expected to result in shortages and higher prices for all. Forest rangers were worried about fire hazards; outdoors enthusiasts, about the loss of fishing and boating opportunities; and homeowners, about keeping lawns and gardens green. Although long-term solutions such as weather modification and better irrigation techniques were being discussed, no amount of talk or money could change the fact that many reservoirs had gone dry, and there was no chance of any change in that condition until the end of the year. No one had dared to consider the consequences of a third drought year.

Public Opinion in California

In March, the California Poll conducted a representative statewide survey of 962 California residents and published the results in newspapers throughout the state. (The California Poll, which had operated since 1947, was an independent media-sponsored, public opinion news service which regularly carried out personal interview surveys on socially significant issues.) Eighty-five percent of those surveyed believed the drought was either "extremely serious" or "somewhat serious." When asked which user class should be cut the most if mandatory rationing became necessary, respondents replied as follows:

User class	% saying cut this group most
Business and industry	50
Households	33
Health and safety	3
Agriculture	3
No opinion	11

With regard to reduction of household water usage by 25 percent, only 10 percent of respondents said it would cause severe problems: however, 51 percent said a 50 percent cutback would cause severe problems. Finally, 93 percent claimed to be practicing some form of water conservation, such as using less water for bathing (70 percent), watering lawns less (67 percent), and washing cars less frequently (58 percent). Twenty-four percent claimed to have installed devices in their toilet tanks to reduce the amount of water used to flush, and 16 percent said they had installed water flow restrictors to reduce the rate of water flow in showers.

PALO ALTO AND THE SAN FRANCISCO BAY AREA

The population of the City of San Francisco was 700,000, and that of the nine-county San Francisco Bay Area totalled some 4.5 million. The Bay Area's generally mild climate had an average temperature range of from 54°F to 77°F in summer and from 39°F to 58°F in winter. The average annual rainfall of 15.5 inches occurred mainly from October through March. It almost never rained in June, July, and August. For the past two years, the rainfall had been less than one half of normal.

Palo Alto, a city of 55,000 people located about 35 miles south of San Francisco and 15 miles north of San Jose, was one of a number of cities which formed an extensive urban corridor along the length of the San Francisco Peninsula (*Exhibit 1*). Palo Alto residents tended to be highly educated and had a median income level among the highest in the nation. They took an active interest in city affairs, and their city government was considered to be very well run. The *Palo Alto Times,* with a circulation of 50,000 in Palo Alto, Los Altos, Menlo Park, Mountain View, and the surrounding area, reported extensively on the actions of the local city governments. Palo Alto fell within the circulation area of the *San Francisco Chronicle,* the *San Francisco Examiner,* and the *San Jose Mercury-News.* City residents could receive broadcasts from six VHF television and 58 radio stations.

Adjacent to the city, but not within city limits, was Stanford University. The presence of Stanford, as well as other factors, had stimulated the development of a high technology emphasis in many companies located in Palo Alto. Firms such as Hewlett-Packard, Varian, and Syntex had headquarters offices, research centers, and manufacturing operations in the city. The business community of Palo Alto had in the past been supportive of most community projects and had also demonstrated an effective response to the initial water conservation program. Civic groups, such as the Chamber of Commerce, had also been supportive of community conservation projects.

EXHIBIT 1 MAP OF SAN FRANCISCO BAY AREA SHOWING PIPELINES AND RESERVOIRS

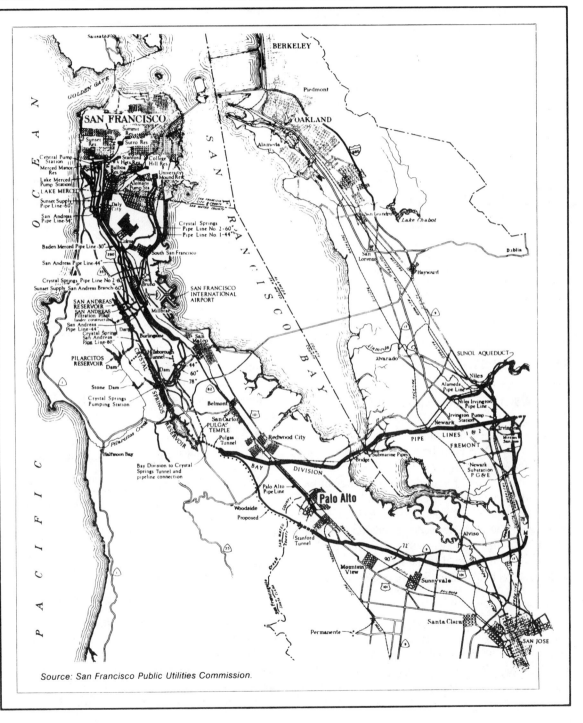

Source: San Francisco Public Utilities Commission.

EXHIBIT 2 PALO ALTO UTILITIES: PARTIAL ORGANIZATION CHART

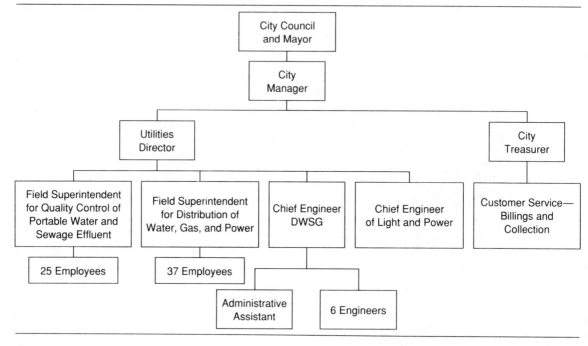

THE WATER SYSTEM IN PALO ALTO

The Palo Alto Department of Water, Sewage and Gas (DWSG) was responsible for the planning, production, and marketing of the water supply service of the city.[1] This department was directly responsible to the Utilities Director, who in turn was responsible to the City Manager (see *Exhibit 2*).

Mr. Jay, the Chief Engineer, was in charge of the operations of the DWSG. He supervised an administrative assistant plus a planning and design team of six people. The customer service department of the city was divided into two parts: first, the clerical function, which reported to the City Treasurer; and second, the technical function (complaints regarding

quality or quantity of the water supply), which was administered by the field supervisors.

In connection with the water supply function, the DWSG had three goals:

1. To serve the populace with an adequate supply of drinking water for domestic, industrial, commercial, and public needs.
2. To provide this service at rates comparable to those charged by the utilities of neighboring cities and towns.
3. To provide revenue to the general fund of Palo Alto by operating efficiently and earning a reasonable (5 percent–8 percent) return on investment. (Profit maximization was *not* a goal, nor was more than a prudent return on investment sought.)

These broad goals had been effectively translated into measurable operating goals. Examples stated by the DWSG were: (1) The DWSG strived to maintain water pressure within narrow tolerances. (Numerical standards were set and monitored.) (2) There was a constant monitoring of the quality of the potable

---

[1]The City of Palo Alto supplied electricity, gas, and water to all residents and commercial or industrial customers in the city. One monthly bill for all three utility services was mailed to all customers by the city. Usage and billing rates for each utility were separately itemized. In addition, the City of Palo Alto also provided garbage collection, but this service was administered and billed separately from the other three services.

water supplied, which was checked against a pre-set quality standard. (3) The customer service department had a goal of 15-minute response time to a customer complaint. Currently a service crew arrived on the scene to investigate a complaint within 30 minutes of notification.

In addition, the DWSG provided such complementary services as technical advice on methods and new devices that could be employed by industrial and manufacturing customers to conserve water and consequently reduce costs. Mr. Jay and his staff had worked successfully with a number of local companies in developing efficient water usage programs well before the current crisis arose. In recent years, a number of local companies had achieved significant reductions in water consumption by recycling water used for cooling, by watering grounds at night when less evaporation took place, and by preventive maintenance programs.

Palo Alto's Water Supply

The source of supply for Palo Alto was the San Francisco Water Department (SFWD) System, which served the City of San Francisco and over 30 communities in the Bay Area. The primary sources for the SFWD were the Hetch Hetchy, Lake Eleanor, and Lake Lloyd Reservoirs in Yosemite National Park nearly 200 miles away. Rain and snow melt in the Yosemite area of the Sierra Nevada Mountain range filled these reservoirs and the water was conveyed to the Bay Area through a series of tunnels and pipelines. The DWSG had a long term contract for water supply with the SFWD. The contract did not specify any guaranteed supply to Palo Alto, but the city had been able to obtain as much water from SFWD as it had needed.[2] The total amount of water supplied by SFWD to Palo Alto was metered, and monthly dollar sales were determined at a pre-set rate. (See *Exhibit 3*).

As an alternative source of supply, the DWSG could draw on groundwater from its own well network. This source, which could supply about 40 percent of current demand, was used as a standby and had been used in the previous year when the supply

---

[2]If there was insufficient water in the SFWD, the contract provided that all users (including the City of San Francisco) would have the amount of water supplied cut back by a uniform percentage of the previous year's usage.

EXHIBIT 3
WATER SUPPLIED BY SFWD TO DWSG 1971–76
Million Cubic Feet/Month

	1971	1972	1973	1974	1975	1976	Average
January	40	46	47	45	48	52	46
February	50	46	45	45	52	58	49
March	45	52	44	46	47	55	48
April	60	71	60	54	53	67[1]	61
May	66	83	79	74	67	82[1]	75
June	86	92	94	94	100[2]	98	94
July	93	95	104	89	99[2]	101	97
August	98	100	95	95	100[2]	97	98
September	92	90	89	100	89	82	90
October	73	71	71	72	73	67	71
November	65	49	54	63	58	66	59
December	48	44	45	48	56	50	49
Average	68	70	69	69	70	73	70

[1]Includes 5 and 7 million cubic feet supplied from groundwater in April and May respectively.
[2]Original data adjusted by summing three months supply and spreading equally to each month.
Source: DWSG records.

from San Francisco was reduced because of a short strike by city workers. The quality of groundwater was inferior to that supplied by the SFWD and required a considerable amount of softening. Prior to 1962, when Palo Alto began receiving its entire water supply from the SFWD, the DWSG had used the well system as its source of supply. At that time, the groundwater table was considerably drawn down, a condition that led to problems of subsidence and fears of salt water intrusions into the aquifers (water bearing ground). The latter was a very real and present threat, since some intrusion had already occurred on the eastern side of the San Francisco Bay. Prolonged use of the ground well system would threaten to "sink" neighboring cities.

The Demand for Water

Because the city's population was stable, the demand for water in Palo Alto had been practically static for several years (*Exhibit 3*); no increase in demand was projected in the future.

The DWSG categorized its customers by usage into the following categories: domestic, commercial, industrial, and public. The domestic consumers were further broken down into single family and multiple family (apartment and condominium type) units. In the latter case, each family was not metered separately; instead the complex as a whole was metered. Customer data are shown in *Exhibits 4* and *5*.

Pricing Policy

The pricing policy for water in Palo Alto was based on the following criteria:

1. Providing an equitable allocation of revenues and cost for the various classes of customers.
2. Providing a reasonable return on investment.
3. Providing the minimum basic requirement of a family for water at the lowest possible price (this was termed a lifeline rate).
4. Encouraging conservation.

The level of prices was based primarily on the cost of the supply from SFWD (which accounted for

EXHIBIT 4 NUMBER OF CUSTOMERS AND ANNUAL WATER USAGE BY USER CLASS

	Number of customers, fiscal year ending June 30					
	1971	1972	1973	1974	1975	1976
Single family	14,083	14,150	14,178	14,146	14,251	14,268
Multifamily	1,235	1,261	1,281	1,240	1,252	1,253
Commercial	1,321	1,332	1,425	1,490	1,496	1,513
Industrial	227	228	265	271	272	271
Public facility	198	200	218	213	208	203
City	121	124	71	207	259	260
Total	17,185	17,295	17,438	17,567	17,738	17,768
	Annual CCF per customer*					
Single family	224	236	225	209	210	204**
Multifamily	435	415	398	410	431	413**
Commercial	709	768	744	662	890	855**
Industrial	7,886	7,835	7,410	7,734	8,211	8,229**
Public facility	3,924	4,144	3,495	4,319	2,601	2,827**
City	2,571	2,608	3,426	1,497	1,212	991**
Total	436	452	444	443	448	455**

*Water consumption is measured in terms of "units" of one hundred cubic feet. One unit = 1 CCF = 748 gallons.
**Estimated.
Source: DWSG.

EXHIBIT 5   WATER DEMAND IN PALO ALTO—MONTHLY AND QUARTERLY AVERAGE FOR 1975–76
Thousands of Units (1 unit = 1 CCF)

	Quarter I				Quarter II				Quarter III				Quarter IV			
	Jan.	Feb.	Mar.	Tot.	Apr.	May	June	Tot.	July	Aug.	Sept.	Tot.	Oct.	Nov.	Dec.	Tot.
Industrial	146	170	163	479	168	183	196	537	213	216	197	626	201	177	156	534
Public facility	42	45	45	132	50	66	84	200	86	85	85	256	68	55	44	167
City departments	16	22	16	54	14	32	42	88	46	41	39	126	24	23	16	63
Domestic single family	180	163	167	510	190	273	379	842	406	363	361	1130	243	194	176	613
Domestic multifamily	41	43	38	122	39	42	52	133	54	51	53	158	43	40	40	123
Commercial	77	88	83	248	75	90	110	275	123	120	110	353	93	79	71	243
Total	502	531	512	1545	536	686	863	2075	928	876	845	2649	672	568	503	1743

Source: Derived from DWSG—Monthly Sales Report.

approximately 63 percent of total revenue). Other costs such as distribution, administration, and general expenses accounted for approximately 19 percent of revenues.

The scale of charges was approved by the City Council, based on the DWSG's recommendation. The current scale of charges had been put into effect nine months earlier. Previously the scale of charges had been such that the marginal cost decreased with increased consumption. The new structure made the unit price greater as consumption increased, so that a user of more than 1,000 CCF (1 CCF = hundred cubic feet) per month would pay about 10 percent more per CCF above 1,000 than would a user of 50 CCF per month. In addition, a general price increase of 8 percent was made. Careful analysis had shown that demand for water was not materially affected by this pricing strategy.

The extent to which DWSG met its goal of maintaining its prices at levels comparable to those of neighboring utilities is shown in *Exhibit 6*. The average residential water bill was 4 percent above to 45 percent below adjacent cities, and average industrial bills were 6 percent above to 32 percent below adjacent cities.

THE WATER SHORTAGE PROBLEM

Despite the two years of record drought, on January 6, the general manager of the San Francisco Water Department (SFWD) informed Mr. Jay in Palo Alto that no curtailment of local water use would be necessary. Mr. Jay was somewhat surprised, therefore, when two weeks later, he heard on the radio that Bay Area suburban users would need to cut water consumption by 10 percent. The need for reduced

EXHIBIT 6   AVERAGE MONTHLY WATER BILL FOR PALO ALTO AND OTHER BAY AREA CITIES

	Usage* (CCF)	Palo Alto	San Jose	Mountain View	Sunnyvale	San Mateo	San Francisco
Residential	18	$ 8.00	$ 8.14	$ 7.66	$ 11.71	$ 9.31	$ 7.71
Commercial	60	22.78	25.84	24.05	34.41	31.52	24.61
Industrial	630	224.58	238.97	238.70	289.81	296.74	241.65
Industrial large (1)	2,500	889.33	938.50	940.50	886.47	1,167.69	950.65
Industrial large (2)	5,000	1,784.78	1,883.00	1,761.00	1,574.04	2,338.20	1,827.40
Industrial large (3)	10,000	3,567.28	3,751.00	3,329.70	2,909.66	4,661.25	3,496.20

*Average usage in Palo Alto for different user classes.
Source: DWSG Staff Report 3/18/76.

water usage immediately received extensive coverage in the *Palo Alto Times* and the San Francisco newspapers.

Palo Alto's Water Conservation Program

Following the SFWD's request of a voluntary curtailment of 10 percent in water consumption, the DWSG developed a conservation program aimed at all users, with special emphasis on domestic and industrial users. The thrust of the campaign was the conservation of water for the benefit of the community in general. After the Palo Alto City Council had adopted a resolution on water usage curtailment, all Palo Alto residents were sent a message from the Mayor with some informational materials (*Exhibit 7*) and two water flow restrictors.[3] The industrial water conservation program is outlined in *Exhibit 8*.

Mr. Jay felt that it was too early to assess the long run effect that DWSG's campaign would have. However, owing to the extraordinary publicity given to the water shortage problem by the press as well as radio and television, the community was well aware of the problem; it had reacted by reducing consumption 17 percent compared to 1976, since the emergency of the water shortage problem. The figures, in fact, were so satisfactory that there was a temptation to complacency. However, other resource crises had shown the public's memory to be very short, and Mr. Jay feared that if the issues were no longer of interest to the media, the public would very rapidly return to its previous levels of consumption. The current shortage was clearly not just a short term problem. Because there was little expectation of significant amounts of additional rainfall before summer, the water shortage problem would probably last until the end of the current year at least.

Mr. Jay knew that 70 percent more water usage occurred in the summer months when people tended their gardens and watered their lawns, and companies maintained the extensive landscaping around their factories, laboratories, and research centers (see *Exhibit 5*). He wondered whether those who conserved water when it was supposed to rain would also conserve when it was not supposed to rain. In addition, he felt that San Francisco would soon raise the water reduction order to at least 25 percent less than the previous year's consumption.

The only comfort Mr. Jay had—which was not much—was that his colleagues in Menlo Park, Mountain View, and the other Bay Area cities served by the San Francisco Water Department and the City of San Francisco itself were faced with the same problem. Even worse off were some San Francisco communities that did not use the SFWD System; for example, Marin County, just north of San Francisco, faced a 57 percent reduction target. Because there were no Federal, State, or County conservation goals, each area user (or groups of users) had to set its own goals in accordance with its perception of its own demand and supply condition. Mr. Jay knew there were literally hundreds of officials who needed to design programs in response to the drought; and although he personally knew and had communicated with many of them, none had solutions to the problem.

The Need for Further Conservation Efforts

Though there was awareness of a water shortage problem in the community, Mr. Jay was concerned that the nature of the problem might not have been fully understood. Thus, he wanted to develop a plan that would ensure that the public had the correct perception of the long term nature of the problem and was provided with the information, motivation, and methodology they needed to help overcome the problem. Mr. Jay had a budget of $12,000 for a water conservation program. Nearly $7,000 had already been invested in the current campaign.

The Chief Engineer had to devise and implement a second water conservation plan that would reinforce the impact of the initial conservation campaign and encourage greater conservation in the immediate future. Although some had suggested a "mandatory" water conservation program, he was not sure that the City Council or the public would accept an extreme approach. Even in a mandatory program, allocations

---

[3] A water flow restrictor, a disc installed on the pipe leading to the shower head, reduced the flow of water by as much as half when showers were taken.

EXHIBIT 7   WATER CONSERVATION TIPS

YOUR PERSONALIZED WATER SAVING PLAN

Use the chart below to determine where the water is used in your house each day and where you want to cut back.

How many times a day do you use water ??

Directions:

1. Locate in the "water use" column all the ways you use water.

2. On the row next to each water use write the number of times per day you use water in that way.

3. Multiply the number of gallons indicated for that water use by the number of times per day. Enter the answer in the "gallons per day" column.

4. After you finish filling in the "gallons per day" column, add up the total number of gallons in that column.

5. The total gallons per day can be used to devise your own <u>water saving plan</u>. If you wish to save 10% of the water you use, multiply the total by .10. (For example: a family of four found that they used 563 gallons per day. 563 x 0.10 = 56 gallons per day) The total for your water saving plan should be 10% less than your old total (in this example, 563 - 56 = 507).

6. Now go back to the chart and figure out how you can save that number of gallons. Put the ways you plan to use your water in the columns under "water saving plan". For example, the family of four took four showers per day. For their water saving plan they decided to insert a flow restrictor in their shower. The first line in the chart is what their entries for "shower" would look like.

WATER SAVING PLAN

Water Use		Typical Gallons per use	No. of times per day	Gals. per day	Water Saving Plan # of times per day	Gallons per day
Example Shower	Normal, water running	25	4	100		
	Flow restrictor, water running	17			4	68
	Wet down, soap up, rinse off	4				
Shower	Normal, water running	25				
	Flow restrictor, water running	17				
	Wet down, soap up, rinse off	4				
Bath	Full	36				
	Minimal water level	11				
Brushing Teeth	Tap running	10				
	Wet brush, rinse briefly	½				
Shaving	Tap running	20				
	Fill basin	1				
Dishwashing	Tap running	30				
	Wash & rinse in dish pan or sink	5				
Automatic Dishwasher	Full cycle	16				
	Short cycle	7				
Washing Hands	Tap running	2				
	Fill basin	1				
Toilet Flushing	Normal	5				
	Water saving toilet	3				
	Toilet with displacement bottles	4				
Other						
			No. of times per week			
Washing Machine	Full cycle, top water level	8*				
	Short cycle, minimum water level	4*				
			No. of min. per week			
Outdoor Watering	Average hose (10 gallons per minute)	1*				

Note: To compare this with your utility bill, 748 gallons are equal to one unit.

Total gallons per day _____
10% saving (total gallons x .10) _____
Water saving goal _____

Water saving total _____

* The figures are the average per day for once a week use.

EXHIBIT 8 INDUSTRIAL WATER CONSERVATION PROGRAM

Industrial Water Conservation Program

- Flushometers – Set the rate of closing of these devices to use only that amount of water required for a proper flush of the apparatus served.

- Flow Restrictors – Install these devices wherever possible to limit flow to showers, lavatory basins, wash sinks, etc.

- Faucet Aerators – Install these devices on sinks, lavatory basins and where rinsing is commonly done.

- Area Wash Downs – The use of the wastewater stream to convey wastes to the Regional Water Quality Control Plant is still looked upon with favor, but the use of potable water to wash leaves and debris from lawns and parking lots is not. This job of cleanup can be achieved with more environmental favor by use of brooms or air blowers.

- Fountains – The use of ornamental fountains during periods of drought is a questionable use of water. If used at all, these facilities should utilize recycled water in a nonwasteful manner.

- Cooling Waters – If cooling waters are used in quantity then cooling tower should be utilized. If cooling tower wastewaters are seriously degraded, they should go to sanitary sewer after filing for industrial waste permit. Nondegraded water may pass to storm sewer or be used for irrigation.

- Rinse Baths – If possible, use the cascade rinse approach to minimize water waste. If water is not seriously degraded, consider storing it for irrigation of landscaping.

- Landscape Irrigation – Serious consideration should be given to converting shrubbery irrigation to the drip method. This method can cut use of water for this purpose by 20 to 50 percent. If this system is operated on a time clock, an overriding tensiometer may be installed to limit irrigation to times when soil moisture content is low.

- Turf Irrigation – Sprinklers

  - Pressure at the heads should be proper (normally 35 psi). Excess pressure may cause atomization and hence waste due to evaporation and wind drift

  - Sprinkling in the rain is of no real value to either the turf, the storm sewer system, the water conservation program, or the pocket book, but is a regular activity engaged in by many of the industries on the hill. A good cure for this illness is the installation of a tensiometer, moisture sensory device to override the time-clock programming sprinkler irrigation. It is claimed that a savings of 25 percent or more may be achieved by irrigating when water is needed instead of when the clock says "go". These devices have been used successfully for many years to control irrigation of citrus groves in Southern California. Recent installations have been made in Palm Park in Redwood City, and four more are due to be installed in the Redwood Shores development.

for different user classes would have to be made and decisions about the watering of lawns, the use of swimming pools, and how to treat unmetered apartment dwellers would be required.[4] Also, it was very unlikely that the City Council would approve a policy banning the watering of lawns and, even if approved, the enforcement of such a ban would be exceedingly difficult.

---

[4]Typically, apartment buildings had one central water meter so that it was not possible to determine how much water was being used by each separate unit.

As Mr. Jay sat pondering the problem and looking out of his window at the rain, his telephone rang with the news that the San Francisco Water Department had imposed a 25 percent mandatory reduction in water consumption throughout its service area. Mr. Jay realized he had a few weeks to prepare a water conservation plan for the City Council to discuss and hopefully, adopt at its March 31 meeting. In presenting this plan, the Chief Engineer knew that not only would he need to defend it against alternative proposals, but he would also have to indicate why he believed that his plan would work.

Kirin Brewery Co., Ltd.: The Dry Beer War

Dominique Turpin
Christopher H. Lovelock
Joyce Miller

On February 22, 1988, Kirin Brewery decided to launch its own dry beer to compete with Asahi's Super Dry in the Japanese beer market. Kirin's decision to launch "Kirin Dry" was backed by strong consumer pressure. In liquor stores, more and more regular Kirin consumers were asking for Kirin's dry beer, and disappointed customers were switching to Asahi's Super Dry. Kirin's executives had anticipated that both Suntory and Sapporo would jump at the new opportunities created by Asahi to attack Kirin and gain a larger share of the beer market by developing the dry niche. In fact, a few days after the introduction of Kirin Dry, both Sapporo and Suntory launched their own dry beers. By early autumn, the market for dry beer had expanded enormously, and Asahi was currently selling half of the dry beer produced in Japan.

In late September 1988, Kazuhisa Tani, who headed Kirin's Beer Division, organized a meeting with several managers from the Marketing and Corporate Planning departments. After reviewing Kirin's performance, Tani remarked:

Kirin may have lost this summer's battle, but we are still fighting the war. Kirin must swallow its pride and commit itself to the dry beer competition, because the market is truly different now. It's all part of the game—even if dry beer triumphs enough to dislodge the old standbys, lager and draft. Campaigning for the 1989 sales year starts now. We have to be ready for the next round of the fight.

THE JAPANESE BEER INDUSTRY

The beer industry in Japan was born in 1853 when a doctor "test-brewed" some beer at home using the description in a Dutch book. Although Shozaburo Shibuya was said to have been the first Japanese to brew and sell beer as a business in 1872, it was not until the Sino-Japanese War (1937–41), and then World War II, that millions of Japanese people, mostly soldiers, enjoyed their first taste of beer.

By 1987, beer was a popular beverage throughout Japan, representing 67% of all alcoholic beverages consumed. It was followed by Japanese sake, 17.7%; Shochu (a white spirit), 7%; and whisky and brandy, 4%. Per capita consumption of beer had doubled from 20.2 liters in 1965 to 43.8 liters, while total consumption of all alcoholic beverages had grown from 36.3 liters to 65.3 liters. Japan was the fourth largest beer market in the world, with an annual per capita consumption of just under 500 million kiloliters (kl). However, international comparative data ranked the Japanese as the 28th greatest consumers of beer in the world on a per capita basis, with a consumption less than half the American figure and under one-third that of Germany, Czechoslovakia, Denmark, and New Zealand.

Production

The production and sale of beer were heavily influenced by seasonality, with 36% of sales made during the three months of June to August. Kirin's production manager estimated that the process of brewing beer was similar among competitors. But economies of scale could be significant.

The production of beer was controlled by the state through a licensing system, which made it difficult for newcomers to enter the market. According to Kenji Yamamoto, Deputy Manager in Kirin's Beer Division, "Investment in production is still dictated by market share, and today, one point market share is worth ¥5 billion in terms of marginal profits.[1]" In 1987, Kirin had 14 brewing plants, while Sapporo, Asahi, and Suntory had 10, 6, and 3 plants respectively. Yamamoto believed that its extensive network of production facilities gave Kirin a logistical cost advantage. Also, most of Kirin's breweries were built close to Japan's largest cities to ensure freshness, an element that had become a major selling point for many Japanese consumers. Yamamoto noted, "For beer lovers, the fresher, the better."

Each brewery had an average production capacity of 250,000 kl. Kirin executives estimated that in 1987, building a new brewery would represent a ¥50 billion investment (including the price of land). However, around Tokyo, such a construction could require an investment of up to ¥80–90 billion.

Product Categories and Market Segmentation

The Japanese beer market was divided into two major categories: "lager" and "draft." By international standards, lager was a beer with a long brewing process. However, in Japan, consumers regarded lager as a beer pasteurized by heat, while draft beer (also called "nama" in Japan) was unpasteurized under strict microbiological control, a technique called microfiltration. While draft beer represented 9% of the total beer market in 1974 (vs. 91% for lager), its share had grown to 20% in 1980. By 1987, draft accounted for 42%, lager for 51%, with the balance going to malts, dry, light, and foreign beers. Kirin held over 90% of the lager category, while sales of draft were split among the four brewers (refer to *Exhibit 1*). Kirin's Lager was by far the best-selling beer in Japan, and the firm's dominant position over the past 40 years had been built almost exclusively on this single product.

Foreign beer accounted for 3% of the total beer market. All the major Japanese brewers had tied up with large foreign brewers to distribute and brew their brands in Japan. Budweiser (from the US), brewed and distributed in Japan by Suntory, was the most popular foreign brand with the equivalent of 3.1 million cases[2] sold in 1987. Heineken (from the Netherlands) had a similar agreement with Kirin and was the second best-selling brand. Beer imports, primarily from the US, West Germany, France, and Denmark, had doubled in volume between 1984 and 1987, reaching 22.4 million liters.

The total adult population (aged 20 years old and over) in Japan was increasing at an average annual rate of 1.2%. The population of males aged 40 and over (regarded by Japanese brewers as the "heavy user" segment) had been growing more rapidly, at an average annual rate of 1.4%. "Heavy users," Asahi's key target for Super Dry, were defined as consumers drinking more than the equivalent of 8 regular (633 ml) bottles of beer each week. They represented 15% of the beer-drinking population and accounted for 50% of beer consumption. "Middle users" (15% of beer drinkers) consumed the equivalent of 3 to 8 bottles of beer weekly. Finally, "light users" (70% of beer drinkers) consumed fewer than 3 bottles each week. "Middle and light users" each represented about 25% of the volume of beer con-

---

[1]Yen (¥) exchange rate: ¥ 1,000 = US$7.25 = £ 4.30.

[2]One case contained 20 bottles of 633 ml (21.4 oz) each.

EXHIBIT 1
BEER SALES BY JAPANESE BREWERS BY SEGMENT, 1986–1988
(In Kiloliters)

	Lager	Draft	Dry	All malts	Total*
1986					
Kirin	2,352,900	388,800	0	22,100	2,763,800
Asahi	71,400	436,100	0	2,500	510,000
Sapporo	207,800	783,200	0	33,500	1,024,500
Suntory	0	408,200	0	41,500	449,700
	2,632,100	2,016,300	—	99,600	4,748,000
1987					
Kirin	2,491,800	479,000	0	42,000	3,012,800
Asahi	60,200	441,900	165,000	19,200	686,300
Sapporo	170,400	886,500	0	33,900	1,090,800
Suntory	0	394,800	0	110,000	504,800
	2,722,400	2,202,200	165,000	205,100	5,294,700
1988**					
Kirin	2,001,600	245,500	501,800	37,900	2,786,800
Asahi	12,500	210,800	943,100	14,000	1,180,400
Sapporo	105,800	712,300	275,200	38,700	1,132,000
Suntory	0	234,000	182,000	89,000	505,000
	2,119,900	1,402,600	1,902,100	179,600	5,604,200

*Totals exclude sales of light beer (15,000 kl) and imported foreign beers (32,000 kl).
**Projections for 12 months as of late September 1988.
Source: Kirin Brewery Co., Ltd.

sumed. In Japan, less than 10% of the total population never drank beer.

One notable trend was the growing number of female beer drinkers. Japanese women tended to be more health and weight conscious than men. To meet the needs of this segment, as well as to increase daytime consumption, Kirin had introduced Kirin Beer Light in 1980 and Kirin Palm Can in 1985. Kirin Beer Light had a lower alcohol content and attractive packaging that differentiated it from Kirin's other beer products. During the 1987 season, sales of light beer represented 0.3% of Kirin total beer revenues versus 83% for lager.

In Japan, 70% of the beer volume sold was consumed at home versus 30% in bars and restaurants. The Japanese associated no class connotation with beer, and it was quaffed with equal enthusiasm every-

where from four-stool diners to elite restaurants. However, consumption patterns were somewhat different from many Western countries. Most beer was consumed after 6:00 pm, before dinner, after the traditional "ofuro" (Japanese bath), or after sports. A Kirin executive explained:

Drinking together after working hours is as much a part of Japanese business as coming to work on time. However, most Japanese feel guilty drinking beer during the day on workdays. Because we Japanese have a different enzymology (enzymes in the human body), we tend to blush very quickly after a drink or two. If employees have a beer during the day, their working colleagues would notice immediately, and this could be quite an embarrassing situation.

Japanese consumers considered beer to be a light casual drink, while wine was perceived as light but more formal. Kirin's consumer research showed that beer was seen as a healthy and natural drink because it was brewed with no artificial additives. Shochu, another popular drink, was also considered casual, but it was a strong drink and was losing its popularity. The consumption of shochu, a distilled spirit, had experienced a major boom from 1982 to 1987. However, shochu was now seen by industry analysts as a fashion fad, and some predicted that the Super Dry boom could be the same.

COMPETITION AND MARKETING ACTIVITIES

The Japanese beer market was an oligopoly with four companies (Kirin, Asahi, Suntory, and Sapporo) representing over 99% of the total sales volume. Two small brewers, Hokkaido Asahi and Orion, operated on a local basis only—on the northern island of Hokkaido and in Okinawa in the most southern part of Japan, respectively.

Kirin Brewery

Kirin was the top brewer in Japan and the fourth largest in the world after Anheuser-Busch and Miller of the USA and Heineken of the Netherlands. Kirin's 1987 sales amounted to ¥1,300 billion with profits of ¥31 billion. Kirin traced its origins back to 1870 when an American entrepreneur, W. Copeland, established Spring Valley, 40 kilometers south of Tokyo. The brewery was active until 1884. The organization was subsequently revamped, and operations resumed under the management of Japan Brewery Company, Ltd., which was taken over by Kirin Brewery Company, Ltd. in 1907. Building on its predecessor's philosophy, Kirin established the management tenets that still guided the company 80 years later: "Quality First" and "Sound Management."

In 1954, Kirin captured top share in the beer industry from Sapporo Breweries. However, Asahi, Kirin, and Sapporo remained close competitors with roughly one-third of the market each (refer to *Exhibit 2*). Since the 1950s, as far as the public was con-

cerned, "Beer meant Kirin." In 1966, Kirin's market share passed 50%. But Kirin pushed its advantage even further, seizing a 63% share of the Japanese beer market in 1979. At this point, under the provision of the Japanese Anti-Monopoly Law, the Fair Trade Commission threatened legislation to break Kirin Brewery into two separate companies. In the end, the Kirin organization remained intact.

In 1971, Kirin began to diversify its operations. Through an agreement with the Canadian firm, J.E. Seagrams & Sons, Kirin began to import liquor produced overseas, including Chivas Regal. Five years later, a joint venture in Australia was established, and through a domestic venture, Kirin began to market Koiwai food products. In 1977, Kirin established KW Inc. to bottle and market Coca-Cola in the US, and later created Kirin USA, Inc. Kirin also planned to expand its presence in the US market using beer brewed in Canada by Molson Ltd. In addition, Kirin had tied up with Heineken N.V., Europe's largest beer brewer, and the company had set up several joint ventures in the United States in the field of biotechnology. In 1987, Kirin arranged to exchange information and technology with several organizations in Czechoslovakia.

Despite its diversification into soft drinks, dairy products, whisky, and biotechnology, Kirin was still heavily dependent on beer. Kirin's president elaborated, "In 1987, beer represented 93% of our sales volume. This makes us vulnerable to Asahi's recent attack. We need to review the market situation and also to react adequately to Asahi's challenge."

Sapporo Breweries Ltd.

Sapporo had once been the dominant player in the market. However, it had gradually lost share to its three competitors. In 1987, it was the second largest brewer in Japan with a 20% share of the domestic market. Sapporo had a dominant position in the draft segment, holding a 40% share (refer to *Exhibit 1*). Although Sapporo had diversified into soft drinks, wine, and imported liquors such as J&B whisky, beer still accounted for 94% of the company's total revenues.

EXHIBIT 2

COMPARATIVE MARKET SHARES IN THE JAPANESE BEER
INDUSTRY, 1949–1987

Year	Brewer				
	Asahi	Kirin	Sapporo	Suntory	Takara
1949	36.1%	25.3%	38.6%	—%	—%
1950	33.5	29.5	37.0	—	—
1951	34.5	29.5	36.0	—	—
1952	32.5	33.0	34.5	—	—
1953	33.3	33.2	33.5	—	—
1954	31.5	37.1	31.4	—	—
1955	31.7	36.9	31.4	—	—
1956	31.1	41.7	27.2	—	—
1957	30.7	42.1	26.2	—	1.0
1958	30.9	39.9	27.5	—	1.7
1959	29.3	42.4	26.5	—	1.8
1960	27.2	44.7	26.0	—	2.1
1961	28.0	41.6	27.8	—	2.6
1962	26.4	45.0	26.4	—	2.2
1963	24.3	46.5	26.3	0.9	2.0
1964	25.5	46.2	25.2	1.2	1.9
1965	23.2	47.7	25.3	1.9	1.9
1966	22.2	50.8	23.8	1.7	1.5
1967	22.0	49.4	25.0	3.2	0.4
1968	20.2	51.2	24.4	4.2	—
1969	19.0	53.3	23.2	4.5	—
1970	17.3	55.4	23.0	4.3	—
1971	14.9	58.9	22.0	4.2	—
1972	14.1	60.1	21.3	4.5	—
1973	13.6	61.4	20.3	4.7	—
1974	13.1	62.6	19.5	4.8	—
1975	13.5	60.8	20.2	5.5	—
1976	11.8	63.8	18.4	6.0	—
1977	12.1	61.9	19.5	6.5	—
1978	11.6	62.1	19.6	6.7	—
1979	11.1	62.9	19.2	6.8	—
1980	11.0	62.2	19.7	7.1	—
1981	10.3	62.6	20.1	7.0	—
1982	10.0	62.3	19.9	7.8	—
1983	10.1	61.3	20.0	8.6	—
1984	9.9	61.7	19.5	8.9	—
1985	9.6	61.4	19.8	9.2	—
1986	10.4	59.6	20.4	9.4	—
1987	12.9	57.0	20.5	9.6	—

Source: Figures up to 1981: estimated by the Brewers Association of Japan. 1982–1987: case-writer's estimates.

Suntory Ltd.

Established in 1899 by Shinjiro Torii, the father of the firm's current president, Suntory was the major producer of whisky in Japan as well as a leading importer of Scotch whiskeys, bourbons, whiskeys, cognacs, wines, liqueurs, beers, etc. In 1986, Suntory had total sales of ¥625.8 billion and was credited with a 63% share of the Japanese whisky market. In comparison, Kirin-Seagram (the third largest whisky company) held a 7.6% share and Nikka Whisky (the second largest local whisky producer) had a 21% share.

Suntory was a privately held company headed by Keizo Saji, who had a reputation for an aggressive management style. In 1960, Saji had turned his attention to beer making, since Suntory had reached a virtual monopoly position in whisky. Most beers available in Japan at that time were German-style lager beers, so Suntory began searching for alternatives. After considerable research, Saji concluded that beer produced under strict microbiological control—similar to Danish-style beer—would have a "cleaner and milder" flavor and be a better match for Japanese cuisine. Suntory's first beer went on the market in 1963. Four years later, the company began producing only unpasteurized bottled and canned draft beer. Suntory had gradually caught up to Asahi in terms of market share. By the end of the 1987 season, Suntory had captured 9.6% of the total beer market. The company focused on the draft segment and was the leading brand in the "all malts" draft sub-segment (refer to *Exhibit 1*).

In addition to brewing its own beers, Suntory produced and marketed several foreign beers in Japan through licensing agreements with Anheuser-Busch Co., Inc. of the United States and Carlsberg, a Danish brewer. Since 1984, Suntory had also brewed beer in China. In fiscal year 1986, beer represented 27% of Suntory's total revenues.

Asahi Breweries Ltd.

Asahi was the third largest brewer in Japan in 1987. The company had gradually lost ground to Kirin, Sapporo, and Suntory, falling below 10% market share in 1985. While sales had grown substantially between 1976 and 1986, net profits declined from ¥2.13 billion in 1976 to ¥1.51 billion in 1986, but climbed up again in 1987. An Asahi manager explained:

In the 1970s, our company was the prisoner of a vicious circle. Sales were gradually slowing down, resulting in slower inventory turnovers and changing tastes, which affected our sales and our image. Also, since consumers did not have a high opinion of our products, retailers did not push our products, no matter how much effort our salesmen put in the trade. The salesmen blamed the engineers for not turning out good products, and the engineers blamed the salesmen for not being able to sell a product that they thought was as good as the competition.

To overcome Asahi's declining market share, management pushed to reduce the dependence on beer by expanding sales of soft drinks, foods, and pharmaceuticals. Asahi had, in fact, become less dependent on beer than both Kirin and Sapporo. In 1987, soft drinks represented 25% of Asahi's total sales. On the basis of field research indicating that consumer preference was shifting from the bitter and richer taste of Kirin's Lager to a sharper draft taste, Asahi's Marketing Department proposed changing the taste of the company's draft beer. Launched in early 1986, the new Asahi Draft "koku-kire" (rich and sharp) got off to a smooth start. However, Asahi's share of the total beer market continued to drop, and the number of retailers carrying the Asahi brand was also declining.

Marketing Activities

Marketing expenditures by the four brewers had increased sharply, rising from ¥140 billion in 1984 to ¥196 billion in 1987, partly as a result of Asahi's launch of Super Dry (refer to *Exhibit 3*). Typically, 80% of all marketing expenditures were made between January and May.

Advertising and Promotion For Kuichi Matsui, the General Manager of Asahi's Marketing Department, advertising was crucial in Japan's highly competitive marketplace "where neon is king and gimmickry is commonplace." Matsui was referring to a "packaging war" that occurred between 1984 and 1986 when various "gadget products," such as the Suntory Penguins and the Kirin Beer Shuttle, had been used to attract consumer attention. By 1987, Matsui felt that consumers had become bored with such sales tactics.

Pricing The National Tax Agency advised Japanese brewers on the appropriate prices for alcoholic beverages. In Japan, beer was the most heavily taxed

EXHIBIT 3

COMPARATIVE MARKETING EXPENDITURES OF JAPANESE BREWERS, 1984–1987

(In billions of Yen)

	Advertising expenses	Promotion expenses	Total marketing expenses	As % of beer sales*
Kirin				
1983	11.4	18.1	29.5	2.7
1984	15.9	21.7	37.6	3.2
1985	13.9	21.4	35.3	2.9
1986	15.9	28.1	44.0	3.5
1987**	18.4	35.2	53.6	4.2
Asahi				
1983	7.9	7.5	15.4	7.1
1984	8.9	10.0	18.9	8.4
1985	7.9	10.9	18.8	7.9
1986	11.7	13.8	25.5	9.8
1987**	18.9	19.2	38.1	11.0
Sapporo				
1983	8.6	4.9	13.5	3.7
1984	11.0	5.5	16.5	4.3
1985	12.1	6.0	18.1	4.5
1986	13.3	7.8	21.1	4.8
1987**	15.1	8.7	23.8	5.1
Suntory				
1983	27.9	39.6	67.5	7.9
1984	26.7	39.8	66.5	8.7
1985	22.8	39.6	62.4	8.1
1986	22.9	46.6	69.5	9.2
1987**	27.1	53.6	80.7	10.3

*Beer as a percentage of total sales (1984–1987): Kirin: 93%; Asahi: 79%; Sapporo: 94%; Suntory: 28%.
**Estimated.
Source: Dentsu Inc., 1987.

alcoholic beverage, at a rate of 46.9% (vs. 36.3% for whiskeys and brandies and 17–20% for sakes and shochus). This meant that when a consumer paid ¥300 for a regular 633 ml bottle of beer, ¥140.7 was collected by the state. Kirin executives estimated that profits increased by ¥4 billion for each yen in price increase.

Distribution   The brewers sold beer to the consumer through a group of primary wholesalers. In turn, some of these sold to sub-wholesalers, who distributed products through a large number of retail outlets. Wholesalers and retailers were both licensed by the state, which strictly limited the issue of new licenses. Most distributors in the Kanto (Greater Tokyo) dealt with all four brewers, while exclusive distributors had a stronger position in the Kansai region (Western Japan). The number of sub-wholesalers was declining; developing personal relationships with the wholesalers was still a key success factor for brewers. In 1987, more than 1,800 wholesalers distributed beer and other alcoholic beverages.

Kirin worked with 800 of these and had exclusive agreements with 70% of them.

Distribution was said to be a major barrier of entry for new entrants. As the executive of a Danish brewery explained:

It's pretty difficult to distribute beer in a country with more than one million bars, pubs, and restaurants, and hundreds of thousands of stores in huge cities with virtually no street names. Tying up with a local player is almost a prerequisite. To establish our own distribution network through primary wholesalers, secondary wholesalers, and sometimes tertiary wholesalers would probably take us at least 10 years.

Retailers were liquor store owners who sold to consumers as well as to neighborhood bars and restaurants. Typically, retailers independently selected which beer to sell according to the popularity of each brand. However, each major brewer had a merchandising sales force to ensure that the company's products were effectively displayed in the stores.

Junichi Nakamura, a 54-year-old retailer in the Shinagawa and one of the 130,000 liquor store owners in Japan, wondered how successful Asahi's Super Dry would be in the long run. He was used to seeing some 40 kinds of new beer packaging arrive on his shelves every year, then disappear after a few months because the brewers launched new products one after another and gave up quickly when a new product did not sell well. Nakamura also wondered if many consumers could really tell the difference between Asahi Dry and other regular beers.

ASAHI SUPER DRY

In the spring of 1986, Hirotaro Higuchi took over the presidency of Asahi Breweries, replacing Tsutomu Murai, who was appointed as the company's chairman. Higuchi intended to pursue the objective set earlier by Murai; namely, to turn Asahi into a truly customer-oriented company. His ultimate objective was to restore Asahi's market share to the level the company had enjoyed right after World War II, when Asahi competed neck-and-neck with Sapporo and Kirin.

Higuchi felt that over the past 30 years, Asahi had developed a corporate culture where everyone blamed someone else for the annual loss of market share. His first step was to change the perception of Asahi Beer within the company. Higuchi's new corporate philosophy emphasized quality first, followed by customer orientation, respect for each other, labor-management conciliation, cooperation with the trade, and social responsibility. A corporate booklet with 10 commandments was distributed to all employees as a guide to daily behavior. These "commandments" were also read aloud at work each morning so that every employee would understand Asahi's new direction.

To change Asahi's image, Higuchi decided to develop new packaging. All beers carrying the old-fashioned imperial flag were recalled from the retailers' shelves. Higuchi aimed to send the trade, the public, and the competition a strong message that Asahi had changed significantly. As well, he implemented a "Quality First" policy and instructed the Purchasing Department to use only the best raw materials, even if this meant higher costs. Finally, Higuchi decided that the company would increase its advertising and promotional expenditures, even at the risk of eating up all net profits.

When Higuchi discussed the "dry" concept for the first time with 12 Asahi executives in the fall of 1986, no one really supported the idea. Higuchi recalled that his production director went so far as to say, "We can't produce a dry beer, this is nonsense to me." The marketing people explained that the meaning of the word "dry" was important, "Dry suggests something new, decisive, and bold. We found out that a 'wet' person is very strongly attached to family, the company, and friends, while a 'dry' type is more individualistic."

Higuchi felt that he should postpone the launch of Super Dry until the new Asahi draft had established a stronger position in the market. Yet, young managers in the Marketing, R&D, and Production departments were quite comfortable with the concept of Super Dry. As well, the production engineers indicated that "dry beer" would not require a major breakthrough in production technology. A young marketing executive had told Higuchi, "I think that the 'dry' concept is viable, but I can't tell you how much we can expect to sell."

The Launch of Super Dry

By early 1987, the R&D department had managed to develop a "dry" beer. Meanwhile, the Marketing Department had gathered more data using "hands-on" test markets to determine favorable consumer attitudes. They had developed a comprehensive marketing plan and set a first-year sales target of 800,000 cases. On March 17, 1987, Asahi's "Super Dry" beer was officially launched.

Super Dry was designed as a draft beer targeted at heavy drinkers. Made with less residual sugar, the beer was less sweet. It contained 0.5% more alcohol than the 4.5% regular draft beers, and had been defined as much sharper and softer than traditional draft beers (refer to *Exhibit 4*). Super Dry was made using the best hops from Czechoslovakia and Germany, and malts from the United States, Canada, and Australia. Asahi's production engineers had shortened the time from production to consumption to an average of 20 days, while other brewers operated on a 23–25 day cycle. The Super Dry silver label with Asahi's new logo and modern lettering reinforced the image of a truly different product.

Asahi's marketing budget had been increased from ¥25.5 billion in 1986 to ¥38.1 billion (refer to *Exhibit 3*), and ¥4.2 billion was spent on advertising to promote Super Dry in 1987. Hakuhodo, Japan's second largest advertising company, designed a campaign featuring Nobuhiko Ochiai, a former US oilman who had become a respected international journalist. To launch Super Dry, Asahi ran full-page advertisements in all five major dailies. The ads were spread across three weeks: a "coming soon" preview, a "debuts today" announcement, and a "have you tried it yet?" follow-up ad. Television commercials were double the normal volume for a new product campaign. Asahi also distributed free samples to a million people throughout Japan. In addition to its 500 salespeople (vs. 520 for Kirin), Asahi had set up sales teams with 1,000 "field ladies" to promote and merchandise the new product at the retail level and collect additional marketing data from consumers regarding preference, purchase habits, and so on.

In the fall of 1987, while the beer market in Japan had grown by 7%, Asahi's total sales had soared by 34%, mainly thanks to Super Dry.

KIRIN'S RESPONSE TO ASAHI

Asahi's performance had had the effect of a small earthquake within the Kirin organization, and various teams were put to work to generate alternatives to meet the Asahi challenge. In late October 1987, Kirin's President, Hideyo Motoyama, called a special meeting of the Beer Division's executives to decide Kirin's strategy for the 1988 beer season. The outcome of this meeting included decisions to launch three new products—Kirin Dry, Kirin Fine Malt, and Kirin Fine Draft—to relaunch Kirin Beer as Kirin Lager Beer, and to make a price cut.

The objective in launching Kirin Dry was to respond to consumers' needs, fill the niche created by Asahi, and beat Asahi on its own turf with a superior product. The Kirin Dry concept was similar to Asahi's Super Dry. The new product had 5% more alcohol than regular beer, the same number of calories, and a drier, less sweet taste. Kirin's Dry (like the dry beers launched by Suntory and Sapporo) used the same silver packaging that Asahi had used for its Super Dry and contained the following message in English:

EXHIBIT 4
POSITIONING MAP FOR KIRIN'S PRODUCTS

Source: Kirin Brewery Co., Ltd.

Our superior fermentation technology and carefully selected hops have produced a beer with an exceptionally delicate taste, well-balanced with a dry finish. The connoisseur's beer, "KIRIN DRY," will add a new taste of pleasure to your day.

Kirin Dry was offered in 633 ml and 500 ml bottles and in 500 ml and 350 ml cans. Asahi's Super Dry was sold in 633 ml, 500 ml, and 334 ml bottles, in 350 ml, 250 ml, and 135 ml cans as well as in 2, 3 and 10 liter barrels for on-premises outlets.

On April 20, 1988, Kirin announced that it would cut the price on one of its mainline products, 500 ml cans, citing an increase in foreign exchange gains due to the appreciation of the yen as the reason. Kirin had indeed saved ¥3.4 billion over the past two years on imported hops and malt used in the brewing process. The result for the consumer was a reduction in the retail price of a 500 ml can of beer from ¥280 to ¥270. A Goldman, Sachs & Co. analyst commented:

The major reason for Kirin's action was to restore its market share under the impact of increased competition from Asahi's Super Dry. Kirin's price cut was immediately followed by Asahi and Sapporo. These cuts (all ¥10 per can) were the first changes in 26 years. The Kirin people believed that the impact of such a price cut would be minimal, while Sapporo and Asahi would each suffer damage in the range of ¥300 million by following Kirin down in price.

Real competition in dry beer is starting now. We believe that distribution capability and financial resources to back strong advertising campaigns will dictate that Kirin wins in view of its larger size.

Kirin's management decided to change the name as well as the packaging of Kirin's regular beer from Kirin Beer to Kirin LAGER Beer, with a large red "LAGER" printed on all labels. In mid-June 1988, just before the summer season, Kirin launched "Kirin Fine Malt" and "Kirin Fine Draft," both positioned as "after-dry" products to reinforce Kirin's presence in the draft segment and to signal an end to the dry beer boom. Kirin Fine Malt was first introduced in some local areas and launched nationally a few months later.

Reorganization at Kirin

In early 1988, Kirin's president appointed Kazuhisa Tani to head a task force to recommend and implement a new corporate strategy for Kirin's Beer Division. Tani had broad responsibilities for marketing and corporate planning, and he reported directly to Motoyama.

Tani had joined Kirin Brewery in 1962 right after graduating from university. He had first worked as a controller in the Amagasaki brewery before joining headquarters in 1971 to work in Kirin's joint venture with Seagram's. From 1982 until early 1988, Tani had headed Kirin-Seagram, apart from one year at the MIT-Sloan School of Management in the United States to earn an MS degree. Kirin-Seagram was considered to be much more market-oriented than the conservative Kirin organization, and Motoyama expected that Tani would be able to transfer some of the entrepreneurial spirit of the joint venture.

Tani recommended the development and the introduction of two new management control systems: MRS (management reporting system) and ME (marketing engineering). MRS was a system to evaluate each salesperson's performance in relation to sales volumes and expenses. The ME system involved developing a marketing database for the brand managers. Under the new organization of the Beer Division, headquarters and the breweries were cost centers, and the only profit centers were the sales branches, with brand managers responsible for the profitability of their own operations.

In the spring of 1988, Tani recommended accelerating the plan to expand the sales network from 17 branches to 40 additional sales offices, and to increase the sales force from 550 to 800 by 1990. Tani also pressed to speed up the development of the KIC (Kirin Intelligence & Communication) network, which would enable Kirin to monitor the market more closely. Information technology had been a central theme of Kirin's 1981 diversification plan. In May 1985, Kirin became the first Japanese brewer to offer a line of computers (the KN line) to wholesalers and retailers throughout Japan. The KIC project aimed to install on-line computers in an additional 350 liquor wholesalers and 1,000 retail stores by

1990, providing them with a variety of speedy services, such as cash register, inventory control, sales data, and invoicing. The computer network would also provide Kirin's management with immediate feedback on the rotation of stocks and daily sales trends for all Kirin products as well as those of the competitors.

THE DRY WAR

The simultaneous introduction of dry products by Kirin, Sapporo, and Suntory triggered an immediate marketing war. None of these dry beers were clearly differentiated from Asahi's Super Dry in concept, taste, or packaging, which led Asahi to request that its competitors modify both the packaging and the concept of their dry beers.

Asahi's rising voice against "unfair competition" attracted the attention of the press, and the dry war suddenly became a national affair. While Asahi and its competitors were fighting through the intermediary of the press, an advertising war was also taking place. Asahi was massively advertising Super Dry using journalist Nobuhiko Ochiai as the central character of its campaign. Meanwhile, Kirin had signed up the Hollywood actor Gene Hackman for its Kirin Dry campaign around the theme: "I'm so happy I could cry Dry, Dry!" Suntory had developed an advertising campaign featuring Mike Tyson, the world boxing superchampion: " Hi, I'm Mike Tyson. I like Suntory DRY." A Suntory manager explained that Tyson had been chosen "to communicate the power and the punch of dry beer." Finally, Sapporo had signed up Japanese sports celebrities for its Sapporo Dry campaign.

Suntory and Sapporo had followed Kirin's strategy, advertising and aggressively pushing for their traditional products: "100% Malt" for Suntory and "Black Label" for Sapporo. The four brewers had increased their advertising budgets by an average of 20% over the previous year, exposing consumers to more beer advertising than they had probably seen in their entire lives. Although consumers had been somewhat confused at first by the dry war, they did realize that Asahi was the original inventor of the dry beer concept. A liquor store owner in Tokyo commented:

Japanese consumers are fascinated by this all-out marketing war. They enjoy reading about the battle for market share in their newspapers. They also like watching hired hands (Mike Tyson vs. Gene Hackman, for example) fight it out in a deluge of TV and print ads. Keeping up-to-date dominates the chats in my store. Employees also discuss the beer war with their colleagues. When I deliver beer to the neighboring bars and restaurants, I can hear people expressing opinions on possible upcoming trends. People wonder what will happen next. It's a social phenomenon.

The Situation in Autumn 1988

By summer's end, when beer consumption typically began to decline, Asahi had clearly won the dry beer sweepstakes. In the beer industry, where a hit product reached sales of 1 million cases in its first year, the 13.5 million cases achieved by Super Dry was an amazing success. Asahi had reached three major milestones that would have been unthinkable a scant 16 months earlier. For the first time in two decades, Asahi's share of total beer sales in Japan had broken the 20% market share barrier. In August 1988, Asahi confirmed that after 23 years it had overtaken Sapporo as Japan's second largest brewery. Asahi was now selling half of the dry beer produced in Japan.

In July 1988, Kirin was actually producing more dry beer than Asahi, although Asahi's sales of the new product remained larger by a slim margin. At this time, total beer sales were 1% lower than the year before. The summer's relatively cool, rainy weather had been bad for beer sales, but ironically good for Asahi. A month later, dry beer accounted for a heady 34% of total beer sales, while lager had 38% and draft, 25%. Yoshio Matsuda from the Brewers Association of Japan remarked:

This is an amazing phenomenon. Just think—in the US it took 18 years for light beers to obtain a 25% share of the total beer market, and it took Asahi only 16 months to achieve a similar result in Japan. Only a year earlier, 51% of all beer sold in Japan was lager and 42% was draft. The good weather in August and September put a new kick in the beer industry and by early October 1988, the market had grown by 7.6%. Meanwhile, Asahi sales had shot up by 72%. I think that the rapid growth of the dry beer market was due to three factors. First, Super Dry was a unique concept and a well-accepted taste, based on extensive marketing research. Second, having the total participation of the four major breweries involved in an advertising war with massive budgets developed awareness and interest in the dry segment. Third, Japanese consumers are inclined to quickly follow fashion trends.

However, other factors had played an important part in Asahi's success. Sales activities had aimed at promoting fresh product rotation. Over the past year, Asahi increased its capital investment in plant and equipment by 50%. By 1988, its production capacity was 2.5 times the level it was in 1986.

The dry war had social consequences as well. Since August, many liquor store owners had placed apologetic signs on their doors saying they were out of Super Dry beer. The press had also reported that Asahi's president had asked his employees not to buy Super Dry because every precious drop had to be reserved for its customers. An Asahi manager acknowledged that the company's success was also an issue:

This summer we had a major problem with capacity. We were planning to sell 13.5 million cases in 1988, but we are only at the end of September and we have already sold more than 83 million! Right now, we have 3 plants producing beer only and 5 plants producing both beer and juice. To meet the demand during the summer, we had to stop producing juice and turn all these plants into breweries. Asahi is now devoting nearly all of its brewing capacity to Super Dry. Despite these efforts, we could cope with only 70% of the demand for dry beer. Moreover, we don't have enough capacity to brew Coors locally, as originally agreed under Asahi's 5-year 1987 licensing pact with Adolph Coors. Last June, our capacity crunch was so severe that we arranged to import the Coors we couldn't brew in Japan. To meet the bare minimum of our licensing agreement, Asahi—at a cost of $2.3 million—chartered 15 Boeing 747 jumbo jet freighters to transport 141,450 cases of Coors and Coors Light in 12-oz. cans and bottles from Golden, Colorado, over a period of 3 months. We now have to decide whether to invest in building one or two new breweries, since we expect industry sales to grow at around 7% annually over the next 3 years.

The dry war that had been taking place in Japan had also attracted the attention of the large foreign brewers. The Miller Brewing Company, for instance, had recently begun conducting market research on dry products in the United States.

New Competitive Moves in Japan

In the fall of 1988, the future of the dry boom remained uncertain. Asahi had recently published the results of a marketing survey called "The Asahi Super Dry Era," concluding that Super Dry was here to stay. However, Asahi's competitors were more divided about the future of the dry segment. In 1988, each major brewer was strong in a different type of beer. Kirin's best-seller was lager, Asahi had dry, and Sapporo had draft. Looking at Asahi's success, Kazuo Arakawa, Sapporo's executive vice president, said, "Asahi helped Sapporo by jolting Kirin. Dry beer has gotten people talking about beer, has widened the range of products available, and generally invigorated the market."

Taking advantage of the turbulent environment created by the dry war, all brewers were launching new products to prepare for what Sapporo executives called the "after-dry era." Japanese consumers now had a wide choice of beers available, varying from 4.5–9% in alcohol content. Sapporo had recently launched its "On-the-Rocks Beer," a high-alcohol (9%) beer that was meant to be sipped over ice, like whiskey. Sapporo had also announced its "Winter's Tale" beer to be sold only from November to February. Suntory had launched "5.5," a dry beer with a higher alcohol content (5.5% vs. 5% for regular dry beers).

Ken Takanashi, a Suntory manager, believed that Suntory's "malts" could be a particular threat to Asahi Super Dry. He explained, "Malts were a hit last year until being eclipsed by the dry war along with lager and draft, but as of August they seem to be bubbling again." To counter an expansion of the malt sub-segment, Kirin had introduced Kirin Fine Malt (a 100% malt beer) in June 1988, initially on a regional basis, then nationally in the fall of 1988. Kirin Fine Malt was positioned as a new draft beer.

Defining Kirin's New Product Line Strategy

In late September 1988, Kazuhisa Tani met with several managers from the Marketing and Corporate Planning departments. After reviewing Kirin's performance relative to the competition in each of the major categories of beer (refer to *Exhibits 1* and *5*), he asked his product managers to put forward their proposals for new products.

Messrs. Fukuyama and Makita, respectively in charge of R&D and Marketing for the Beer Division, presented two new products. Malt Dry was a 100% malt draft beer with a 5% alcohol content, which would occupy a unique position in the market. In Makita's opinion, Malt Dry was a new concept serving the two fastest growing segments of the market: dry and all malt. Kirin Cool was an extra smooth beer with a 4.5% alcohol content and a softer taste, targeted at men and women aged 20–25. It was positioned in the "soft and smooth segment" of the market (refer to *Exhibit 4*). Kirin Cool's unique selling proposition was "a taste never before experienced."

Makita also indicated that Kirin Fine Pilsner was

ready to be launched. Positioned in the "rich and smooth" segment, Kirin Fine Pilsner would be targeted at people in their twenties and thirties. Its unique selling proposition was "a new standard beer with creamy froth like a velvet touch." The Corporate Planning Department favored launching all three products in the next year, reasoning that a full-line strategy would give Kirin complete coverage of the market. Makita was not convinced:

With so many new products on the market, we run the risk of confusing the consumer. Moreover, the launch of each new product will cost us at least ¥1 billion. For next year, I would personally favor launching "Malt Dry" and *only* "Malt Dry."

Ryosuke Murata, also from the Marketing Department, disagreed:

I don't think that we should launch a new dry beer. We should get away from this segment and prepare for the after-dry era. I am in favor of pushing Kirin Lager more aggressively. After all, it's still our best-selling product, and it has a rich thick taste with a fine aroma.

EXHIBIT 5 COMPARATIVE PERFORMANCE OF JAPANESE BREWERS, 1987–1988

	Comparative market shares by segment							
	Lager		Draft		Dry		All malts	
	1987	1988*	1987	1988*	1987	1988*	1987	1988*
Kirin	91.5%	94.4%	21.8%	21.5%	0%	26.4%	20.5%	29.6%
Asahi	2.2	0.6	20.1	14.3	100	49.6	9.4	7.0
Sapporo	6.3	5.0	40.2	48.3	0	14.5	16.5	19.2
Suntory	0	0	17.9	15.9	0	9.5	53.6	44.2
Total	100%	100%	100%	100%	100%	100%	100%	100%

	Comparative product mix by brewer									
	Lager		Draft		Dry		All malts		Total	
	1987	1988*	1987	1988*	1987	1988*	1987	1988*	1987	1988*
Kirin	82.7%	69.6%	15.9%	11.0%	0%	17.4%	1.4%	2.1%	100%	100%
Asahi	8.8	1.1	64.4	17.9	24	79.9	2.8	1.2	100	100
Sapporo	15.6	9.3	81.3	62.9	0	24.3	3.1	3.4	100	100
Suntory	0	0	78.2	46.3	0	36.0	21.8	17.6	100	100

*As of September 1988.
Source: Kirin Brewery Co., Ltd., 1988.

Makita presented a final proposal concerning Kirin Fine Draft, which aimed to reposition Kirin in the draft segment by "re-creating the taste in beer halls."

Tani also had in front of him some new marketing data collected by the Mitsubishi Research Institute (refer to *Exhibit 6*) as well as some data on dry beer blind tests in which consumers had been asked to compare competitive products according to different attributes (refer to *Exhibit 7*). It was now time to make a decision on Kirin's product strategy and develop a marketing plan for 1989.

EXHIBIT 6
RESULTS FROM THE MITSUBISHI RESEARCH INSTITUTE CONCERNING CONSUMER OPINIONS ON DRY BEER IN JAPAN

Survey design

Area: Tokyo
Timing: September 1988
Sample: 504 people (all beer drinkers)

Question 1: "What is your favorite type of beer?"

Responses by sex

	Men	Women	Total
Lager	15.8%	6.0%	12.1%
Draft	20.9	20.2	20.6
Dry	55.6	65.6	59.3
All malts	4.9	4.9	4.9
Light	1.3	2.2	1.6

Responses by age bracket

	20s	30s	40s	50s
Lager	6.2%	9.2%	17.0%	27.3%
Draft	21.2	20.9	20.6	18.2
Dry	61.6	63.8	54.6	50.0
All malts	7.5	3.7	4.3	2.3
Light	2.7	1.2	0.7	2.3

Question 2: "What made you drink dry beer?"

I saw some commercials on TV	64.0%
I read an article about it	37.7
I saw it in a store	14.3
I read some comparative studies	36.2
It's available at home	34.2
People around me drink it	36.2

Question 3: "What made you drink . . ."

	Asahi Super Dry?	Kirin Dry?	Sapporo Dry?	Suntory Dry?
I saw some commercials on TV	63.4%	62.8%	72.0%	76.2%
I read an article about it	38.8	35.9	38.0	33.3

(Continued on next page)

EXHIBIT 6   *(Continued)*

Question 3: "What made you drink . . ."

	Asahi Super Dry?	Kirin Dry?	Sapporo Dry?	Suntory Dry?
I saw it in a store	14.6%	12.8%	12.0%	28.6%
I read some comparative studies	34.8	37.2	38.0	42.9
It's available at home	35.1	30.8	32.0	38.4
People around me drink it	34.8	37.2	38.0	42.9

Question 4: "Why do you think beer-drinking attitudes changed?"

Preferences have changed	12.7%
New products have been introduced	68.8
People make comparisons	18.5
Newspapers and magazines reported on it	30.2
Lifestyles have changed	16.0

Question 5: "What were your impressions when you first tasted a dry beer?"

It tastes different	28.0%
It has good body	30.8
It has a sharp taste	38.1
It has a smooth taste	35.6
It has more alcohol	20.3
It tastes like other beers	17.8
It is trendy	15.1
It has a good label and a good name	15.3
Others	2.9

Question 6: "What do you mean by 'beer with good body'?"

A sharp beer	22.9%
A thick beer	52.2
A bitter beer	30.4
A sweet beer	18.8
A good feeling in the throat	19.0
It smells good	17.0
A stronger beer	14.4
The real beer	57.5
Others	2.4

Question 7: "What type of beer do you associate most with this concept of good body?"

Lager	14.0%
Draft	17.8
Dry	28.5
All malts	20.6
Light	0.2
Black	11.7
Others	1.6

EXHIBIT 6   *(Continued)*

Question 8: "What do you mean by 'a sharp beer'?"

A good feeling in the throat	60.1%
A pure taste	38.5
Bitterness disappears rapidly	51.6
No bitterness	20.0
A beer with a higher degree of fermentation	24.3
A stronger beer	14.6

Question 9: "With what kind of beer do you associate most with this concept of sharpness?"

Lager	5.5%
Draft	21.9
Dry	55.1
All malts	4.7
Light	3.8
Black	0.2
Others	1.6

Question 10: "Do you think that your consumption of dry beer will increase or decrease?"

Will decrease	23.2%
Will remain stable	48.7
Will increase	25.2

Question 11: "Why will your consumption of dry beer decrease?"

It is not my taste	44.6%
I don't see any difference from other beers	8.0
I don't drink it because it is a fad	4.5
People around me don't drink it	8.9
It does not taste good	28.6
I'm getting tired of it	28.6
That's the way it is	25.0
Other reasons	10.7

Question 12: "Why will your consumption of dry beer increase?"

I like the taste	52.2%
People around me drink it	17.6
It's trendy	21.3
I'd like to try other beers	19.1
It tastes good	63.2
It's available at home	25.7
I'm tired of other beers	5.1
Other reasons	8.1

Note: Multiple responses to questions 2–12 add to more than 100%.
Source: Mitsubishi Research Institute, September 1988.

EXHIBIT 7
BLIND TESTS FOR DIFFERENT BEERS

Survey design			

Area:	Tokyo
Timing:	September 1988
Sample:	450 people (all beer drinkers)

	Product		
Attribute	**Kirin Lager**	**Asahi Dry**	**Sapporo Draft**
Flavor	100*	99.4	98.8
Bitterness	100	92.6	94.9
Softness	100	113.3	113.0
Lightness	100	116.0	114.5
Richness	100	88.1	91.7
Carbonization	100	99.3	97.0

*Index: A higher figure than 100 indicates rated better than Kirin; a lower figure indicates rated worse.

Source: Kirin Brewery Co., Ltd.

Norton Company

Francis Aguilar

Subject to the business-cycle swings of the capital goods industry, Norton Company experienced the usual drop in sales during the economic downturn of 1975. What was unusual for Norton was its ability on this occasion to sustain profits, compared with the customary plunge in earnings whenever the economy dipped. Robert Cushman, president and chief executive officer of Norton, saw this performance as evidence of the growing effectiveness of the company's strategic planning.

By 1976, five years' efforts had gone into developing planning activities that could help top management shape strategies for the firm's diversified business operations. Cushman was pleased with the results of these efforts: "Our strategic planning has made a tremendous difference in the way the company is now managed. It gives us a much-needed handle to evaluate strategies for each of our many businesses."

One of the difficult strategic planning decisions faced by top management in 1976 concerned a reevaluation of the long-term strategy for the coated abrasives business operations in the United States. This situation is described later on in the case, following a general explanation of the strategic planning process at Norton and how it came to be.

COMPANY BACKGROUND

Norton Company, headquartered in Worcester, Massachusetts, was a multinational industrial manufacturer with 85 plant locations in 21 countries. The firm employed almost 19,000 persons.

As the world's largest abrasives manufacturer, Norton produced both abrasive grain raw materials and finished products. The latter included such items as sandpaper and grinding wheels. The company also produced a wide range of other industrial products including industrial ceramics, sealants, catalyst carriers, and tower packings for the chemical process industries, engineered plastic components, tubing and related products for medical applications and for food processing, and industrial safety products. In 1975, these other products accounted for about 27%

of the reported total sales of $548 million.[1] *Exhibit 1* contains a five-year summary of Norton's financial results.

Organization

Norton Company was organized into low-growth and high-growth product groups. This organizational structure reflected two basic corporate objectives. The first was to remain the worldwide leader in abrasives. The second was to improve profitability through a "limited number of diversified product lines and without conglomeration."[2]

When introducing this structure in 1971, Cushman had remarked: "As you look at Norton Company you see two major areas of business: our traditional abrasives products, which are good cash generators but have low growth, and our newer nonabrasive lines, which need cash but have a high growth potential. We need a different type of manager to run each business."[3]

Harry Duane, age 45, headed the abrasives group. His job was characterized as "running a large, cyclical-prone, slow-growth business with stiff competition in many different markets." Successful performance in this business was said to depend on careful cost control, keeping products up to date, and holding established markets. Duane had had experience in the abrasives business abroad as well as in the United States since joining Norton in 1957.

Donald R. Melville, age 50, headed Norton's diversified products business group. He had joined the company in 1967 as vice president of marketing after having served in various marketing capacities with Continental Can Company, Scott Paper Company,

and Dunlop Tire & Rubber. As reported in *Business Week*: "Melville's management style relies on creating an entrepreneurial atmosphere. . . . 'In the case of abrasives,' says Melville, 'you compensate your people on the basis of whether or not they make that month's budget. In diversified products, you don't care as much about a month's budget—you try to double your sales in 12 months.' "

The 1976 company organization structure is shown in *Exhibit 2*.

Concepts for Strategic Planning

In 1967, as executive vice president in charge of companywide operations, Cushman faced the problem of assessing the role that each of some 75 product lines was to play in Norton's future. Conventional corporate long-range planning then in use at Norton was found wanting for this task. Cushman consequently began to search for more appropriate ways to plan multibusiness operations. He later remarked:

During the early 1960s, Peter Drucker—widely known spokesman, critic, and analyst to business—began to describe business in terms of certain variables which seemed to determine a company's future. But it was Fred Borch, marketing vice president of the highly diversified General Electric, who in 1960 asked the key question and then assigned two members of his staff, Jack McKitterick and Dr. Sidney Schoeffler, to find the answer. "Why is it," he said, "that through the years some of our businesses fail while others succeed? There must be certain decisions, strategies, or factors which lead to certain results. With hundreds of products ranging from electric pencil sharpeners to diesel engines and nuclear plants, it is difficult to do an effective job of planning. It is, in fact, impossible for management to have a direct, personal feeling and knowledge about so many business environments. We need better guidelines."

In 1967, Dr. Schoeffler was invited to Norton to describe the results of G.E.'s profitability optimization study. Based on sophisticated multiple regression analyses covering 10 years' experience for 150 product lines at General Electric, Dr. Schoeffler had been able to identify some 37 factors that accounted for more than 80% of the variations in profit results. The findings showed how profitability varied with

---

[1] On September 9, 1976, Norton Company announced an agreement in principle to merge with Christensen, Inc., for stock valued at $100 million. Christensen, with 1975 sales of $118 million and net income of $9.5 million, manufactured diamond-drilling bits and coring bits for the petroleum and mining industries. With Christensen, nonabrasive products would account for about 40% of total sales.

[2] The Norton Company annual report for 1975 also highlighted three other corporate objectives: "(1) to maintain responsible corporate citizenship. . .which at times means accepting lower profits; (2) to maintain a superior employee working environment, and (3) to enhance the value of Norton stock."

[3] *Business Week*, August 7, 1971.

EXHIBIT 1   FIVE-YEAR FINANCIAL SUMMARY
(In Millions)

	1971	1972	1973	1974	1975
Net sales	$346	$374	$475	$558	$548
Net income[a]	$ 11.4	$ 14.5	$ 25.4	$ 21.6	$ 20.9
Net income, excluding effect of foreign currency exchange rate changes[a]	$ 10.3	$ 15.0	$ 21.3	$ 25.1	$ 24.8
By line of business					
Abrasives					
Sales, %	70	75	75	75	73
Net income, %	85	87	89	76	70
Diversified products					
Sales, %	30	25	25	25	27
Net income, %	15	13	11	24	30
By subsidiaries outside the U.S.					
Sales, %	41	41	42	45	49
Net income, %	39	33	56	56	40
Working capital	$148	$151	$155	$159	$200
Total debt	$ 69	$ 65	$ 66	$102	$112
Shareholders' equity	$211	$218	$232	$244	$255
Operating and financial ratios					
Net income as % of sales	3.3	3.9	5.3	3.9	3.8
Net income as % of equity	5.4	6.7	10.9	8.8	8.2
Current ratio	3.7	3.6	2.9	2.3	3.3
Total debt to equity, %	33	30	29	42	44
Per share statistics[b]					
Net income[a]	$ 2.12	$ 2.70	$ 4.70	$ 4.02	$ 3.85
Net income, excluding effect of foreign currency exchange rate changes[a]	$ 1.92	$ 2.80	$ 3.94	$ 4.68	$ 4.57
Dividends	$ 1.50	$ 1.50	$ 1.50	$ 1.575	$ 1.70
Stock price (NYSE)	$27–$37	$32–$39	$23–$36	$19–$29	$21–$29

[a]Exchange gains and losses resulting from the translation of foreign currency financial statements were included for the first time in the 1975 annual report, thus determining net income in accordance with a new procedure recommended by the Financial Accounting Standards Board (FASB). The net income results excluding foreign currency effects conform to prior reporting practices used at Norton and generally throughout the industry.
[b]The average number of shares of common stock outstanding varied between 5.37 million and 5.67 million during this period.
Source: Annual reports and *Moody's Industrial Manual,* 1975.

respect to such factors as market share, market growth rate, and the level of investments required. The findings also showed how profitability varied with respect to policies on such matters as research and development as a percent of sales, marketing expenditures, product quality, and pricing.[4] Cushman

---

[4]Examples of profit determinants would include: (1) high marketing expenditures damage profitability when product quality is low; (2) high R&D spending hurts profitability when market share is small but increases ROI when market share is high; and (3) high marketing expenditures hurt ROI in investment-intensive businesses.

was struck with the relevance and concreteness of the resulting guidelines.

In his search for better guidelines, Cushman also became interested in the work of Bruce Henderson, founder and president of the Boston Consulting Group. Based on the premise that costs decreased with experience in a predictable manner, Henderson held that the firm with the greatest volume should have the lowest costs for a given product line. Market share served as a measure of relative volume for planning purposes.

The cash flows associated with growth and mature

EXHIBIT 2 COMPANY ORGANIZATION STRUCTURE, 1976

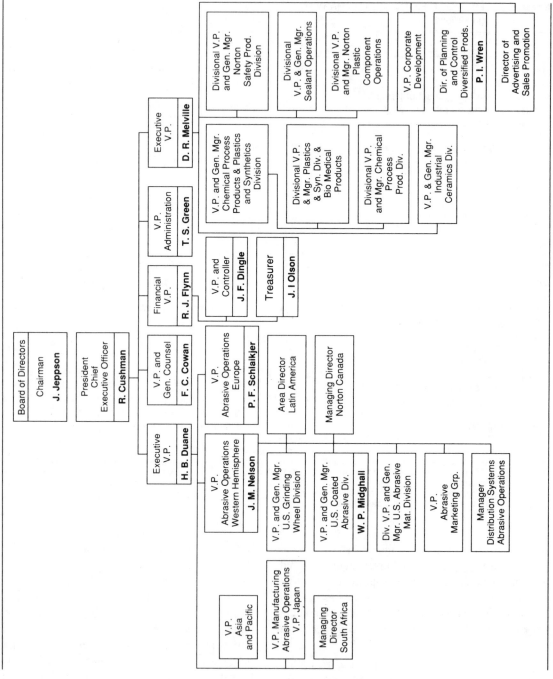

industries constituted a second element of Henderson's approach. Product lines with leading market shares in mature industries were generators of surplus cash; those in growth industries represented the potential cash generators for future years. For diversified business operations, Henderson urged that attention be given in strategic planning to the creation of a portfolio in which some product lines could generate sufficient cash throwoff to nourish the development and growth of other product lines in growing markets.

STRATEGIC PLANNING AT NORTON

The basic building block for planning continued to be the strategy analysis for individual product lines. This analysis considered a wide range of business factors such as competitive conditions, technology, and future trends, and concluded with a proposed course of action over time. Each strategy was prepared by the manager holding profit responsibility for the product line, and it was then evaluated by group and corporate line management. The customary analysis and review of strategy was extended to include two additional tests based on the somewhat related sets of concepts described above.

One of these additional tests concerned the intrinsic profit potential for a business. Based on experimental data for a wide range of businesses (such as had been generated for General Electric), Norton was able to measure the profit level appropriate for a business as it existed. It was also able to measure how profits and cash flows might be increased under alternative strategies. These financial norms helped management to evaluate how well a business was being run and how much additional potential it had.

A business strategy was also evaluated in the context of total corporate cash flows. The strategy had to conform to the overall availabilities of or needs for cash. For this purpose, market share performance served as a major controlling device. In broad terms, businesses were assigned the task of building, holding, or harvesting market share. *Building strategies* were based on active efforts to increase market share by means of new product introductions, added marketing programs, and so forth. Such strategies customarily called for cash inputs. *Holding strategies* were aimed at maintaining the existing level of market share. Net cash flows might be negative for rapidly growing markets and positive for slow growing markets. *Harvesting strategies* sought to achieve earnings and cash flows by permitting market share to decline.

In line with this approach, Norton's operations had been divided into some 60 businesses whose characteristics were sufficiently different to warrant the development of individual business strategies. These subdivisions were known as substrategic business units. Combinations of these substrategic business units were grouped into about 30 strategic business units for purposes of top management review.

Strategy Guidance Committee

In April 1972, Cushman formed a top-management committee to assist in the evaluation of these business strategies. As Cushman later reported to the Norton board:

The function of the Strategy Guidance Committee is to review at appropriate levels the strategy of each business unit to make certain it does fit corporate objectives, and to monitor how effectively its strategy is being carried out. It provides the executive, regional, and division manager an opportunity for an "outside" peer group to examine and advise.

The committee totals twelve: the president, the executive vice president, the regional vice presidents, the financial vice president, the controller, the vice president of corporate development and Graham Wren as secretary. Depending on the circumstances, business units are reviewed on a two-year cycle. Well-documented strategies along standard lines are sent to members for review before meetings.

Each strategic business unit was responsible for preparing a strategy book for review. Copies of this book were distributed to members of the Strategy Guidance Committee at least one week prior to the scheduled review. To focus attention on the critical issues, Cushman set the following ground rules for the review session:

No formal presentation is required at the meeting because each committee member is expected to have thoroughly studied the strategy book. Discussion during the meeting will generally center around these questions:

1. Questions of facts, trends, and assumptions as presented in the strategy book.
2. Questions as to the appropriateness of the mission of the business in terms of build, maintain, or harvest.
3. Questions as to the appropriateness of the strategy in the context of the facts and mission.
4. Questions suggested by PIMS [Profit Impact Marketing Strategies] analysis.
5. How does the business unit and its strategy fit and relate to similar businesses within Norton (e.g., coated abrasives Europe vs. coated abrasives worldwide)?
6. How does the business unit and its strategy fit within the corporate portfolio and strategy?

Involvement of Line Managers

The involvement of key line managers in the Strategy Guidance Committee and the methodology used in generating the strategy books gave a distinct line orientation to planning at Norton. Management for each business unit had to take a position concerning its mission, strengths and weaknesses, likely competitive developments, trends, and finally its strategy. The analysis and recommendations had to stand the test of critical evaluation by an experienced and involved top management.

Although Cushman was pleased with the planning tools Norton had developed, he felt that the deep involvement of line managers in both the formulation and review of strategies served to prevent a mechanical or otherwise undue reliance on the planning tools themselves. He believed it highly desirable that an operating manager's gut feeling remain an important input to strategic planning.

Other Elements Related to Strategic Planning

In 1976 detailed cash flow models that could be used to support and extend the analysis described above were being completed. Several Norton managers remarked that these models would contribute importantly to the strategic planning efforts.

In addition, Norton's incentive system was designed to motivate managers in carrying out their assigned strategic moves—whether to build, maintain, or harvest their businesses. Cushman reported the use of over 50 different custom-tailored plans for this purpose.

Finally, Cushman's deep-seated involvement in the strategic planning process and the respect he commanded from other senior-level managers at Norton undoubtedly influenced this process in major ways.

COATED ABRASIVES DOMESTIC

One of the difficult cases for consideration by the Strategy Guidance Committee in 1976 concerned a reevaluation of the strategy to be followed for the U.S. coated abrasives business. Coated Abrasives Domestic (CAD), one of Norton's larger operating divisions, then had a history of declining market share and profitability.

In 1974, Norton management had decided to stem further loss of market share by a major restructuring of the CAD division. During the ensuing two years, market share and profitability continued to decline. These unfavorable results raised important questions about the merits of the earlier decision. The case for holding market share (then the strategy) was further challenged by the recommendations resulting from the PIMS regression analysis. The PIMS report had concluded that the CAD business should be moderately harvested (market share permitted to decline) for its cash throwoff.

The remainder of this case presents excerpts from information presented to the Strategy Guidance Committee or otherwise known by its members concerning CAD. (Data used in the following sections have been disguised.)

The Abrasives Market

Abrasive finished products were generally classified as bonded or coated. *Bonded abrasives* were basic tools used in almost every industry that required shaping, cutting, or finishing of materials. Some of the major uses were in foundries and steel mills for rough grinding of castings and surface conditioning of steels and alloys; in metal fabrication for such products as automobiles and household appliances; in tool and die shops; in the manufacture of bearings; and in the paper and pulp industry. Norton produced more than 250,000 types and sizes of grinding wheels and other bonded abrasive products.

Coated abrasives, which included sandpaper and emery cloth, were widely used throughout the metal-working and woodworking industries, and in service industries such as floor surfacing and automobile refinishing. Norton produced more than 38,000 different items in the form of sheets, belts, rolls, discs, and specialties. The most common form of coated abrasives was the endless belt, some major applications of which included the grinding and finishing of automobiles and appliance parts, the precision grinding and polishing of stainless and alloy steel, and the sanding of furniture, plywood, and particle board.

The overlap of customers' requirements for bonded and coated abrasives varied from industry to industry. For example, the woodworking industry used coated abrasives almost exclusively. In contrast, the auto industry purchased large quantities of both bonded abrasives (e.g., for grinding engine parts) and coated abrasives (e.g., for finishing bodies). Industrial distributors, which accounted for a large portion of Norton's abrasive sales, usually carried both bonded and coated abrasive products. Both Norton and Carborundum offered full lines of bonded and coated abrasive products; 3M competed only in coated abrasives.

In management's opinion, the principal factors contributing to a favorable market position in this industry included quality and reliability of product, completeness of product line, nonpatented technological know-how, substantial capital investment, length of experience in the business, familiarity and reputation of name, strength of marketing network, technical service, delivery, reliability, and price. In 1975, no single customer, including the U.S. government, accounted for as much as 5% of Norton's net sales.

CAD in the Corporate Context

As was customary, the meeting of the Strategy Guidance Committee to review the CAD strategy was opened by Graham Wren, secretary of the committee, with a short presentation showing where the product line in question fit in the Norton portfolio of businesses. The first chart he presented contained an overview of the market share strategies for 31 strategic business units, as summarized in *Exhibit 3*.

Separate charts showed the ranking of all business units with respect to return on net assets (RONA), return on sales (ROS), and asset turnover ratio for 1974, 1975, and the average for the two years. CAD placed in the ranking as follows:

	Rank among 31	CAD 1974–1975 (avg.)	Norton 1974–1975 (avg.)
RONA	27	6.0	10
ROS	26	3.5	6
Asset turnover	23	1.7	1.9

A growth-share matrix showed CAD to lie well in the undesirable low-growth, smaller-than-competitor quadrant (see *Exhibit 4*). A product experiencing low growth and low market share (relative to the industry leader) would likely be a net user of cash with little promise for future payoff.

Finally, the committee's cash generation versus market share corporate test was applied to the CAD proposed strategy. As shown in *Exhibit 5*, the combination of maintaining market share at its present level and generating cash was acceptable.

CAD STRATEGY PLAN

Paul Midghall, vice president and general manager for Norton's U.S. Coated Abrasives Division, was the principal architect of the strategic plan to maintain market share. His reasoning as laid out in the 1976 strategy book for CAD began with a statement of the division's role and strategy:

EXHIBIT 3

SUMMARY OF MARKET SHARE STRATEGIES FOR THE NORTON PORTFOLIO
OF BUSINESSES
(In Millions)

Market share strategy	Sales	Abrasive operations	Diversified products
Build	$ 96	Note: In the actual presentation, each strategic business was listed under its appropriate category. For example, CAD and 15 other business units were listed in the abrasives column for the maintain strategy.	
Build/maintain	135		
Maintain	257		
Maintain/harvest	60		
Harvest	0		
Total	$548	$400	$148

Mission—Cash Generation

Norton's long-term objective is to allocate resources to high-growth opportunities while maintaining total world abrasives leadership. CAD's role within that corporate objective is: to be a long-term cash generator; to act as the technical focal point for coated abrasives operations worldwide.

Strategy—Restructure and Maintain

To meet that objective, CAD has in the last two years radically restructured its operations. Its strategy now is to complete the restructuring, to consolidate the organization into a confidant, coherent team, and to pursue market segmentation based on the strengths which have emerged from restructuring. To understand how this strategy evolved, one must turn to CAD's history.

The strategy report went on to identify the reasons for the earlier deterioration of market share and profitability. These included:

1. Inadequate reinvestment in the basic coated abrasives business in favor of investments which attempted to build allied businesses.[5]
2. High wage rates and fringe benefits coupled with low productivity and poor work conditions.
3. High overheads.

---

[5]According to Duane, coated abrasives and the other allied businesses had been organized in a single profit center at that time. The focus of attention had been on the total unit's overall performance. With this approach to strategy analysis, each major product line was examined separately.

EXHIBIT 4

NORTON PORTFOLIO OF BUSINESSES ON
GROWTH-SHARE MATRIX

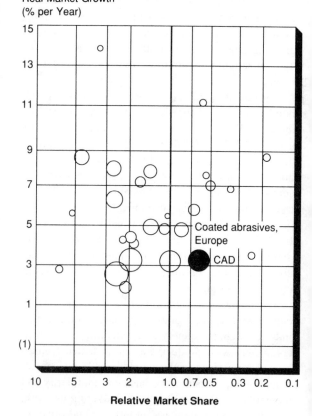

Real Market Growth
(% per Year)

Relative Market Share

Note: Balloon areas are proportional to sales.

EXHIBIT 5
CASH GENERATION—MARKET SHARE STRATEGY TEST

	Market share strategy		
Cash generation	Build	Maintain	Harvest
Uses cash	A/?	U	U
Provides own cash	A/?	U	U
Disengages cash	A	Aª	A

ª CAD followed a maintain strategy along with disengagement of cash, which was an acceptable combination.
Note: A = The combination is an acceptable strategy.
? = The combination is a questionable strategy.
U = The combination is an unacceptable strategy.

4. Premium pricing without compensating benefits to the customer.
5. A labor strike in 1966.

Serious attempts to reverse the negative trends for CAD had proved unsuccessful, and in late 1973 management decided a major change had to be made in the business. The strategy report reviewed the alternative strategies that had been considered earlier.

By late 1973, CAD's condition demanded positive action; share had dropped to 26% and RONA to 7.5%. A fundamental change had to occur. The principal options were:

1. *Sell, liquidate, or harvest.* These alternatives were eliminated because: (a) a viable coated abrasives business was deemed important to worldwide coated abrasives business; (b) a viable coated abrasives business was judged important to U.S. bonded abrasives business.
2. *Attempt to regain lost share and with it volume to cover fixed expenses.* In a mature industry, with the major competitors financially secure and firmly entrenched, such a strategy was judged too expensive.
3. *Greater price realization.* We already maintained a high overall price level, and 3M was the price leader in the industry. In late 1974, Norton tried to lead prices up dramatically to restore profitability, but the rest of the industry did not follow.

Alternative—Comprehensive Cost Reduction

A new cost structure was the only reasonable choice for a radical change. We had to scale down to a cost level consistent with our volume and our position in the industry.

In 1974, a decision to restructure the CAD business by making major cost reductions was made by Norton's executive committee and approved by its board of directors. This move was intended to make CAD more competitive so that it could prevent further erosion of its market share.

Restructuring

The strategy review of 1974 had identified many areas for cost reduction. These touched on almost every segment of operations and included: moving labor-intensive manufacturing operations from New York to Texas; combining the coated abrasives sales force with that for bonded abrasives (e.g., grinding wheels); and reducing fixed assets. The product line would also be reduced. Earlier, about 4,000 product items out of some 20,000 (20%) had accounted for 87% of sales.

During the two-year period 1974–1975, over $2 million had been invested to implement the restructuring. The changes were eventually expected to result in $9 million annual direct recurring savings, raising RONA by about 8 percentage points to a total of 14%. (It was estimated that 3M had a RONA of 17% to 20% in coated abrasives.) The number of employees for CAD had declined from 2,000 to 1,300 by 1976.

CAD's Future Environment

The U.S. coated abrasives industry was expected to experience low growth and gradual changes as a rule. The strategy book forecasted long-term growth at 2.5% per annum. Industrial markets, which constituted 75% of Norton's CAD business, were expected to grow even more slowly. Because of the depressed level of business operations in early 1976, annual growth for industrial markets was forecasted to spurt to about 7% until 1980.

An investment advisory report issued by Loeb Rhoads some months later in August 1976 had this to say about future prospects for the industry as a whole, including bonded and coated products.

We have believed for some time that there were fair prospects for higher profitability in abrasives on a secular and not just a cyclical basis, merely because profitability had been poor for a long enough (seven to nine years') time. In a product that is basic to economic activity and that is capital intensive, and where no unusual reason can be discerned for the poor return on investment, such as foreign competition or technological change, e.g., a lengthy period of poor profitability generally will lead to changes by industry factors designed to improve returns. . . . At some point supply and demand come into a better balance, which then supports firmer pricing. And in fact. . . pricing had improved significantly since late 1974 despite declining demand in real terms.

Product technology was expected to change slowly, but in important ways. The strategy book noted:

The advent of Norzon grain, new resin bonds, and synthetic backings illustrates the fact that although coated abrasives

may be a mature product, it is not a commodity product. Technological evolution is slow but continuous, and a competitor who fails to keep abreast cannot survive.

While product development exhibits highly visible evolution, process development is inconspicuous. No major changes have occurred, or are expected, in manufacturing technology.

Capacity in all segments of manufacturing will be adequate to fill demand well into the 1980s.

The U.S. coated abrasive market was said to have "healthy, strong, rational competition." With the exception of 3M, the return of most competitors was thought to be below the U.S. industrial average. *Exhibit 6* shows sales and market shares for the principal competitors.

CAD Strategy for 1976

The proposed CAD strategy for 1976 contained two principal elements. One element was a continuation of the restructuring and cost cutting that had begun in 1974. CAD management estimated that about 75% of this program had been put into effect and that two

EXHIBIT 6
U.S. COATED ABRASIVES MARKET SHARE ESTIMATES

	1975 sales, millions	Market share, %	
		1975	1973
3M	$ 99	34	32
Norton	76	26	27
Carborundum	40	14	15
Armak	23	8	8
Other U.S.	35	12	12
Foreign	21	7	7
Total industry	$294	100%	100%

Market segment	Metalworking[a]	Woodworking	General trade[b]
Market potential, 1975, millions	$130	$36	$81
Estimated market share, 1975, %			
3M	30	27	65
Norton	29	26	20
Carborundum	22	10	11

[a]Includes primary metals, fabricated metals, and transportation equipment (autos, aircraft) industries.
[b]Includes hardware retail and automobile finishing businesses.

more years would be required to complete the steps under way.

The second element of the strategy was to focus on those market segments in which Norton had competitive advantage. Detailed share growth balloon charts, such as shown in *Exhibit 7*, were used to identify specific sectors for attention.

To foster product innovation, the 1976 plan had introduced a recommendation to expand R&D ef-

forts. Twenty-two people had been assigned to CAD product development in 1975.

These strategic moves were predicted to produce favorable results. The CAD report identified the unit's future strengths to include: variable costs to be among the lowest in the industry; distribution channel relations to be among the best, especially with the close tie between coated and bonded abrasives; and a technological edge on new products (e.g., Nor-

EXHIBIT 7
CAD GROWTH-SHARE MATRICES

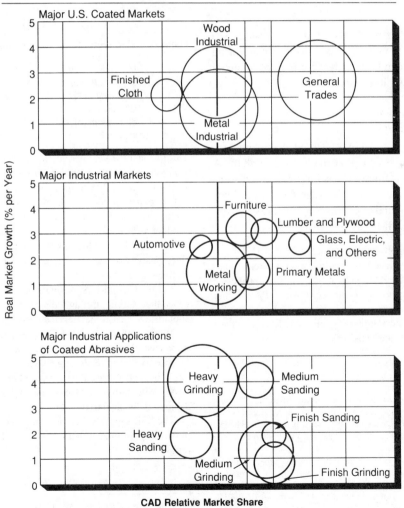

Note: Balloon areas are proportional to Norton's sales.

EXHIBIT 8 SUMMARY OF FINANCIAL RESULTS

	Actual					Expected[a]				
	1971	**1972**	**1973**	**1974**	**1975**	**1976**	**1977**	**1978**	**1979**	**1980**
Market share, %	29	28	27	26	25.5	26	27	27.5	27.5	27.5
Net sales (index)	77	90	107	120	100	108	128	150	160	180
Net income (index)	215	220	310	230	100	140	480	760	810	950
Percent return on sales (c/b)	4.4	3.9	4.6	3.0	1.6	2.0	6.0	8.0	8.0	8.0
Percent RONA	8	8	7.5	7	5	4.5	8	13	13	13
Funds generated, $ millions						(4.7)	0.5	2.5	3.4	1.3

[a] 7% inflation per annum assumed.
Note: Numbers are disguised.

zon). The ultimate result, the report forecasted, was the generation of more than $7 million cash during 1977–1980. Excerpts from the summary of financial results are shown in *Exhibit 8*.

The PIMS Report

The PIMS analysis[6] for CAD resulted in a recommendation at variance with that made by Midghall. A summary of these findings was included in the strategy book submitted to the Strategy Guidance Committee. The remainder of this section presents excerpts from the PIMS analysis.

The 1975 PAR report[7] indicates that the Coated-U.S. business is a below-average business in a weak strategic position with a *pre-tax* PAR-ROI of 12.0%. The business's operating performance has been very close to PAR with a 1973–75 average *pre-tax* actual ROI of 12.2%.

The major factors impacting on PAR-ROI and their individual impacts are listed below.[8]

Major negative factors		Major positive factors	
(1.5)	Marketing only expense/sales	1.8	Sales direct to end users
(1.7)	Capacity utilization		
(4.1)	Effective use of investments		

During the three-year period, the *marketing less sales force expenses/sales* ratio averaged 6% compared with the 4.1% PIMS average. PIMS findings acknowledge that high marketing expenses hurt profitability when relative product quality is low; i.e., it doesn't pay to market heavily a product with equivalent or inferior product quality. The average relative product quality for the business over the three years was estimated as follows: 10% superior, 75% equivalent, and 15% inferior.

For the Coated-U.S. business, the positive impact indicates that selling through distributors instead of direct should lower customer service costs.

Whether the Coated-U.S. business objective is to optimize cash flow or ROI over the long term, the Strategy Sensitivity Report (SSR) suggests a *moderate harvest* strategy. The SSR is based upon how other participating businesses with similar business characteristics have acted to achieve their objectives.

The SSR suggests that the following strategy should be pursued to optimize either cash flow or ROI over the long term.

---

[6] As a subscriber to the services of the Strategic Planning Institute, Norton received analysis reports on a regular basis for several of its major businesses. These reports were circulated to divisional and corporate managers concerned with the business in question.

[7] The PAR report specified the return on investment that was normal for a business, given the characteristics of its market, competition, technology, and cost structure.

[8] The figures represent the impact of that factor on PAR-ROI. For example, the higher marketing (excluding sales force) expenses/sales ratio noted in the following paragraph when comparing CAD with all PIMS businesses was said to have an effect of

reducing the PAR-ROI by 1.5%. In contrast, by selling directly to the end users, PAR-ROI was increased by 1.8% compared with all PIMS businesses.

1. *Prices*—Prices relative to competition should be maintained.
2. *Working capital/sales*—The SSR suggests that this ratio be lowered significantly to about 25% through primarily reduced inventory levels.
3. *Vertical integration*—Over the long term, the degree of vertical integration should be reduced.
4. *Fixed capital*—Don't add large segments of capacity, and maintain capacity utilization at the 80% level.
5. *R&D marketing expenses*—The SSR recommends that R&D expenditures should be reduced; and consequently, the relative product quality remains inferior. Also, the product should be marketed less energetically during the implementation phase.

The result from this strategy is (1) a gradual loss of market share from 26% to 21%; (2) an average ROI of 24% vs. the current PAR-ROI of 12%; and (3) a ten-year discounted cash flow value of $2.33 million.

A study was undertaken to compare the PAR-ROI of this business in its steady-state environment (after the recommended strategy has been implemented—1978–1980) with the 1973–1975 PAR-ROI. The results indicate that the strategy is successful in moving this business into a much better strategic position. The pre-tax PAR-ROI increases from 12% to 24%.

The major factors that had a significant impact on the improved PAR-ROI are *relative pay scale* and *use of investments*. These two factors account for a majority of the 12 percentage point increase in PAR-ROI.

The general message from the SSR for the *restructured* Coated-U.S. business is the same as for the *current* business; i.e., if the objective is to manage the business for cash flow or ROI, a *moderate harvest strategy* is recommended by PIMS.

Management Considerations

Norton's top managers recognized how difficult it was for them to remain objective when deciding the fate of a core part of the company's traditional business. As John Nelson, vice president of abrasive operations, western hemisphere, remarked:

There is no question that this decision has been an emotional one for me and probably for others, as well. It would be difficult to turn our backs on CAD. Yet, if the business cannot produce the target return on net assets, I think we are prepared to take the appropriate actions.

I do not think that we are likely to close shop on United States coated abrasives. It is too important to other parts of our business to go that far. For example, coated abrasives strengthens our sales of bonded abrasives and is a plus to our distribution system in the United States. It also provides us with a bigger base for R&D on coated abrasives. This benefits our overseas coated abrasive operations. Nonetheless, whether to stay with our earlier decision to maintain market share or to harvest the business was and still is very much at issue.

Both Duane and Nelson remarked that the choice of strategy in 1973–1974 had been predicated on the belief that the industry could support a profitable #2 and Norton could play that role with its existing market share. The continued loss of market share was a cause of concern to them and to other members of the Strategy Guidance Committee, as noted in the minutes for the CAD review session of June 7, 1976:

In the shorter term period of late 1973 to the first quarter of 1976, CAD market share dropped from 27% to 25%. Some of this drop was due to international de-emphasis of the general trades segment. However, there was also an unintentional loss in the industrial segment. The key question is whether this short-term market share decline in the industrial area can be stopped and reversed.

The PIMS recommendations for an alternate strategy also served to raise questions about the soundness of the present approach. One Norton executive put the relative impact of PIMS in context with the following observation: "We are still learning how to use PIMS. At present, we consider it a useful input, among many, to our thinking. We would not reverse divisional management's position on the basis of PIMS alone."

Donald Melville, executive vice president of diversified products, made the following comment about the CAD issue.

You have to consider the dynamics of Norton's situation in 1976. We have done a lot to restructure the company, and the results in 1975—a bad recession year for abrasives—show our progress. But we are not yet in a position where we can harvest a major segment of our abrasives business, because that is the major guts of our company.

By the early '80s our restructuring should be complete, and we will not be so dependent on abrasives. If we were faced with the decision in say 1982, instead of 1976, we could and probably should be willing to harvest CAD. In the meantime, we might as well repair CAD, because if we succeed, then we won't have to harvest it in the '80s. And if we fail, we will have lost very little.

A relative newcomer to the top management ranks at Norton, Richard Flynn,[9] financial vice president, made the following comments about Norton's approach to strategic planning:

---

[9]Richard Flynn joined Norton Company in January 1974 as financial vice president and member of the board of directors and the executive committee. He had been president of the Riley Stoker Corporation, a subsidiary of the Riley Company, manufacturers of steam-generating and fuel-burning equipment. He previously held executive positions with Ling-Temco-Vought and Collins Radio.

However the Strategy Guidance Committee finally decides on this matter, I think they are at least addressing the right issues, and that itself is something.

The wide use of profit centers in large U.S. corporations has often led to bad analysis when different products were lumped together. Corporatewide planning did not help the situation. Looking at a single product line family, as we are doing for U.S. coated abrasives, gives management much more meaningful data to work with.

The other thing I like about Norton's strategic planning is that we are doing it repeatedly during the year. This means that we are always called on to think strategy. Looking at different businesses at different times enables us to take on different perspectives to our strategic thinking. This sometimes helps us to gain new insights for other businesses.

All in all, the strategic planning sessions have been very effective in helping top management to think about and to deal with business strategies.

PART TEN

Organizing and Implementing the Marketing Effort

Excellence in organizing and implementing the marketing effort is a characteristic of outstanding firms. Organizing the marketing effort requires more than just deciding how to structure the marketing department and assigning specific responsibilities to specific individuals. It includes developing a strong consumer orientation throughout the institution, examining marketing's role in the overall organization, and facilitating marketing's interaction with other functional areas of management.

TOWARD A MARKETING ORIENTATION

Meaningful implementation requires a marketing orientation throughout the organization, starting with the chief executive officer. Managers at all levels in each function must understand what marketing is and how it can contribute to the organization. Employees must be service-oriented and prepared to act as if they were users instead of providers of the product.

Once market sensitivity has been achieved, maintaining such an orientation is a continuous process. Long-run vitality requires responsiveness to change and maintenance of the external perspective that market-focused management brings.

Marketing is a demanding discipline; even successful organizations face the danger of slipping back into an inward-looking or product orientation. Executives must constantly be aware of the indicators of product-oriented management. Not tailoring marketing strategies to meet segment needs and seeing the product as being inherently desirable for the target market may cause the organization to blame lack of customer interest in the offering on

511

ignorance or lack of motivation. Consequently, management places too much emphasis on communication strategies, and uses research, not to understand consumer needs, but to confirm management beliefs. Similarly, generic competition is largely ignored in a product-oriented firm. Successful implementation requires that a business maintain a market orientation at all levels and throughout all functional and management areas that interact directly or indirectly with consumers.

Working with Other Areas

Marketing is just one of several major management functions. Although the importance of these functions varies by the nature of the organization and the types of products offered, successful design and implementation of marketing programs require cooperation and coordination across functional areas. For example, a marketing organization requires that the finance and control functions provide financial information on a product or market basis so that decisions about changes can be made in a sound way. A good manufacturer needs to know the difference in costs if it offers additional flavors or package sizes; a restaurant should know both the incremental and allocated costs of opening early for breakfast. Because financial executives often have an oversight role on substantial investments and expenditures, they must be educated by the marketing managers to the need to spend funds on intangibles such as market research and advertising, which are not capitalized as assets on the balance sheet and whose value is realized only after the money is spent.

Coordination with all functional areas is important, but cooperation with the management of production and operations is of particular concern. Especially in a service industry, marketing and operations should be seen as mutually supportive functions. Developing customer demand for a product that cannot subsequently be produced is as harmful as efficiently providing a product nobody needs and for which there is no potential to develop a demand. Successful products make sense from the vantage point of both operations and marketing.

Nevertheless, there are fundamental differences in orientation between marketing and production (or operations) that management must bridge in order to achieve competitive and market success. Marketing management is oriented externally to the needs of the customers and to threats from competition. In response, it tends to offer a wide range of products and to want to update them frequently. Success is defined in terms of customer satisfaction and product utilization. Operations, or manufacturing management, on the other hand, is internally oriented. It wants to offer a few standardized products and is reluctant to make changes. It emphasizes producing these products in an efficient manner. Success tends to be measured in terms of cost minimization and achievement of operating standards that may have no relation to customer concerns. Often there is little recognition that the organization currently or potentially faces either direct or generic competition.

Ultimately, success of a marketing program depends upon the people who come in direct contact with the users; these people are often operations, not marketing, personnel. Many organizations—such as hotels, restaurants, and airlines—produce the final product as it is being consumed. As a result, the marketing function in a service organization must be closely interrelated with, and dependent on, the personnel and operations functions and the people, procedures, and facilities administered by these functions.

Assigning Responsibility

In any organization, the best-laid plans will undoubtedly go astray unless implementation process is carefully spelled out. As noted in the section on strategic market planning, a marketing action plan should specify:

1. A detailed breakdown of required activities
2. Responsibility by name
3. An activity schedule in milestone format
4. Tangible and intangible results expected from each activity

Let's look at each of these in slightly more detail.

Breakdown of Required Activities Implementing a marketing program requires coordinating a wide array of activities, usually across the full breadth of the marketing mix. The key to ensuring that all needed tasks are properly executed is to start by identifying all the necessary steps that have to be performed. Large and complex tasks become more manageable when broken down into smaller subtasks. The big packaged goods companies, such as Procter & Gamble, are known for their legendary attention to detail in implementation.

Responsibility by Name For planned tasks to be implemented, they must be assigned to a specific person—not just to a department or an advertising agency. How many marketing programs, one wonders, have come unstuck because a key task went undone? By the time a subordinate says, "Oh, I didn't know I was supposed to do that; I assumed it was Leslie's responsibility," the manager has more than just a personnel problem to worry about—an entire campaign may be at risk (and his or her own job with it). Wise managers do not just assign a job to anyone; they think carefully about matching the nature of the task at hand to the capabilities of a particular individual. The manager must also ensure that the assigned person has the needed time, money, and support services to complete the task properly and on schedule. Certain tasks—such as research studies, advertising campaigns, and creation of new packaging designs—may be delegated to outside suppliers. But the careful manager will want to make sure that named individuals within those firms have been assigned specific responsibilities.

Activity Schedule in Milestone Format   Implementation of a strategy requires that steps be taken in a carefully designed sequence. Certain actions are prerequisites to others that follow later. For instance, product samples may be needed before the sales force can call on distributors. Management of complex projects is often aided by various charting techniques. These range from simple Gantt charts, depicting what activities will be happening during what time periods, to more sophisticated approaches that clarify the interrelationship between specific activities. Critical path analysis is valuable not only in determining the sequence of activities and the length of time that each will consume but also in identifying what structuring of those activities will result in the shortest total elapsed time for the project. (Probability estimates of time to completion can be added as well.) Critical path scheduling enables the manager to decide which activities must be performed in sequence and which can be performed in parallel.

Results Expected from Each Activity   Personnel involved in a large project often tend to feel like cogs in a giant machine. What are they contributing to the total scheme of things? What does it matter if they cut a few corners or complete the work a week or so after the so-called deadline? By spelling out the tangible and intangible results expected from each activity, the project manager can clarify to all participants what the nature of their contribution actually is. This understanding may provide added motivation. To the extent that commercial security allows management to let all participants know that they are part of a team, that completion of their work by a given date is essential to the work of another group, and that each group is making a contribution to the success of a larger activity, all participants are likely to perform better and more responsibily.

THE MARKETING ORGANIZATIONAL STRUCTURE

The effectiveness of marketing efforts depends on how well matched the marketing department is to both the external environment and the company's internal characteristics. No single organizational structure can be effective in all settings, and the structure of a marketing department may have to be changed as the corporation evolves.

Marketing departments are generally structured in one of two major ways (*Exhibit 1*). A *functional system* groups together people who carry out similar marketing functions. Thus all those working on advertising would be in one group, those involved in field sales in a second, those responsible for pricing in a third, and so forth. By contrast, a *decentralized product-manager system* focuses on grouping together managers on the basis of a series of different products. Some have found that a product-manager system provides too much focus on the product and not enough on the market segments served. Consequently, they have turned to a market-centered system, which is a variant

EXHIBIT 1   ORGANIZING AND IMPLEMENTING THE MARKETING EFFORT

```
                            ┌─────────────────┐
                            │ Market manager  │
                            └─────────────────┘
        ┌──────────────┬──────────────┬──────────────┬──────────────┐
   ┌─────────┐   ┌─────────┐    ┌─────────┐    ┌──────────────┐
   │ Market  │   │Promotion│    │ Pricing │    │   Product    │
   │ research│   │         │    │         │    │ development  │
   └─────────┘   └─────────┘    └─────────┘    └──────────────┘
        ┌──────────────┬──────────────┐
   ┌─────────────┐ ┌─────────┐  ┌──────────────┐
   │ Advertising │ │ Personal│  │ Distribution │
   │             │ │ selling │  │              │
   └─────────────┘ └─────────┘  └──────────────┘
```

Functional Organization for Marketing

```
                            ┌─────────────────┐
                            │ Market manager  │
                            └─────────────────┘
        ┌──────────────┬──────────────┬──────────────┬──────────────┐
   ┌─────────┐   ┌─────────┐    ┌─────────────┐  ┌─────────┐
   │ Personal│   │ Market  │    │ Advertising │  │Promotion│
   │ selling │   │ research│    │             │  │         │
   └─────────┘   └─────────┘    └─────────────┘  └─────────┘
        ┌──────────────┬──────────────┐
   ┌─────────────┐ ┌─────────────┐ ┌─────────────┐
   │  Product    │ │  Product    │ │  Product    │
   │  manager,   │ │  manager,   │ │  manager,   │
   │  product A  │ │  product B  │ │  product C  │
   └─────────────┘ └─────────────┘ └─────────────┘
```

Product Organization for Marketing

of the product-manager structure except that the marketing department is subdivided by market served rather than by product. For example, a computer company's marketing organization may be structured by customer type (financial firms, manufacturing applications, etc.) rather than by size or model of computer.

Functional Organization

Functional organizations are structured to facilitate development of expertise in such important functional areas as advertising, promotion, new product development, and market research. Mastery of these functions is often critical for marketing success. A functional organizational structure is relatively easy to administer and is most appropriate when the company faces similar markets and offers broadly similar products. However, it is relatively difficult in such organizations to undertake detailed planning for specific goods and services. Coordination by senior management is needed to make sure overall marketing goals are being met. This can be particularly difficult in fast-changing, highly competitive markets.

Product Management

The purpose of a product-management system is to provide focus on the needs of individual products (or markets in a market-centered system) in a complex, competitive multiproduct environment. A company's product managers are expected to be the resident experts on their assigned products. They are expected to develop marketing plans, monitor performance and competitive activities, understand the impact of all marketing actions, and coordinate the activities of functional specialists to develop and implement the marketing plan. The key advantages of the product-manager system are its concentration on individual products and markets and its ability to provide a quick response to changing conditions. But there are disadvantages as well. The product managers usually have responsibility for, but limited authority over, the functional experts whose assistance they require. Since senior management needs to integrate and review the plans that product managers prepare, functional departments often see product managers as coordinators with limited power. At the same time, since the path to senior management often involves promotion through a series of increasingly more significant products, the opportunity to develop functional expertise in the company is limited. Thus, product managers may not have time to develop the skills required to judge and manage work in such important functional areas as advertising. Moreover, the most talented functional experts may choose to move to companies that use a functional structure which, they may feel, better suits their talents and their own chances for promotion.

The choice between a functional system and a product-manager (or market-centered) system has long been a topic of debate in marketing. Each system has its strength and weaknesses. Companies rarely install one of these frameworks in a "pure" form, tending to modify the basic structure to meet their own needs. In complex situations, combined product-market manager systems are sometimes needed.

MANAGING NEW VENTURES

Successful new ventures are critically dependent on the people who lead the enterprise. Because these businesses are often small, the abilities and efforts of the individuals involved are critical. The willingness of such individuals to devote long hours and their full intellectual capacities is often a key strength of a start-up business.

While new ventures are occasionally begun with a large team of people, one or two individuals are usually the key or lead entrepreneurs in the project. As with all aspects of a new business, leaders must evaluate themselves on an objective, realistic basis. All entrepreneurs should know their own entrepreneurial strengths *and* weaknesses—what skills and experiences they already have and which ones need to be acquired to make a particular venture succeed. Except in the smallest of ventures, the entrepreneur should also have a highly committed and motivated team of coworkers. These people should be chosen for reasons other than friendship. Their skills and experience should complement the founder's, according to the needs of the business.

Just as there is no single personality type or skill base that ensures success in any field—from being the CEO of a multibillion-dollar corporation to managing a restaurant—successful entrepreneurs do not fit a common mold. On the other hand, we can identify some characteristics that seem important for entrepreneurs to have. These include:

- *A high level of drive and energy.* New ventures are only for those who are willing to work extremely hard.
- *The self-confidence to take carefully calculated, moderate risks.* The successful entrepreneur is not reckless but is willing to take risks.
- *A conception that money is a way of keeping score and a tool for growth.* Money is necessary both to satisfy the needs of investors and to fund growth, but seldom is a short-term payout available.
- *Unusual skill in motivating and obtaining productive collaboration from other people.* New enterprises are resource-constrained so that extra efforts from people are always needed.
- *High but realistic and achievable goals.* Impossible goals only lead to frustration, but realistic, demanding goals stimulate new venture management.
- *The ability to learn from their own failures.* Few new enterprises do everything right. But many mistakes, if recognized, are correctable and can lead to improvements in business functioning.
- *A long-term vision of the enterprise.*

Few entrepreneurs have strength in all these areas, but they will in many of them. They will also recognize their own shortcomings and seek ways to limit their impact.

Competitive Advantages of Small Businesses

New businesses are typically small, so they often lack the resources necessary to sustain themselves when projects get delayed or market demand does not develop as planned. Their lack of money often limits their ability to do proper research—both technical and market oriented—so entrepreneurs tend to live with a higher degree of risk than managers in large companies. Even when new ventures are successful in market terms, they can fail because they run out of cash to fund their growth—suppliers and employees need to be paid well before customers receive the goods and, more importantly, pay their bills. But being small in size also has its advantages. The new venture team can be very carefully selected, and the members often work together directly without many layers of bureaucracy. Decision making can be fast and related directly to the problem or opportunity at hand.

Additionally, small businesses can be very low-cost operations. The combination of concentrating on a specialized market segment and offering a limited product line can lead to reduced costs for attentive managers. While such a viewpoint seems counter to the notion of economies of scale, this notion assumes all other factors are equal. In a tightly managed, low-overhead small business they often are not.

While small businesses always have to be wary that their success will provoke retaliation from competitors, their small size can often assist them in finding ways to outmaneuver their competitors. One area is the development of market concepts that would not be attractive for larger businesses. For example, the competitive edge of one small company that we will call Emergency Parts Service, Inc. (EPS) was to specialize in locating and shipping urgently needed spare parts in 24 hours. Very few large manufacturers or distributors of spare parts could consistently fill orders on such short notice. One premise underlying EPS's business plan was to avoid head-on competition with large parts manufacturers and industrial supply houses. Since competitors did not attempt to fill emergency needs (except for "standard" items) within 24 hours, this position was protected. In general, a successful new venture strategist should be able to come up with creative designs in the first place and then be able to continue to keep them aligned with changes in the firm's environment. EPS, for example, exploited the fact that large parts manufacturers and distributors were slow in filling single-item orders on a very short notice, since such orders were unprofitable for them to process. Moreover, competitors' cost structures were unlikely to change in ways that would allow them to take this market away from EPS. In this case, EPS's existence may be of benefit to the larger companies, since it satisfies customers in emergency situations.

A second area in which a small business can outmaneuver larger businesses is in the choice of a specific niche or market segment to serve. EPS chose, as its niche, manufacturing concerns that need parts in a hurry, at virtually any cost. This is a small segment but, nevertheless, it can generate considerable revenue. Price is not a major concern to customers because of the urgency involved. On the other hand, small niches can grow into large markets, as the success of Federal Express demonstrates.

Small businesses can also develop unique capabilities that are difficult for its larger competitors to duplicate. These include technical know-how, customer knowledge, and supplier contacts. EPS, for instance, established contacts with parts suppliers around the world and constructed air freight arrangements that allowed it to deliver needed items in 24 hours to virtually any place around the world.

GOOD PRACTICE IN MARKETING

There are no magic formulas for good practice in marketing or sure-fire formulas for success. But there are some areas that need to be emphasized, including a consumer orientation throughout the firm and a supportive relationship among the functional areas based on mutual trust and respect.

Particularly important in successfully executing marketing strategies is the establishment of a clear, powerful, shared theme, a vision of what the company does and how with regard to marketing. For example, a company may emphasize customer service so that no customer problem, however small, is disregarded. Products are to be highly reliable, and virtually instantaneous service is provided nationwide, 24 hours a day, every day of the week. All personnel then know that customer satisfaction comes first in decision making.

Success also requires a high degree of competence in carrying out the marketing mix functions—advertising, pricing, and distributing the product. Often a company will have one or a few selected functions in which it excels. One consumer goods firm, for example, dominates its markets through its skill in obtaining display space in stores for its heavily advertised branded products.

In addition to skills in the marketing mix functions themselves, there needs to be a program to coordinate the functions. In other words, management must make sure the elements operate as an integrated marketing mix, not as individual components. For example, one organization's mail-order campaign to sell Christmas gifts was enormously successful in generating orders but produced huge embarrassment to the company when stocks were exhausted early in the campaign, because of someone's failure to ensure access to adequate supplies.

Good implementation requires the development of a monitoring system to measure and control the results of marketing activities. The marketing plan can be the basis of a management control system. As discussed earlier, an action plan can detail the specific activities that need to be carried out and list responsibilities, or targets, by name or functional area. The established targets then become the basis for control so that deviations in performance are identified and corrective action, when necessary, is taken. By monitoring against these targets on a continuing basis, usually monthly or quarterly, management has time to make changes before the situation deteriorates to a crisis condition. It would seem easy for managers to get information to keep track of how well they are doing. Nevertheless, many marketing departments do not have reliable, understandable monitoring mechanisms. The marketing strategy may set the direction and excellent execution may carry the organization along, but a reliable, timely monitoring and control system is needed to make sure the program is on the right path.

SUMMARY

Marketing is concerned not only with the grand design of strategy but also with the implementation of programs and the execution of myriad necessary details.

A continuing challenge for any business is to organize its marketing efforts in ways that efficiently leverage its competitive standing in the marketplace.

Decisions on whether to structure the marketing organization by marketing function, products, markets, or geographic areas (or a combination of these alternatives) should reflect an understanding of the key success factors underlying the strategy selected by the firm.

Within any firm, marketing has to develop a means of coexisting with other functional areas of management, whose concerns often tend to be cost- and efficiency-centered rather than driven by a desire to satisfy customer needs in a competitive marketplace. One of the responsibilities of the general manager is to act as arbiter in interfunctional disputes, balancing the concerns of both sides. Clearly, this requires that the general manager have a good understanding of all functions.

The organizational structure and procedures to be adopted should reflect the nature of both the firm and its environment. No firm can afford to allow its organization to be cast in concrete. As the role of marketing evolves, and as changes take place in products, markets, and the competition, so should organizational frameworks be allowed to evolve in response.

Dunfey Hotels Corporation

Robert J. Kopp
Christopher H. Lovelock

"THE DUNFEY CHAIN: A SAVIOR OF DYING HOTELS" ran the headline above a half-page story in the financial section of the Sunday *New York Times* for June 22, 1980. The story began:

Suburban motor hotels. Sprawling convention hotels. Small and elegant city hotels. Foreign hotels. At first glance, the collection of properties under the Dunfey name seems an unmanageable mishmash.

Yet the Dunfey Hotels Corporation, which within the last year and a half has put together such a chain of unlikely properties, is getting to be known as a comer in the lodging industry, with a knack for taking over aging hotels and returning them to profitability. In fact, Dunfey is a success story on top of a success story.

Success story No. 1 goes back to the 1950s and features the Dunfeys, an Irish-American family of eight brothers from Hampton, N.H. The Dunfey boys, who started with a hot dog stand at Hampton Beach, built a multimillion-dollar New England hotel and restaurant chain.

Success story No. 2 stars Jon Canas, brought in by the Dunfeys as chief operating officer and executive vice president in 1975. Mr. Canas. . .is a marketing man who is

not afraid to step in to operate a hotel where others have faltered. With Mr. Canas on board, Dunfey has become one of the nation's fastest growing hotel chains.

COMPANY HISTORY

After being discharged from military service shortly after World War II, John and William Dunfey opened a clam and hot dog stand on the boardwalk at Hampton Beach, New Hampshire. Soon John and William were joined in the business by four younger brothers. In 1954, the six brothers formed a partnership with their mother, and purchased Lamie's Tavern in Hampton, N.H., three miles from the original business in Hampton Beach.

In 1958, the family business headed in a new direction when a 32-room motor inn was constructed adjacent to Lamie's Tavern. Further acquisition followed. By 1968, Dunfey Family Corporation, as the firm was then known, either owned or managed 18 hotels in the eastern U.S. Many of these properties, including the original Lamie's Motor Inn, were operated as franchises of Sheraton Hotels, the nation's largest hotel corporation.

In 1969, Dunfey Family Corporation made two new moves. First, Dunfey's Tavern Restaurants were opened in four of the company's New England properties. Second, the company acquired its first downtown hotel by purchasing the historic Parker House in Boston. The experience gained in succeeding years in renovating and repositioning the Parker House was to play an important role in shaping the future growth strategy for the Dunfey hotel business.

Injection of New Capital and Management

To finance further expansion following the purchase of the Parker House, the Dunfey family sold the company to the Aetna Life Insurance Co. in 1970. Six years later it was acquired from Aetna by Aer Lingus, the national airline of Ireland. But throughout these changes in ownership, the Dunfey family maintained managerial control over the business, with Jack Dunfey continuing on as the chief executive officer.

During the early 1970s, a number of professional managers were hired. They included Jon Canas, who joined the company in 1975 as vice president of sales and marketing. Canas, a Frenchman by birth, had been educated at the Cornell School for Hotel Administration and also held an MBA from Northeastern University; he had worked for six years with the Sheraton Corporation, where his most recent position had been vice president of sales and marketing for Sheraton's two international divisions—Europe/Africa/Middle East and Hawaii/Far East/Pacific.

A New Approach to Planning

Canas recalled how his experience with Sheraton had led him to develop a planning approach based on market segmentation for marketing widely diverse hotels:

About four years before coming to Dunfey, I was assigned the position of sales director of Sheraton's Hawaii Division, consisting at that time of seven hotels. Since I had no previous experience in the day-to-day operation of the selling function as such, I decided to approach the job from a planning point of view. I began immediately to ask those questions, the answers to which would result in a better understanding of the market: Why do people come to Hawaii? What kind of hotel experience are they looking for? What does competition currently offer? Are there segments of consumers who differ in their needs for the level and quality of service? The more I worked on it, the more I could see practical solutions evolving out of this approach.

In Hawaii, at that time, virtually the only thing standardized about the Sheraton properties was the Sheraton name. The individual hotels varied widely in terms of size, age, location, rates and types of customers. Faced with marketing such a diverse portfolio of properties, I was forced into understanding market segmentation. In the hotel business, this translates into offering different types of hotels for different types of customers . . . the idea really isn't revolutionary but you must remember that it ran against the tide of an industrywide move toward standardization of the "product"—a move which was clearly at the heart of the corporate strategies of most chains. . . .We were very successful in Hawaii. Not only did current properties perform well, but two years later our territory was expanded to include several new and existing hotels in the Far East and Pacific.

When the Dunfey opportunity came up, a friend of mine in the industry told me that, as a group, the Dunfey properties were "a mixed bag" of hotels, widely diverse in location and service level. Several had generally reached the end of their life cycle. I could see some similarities with the Hawaii situation. I took the job partially to see whether the planning approach I had developed was really successful or whether I had just been lucky in Hawaii.

Dunfey Hotel Properties

Since purchasing the Parker House, the Dunfeys had continued to acquire additional properties and management contracts as the opportunities presented themselves.[1] In 1972, for instance, when Aetna Life Insurance acquired Royal Coach Motor Inns, Dunfey was hired to manage four units of this chain, each located on a major suburban highway in Atlanta, Dallas, Houston, and San Mateo, California, respec-

---

[1]Between 1975 and 1980, the company had discontinued its relationship with twelve units. This turnover included properties that no longer fit in with the Dunfey product line, either because of product, market, or owners' objectives. The properties replacing them tended to be larger and more important hotels.

tively. Each was built in an exterior style reminiscent of sixteenth century English Tudor, set off against a round, stonefaced, castellated tower, while the hotel interiors were decorated in a Scottish clan theme. The previous owners had gone bankrupt.

By mid-1980, Dunfey Hotels fully or partially owned, leased, or managed 22 properties in the United States and Europe, containing a total of 8,950 rooms (*Exhibit 1*). Fourteen of these properties had been part of the Dunfey organization for six years or more. Each hotel was managed by a general manager who headed an executive operating committee (EOC) of department heads.

The Dunfey inns and hotels were divided into four groups, each directed by a group director of operations. (*Exhibit 2* shows a corporate organization chart.) These groups were as follows:

1. Dunfey Classic & Luxury Hotels (four properties: the Parker House, Boston; the Ambassador East, Chicago; the Berkshire Place, New York; and the Marquette, Minneapolis).
2. Dunfey Major Meeting & Convention Hotels (seven properties, located in Atlanta, Dallas, Houston, Cape Cod, San Mateo, New York, and Washington).

EXHIBIT 1 PROPERTIES OWNED OR MANAGED BY DUNFEY HOTELS, OCTOBER 1980

Group	Type	Property	Location	Year acquired	Status*	No. of rooms
1	Classic hotels	Ambassador East	Chicago, IL	1977	P	300
		Berkshire Place	New York, NY	1978	P	500
		Marquette	Minneapolis, MN	1979	M	270
		Parker House	Boston, MA	1969	F	550
2	Meeting and convention hotels	Dunfey Atlanta Hotel	Atlanta, GA	1971	F	400
		Dunfey Dallas Hotel	Dallas, TX	1971	F	650
		Dunfey Houston Hotel	Houston, TX	1971	L	450
		Dunfey San Mateo Hotel	San Mateo, CA	1971	F	300
		Dunfey Hyannis Resort & Conference Center	Cape Cod, MA	1972	F	250
	Other metropolitan hotels	New York Statler	New York, NY	1979	P	1,800
		The Shoreham	Washington, D.C.	1979	P	900
3	Inns	Howard Johnson's Motor Inn	Newton, MA	1970	L	275
		Sheraton Inn and Lamie's Tavern	Hampton, NH	1958	F	30
		Sheraton Lexington	Lexington, MA	1967	F	120
		Sheraton N.E. Philadelphia	Philadelphia, PA	1973	F	200
		Sheraton Tobacco Valley	Windsor, CT	1968	F	130
		Sheraton Wayfarer	Manchester, NH	1962	F	200
	Airport hotels	Sheraton Airport Inn	Philadelphia, PA	1974	M	350
		Sheraton Inn	South Portland, ME	1973	F	130
		Sheraton Airport Inn	Warwick, RI	1973	F	125
4	International hotels	London Tara Hotel	London, England	1976	F	850
		Hotel Commodore	Paris, France	1979	L	170
Total:	22 hotels					8,950 rooms

*Key: F = Fully owned by Dunfey Hotels.
P = Partially owned by Dunfey Hotels (joint venture with management contract).
L = Leased by Dunfey Hotels.
M = Strictly management contract.
Source: Company records.

EXHIBIT 2 PARTIAL ORGANIZATION CHART, JUNE 1976

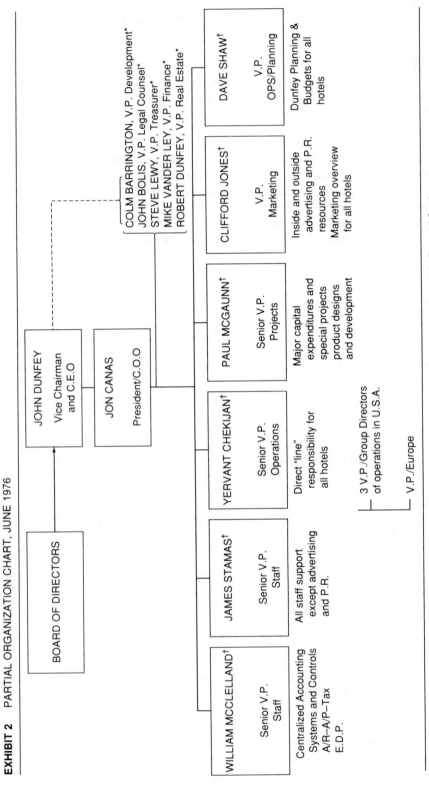

*Member of the Finance Review Committee, which also includes the Vice Chairman, President, and DAVE JUNE, V.P. Financial Services.
†Member of the Corporate Executive Operating Committee, which also includes the President.
Source: Company records.

524

3. Dunfey Inns and Airport Hotels (nine properties, located in New England and Pennsylvania).
4. International Hotels (two properties, located in London and Paris).

Some of the airport hotels and motor inns were affiliated, for marketing purposes only, with another chain (Sheraton or Howard Johnson). Although this affiliation had the advantage of linking the inns to national advertising campaigns and toll-free telephone reservations numbers, it did nothing for the visibility of the Dunfey organization.

Between 1974 and 1979, average occupancy, systemwide, increased from 56% to 72%. A financial summary, showing total revenues and operating profits for all U.S. units in the Dunfey organization both owned and managed, appears below.

DUNFEY HOTELS CORPORATION FINANCIAL SUMMARY (U.S. UNITS ONLY)

Year	Total revenues	Operating profit
1976	$ 58 million	$ 7 million
1977	72 million	9 million
1978	88 million	16 million
1979	120 million	21 million
1980 (est.)	165 million	34 million

Jon Canas and the Dunfey "System"

When Canas joined Dunfey in May 1975, the company had a marketing staff, but not an organized marketing effort. Recalled Canas:

The operation was characterized by extremely tight cost control, declining occupancy and declining market share. Internally, many units were perceived to be at the end of their life cycle. We moved quickly to take some specific actions which paid off, and we were helped along by an improving economy beginning in 1976. Groups sales doubled in three years and occupancy went from below the industry average to above.

In reviewing the specific areas of the business that the company had concentrated on, Canas divided the years 1975–80 into three distinct periods:

Our greatest need during 1975 and 1976 was to build occupancy. I don't have to tell you that profit in the hotel

business comes from selling rooms, and we did everything possible to "keep the lights on" as they say in the industry. This meant going after any and all types of business, including lower rated (in terms of revenue-per-room night) market segments. As an example, we found early success in attracting what we call "training and destiny" business. This is primarily in-residence programs centered around training sessions, often lasting five to eight weeks. One example would be a flight attendant training program by an airline. Such programs are typically repeated many times over the course of a year by the same company, and effectively amount to an extended rental of space in the hotel. The meetings are planned far in advance and don't require elaborate arrangements such as banquet facilities; demand is fairly price sensitive. Of course, as occupancy began to improve, we instituted a policy of actively pursuing higher rated segments and gradually substituting this new business for the lower rated segments.

During 1977 and 1978, we embarked on a major program to improve the overall appearance of our properties. In most cases this involved renovating, restoring, repositioning and remarketing individual properties. Basically, we made the decision to *reject* the life cycle assumptions which prevailed in the firm at the time. The Parker House in Boston is a good example of this philosophy. The Parker House was an old property, which had a deteriorating and outdated physical plant, declining occupancy, and had been given up on by the previous management. We saw an opportunity in the hotel's heritage—and the fact that it occupied an excellent location in a metropolitan area where quality lodging was in short supply. The result of this renovation was dramatic increases in occupancy and profitability.

Now as room occupancy rates topped-out on a companywide basis, we sought revenue in other departments. We went into a very creative period where new restaurants and lounges were created. We didn't just open a room, we created a *concept*. A key product of our "creative period" is the Tingles lounges and discotheques located in several of our hotels; these discos were unique in that the sound, loud over the dance floor, but softer at surrounding tables, allowed people to sit, relax, and converse. As an example of the impact on revenue, the conversion of the lounge in the Atlanta Hotel to a Tingles, took food and beverage revenue from $8–9,000 per week to over $25,000 weekly in that room.

In 1979 we entered a new phase. With both room and food and beverage (F&B) revenues peaking, we turned our attention to better cost management to maintain profit growth. We brought in an outside consulting firm to help us develop a rather sophisticated cost management/payroll efficiency system. The system was tested at the Parker House in 1977–78 and was expanded to our other units in 1978–79. In addition, we sought cost savings in centralized purchasing and in better heat, light, and power management.

So in looking back, I suppose you could say we concentrated our efforts on different areas of the business at different times. We were consciously trying to improve the "state of the art" in all areas of the hotel business, and I think the results show that we succeeded.

The situation facing Dunfey in 1975 was surprisingly similar to that of the Sheraton situation in Hawaii when I became sales manager; the mixed bag of food and lodging businesses grouped under the Dunfey corporate name ran the gamut from small, outlying motels to larger urban hotels. In fact, unlike Sheraton, the Dunfey group lacked a common name and identity—there were Sheraton, a Howard Johnson's, a group of four hotels purchased from Royal Coach renamed Dunfey Hotels, as well as several properties which stood alone in terms of identification. Thus, it was out of a need to simplify the management task that the Dunfey Planning Process and the Dunfey Management Approach evolved.

In essence, our approach to marketing planning is based on the belief that there exists a unique strategy or market position for each property which will maximize revenues in the long term. While other hoteliers were focusing on product efficiency and standardization, at Dunfey our commonality became the planning process. Of course, we've come a long way since 1975. In particular, we have grouped our hotels in a way where we can take advantage of some economies of scale in marketing. However, our basic approach is still at the individual hotel marketing level.

THE DUNFEY PLANNING PROCESS

As a first step toward development of a management system for all the Dunfey properties, Canas had drafted a series of internal documents. "The Dunfey Management Approach" and "The Way We Work" enunciated a management philosophy based on the conviction that each hotel had to recognize and satisfy certain needs from its customers, owners, and employees. The third document, titled "The Dunfey Planning Process," laid out a clearly defined system of annual and quadrimester (four-month) planning,

dealing with objectives and strategies relating to customers, owners, and employees.

Canas believed that the planning system for any given unit must begin with the needs of one or more clearly identified customer segments which, when related to the nature and extent of competition, served to determine the positioning the hotel would have in the marketplace. Time and again, remarked Canas, he had seen chains, which had standardized their offerings against certain market segments, expand unsuccessfully into geographic areas that already had an excess of hotel rooms serving those same segments.

He emphasized that profitability in the hotel business was primarily based on the revenue side and stressed the importance of good rooms merchandising through a specific planning process which was evaluated with the help of a performance measure he called Room Sales Efficiency (RSE).[2]

The key to good rooms merchandising and to good cost control, he said, was accurate forecasting of demand at all times of the week and all seasons of the year.

Every year, the management of each Dunfey hotel had to prepare both an annual plan and a series of three quadrimester (four-month) plans, referred to as Q-Plans. The planning process for each hotel proceeded through four basic steps, supported by appropriate documentation.

1. Assess supply-demand relationship—by examining the type (conventions, tourists, business travelers, etc.) and quantity of customers available in a given geographic market. A careful evaluation was made of the positioning of competitive hotels against each segment.
2. Determine where Dunfey *should be* in terms of the market position of the hotel as a whole, and each food and beverage outlet within that hotel.
3. Identify the gap between where the hotel is currently positioned and the desired position.
4. Structure the measures required to move the hotel

---

[2]RSE equals the total room sales revenue received during a period divided by the total revenues that could have been obtained if all available rooms had been sold at the maximum price.

and F&B outlets toward the desired market position. Requests for capital expenditures—to add to or improve facilities—were a key element of Step 4.

The outcome of Steps, 2, 3, and 4 was a "Mission Statement" for each hotel which had as its input the supply/demand relationship, and as its output a set of specific operating objectives for all members of the field operations team.

Exhibit 3 summarizes the planning process. In essence, broad strategic goals embodied in the Mission Statement were "stepped down" into key result areas (KRAs)—specific action steps to be undertaken in support of unit or departmental objectives—via a series of annual planning forms referred to as Y1s (unit objectives and strategies), Y2s (departmental objectives and strategies), and Y3s (specific goals for each unit and department objective). These goals formed the basis for the employees' incentive plan.

EXHIBIT 3
DUNFEY HOTELS CORPORATION: DUNFEY HOTELS UNIT PLANNING PROCESS

Objective:	Corporate Planning Committee (CPC) to provide corporate input and direction for each unit's 1981 Mission and Annual Plan; the CPC includes the Corporate Executive Committee—see *Exhibit 2*—plus, as appropriate, Vice President–Sales, Corporate Food and Beverage Director, and the relevant Group Director of Operations (GDO).

A. For the CPC to do this, it needs:
    1. Marketing Assessment, which includes:
        a. 1–3 page summary of supply/demand analysis.
        b. 1-page report to indicate if supply/demand findings call for a significant change in strategies or product.
        c. Historical and Proposed (1981) Market Segmentation and F&B and total revenues.

    2. Financial Assessment, which includes:
        a. 1 page outlining:
            (1) Corporate objectives for the unit.
            (2) Are we meeting corporate objectives (if not, why)?
        b. Historical Financial Summary for 3–5 years showing financial results and key statistics.

    3. Outside Owners' Assessment,* which includes:
        a. Page outlining outside owners' objectives.
        b. Assessment of current results.

B. The CPC will review the above material resulting in a memorandum to the GDO and unit EOC outlining:

	1. Unit is on track and should not change direction.
O.K. to proceed to items C and D	2. Unit is on track except for certain items (outlined) which should be corrected (no major direction change).
Not O.K. to proceed to C and D	3. Unit is off track seriously—people will be assigned to assist in making major direction changes.

C. The Director of Marketing and GDO will then write the Unit Mission Statement and send it to the units (after CPC has approved the wording).

D. Unit EOC will then prepare Y-1, Y-2, and Y-3 (GDO and corporate staff must review and approve).

E. CPC will have final approval on Item D.

*For properties managed by Dunfey Hotels for outside owners.

EXHIBIT 3 *(Continued)*

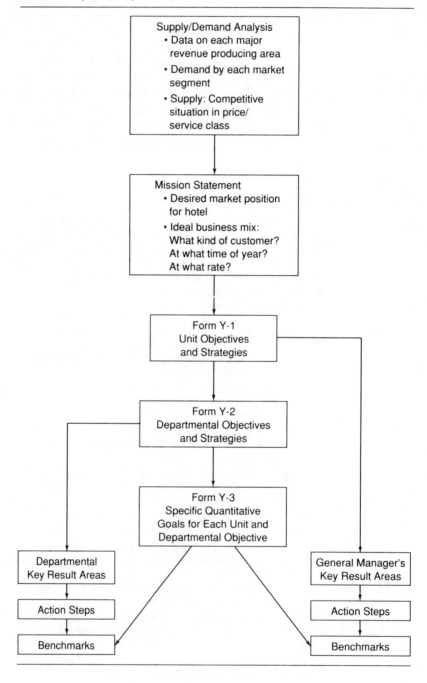

Similar planning efforts, with a shorter-term focus, were undertaken each quadrimester; these were referred to as "Q-Plans."

The planning process for each unit (hotel) was carried out by that unit's executive operating committee (EOC) with the participation of the corporate planning committee (CPC). The unit EOC usually consisted of the general manager (GM), assistant general manager or resident manager, sales director, rooms manager, food and beverage (F&B) manager, and personnel director. The CPC comprised Jon Canas, the controller, and five vice presidents in charge of operations, staff report, product design, profit planning, and marketing. The CPC was assisted in its review of individual unit plans by the vice president–sales, the corporate F&B director, and the relevant group director of operations.

Each group director of operations was responsible for coordinating the preparation of key planning documents by each of the unit EOCs in his group of hotels. The various documents were submitted to the corporate planning committee for approval in a succession of steps carried out from July 1 to November 1 of each year. Units were required to submit an outline of their preliminary thinking in July in order that the CPC could provide early feedback on the appropriateness of tentative plans.

Based on these early submissions, the CPC had, by early August, classified individual hotel plans as:

- "Green," signifying that the unit was on track and should not change direction
- "Yellow," signifying that the unit was on track except for certain items (outlined) which should be corrected (no major direction change)
- "Red," indicating that the unit was seriously off track—corporate staff would be assigned to assist in making major direction changes

Each unit EOC, working with their group director, was required to prepare a Mission Statement addressing the following questions:

- What type of customer are we aiming for?
- Where do we stand versus the competition?
- What are we trying to be?
- Where should we focus our efforts to satisfy targeted customers, as well as dealing with owners' corporate needs and also employees' needs?

The hotel business, noted Canas, was operations oriented, involving a multitude of basic activities that must be carried out over and over again, yet could be done in a number of different ways. He continued:

We believe that people carry out functions in different ways depending on the purpose they have in mind. The GM may have one purpose, the F&B manager another—and neither may be in concert with the corporation. So, as simplistic as it sounds, the Mission Statement integrates the activity of unit and corporate management. Any management team that has succeeded in crystallizing and communicating the mission of the hotel will find the various departments pulling together, in the same direction, to create the sought-after hotel experience for the customer. It provides more fulfillment for the employees and better results for the owners and the corporation. Also, the process helps achieve agreement between corporate and unit management.

The Ideal Business Mix

"The most important part of the mission," Canas noted, "deals with what we call the IBM—ideal business mix. This defines the customer segments we will direct our sales efforts toward at various times of the year." He elaborated:

There are many ways to segment the market. The first, of course, is the way we categorize business on our control reports: for instance, pure transient, regular corporate group, bus tours, and so forth. In addition, we segment our marketing effort by geography and by industry, and we assign sales coverage to whatever groupings seem to make sense for a particular area.

The point is that, once we identify our desired segments, it becomes a simpler task to set objectives for the operating departments—such as sales, rooms, and food and beverages. We've found that certain segments of the market tend to have common needs—or "reason to buy." Very often the marketing challenge is to define these needs: Is the customer primarily interested in price, in location, in facilities, in social status—or is he just looking for a hotel consistent with his personal tastes in furnishings and food?

The ideal business mix also carried implications for our capital spending and renovations and maintenance decisions. We often say, "We could reach this segment *if* we had certain facilities." The *if* here is important: we may have an intended market position, but we must have programs and facilities to reach it. The restoration and revitalization of the Parker House taught us a lot about repositioning—a lesson we have been able to apply to other properties in the chain.

After we have outlined our goals by type of customer, amount of room nights, period of year, and rates, then we ask two further questions: (1) How do we market—how do we reach these customers? And (2) How do we deliver? (And delivery at a *profit?*)

Our Rooms Merchandising Plan and the supporting Account Coverage Program guide our sales efforts. As part of the Rooms Merchandising Plan, you have your ideal business mix prioritized by segments and by lead time in their respective buy decision. If, for example, a convention cancels 9 months ahead of time, then you go after alternative segments. It's like starting all over again. But, at least you will have identified in advance where you are going to go to make up that business.

Most hotels hire a sales manager and tell him or her to "fill the rooms." This usually works in the short term, but is not a good business approach in the long term. Customers contribute to the atmosphere of hotel experience; you should choose your clientele selectively to match your market position. In our system we specify: (1) a certain kind of customer at (2) a certain time of year at (3) a certain rate.

With the Rooms Merchandising Plan you know what to ask sales and reservations people to do. In general, in the industry, salespeople often don't know who to see, they don't know how many rooms are available, and they don't know what rate to charge. At Dunfey we provide these guidelines as closely as possible in order to maximize our profitability and productivity.

In general, we find there is an inverse relationship in the lead time between the buy decision and consumption by various market segments and the rate we can get. In other words, the farther in advance groups book, the cheaper the rate usually it. So, most hotels used to book business way in advance, without consideration of more desirable business which could be booked later on.

So, the moral for the periods of time where we anticipate strong demand—and since we have a limited supply of rooms—is that we shouldn't sell on a first-come, first-served basis. For better profits, we plan the IBM proportion which is set aside for long lead time groups and for shorter lead time groups, and then save some capacity for higher rated walk-in business.

When business for the future begins to pick up, we try to monitor whether we're attracting our target customers. We want to build our business with the correct market segments—not just fill rooms—because we're building an image for the future and the profile of customers to take in has a tremendous impact on the position of the hotel. Of course, when occupancy is very low, oftentimes we will sell rooms to less desirable segments, but as we build occupancy, we can become more selective in our marketing.

Now, talking about the Account Coverage Program, in a lot of cases we find that 20 percent of the accounts give us 80 percent of the business. Therefore, it is important to identify, qualify and quantify all our accounts to set proper sales priorities. It also allows us to know what accounts we'll have to approach to get what business. Moreover, we identify what "buy decisions" exist for each individual account. For instance, for corporate groups it's usually either a "price buy," a "location buy," or a "facilities buy."

Also, our sales department provides a significant amount of information and feedback on our supply-demand studies. Through the direct salespeople we know what to sell, to whom, and at what rates. We truly see "need satisfaction" as a sales approach to sell and get repeat sales.

A MANAGEMENT ISOLATION MEETING

An isolation meeting—so designated because the participants were isolated from the interruptions of the home office—was held in the early fall of 1979 to discuss the status of the 1980 planning process and to reinforce understanding of the Dunfey management philosophies among the top 15 corporate operations and marketing executives.

Jon Canas opened the meeting by reiterating some of the basic percepts of the Dunfey Management Approach:

The Dunfey Management Approach is companywide. It not only includes the concepts inherent in the way we look at our business, but also includes the process and the systems through which we operate. We must have agreement at top on our philosophies. That means amongst all of us. And then we must attempt to achieve concurrence at lower levels.

What we're saying is that the traditional "get results and we don't care how you do it" doesn't work at Dunfey. We *do care* how you do it! We're concerned with the manner in which results are obtained.

The mission becomes the point of reference for the selection of unit objectives and strategies. The process to be followed by the EOC is to ask: "If we were totally successful in reaching our mission, what are the desirable things that would happen, or desirable conditions that would prevail (positive indicators of success), and what are the undesirable conditions that should be eliminated (negative indicators of success)?"

It's here that we should use the scenario approach: That is, take any aspect of the operation—such as the guest experience at the front desk—and talk through what would happen if we were successful. Each department and facet of the business should be able to visualize what the operation would look like if fully successful. Out of this come the specific action steps that we can focus on as our key result areas—KRAs.

Each department must understand what was expected of it, continued Canas, and how it contributed to the whole. "Sometimes," he observed, "we move too fast from the mission to our planning structure without understanding the implications of what we're doing."

Pushing the Dunfey Approach Down the Organization

Following a brief discussion of the basic approach, Canas turned to his area of principal concern.

Overall, I think you will agree we have been successful in establishing the Dunfey business philosophy among members of the organization down through the level of the EOCs of each hotel.

The challenge I want to discuss with you today is in modifying the behavior of people farther down in the organization. In order to convey our philosophy and our approach to the customer, we must push a commitment to our management style down to the very lowest levels of the organization. This is a particular problem when, like us, you take on many new people during the year.

Also, we have had some areas of confusion, such as in defining KRAs. When we talk about key result areas, we're talking about the 20 percent of items against which we can devote effort which will account for 80 percent of the success in reaching our goals. A good selection of KRAs requires a narrow focus and clear delineation of those few key areas which will make the biggest difference in our results at the end of the year.

Now, for instance, if the food and beverage manager gives us 36 things he wants to do, these are *not* KRAs. Most of these are just doing his job; after we get through those, there are probably one or two KRAs which we can

identify which will really make a quantum improvement in his operations. If he works 14 hours a day and doesn't accomplish his KRAs, he has failed. But if a manager has a list of 17 KRAs, he just doesn't understand our planning process!

Yervant Chekijian, at the time group director of operations for the three Dunfey Classic Hotels, caught Canas's eye and offered an illustration:

I can point to an example of this at the Ambassador East. The engineers had many KRAs but I noticed the stoppers in the sinks weren't working. I asked them to get to the basic problems like stoppers in the sink before they submitted a bunch of lofty KRAs. And I mentioned to them that they shouldn't just say they're going to fix the stoppers, they should propose an action plan as follows:

1. Inspection.
2. Locate the problems.
3. Define the scope of work.
4. Allocate man-hours.
5. Commit to having the job completed by a specific date.

Canas nodded agreement and added:

What we need is a scenario documented for each member of the operating team. We need to describe a certain level of service, start selling some standards of guest expectations, and relate the scenarios to these. Otherwise, the people we are dealing with at the lower levels easily forget the basics that we are expecting from them.

Canas turned toward the group directors of operations. "I guess you could say that our planning process and programs have given Dunfey people a common language. It also means we can transfer people from property to property and they will know the system." He went on to say, "one of the things I need to know is how well this planning process is actually being implemented by the EOC in each of our hotels."

Yervant Chekijian answered:

At the Parker house, the EOC meets on a weekly basis to go through the Q-Plan and review benchmarks. At the Ambassador East, on the other hand, they work with me but they have a tendency to be overwhelmed by what happens during the day—putting out fires, if you will. They usually "intend" to use the plan when things are "normal." One general manager did the plan three times—over and over again—threw up his hands, and asked me if he should get back to work. My answer was "How can you work without a plan?"

A regional director of sales observed that in some ways the plan was "sophisticated—even scary—but it's very natural when you get into it." Chekijian responded that the plan would not get used if its content wasn't real. The group directors, he said, must be responsible for ensuring that individual hotels not only understood the plan but had also proposed realistic goals and action steps.

Canas then turned the discussion toward the questions of contingency planning:

We didn't predict the slowdown in business resulting from the 1979 gasoline shortages until nine months into the year. Very frankly, the oil crisis just wasn't predicted, so we didn't have a "Plan B" in marketing. However, we have one in cost control, which is a lot easier to implement. Another question is, How do you build in sales flexibility when rooms merchandising calls for such advance bookings?

Jurgen Demisch, group director of operations for Dunfey's Inns division, offered a solution: "If sales aren't coming in, we can go to the sales force and ask them to use their account coverage program and get more business from the segments lower down the list."

"So, what you're saying," responded Canas, "is that we already have a system. We have sales actions plans, pricing flexibility, ability to cut costs over a 30-day period, and an account coverage program. What we need now is to fully learn to use these things."

"Overall, I see our planning as an evolutionary process," remarked Demisch. "As people learn to work with the plan, they become Dunfeyized, and then when these people are promoted, they can get into the plan from day one at any new property."

"We must get the planning process down to the third level: to restaurant managers, engineers, etc.—down the organization," Canas emphasized "What I think we need for your division, Jurgen, is a simplification of The Way We Work. All the ingredients must be there and we don't want to short-circuit it—but Jurgen, we must find a way to have a simplified planning process for a division like yours where you take in so many new people in a short period of time.

After all, the basic objective is to be professional innkeepers."

Chuck Barren, group director of operations for several medium-sized hotels, entered the discussion:

At Hyannis we have a very structured, Dunfeyized team. They are using the planning process and they're moving on without looking back to where they were. We've had a new sales manager in there for 10 days and he already has an excellent plan for the first quarter. The planning system was readily applied here and worked very well.

Baltimore was initially a distress property, and we said, "Do we really want to work from a checklist?" After three months, we went into the planning process. The owners sat in at our planning meetings and it really helped *them* understand our side of the business and to set mutual objectives.

It's clear that the planning process tends to break down where we don't have Dunfeyized people. And where this occurs, we should have a checklist or a simplified version of the plan to use in situations like takeovers.

Conclusion of Meeting

In answer to a question from one participant, Canas conceded that Dunfey had indeed developed its own management language, which made it hard to acculturate new people, and especially to bring in top management people at the operations level. On the other hand, he felt that the Dunfey process still allowed individual styles to come through, and in fact, called on the creativity of each manager. "The process provides no solutions," he stated, "only managers do!"

Before the meeting adjourned Canas reiterated the essence of the corporate operating mission, which he read to participants:

To create and/or maintain the structure that provides for the appropriate satisfaction of specifically defined needs of targeted customers, owners, and employees.

He added:

The key here is that we're talking about a structure—and a structure has strength. It has durability. It's an entity which must be full and self-supporting. The structure is our management philosophy and our planning process which, when implemented properly, will provide for the needs of owners, employees, and customers.

Knowles Products: Brand Management System

Charles B. Weinberg

In early 1989, Clive Langdon, Group Vice President—Pharmaceutical Products of Knowles Products, was reviewing a specially commissioned report on his division's brand management system. Knowles, a major marketer of a well-known brand of analgesic and a number of personal care products and owner of a Southern U.S. chain of franchised drug stores, has used a brand management system for more than a decade. This system had worked well for Knowles; however, it seemed to Langdon that a review of this system was appropriate. Consequently, in September he had asked Leslie Nome, a well-regarded marketing consultant, to conduct such a review. After some discussion, Langdon and Nome agreed that the first stage of the project should be to document the way that brand management system operated at Knowles. Langdon was reviewing that report in anticipation of a meeting the next morning with Nome.

COMPANY BACKGROUND

In the early 1900s Jason Knowles, a pharmacist by training and a traveling salesman by profession, de-

veloped a patent medicine that he claimed was beneficial for relieving a variety of ills. Over time, the claims moderated but Knowles' products, sold primarily in tablet form, gained popularity as a headache remedy. Descendants of the original family maintained control of the company until the late 1970s, when the stock was first publicly offered.

PRODUCT LINE

Prior to going public in 1978, the firm had essentially been a one-product company. Although Knowles analgesic was sold in liquid and tablet form and combined with other ingredients to produce such products as cough syrups and cold remedies, the focus was always on Knowles pills and their promised relief from headaches. Some other brands had been introduced but none had ever accounted for more than 10 percent of corporate sales.

In the late 1970s, Knowles management had begun to plan a major expansion of its product line. In 1980, the company announced a program for growth marked by expansion in four major directions:

1. Health-related products
2. Personal care products
3. Franchised drugstores
4. International markets

533

In the immediately ensuing years, Knowles acquired three companies, each with a major well-known brand name of health related product (an upset stomach remedy, a muscle relaxant, and a treatment for athlete's foot). In addition, Knowles also acquired several small companies that marketed specialty personal care products, such as a dandruff shampoo and a denture cleaner. In the six years ending in 1986, Knowles acquired companies with a total of fifteen significant brand names and introduced three new internally developed brands as well. Although selling a variety of pharmaceutical and personal care products, the majority of the company's sales was made through supermarkets. In 1986, senior management decided to cease acquiring new companies and concentrate on internal development.

In 1984, Knowles acquired a chain of drugstores, named Southern Star, located in Florida and Georgia. About half of Southern Star's outlets were franchised; the rest were wholly owned. Although some additional smaller acquisitions were made, expansion of the Southern Star was accomplished primarily through opening new outlets and increasing sales per store.

Knowles' analgesics had been sold in Western Europe for almost thirty years. Several of the new brands were also manufactured in Europe or Asia, but most overseas markets were served through export sales.

Overall corporate sales had increased by more than tenfold in the past decade to $1.3 billion in 1988. However, profits had not kept pace. *Exhibit 1* summarizes corporate performance by line of business. An abridged organization chart for Knowles Products is given in *Exhibit 2*.

THE BRAND MANAGEMENT SYSTEM

Knowles had been organized on a product management system, particularly in the Pharmaceutical Products division, as shown in *Exhibit 3*. There were five job levels in the brand system: brand assistant (BA), assistant brand manager (ABM), brand manager (BM), associate marketing manager (AMM), and marketing manager (MM). The focus of Nome's initial report was on the brand manager and lower levels, i.e., assistant brand manager and brand assistant. (See *Exhibit 4, 5,* and *6,* for relevant job descriptions.)

Although Nome's report did not deal extensively with the MM and AMM levels of management, these managers played a critical role in brand management. The MM managed all aspects of marketing, except sales execution, for the division. This manager's key objectives were not only achievement of short-term volume and profit goals but also development, testing, and expansion of new products, improved products, and line extensions. These latter goals were

EXHIBIT 1
KNOWLES PRODUCTS: CORPORATE PERFORMANCE
(by line of business; $ millions)

	1988	1987	1986	1985	1984	1983
Net sales:						
Consumer products						
Pharmaceuticals	513	461	399	338	339	251
Personal care	110	94	86	67	39	31
Subtotal	623	555	485	405	378	282
Drugstores	690	678	596	403	240	—
Total	1313	1233	1081	808	618	282
Net income:						
Consumer products	53	49	41	39	32	29
Drugstores	20	18	16	10	7	—
Total	73	67	57	49	39	29

EXHIBIT 2 PARTIAL ORGANIZATION DIAGRAM FOR KNOWLES PRODUCTS

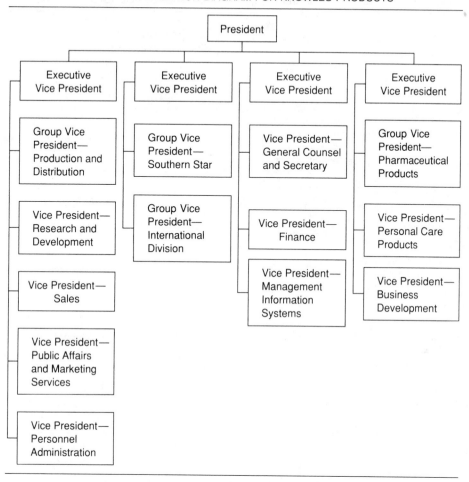

emphasized by top management to ensure continued corporate growth. The AMMs largely served coordinating, controlling, training, and strategic overview roles between the AM and BMs. They also had final decision-making authority on promotion activities within existing budgets, and handled many of the administrative jobs in the advertising department.

The entry-level job was that of BA. The BA was primarily responsible for monitoring the product budget, developing sales promotions, and analyzing marketing information (e.g., sales data from the com-

pany's management information system, consumption data from the A. C. Nielsen Company, and additional data from other outside market research services). New projects were added as competence was gained until the BA was sent out for "sales training," a 12-week field sales assignment.

Promotion to ABM followed this selling experience. Emphasis was placed upon learning advertising copy and media, developing long-term business-building programs, and assisting and helping train the BA in the area of sales promotion. ABM was a

EXHIBIT 3   KNOWLES' MARKETING ORGANIZATION, PHARMACEUTICAL PRODUCTS DIVISION

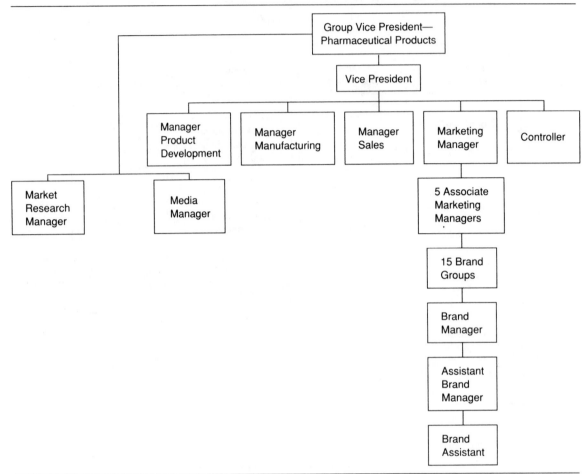

transition job which could last from one to two and a half years, depending on the capabilities of the person and the needs of the company.

When the ABM was promoted to BM, he or she was given overall marketing responsibility for one or more products, including planning, forecasting, and controlling volume and spending for these products. He or she also supervised ABMs and BAs. Due to rotation and normal turnover, not all brand groups were fully staffed with a BA and ABM.

In terms of day-by-day operations, the brand management group considered the other functions as "staff" to them. Nonetheless, brand management had no direct authority over sales, manufacturing, market research, and product development. But it did have the responsibility to obtain from staff the inputs necessary for successful marketing. Each functional group, for this purpose, had a representative designated to deal with the brand manager. An integral part of this system of "responsibility without direct authority" was the fact that brand management controlled budgets for areas such as market research and package design and represented staff's channel to top management. For example, a departmental request

EXHIBIT 4 JOB DESCRIPTION—BRAND MANAGER

Function: *To contribute to the overall growth of Knowles through development, recommendation, and implementation of effective marketing programs capable of building brand volume, share, and profit for assigned brands. The brand manager is charged to:*

1 Provide management with relevant data regarding the state of the business, serving as management's antennae in the category to identify problems and opportunities.

2 Develop recommendations which are designed to stimulate brand growth.

3 See that all programs are coordinated and run properly, serving as the focal point for all brand-related activity.

4 Ensure that brand personnel learn the skills to handle multifaceted responsibilities of the job.

The brand manager's specific marketing responsibilities are as follows:

1 *Product.* Ensure that the product and package are superior to competition within cost constraints demanded by the marketplace and profit considerations. Requires consumer usage/attitude and product research, establishment of product improvement objectives, and periodic review of progress toward these objectives.

2 *Positioning.* Position the product to maximize volume within the existing consumer and competitive environments. Periodically review marketing strategy in light of changing consumer needs, wants, and attitudes and competitive product positionings and sales. Develop and test alternative copy and promotion strategies attuned to the marketing strategy to improve the brand's overall positioning.

3 *Copy.* Ensure that copy provides the optimum selling power. Demands an ongoing effort in development and testing of new copy pools, different executional formats, and alternative copy strategies.

4 *Media.* Ensure that media plans are designed to deliver advertising in the most effective and efficient manner against the brand's target audience. Requires periodic review of target audience criterion and testing of alternative mixes of media vehicles within budget constraints, as well as testing of different media weights.

5 *Promotion.* Plan, execute, and evaluate, with the assistance of the sales department, consumer and trade promotions, which are cost-effective in increasing brand volume. Demands testing of a variety of promotions each fiscal year and testing, on a periodic basis, alternative annual promotion levels and/or alternative consumer/trade promotion splits within existing budgets.

6 *Volume/Control.* Make adjustments as necessary in fiscal year plans to deliver volume base.

The brand manager's specific management information responsibilities are to identify, analyze, and recommend actions in response to significant developments in the following areas:

1 Realized volume versus budgeted level

2 Competitive developments

3 Product and package problems

4 Problem markets

5 Implementation delays and cost overruns

6 Legislative and regulatory activities

---

for information or specific action was typically directed to the brand manager who not only had to concur but was the interface with top management. (See *Exhibit 7.*)

Excerpts from interviews with several brand managers are given in the Appendix at the end of the case.

Corporate Atmosphere

Nome considered Knowles to be an almost classic example of brand management. Brand managers

played a "line management" role within the marketing function at Knowles. The reasoning for this was that the BM had direct responsibility for the most critical marketing factor—advertising—and had the broadest exposure to the operations of the company and the best overall perspective on his product and markets.

Brand managers were able to accomplish their goals through other people by using their control over the product budget, their position as coordinator of all information, and their interpersonal skills. They had to be successful "at getting others to do the job."

EXHIBIT 5   JOB DESCRIPTION—ASSISTANT BRAND MANAGER

Marketing Responsibilities:

1 *Business Building Plans.*   Develop, recommend, and execute those key projects which, long term, will have a major effect on the shipments and consumption of the brand. Examples of these are the introduction of new sizes/products, major distribution building programs, or major trial-generating promotions.

2 *Copy.*   Work with the brand manager in providing direction to the advertising agency in the development of new executional formats (based on current strategy) and the testing of new copy strategies/executions. Also, work with technical and legal to obtain copy clearance/claim support.

3 *Media.*   In conjunction with the brand manager, provide the agency with direction on new ways to more efficiently reach the brand's target audience. This may take the form of media mix tests or testing of different media levels.

4 *Product.*   Ensure that a product which fulfills consumer needs and wants is marketed within cost constraints.

5 *Market Research Planning and Analysis.*   Initiate and analyze those market research projects which will yield information upon which the brand may act to improve current market position or correct an ongoing problem.

6 *Package Design.*   Ensure that the package in the marketplace is appealing and eye-catching, and connotes those attributes of the product most important to consumers.

Management Information:

1 *Market Research.*   Analyze research and recommend next steps to correct any problems or capitalize on any opportunities.

2 *Media.*   Analyze results of media testing and recommend action to be taken.

3 *Schedule Changes.*   Inform brand manager of delays in the progress of key projects in order that management may be apprised of the delay and the reason why.

But there was even more to the essential nature of the brand manager's job, a perspective that can only be expressed by senior management. These people looked upon brand managers as individuals who could be expected to ask the types of questions a top manager might ask, gather the facts necessary to make a decision, and then recommend a course of action in a very succinct memo. The net effect was that top management's job of managing the marketing of a large number of diverse brands in diverse categories became easier and more effective. The system assured that all brands, even those with small sales, were given attention and that a variety of marketing approaches designed to stimulate growth would at least be explored and recommended.

The power of the brand managers rested largely in their authority to ask questions anywhere in the company and demand carefully thought out, responsible answers, as long as the questions and answers were limited to matters which either directly affected the consumer of their product or affected their brand's contribution margin (revenue less manufacturing and shipping costs and brokerage commis-

sion). In addition, successful brand managers had informal authority arising from their superior knowledge, as compared to that of a functional specialist's, of all consumer aspects of their product, and they had the power to discuss their recommendations (in writing, usually) with top management.

Selection and Screening

Typically, brand assistants were recent MBAs from leading business schools with minimum work experience. (See *Exhibit 8* for a sample recruitment ad.) In recent years, Knowles had hired some graduates with advertising experience as well as some transferees from other company departments, but these were exceptions. Brand managers were almost always promoted from within. In initial hiring, Knowles sought individuals who were intelligent, trainable, competitive, aggressive, and hard-working. Ideal candidates had qualities which were generalized as: analytical ability; communications skills; the ability to plan, organize, and follow through; the ability to work well with others; leadership, resourcefulness, and ingenu-

EXHIBIT 6   JOB DESCRIPTION—BRAND ASSISTANT

Marketing Responsibilities:

   1 *Sales Promotion.* Plan, in consultation with other brand group members and the sales department, national and test promotions. Write promotion recommendations and issue related feasibility requests and production orders. Implement consumer-oriented portions of promotions (e.g., coupon copy and media, sample drops, etc.) and oversee and/or cooperate with sales department in implementing trade-oriented portions of promotions. Budget and evaluate promotions.

   2 *Budget Administration and Control.* Review and code invoices. Reconcile the budget with accounting on quarterly basis. Close out budget with accounting at the end of the fiscal year.

   3 *Market Analysis.* Analyze Nielsen data and write bimonthly Nielsen reports. Audit other sources of market information (monthly shipment reports, scanner data, etc.) and write analytical reports as necessary.

   4 *Shipment Estimates.* Prepare monthly shipment estimate which forecasts next three months' shipments with supporting rationale.

   5 *Competitive Activity.* Monitor competitive activity reported by sales (promotion and pricing activity), agency (competitive and media spending), and other sources (periodicals, etc.). Write reports on significant developments.

   6 *Public Relations.* Cooperate with consumer services in handling special consumer-oriented problems which fall outside normal consumer services activities. Work with research services (home economists) and public affairs on brand-related consumer information projects.

Other areas where brand assistant may contribute, depending upon individual brand assignments, include package design and business-building tests.

Management Information: Report to brand manager on:

1 *Competitive Activity.*	Significant competitive developments.	
2 *Budget Variance.*	Any variations from budget forecasts.	
3 *Promotion Problems.*	Any problems with implementation of promotions.	
4 *Consumer Relations.*	Any product problems which threaten volume.	

ity; decision-making skills; drive and determination; and maturity.

Training

The introduction for the new brand assistant was strenuous. Although the initial jobs might range from planning promotions to writing market research summaries, there was a lot of arduous "number crunching." Hours were long, often including weekends. There were no shortcuts or special courses and readings that could bypass this breaking-in period. Nor was there much sympathy for the neophyte. Everyone in brand management had been through the same experience, recognized its necessity, and knew the work could be done. "Help" was mainly in the form of providing initial direction, pointing out errors, and suggesting new projects as competence increased. The newer projects were invariably more interesting and challenging, which provided additional incentive to master the earlier tasks. And as new BAs were

hired, the more mundane jobs could be passed down.

The purpose of this training was to internalize certain "first principles" which were considered necessary to maintain the brand management system:

1. *All information could be derived from numerical data*: Brand people had minimal contact with either customers or suppliers. Customers were normally represented by market research findings and sales results. Suppliers were represented by specific liaison people. Thus there always had to be an analytic justification for a project or program. Results needed to be summarized in terms of cases of product and net revenue (minus all costs except advertising).

2. *Concern for mistakes*: Brand people were trained to be detail-oriented and concerned about not making errors. No mistake, particularly in a memo, was too small to be noticed. The feedback was intense since memos were commented on in writing as they were passed up and down the

distribution chain. If anyone found a mistake, then everyone who missed it was embarrassed.

3. *Brand manager's budget as a control system*: This principle was a bit deceptive, however. While some staff groups—market research, sales merchandising, and package design—were dependent upon brand management for funding of projects, brand management did not use the budgets as a club. The range of interrelationships between brand management and staff was too involved to be reduced to the single lever of money control.

4. *Career success required "the Knowles style":*

EXHIBIT 7 INTERFACE MATRIX

Brand manager responsibilities	Work with these departments	Brand role
Product or package improvement	Sales, R&D market research, manufacturing, and controller	(a) Development objectives for product or package development. (b) Approve aesthetics. (c) Develop consumer research objectives, fund research and summarize results. (d) Determine unit profit potential and return on investment. (e) Recommend test market to management. (f) Write manufacturing production orders for test market production of product. (g) Analyze test market results and recommend national expansion.
Positioning	Advertising agency, market research, and legal	(a) Develop alternative positionings. (b) Develop consumer research objectives and fund research. (c) Analyze research results and recommend test market. (d) Analyze test market results and recommend national expansion.
Copy	Advertising agency, market research, and legal	(a) Review agency copy submissions and select copy to be presented to management. (b) Approve final production for on-air copy testing. (c) Analyze copy test results. (d) Recommend national airing of copy.
Media	Advertising agency and media services	(a) Review agency media objectives and strategies and recommend alternatives. (b) Review and modify agency media plans with help of media services. (c) Forward agency media plan to management. (d) With help of media services monitor implementation of media plan.
Sales promotion	Sales, manufacturing, promotion development, and legal	(a) Develop national promotion plan with help of sales department. (b) Recommend plan to management. (c) Write manufacturing production order for production of sales promotion product. (d) Implement consumer portion of promotion (i.e., coupons, samples, etc.) and fund all trade allowances and consumer promotions.
Volume control	Sales	(a) Monitor shipments. (b) If undershipment of objectives seems possible, recommend remedial marketing efforts.

EXHIBIT 8
SAMPLE RECRUITING ADVERTISEMENT

Marketing Careers with
One of the Nation's
Leading Companies

Knowles Corporation manufactures and markets over 15 major consumer brands. Many are among the country's market leaders.

A limited number of entry-level positions are available as BRAND ASSISTANT, working within a Brand Group which has responsibility for one or more individual products and is the driving force behind them.

As a Brand Assistant, you will be assigned to a specific product. Your Brand Manager will give you immediate responsibility for a variety of projects and then look to you for leadership, ideas, and results. Some examples of your assignments will be: planning, executing, and evaluating promotions; analyzing business performance; planning and executing a sales presentation for a new market initiative; developing new packaging; and helping to manage your brand's budget.

In addition to individual projects, you will be broadly exposed to all aspects of Brand Management. As you contribute to the management of your brand and demonstrate your ability to handle additional responsibility, you will be assigned more complex and important projects. Your Brand Manager is responsible for your training and will work very hard to accelerate your personal development. The emphasis, however, is always on you . . . your thinking, your ideas, your contributions. Management career development is excellent. At Knowles, promotion is always from within, and based upon individual performance and contribution.

If you are about to obtain an MBA degree or equivalent and are just starting your career, if you have a background of achievement and can exhibit good analytical and communication skills, and if you are interested in talking further with us, send your resume to:

CORPORATE RECRUITING MANAGER
KNOWLES CORPORATION

The Knowles style contributed to the climate and mystique which made brand management successful. This style included memo format, job concept, and attitude. Memos conformed to a particular writing style and format and were not supposed to exceed two pages without an attached summary. Brand people had to be the resident experts on everything affecting their products. Brand managers thought of themselves as the general managers of a very small company. Nonetheless, brand people had to maintain their aggressive, competitive attitude without hurting their relations with staff. The BA might achieve a basic competence in one or two years. The competence was recognized by the addition of more complex assignments. As the BA's credibility and influence increased with the staff, he or she conformed more and more to the corporate style. BMs estimated that they spent as much as 25 percent of their time training BAs and ABMs. In fact, the entire brand management system was a training program. There was no such thing as an old BM; there was no place for the person who didn't want to be promoted.

MANAGEMENT INFORMATION SYSTEMS

The BM used current data almost exclusively, even though comprehensive historical files were maintained. Meetings were usually frequent and short.

Memos were passed through for comment and review by the BM. Magazines might be scanned for ideas but were seldom read. For many BMs, only the Nielsen chart books, the product fact book, and project folders were kept within easy reach.

Tests were used extensively to determine the accuracy of the information routinely received so that results could be optimized and problems avoided. Brand people went out into the field infrequently, yet they had a strong perception about what was happening through their tests and the management information system.

Emphasis had to be placed on the management information system because the BM changed products about every two years and thus lost personal contacts in the agency and staff groups who tended to remain with the products.

RELATIONSHIP WITH THE "BIG FIVE"

The five groups which brand management dealt with regularly were the advertising agency, sales, market research, manufacturing, and product development. With each group, there were conflicts which the BM had to resolve. These conflicts might include work priorities, differences of opinion about strategy or objectives, or disagreements over project timing. Brand managers sometimes argued that they had the responsibility for volume and spending without explicit authority to force staff compliance. These other departments, however, saw brand management as more in control due to its final authority to make recommendations to top management as well as its role in setting initial objectives. The other departments would have preferred a better understanding (by brand management) of their role and problems, yet essentially believed in the brand system as the best way to run the company.

ROTATION AND PROMOTION

Brand people were expected to shift products about every two years. Due to attrition, new hires, and promotions, the time could vary but seldom exceeded three years. It took a BM several months to become familiar with a new assignment and perhaps a year to implement a major strategy. Thus, the typical BM was working on a predecessor's strategy for much of his or her tenure.

Performance was judged on a number of bases:

1. Did the BM prepare a sound annual marketing plan and was he or she able to sell it to management?
2. How well did the product perform against the volume objective in the marketplace (regardless of who prepared the budget)?
3. What sort of major improvements or line extensions were proposed (though not necessarily implemented)?
4. How well did he or she train others?

In addition, part of a BM's evaluation was based on such factors as: communication, analysis, thoroughness, prioritization, productivity, organization, leadership, work with others, responsibility, ability to accept criticism, motivation, maturity, capacity, judgment, and attitude.

SUMMARY

Brand management at Knowles was a total system. The climate, selection, training, and promotion all tended to encourage the "best and brightest" people to dedicate themselves to making a product successful.

The people were supported by a management information system and organized structure that allowed them to be trained on the job and rotate from product to product at frequent intervals. The products were all marketed in a similar enough way, e.g., advertising, sales promotion, supermarkets, and retail drug outlets, that the system and organization were the same for each.

The strength of the system lay in the fact that each product had a "champion" who attempted to achieve volume and share objectives, as predicted in an annual plan. The short term was not sacrificed for the long term since the long term generally represented the incumbent's proposed strategy and ongoing business-building tests, and the short term represented a predecessor's strategy. In addition, a pool of potential general management talent was being established and utilized as experienced managers were promoted and new employees added.

Selected Portions of Interviews with Brand Managers

Question 1: You typically hire business school graduates with a small amount of work experience. What do you look for and how would you describe their jobs as BAs?

Brand Manager No. 1: I find it takes several months for a BA to become acclimated. New people are usually too theoretically oriented; at this level, pragmatic application of judgment to problems is more important. The most important thing for a BA to learn is to pay attention to details. Even "typos" have a dollar impact. The BA should learn to think things through comprehensively.

The BA begins working about ten hours per day plus homework, but the time goes down as the job is learned. All marketers are pretty much alike—aggressive, detail-minded—and that's what we look for here.

BM No. 2: The biggest problem a new BA has is to learn how to juggle projects and determine priorities. Business schools teach sequential problem solving but "Brand" requires juggling 15 trivial things and 1 major one. The BA's initial problem is establishing credibility. Brand management requires a mixture of talents but no one specific personality is appropriate. Some brand people do consider themselves "prima donnas."

BM No. 3: The BA's problem is simply a lack of experience with our system. The system relies on numbers, and the numbers come from the BA. The BA is constantly calculating and must think in analytic terms. The BA must work very hard, develop rapidly, and learn what brand management is all about. It takes two to six months for the BA to have a good grasp of the job and become acclimated to the system. All training is on-the-job.

Question No. 2: What is the relationship between brand management and the other departments?

BM No. 1: Brand mangers are considered with respect by the advertising agency but brand managers are committed to the agency because the BM cannot fire the agency. Most of the people in other departments do not want to move as fast as brand management. It is a problem conveying the urgency and importance of timing. The BM is responsible for planning, and the other departments for advice and/or execution.

Knowledge is power and the BM is the resident expert on his or her products.

BM. No. 2: Brand management is more a line than a staff function.

Brand management has responsibility for achieving volume objectives and keeping profit/case close to target level, but brand management has no direct authority over many other departments which impact on the ability to achieve objectives.

Senior management recognizes that sometimes performance is beyond the control of brand managers.

BM No. 3: Brand managers control the money. Many other departments must rely upon brand management for direction and project funding. The advertising agency has account executives who deal with brand people and the agency's creative and media departments. The agency presents a national media plan once a year. Since the marketing budget is mainly advertising, brand and agency personnel write the request. Sales promotions are originated by brand management and proposed to the sales department.

Brand management recommends and analyzes market research and test markets. The purpose of these is to avoid "national blunders" although the risk is relatively small with ongoing products.

Question 3: How do brand managers spend their time?

BM No. 1: Daily activities are coordination, fielding short questions with answers on the telephone, and commenting on memos passing through. Wide variation exists, but a day might have one hour for thinking and strategy, one hour for standard reports, one hour for the "In/Out basket," two hours on the phone, one hour with subordinates, and two hours in meetings.

Dealings are mainly with the "Big Five": the account executive at the advertising agency; sales; the manufacturing coordinator; market research; and the product development specialists.

On the average, the BM travels to the field once every three months. Brand management's job is to study the product, determine what is needed, and prioritize projects. The budget for this is set once a year.

BM No. 2: The most important job of a brand manager is the budget request and appropriation. Once each year, a two- to three-hour meeting is held which lays out how and why money is to be spent for the next year. During the period preceding this meeting, much of a BM's time may be spent with the agency. During the remainder of the year, the time falls off with the time spent in once-a-week meetings and telephone calls.

The second major job is the Brand Improvement Objectives meeting which is also held once a year. Brand works with R&D to develop both short-term and long-term product development plans.

Brand strategies require 1½ to 2 years to implement. Long-range planning is important because few changes can be made in the short term due to long lead times in production and media planning.

Most of the BM's time is spent on specific projects.

Heavy use is made of the telephone and many short meetings are held, usually with six people or less.

Brand management has a meeting with the Product Development Center every two weeks.

Question 4: How often does a brand manager change brands?

BM No. 1: All brand people are interchangeable, although it takes about two to four months to become the most knowledgeable. You spend one to two years on a brand.

BM No. 2: Rotation is caused by promotions and departures and occurs every 1½ to 2 years. Continuity is provided by the staggered rotation of BAs, ABMs, and BMs. Once you rotate, you usually do not have time to find out how your old product is doing.

Federal Express Quality Improvement Program

Christopher H. Lovelock

"The first year of our quality improvement program was really a great success. But the last six months have been tough," said Thomas R. Oliver, shaking his head ruefully. Oliver, senior vice president for sales and customer service, was talking about some of the challenges facing Federal Express as it sought to maintain momentum on quality improvement efforts in early 1990.

Last August, we merged with Flying Tigers, which has proved to be more difficult than anyone anticipated in terms of impacting service. In September, Hurricane Hugo, perhaps the most powerful storm of the century, disrupted our operations in the southeastern United States. Then there was the San Francisco earthquake in October. In December, the Mount Redoubt volcano in Alaska began erupting a hugh ash cloud, which totally dislocated our international flights through Anchorage. That volcano's still erupting on and off. The Friday before Christmas, the coldest weather seen in Memphis in the past 50 years caused burst water pipes and a computer foul-up that shut down our Superhub sorting operation. And now we're facing a profit crunch.

Our revenues are way up, but we've incurred very heavy costs from the Tiger purchase and the continued expansion of our international operations.

Oliver pushed the company newspaper *Update* across the table. "Earnings Drop: Costs to Be Controlled" read the headline. He explained that Federal's third quarter profits for the fiscal year (FY) 1990 were down by 79% to $5.2 million on revenues of $1.7 billion (up 35% over last year). Then he added:

A going concern that is doing reasonably well but not making the desired level of profit can experience a big courage gap on the quality issue. People know what it costs to train management, to train employees, to continuously train new hires, to give people "time around the clock" to work quality issues, and to organize the implementation of the various ideas that emerge. Yet, they aren't clear about the benefits. I want to ensure that last year's interest in quality doesn't get preempted by this year's interest in cutting costs.

THE EVOLUTION OF A LEGEND

Few companies had achieved legendary status as quickly as Federal Express. People loved to tell stories about the firm, incorporated in 1971 by Frederick

W. Smith, Jr., then aged 27. The earliest story told how Smith had sketched out the concept of a national hub-and-spoke airfreight network in a paper written while an undergraduate at Yale. The professor told Smith that his concept was interesting but infeasible because of competition and regulation, and gave the young man a "C" grade. But after service in Vietnam, Smith went on to turn his dream into reality, basing the hub in his home town of Memphis, Tennessee.

The concept was simple. Federal Express couriers, based in cities around the country, would pick up packages and take them to a local station, from where they would be flown by air to a central hub. Memphis was selected since it was centrally located in the US and airport operations were rarely disrupted by bad weather. At the hub, packages would be unloaded, sorted, reloaded, and flown to their destinations, where they would be delivered by couriers driving Federal Express vans. Because of federal regulations, the new airline had to be chartered as an air taxi operator and was restricted to aircraft with a carrying capacity of 7,200 pounds. Initially, Federal flew Dassault Falcons, French-built executive jets converted into minifreighters.

On an April night in 1973, 14 Falcons took off from cities around the US and flew to Memphis. In total, they carried 186 packages. Not surprisingly, the company lost money heavily in its early years. But aided by aggressive sales and clever advertising, package volume built steadily and by 1976 the firm was profitable. Thereafter, growth in revenues, profits, and package volume was rapid: *(see table at bottom of page)*

With the 1978 deregulation of the airfreight industry (for which Smith had lobbied heavily), Federal went public and bought larger aircraft. Having redefined service as "all actions and reactions that customers perceive they have purchased," management began a major investment in information technology, creating an online order-entry system known as COSMOS. This was designed to provide superior customer service in the face of increasing competition from UPS, Emery, the US Postal Service, and other express delivery firms.

Federal's early advertising slogan "When it absolutely, positively has to be there overnight" became almost a national byword. By FY 1985, Federal's sales exceeded $2 billion and its advertising jabbed fun at the competition, asking provocatively "Why fool around with anybody else?" Later, to emphasize its role as a tool for JIT (just-in-time) inventory management procedures, the company began using the slogan "It's not just a package, it's your business."

Following the purchase of Flying Tigers in August 1989, analysts forecast that Federal's total revenues for FY 1990 could exceed $7 billion. By now the company was an American institution. Its vans with their distinctive purple, orange, and white colors were everywhere; its aircraft could be seen at most airports; and the verb "to Fedex" (meaning to ship a package overnight) had become as much a generic expression for office workers as the term "to Xerox."

For 19 years, Federal Express had had a single leader, its chairman, Fred Smith, who was still only 46 years old. Outside management experts noted that it was unusual for an entrepreneur whose company had grown so large, so fast, to continue to lead the firm. Smith appeared to have a remarkable ability to supply vision, inspire loyalty, and create a climate in

FISCAL YEAR ENDING MAY 31

	1976	1981	1986	1988	1989[1]	1990[2]
Annual revenues ($mn)	75	589	2,573	3,883	5,167	7,000
Annual net income ($mn)	4	58	132	188	185	110
Av. dly. express packages (000)	15	87	550	878	1,059	1,250
Av. dly. heavyweight vol. (000 lbs)[3]	—	—	—	—	4,019	3,300

[1]Includes Tiger International operations for the last four months.
[2]Projections.
[3]1,000 lbs = 0.454 metric tonnes. = 454 kilograms.

which innovation and risk taking were encouraged and rewarded. Although the Federal Express Manager's Guide ran to 186 pages, Smith's core philosophy for the corporation was simple:

Federal Express, from its inception, has put its people first, both because it is right to do so and because it is good business as well. Our corporate philosophy is succinctly stated: People–Service–Profits

Line Haul Operations

Federal's operating concept of a hub in Memphis, served by aircraft flying spokelike routes from cities all around the US, had been only slightly modified over the years. But the technology and scale of the operation had changed dramatically. The sorting facility at Memphis International Airport had been enormously expanded. The Superhub, as it was known, now covered some 23 acres (100,000 m³), consisting of a matrix of 83 conveyor belts moving at right angles to one another. Aircraft arrived at Memphis almost continuously between 11:00 pm and 1:15 am. Using specially designed equipment, a crew of 14 workers could unload 44,000 pounds (20 tonnes) of freight from a Boeing 727 in 12 minutes.

The freight began its journey through the Superhub on a wide belt, known as the Primary Matrix, moving at 10 mph (16 km/h). Watching the packages rush by on this belt and then be diverted by guide arms into specific sort areas reminded one visitor of seeing a mountain torrent in full flood. Although the sort was assisted by computers, much of the process was labor intensive and expected to remain so. Once reloaded, the aircraft left Memphis between 2:15 and 3:45 a.m.

Regional domestic sorting facilities had been established; packages traveling between two East coast cities were sorted in Newark, New Jersey, rather than being sent to Memphis, while packages traveling between West Coast destinations were sorted in Oakland, California. A second national hub had been opened in Indianapolis, southeast of Chicago. These facilities were served by large trucks as well as by aircraft; packages traveling shorter distances were frequently transported entirely by truck.

Since 1979, Federal had offered service to and

within Canada. In 1985, the company inaugurated international service and began to build up a network of routes around the world. A European hub was established in Brussels, the capital of Belgium (and administrative center of the 12-nation European Community). Federal planned to build up significant intra-European business as well as transatlantic volume. Overseas expansion was aided by the purchase of existing courier firms in each national market (nine were purchased in FY 1989).

In December 1988, Smith announced what the press described as "an ambitious and highly risky plan" to pay $895 million for Tiger International, Inc., the world's largest heavy cargo airline, best known for its Flying Tiger airfreight service. Although Tiger had some domestic business, most of its revenues came from international services. The merger was a key step toward realizing Smith's goal of making Federal "the world's premier priority logistics company." Six "Freight Movement Centers"—located in Anchorage, Memphis, Chicago, New York, Brussels and Tokyo—now coordinated Federal's international traffic, which was expected to generate 30% of the firm's revenues in FY 1990.

A major benefit was Tiger's overseas operating rights, including landing rights in Japan. The merger allowed Federal to operate its own aircraft on routes where transportation had formerly been contracted out to other carriers. It also catapulted Federal into the heavy cargo business; previously, the firm had limited most packages to 150 pounds (68 kg) maximum weight, as well as imposing length and girth restrictions. Another important asset was Tiger's fleet of aircraft, including 21 Boeing 747s. However, these benefits came at the cost of taking on significant debt at a time when margins were being squeezed by price competition and heavy upfront costs were being incurred due to overseas expansion. There was also the challenge of merging two sharply different corporate cultures.

The Scope of the Operation in 1990

By 1990, Federal Express was one of the world's largest airlines, with a fleet of some 350 aircraft. This fleet comprised 170 trunk line aircraft (21 Boeing

747s, 25 McDonnell-Douglas DC-10s, 118 Boeing 727s, and 6DC-8s) and another 180 feeder aircraft used for shorter-distance operations. The firm served 119 countries and had 1,530 staffed facilities worldwide. Some four-fifths of its 86,000 employees were based in the United States, including 17,300 employees in Memphis. Federal operated over 20,000 vans and almost 2,000 large trucks in the US, plus another 6,300 vehicles in international locations.

A visitor to Memphis might be surprised to see a large fleet of snowplows and other snow-removal vehicles sporting Federal Express colors. The company had purchased this equipment in 1988 after a heavy snowstorm—unusual for Memphis, which had almost no snow removal equipment—had badly disrupted operations one night. "We only need this equipment about one night every two years," explained a company official. "But when we need it, we really need it!"

The average daily volume for express packages (up to 150 pounds in the US) was around 1.25 million. Federal's average package weighed 5.4 pounds (2.5 kg) and yielded a revenue of over $16; a significant price increase would take effect on April 1, 1990. Document shipments weighing just a few ounces (100–200g) had a declining share of package volume; the Fedex Overnight Letter represented 37% of all express packages in FY 1989, down from 40% two years earlier. The company offered three levels of delivery speed in the United States: Priority Overnight (next business morning by 10:30 a.m. in most locations); Standard Overnight (next business day for shipments of 5 pounds or less, with delivery before 3:00 p.m. in most locations); and Standard Air (second business day). Federal's rates tended to be more expensive than most of its US competitors.

For heavyweight shipments, the average daily volume was around 5,000 units. These shipments weighed an average of almost 800 pounds (360 kg) each—some were so large that they required an entire aircraft—so they were handled separately from the normal hub-sorting operations. The revenue for each shipment ranged widely but the average was around $850.

The express package industry was consolidating and the company's chief operating officer, James L. Barksdale, described the challenge facing its 1,300 sales professionals: "We're in a tough business. Our competitors are tough, mean, go-getting folks. They are not a bunch of idiots. I wish they were." Within the US, the key players were Federal Express (with about 45–50% of the market), UPS (15%), Airborne (10–15%), Emery/Purolator (5%), US Postal Service (10%), and others (5%). Federal had purchased Purolator's Indianapolis hub. Overseas, Federal faced UPS, Emery, DHL, and Australian-owned TNT, plus the express divisions of national postal services and airline freight and package services.

INFORMATION TECHNOLOGY

For Federal Express, information about each package was seen as just as important as the package itself. Information also played a key role in achieving the most effective utilization of the entire physical operation. Dr. Ron J. Ponder, senior vice president for information and telecommunications, described the line-haul operations (package sorting and transportation) as one of several parallel fibers running through the entire business. The others included a series of major information networks. "We run three data processing houses at Federal," explained Ponder, a former business school professor. "There are the traditional commercial revenue systems that every company has; a line-haul flight operations system that is unique to airlines; and COSMOS, our customer service house."

To me, quality is everything we do. Our goal for availability—communication and systems—is 99.8%. We've cranked that up during the last ten years from about 88%. Each year, we keep raising the bar. We're running some of the highest systems availability numbers in North America. Most companies are happy at 95% or 96%.

Our computer center is now one of the largest in the world under one roof, and we have the highest transaction rates of any shop in North America on a daily basis. Last month, we had 320 million transactions from all over the world go through our computer systems. We measure each one of them. Less than 86,000 exceeded our standard internal compute time of one second, which you have to have to run these massive parallel systems. Each morning at

8:30, we have a conference call in this division with perhaps 50 people in on it. We start off with any problems we've had in the last 24 hours.

In addition to overseeing the systems, I do the strategic architectural planning that lets this company use technology to the greatest possible advantage for customer satisfaction and competitive superiority, and for reducing operational costs to improve productivity.

Ponder believed that Federal Express had a sharply different view of technology from most companies.

Technology transfer—or being able to absorb new technology—is a cultural thing that we've built in here. One of the keys to our success is that we constantly embrace new technology. For most companies, that's very painful and they don't like it. It's painful to leave what works and is cheap for new, expensive, unknown approaches. So they don't do it. At Federal, we would rather get an innovation a year earlier and develop backup systems to counter a relatively high failure rate than to wait until the failure rate—and the price—have been reduced to more "acceptable" levels. Most folks prefer to wait until a technology matures.

You can view technology as a wave in the ocean, washing in debris. Most people concentrate on the debris that floats in. "Oh, isn't this neat!" they'll say of some device. "Where can I use it?" And that's where I think they mess up. I view technology as the wave itself, not the individual things that are brought to shore. We knew what we wanted to do ten years ago, but the technology wasn't there. So we were waiting for the wave and constantly prodding manufacturers to create what we needed as that wave rolled in.

Asked what new waves Federal Express was watching, Ponder listed battery technology, continued miniaturization, the maturing of relational databases (essential to maintaining detailed customer files) and, most importantly, a new generation of computer hardware and software using RISC (Reduced Instruction Set Computing) architecture. The net effect would be more computing power and faster access to information for less money.

COSMOS and DADS

Federal prided itself on having one of the most sophisticated customer service systems in the world.

COSMOS (Customer, Operations, Service, Master On-line System) was first installed in 1979 and had been constantly upgraded to cope with the more than 260,000 calls now received, on average, each working day. COSMOS had evolved into a worldwide electronic network that transmitted critical package information to Memphis. Its major components were an order-entry system for customers to request package pickups, a continuously updated record of each package's progress through the Fedex system that could be used to trace a missing package, financial records for billing purposes, and a huge relational database that could also be used for marketing analysis and planning.

The system worked in much the same way around the world. In the US, customers had a choice between requesting a pickup or, for a reduced fee, of dropping off a package at a drop-box or at one of Federal's business service centers. To request a pickup, customers telephoned a toll-free number that connected to a customer service agent (CSA) at one of 17 call centers around the nation. Calls could be diverted from one center to another to maintain the company's response-time standards. Since most calls were received in the mid to late afternoon, peak volumes could be shifted to centers in other time zones. The CSA requested the shipper's account number, which was entered on an electronic order blank on the video screen (refer to *Exhibit 1*). Armed with this information, the system automatically provided the CSA with the account name, address, phone number, pickup location, contact name, and other relevant data.

An alternative method was to call a special Automatic Pickup number. In response to the promptings of a recorded voice, callers used the buttons on their touch-tone telephones to enter their account numbers and then, as a cross-check, their postal zip code, followed by the number of packages being shipped. The voice would then provide a confirmation number and latest pickup time. These service requests were transmitted automatically to the nearest origin station.

Federal was also testing a custom-designed desktop unit, smaller than a telephone, called "Hello Federal." This device had a full alpha-numeric keypad,

EXHIBIT 1   CONTENTS OF FEDERAL EXPRESS DISPATCH REQUEST SCREEN

Customer Information

Location ID_____ Zip Code_____ Pickup Time_____ Cutoff _____

Account # _____ Company Name_____

Address_____

City _____ State_____ Type of Account_____

Contact person_____ Phone # _____ Extension _____ Close time_____

Remarks to Courier_____

Local Area Promotions_____

Package Information

Pickup Day_____ Total Packages_____ Total Weight_____ Rate_____

Time Package ready_____ Supplies Requested_____ Commodity Shipped_____

Remarks by CSA_____

Dispatcher's Remarks_____

Dispatcher's #_____ Exeptions_____ Credit Approved_____

Courier's #_____ Time_____ Date _____

Note: The screen display has been clarified and simplified for purposes of case presentation, with abbreviations written out in full.

When a customer called Federal Express, the customer service agent first asked the caller for a Federal Express account number. When this was typed in, most other customer information (other than details of the caller's request, e.g., pickup) was automatically retrieved from the computer's memory and displayed on the screen, from where it could be verified with the caller.

an adjustable LCD screen, and buttons to press for pickup, package tracing information, and requests for airbills and packaging. The requested information was displayed on the screen; no voice communication was needed. Since each unit was programmed with the shipper's account number, it was not necessary to provide account identification when calling. If the tests proved successful, the company planned to offer a "Hello Federal" unit free to any customer shipping a predefined volume of packages three or more days per week.

Once a pickup request was received, the CSA entered shipping information through COSMOS to alert the dispatch center nearest to the pickup location. The message was received by the dispatch center's DADS (Digitally Assisted Dispatch System) computer which, in turn, sent the information to a courier. The request was displayed on a small DADS video screen in the courier's van or on a portable unit the size of a slim briefcase used by walking couriers.

One customer, a management consultant working out of a home office, testified to the efficiency of the system:

It was only the second time that I had used the Automatic Pickup service and I still didn't have 100% confidence in it, but I knew that it was a little faster than talking to a CSA in a call center and I was in a hurry. I had just finished a report for one client and was about to leave for the airport on a visit to another client. So I sealed up the report, phoned for a cab, and then called the Automatic Pickup number to place my order. The taxi arrived in five minutes, which was pretty good. As I was getting into the cab, what should roll up but the Federal Express van to pick up my package. I was so astonished that I got out of the cab and asked the courier how he had arrived so quickly. "I was driving on the next street," he said, "when your request came up on my screen."

Tracking the Package through the Federal Express System

Each airbill contained a unique 10-digit bar code label which was scanned by an infrared light pen every time the package changed hands. The first scan, known as PUPS (Pick Up Package Scan), took place at the pickup location. Using a hand-held terminal called a COSMOS IIB SuperTracker (a little bigger than the remote control for a TV set), the courier scanned the bar code and then entered on a key pad the type of service, handling code, and destination zip code. The SuperTracker recorded this information, added the time of pickup, and responded on its LCD display with a routing and sorting code which the courier then handwrote on the package. Dr. Ponder noted, "Miniaturization has enabled us to stretch the communications system right to the customer's doorstep."

On returning to the van, the courier plugged the SuperTracker into a shoe within the dispatch computer, which transmitted its information to COSMOS. In many overseas countries, this data transfer took place when the van returned to its station. Once unloaded, each package received a Station Outbound Package Scan (SOPS) before being reloaded into a container for transport to a sorting hub. Any exceptions, such as packages that were damaged or missed the aircraft, received a PM eXception (PMX) scan. These data were then transmitted to COSMOS. Similar scans were made at several other points (refer to *Exhibit 2*).

Finally, at the delivery point, the package received a Proof of Delivery Scan (PODS). The courier entered the recipient's first initial and last name, as well as a code for delivery location, and the SuperTracker automatically recorded the time. If the package were delivered to an alternative location (for instance, a neighboring building) or no one was available to accept delivery, it received instead a Delivery EXception (DEX) scan and full details were entered.

The records provided by these scans enabled Federal to offer full custodial care of all packages. A trace of a missing package would reveal in seconds the time and location of the latest scan. No competitor could match this level of tracing capability. Said Ponder, "The notion of picking up and delivering a package without being able to offer the customer total information on it is totally unacceptable to us."

Automated Systems for High-Volume Customers

Federal had formed a team called Customer Automation to assist customers in managing their shipments more effectively. The result was a family of automated shipping and invoicing systems designed to reduce paperwork and tie the company more closely to its large-volume customers.

Tape Invoice offered customers a weekly invoice on magnetic tape, instead of paper. By running the invoice tape on the computer, customers could analyze Federal Express shipping information any way they wished. Such data could be fed directly into the firm's accounting system.

Powership 2 was a shipment management system that streamlined package preparation and billing. Federal provided customers with an electronic weighing scale, microcomputer terminal, bar code scanner, and printer at no charge; all the customer paid was telephone charges. The system eliminated the need for airbills and express manifests, and could be programmed to store up to 32,000 recipient names and addresses. The printer could generate barcoded address labels. Powership 2 rated packages with the right charges, automatically combining package weights by destination to provide volume discounts. Daily invoices could be prepared automatically, as could customized management reports. Customers could trace their own packages through COSMOS.

Powership Plus allowed customers to link their computers with Federal Express's tracking and invoicing systems. If the package weight were known (which was true for many mail order items) users could quote shipping rates, delivery schedules, and tracking numbers to their own customers at the very

EXHIBIT 2   PHYSICAL FLOWS AND INFORMATION FLOWS FOR FEDERAL EXPRESS PACKAGES

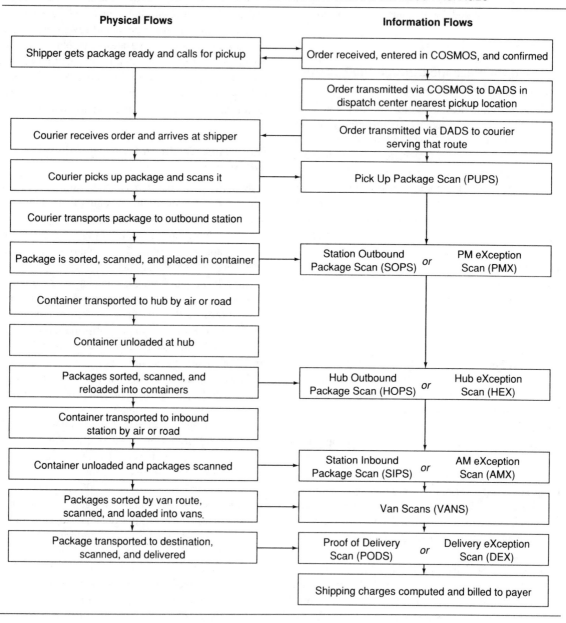

Physical Flows — Information Flows

Physical Flows	Information Flows
Shipper gets package ready and calls for pickup	Order received, entered in COSMOS, and confirmed
	Order transmitted via COSMOS to DADS in dispatch center nearest pickup location
Courier receives order and arrives at shipper	Order transmitted via DADS to courier serving that route
Courier picks up package and scans it	Pick Up Package Scan (PUPS)
Courier transports package to outbound station	
Package is sorted, scanned, and placed in container	Station Outbound Package Scan (SOPS) *or* PM eXception Scan (PMX)
Container transported to hub by air or road	
Container unloaded at hub	
Packages sorted, scanned, and reloaded into containers	Hub Outbound Package Scan (HOPS) *or* Hub eXception Scan (HEX)
Container transported to inbound station by air or road	
Container unloaded and packages scanned	Station Inbound Package Scan (SIPS) *or* AM eXception Scan (AMX)
Packages sorted by van route, scanned, and loaded into vans	Van Scans (VANS)
Package transported to destination, scanned, and delivered	Proof of Delivery Scan (PODS) *or* Delivery eXception Scan (DEX)
	Shipping charges computed and billed to payer

time they entered the purchase order. Next, they transmitted information directly to the warehouse, where the barcoded address label could be printed and applied. When each night's shipping was complete, users would transmit their shipping data to Federal. At the end of the week, they would send Federal Express a computer tape containing the week's shipping data, plus a check for the total shipping charges.

NEW QUALITY INITIATIVES

Quality had been implicit in Federal's efforts from the beginning. In 1975, its advertising claimed "Federal Express. Twice as Good as the Best in the Business" (a slogan comparing Federal's performance against its then leading competitor, Emery Air Freight). The firm's emphasis on reliability was captured in its classic slogan, "Absolutely, Positively Overnight." Management had long recognized the connection between doing things right the first time and improving productivity: "Q = P" (quality equals productivity) was the internal rallying cry.

Employee Orientation

As chairman, Fred Smith constantly set goals of improving reliability, productivity, and financial performance to promote the corporate imperative of People–Service–Profits. Particular attention was paid to leading and motivating employees. Regular communication with employees had always been a corporate priority. As the company grew in numbers and geographic scope, increasing reliance came to be placed on the use of videotaped messages for both communication and training. In 1987, Federal launched FXTV, a real-time business television network broadcasting daily by satellite to over 700 locations in the US and Canada from studios in Memphis. Satellite hookups with overseas locations were arranged for special occasions. Each month, FXTV produced about 20 hours of broadcast TV, plus 10–15 hours of videotape.

Since 1985, a confidential employee survey had been conducted annually called Survey Feedback Ac-

tion (SFA). It consisted of 26 statements with which the employee was asked to agree or disagree on a 5-point scale ranging from "strongly agree" to "strongly disagree." Scores were reported for employee work groups, not for individuals. The first ten questions (refer to *Exhibit 3*) related to employees' views of their managers. The percentage of favorable responses on these items constituted what was known as the SFA Leadership Index.

The full SFA Index represented the percentage of positive responses on all 26 items, including questions on pay, working conditions, views on senior management, and feelings about the company. Other companies administered the same survey, so scores could be compared with those from employees in other firms. Federal had consistently obtained above-average ratings.

In 1983, Smith initiated "Bravo Zulu" awards (from the US Navy signal flags for BZ, meaning "Well done!"), which allowed managers to provide instant recognition to employees for excellent service within the company. Stickers bearing the signal flags could be placed on paperwork or a memo; managers also had authority to issue a Bravo Zulu voucher worth up to $100.

Outstanding examples of customer service were celebrated with Golden Falcon awards, consisting of a gold pin and ten shares of Federal Express stock

EXHIBIT 3
SURVEY FEEDBACK ACTION PROGRAM:
COMPONENTS OF LEADERSHIP INDEX

1. I can tell my manager what I think.
2. My manager tells me what is expected.
3. Favoritism is not a problem in my work group.
4. My manager helps us do our job better.
5. My manager listens to my concerns.
6. My manager asks for my ideas about work.
7. My manager tells me when I do a good job.
8. My manager treats me with respect.
9. My manager keeps me informed.
10. My manager does not interfere.

Note: The above sentences paraphrase the actual wording used in compiling the Leadership Index. Employees were asked to review each statement carefully and then to express their agreement or disagreement with that statement on a 5-point scale.

(worth about $500 in early 1990). About 20 such awards were made each year. Nominees were often identified by customer calls or letters; a typical example might concern extraordinary effort in tracking down and delivering a missing package. Golden Falcon and Bravo Zulu awards, and the stories behind them, were publicized to motivate employees and create corporate legends.

An Unsuccessful First Look at Quality Training

It was not until 1985, when Smith and senior officers became concerned about a possible slowdown in the business and decline in profitability, that the company first addressed quality improvement techniques at the corporate level. Smith hired a consultant to conduct an off-site meeting with top management, but it was not a success. As Tom Oliver recalled, "Everyone walked away with a calculator and a statistics book, but our interest had not been captured." Some improvements were made, but the idea lost momentum. Smith was soon preoccupied with the problems of ZapMail, the company's same-day facsimile service, which was discontinued in 1986 with a write-off of some $360 million—the company's first major setback since its start-up days.

Two and a half years passed, during which the feared slowdown was replaced by a period of explosive growth. By mid-1987, the sales and customer service division was struggling with service problems that were becoming increasingly serious as the company continued to expand. As senior vice president of the division, Oliver decided it was high time to re-explore the quality issue.

Working with ODI

Disappointed with the previous statistically based approach to quality improvement, Oliver selected Organizational Dynamics, Inc. (ODI), an international consulting firm headquartered in Burlington, Massachusetts. ODI's great advantage, from Oliver's perspective, was that it paid little attention to statistical techniques but a lot more to the thought processes and involvement of people within the company in developing quality programs.

ODI began by designing and leading quality planning workshops for senior executives from all divisions. The product of each workshop was a series of action plans, setting priorities for problems needing resolution. Next, ODI focused on the sales and customer service division. Under the leadership of ODI vice president Rob Evans, the consultants trained all managers in the division to understand the quality process, then began training employees and creating quality action teams. ODI also trained facilitators from other divisions, including ground operations. A key goal was to get people to analyze what were often complex problems, rather than shooting from the hip with instant solutions. Different versions of the programs were developed for managers and employees.

The Quality Advantage Program began with a module on "The Meaning of Quality," introducing five pillars on which a quality organization must be built:

- *Customer focus*—a commitment to meeting customer needs
- *Total involvement*—"improving quality is everyone's job"
- *Measurement*—where and when to take action; documenting progress
- *Systematic support*—applying strategic planning, budgeting, and performance management to quality improvement efforts
- *Continuous improvement*—always reaching for new and better ways to perform one's job

"The Cost of Quality" module identified the costs of not doing quality work—rework, waste, unnecessary overtime, and job dissatisfaction. The goal was to help participants estimate their own cost of quality, break this down into avoidable and necessary costs, and then plan ways to reduce avoidable costs. The third module, "You and Your Customer," described the customer-supplier chain and helped participants to see that everyone in Federal Express was both a customer and a supplier. Participants learned to identify their own key customers and suppliers within the company, as well as how they were linked, and then to align customer needs and supplier capabilities in order to meet agreed requirements.

The "Continuous Improvement" module emphasized that it was everyone's responsibility to fix and prevent problems, showed how to identify early warning signals, and required that everyone strive to meet customer needs in innovative ways. The fifth module, "Making Quality Happen," was directed at managers, supervisors, and professionals; it described how to take a leadership role to implement quality programs.

A separate program, Quality Action Teams (QATs), focused on how to implement quality improvement. ODI taught a problem-solving process consisting of four phases: focusing on a particular problem or opportunity, analyzing data, developing solutions and action plans, and executing plans for implementing solutions. To help the QATs perform each of these tasks, ODI taught participants how to apply 20 problem-solving tools, including fishbone analysis, flowcharting, and cost-benefit analysis.

Setting Goals for People–Service–Profits

By June 1988 (the beginning of fiscal year 1989), Oliver had concluded that to make quality improvement work for customer service, it was critical to involve domestic ground operations. Most problems at Federal were cross-divisional in nature, in the sense that one division created a certain output and passed it on to the next one. The next division's problems were often directly related to what had happened earlier up the line. Commenting on this, Oliver noted:

We were able to put across the idea that one of the big difficulties in getting cross-divisional cooperation was the multiplicity of different goals. These goals might individually maximize the performance of each division, but collectively resulted in a deterioration of performance for the system. We realized that the more each unit tried to maximize its own performance, the more it tended to send difficult problems downstream. So we concluded that what we needed for Federal Express were three very simple goals.

First, we took the existing SFA Leadership Index. The

leadership a manager provides has a tremendous impact on the positive attitudes of the employees. We determined to use this index as the single goal in our people management process and established a goal of 72 for FY 1989, up from 71 the previous year.

People–Service–Profits implied a profit goal, so we set a goal of a 10% operating margin on the domestic business. That goal was irrespective of individual department performance. Service had historically been defined in terms of couriers' on-time delivery efforts, what percentage of packages were delivered by 10:30 am. There were a lot of problems with that service level measure: specifically, we could get that package delivered by 10:30 am on the wrong date! It was also a limited measure, suggesting that Federal could be successful simply by delivering packages on time. That was no longer true!

We found that the information associated with packages had as much to do with customer satisfaction as did delivery. For instance, "don't know" answers to questions upset customers. As we reviewed customer correspondence, we found that the angriest of all the letters we got were those where our information processes failed us as opposed to those where we didn't deliver on time. What was needed was a broader measure that also addressed other shortcomings that upset customers, such as failure to answer the phone quickly and damaged packages.

ODI stressed the danger of using percentages as targets. In an organization as large as Federal Express, delivering 99% of packages on time or having 99.9% of all flights land safely would still lead to horrendous problems. Instead, ODI approached quality from the standpoint of zero failures. Oliver emphasized:

It's only when you examine the types of failures, the number that occur of each type, and the reasons why, that you begin to improve the quality of your service. For us, the trick was to express quality failures in absolute numbers. That led us to develop the Service Quality Index, or SQI, which takes each of 12 different events that occur every day, takes the numbers of those events and multiplies them by a weight from one to ten points, based on the amount of aggravation caused to customers—as evidenced by their tendency to write to Federal Express and complain about them. Fred Smith calls it our "hierarchy of horrors."

The SQI, pronounced "sky," was computed as a daily average. (*Exhibit 4* shows its 12 components.) Like a golf score, the lower the index, the better

EXHIBIT 4 SERVICE QUALITY INDEX (SQI) FY 1990 GOALS VS. ACTUAL FOR FIRST NINE MONTHS

Beginning in FY 1989, the overall quality of service was measured by the Service Quality Index (SQI). This index, which was based on the findings of extensive customer research, weighted service failures from the customer's perspective, and comprised the 12 components shown below.

Failure type	Weighting factor	FY 1990 goals (June 1989–May 1990)		June 1989–Feb. 1990
		Goal for average daily occurrences	Weighted daily failure points	Actual average daily failure points
Right-day late service failures	1	22,000	22,000	*33,561
Wrong-day late service failures	5	11,522	57,606	*74,674
Traces (not answered by COSMOS)	1	4,170	4,170	5,165
Complaints reopened by customers	5	851	4,255	2,330
Missing proofs of delivery (PODs)	1	4,959	4,959	6,260
Invoice adjustments requested	1	12,852	12,852	11,921
Missed pickups	10	152	1,526	1,548
Lost packages	10	72	725	1,102
Damaged packages	10	181	1,815	2,868
Delay minutes/aircraft (0 based)	5	327	1,635	16,821
Overgoods	5	327	1,635	1,788
Abandoned calls	1	4,782	4,782	8,073
Total average daily failure points (SQI)			125,000	166,111

*Estimated.
Note: SQI points were reported on a daily basis, as well as on a weekly, monthly, or year-to-date daily average.

the performance. Based on internal records, it was calculated that the average score during FY 1988 (which ended on May 31, 1988) would have been 152,000 points per day—out of a potential maximum of 40 million per day if everything possible had gone wrong. The goal set for FY 1989 was the same— 152,000 points—but since package volumes were expected to rise by 20%, this goal actually represented a 20% improvement. Employees were urged to "Reach for the SQI!"

To reinforce the significance of these three corporate-wide goals, senior management tied the entire management bonus process to achievement of the three goals. Simply put, there would be no bonus for any manager at the end of FY 1989 unless the company achieved all three goals. "Needless to say, that caught everyone's imagination." Oliver smiled wryly and continued:

It was very different from our previous approach of having managers' bonuses based on their ability to meet individual management-by-objective goals without regard to whether that did or didn't help the corporate process. In the actual unfolding, fiscal year 1989 turned out to be the best year we had had in a long, long time. We achieved the profit goal despite some difficult circumstances, and the SQI came in at 133,000 points. The Leadership Index reached 76. It was the largest single jump in the history of the SFA process, in terms of managers' relationships with employees.

ODI's Evans believed that one reason for the SQI successes was that Federal had set up 12 QATs, each of which focused on a specific SQI category. As CEO, Fred Smith provided active support and encouragement. Most teams were headed by a vice president. Results were posted weekly, and every three months each QAT reported out to Smith, Barksdale, and other senior executives. Quarterly awards were given in four categories:

1. Greatest impact on SQI results;
2. Best use of the quality process (using tools that had been taught);
3. Best understanding of root causes (identifying and working on underlying problems rather than superficial effects); and
4. Best use of line employees (gathering information from the people closest to the process who knew it best).

Activities during FY 1990

While training continued, efforts were made to facilitate a bottom-up movement in quality improvement. John West, manager of quality improvement, saw his job as a catalyst to bring about shared approaches to problem solving. West coordinated training efforts with ODI and had established a network of quality professionals in each of Federal's ten divisions. These people form a quality advisory board which met biweekly to discuss failures and successes.

One of the professionals was Linda Griffin, senior quality administrator for domestic ground operations, which had 40,000 employees working out of 600 stations. Griffin felt that while the quality program had enjoyed many "surface" successes, the challenge was to coordinate the replication of these successes by getting people to describe what they had actually done and how they did it, as opposed to simply talking about the results. Forms and electronic mail systems had been created to make it easy to record this information, while a reward system encouraged people to turn in details of their successes. Said Griffin:

Recognition programs have a mutual benefit. They motivate and reward employees and create some peer pressure. At the same time, management gets to see the value of the training programs, which reinforces the belief that training is the right thing to do.

One replicated success concerned a sorting table designed by employees in the Phoenix station to prevent missorts caused by envelopes sliding into the wrong destination pile. They sent a videotape of the table design to the company's industrial engineers, who developed several versions of the sort table for different-sized stations. Couriers in a QAT at another station were frustrated with the problems (such as missed pickups) caused when the regular courier on a route had to be replaced by a substitute unfamiliar with obscure addresses, building entrances, location of freight elevators, and pickup or delivery locations on different floors. So they designed an informational booklet describing each route. The result was a sharp increase in on-time delivery and productivity. This idea had now been incorporated in the "Policy and Procedures" manual for all stations.

Sharing success stories was seen as a way to get more people involved in QATs and to improve working relations within the company through customer-supplier alignments. West commented:

People tend to gravitate toward QATs, which are more fun. We really have to push the notion of customer-supplier alignment. People and departments don't always work well together. W. Edwards Deming, the American quality pioneer, claims that about 95% of quality problems are management problems, because of the way the system was designed.

Federal's satellite broadcast network, FXTV, was employed in both a sharing and training role. Rob Evans participated in a program entitled "Customer/ Supplier Alignment: The First Step in Quality," designed to reinforce earlier quality training. Evans began his segment of the live broadcast by reminding viewers of the "Right Things Right" grid, a simple four-cell matrix developed by ODI.

That grid is a simple way to look at the work we do from two different angles. The first angle is *how* we do the work we do. Either we do things wrong or we do things right. The second angle has to do with *what* work we actually do, doing the right things or the wrong things. When we put these two together, we have four possibilities. We could be doing the right things wrong; that's the old way of looking at quality problems and, of course, that happens. We could be doing the wrong things wrong, really wasting our time. Or we could be doing the wrong things right, things that don't matter to our customers, internal or external, but doing a very good job of them. The fourth possibility is doing right things right. This is the only one that adds value to our customers and our company.

In a quality organization, people spend the great majority of their time doing the right things right. What we've found at ODI is that most managers spend 45–60% of their time doing the right things right, but the rest is wasted—time, effort, money. Of that wasted time, about half seems to fall into the wrong-things-right category.

Pressures and Distractions

Top management was delighted by improvements in SQI and other measures during FY 1989, but then the picture changed dramatically. The average daily SQI goal of 125,000 points for FY 1990 (on a higher package volume) was ravaged by the dislocations of the Tiger merger and a series of natural disasters during the fall and winter. Mount Redoubt's volcanic ash cloud grounded five of Federal's 747s at the Anchorage hub in Alaska for two days and forced subsequent Far East flights to operate through Seattle, using more fuel and carrying less freight. The computer shutdown at the Memphis Superhub on December 22 resulted in manual sorting, delayed deliveries, and an average daily SQI for that week of 613,842. At the end of February, the year-to-date daily average stood at 166,111.

Meantime, a sharp earnings decline had led to companywide cost reduction efforts, including some impacting quality facilitation. Some outside financial analysts had suggested that the company's financial situation made it vulnerable to a takeover. Tom Oliver was very concerned that the momentum of the quality improvement efforts not be lost.

Most companies need four to five years of continuous effort before employees and managers alike really understand that this is *the* way to approach problems. The fact that we had some initial successes was certainly positive, but by no means have we gotten it to the point where if you scratch an employee, you're going to get a quality-related response. And that's especially true of first-level management, who feel tremendous pressure to achieve budget-related financial results.

We've found that the SQI process works really well for the corporation as a whole, but Federal Express doesn't have the ability to develop a precise tracking of these events down to individual locations, so our station-level goals tend to stay related to the service level measurement (on-time deliveries) instead of the broader SQI perspective. We're trying to work aggressively on measurement systems so that Federal can use that information more precisely in measuring and managing the performance of first-line managers. Feedback is critical in any quality process.

Much remains to be done. But it always comes back to these questions: Is it financially feasible to spend the dollars and take the time to train the people? Will we spend the time and money to let them work the issues after they are trained? Are investments in quality high enough in the corporation's competing priorities? In the sales and customer service division's case, feedback systems require substantial investments in data systems resources. We want to make them, but we're always fighting the allocation process.

Right now, everyone is trying to minimize their own costs and efficiency; in the process, they're sending enormous costs downstream. The tendency in corporate management is to seek good budgets and financial controls for every individual unit in your operation. A well-managed corporation has a very strong financial system—but a strong, department-oriented financial system is precisely what you're trying to get around when you're attempting to approach things from a systemic quality and cost viewpoint. You must expend money at the source of the problem to eliminate the waste expenses later in the process. But people won't do it, because they don't get the benefits; some other department and the customers do.

Almost every change we've made in Federal's services has no measurable ROI (return on investment). You cannot, in effect, prove the reductions in cost because they're systemic reductions, as opposed to individual area reductions. In any case, changes in the quality of service impact customer revenues as much or more than they impact costs. In the final event, one needs to make these decisions based on the impact on customers and on the system, as opposed to precisely measured return-on-investment calculations.

Oliver glanced at the clock. It was almost time for another senior executive meeting on cutting costs. ODI had submitted a proposal for the next phase of the quality training program, and there were numerous internal projects as well. His best estimate was that future training and other key quality initiatives would, if properly funded, cost as much as $200 per employee in the first year and half of that in subsequent years. "It all comes down to that courage gap," he said to himself as he gathered up his papers and strode out of the office.

Alias Research Inc.

Douglas Snetsinger
Susan Spencer

"I can't believe they did it again!" exclaimed Isaac Babbs, district sales manager for the southwestern United States for Alias Research Inc. For the fourth time in 1990 he had lost a sale to Wavefront, his major competitor in the animation software market. He had worked on this sale for a month and he felt confident that the prospective customer was ready to buy Alias' $100,000 software. But Wavefront had stepped in at the last moment, cut their price from $55,000 to $25,000, and obtained the sale. Wavefront, a California-based company, seemed determined to dominate the region, while Alias, based in Toronto, was at least equally determined to make further inroads into the California market. "How does Toronto expect me to compete if they won't give me some flexibility on pricing?" Babbs lamented as he thought about Alias' rigidly enforced policy of not permitting any price discounting on its products. With a sigh of resignation, he reached for the phone to call Toronto and let them know that another sale was lost to a price-cutting competitor.

THE HIGH-END GRAPHICS MARKET

Alias Research Inc., a software company located in Toronto, was a recognized market leader in high-end, three-dimensional (3D) computer graphics. Its product, ALIAS, was used in film animation, industrial design, architecture, education, medical and scientific visualization, packaging and product design, flight or space simulation, and a number of other applications. Seventy percent of the world's automobile manufacturers used ALIAS in their design processes. Some of its customers in other industries included Goodyear, Timex, Kraft, Motorola, Northern Telecom, Johnson & Johnson, and Industrial Light and Magic. Alias had sales offices in Boston, Princeton, Los Angeles, Chicago, and Detroit, as well as in France and Germany. The corporate officers for Alias are listed in *Exhibit 1*.

The total size of the market served by Alias was estimated at $81 million (U.S.) in 1990, of which Alias held a 15% share. Industry experts had forecast that the market would increase to $300 million by 1992. Virtually all of the growth was in the field of industrial design, which currently accounted for 40% of the market. The remaining 60% was in the animation field, which was growing at a rate of only 1%

559

EXHIBIT 1
ALIAS RESEARCH INC.—EXECUTIVE OFFICERS AND DIRECTORS

Name	Age*	Position
Stephen R. B. Bingham	40	President, Chief Executive Officer and Chairman of the Board of Directors
Susan I. McKenna	31	Executive Vice-President and Director
William J. McClintock	38	Vice-President Finance, Secretary, Treasurer, and Chief Financial Officer
Arthur W. Bell	34	Vice-President Marketing
Martin I. Tuori	38	Vice-President Research and Development
Gregory S. Hill	35	Vice-President Business Development
David N. Macrae	34	Vice-President Sales
Brian J. Conway	31	Director
William S. Kaiser	34	Director
Barry L. Stephens	50	Director

*Ages are as of July 1990.

each year. The animation market was saturated with a variety of competing products.

Alias' three main competitors were Wavefront Technologies, Thompson Digital Image (TDI), and Evans and Sutherland Computer Corporation (E&S). Originally a private custom software builder, Wavefront entered the video animation market in 1985 at approximately the same time as Alias. It had recently modified its package to provide some industrial design capability. However, Wavefront's product did not easily translate into manufacturable designs, and it required extensive training before any of its advanced tools could be properly used. Wavefront's major advantage was that their product could be run on many different types of computers, as opposed to Alias' which could only be run on Silicon Graphics hardware or IBM workstations.

Based in Paris, France, Thompson Digital Image (TDI) was Alias' principal competitor in the European market. TDI was a subsidiary of the Thompson Group, though 56% of TDI was owned by the French government. TDI's primary market, accounting for 80% of sales, was the video animation market. It was estimated that TDI had approximately 20 clients in the video post-production industry. TDI was also pursuing industrial design customers and had been successful with some leading French firms including Renault, the automobile manufacturer. TDI was cur-

rently overhauling its design software based on a similar technology to the Alias product.

Evans and Sutherland (E&S) was a large, multidivisional computer hardware and software company with total sales of $129 million (U.S.). Based in Salt Lake City, they were engaged in the development of interactive super-computers for large-scale scientific and technical computations, modelling, and simulations. The Graphics Products Group designed and built high performance three-dimensional graphics hardware and specialized software. E&S's closest product to ALIAS was the Conceptual Design and Rendering System, a turn-key, computer-aided design system that was introduced in 1988. The system was developed in partnership with Ford and Chrysler. It was based on Alias-type technology and was priced at $200,000 (U.S.) to $250,000 (U.S.) and ran only on proprietary hardware manufactured by E&S.

ALIAS HISTORY

The Beginning

Alias Research Inc. was founded in 1983 by Stephen Bingham, Nigel McGrath, Susan McKenna, and David Springer. With few resources, they borrowed $500,000 of computer graphic equipment from McGrath's company and rented an office in an old elevator shaft for $150 per month. Though starting small in scope, the owners of this fledgling company had a big dream: to create an easy-to-use software package that would produce realistic 3D video animation for the advertising industry post-production houses.

Many companies in this industry had difficulty raising start-up funds and Alias was no exception. The problem was that it required substantial time and effort to develop software to the point where it was "debugged" and ready to be sold to customers. As much as 150 person-years of research and development effort might go into making the first working piece of software. Thus, investors were reluctant to provide funds on promises, as opposed to finished products.

However, Alias was able to obtain a $61,000 grant from the National Research Council, which, when combined with the limited funds of the founders, allowed work to begin. Other financial support was gained from the federal government through Scientific Research Tax Credits (SRTCs). A SRTC was actually a contract that allowed an investor to hire Alias to do a specified amount of research, in return for which the investor would get a tax credit for their own company. This sort of arrangement yielded two benefits for Alias. It provided much needed start-up funding and it allowed the four founders to maintain control of the company. It also allowed Alias to earn money by doing the research that was required for its own project.

Development of the software continued until mid-1985. One of the early decisions made was building the software based on a relatively new form of modelling technique which used cardinal splines rather than traditional polygonal lines.[1] Silicon Graphics, a small hardware firm based in California, produced a workstation that was specifically designed to work with spline technology. Silicon Graphics soon became a staunch supporter of Alias as they saw the opportunity for enhanced applications for their workstation.

The product, ALIAS, was unveiled at the Special Interest Group on Graphics (SIGGRAPH) show in July of 1985. The annual SIGGRAPH show was attended by many people who were involved in design (for example, designing products, labels, packages) and by many people who could help the designers (for example, software companies like Alias). For a company like Alias, the SIGGRAPH show provided an important opportunity to introduce and market new products. Many of the Alias group would attend the show and work long hours to generate leads for the ALIAS system. In fact, sales of ALIAS could often be traced to an initial meeting at the SIGGRAPH show.

The first sale, to a post-production house, came on July 15th. Then the unexpected occurred; General Motors Inc. (GM) expressed an interest in buying a system. GM was looking for a system that was compatible with their spline-based computer-aided-design (CAD) systems, and ALIAS was the only spline-based system available. Initially, the Alias group were reluctant to enter this new market; industrial design applications had not been part of the corporate objective and seemed too distant from their animation market. Further, GM wanted the package to run on basis-splines (b-splines)[2] which would require yet another significant investment by Alias in research and development (R&D). However, when GM kept dropping broad hints about 20 systems, potentially representing millions of dollars of revenue, Alias decided to go ahead and, in November 1985, the deal with GM was signed.

Once again, money was required to finance the research. However, Alias now had a major customer, more or less in hand, which reduced the risk of the venture in the eyes of potential investors. Early in 1986, Crownx, a venture capital company associated with Crown Life, invested $1.2 million for a 20% stake in Alias.

[1] A cardinal spline is based on the first derivative of the modelling equation, while polygonal lines are based on the actual equation. The results that were achieved from cardinal splines, in terms of computer graphics, were a much smoother, more realistic line or surface than had been possible from a polygonal line.

[2] B-splines are based on the second derivative of the modelling equation and were generally regarded as producing the smoothest lines and surfaces available in computer graphics.

By early 1986, the company had sold ALIAS to a number of firms. Most of the sales were to small production houses in the video animation market, but sales were also made to Kraft, Motorola, and NASA. By the middle of 1986, there were 70 people working for the company, of whom 40 were programmers, Morale was high and the employees were beginning to see the fruits of their labours in print and on video. The work environment was flexible and relaxed—purposely designed to facilitate and stimulate creativity. Improvements and upgrades to the original package were constantly being developed, and a new release of the software (with a b-spline base) was planned for mid-1986. Staff increased to 80 in April of 1987, with the opening of three sales offices in the United States. In the same year, almost $3 million in new venture capital was received from two American companies. Everything was moving quickly and the people at Alias were looking forward to a promising future.

The Downturn

The development of ALIAS/2 (using b-splines) took much longer than had been expected and the product was not released until late in 1986. Initial sales were strong, but a problem was discovered with the new system. The final rendered picture was not matched to the original design on a consistent or reliable basis. While Alias could fix the bug on the installed systems on a patchwork basis, the sales force would find it next to impossible to sell new installations of ALIAS/2 until the problem was solved. The company immediately pulled members of the marketing and R&D staff together with a product management group to fix the software.

The first half of 1987 saw the beginnings of what was to become a major downturn in the animation industry as a whole. Premium, high-end systems, like those of Alias, were particularly affected by the slump. At the same time, personnel changes and budget cuts at GM had reduced the number of systems purchased from the expected number of 20 to only 4. Some of the new investors in Alias were dissatisfied with the company's performance and were demanding cuts in investment, particularly on R&D spending and personnel. Mr. Bingham and the other original owners still retained control and resisted the pressure. However, by late summer of 1987, Alias was forced to lay off 12 employees from marketing and administration.

The Recovery

Following the layoffs, quarterly company meetings were instituted in which the status of the company as a whole, plans for the future, and the past quarter's performance were reviewed with all employees. Day-long meetings of the management team (vice-president level and above) were held monthly. Efforts at clearing the lines of communication between departments were made to build a more cohesive team atmosphere than had existed previously. Although the culture of the company remained informal, the methods of control and the way of doing business became more formalized, with more attention being paid to earnings and profit. Although Alias experienced an operating loss in fiscal 1989, it was considerably less than in fiscal 1988 (the corporate year end is January 31).

In the summer of 1989, for the first time in two years the company began to hire people for new positions. A new vice-president of finance, Bill McClintock, took over the financial aspects of the company and tightened the purse strings on all expenditures. Staff were added to R&D, customer support, and marketing. For over two years, marketing of ALIAS had been handled primarily by the vice-president of marketing and communications, Arthur Bell. People were now hired to fill the positions of product manager, CAD marketing manager, distributor marketing manager, and communications manager. These people came from a variety of different backgrounds, not necessarily in computer-related industries. Mr. Bell, who was very enthusiastic about his new recruits, commented:

So often, people who market software come directly out of R&D, or they are engineers. They are way too "techi" for most of our customers, who are designers. I wanted people who understood marketing, but who did not necessarily know computers. Peter Goldie (formerly senior brand manager for Crisco at Procter & Gamble) understands shelf space and everything that leads up to getting that shelf space. No one knows it better. He knows how to market, no matter what, and he can do that for us.

Perhaps most important of all were the changes made to the software itself. Because of all the "bugs" in ALIAS/2, R&D immediately went to work on a "bug-fix" version, known as ALIAS/2.1. Other versions followed, which in some cases included only bug-fix material, and in other cases, included new applications or improved processes. By the summer of 1989, Version 2.4.2 was being used by most Alias customers. At that time, Alias had $3 million in the bank. The income statements for 1988 to 1990 are provided in *Exhibit 2*.

Alias Culture

The culture at Alias was by design relaxed and informal. Everyone, from the programmer in the R&D department to the president, appeared in jeans most of the time. Suits were worn only when people were expected from outside the company. In the words of Bill McClintock: "There are very few 'ties' around here, never mind 'suits,' and that is the way it should be." Friday was known as "shorts day," and throughout the summer, anyone not wearing shorts on a Friday had better have been expecting company.

Employees referred to themselves as "Alians," and the term was expressed with affection and pride. A friendly rivalry existed between the R&D and the administrative sides of the company, each housed in separate sections of the office. Employee birthdays

EXHIBIT 2
ALIAS RESEARCH INC.—CONSOLIDATED STATEMENT
OF OPERATIONS ($000 U.S.)

	1988	1989	1990	First three months of fiscal 1991
Revenue:				
Products	5,709	6,466	10,962	3,106
Maintenance and services	451	774	1,044	271
Total revenue	6,160	7,240	12,006	3,377
Costs and expenses:				
Direct cost of products*	2,861	2,131	1,810	336
Direct cost of maintenance and services	448	509	615	198
General and administration	842	910	1,956	533
Sales and marketing	1,716	2,172	3,527	1,100
Research and development	1,150	954	973	525
Depreciation and amortization	480	500	560	145
Total costs and expenses	7,497	7,176	9,441	2,837
Operating income (loss)	(1,337)	64	2,565	540
Interest income (expense)	(39)	(20)	134	73
Other income (expense)	13	(9)	163	13
Income (loss) before income taxes	(1,363)	35	2,862	626
Provision for (recovery) income taxes	(43)	0	1,229	258
Net income (loss)	(1,320)	35	1,633	368

*Hardware purchased for resale.

were celebrated by all, with cake, drinks, and the occasional Elvis impersonator supplied by the company. Team spirit abounded and everyone regarded it as a great place to work. This was reflected in an article that appeared in the August 1990 *Report on Business Magazine* which described the company, its culture, and the software industry (*Appendix 1*).

ALIAS MARKETING

In many ways, marketing software is unlike marketing any other product. For example, security is a serious problem. Once the product has been sold, it is always possible that the product will be copied or even copied and resold. Once the product has been purchased, customers have to be kept up to date on new developments. When new versions and developments occur, the decision needs to be made whether current customers should be given free upgrades or not. Selling expenses are very high in the industry. Customers are geographically dispersed and sales are often achieved over an extended period and with the support of a number of individuals. As was the case with the Isaac Babbs sale that fell through, or the GM installations that were slow in coming, significant resources were invested in a potential sale which might evaporate at the most inopportune time.

Having a professional marketing and sales team was critical. As well, knowing how much to spend on marketing and in what areas was a perplexing task. Another difficult task was deciding how much R&D should be spent and on what projects. The company needed to determine how much customer service and support to provide and at what price, if any, to charge for that support and service. The potentially crippling problem of bugs needed to be considered and what actions were to be taken if, and when, they occurred. How should the product be priced in the first place? Should all the R&D, marketing, and overhead be factored into the price? How flexible should the company be with its pricing strategy?

The ALIAS Product

When a data tape containing the ALIAS product left Toronto, it contained a "hole" or a missing line of code which must be filled in before the software would operate. This line of code, called an encryption string, was twelve digits long and could contain numbers, punctuation marks, and upper or lower case letters. The string was unique to one tape of software and to the one piece of hardware upon which it would run. In other words, the same data tape could not be used to start up several different machines.

When customers purchased the software, they purchased customer support for that software. Phone support was provided 12 hours a day, as well as free upgrades and bug-fixes for a period of one year. The support contract had to be renewed each year by the customer if continuing support was to be received. No services were provided until the contract was renewed and payment was received.

A major advantage with the ALIAS system over other software was that ALIAS was easy to learn and easy to use. See *Exhibit 3* for a comparison of Alias and Wavefront products. Those who were not computer literate, and even those who regarded computers with suspicion, were able to make use of most of the system's tools after only a few days of training. Like Apple products, ALIAS was menu-driven, and most "drawing" was done with the aid of a mouse. Once the design, or "modelling" process was finished, the information could be sent to a variety of media. The information could be fed to a plotter, which gives a flat wireframe picture of the object, or it could be directly linked to a CAD machine, which was then used to construct the object from the computerized data. Other options included creating a surface and background for the object and outputting the picture or pictures to slides or videotapes, or even to a stereolithography vat[3] where a plastic prototype is created. In any case, ALIAS shortened the time between the conception of an idea and its appearance on the market, be that idea a car, a building, a piece of jewellery, or a special effect for a movie.

Customers, in general, had responded favourably

---

[3] A stereolithography vat is a vat filled with molten plastic and equipped with a pinpoint laser. The path that the laser takes is determined by the instructions in ALIAS. The result is a perfectly proportioned, solid, three-dimensional plastic model of the original computerized design.

EXHIBIT 3
A COMPARISION OF WAVEFRONT AND ALIAS

Dimension	Wavefront	Alias
Ease of use	Not easy Requires substantial training to use advanced functions	Pioneer in the development and improvement of making the product easy to use
Price	Negotiable Approximately U.S. $55,000 Discounts as much as 50% to make a sale	Fixed Base price is approximately U.S. $65,000 Discounts to educators and co-developers only
Primary market	Animation Some industrial features recently added	Industrial design but also has found wide application in animation
Basic technology	Polygonal lines	Basis splines
Hardware	Runs on many different kinds of hardware	Dedicated to Silicon Graphics and IBM workstations (industry standards)

Source: Company Records.

to the flexibility and ease of use of ALIAS and its convenient access to a wide range of powerful options. Designers had liked the way ALIAS reduced the time between the conception of their ideas and having prototypes built, as well as having the capability of examining more iterations, improvements, and changes at the early stage of product development. Engineers had found that ALIAS provided a precise reading and measurement of designers' concepts and took advantage of its ability to directly link into CAD/CAM systems.

The fundamental source of ALIAS's strength had been as a communication tool. It had given designers and engineers a common language to speak, and in the process, sped up the design-to-market cycle. The enthusiastic response of designers and engineers had led to the steady shift of Alias' revenue from animation into industrial design markets (*Exhibit 4*). While this trend was expected to continue, there are no plans to abandon the animation market.

Marketing and Sales

Alias promoted its products through participation in trade shows like SIGGRAPH, an annual world demonstration tour, articles and advertisements in industry publications, live demonstrations, television advertising, and sponsorship of cultural events. These activities were augmented by print and videotape sales support materials. A direct sales force was em-

EXHIBIT 4
ALIAS RESEARCH INC.—SALES HISTORY BY LINE OF BUSINESS ($000 U.S.)

	1987	1988	1989	1990
Industrial design market:				
Sales	790	3,374	5,320	10,186
Percent of revenue	17%	55%	73%	85%
Animation market:				
Sales	3,970	2,786	1,920	1,820
Percent of revenue	83%	45%	27%	15%
Total sales	4,760	6,160	7,240	12,006

ployed in North America and Europe. This group, which also managed Alias' distributor and dealer network, consisted of 19 people. There were sales offices in five cities in the United States, as well as in France and Germany. Alias' network of 16 dealers and distributors represented the product in 11 countries. This network generally specialized in design and engineering hardware and software complementary to the ALIAS product.

Pricing the Product

As is shown in the consolidated income statement for 1990 (*Exhibit 2*), the direct costs of sales amounted to only 20% of revenue. Almost all of the direct costs were for hardware purchased for resale, for maintenance, and for other services. The direct cost of the software was negligible. Using a cost-based approach to pricing would give Alias substantial room to maneuver on price. However, that was not their approach.

The approach used was to price the software at parity to the hardware upon which it was mounted. For example, a Silicon Graphics Personal IRIS Workstation cost the customer approximately $100,000 (U.S.). The ALIAS tape installed on that workstation would cost another $100,000 (U.S.). This method of pricing put ALIAS at or near the top of what the market would bear. A stripped-down version of ALIAS could sell for as little as $65,000 (U.S.), while the version with every option could run as high as $150,000 (U.S.). Once a system was installed, further options could be added at a cost of $10,000 (U.S.) to $30,000 (U.S.) per option. Customer support was provided on a two-tier pricing schedule. The first tier, which included software release updates and installation only, was provided for an annual fee equal to 10% of the then current software price. A second tier, in addition to incorporating the services of the first tier, provided hotline support and could be purchased for an annual fee of 15% of the then current software price. Training and consultant services were provided on a per day or per task rate (usually about U.S. $500 per person per day).

BACK TO THE FIELD

As Isaac Babbs drove down Highway #1 on the California coast to meet a new prospect at Boeing his thoughts wandered back to his telephone call with Arthur Bell. Arthur had expressed his disappointment over the lost sale, but had refused to make any changes in the pricing policy.

Isaac Babbs had a lot of confidence in the company. Alias management had made some tough calls over the history of the company and been proven right. However, Toronto was a long way from California and he felt he knew his customers better than anyone did. He disliked losing any sale, and he was still smarting from this last one. He understood why Alias had not engaged in price cutting in the past, but he was unsure if he could continue to compete against aggressive price-cutters, like Wavefront. Maybe it was time for a change. How many times had he heard about what a flexible company Alias was, he thought. Perhaps the pricing policy was the correct one, but he could not help worrying over the long-term implications of this rigid policy.

Arthur Bell had been disappointed to have received the news from Babbs. Babbs was one of his best field representatives and had been very successful in cultivating the lucrative southwestern market. Arthur Bell respected Babbs's opinions and was not pleased to hear about his concern over the lost sales and the inflexible pricing policy. The morale and commitment of any member of the sales force could not be treated lightly. Mr. Bell wondered if he came across as too intransigent on the issue of pricing. Perhaps it was time to review the pricing policy and bring it forward at the next management meeting. As he began preparing the memo Stephen Bingham, the president walked by. Arthur told him about the California incident and his interest in putting the pricing policy on the agenda. "Sure let's take a look at the issue," said Stephen. "I think our current pricing policy is just fine, but I am prepared to listen. However, I don't think we can look at price in isolation from the other marketing policies. It would be more useful if it was in the context of a review of the entire marketing program."

APPENDIX 1   EXCERPTS

Daniel Stoffman, "Big Dreams, No Backers," *Report on Business Magazine,* August 1990, pp. 47–51.

- Unlike cars or clothes or bread, no raw material is required to manufacture software. It is purely a creation of the mind, which is why it (Alias) attracts people that include a former comedian, a French horn player, and a former cabinet-maker.

- When the Honda Accord became the first car made by a foreign manufacturer to head the U.S. best-seller list last year, it was more than just another triumph for Japanese industry. Only a few insiders knew that it was also a triumph for Alias. All of Honda's cars, like those of BMW and Volvo, are designed on three-dimensional graphics software created at Alias.

- Canada produces almost no original industrial design—there is no such thing as a Canadian-designed car—but the eccentrics at Alias have created a wonderful tool for industrial designers. Until their software was developed in 1985, these designers did their work the old-fashioned way—with pencil and paper and clay models. Now the designers for such Alias customers as Timex, Motorola, Mitsubishi, British Telecom, and Goodyear can create moving, three-dimensional designs on their computer screens. The models are so realistic that a designer can see how light will reflect off a watch face or a car body long before the actual objects exist. Using Alias software can shave precious months, even years, off the time it takes to create a product.

- Good software is a living thing, constantly growing and adapting to meet its users' needs. That means long nights in front of computer screens. The Alias office contains two eating areas because software developers don't have time to go out for lunch or dinner. On a typical evening, the company will order in large quantities of chicken or pizza. Then the denizens of the factory might amuse themselves for a while playing the latest computer games or reading. A favorite writer at Alias is Vancouverite William Gibson, who writes science fiction novels about "cyberpunks" with computer chips embedded in their brains.

- In the software industry, tiny companies can grow into billion-dollar giants like Lotus and Microsoft almost overnight. That's exactly the sort of future the president, Stephen Bingham, has in mind for Alias, and he is off to an impressive start. Sales were just $12 million last year, but more than a third of those sales were to the Japanese—not known to deal with bantam-weights unless they have very good reasons to do so. The company even managed to forge a strategic alliance with mighty IBM. But for all its successes, there is no guarantee that Alias will make it. In fact, the odds are stacked against it. Software companies in Canada are starved for capital. Without money they can't grow, and in this business if you don't grow fast, you're dead.

- The sale is only part of the story. After you sell someone a $150,000 hardware and software package, you don't just wander off in search of the next customer. Software must be continually enhanced, and most of the enhancements are suggested by the users. Alias personnel meets regularly with their biggest customers. Investing in software is a commitment, and customers are anxious to know where the company is going long term. Several have visited Alias's offices. "The Japanese were impressed that we can turn out so much new technology so quickly," Mr. Bingham says. "A visitor from Honda said we had 20 people doing the work of 200."

- Alias got early support from Montreal "angel" Jim Muir, a friend of one of the partners, and Crownx Inc. of Toronto. Two Boston-based venture capitalists who specialize in high-tech also chipped in. But the company's growth has been largely financed through its own sales. Banks have so far refused to offer more than a small line of credit, saying they do not wish to finance foreign receivables which are the only kind Alias has. Banks also like to have collateral in case a loan goes sour—and by collateral they mean some real estate or a yard full of steel ingots. They don't mean a numeric code on a computer disc—software—which is where the wealth of a company like Alias resides.

- It's not hard to understand why lenders shy away from technology companies. Just look at the record of those high-tech darlings of the '70s—companies like Mitel and Lumonics. More recently, Canada's biggest software firm, Cognos, lost $17 million in fiscal 1990 after several years of good earnings. From an investor's viewpoint, the problem is the rapid rate of change. One banker notes: "In a traditional borrowing relationship, you might analyze the company's record over the last five years. With high-tech companies, I look at the last five quarters. They go through the same cycles as a traditional firm but they do it at an accelerated pace. The products they were selling two years ago are now all obsolete and they've got new products."

The Lively Arts at Hanson, I

Kenneth Shachmut
Charles B. Weinberg

"I'm very frustrated about our attendance figures," noted Barbara Lynn, associate director of the Office of Public Events at Hanson University, a well-known privately funded university in Southern California. "Our programming is high quality, and for the whole season we have only about 30,000 seats to sell, but we have a significant seasonal attendance problem. Our Spring quarter attendance has been running at only 50 percent of capacity over the last few years, down from about 85 percent in the Fall. Winter quarter figures are just marginally better than those for Spring, averaging about 60 percent."

Both she and Tom Bacon, who was finishing his fourth year as director of the Office of Public Events, regarded this seasonal attendance pattern as their most pressing management problem in May 1982 as they contemplated possible remedies for the upcoming 1982–83 season and beyond.

Reprinted from *Stanford Business Cases 1985* with permission of the publishers, Stanford University Graduate School of Business. Copyrighted © 1985 by the Board of Trustees of the Leland Stanford Junior University. Revised 1992.

PROGRAM CHANGES

Over the past three seasons, Mr. Bacon had implemented a number of changes in the "Arts at Hanson" program. Attendance as a percentage of capacity had increased from 54 percent in the three academic years 1976–79 to 68 percent in the most recent three years. These changes are summarized below:

Programming

The number of performances was reduced from 41 in 1978–79 to 31 for the 1979–80 season. This figure rose again to 36 in 1980–81 and was reduced once more to 25 in 1981–82. Additionally, Bacon had attempted to make the program commercially more viable during the last three seasons than it had been previously. He accomplished this by scheduling relatively more performances by string quartets and guitarists, which usually did very well at Hanson. Attendance data by type of programming for the period from Fall 1979 to Spring 1982 were: guitar—104 percent of capacity, chamber music—79 percent, jazz—75 percent, dance—62 percent, and young concert artists—51 percent. Detailed attendance statistics are shown in *Exhibit 1*.

EXHIBIT 1   1981–1982 ATTENDANCE, STATISTICS FOR LIVELY ARTS

	Percent of capacity*				
	Student	Nonstudent	Total	Capacity	Day
Fall					
Performance:					
Sour Cream (CM)	49%	55%	104%	720	Tuesday
LA 4 (Jazz)	39	59	98	1,694	Friday
Hartford Ballet 1 (Dance)	38	28	66	1,694	Thursday
Hartford Ballet 2	27	27	54	1,694	Friday
Contemporary Chamber Ensemble	19	19	38	720	Friday
Guarneri Quartet 1 (CM)	49	63	112	720	Tuesday
Guarneri Quartet 2	53	62	115	720	Friday
Guarneri Quartet 3	50	71	121	720	Sunday
Ron Thomas (YCA)	22	37	59	350	Friday
Paco de Lucia (Guitar)	39	69	108	1,085	Friday
Breakdown (average figures):					
Chamber Music (5)	44%	54%	98%	720	
Guitar (1)	39	69	108	1,085	
Jazz (1)	39	59	98	1,694	
Dance (2)	33	28	60	1,694	
Young Concert Artist (1)	22	37	59	350	
Totals (10)	38	48	86	10,117	
Winter					
Performance:					
AMAN! (Dance)	31%	69%	100%	1,694	Friday
Music by Three (YCA)	14	37	51	350	Friday
Nicanor Zabaleta (Harp)	38	66	104	720	Friday
Pilobolus Dance Theater 1	6	37	43	1,694	Thursday
Pilobolus Dance Theater 2	26	25	51	1,694	Friday
Tel Aviv Quartet (CM)	19	64	83	720	Friday
Fernando Valente (Harpsichord)	26	68	94	720	Friday
Hiroko Yajima (YCA)	7	41	48	350	Friday
Murray Dance Company 1	7	12	19	1,694	Thursday
Murray Dance Company 2	22	21	43	1,694	Friday
Music from Marlboro (CM)	14	52	66	720	Friday
Breakdown (average figures):					
Chamber Music (2)	17%	58%	75%	720	
Dance (5)	18	33	51	1,694	
Young Concert Artist (2)	11	39	50	350	
Other (2)	32	67	99	720	
Totals (11)	19	41	60	12,050	
Spring					
Performance:					
Mummenschanz (Mime)	17%	26%	43%	1,694	Tuesday
Early Music Consort of London (CM)	35	69	104	720	Friday
Paul Winter Consort (Jazz)	21	24	45	1,694	Friday
Arthur Renner (YCA)	11	51	62	350	Friday
Breakdown (not applicable):					
Totals (4)	21%	34%	55%	4,458	

*Chamber Music events were held in the 720-seat hall, Dance and Jazz in the 1,694-seat hall, and the Young Concert Artist series in the 350-seat hall. For the Guitar Concert, the balcony and back rows of the 1,694-seat hall were not made available for sale, leaving a capacity of 1,085 seats. Other events were scheduled for either the 720- or 1,694-seat hall depending upon the nature of the event. The average production cost per performance was $3,000 in 1981–82.

Personnel

The size of Mr. Bacon's staff was increased, permitting more and more effective promotional activities. Even with this increase, however, the total time devoted to the program was not greatly in excess of one person-year, due to the fact that the Office of Public Events was responsible for managing four other University programs in addition to the Arts program during the school year.

The first of these programs was general administration (mainly scheduling) of all public events on the Hanson campus. This function required considerable time and represented a steady workload throughout the academic year. Second, the office was responsible for coordinating all university public ceremonies. Most significant of these was the annual Commencement exercise, conducted during June. Although some aspects of Commencement required advance planning and coordination, by far the biggest push came in the two months immediately preceding the event. The third major responsibility of the office was coordination of various university lecture programs, including several endowed lectures. As with general administration, the lecture series imposed a relatively steady workload throughout the year.

In addition, Mr. Bacon was responsible for a travel film and lecture series which ran throughout the academic year. Also, during the summer, he scheduled a number of "commercial" attractions (for example, the Preservation Hall Jazz Band) for community enjoyment.

The university administration considered all of these activities to be important in helping fulfill the multiple goals of a major university in the community. Tom Bacon knew that whatever new marketing moves he attempted for the "Arts at Hanson" must be accomplished within strict personnel time constraints.

PROMOTIONAL CHANGES
Name

The name of the program was changed to "The *Lively Arts at Hanson*" for the 1979–80 season, in order, hopefully, to attract more attention to the program and to identify it more positively as a *performing* arts program. This new name was incorporated in a redesigned logo used in all media advertising.

Brochure

The season brochure (now entitled "The Lively Arts at Hanson") was made much more elaborate and eye-catching, starting with the 1979–80 season. Its physical size was doubled (to 8½ by 11 inches) and it was printed in three colors on glossy paper stock. These changes increased the costs substantially. By the current year the total cost of the brochure (45,000 copies printed, of which 30,000 were mailed and 15,000 bulk distributed) had risen to $16,800 (including mailing costs) from approximately $6,500 three years earlier.

The brochure included listings for not only the Lively Arts program, but also performances by various university departments (e.g., drama and music departments). These nonprofessional performances were clearly separated from the Lively Arts offerings within the brochure. In addition, the sponsoring departments were required to fully absorb their pro rata share—$2,000—of total brochure costs. Mr. Bacon planned to maintain this policy into the foreseeable future.

The brochure was sent out to a composite mailing list at the beginning of each season in early September. The mailing list was actually composed of three individual lists. The first list included approximately 15,000 individuals who had previously purchased Lively Arts season tickets, who had purchased individual tickets by check (from which a name and address was obtained), or who had specifically requested to be put on the list (by filling out cards available at all performances).

A second list (about 6,000)—the so-called "Sunset Hills Cultural List"—was obtained from the Council for the Arts in Sunset Hills (a large suburban community adjacent to Hanson). The remainder of the mailed brochures (approximately 9,000 for 1981–82) was sent to local Hanson alumni, priority being determined by proximity of residence to the university campus.

These three lists were not cross-checked against each other for duplication. A spokesperson from University Computing Services, which maintained the lists, said that due to their different coding systems, reprogramming and integrating the lists would be costly and time-consuming. Overall, Mr. Bacon had no good feeling for the extent to which duplication existed within the lists. However, he noted that he personally received three mailed copies of the brochure each year.

In addition to program information, the annual brochure included a calendar of all performances (professional and nonprofessional), season ticket information, and ticket order forms for all performances.

Additional Brochures

Supplemental one-page brochures in a postcard format were mailed at the beginning of Winter and Spring quarters to the Lively Arts mailing list, briefly outlining the upcoming quarterly program offerings.

Posters and Flyers

When available from the performers' agents, posters and flyers were distributed around the Hanson campus on centrally located information kiosks, in dormitories, and other places about two weeks prior to each performance. Depending upon availability, additional posters were distributed to other college campuses in the area and to willing local merchants. These posters were of varied quality and Public Events staff had no control over their format. Typically the posters included a blank area at the bottom in which was printed program time and location information. The posters did not include the Lively Arts logo or any other mention of the program itself.

Advertising and Other Promotional Activities

Each performance was advertised for about two weeks prior to the performance itself in the local press and, for some performances, on classical music

radio stations. Typical newspaper sources were the *Hanson Daily, Los Angeles Times, Sunset Hills News,* and *Orange County Crier.* Additionally, miscellaneous promotional pieces such as Lively Arts bookmarks were printed in large quantities and made widely available on campus at the beginning of each season. Total approximate promotional expenditures are presented in *Exhibit 2.*

Pricing

Greater flexibility was introduced to the pricing scheme, with price levels varying across different performances according to program cost, expected drawing power of individual performers, and other factors. For example, the best nonstudent tickets for the Murray Dance Company sold for $9.00, while the Tel Aviv Quartet seats went for $7.00, and Young Concert Artist series performances sold at $5.00 for nonstudents. Additionally, the overall price level was increased to an average ticket price paid (including student and season discounts) of $4.97 for 1981–82, compared to $4.01 two years earlier.

STUDENT PROMOTIONS
Student Introductory Program (SIP)

Under this program, initiated two years ago, each new Hanson undergraduate or graduate student was given a free pass to any one performance during the Fall quarter and also a coupon allowing that student to buy a ticket at 75 cents for any other performance during the year.

Response to the initial free ticket was good, but only a very limited number of students exercised the follow-up 75-cent option. Consequently, the 75-cent coupon was discontinued after only one season. The initial free SIP ticket had been maintained up to the present time, however.

Student Discount Tickets

The price of a ticket to any performance for students was set substantially below the average nonstudent ticket price. During the just completed season the

EXHIBIT 2
APPROXIMATE PROMOTIONAL EXPENDITURES—1981–1982 SEASON

Annual costs:			
Season brochure*	$16,800		
Program covers	1,200		
Promotional material (bookmarks, surveys, etc.)	1,650		
			$19,650
Fall quarter costs:			
Advertising			
Newspaper	$ 7,500		
Radio	900		
Other	300	$ 8,700	
Posters & flyers		600	
Other		300	
			$ 9,600
Winter quarter costs:			
Advertising			
Newspaper	$ 7,650		
Radio	1,050		
Other	450	$ 9,150	
Posters & flyers		600	
Winter brochure*		3,150	
Other		450	
			$13,350
Spring quarter costs (estimate):			
Advertising			
Newspaper	$ 3,750		
Radio	750		
Other	150	$ 4,650	
Posters & flyers		300	
Spring brochure*		1,350	
Other		150	
			$ 6,450
Total promotional costs			$49,050

*Includes mailing cost.

student price was $4.50 per ticket. Mr. Bacon felt that this price level was appropriate and equitable and he desired to maintain it as long as possible.

OVERALL ACCOMPLISHMENTS

Tom Bacon was convinced that the program changes represented significant accomplishments for "The Lively Arts at Hanson," notwithstanding the existence of several persistent problems. Overall, he felt there were two major accomplishments:

- Total program attendance had risen steadily from 1976–77 to 1979–80, declining in the recession year 1980–81. Further declines in the total attendance for 1981–82 were believed to be due principally to the reduced number of performances.
- Average percentage attendance for Fall quarter had increased markedly from 68 percent in 1976–78 to 85 percent in 1979–81. Mr. Bacon attributed this increase to a combination of successful marketing innovations initiated in Fall quarter 1979. These included the expanded brochure, more successful programming, and the SIP program.

Together these accomplishments convinced Mr. Bacon and Ms. Lynn that the Lively Arts was an extremely viable program with a growing base of supporters.

PROGRAM ATTENDANCE

In May 1982, Mr. Bacon was undertaking a reappraisal of the entire Lively Arts marketing program employed over the past three years to determine what changes, if any, might be warranted. Although he felt strongly that many of his program changes had been successful, he still faced significant problems. Most worrisome of these was a marked pattern of seasonal attendance. While Fall quarter audiences had been very good, averaging nearly 85 percent of capacity, the comparable figures for Winter and Spring quarters were 60 percent and 50 percent, respectively. To compound this difficulty Mr. Bacon noted that student attendance had slipped from a high of over 45 percent of the audience during the 1979–80 season to an all-time low of 32 percent for the past Winter quarter (*Exhibits 1* and *3*).

Mr. Bacon was concerned about both of these trends:

"The Lively Arts at Hanson" presents first-rate artists in a varied program that should appeal to a broad base of individuals. Look at this season's offerings, for example: The Guarneri and Tel Aviv string quartets; Music from Marlboro; AMAN! (a folk dance group); Pilobolus and the Murray Louis Company in dance; the Early Music Consort of London. These artists are representative of the best in their fields.

Our Young Concert Artist series brings some of the most promising young talents in the world to the Hanson audience. These are the artists who will be at the top of their profession in a few years. Already they have received laudatory reviews by major music critics. Moreover, our prices are quite low compared to what one would have to pay to see comparable performers in Los Angeles. The average nonstudent ticket price this year was only about $6.00–9.00. Most city performances cost twice that much.

Student attendance also bothers me. As a group, Hanson students should be very interested in the Lively Arts program. However, from a number of sources, I have the strong impression that they're really not as aware of our program as I would like. For example, take the Student

EXHIBIT 3 ATTENDANCE BY QUARTERS

	1976–77	1977–78	1978–79	1979–80	1980–81	1981–82
Fall:						
Total attendance	5,211	7,448	7,768	14,168	13,298	8,869
Student attendance	NA	2,694	3,123	5,349	4,833	2,726
No. of performances	6	9	13	13	14	10
Winter:						
Total attendance	7,355	8,542	6,645	8,070	6,765	7,216
Student attendance	NA	3,434	2,590	2,905	2,395	2,318
No. of performances	11	8	14	10	14	11
Spring:						
Total attendance	2,160	3,099	9,226	4,667	4,048	2,456
Student attendance	NA	1,102	3,437	1,720	1,529	938
No. of performances	3	8	14	8	8	4
Total:						
Total attendance	14,726	19,089	23,639	26,905	24,111	18,541
Student attendance	NA	7,230	9,150	9,974	8,757	5,982
No. of performances	20	25	41	31	36	25

Note: SIP coupon attendance in the Fall terms of 1979, 1980, and 1981 was 1,666, 1,363, and 1,221 respectively and is counted in total but not student attendance. SIP coupons accounted for 253 students in the Winter and 155 students in the Spring terms of 1979–80.

Introductory Program (SIP). By and large, new students were very willing to take a complimentary ticket, but very few of them exercised the option to purchase a second ticket for 75 cents plus the SIP coupon, as our statistics show.

There are other indications as well. Not concrete to be sure, but present nevertheless. Somehow we have to get through to the students that "The Lively Arts at Hanson" is something very special and very professional, to be distinguished from the whole host of other performance activities with which we must compete for their attention on campus.

"The Lively Arts at Hanson" was not alone in facing a seasonal attendance problem. The performing arts program at State University experienced similar difficulties. Mr. Bacon's counterpart at State U. commented that she had had some success in combating this problem by scheduling relatively more "light" and fewer "heavy" performances during Spring quarter, her toughest attendance period. The "light" category encompassed performances which typically sold well at State U., including string quartets, early music, and anything by Bach. "Heavy," on the other hand, included contemporary music and vocalists, which were always difficult to sell. The State U. manager also tended to favor more well-known performers in the Spring.

PROGRAM GOALS

Mr. Bacon felt strongly that the program had—and must of necessity have—multiple goals reflecting the multiple dimensions of managing an arts program. For purposes of control and evaluation of the program's progress, Mr. Bacon decided after much thoughtful consideration that the following four goals were paramount:

- Establish "The Lively Arts at Hanson" as a major source of first-rate performing arts talent for the extended county community as well as for the immediate Hanson University community.
- Run the series on a close-to-breakeven basis, incurring only a minimal deficit as approved by the university administration.
- Keep prices as low as possible in order to make performances widely accessible.

- Target the total season for overall attendance at 75–80 percent of capacity. Further, maintain the following overall audience proportions: students, 35 percent; nonstudents, 65 percent.

PROGRAMMING DIFFICULTIES

In order to achieve the first of these goals, which he and his staff felt was probably the most important, Mr. Bacon knew it would be imperative to continue to present a varied program of artists each season. This was difficult for two reasons. First, the scheduling problems were impressive. Not only did Mr. Bacon have to book the artists more than a year in advance in most cases, but also he had to compete with various departmental and student arts productions (e.g., music department concerts, drama department, and theatrical club productions) for a very limited number of available auditoriums on campus and suitable dates.

However, even more troublesome was a second factor. By maintaining a varied program, Mr. Bacon was including each season a number of performance types which did not seem to do very well in drawing large audiences, such as the Young Artist series and dance in general. He had broken down his quarterly attendance statistics for the past three seasons and was upset by them. He knew that he would have to try to ameliorate the contrasts in attendance statistics by performance type for the upcoming season if possible, but he wasn't sure of the best way to go about it.

SEGMENTATION

Barbara Lynn, who had been working in the Office of Public Events for two years, had some strong feelings about the potential audience:

I think we have, basically, three groups of people who come out to our performances. First there are the students—mostly from Hanson, but some from neighboring colleges and secondary schools as well. Our sources on campus seem to indicate that Hanson students are not very aware of our program. The students have heard of the Guarneri Quartet—and they know they will be performing—but they don't seem to know that the "Lively Arts" is bringing the Guarneri to campus. I don't know, but maybe our posters and *Hanson Daily* advertising aren't doing the job. They sure cost enough, though!

Second is the group I like to call "Hanson affiliated": University faculty and staff members and their spouses. We haven't made any special attempt to get them interested, but feel they should respond to the advertising both on campus and in the local press.

Finally we've got the community at large—mostly in and around Hanson and Sunset Hills. Many of these people receive our annual brochure and the subsequent quarterly postcard mailings. In addition, they probably read both the *Los Angeles Times* and the *Sunset Hills News,* in which we advertise regularly. They're all great fans in the Fall, but when we have to compete with spring weather their loyalty runs thin. Their allegiance during the Winter is also poor.

There are other groups, too. For example, local music teachers and their pupils; maybe even some of the companies up in the Hanson Industrial Park. We could probably do a lot here in the way of group discounts. This also might apply to faculty and staff—especially those living nearby on University land. I've got a million ideas I'd like to try out, but not nearly enough time. Especially now, with Commencement to worry about. . . .

IMAGE ADVERTISING

Both Ms. Lynn and Mr. Bacon were concerned that the perceived image of "The Lively Arts at Hanson" was not as good as it could be. Precise information was not available on this issue, but a number of informal sources supported this belief:

- The manager of the Campus Ticket Office reported that very few buyers ever mentioned the program when purchasing individual performance tickets. Additionally, she said that over the past few years only one of the many students who had worked part time in the ticket office had heard of the program before beginning work.
- Informal pollings of students in the Hanson Graduate School of Business indicated that only 5–10 percent of them had heard of the program before studying an earlier version of this case in class.

These and other indicators led Mr. Bacon and Ms. Lynn to consider the possibility of an image advertising campaign during the summer in the local press as well as on campus at the beginning of the academic year in September. Lynn also thought that students in Hanson's several graduate professional schools (Business, Law, Medicine, and Education), might be a good target segment. She reasoned that these students were much more dedicated to a particular field than were undergraduates, and therefore probably were less involved in competing general university activities, of which there were many.

Also, professional school students were generally more isolated from the university at large, she thought, and therefore less likely to be aware of the Lively Arts program. Finally, many of the professional school students were married; Lynn felt that the combination of easily accessible, low priced, high quality performing arts entertainment should have tremendous appeal to young professionals on a student budget.

AUDIENCE QUESTIONNAIRE

In order to try to get a handle on some of the characteristics of the audience and formulate an appropriate marketing plan for next year, Lively Arts staff had prepared an audience survey. This questionnaire was distributed to most of the audience at 10 of the Winter quarter performances. A random sample of about 100 (when less than 100 questionnaires were turned in, the whole group was used) was selected from each performance (in all, over 850 responses were sampled) and the results were analyzed using the computer program available through the university computer center.

By mid-May Mr. Bacon had the results of his analysis (*Exhibit 4*). By and large the questionnaire reconfirmed many intuitive feelings he and his staff had had prior to the survey. But they gained several new insights as well. As a result of the questionnaire, Mr. Bacon was seriously rethinking some of his marketing strategies for next season.

THE 1982–83 SEASON

Due to the long-range planning horizon implicit in arranging bookings for performing artists, the 1982–

EXHIBIT 4
AUDIENCE PROFILE

	Students*	Nonstudents
Median:		
Age group	18–24	35–44
Number of children	0	1
Education level	4 years college	graduate work
Annual family income	—	$25–49 K
Hanson affiliation:		
Students	73%	3%
Faculty	—	10
Staff	1	9
Alumni	3	15
Place of residence		
Hanson	44%	10%
Sunset Hills	26	35
Verona	1	2
Mateo Park	8	15
Parkside/Vista Valley	1	5
Verdes/Verdes Hills	2	7
Ocean View	5	5
Other	13	21
Performing arts performances attended in Hanson within the past year:		
1–3	64%	49%
4–7	27	27
8–10	4	10
Over 10	5	13
Time of ticket purchase:†		
At the door	19%	12%
Day of performance	11	9
1–3 days before	23	12
4–7 days before	16	11
2–3 weeks before	11	12
1 or more months before	20	45
Lively Arts at Hanson:		
Current subscribers	8%	34%
Received brochure in mail	21	56
Information sources for this performance:		
Brochure by mail	15%	48%
Newspaper advertising	34%	27
Newspaper story	9	14
Poster or flyer	42	14
Word of mouth	46	29

EXHIBIT 4 (*continued*)

	Students*	Nonstudents
Sources usually consulted for upcoming arts events:		
Hanson Daily	725%	27%
Campus Report	12	17
Hanson Observer	9	14
Los Angeles Times	32	46
Sunset Hills News	21	54
KNFC/KIBC	18	17
KKBM	13	18
Listen to classical music radio regularly	57%	73%
Station most often listened to:		
KKBM	20%	37%
KNFC/KIBC	39	40
Performance preferences:		
Theater	81%	77%
Contemporary music	41	33
Symphony	63	68
Modern dance	58	51
Instrumental recitals	47	51
Opera	25	32
Chamber music	47	55
Ballet	58	62
Vocal recitals	11	17
Factors important in deciding to attend a performance:		
Name of performers	68%	75%
Repertoire	79	87
Ticket price	68	49
Find hall easily	28	29

*Student/Nonstudent categories were developed according to the response to an occupation question. About 80% of respondents were nonstudents.

†Among nonstudents attending 1 to 3 performances, 30% bought their tickets at the door or on the day of the performance; among nonstudents attending 4 or more performances, the comparable percentage was 11%. For students, the percentage was about 30%, regardless of attendance level.

Source: Audience survey questionnaire.

83 season was already scheduled (*Exhibit 5*). Of the 26 performances, 9 were scheduled for the fall quarter, 10 for winter, and 7 for spring. Within this programming context, Mr. Bacon sought to use all the market information he had gathered during the season to formulate a well-integrated, *specific* marketing plan.

To operationalize his strategic planning, he thought it would be a good idea to set a specific attendance objective. After much thought he decided upon a season attendance goal of 75 percent, with a 35–65 percent student/nonstudent mix. This was clearly a stretch target, but by setting his overall season goal high, Bacon hoped to really come to grips with his historically most pressing problem: seasonal attendance. He further thought that, at a minimum, his plan should address the following issues:

• *Brochures* Was the "lavish" annual brochure with quarterly postcard follow-ups sufficient, or should *each* quarterly mailing be more like the current annual elaborate brochure?

EXHIBIT 5
1982–83 SEASON SCHEDULE

Fall quarter:

October 22	Chamber Music Society of Lincoln Center
October 28	"Are You Now or Have You Ever Been?" (drama)
October 29	Oba Koso (Nigerian opera)
November 5	Roman de Fauvel (medieval secular music drama)
November 9	Music from Marlboro (chamber music)
November 12	Young Concert Artist
November 14, 16, 19	Guarneri String Quartet—Beethoven Quartet Series (chamber music)

Winter quarter:

January 18	"An Evening of George Orwell" with Jose Ferrer (celebrity)
January 21	Young Concert Artist
February 1, 2, 3	Eliot Feld Ballet Company (dance)
February 11	Young Concert Artist
February 18	Bach Aria Group (chamber music)
February 22, 25, 27	Guarneri String Quartet—Beethoven Quartet Series (chamber music)

Spring quarter:

April 1	Narciso Yepes (guitar)
April 7, 8	Utah Repertory Dance Company
April 15	Young Concert Artist
April 17	American Brass Quintet (chamber music)
April 24, 26	Fine Arts Quartet (with viola)—Mozart Quintet Series (chamber music)

- *Advertising* How should he allocate his advertising budget? What media should he expand? Contract? Why? What were the possibilities of image advertising over the summer to develop latent demand?
- *Pricing* How might he alter his pricing policy further? What level of prices would be tolerable and consistent with his goals?
- *Season Tickets* Was the "choose-your-own" program[1] viable? Why or why not? What might be employed as an alternative? For example, should the six Guarneri Quartet performances by packaged as a series to be sold at a discount?
- *Segmentation* What would be an effective way to

target his marketing pitch at each of the segments that Ms. Lynn had identified? Were there other viable segmentation possibilities?

As Mr. Bacon mulled over these issues he recognized that his total promotional budget could not exceed about $50,000 for the forthcoming season. To assist in formulating the marketing plan, Ms. Lynn had put together an estimate of the major advertising, brochure, and other promotional expense items for the forthcoming season (*Exhibit 6*). Mr. Bacon also thought it would not be too early to begin formulating some strategy regarding the more long-term issue of programming selection (i.e., how many of what type of performances to schedule when?). Although he wanted to maintain program diversity, he knew that university financial pressures would force his program's funding implications into prominence in future interdepartmental budget battles.

---

[1] The "choose-your-own" program allowed season ticket purchasers to structure their own discount season, choosing only those performances they wished to attend, as long as a minimum number of performances was selected.

EXHIBIT 6
ESTIMATED MARKETING EXPENSES—FORTHCOMING SEASON

Newspaper ad rates costs quoted are "per column-inch" for each time the ad is run:

Sunset Hills News	$11.00	
	8.50	(if there are no changes and the ad is run a minimum of four times)
Orange County Crier	17.25	
Hanson Daily	5.00	
Los Angeles Times	54.00	

Radio ad rates—costs for a 30-second announcement:

KKBM	$43.00
KIBC/KNFC	24.00
KBIG	36.50

Lively Arts brochure—annual:

Typesetting	$165 per page		
Printing	150 per page		
Fixed cost (plates)			
Variable cost per page:			
First 10,000 copies	$.022		
Next 20,000 copies	.007		
Next 30,000 copies	.005		
Labels and bulk mailing	.11 per brochure		
Typesetting	$165 × 20 pages		$ 3,300
Printing:			
Fixed (plates)		$3,000	
Variable			
$.022 × 10,000 × 20		4,400	
$.007 × 20,000 × 20		2,800	
$.005 × 15,000 × 20		1,500	11,700
Labels and bulk mailing	$.11 × 30,000		3,300
			15,000

Winter and Spring quarter brochures ("snake mailers"):

Printing	
Fixed cost (plate)	$15.00
Variable cost per item:	
First 25,000	.03
Next 50,000	.022
Labels and bulk mailing	.09 each
Bookmarks:	
Printing	$ .019 each

Notes: (1) A typical Lively Arts ad was 2 columns wide and 3 inches long, or 6 column-inches. In the *Sunset Hills News* these ads typically ran for about two weeks prior to the performance.

(2) *Los Angeles Times* advertising was restricted to the Sunday "Datebook" section.

(3) For the recently completed season the brochure was 20 pages; 45,000 copies were printed and 30,000 bulk-mailed at a total cost (including mailing) of $16,800.

Glossary of Selected Marketing and Management Terms

advertising Any paid form of nonpersonal presentation and promotion of a product or organization by an identified sponsor.

agent A business unit that negotiates purchases or sales (or both) of goods and services. Agents are commonly remunerated by payment of a commission or fee.

attitudes Enduring systems of positive or negative evaluations of, or emotional feelings toward, an object.

augmented product The core product plus any additional services and benefits that may be supplied.

backward integration Obtaining ownership or increased control of an organization's supply systems (see also *forward integration* and *vertical integration*).

benefit segmentation Dividing the population into different groups on the basis of the benefits they want or require and the costs they wish to avoid.

billings The total charges for advertising space or time, production, and other services provided by an advertising agency to its client.

bottom-up planning Designing, developing and implementing of programs by middle-level and lower-level managers and other personnel who work out the details and follow through on them (see also *top-down planning*).

brand A name, term, sign, symbol, design, or combination of these that seeks to identify the product of an organization and differentiate it from those of competitors.

branding The process of creating, assigning, and publicizing a brand name, term, sign, symbol, etc., to one or more products.

breakeven The volume of sales necessary, at a specific price, for a seller to recover all relevant costs of a product.

broker See *agent*.

cannibalization The erosion of sales of an existing product by a new product marketed by the same firm.

cash cow A product in the mature or declining stage of the product life cycle that can be "milked" for as much profit as possible.

catchment area (or primary market area) The geographic region or area from which the bulk of an organization's customers are drawn.

centralized management The decision-making power concentrated among a relatively small number of managers at the head office (see also *decentralized management*).

chain store One of a group of centrally owned retail stores of similar type with some degree of centralized control over operations.

channels of distribution See *distribution or delivery system*.

clutter See *noise*.

cognitive dissonance Perceived inconsistency within an individual's own beliefs or attitudes or between these and one's behavior. A person will attempt to reduce the dissonance through changes in either behavior or cognition.

commodity A generic product category or product that cannot be distinguished by potential customers from similar products offered by competitors.

communication The transmission of a message from a sender (or source) to a receiver (or recipient).

communication medium The personal or impersonal channel through which a message is transmitted to an audience or individual (see also *mass media*).

communication mix The combination of elements (personal selling, media advertising, signage, public relations, publicity, and onsite display) used by an organization to communicate its message(s) to its target market(s).

comparative advertising Advertising messages that make specific brand comparisons using actual product names (sometimes referred to as "knocking copy" when the comparisons are sharply unfavorable).

competition See *direct competitor* and *generic competitor*.

concentrated marketing strategy The efforts, in a segmented market, of an organization that is focusing on one target group and designing its marketing strategy specifically to reach that group, rather than trying to be all things to all people.

consignment sales Sales not completed until products placed by a supplier with a retailer are resold to customers, at which point payment becomes due from the retailer to the supplier.

consumers Individuals or households or organizations that are current or prospective purchasers or users of goods and services.

contingency budget Funds set aside in advance to finance contingency plans and respond to unanticipated events.

contingency plans Plans, prepared in advance, outlining a course of action to deal with situations that might potentially arise.

contribution (or gross contribution) The monetary difference between total sales revenues (gross income) and variable expenses (see also *margin*).

convenience products Products the consumer usually purchases frequently, immediately, and with a minimum effort in comparison and shopping (see also *shopping products* and *speciality products*).

convenience store A small store, with a limited stock of groceries and household products, that remains open for long hours.

cooperative advertising Local or regional advertising whose costs are shared jointly by a national advertiser and a retail or wholesale institution.

copy testing A preliminary test of alternative advertising copy appeals or selling messages to assess their relative effectiveness for specific audiences.

core product The central elements of a product that serve a basic consumer or societal need (see also *augmented product*).

cost center An organizational unit whose costs are clearly identifiable.

cost-per-thousand The cost of advertising for each 1,000 homes reached in TV or radio, or for each 1,000 circulated copies of a publication (often abbreviated CPM).

coupons Certificates that are mailed, handed out, or incorporated in print advertising and that entitle the bearer to a specified monetary savings on a purchase of a specific product.

crisis management The result of the occurrence of an unexpected event for which management has not prepared and that requires immediate action (see also *contingency plans*).

cross-sectional data or study Research information gathered from a whole population (or a representative sample of that population) at a single point in time (see also *longitudinal data*).

cumulative audience ("Cume") The net unduplicated radio or TV audience delivered by a specific program in a particular time slot over a measured period of time usually one to four weeks.

customer service A collective term that describes all the supplementary services provided by an organization to satisfy customers and combat competitors, such as technical aid, information, order taking, complaint handling, refunds, or substitutions.

decentralized management The result of the dispersion of decision-making power to relevant personnel at lower levels within an organization (see also *centralized management*).

decision-making unit (DMU) An individual or group of individuals involved in making decisions on the purchase of a specific product.

demographic segmentation Categorizing or differentiating people based on demographic variables such as age, sex, religion, income, etc.

differentiated marketing strategy   Developing different products and/or marketing programs for each market segment that the organization plans to serve.

direct competitor   An organization offering a product that meets similar consumer needs and is broadly similar in substance or process to one's own product.

direct selling   Selling to the end user by the producer without use of retail or wholesale intermediaries.

discretionary income   Funds remaining to an individual or household after paying for necessities out of disposable income (see *disposable income*, below).

disposable income   Personal (or household) income remaining after deduction of income taxes and compulsory payments such as social security.

dissonance   See *cognitive dissonance*.

distribution or delivery system   The combination of internal organizational resources and external intermediaries employed to move a product from production or creation to the final consumer. Goods necessarily move through physical distribution channels, involving transportation, storage, and display. Services may be delivered to the customer directly at the production site, or, in certain instances, transmitted electronically.

diversification   The process of entering new markets with one or more products that are new to the organization.

drive time   The weekday commute hours when many motorists are listening to their car radios.

durable goods   Goods such as appliances, furniture, and automobiles that are expected to last several years or more.

elasticity of demand (to price)   The responsiveness of sales volume to a change in price. Demand is said to be *price inelastic* when raising (or lowering) price by a certain percentage has a proportionately smaller impact on sales volume, and *price elastic* when the impact on volume is proportionately greater than the price change.

evoked set   The array of specific brands for a product category consciously considered by a consumer in making a purchase decision.

experiment   An attempt to measure cause-and-effect relationships under controlled or natural conditions.

fixed costs   Costs that remain unchanged in total for a given time period despite wide fluctuations in activity, such as property taxes, executive salaries, rent insurance, and depreciation (see also *variable costs*).

flight of advertising   A part of an advertising campaign that is divided into groups of ads, with periods of time between each group.

focus-group   interviews   A   small-group-discussion method of obtaining qualitative information from individuals who are broadly representative of the target market.

forward integration   Obtaining ownership or increased control of the means by which an organization distributes its products to end users (see also *backward integration* and *vertical integration*).

four Ps   See *marketing mix*.

franchise   The licensing of a production and distribution business, dealership, or complete business format where one organization authorizes a number of independent outlets to market a product or service and engage in a business using the franchisor's trade names and methods of operation.

frequency   The number of times an accumulated audience has the opportunity to be exposed to the same advertising messages within a measured period of time.

generic competitor   An organization offering a product that, while possibly different in substance or process, is capable of satisfying the same general consumer needs as one's own product (see also *direct competitor*).

geographic segmentation   Segmentation of a market on the basis of region, city metropolitan area size, population density, climate, or terrain.

gross rating points (GRPs)   A measurement of advertising impact derived by multiplying the number of persons exposed to an advertisement by the average number of exposures per person (see also *reach* and *frequency*).

horizontal integration   The process of obtaining ownership or increased control of one's competitors (see also *vertical integration*).

impulse purchase   A purchase decision made on the spur of the moment without prior planning.

industrial/institutional marketing   Selling goods and services to corporate, institutional, or government purchasers as opposed to individuals and households.

intermediary   An organization or individual that serves as a go-between, or facilitator, between producer, marketer, and customer.

knocking copy   See *comparative advertising*.

list price   The price shown on the marketer's sales list and used as the basis for computing discounts.

longitudinal data or study   Research information gathered over time (usually at periodic intervals) from the same population or sample; this allows the researcher to monitor individual changes among participants in the study.

loss leaders   A product of known or accepted quality

priced at a loss or no profit for the purpose of attracting consumers who may then purchase other regularly priced products.

manufacturer's agent/representative An intermediary who handles noncompeting but related lines of goods usually on an extended contractual basis within an exclusive territory.

margin The difference between the selling price of a product and its production cost (for a manufacturer or service provider) or purchase cost (for a wholesaler or retailer). The margin may be expressed in monetary units or as a percentage of the selling price.

markdown A reduction in the originally established price of a product.

market The set of all current and potential consumers of a particular product.

market aggregation See *undifferentiated marketing strategy*.

market definition An attempt by the organization to determine which segment of the market its operations are or should be serving.

market development An organization's marketing of its current line of products to new markets or segments.

market niche A segment of a market where there is demand for a product with specific attributes distinguishing it from competing offerings.

market penetration An organization's attempt to increase consumption of its current products in its current markets.

market potential A calculation of maximum possible sales (in units or currency values), or usage opportunities in a defined territorial area for all marketers of a product during a stated period of time.

market segment A homogeneous subset of the target market that may require a marketing plan tailored to the segment's distinctive characteristics.

market segmentation The process of identifying distinctive submarkets or segments within the target market.

market share The ratio of an organization's sales volume for a particular product category to total market volume on either an actual or potential basis.

marketing audit A systematic, critical, unbiased, and comprehensive review and appraisal of an organization's or subunit's marketing objectives, strategies, policies, and activities.

marketing mix The four basic ingredients (or elements) in a marketing program that influence consumers' decisions on whether or not to patronize the organization.

These four elements are product, price, distribution or delivery systems, and communication. (Note: Some people use the phrase the *four Ps*—product, price, place, and promotion—to describe the elements of the marketing mix, but we regard the terms "place" and "promotion" as too narrow and potentially misleading.)

marketing planning The tasks of setting up objectives for marketing activity and of determining and scheduling the steps necessary to achieve such objectives.

marketing research The systematic gathering, recording, and analyzing of data to provide information for marketing decision making.

markup The amount by which a seller increases the selling price of a product over its original purchase price; markup is generally computed as a percentage of the final selling price rather than of the original price.

mass media Informational networks, reaching large numbers of people, that carry news, features, editorial opinion, and advertising—specifically newspapers, magazines, radio, and television; the term can also be applied to other communication vehicles, such as billboards, poster sites, and mail service, that can be used to convey marketing messages to large numbers of people.

members Individuals who join nonprofit organizations and pay dues or support the organization on a periodic basis with funds, services, or their time and efforts.

merchandising Selecting, displaying, and promoting products in a retail store or other distribution outlet.

national account A customer operating over extended geographic areas whose service and sales needs are typically coordinated out of a head office.

noise (or clutter) Conflicting, counter, or unrelated communications that detract from an advertiser's ability to communicate a specific message to members of a target audience.

nondurable goods Consumer goods such as food, health and beauty aids, and items that are consumed or otherwise used up relatively quickly (see also *durable goods*).

opinion leader An individual who influences other people's purchase and consumption behavior.

opportunity cost The maximum benefit foregone by using scarce resources (e.g., money, management time, physical facilities) for one purpose instead of the next best alternative.

penetration strategy An aggressive marketing strategy, based upon low price and heavy advertising and promotional expenditures, that is designed to gain quickly a large share of the market for a specific product.

point-of-sale advertising Promotional displays used by retailers at in-store locations, such as shelf, window, counter, aisle, or checkout, to promote specific products (also known as point-of-purchase, or P-O-P, advertising).

price Defined narrowly as the monetary cost to the purchaser of obtaining a product; more broadly it includes other monetary outlays associated with purchasing and using the product, as well as all nonmonetary costs associated with purchase and use of a good or service (or adoption of a social behavior), such as time and physical and psychological effort.

price elasticity See *elasticity of demand.*

price leader A firm whose pricing policies are followed by other companies in the same industry.

pricing strategy The mix of monetary price level charged to the final purchaser, terms and methods of payment (e.g., checks, credit cards, exact change), and discounts offered to both intermediaries and final purchasers.

primary data Information the researcher collects through observation, experimentation, or survey research (see also *secondary data*).

primary demand The current level of demand for all sources for the entire product class in question.

prime time The evening hours of broadcasting (8:00 p.m.–11:00 p.m.) when audience size is usually the largest and advertising rates are highest.

private label brands Brands owned by retailers or other channel intermediaries, as distinct from manufacturers' brands.

proactive selling Actively seeking out prospective customers (see also *reactive selling*).

product What the organization offers to prospective customers for their acquisition, use, consumption, or adoption; the term includes physical goods, services, and social behaviors or causes (such as driving safely, giving blood, etc.).

product class A group of products that serves the same general function or fulfills the same basic need.

product development The process of developing or acquiring new or improved products for an organization's current market (see also *diversification*).

product differentiation Creating and communicating product attributes that cause consumers to perceive the product as being different from the other offerings on the market.

product life cycle The movement of a product from introduction ("birth") through growth, maturity, and decline to eventual termination; each of these phases requires a distinctive marketing strategy.

product line All the products marketed by a given organization, sometimes subdivided into sets of product lines.

product portfolio Mix of products offered by an organization, grouped with reference to market share, cash flow, and growth characteristics.

product recall Retrieval by the manufacturer of products (usually defective) that are already in the hands of customers and/or channel intermediaries.

profit center An organizational unit whose revenues and costs are clearly identifiable and whose management is held responsible for controlling both sides of the income statement.

promotional activities Various nonrecurrent selling efforts, usually of a short-term nature, such as contests, discount coupons, special displays, and introductory offers.

psychographic segmentation Dividing the market into segments using variables such as people's life styles, values, attitudes, personalities, and interests.

public relations The managing of public perceptions of an organization and its products by making available news about the organization to the media, or by interacting directly with opinion leaders.

publicity The end result of the staging and publicizing of special events and activities to attract community attention, often via the news media.

pull strategy A marketing strategy based upon heavy advertising by the manufacturer to potential end users, with the objective of "pulling" the product through the channels of distribution (see also *push strategy*).

push strategy A marketing strategy in which the channels of distribution take major responsibility for promotional and personal selling efforts to end users, designed to "push" the product out of the store (see also *pull strategy*).

reach The number (or percentage) of target audience members who are exposed to an advertising campaign at least once.

reactive selling Letting customers take the initiative in seeking out the vendor, who then tries to complete the transaction (see also *proactive selling*).

roll out The process of extending distribution and advertising/promotion for a new product from a limited geographic area to a wider (or national) area.

secondary data Existing information in an accessible form that can be used to provide insights for management decision making or serve as inputs to new primary data collection efforts (see also *primary data*).

shopping products Products that the consumer, in the process of selection and purchase, characteristically compares on such bases as suitability, quality, price, and style (see also *convenience products* and *specialty products*).

specialty products Products with unique characteristics and/or brand identification for which a significant group of buyers are habitually willing to make a special purchasing effort (see also *convenience products* and *shopping products*).

spot advertising The purchase of TV or radio time on a station-by-station or market-by-market basis rather than networkwide.

stockkeeping unit (SKU) The lowest level of disaggregation at which a product can be ordered; it reflects size, style, color, and other distinctive variations.

store audit Retail and wholesale audits that track the movement of goods through the distribution channel to provide manufacturers with sales and market share data (see also *marketing audit*).

strategic business (management) unit (SBU/SMU) A unit within a larger organization that is essentially treated as a separate entity and established as an independent profit center, usually with a distinct mission, objective, competitive environment, and managerial requirements (see also *profit center*).

target market That portion of the total market the organization has selected to serve.

target marketing Focusing the marketing efforts on specific segments within the total market.

telemarketing Use of the telephone as a tool for marketing communication (e.g., sales and advertising) and as a channel for proactive account management.

test marketing Evaluating customer response to a new product by putting it on the market in a limited geographic area.

third-party payers Persons or organizations that provide the funding for projects, products, or services that benefit the user, or consumer.

time-series data See *longitudinal data*.

top-down planning Designing programs to be implemented by top-level management; participation filters down to the lower levels (see also *bottom-up planning*).

trademark A brand or part of a brand that is given legal protection and whose use is restricted to its owner.

trading up Encouraging current or prospective customers to purchase a more expensive version of a given product.

transit (or bus) card An advertisement mounted inside a public transit vehicle.

undifferentiated marketing strategy A plan whereby the organization treats the market as an aggregate and designs its products and marketing program to appeal to the greatest number of consumers possible.

usage segmentation Subdividing the total consumer market on the basis of where, when, why, and in what quantities the product is used.

value pricing Establishing price levels on the basis of how the buyer perceives the value of the product rather than on the basis of the costs to be recovered by the seller.

variable costs Costs that change in direct proportion to changes in activity, such as materials and parts, sales commissions, and certain labor and supplies (see also *fixed costs*).

vertical integration The process of purchasing or acquiring control over one's suppliers (see *backward integration*), or one's distributors (see *forward integration* and *horizontal integration*), or both.

wholesaler A business unit in the channel of distribution which buys goods or services from producers and resells them to other merchants or to institutional purchasers but not to household consumers.

Financial and Economic Analysis in Marketing

A financial or economic analysis is necessary to evaluate all major courses of action in marketing. Introducing a new product, entering a new market, changing price, or increasing the size of the sales force are all decisions that can have significant financial consequences.

In this appendix, we review some of the basic concepts of financial and economic analysis as applied to marketing decision making. We concentrate on simplified situations in order to focus on the key issues.

COSTS, PRICE, AND CONTRIBUTION

Variable costs (VC) change with the volume of the product produced or sold. For a manufacturer, variable costs typically would include the costs of materials and labor; as more units are manufactured, total variable costs increase. Variable costs are usually expressed as VC per unit. This is often a good representation of the way such costs vary over the relevant range of sales for marketing and decision making.

Fixed costs (FC) do not change with the volume and are those which would still be incurred, at least in the short run, even if no products were manufac-

tured or sold. Fixed costs can include the rental of a building, the cost of display cases, the advertising budget, and other expenses which would not change, once committed, irrespective of the volume sold or produced. See *Exhibit 1* for an example of variable and fixed costs.

Although in many analyses the two major cost categories are fixed and variable, in some situations a third type of cost, *semi-variable cost* (SVC), is important. Semi-variable costs tend to vary with the *capacity* to provide volume (often in stepwise fashion) as opposed to directly with volume itself. Such costs are particularly prevalent in service industries. For instance an airline might incur a semi-variable cost of $900 per flight (for fuel, salaries, and landing fees) when adding an extra flight a day on its Orlando to New York schedule; its variable cost might be only $6 per passenger boarded (for refreshments and ticketing costs). For theatre companies, the cost of running another performance of a show and for a retail store, the cost of opening an additional day are semi-variable costs. For a manufacturer, the decision to add an overtime shift to meet anticipated demand can involve semi-variable costs. Although we will not consider semi-variable costs explicitly in the remainder of this appendix, they are often quite im-

EXHIBIT 1
RELATIONSHIP OF VARIABLE AND FIXED COSTS

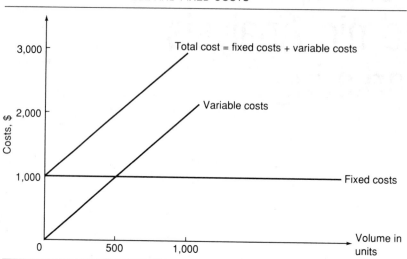

portant and need to be considered in an economic analysis of alternatives.

Price (P) per unit is the revenue obtained per unit, net of any discount offered to others in the distribution channel. Price per unit times *volume* (V) sold gives the total (or gross) revenue realized by the seller.

Contribution or margin per unit is the difference between price per unit and variable cost per unit, i.e.,

Unit contribution = P per unit − VC per unit

Similarly, total (or gross) contributions is the product of unit contribution times volume. Net contribution is equal to unit contribution times volume less fixed cost, i.e.,

Net contribution = [(P − VC) × (V)] − FC

To illustrate these concepts, consider the example of a fruit packer who is thinking of setting up a small factory to produce frozen raspberry juice. Rental costs of the factory and facilities, including such factors as utilities, insurance, and property taxes, are $150,000 annually. Sales force, advertising, market-ing, and other management operating costs are $200,000 per year. The costs of leasing specialized packing and freezing machinery, which has a useful life of five years, is $100,000 annually. The cost of raw materials and labor is $15 per case (12 large cans) of frozen raspberry juice. If the selling price of frozen raspberry juice is $37.50 per case, then we could calculate the following:

Fixed costs	= $150,000 + $200,000
	+ $100,000
	= $450,000
Variable costs per case	= $15
Selling price per unit	= $37.50
Unit contribution	= $37.50 − $15.00
	= $22.50

If the company expects to sell 24,000 cases in a year, then estimated costs and revenues would be as follows:

Total VC	= 24,000 × $15 = $360,000
Total revenue	= 24,000 × $37.50 = $900,000
Total contribution	= $540,000
Net contribution	= $540,000 − $450,000
	= $90,000

Next we shall examine some concepts that can be used to help evaluate the economics of deciding whether to set up the frozen raspberry juice factory.

BREAKEVEN ANALYSIS AND PROFITABILITY

Breakeven analysis allows management to calculate the level of sales required to cover the fixed costs of making any significant marketing change (see *Exhibit 2*). The breakeven volume is found by dividing the fixed costs by the unit contribution, i.e.,

$$\text{Breakeven volume (in units)} = \frac{\text{fixed costs}}{\text{unit contribution}}$$

In the case of the raspberry juice packer, the breakeven volume is

$$\frac{\$450,000}{\$22.50} = 20,000 \text{ cases}$$

If the alternative being examined involves a change from a current one, then the fixed cost component of the breakeven calculation is replaced by the amount of the change in the fixed costs. The importance of breakeven calculation is that it puts the focus on the profitability of a product, not just its sales volume.

One test of a marketing initiative is the feasibility of attaining the breakeven volume. If the current market size is 50,000 cases, then selling 20,000 cases means getting a 40% market share unless the market is expected to grow rapidly. If high market share is necessary for success, then competitive reaction must be carefully considered.

For many marketing alternatives, such as the introduction of a new product, it would be unreasonable to expect the project to achieve breakeven in its first year. In such a case management may look at the feasibility of attaining breakeven within two, three, or more years.

While public and nonprofit organizations may seek to obtain only a breakeven volume, most busi-

EXHIBIT 2
BREAKEVEN ANALYSIS

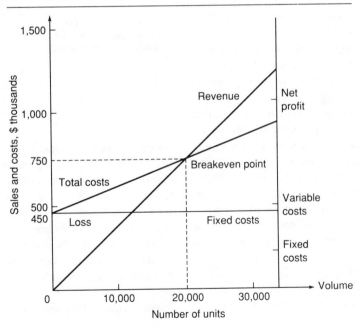

nesses would not go ahead with a project unless a profit was likely. While the profit required can be set in many ways, one alternative is to specify it as a percentage of the investment required. Target profitability volume in units can be calculated as follows:

$$\frac{\text{Target profitability}}{\text{volume (in units)}} = \frac{\text{fixed costs} + \text{target profit}}{\text{unit contribution}}$$

For example, if the raspberry juice producer had to invest $1 million to establish this business and set a target profit of 18% on the investment, then the number of units it would need to sell to achieve target profitability is calculated as follows:

$$\frac{\$450,000 + \$180,000}{\$22.50} = 28,000 \text{ cases}$$

Conditional Sales Forecasts and Response Functions

In many ways, a breakeven analysis evaluates a marketing program from a different perspective than that used in formulating the plan itself. The breakeven analysis produces a target volume and asks how feasible is its accomplishment. In contrast, the development of a marketing plan forecasts that a certain level of sales is expected if the specified plan is implemented. In other words, sales are a function of a specific marketing plan. More succinctly, and in the context of the marketing mix, we can say that the plan represents a *conditional sales forecast* in that the sales are conditional on a particular marketing mix. A response function is the part of the conditional sales forecast that explicitly links a response to one or more elements of the marketing mix.

Take, for instance, the example of advertising expenditure level for the management of a regional movie chain. In the present marketing plan, a monthly advertising expenditure of $20,000 is expected to result in attendance of 60,000 people. However, increasing the ad budget by 50% to $30,000 is expected to increase the number of attendees to 66,000; increasing advertising by another $10,000 is

expected, based on tests in other regions of the country, to raise attendance to 68,000 people. On the other hand, reducing advertising by $10,000 from the present budget of $20,000 is expected to reduce admissions to 50,000 people. Given these estimates then, a forecast of sales conditional on advertising would be as follows:

Advertising budget	Estimated attendance
$10,000	50,000
$20,000	60,000
$30,000	66,000
$40,000	68,000

As can be seen in *Exhibit 3*, attendance is much more sensitive to decreases than to increases in advertising. The profitability of changing the advertising level depends upon the contribution per ticket sold. If in this case the contribution were $3 per ticket sold, the following profitability analysis would help management to make a decision about the advertising budget:

(1) Advertising budget	(2) Estimated attendance	(3) Contribution before advertising, [$3 × (2)]	(4) Contribution after advertising, [(3) − (1)]
$10,000	50,000	$150,000	$140,000
$20,000	60,000	$180,000	$160,000
$30,000	60,000	$198,000	$168,000
$40,000	68,000	$204,000	$164,000

As can be seen, the most profitable level of sales is obtained when advertising spending is $30,000 for a contribution, after allowing for the expense of advertising, of $168,000. It is evident from looking at the data that the highest level of sales is not the most profitable level in this case.

This section has illustrated one form of profitability analysis. At times more complex techniques may be needed to adjust for the time value of money, to allow for risk and uncertainty, and to account for possible competitive response.

EXHIBIT 3
ADVERTISING RESPONSE FUNCTION

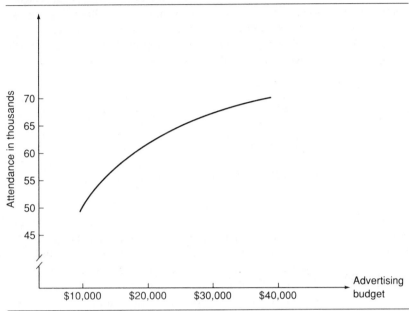

Uncertainty

Marketing managers develop marketing plans with the expectation that certain sales outcomes will be achieved. But they cannot be certain of those outcomes. A furniture manufacturer may find that a particular advertising campaign was not as effective as anticipated or an amusement park operator may do better than planned due to unusually pleasant weather. Competitors may also take actions which keep firms from reaching their goals. Thus, a new brand of shampoo may achieve a promising 10% market share in its test markets, but only a 4% share when an established competitor engages in extensive promotional activity during the new brand's national launch.

There is no simple way to account for uncertainty. A good first step, however, is to identify the major sources of uncertainty in the marketing plan. In gen-

eral, any uncertainties that have a significant impact on the final outcome need to be considered in depth. While no risk factor can be totally ignored, concentration should be placed on the critical ones. Market research may help to narrow the range of uncertainty.

One test of a marketing strategy is to examine its robustness in the face of difficulties. Consider, for example, an airline opening a new route using jumbo jets. The strategy would be robust if the airline could profitably substitute a smaller plane on the new route, using the jumbo jet on the charter market if traffic were not to develop as expected.

All risk cannot be eliminated from marketing decisions, but it can be reduced. While many approaches are available to deal with uncertainty, we will mention just two here. The first is to estimate a range of possible outcomes of a particular decision and determine if management is willing to live with the resulting risk. A typical approach is to construct three scenarios—optimistic, expected or most likely, and pessimistic. For example, suppose a shampoo marketer has developed a new line of shampoos to appeal to men whose hair is graying. To market the line, the company will need to invest in advertising and promotion. The company thinks it will sell 50,000 tubes annually, with a contribution margin of $2 per unit. However, if the product catches on, sales could go as high as 100,000 tubes. On the other hand, the product could make no headway at all in the market and sell only 10,000 units. Profitability under these three scenarios would be as follows:

	Optimistic	Most likely	Pessimistic
Sales, units	100,000	50,000	10,000
Contribution	$200,000	$100,000	$ 20,000
Fixed costs	$ 75,000	$ 75,000	$ 75,000
Net profit (loss)	$125,000	$ 25,000	$(55,000)

The company might look at these data and conclude that it could not afford a loss of $55,000 and would reject the project, at least in its present form, or it might feel that the chances of a profit are so much greater than the chances of a loss that the new shampoo should be launched. If it were to pursue this second course of action, the company would, of course, do whatever it could to prevent the pessimistic scenario.

A second approach to dealing with uncertainty is to try to estimate the proability of each outcome and then calculate an expected value. If the expected value is positive, then the company goes ahead with the project, assuming, naturally, that the firm has the funds required to invest in the project and that no better opportunities are available. While many pages could be devoted to a discussion of expected value, a common sense example is sufficient, for our purposes, to convey its meaning and illustrate its calculation. Suppose you make a bet with a somewhat naïve friend, saying that you will pay him $1 if a tossed coin comes out heads, but he will pay you $2 if the coin is tails. In the long run, half the coin tosses will result in heads and half in tails (assuming the coin is fair). So half the time you will pay a dollar and half the time you will win $2. Your expected value is therefore $0.50, calculated as follows:

$$\tfrac{1}{2}(-\$1) \quad + \quad \tfrac{1}{2}(\$2) \quad = -\$0.50 + \$1$$
$$= \quad \$0.50$$

Probabilities are not so easy to determine for management decisions, but market research and test marketing do help. To return to the shampoo marketer, suppose the company estimated that there was a 10% chance of the optimistic scenario, a 10% chance of the pessimistic, and an 80% chance of the most likely sales outcome. Then the expected profit from the new shampoo would be

$$0.10(\$125,000) + 0.80(25,000)$$
$$+ 0.10(-\$55,000) = \$27,000$$

In this case, the new product launch has a positive expected value, so it looks like the firm should go ahead with its plans.

Uncertainty is a reality for a manager. To consider only the most optimistic outcomes would be foolhardy, but to consider only the worst results would paralyze a company into inaction. Approaches such as those discussed here, which try to balance risk against profit, help managers make decisions in the face of an uncertain environment.

Longer Time Horizons

For some marketers, the time between taking an action and its impact on sales is very short. For example, when a fast food chain advertises a special free drink with each hamburger ordered for one week only, then the company's return is almost immediate. Other actions, however, involve a longer time frame, and it may be years before an investment earns its full return. For example, if the fast food chain opened a new store, it might take several years before the store became profitable and even longer before the store's full potential was realized. To be more concrete, suppose opening the new store involved an investment of $90,000 on the company's part and produced a loss of $10,000 for the first year and an expected profit of $60,000 in each of the next two years. The company treasurer insists that all projects must pay for themselves within three years. Should the company open this new store?

The problem in answering this question is that money received a year or two from now is worth less than money available now. If you have money now, you can invest it and earn interest. If you do not have it now, you can try to borrow it from the bank and pay the banker interest. Suppose you go to a bank and the loan officer offers to lend you $90,000 now if you pay the bank $100,000 a year from now. Then, in financial terms, the "present value discount factor" is 0.90 now. Similarly, a dollar paid two years from now is worth $0.81; calculated as $(0,90)(0.90) = \$0.81$. Using this notion of "present value," here is how we might calculate the return on the $90,000 investment in a new store:

Years from Now	Profit	Discount Factor	Value Now
1	− $10,000	0.90	− $ 9,000
2	60,000	(0.90)(0.90) = (0.81)	48,600
3	60,000	(0.90)(0.90)(0.90) = (0.729)	43,740
			$83,340

The return of $83,340 is less than the required investment of $90,000, so on economic grounds the company should not proceed with the investment.

How could the company change this outcome? If a longer time horizon for cost recovery were permitted, then perhaps the project would be viable. Another alternative would be to upgrade the value of future returns by attempting, for example, to borrow money more cheaply.

These actions require a careful consideration of the company's financial policies, particularly with regard to setting the terms for judging marketing plans that involve both expenditures and returns over several years. In this brief discussion we can only suggest the need for considering both the short- and long-term effects of marketing actions and point out that some way needs to be established for placing a value on future returns. Such policies generally involve deciding on a time horizon over which to measure returns and a means to discount the value of future returns.

CONCLUSION

Financial and economic analysis is an important part of the evaluation of all significant marketing alternatives. This section provides an introduction to some of the basic approaches that will be helpful in the cases included in this book. No one form of analysis, however, is sufficient to evaluate a course of action; the soundness of a plan must be judged against multiple criteria.

FINANCIAL AND ECONOMIC EXERCISES

1. Bengy Manufacturing, located in the Tucson, Arizona area, enjoys a 4% share of a total market of 75,000 emergency power generators that are sold in the southwest each year. Bengy offers its retailers and wholesalers a combined margin of 35% on a retail price of $2,000 per generator.

   Debra Stern, Bengy's controller, estimates that variable production costs amount to $785 per generator and fixed manufacturing costs total $260,000 per year. In addition, shipping and packaging costs of $40 per unit must be paid by Bengy. Management costs are $85,000 and the annual advertising budget is $80,000. The company employs one sales representative at a salary of $60,000 a year.

A. What are Bengy's fixed costs?

B. What are Bengy's variable costs per unit?

C. What is the unit contribution?

D. What is the breakeven volume for Bengy (in units)?

E. What market share is needed to achieve this volume?

F. What are Bengy's current profits?

G. If establishing the Bengy company involved an investment of $1,100,000 and the company requires a return of 18% on its capital, is the generator line still profitable? Justify your answer.

H. What are the profits after allowing for the required return on capital?

I. Ted Rastelli, the firm's vice-president for marketing, estimates Bengy can sell 4% more generators than it does presently by increasing its advertising budget from $80,000 to $100,000. Alternatively if he reduces the advertising budget by $20,000, he expects to sell 75 fewer units. Should Bengy raise or lower its advertising budget? Why?

J. What would the breakeven level (in units) be if the advertising budget were raised?

K. What would the breakeven level (in units) be if the advertising budget were lowered?

L. As an alternative to the change in advertising, Bengy is considering offering one free safety light with every generator sold. These safety lights cost Bengy $50 each. If this offer can increase generator sales by 150 units, what would be the change in total profits?

2. The Blume-James Doll Corporation has completed development of a new line of realistically proportioned dolls. It expects to sell 15,000 of these dolls in the first year, 25,000 in the second.

The following financial and sales data have been assembled:

Retail selling price	$60
Retail margin	50%
Materials cost/unit	$4.50
Labor cost/unit	$6.25
Packaging cost/unit	$0.25
Sales force salaries/expenses	$145,000
Manufacturing overhead, allocated (per unit)	$3.80
Administrative expenses	$68,000
Sales promotion, first year only	$35,000

Prepare a two-year financial summary for the new doll including: variable cost per unit, contribution per unit, total contribution, total fixed costs, breakeven volume, gross margin and net profit.

3. Madson Gloves (MG) is considering the addition of a new line of water proof gloves ("Water Smart") next year to its existing brand, "Stay Dry." First-year sales of the new line are projected at 300,000 pairs. *Exhibit 1* provides price and cost data. The sources of these sales are expected to be 20% from new customers, 40% from competitors' customers and 40% (of the 300,000) from previous buyers of MG's other brand, Stay Dry. Sales of Stay Dry totalled 200,000 pair this year and are expected to remain at this level if the new line is not introduced. Rena Aubman, manager of the Gloves Division, is concerned about the cannibalization of Stay Dry sales by the new line. Should the new line be introduced?

4. Locuster Industries (LI) is a major manufacturer of cleaning, baby and personal care products. Jason Flynn, manager of the Personal Care Prod-

EXHIBIT 1
MADSON GLOVES

	Current	Year 1 with new line	
	Stay Dry	Stay Dry	Water Smart
Factory selling price	$22.00	$22.00	$27.50
Variable costs	$14.50	$14.50	$20.00
Fixed costs	$825,000	$645,000	$1,510,000

ucts (PCP) Division, has just had a disturbing conversation with Deborah Cermeil, brand manager for the Quintene line of shampoos and conditioners. The Quintene brand was successfully introduced, two years ago, as an exclusive (professional-formula), "natural" line of hair-care products. However, the market for upscale shampoos and conditioners has matured; competitors are flooding the market and consumers are becoming much more price sensitive.

After reviewing several strategies, Mr. Flynn and Ms. Cermeil narrowed their choice down to two options beyond what Locuster was currently doing. *Exhibit 2* presents data for each of these options.

A. Introduce the Essence line, lower-priced "natural" hair-care products, under the Locuster company name.

B. Manufacture a line of private-label (Style Brand) "natural" hair-care products for a major drug store chain. The Quintene line is still very profitable and will be maintained, so Locuster does not have the capacity to undertake both new projects. In fact, management is uncertain about making *any* changes.

Prepare answers for the following two questions:

A. The PCP Division currently makes a profit of $5.3 million on factory sales of $35 million. Any strategy chosen must maintain this ratio. Based on the net profit percentage, what course of action should be taken?

B. What other factors should influence the PCP Division's choice of strategy?

5. Laura Jeffries, the owner of the Jenifer Beauty Parlour in Washington, D.C., has to decide whether or not to open a second shop in the newly opened Joshua Arms shopping mall in nearby Bethesda, Maryland. If she does so, she would incur a monthly cost of $5,000 for a rental of a fully equipped beauty parlour and would have to sign a minimum one year lease. Since Ms. Jeffries pays her employees on a commission basis, she estimates that each customer who comes to the store will provide a net return (contribution) to her of $5. She thinks it is most likely (about a 75% chance) that the suburban store will attract 1,000 customers a month, but there is a 10% chance that demand could be as low as 600 customers. There's a 15% chance, she thinks, that demand could reach 2,000 customers per month. Based on the experience of other beauty parlour owners, she believes that demand would not reach its full level until the third month of operation. The first two months would likely produce about half the sales of the other months, but would not be a good predictor of ultimate sales.

EXHIBIT 2   LOCUSTER INDUSTRIES

	Current		Projected Year 1			
	Quintene only	Quintene only	Quintene and Essence		Quintene and Style	
Sales (millions bottles)	3.0	2.8	2.0	3.0	2.5	1.8
Retail price	$6.00	$6.50	$6.50	$4.79	$6.50	$3.59
Factory price	$2.90	$3.10	$3.10	$2.25	$3.10	$2.05
Variable cost/bottle	$1.60	$1.70	$1.80	$1.10	$1.80	$1.00
Fixed costs:						
Manufacturing	$ 700,000	$ 700,000	$700,000	$ 700,000	$700,000	$700,000
Administration	600,000	600,000	600,000	600,000	600,000	300,000
Marketing	1,000,000	1,000,000	600,000	1,800,000	800,000	200,000

Should Ms. Jeffries open the beauty parlour at the Joshua Arms mall?

6. Star Airways, a major national airline, was considering operating an airplane shuttle service between Atlanta and Chicago. The airline was to be named Executive Airlines, and all necessary operating arrangements had been made. Operating the airline would cost $900,000 per month for leasing of airplanes, management, and marketing.

In addition, the incremental costs were as follows:

Per Flight:	
Crew pay	$189.22
Fuel	179.38
Airport landing fees	23.76
Airport personnel	21.12*
Per Passenger:	
Food and drinks	1.23
Commissions	1.76
Passenger liability insurance	0.62

* Provided by Star Airways at the stated cost per flight.

Patrick O'Donnell, the manager in charge of Executive Air, believes that at a price of $60 per flight, he can run 12 flights per weekday from 6 A.M. to 6 P.M. (6 each way), at an average of 68 passengers per flight. If Executive Air runs the planes at night or on the weekends, the additional service would have to charge half-price and expect to attract 40 passengers per flight. Executive would run 4 flights each weeknight (2 each way) and 10 flights (5 each way), each weekend day. The entire operation would depend on 2 jet airplanes being totally dedicated to the service.

A. Assuming that no night and weekend flights are run, prepare a monthly income statement for Executive Airlines.

B. Assuming night and weekend flights are to be run also, prepare a monthly income statement for Executive Airlines.

C. What should Mr. O'Donnell do? Why?

Use of Computers for Marketing Decision Making

A student recently commented to one of us that he could not imagine how we studied for our M.B.A. degrees (in the later 1960s) without pocket calculators. The immediate reply was, "Soon, students won't be able to imagine completing their degrees without a personal computer."

In the early days of computer development, some observers predicted that at most the world market for all computers would be a hundred or less. Others suggested that computers would replace managers and lead to sharp reductions in the number of managers. Neither forecast proved accurate—fortunately for all. Instead, computers and computer-based systems have become important aids in managerial analysis and decision making. Computers, when properly used, can lead to better decisions or decisions made more rapidly or more efficiently. Successful computer applications provide help to managers trying to deal with an uncertain, competitive, dynamic environment.

Access to a computer is not necessary for the study of the cases in this book. However, availability of a personal or other computer will reduce the time in which cases can be analyzed, increase the depth of analysis of alternative courses of action, and allow for an examination of a broader set of options. The course instructor will suggest the appropriate level of computer involvement, depending on the objectives of the course, the availability of computers, and your own computer skills.

Computer Aids and Managers

A computer can help in analyzing some, but not all, cases. The optional computer disk that accompanies this book lists the cases for which computer aids are available.

Economic and Profitability Analysis For most students, the first type of computer aid to be used in a marketing course will be a relatively straightforward program to do breakeven and profitability analyses. This kind of program allows the user to evaluate quickly the financial and economic implications of alternative courses of action from a set of assumptions about future demand, price, cost, and other factors. The program asks the user to input such data in a conversational format and then does the calculations necessary to generate income and other statements. The real challenge lies not in running the analysis but in establishing the appropriate assumptions, as will be seen in studying such cases as Co-

597

lumbia Plastics. While set within the context of a spreadsheet program, these programs are specially designed to be easily used by the neophyte. They greatly reduce the computational burden in testing assumptions, thereby allowing a more thorough evaluation of the cases.

For other cases, the computer programs assume some familiarity on the student's part with the use of spreadsheet programs. In these cases, data from a case and its exhibits have been transferred to the computer disk in a framework that makes it easy to analyze case information. For example, in the Crestlight Paper case, data on each sales representative's total sales, gross margin, number of accounts, potential, number of calls, salary, expenses, and commissions are available for use with a spreadsheet program. It is straightforward to calculate quickly such useful facts as each sales representative's profitability, sales per account, calls per account, and ratio of sales to potential. In the Cascade Foods case, data from a test market that examined the sales impact of different price and advertising levels at various stores and times are stored on the computer disk. By combining the data from the different stores and time periods, the effect of different marketing mix strategies can be assessed. More generally, the spreadsheet programs primarily involve application of the four basic arithmetic operations of addition, subtraction, multiplication, and division to tables of case data to derive meaningful information. Only limited knowledge of the use of spreadsheet programs is required; most students can learn to use the programs needed for this book's cases in less than a day. The payoff from this knowledge is the ability to carry out quickly a thorough analysis of case data and to test readily the impact of alternative plans.

Marketing Models Several cases in this book allow the use of specially developed marketing models. These models typically develop some structure that estimates the effect of marketing variables such as price, advertising, and product design on sales. For example, an important issue in the Castle Coffee case is how much money to spend on advertising. A successful analysis requires the manager to estimate the relationship between advertising and sales. While a computer is not necessary for such an analysis, using an appropriately designed computer model will help the manager to specify the nature of that relationship and predict the sales and profit consequences of different advertising levels. Computer models can also help a manager simulate possible market responses to different competitive actions. In the case of Hinesbury Mills, for instance, a competitor introduces a new type of cake mix. Market research data provides information on market segment structure and how people choose cake mixes. A computer simulation of the behavior of cake-mix-buying households can help the manager predict what share of the market the new cake mix will achieve if no action is taken or, alternatively, if the company introduces its own imitative cake mix. This model, in a slightly different form, was used by managers at Hinesbury Mills to help them make a decision. Another model that was implemented by an organization is treated in the "Lively Arts at Hanson" case. A student can use the product planning computer system employed at Hanson University to forecast attendance at performing arts events and help identify which events should be presented and promoted during the year.

Detailed descriptions of these models and the management problems which stimulated their development are given later in this Appendix.

Conclusion

The cases in this book do not require access to a computer. However, the increasing use of personal computers by managers and the potential of computers to help managers suggest the benefits of analyzing the cases with the aid of computers and spreadsheet programs. Some of the cases in this book can be studied at various levels of sophistication with the aid of specially developed computer programs. Remember, however, that the objective of any computer model—simple or sophisticated—is to help analyze and understand a marketing situation. Responsibility for discovering problems and developing, testing, and implementing sound, creative decisions rests with the manager.

Castle Coffee Company, II

William F. Massy
David B. Montgomery
Charles B. Weinberg

Since returning from a one-week management development course a few months before, Adrian Van Tassle had been working with Jack Stillman on the adaptation of a small "marketing planning model" to help him plan Castle Coffee's advertising budget for the coming fiscal year. Stillman, director of research for Castle, was quite experienced in computer models applied to a broad range of management problems. While Stillman had little or no experience in the marketing area, he had welcomed the opportunity to work with Van Tassle.

The model being developed (described in more detail later) was designed to aid a brand manager or advertising manager to determine a reasonable advertising budget for a product. Van Tassle felt that the model might help him to clarify his own thinking, to make sounder decisions, and to communicate better with management.

Inputs Required by the Planning Model

After reviewing the marketing planning model with Jack Stillman, Van Tassle asked Stillman to provide

Reprinted from *Stanford Business Cases 1985* with permission of the publishers, Stanford University Graduate School of Business. Specially revised for inclusion in this book. Copyright © 1985 by the Board of Trustees of the Leland Stanford Junior University.

a list of the basic inputs required by the model. After much tugging at his red mustache and several conferences with Stillman, Van Tassle arrived at a preliminary set of estimates for the basic inputs. The input list and the preliminary estimates are presented in *Exhibit 1*. Some of these factors were obvious; only the ones relating to market share and the advertising plan itself required a lot of thought.

Although Adrian Van Tassle had to develop a quarterly plan, he decided that the best first step would be to determine the size of the annual advertising budget. He felt that developing an annual plan would be relatively easier in that seasonal effects could be ignored and questions of how fast sales and market share respond to advertising could be postponed. In addition, he felt that the experience of developing an annual plan would sharpen his understanding of the model and his ability to use it.

After some thought Van Tassle concluded that if his advertising were reduced to zero for that year, he would lose perhaps half his market share in the first year, cutting it to a mere 2.7 percent. This would result partly from a slackening in consumer demand and partly from an accelerating erosion of Castle's distribution. If a zero rate of advertising were to be continued, he was relatively certain Castle would lose all its distribution, and hence market share. On the other hand, pushing advertising to saturation

EXHIBIT 1
PRELIMINARY VALUES FOR INPUTS TO THE
ADVERTISING PLANNING MODEL
(Annual plan)

EXHIBIT 1
PRELIMINARY VALUES FOR INPUTS TO THE
ADVERTISING PLANNING MODEL
(Annual plan)

Variable	Preliminary value
Number of periods	1
Reference market share	.054
Maintenance advertising per year (millions of dollars)	8.0
Market share at end of year if during the year:	
No advertising	.027
Saturation advertising	.10
20% increase in advertising	.060
Market share in long run with no advertising	0
Media efficiency	1.0
Copy effectiveness	1.0
Contribution ($/unit)	4.50
Brand price ($/unit)	17.20
Initial market share (the March–April result)	.054
Annual product sales (industry sales, in millions of cases)	88
Product price ($/unit)	17.20

might nearly double the company's share, to about 10 percent. "Of course," he commented to Stillman, "that figure could as well be 9 percent or even 11 percent or 12 percent. We've never come close to blitzing the ad budget." He also believed that the most likely result on a 20 percent increase in advertising would be a 6 percent market share (up from 5.4 percent) though here again there was considerable uncertainty. Van Tassle still wasn't sure how quickly this increase would be observed, but he felt that this would surely occur by the fourth quarter after the change.

Van Tassle had run the model using data that represented his plans as they had existed at the beginning of the 1982 fiscal year. At that time, the late spring of 1981, he had estimated the previous period's market share at 5.5 percent; however, the market share report he later received estimated market share (called "Most Recent Market Share" in the computer model) at 5.4 percent. According to the results of the theater tests, the copy effectiveness for the autumn-winter-spring campaign, he had recently

learned, was rated at 0.90. (Curiously, the "old" advertising copy used in the summer of 1981 had been rated at 1.0.) In addition, as compared to last year, Van Tassle now had judgments concerning maximum and minimum shares, a subject he had not thought about last year. In using the advertising planning model, Van Tassle first set the levels of brand advertising at the amounts he had planned for the year, not the amounts actually expended. Given the confusion with the media schedule caused by the abrupt cancellation of 20 percent of Castle's advertising weight during the winter quarter, Van Tassle wondered whether a run of the model with actual expenditures would be meaningful. The inputs and outputs for this run are shown in *Exhibit 2*.

Quarterly Plan Van Tassle next decided to test a quarterly plan. Stillman indicated that some changes in the values of the variables would have to be made. Some were obvious: average sales rate per quarter is the annual rate divided by four. Other changes were more difficult. For example, if there were no advertising for a year, market share would drop by 50 percent (i.e., to 0.027) at the end of the year. Stillman suggested that market share fell off by quarter in approximately the same way that a bank compounded interest—in this case at the rate of 16 percent per quarter. Thus, if there were no advertising for four quarters, market share would drop to approximately 84 percent, 71 percent, 60 percent and 50 percent of the initial value. This seemed to be a reasonable approach, so Van Tassle let Stillman make the calculations which led to the data in *Exhibit 3*. Van Tassle made some trial runs of a quarterly plan, as shown in *Exhibit 4*.

Next Year's Budget Van Tassle gave a final pull to his mustache, and turned to the evaluation of the results of running his model on quarterly data. He expected he would want to make a series of additional runs, including tests of alternative plans for fiscal year 1983 before making his advertising budget presentation and recommendation to management. He expected that use of the model would help clarify his thinking and lead to a better recommendation. He

EXHIBIT 2 RUN OF ADVERTISING PLANNING MODEL (ANNUAL)

```
+-------------------------------------------------------------------+
            +--------------------------------------------+
                        CASTLE COFFEE COMPANY
            +--------------------------------------------+
            This spreadsheet contains two advertising
            planning models to help Mr. Van Tassle plan
            Castle Coffee's advertising budget.

            The first is an ANNUAL plan which may be used
            to determine the size of the annual budget
            and sharpen the understanding of the models.

            The second is a more detailed QUARTERLY plan
            for developing the actual budget.

                    HIT <Home> TO BEGIN.
            Hit <Alt-I> to return to these instructions.
+-------------------------------------------------------------------+
+---SCREEN 1A: Castle Coffee Company -------------- ANNUAL MODEL ----------------+
  Annual Industry Sales
   (millions of cases)          {    88   }   Market Share at YEAR END If . . .
  Maintenance Advert'g $mm       {    $8   }      No Advertising          {    2.70%  }
  Market Share @ Maintenance  {  5.40%  }      20% Incr in Adv'g        {    6.00%  }
  Most Recent Market Share     {  5.40%  }      Saturation Adv'g         {   10.00%  }
  Long Run Shr Without Adv'g   {   .00%  }      Brand Advertising $mm    {    $9.28  }

        YEAR END OUTCOMES* (in thousands)
         Market Share                     5.89%
         Industry Unit Sales             88,000          *Outcomes are based on
         Brand Unit Sales                 5,180          a price of $17.20 and unit
         Brand Dollar Sales             $89,089          contribution of $4.50.
         Gross Contribution (Bef Adv)   $23,308
         Net Contribution (After Adv)   $14,028
         Slope:Net $Contrib/$Adv            .41
+-------------------------------------------------------------------+
  Enter Decisions and Estimates Between { }'s. Hit <F9> to Recalculate.
  Hit <Tab> for Quarterly Model, <PgDn> for Advertising Response Function.
+-------------------------------------------------------------------+
+---SCREEN 1A: Castle Coffee Company -------------- ANNUAL MODEL ----------------+
  Annual Industry Sales
   (millions of cases)          {    88   }   Market Share at YEAR END If . . .
  Maintenance Advert'g $mm       {    $8   }      No Advertising          {    2.70%  }
  Market Share @ Maintenance  {  5.40%  }      20% Incr in Adv'g        {    6.00%  }
  Most Recent Market Share     {  5.40%  }      Saturation Adv'g         {   10.00%  }
  Long Run Shr Without Adv'g   {   .00%  }      Brand Advertising $mm    {    $8.64  }
                                                                         ======

        YEAR END OUTCOMES* (in thousands)
         Market Share                     5.65%
         Industry Unit Sales             88,000          *Outcomes are based on
         Brand Unit Sales                 4,971          a price of $17.20 and unit
         Brand Dollar Sales             $85,499          contribution of $4.50.
         Gross Contribution (Bef Adv)   $22,369
         Net Contribution (After Adv)   $13,729
         Slope:Net $Contrib/$Adv            .48
+-------------------------------------------------------------------+
```

EXHIBIT 3
CHANGES IN PRELIMINARY VALUES OF REFERENCE CASE CONDITIONS FOR
INPUTS TO THE ADVERTISING PLANNING MODEL
(Quarterly plan)

Variable	Preliminary
Number of periods	4
Maintenance advertising per quarter (millions of dollars)	2.0
Market share at end of quarter if during the quarter:	
No advertising	.0454
Saturation advertising	.0686
20% increase in advertising	.0559
Quarterly product sales (industry sales in millions of cases)	22

also hoped that the model would permit him to develop a better presentation so as to more effectively communicate his objectives and assumptions to management. He was not quite sure how to go about pursuing these goals and recognized he would have to develop his own methods of approach as he went along.

Structure of the Model

The advertising planning model available to Van Tassle was designed to help him evaluate the impact of different advertising budget levels primarily on market share. While advertising and other effects on industry sales were also represented in the model, this was not its main focus.

The model was intended to help a manager translate both subjective estimates and data from past events and market research studies about responses to advertising into a systematic framework. The model encompassed enough critical variables to provide acceptable outputs—given reasonable judgment in estimating the variables. Yet at the same time it was not so complex and cluttered that it became difficult for the manager to understand and apply.

Using the Model To use the model, the manager first needed to estimate four quantities (see *Exhibit 5*):

1. If a brand's advertising is reduced to zero, there is a minimum point (min) to which brand share

will fall from its current or initial value by the end of one time period.
2. If a brand's advertising is increased a great deal, to a saturation level, there is a maximum point (max) beyond which sales will not rise by the end of one time period.
3. There is some advertising rate that will maintain current market share, called the maintenance level of advertising.
4. If there is a 20 percent increase in a brand's advertising over the maintenance rate, share would increase to a new level by the end of one time period.

The estimates of these four quantities are used to estimate an advertising response function for one period, as shown in *Exhibit 6*. Algebraically, the relationship can be written as follows:

$$\text{Share} = \text{min} + \frac{(\text{max} - \text{min})(\text{adv})^b}{a + (\text{adv})^b}$$

The min, max, a and b are implicitly determined by the input data. The diagram in *Exhibit 6* shows an S-shaped curve, i.e., at low levels of spending there is very little effect of advertising on share and there are first increasing and then decreasing returns to scale. (This is not required by the equation. If $b > 1$, the curve will be S-shaped, for $0 < b \leq 1$, a concave function. The particular value of b will depend on the estimate provided in response to item 4 above.)

EXHIBIT 4 RUN OF ADVERTISING PLANNING MODEL (QUARTERLY)

```
+---SCREEN 1B: Castle Coffee Company--------------------QUARTERLY MODEL---------+

     Quarterly Industry Sales (millions of cases)        {      22    }
     Maintenance Advertising/Quarter ($ millions)        {       2    }

     Market Share at Maintenance Advertising             {     5.40%  }
     Most Recent Market Share                            {     5.40%  }
     Long Run Market Share With No Advertising           {      .00%  }

     Market Share at END OF QUARTER if . . .
        No Advertising                                   {     4.54%  }
        20% Increase in Advertising                      {     5.59%  }
        Saturation Advertising                           {     6.86%  }

+-----------------------------------------------------------------------------+
              Enter Model Inputs Between (   )'s. Hit <F9> to Recalculate.
              Hit <PgDn> for Decisions, Estimates, and Outcomes.
+-----------------------------------------------------------------------------+
```

```
+---SCREEN 2B: Castle Coffee -----------------------------QUARTERLY MODEL---------+
```

ADVERTISING DECISIONS		Qtr 1	Qtr 2	Qtr 3	Qtr 4	
Brand Advert'g (millions)	{	$1.60	$2.40	$2.88	$2.40	}
SEASONALITY AND OTHER ESTIMATES						
Product Seasonality Index	{	.85	1.00	1.15	1.00	}
Advert'g Maintenance Index	{	.80	1.00	1.20	1.00	}
Media Efficiency Index	{	1.00	1.00	1.00	1.00	}
Copy Effectiveness Index	{	1.00	1.00	1.00	1.00	}
OUTCOMES (000's Unless Noted)						
Market Share		5.40%	5.59%	5.75%	5.88%	
Industry Unit Sales		18,700	22,000	25,300	22,000	
Brand Unit Sales		1,010	1,230	1,455	1,294	
Brand Dollar Sales		$17,369	$21,153	$25,021	$22,265	
Gross Contribution (Bef Adv)		$4,544	$5,534	$6,546	$5,825	
Net Contribution (After Adv)		$2,944	$3,134	$3,666	$3,425	
Cumulative Net Contribution		$2,944	$6,078	$9,744	$13,169	
Slope: Net $Contrib/$Adv		.90	.38	.15	.35	

```
+-----------------------------------------------------------------------------+
       Enter Decisions and Est's Between {   }'s. <F9> for CALC, <Alt-E> for END.
+-----------------------------------------------------------------------------+
+---SCREEN 2B: Castle Coffee -----------------------------QUARTERLY MODEL---------+
```

ADVERTISING DECISIONS		Qtr 1	Qtr 2	Qtr 3	Qtr 4	
Brand Advert'g (millions)	{	$1.60	$2.40	$2.64	$2.40	}
SEASONALITY AND OTHER ESTIMATES				======		
Product Seasonality Index	{	.85	1.00	1.15	1.00	}
Advert'g Maintenance Index	{	.80	1.00	1.20	1.00	}
Media Efficiency Index	{	1.00	1.00	1.00	1.00	}
Copy Effectiveness Index	{	1.00	1.00	1.00	1.00	}
OUTCOMES (000's Unless Noted)						
Market Share		5.40%	5.59%	5.66%	5.81%	
Industry Unit Sales		18,700	22,000	25,300	22,000	
Brand Unit Sales		1,010	1,230	1,431	1,277	
Brand Dollar Sales		$17,369	$21,153	$24,620	$21,972	
Gross Contribution (Bef Adv)		$4,544	$5,534	$6,441	$5,749	
Net Contribution (After Adv)		$2,944	$3,134	$3,801	$3,349	
Cumulative Net Contribution		$2,944	$6,078	$9,879	$13,228	
Slope: Net $Contrib/$Adv		.90	.38	.23	.35	

```
+-----------------------------------------------------------------------------+
```

EXHIBIT 5
INPUTS FOR ESTIMATING SHARE RESPONSE TO ADVERTISING IN ONE PERIOD

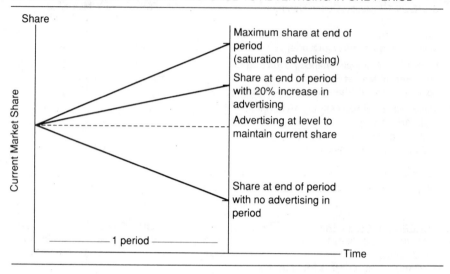

EXHIBIT 6
ADVERTISING RESPONSE FUNCTION

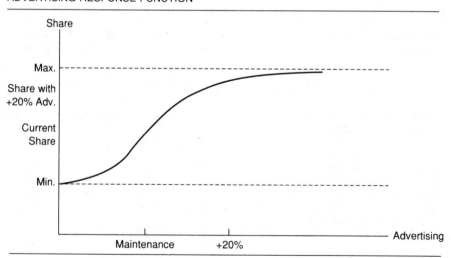

Carryover Effects and Time Delays   To take into account carryover effects and time delays, the model assumes:

1. In the absence of advertising, share would eventually decay to some long run minimum value (long run min). Its value can possibly be zero.
2. The decay in one time period will be a constant fraction of the gap between current share and the long run minimum, i.e., decay is exponential.

The term "persistence" denotes the fraction of the difference between share and long run minimum that is retained each period after decay. Algebraically,

$$\text{Persistence} = \frac{\text{min} - \text{long run min}}{\text{current share} - \text{long run min}}$$

and

$$\begin{aligned}\text{Share }(t) - \text{long run min} &= (\text{persistence}) \\ &[\text{share}(t-1) - \text{long run min}] \\ &+ \frac{(\text{max-min}[\text{adv})(t)]^b}{a + [\text{adv}(t)]^b}\end{aligned}$$

This is a simple, dynamic model. Share is based on a carryover from last period's share plus the effect of current advertising. It is explainable and it behaves reasonably.

To adjust advertising for media and copy, two time-varying indices are constructed: (1) a media efficiency index and (2) a copy effectiveness index. Both will be assumed to have a reference value of 1.0. The model then hypothesizes that the delivered advertising, i.e., the adv(t) that goes into the response function is given by

$$\begin{aligned}\text{adv}(t) = &[\text{media efficiency}(t)] \\ &[\text{copy effectiveness}(t)][\text{adv dollars}(t)]\end{aligned}$$

The media efficiency and copy effectiveness indices can be determined subjectively, but better alternatives exist. Copy testing is helpful; data on media costs and exposures by market segment and relative value of market segments can be used to develop a media index.

Other Factors   Thus far Van Tassle had taken up share responses to advertising, media efficiency, copy effectiveness, and share dynamics. Next he considered product class sales. Two important phenomena here were seasonality and trend. These and any similar effects could be combined into a product class index that varies with time. Thus,

$$\begin{aligned}\text{Product class sales}(t) = &\\ [\text{reference product class sales}]&\\ [\text{product class sales index}(t)]&\end{aligned}$$

Contribution and Slope   Upon looking at the outputs in *Exhibits 2* and *4*, Van Tassle was somewhat puzzled by the rows entitled "Net Contribution (After Adv)" and "Slope: Net (Contrib/$Adv." Stillman explained that slope (marginal profit) and contribution measured two different elements. Contribution measured the aggregate results in only one period; slope estimated the marginal return (marginal revenue—marginal cost) from advertising. In addition, when used for the quarterly model, slope included an estimate of the revenue impact of the carryover effect of advertising; for example, a fraction of the customers attracted to Castle Coffee in one quarter by advertising might repeat purchase in future quarters, so that advertising in one period might have an impact on future profits. This was a particular concern in planning the quarterly budget. Slope attempted to measure this carryover effect by estimating repeat sales in future periods. In the quarterly model, repeat sales for a full year were included in the estimate of slope.

Hinesbury Mills, II

Gerald J. Eskin
Christopher H. Lovelock

The marketing research department at Hinesbury Mills, Inc., a leading foods manufacturer, had been assigned the task of developing a simulation model of the cake-mix market. Hinesbury Mills had recently added a premium cake mix, containing real butter, to its existing standard-mix line, only to see the two major competitors, Allied Foods Corporation and Concorn Kitchens, Inc., counter with ''add-butter'' varieties of mix. These mixes called for consumers to add their own butter, rather than including any shortening in the mix, and retailed at $.79 (the same price as standard mixes) compared to Hinesbury's $1.19 price for its premium cake mix.

Hinesbury's management was concerned about the possible impact of the competition's add-butter lines on its own premium mix. Hinesbury was also undecided as to whether or not it should introduce a line of add-butter mixes of its own; and if so, whether such a line should be allowed to complement or replace the existing premium line.

The objective of the simulation model was to

develop a greater understanding of the purchase decision process and to derive predictions of the future market performance of standard, premium and add-butter lines under differing assumptions. Drawing on management's existing knowledge of the cake-mix market, and also on the transcripts of some recently completed interviews with consumers concerning their cake-buying and making habits, the marketing research department began its task of building the model. Duncan Gateau, manager of marketing research, explained how the model was intended to work.

The Decision Flow Model

The first step in building the model, Gateau noted, was to develop a simple but explicit depiction of the decision flow involved in the purchase of a cake mix by consumers. The resulting flow diagram was based on both managerial experience and information obtained from studying the consumer interview transcripts, and is illustrated in *Exhibit 1*.

In this flow diagram, consumers are shown coming to the market with a perceived need for a particular type of cake mix. They then form a perception of each product's characteristics concerning factors

EXHIBIT 1 DECISION FLOW MODEL

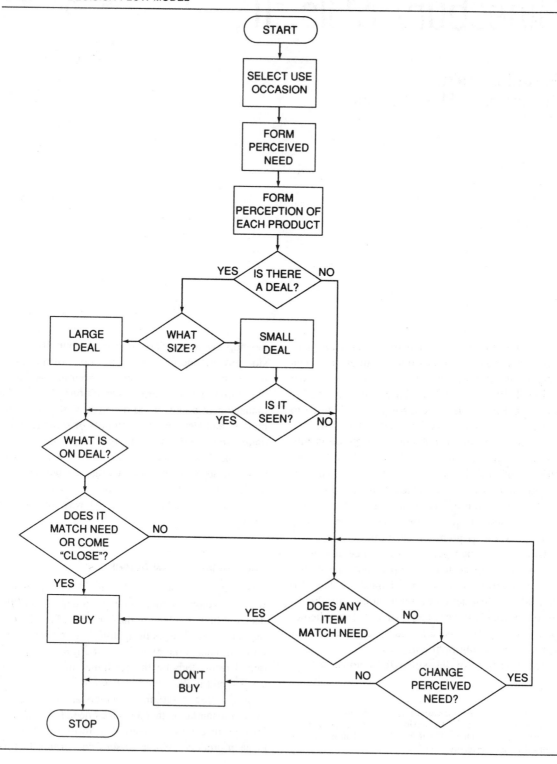

such as quality, taste and texture, and what is actually involved in transforming the mix into a finished cake, etc.

Consumers try to find a product that matches their perceived needs (these needs being related to particular use occasions). Complications arise whenever there are special deals being offered or when consumers cannot find exactly what they are looking for.

In the case of deals, there are several issues to be considered. First, consumers may or may not be aware that a deal is present in the market. Whenever promotional activity is extensive (for example, displays at 3 for $2) it is assumed that all relevant consumers become aware of this fact. These ''Large Deal'' promotions in the model contrast ''Small Deal'' promotions such as ''5 cents off'' which are sometimes missed. Once consumers are aware of a deal, they will determine if it fits their perceived needs. If it fits exactly they will, of course, purchase the item. If not, they will consider the trade-off between the lower price and the fact that the product is not exactly what they want.

Matches are easier in the deal situation because the consumer will always be willing to accept higher quality than originally desired as long as there is no additional cost to this choice. She or he will also be willing to accept lower prices as long as there is no loss in quality associated with this decision.

If no exact match is found to a deal item, it is still possible that the deal item will be purchased. This will occur when the item is ''close enough'' to the perceived need to be attractive at the special price. What is ''close enough'' depends on the use occasion envisioned and the nature of the preference structure. For some special occasions, only an exact match will do, while for snacks, ''almost anything'' will do at a special price. What is ''close enough'' is modeled by a set of decision rules specific to each use occasion and initial need structure. These were subjectively assigned by the model building team after listening to the protocol tapes where consumers talked about how they made such decisions.

If no deal item is purchased, non-deal items will be considered and again the consumer will look for a match between needs and perceived product attributes. If a match is found, a purchase results. If no match is found, the consumer considers which component of her or his perceived need is least important and looks for a product that matches needs in all respects except on this one dimension. The way this search is accomplished in the model is to have the consumer change the perceived need in terms of this ''least important'' dimension and again look for a match. The thing that is ''least important'' will depend on the intended use for the product. For special occasions ''quality'' will never be ''least important'' while for snack use, quality may well play this role. For the snack occasion, the consumer may be unwilling to give up ''low price.''

Perceived Need   In order to ascertain whether or not a purchase will take place, it was necessary to be able to identify all the perceived needs that a consumer might be expected to have, and to relate these to the perceived characteristics of different brands and types of cake mix. The resulting matching process is illustrated in *Exhibit 2*, which is a specially prepared excerpt from a model run.

The Marketing Research staff decided that the basis of the perceived need for a mix was the occasion at which the resulting cake might be served, i.e., the primary use to which the product was to be put. Accordingly, three basic serving occasions were identified.

#1 = Snack
#2 = Everyday family dinner
#3 = Special

Note that each of the consumers in *Exhibit 2* is classified into one of these three primary use categories, and is then assigned a four-digit number describing four other factors which were considered to form part of her or his perceived need. These other factors relate to the quality level desired in the product, the price the consumer is prepared to pay for a product of a given quality, the extent to which she or he desires a convenience product as opposed to one offering a degree of personal involvement, and finally the type of taste and texture desired in the finished

EXHIBIT 2 TRACE OF EXCERPT FROM TYPICAL RUN OF CONSUMERS THROUGH MODEL

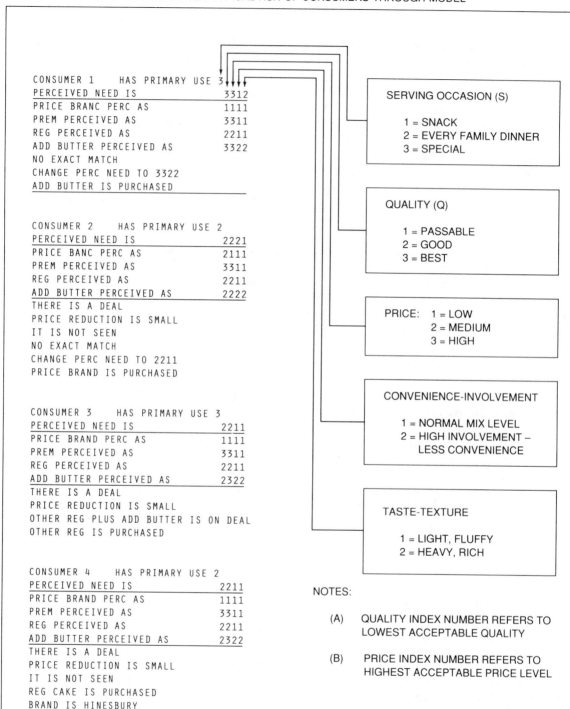

```
CONSUMER 1    HAS PRIMARY USE 3
PERCEIVED NEED IS              3312
PRICE BRANC PERC AS            1111
PREM PERCEIVED AS              3311
REG PERCEIVED AS               2211
ADD BUTTER PERCEIVED AS        3322
NO EXACT MATCH
CHANGE PERC NEED TO 3322
ADD BUTTER IS PURCHASED


CONSUMER 2    HAS PRIMARY USE 2
PERCEIVED NEED IS              2221
PRICE BANC PERC AS             2111
PREM PERCEIVED AS              3311
REG PERCEIVED AS               2211
ADD BUTTER PERCEIVED AS        2222
THERE IS A DEAL
PRICE REDUCTION IS SMALL
IT IS NOT SEEN
NO EXACT MATCH
CHANGE PERC NEED TO 2211
PRICE BRAND IS PURCHASED


CONSUMER 3    HAS PRIMARY USE 3
PERCEIVED NEED IS              2211
PRICE BRAND PERC AS            1111
PREM PERCEIVED AS              3311
REG PERCEIVED AS               2211
ADD BUTTER PERCEIVED AS        2322
THERE IS A DEAL
PRICE REDUCTION IS SMALL
OTHER REG PLUS ADD BUTTER IS ON DEAL
OTHER REG IS PURCHASED


CONSUMER 4    HAS PRIMARY USE 2
PERCEIVED NEED IS              2211
PRICE BRAND PERC AS            1111
PREM PERCEIVED AS              3311
REG PERCEIVED AS               2211
ADD BUTTER PERCEIVED AS        2322
THERE IS A DEAL
PRICE REDUCTION IS SMALL
IT IS NOT SEEN
REG CAKE IS PURCHASED
BRAND IS HINESBURY
```

SERVING OCCASION (S)

1 = SNACK
2 = EVERY FAMILY DINNER
3 = SPECIAL

QUALITY (Q)

1 = PASSABLE
2 = GOOD
3 = BEST

PRICE: 1 = LOW
        2 = MEDIUM
        3 = HIGH

CONVENIENCE-INVOLVEMENT

1 = NORMAL MIX LEVEL
2 = HIGH INVOLVEMENT –
    LESS CONVENIENCE

TASTE-TEXTURE

1 = LIGHT, FLUFFY
2 = HEAVY, RICH

NOTES:

(A) QUALITY INDEX NUMBER REFERS TO
     LOWEST ACCEPTABLE QUALITY

(B) PRICE INDEX NUMBER REFERS TO
     HIGHEST ACCEPTABLE PRICE LEVEL

```
CONSUMER 5     HAS PRIMARY USE 3          CONSUMER 8     HAS PRIMARY USE 2
PERCEIVED NEED IS            2211         PERCEIVED NEED IS            2222
PRICE BRAND PERC AS          2111         PRICE BRAND PERC AS          2111
PREM PERCEIVED AS            3311         PREM PERCEIVED AS            3311
REG PERCEIVED AS             2211         REG PERCEIVED AS             2211
ADD BUTTER PERCEIVED AS      3222         ADD BUTTER PERCEIVED AS      3222
THERE IS A DEAL                           ADD BUTTER IS PURCHASED
PRICE REDUCTION IS SMALL
IT IS NOT SEEN
PRICE BRAND IS PURCHASED
                                          CONSUMER 9     HAS PRIMARY USE 3
                                          PERCEIVED NEED IS            3321
                                          PRICE BRAND PERC AS          2111
CONSUMER 6     HAS PRIMARY USE 3          PREM PERCEIVED AS            3311
PERCEIVED NEED IS            3321         REG PERCEIVED AS             2211
PRICE BRAND PERC AS          2111         ADD BUTTER PERCEIVED AS      3222
PREM PERCEIVED AS            3311         NO EXACT MATCH
REG PERCEIVED AS             2211         CHANGE PERC NEED TO 3311
ADD BUTTER PERCEIVED AS      3222         PREM IS PURCHASED
THERE IS A DEAL
PRICE REDUCTION IS SMALL
IT IS NOT SEEN
NO EXACT MATCH                            CONSUMER 10     HAS PRIMARY USE 3
CHANGE PERC NEED TO 3311                  PERCEIVED NEED IS            2211
PREM IS PURCHASED                         PRICE BRAND PERC AS          2111
                                          PREM PERCEIVED AS            3311
                                          REG PERCEIVED AS             2211
                                          ADD BUTTER PERCEIVED AS      3322
CONSUMER 7     HAS PRIMARY USE 3          REG CAKE IS PURCHASED
PERCEIVED NEED IS            2211         BRAND IS OTHER REG
PRICE BRAND PERC AS          2111
PREM PERCEIVED AS            3311
REG PERCEIVED AS             2211         BRAND SHARES
ADD BUTTER PERCEIVED AS      3322         HINESBURY REG    6.22222E-02
THERE IS A DEAL                           HINESBURY PREM   4.66667E-02
PRICE REDUCTION IS LARGE                  OTHER REG        .186667
OTHER REG PLUS ADD BUTTER IS ON DEAL      ADD BUTTER       9.33333E-02
NO EXACT MATCH                            PRICE BRAND      .124444
OTHER REG IS PURCHASED                    TOTAL PURCHASE   10
```

product. Various classifications were established for each of these factors, as shown below:

    (a) Quality level ("Q")
        1 = Passable
        2 = Good
        3 = Best
    (b) Price level ("P")
        1 = Low
        2 = Medium
        3 = High
    (c) Convenience-involvement ("C")
        1 = Normal cake-mix level
        2 = Desire for high involvement, less convenience
    (d) Taste-texture ("T")
        1 = Light, fluffy
        2 = Heavy, rich

Price and quality are interrelated, in that a consumer wanting a top quality cake would be prepared to pay a high price; alternatively a consumer seeking a low price cake mix would be expected to accept one of passable level of quality. The need for the convenience-involvement index was explained by Gateau as follows: From research findings, it was believed that some consumers were primarily concerned with minimizing the time and effort required to make a cake while others desired the satisfaction obtained from greater personal involvement in the cake-mixing task. The taste-texture classification, while fairly broad, made it possible for the model to reflect varying consumer preferences concerning the consistencies of cakes made from different types of mix.

Interpreting the Trace With the system outlined above, it was theoretically possible to describe any type of consumer. For example, one who wanted a cake to serve for a special occasion (No. 3) and who had a perceived need (listed in the order QPCT) for a mix of good quality (2), with a normal level of convenience (1) and producing a light, fluffy cake (1) would be designated as having primary use No. 3 and perceived need 2211. Note that the perceived need for a good quality (2) implies a willingness to

pay a medium price (2) in order to obtain this quality level. However, it is possible that once in the marketplace, the consumer may succeed in finding a cake which is perceived as being medium quality but which also happens to be offered at a low price; in such a case she or he is predicted to purchase a 2111 cake-mix in preference to one perceived as 2211.

On the basis of consumer test results and managerial judgment, Gateau felt it was realistic to try to describe the product in the same kind of terms. Accordingly, the characteristics of each of the four types of regular cake on the market were categorized against their ability to satisfy consumers' perceived needs. *Regular cake* was taken as the norm and always assigned a code of 2211 (see *Exhibit 2*), namely good quality, medium price, normal convenience-involvement level, and light, fluffy taste-texture.

For other types of cake, there were always some uncertainty components, reflecting varying consumer perceptions. Probabilities were assigned to the occurrence of these components for each type of product. Thus, *private label* mixes might be viewed in the model as being of either passable or good quality, but the other three components were all fixed at level 1. Consequently, they might appear either as 1111 or 2111. *Premium mixes* might be viewed as of either good or best quality, with prices being fixed as high, convenience-involvement as normal, and taste-texture as light and fluffy. Finally, *add-butter* mixes were viewed in the model as high on involvement, and heavy, rich on taste-texture; however, quality perception might be either good or best and price as medium or high.

How the price of *add-butter* was perceived depended on how consumers thought about the extra costs associated with adding their own shortening. The recipe on the box called for adding real *butter* as the shortening agent. If consumers did this and included the cost of butter in their perception of costs, they would view the product as costing about the same as *premium cake*. If butter costs were not included in this perception, the consumer would view the cost of the *add-butter cake* as being the same as *regular cake*. It was possible that some consumers might use margarine in spite of recipe directions.

This might result in a cost perception below premium but above regular. This last possibility was not considered in the model.

Based upon the above four factors, it was assumed by the model-builders that every consumer would have an individual perception of each type or brand of cake mix.

To summarize, feasible values for perceived needs for different types of products were as follows:

Regular cake	2211 (always)
Private label	1111 or 2111
Premium cake	2311 or 3311
Add-butter	2222, 2322, 3222 or 3322

Quantifying the Input Once the design of the model had been formalized, it was necessary to provide the input. Areas requiring quantification were total market profile and presence of a deal or price reduction.

The assignment of consumers into primary use categories was done on a probabilistic basis, reflecting the proportion of total cake mix purchases made for each of the three primary use purposes. Within each of these groups the simulation team then had to quantify perceived needs (e.g., how many of those wanting to serve cake for snacks would require each of the quality/price levels, each convenience level and each texture type). These data were derived from judgments formed after reviewing the tapes on which consumers discussed their cake-buying and making habits. Previous surveys on cake usage were also used as inputs. A summary of the inputs is shown in *Exhibit 3*.

Meantime, the presence of deals or price reductions was simulated by estimating the probabilities of an individual consumer's finding a deal of any sort, of such a deal being large rather than small, of the consumer's noticing only a small price reduction, and of the deal being Hinesbury's rather than Allied's or Concorn's.

Running the Model Next, an artificial random population of consumers was run through the model. *Exhibit 2* shows how ten typical consumers entered the market, what their perceived need was, what their perceptions were of the various brands in the market, whether they were exposed to a deal or not, whether they altered their perceived need based on price, and what each purchase decision was.

A share report based on this trace is then provided. It shows the fraction of purchases by product type and brand. Reported shares total to 56 percent, this being the fraction of the total market accounted for by regular shortening cake produced by major brands.

The remainder (44 percent) is accounted for by foam and specialty cakes and the sale of some minor brands whose purchasing process is not modeled. The shares reported in *Exhibit 2* are not reliable since they are based only on a sample of 10 consumers. To evaluate market performance, large samples (1,000 consumers) need to be used, as shown in *Exhibit 4*. A trace of individual consumers is not produced in this model.

The simulation model can be used to forecast share configurations under a number of product line alternatives,[1] for example (1) Hinesbury with only premium cake (but no add-butter) in its line, (2) Hinesbury replacing premium with add-butter, and (3) Hinesbury also introducing an add-butter product.

Management Request

Marjorie Halstein, the group product manager responsible for cake mix products at Hinesbury Mills, had asked the market research department for an estimate of the market share impact of the three strategies listed. One concern was whether share gains would come from the Hinesbury brands. She and her colleagues wondered how sensitive the results might be to changes in the estimates listed in *Exhibit 3*.

---

[1] When first experimenting with the model, it is desirable to generate identical sequences of numbers on successive runs so that the results may be compared on an equal basis. This is done by generating random numbers in a cyclical pattern. Once the key parameters have been identified, the number sequences may be randomized in order to generate a wider range of results. In the spreadsheet program accompanying this edition, outcomes are calculated on an expected value basis, so the distinction between alternative methods of generating random numbers is no longer needed.

EXHIBIT 3
SUMMARY OF MARKET RESEARCH DATA AND MANAGERIAL ASSUMPTIONS
FOR SIMULATION MODEL

	Occasion		
Use and preference	**Snack**	**Family dinner**	**Special occasion**
Proportion of use for each			
occasion	.15	.50	.35
Characteristics desired:			
Quality			
Passable	.60	.15	.00
Good	.40	.70	.70
Best	.00	.15	.30
Convenience			
Normal	1.00	.65	.55
High involvement,			
less convenience	.00	.35	.45
Taste-texture			
Light, fluffy	.65	.75	.90
Heavy, rich	.35	.25	.10

	Product		
Perception of quality	**Price brand**	**Premium cake**	**Add butter**
Proportion of population perceiving			
product at quality level			
Passable	.50	.00	.00
Good	.50	.40	.50
Best	.00	.60	.50

Other data	
Proportion perceiving add-butter as high priced	.35
Probability of a deal	.50
Probability price reduction is large	.35
Probability that small deal will be seen	.60
Probability Hinesbury is a deal item	.35
Other regular's share of regular cake sales without deals	.75
Total shortening cake's share of total cake-mix market	.56
Others' share of add-butter sales without deals	.75

```
                    HINESBURY MILLS (HBM) SIMULATION MODEL
                    ==========================================
DO YOU WISH TO SEE A DESCRIPTION OF THIS PROGRAM (Y=YES N=NO)? N
                         CHOOSE ONE MARKET SCENARIO
                         --------------------------
1. HBM REG, OTHER REG & ADD-BUTTER, PRICE BRAND
2. HBM REG & PREM, OTHER REG & ADD-BUTTER, PRICE BRAND
3. HBM REG & ADD-BUTTER, OTHER REG & ADD-BUTTER, PRICE BRAND
4. HBM REG & ADD-BUTTER & PREM, OTHER REG & ADD-BUTTER, PRICE BRAND? 2
NUMBER OF CONSUMERS TO BE SIMULATED? 1000
DISPLAY BASE CASE CONDITIONS [1=ON SCREEN 2=ON PRINTER 3=NO]? 3

OPTIONS [1=CHANGE 2=OUTPUT TO SCREEN 3=OUTPUT TO PRINTER 4=EXIT TO MAIN MENU]? 2
                              MARKET SCENARIO 2
                 HBM REG & PREM, OTHER REG & ADD-BUTTER, PRICE BRAND
                 ===================================================
                           CONSUMER CHARACTERISTICS
                           ------------------------
```

1) PROPORTION WHO BUY CAKE FOR USE AS A SNACK		.15
OF THESE, THE PROP. WHO DESIRE: GOOD QUALITY: .40	BEST QUALITY	.00
2) PROPORTION WHO BUY CAKE FOR THE FAMILY DINNER:		.50
OF THESE, THE PROP. WHO DESIRE: GOOD QUALITY: .70	BEST QUALITY	.15
3) OF THOSE WHO BUY CAKE FOR SPECIAL OCCASIONS:		
THE PROP. WHO DESIRE: GOOD QUALITY: .70	BEST QUALITY	.30
4) PROPORTION OF SNACK USERS PREFERRING HIGH CONVENIENCE		1.00
5) PROPORTION OF DINNER USERS PREFERRING HIGH CONVENIENCE		0.65
6) PROPORTION OF SPECIAL USERS PREFERRING HIGH CONVENIENCE		0.55
7) PROPORTION OF SNACK USERS PREFERRING LIGHT-FLUFFY TEXTURE		0.65
8) PROPORTION OF DINNER USERS PREFERRING LIGHT-FLUFFY TEXTURE		0.75
9) PROPORTION OF SPECIAL USERS PREFERRING LIGHT-FLUFFY TEXTURE		0.90
10) PROPORTION WHO PERCEIVE THE PRICE BRAND AS NORMAL QUALITY		0.50
11) PROPORTION WHO PERCEIVE THE PREMIUM CAKE AS BEST QUALITY		0.60
12) PROPORTION WHO PERCEIVE THE ADD-BUTTER CAKE AS BEST QUALITY		0.50
13) PROPORTION WHO PERCEIVE ADD-BUTTER CAKES AS HIGH PRICED		0.35

```
PRESS RETURN TO CONTINUE
                            MARKET CONDITIONS
                            =================
```

14) PROBABILITY OF A DEAL	0.50
15) PROBABILITY THAT A PRICE REDUCTION IS LARGE	0.35
16) PROBABILITY THAT A SMALL DEAL WILL BE SEEN	0.60
17) PROBABILITY THAT HINESBURY IS THE DEAL ITEM	0.35
18) OTHER REGULAR'S SHARE OF REGULAR CAKE SALES WITHOUT DEALS	0.75
19) TOTAL SHORTENING CAKE'S SHARE OF TOTAL CAKE MARKET	0.56
20) OTHERS SHARE OF ADD-BUTTER SALES WITHOUT DEALS	0.75

```
                         CURRENT MODEL CONDITIONS
                         ========================
```

21) CONSUMERS ARE BEING GENERATED IN A CYCLICAL PATTERN	
22) MARKET SCENARIO	2
23) NUMBER OF CONSUMERS SIMULATED	1000

```
                              MARKET SHARES
                              -------------
```

HINESBURY REG	.106	OTHER REG	.190
HINESBURY PREM	.033	OTHER ADD BUTTER	.058
HBM ADD-BUTTER	.000	PRICE BRAND	.173
	TOTAL PURCHASES	942	

```
OPTIONS [1=CHANGE 2=OUTPUT TO SCREEN 3=OUTPUT TO PRINTER 4=EXIT TO MAIN MENU]? 1

ENTER THE LINE NUMBER CORRESPONDING TO THE DATA YOU WISH TO CHANGE.
(SEE LISTING OF BASE CASE FOR LINE NUMBERS)
```

(Continued on next page)

EXHIBIT 4 *(continued)*

IF ALL CHANGES HAVE BEEN COMPLETED PRESS RETURN? 11

PROPORTION WHO PERCEIVE THE PREMIUM CAKE AS BEST QUALITY? .8

ENTER THE LINE NUMBER CORRESPONDING TO THE DATA YOU WISH TO CHANGE.
(SEE LISTING OF BASE CASE FOR LINE NUMBERS)
IF ALL CHANGES HAVE BEEN COMPLETED PRESS RETURN? 12

PROPORTION WHO PERCEIVE THE ADD-BUTTER CAKE AS BEST QUALITY? .3

ENTER THE LINE NUMBER CORRESPONDING TO THE DATA YOU WISH TO CHANGE.
(SEE LISTING OF BASE CASE FOR LINE NUMBERS)
IF ALL CHANGES HAVE BEEN COMPLETED PRESS RETURN?

OPTIONS [1=CHANGE 2=OUTPUT TO SCREEN 3=OUTPUT TO PRINTER 4=EXIT TO MAIN MENU]? 2

MARKET SCENARIO 2
HBM REG & PREM. OTHER REG & ADD-BUTTER, PRICE BRAND
=====================

CONSUMER CHARACTERISTICS
===========================

1) PROPORTION WHO BUY CAKE FOR USE AS A SNACK	.15
OF THESE, THE PROP. WHO DESIRE: GOOD QUALITY: .40 BEST QUALITY	.00
2) PROPORTION WHO BUY CAKE FOR THE FAMILY DINNER:	.50
OF THESE, THE PROP. WHO DESIRE: GOOD QUALITY: .70 BEST QUALITY	.15
3) OF THOSE WHO BUY CAKE FOR SPECIAL OCCASIONS:	
THE PROP. WHO DESIRE: GOOD QUALITY: .70 BEST QUALITY	.30
4) PROPORTION OF SNACK USERS PREFERRING HIGH CONVENIENCE	1.00
5) PROPORTION OF DINNER USERS PREFERRING HIGH CONVENIENCE	0.65
6) PROPORTION OF SPECIAL USERS PREFERRING HIGH CONVENIENCE	0.55
7) PROPORTION OF SNACK USERS PREFERRING LIGHT-FLUFFY TEXTURE	0.65
8) PROPORTION OF DINNER USERS PREFERRING LIGHT-FLUFFY TEXTURE	0.75
9) PROPORTION OF SPECIAL USERS PREFERRING LIGHT-FLUFFY TEXTURE	0.90
10) PROPORTION WHO PERCEIVE THE PRICE BRAND AS NORMAL QUALITY	0.50
11) PROPORTION WHO PERCEIVE THE PREMIUM CAKE AS BEST QUALITY	0.80
12) PROPORTION WHO PERCEIVE THE ADD-BUTTER CAKE AS BEST QUALITY	0.30
13) PROPORTION WHO PERCEIVE ADD-BUTTER CAKES AS HIGH PRICED	0.35

PRESS RETURN TO CONTINUE

MARKET CONDITIONS
----

14) PROBABILITY OF A DEAL	0.50
15) PROBABILITY THAT A PRICE REDUCTION IS LARGE	0.35
16) PROBABILITY THAT A SMALL DEAL WILL BE SEEN	0.60
17) PROBABILITY THAT HINESBURY IS THE DEAL ITEM	0.35
18) OTHER REGULAR'S SHARE OF REGULAR CAKE SALES WITHOUT DEALS	0.75
19) TOTAL SHORTENING CAKE'S SHARE OF TOTAL CAKE MARKET	0.56
20) OTHERS SHARE OF ADD-BUTTER SALES WITHOUT DEALS	0.75

CURRENT MODEL CONDITIONS
----

21) CONSUMERS ARE BEING GENERATED IN A CYCLICAL PATTERN	
22) MARKET SCENARIO	2
23) NUMBER OF CONSUMERS SIMULATED	1000

MARKET SHARES

HINESBURY REG	.105	OTHER REG	.107
HINESBURY PREM	.039	OTHER ADD BUTTER	.055
HBM ADD-BUTTER	.000	PRICE BRAND	.173

TOTAL PURCHASES 952

OPTIONS [1=CHANGE 2=OUTPUT TO SCREEN 3=OUTPUT TO PRINTER 4=EXIT TO MAIN MENU]?

Note: Consumer-characteristics and market-conditions portion of output not reproduced when no changes are made.

The Lively Arts at Hanson, II

Charles B. Weinberg

In the fall of 1983, Tom Bacon and Barbara Lynn of Hanson University's Office of Public Events began planning the 1984–85 season for the Lively Arts at Hanson (LAH) program. In December, they would go to the annual booking meeting in New York, at which time almost all the commitments for 1984–85 would be made.

In preparation, the two managers had prepared a list of events they might wish to schedule for LAH. *Exhibits 1* to *5* list the performers that were being actively considered, a brief description from promotional brochures about the performer, the month the performer was available, and the seating capacity of the hall they would perform in if they were to be booked as part of the LAH program.[1] Each performer listed went on a national or regional tour and would be available for Hanson at different times of the year, although sometimes performers could adjust their schedule to be available at another time.

The LAH season generally ran from October to early May. Most of December and early January were excluded because of winter holidays at the university; much of March, because of spring holidays.

As in the current year, LAH planned to offer approximately 25 performances. In general, performers made only one appearance on campus during a year. However, because of the expense of setup, any dance group that was booked appeared a minimum of two times and usually three times. In addition, the Guarneri String Quartet, which had become virtually a Hanson tradition (and a sellout), performed three times and it was possible to book one other chamber music group for more than one night. Booking too many groups for more than one night would detract from LAH's objective of presenting a mix of events.

It was decided to abandon the "Young Concert Artist" designation for 1984–85. Such as designation seemed to create a self-fulfilling prophecy of low attendance. Consequently, younger artists would not be separately identified but would be described by type of performance.

---

[1]The seating capacity of the large hall was approximately 1,700 (usually 1,694) seats. When the balcony and back rows were closed off, then approximately 1,100 (usually 1,085) seats were available for sale.

617

EXHIBIT 1 CHAMBER MUSIC

Name	Description	Month available	Seating capacity
1 Tokyo String Quartet	Four young musicians who burst on the musical scene eight years ago and are now ranked with the nation's top-flight quartets. "If you care at all about chamber music, you won't want to miss them."	October	720
2 Guarneri String Quartet	The talents of the Guarneri need little description, so supreme is the quartet's playing. Played at the university every year since 1970.	November	720
3 Juilliard String Quartet	As veterans of more than 3,000 sold-out concerts, participants in every major music festival around the world and with a repertory of more than 375 works, it's no wonder that the Juilliard is hailed as one of America's first families of chamber music.	November	720
4 Pittsburgh Symphony Chamber Players with Barry Tuckwell, French Horn	Tuckwell has subjected one of the most difficult instruments to a degree of obedience that approaches perfection. His performance with the principal players of the Pittsburgh Symphony Orchestra provides a delightful evening of music.	January	720
5 Bartok Quartet	Acclaimed worldwide as one of the most distinguished chamber groups on the concert scene. "The sense of ensemble could hardly be more intimate and the tonal blend of the instruments more homogeneous."	January	720
6 Music from Marlboro	Join us for what has become a tradition at Hanson; the annual visit of Music from Marlboro. Performing with the ensemble on its 1979 tour will be Isidore Cohen, famous violinist with the Beaux Arts Trio.	March	720
7 Chilingirian String Quartet	Four polished musicians who produce an elegant, exquisite sound. "Once you've heard them, you'll never forget them."	April	720

Bacon and Lynn were trying to develop a 25 event schedule. They had already scheduled the following 10 performances:

Edward Albee, playwright	October (to open the season)	1 night
Guarneri String Quartet	November	3 nights
Misha and Cipa Dichter, pianists	January	1 night
Nicanor Zabaleta, harpist	February	1 night
Repertory Dance Theater	February	3 nights
Michael Lorimer, guitar	May	1 night

While the financial aspects could not be ignored, at this stage LAH management was more concerned with scheduling a season that would help LAH to meet its nonfinancial objectives. Indeed, the artistic fees of the performers listed in *Exhibits 1* to *5* were such that LAH would have a deficit of between $1,000 and $2,000 if ticket sales were at the historic average level for the type of event. Ticket prices were expected to be in the $9 to $10 range, but the decision on prices would not be required for some time.

In planning for next year, LAH management had available an interactive computer model, called ARTS PLAN, to help forecast attendance and choose events to schedule. A brief report describing this system is included at the end of this case. The system had provided accurate forecasts when previously used by LAH management.

EXHIBIT 2   DANCE

Name	Description	Month available	Seating capacity
1 Bella Lewitzky Dance Company	Lewitzky is a revelation . . . a major choreographer . . . a great dancer . . . a superb teacher. With herself and her company, there is a body awareness that transcends mere muscular discipline.	October	1,700
2 Kathryn Posin Dance Company	One of the bright new stars on the dance horizon. "Posin's choreography is simply brilliant, employing both space and body in fresh, formful ways. She uses a wide range of dance idioms that are molded like putty to her purpose."	October	1,700
3 AMAN*	Colorful, authentic costumes, exotic instruments, and an exciting repertory of more than 70 folk dances from the Balkans, Middle East, North Africa, and the U.S. AMAN, the American International Folk Ballet, has become one of the nation's most respected performing arts companies.	January	1,700
4 Joffrey II	The best small classical ballet company in the country. Their remarkable control and technique will dazzle you.	January	1,700
5 Repertory Dance Theater	Utah's exciting dance company includes in its repertory some 60 works by the greatest names in modern dance. From the classics to exciting new choreography, this company of nine excels in its art.	February	1,700
6 Alvin Ailey American Dance*	Modern, jazz, and classical dance technique which reflects America's heritage, black and white.	March	1,700
7 Pilobolus	An ever-changing flow of linked body shapes that mold and remold in space with skill and sophistication. Pilobolus is gymnastics, acrobatics, applied physics, theories of leverage and contemporary dance!	April	1,700

*Can be considered a "well-known" dance group.

Tom Bacon and Barbara Lynn expected to use ARTS PLAN as an aid in developing next year's schedule. However, from past experience, they knew it was best to develop a limited list of alternative schedules before using the computer system. They also found it more efficient to prepare the fall (October, November, December), winter (January, February, March), and spring (April, May) schedules separately at first, and then, after some test computer runs, to consider a full schedule. One year, when the computer was unavailable, Mr. Bacon and Ms. Lynn simply used the ARTS PLAN forecasting rule (see report at end of case) with a pocket calculator to test scheduling alternatives.

Meeting attendance goals was just one of the tasks that they faced. They had to deal with the pragmatic problems of when performers were available and the need to have a schedule that presented a relatively even number of events in the major months of October, November, January, February, and April. Beyond this, the programming schedule also had to help achieve the goal of establishing LAH as a major source of first-rate performing art talent in a variety of fields.

EXCERPTS FROM A REPORT DESCRIBING THE DEVELOPMENT AND USE OF ARTS PLAN

To gain a better understanding of the factors influencing attendance at LAH events, LAH management

EXHIBIT 3 GUITAR

Name	Description	Month available	Seating capacity*
1 Eugenia Zukerman, flutist/Carlos Bonell, guitarist	Zukerman, one of the finest flutists to be found anywhere, teams up with Bonell, one of Europe's leading guitarists, for a program of works primarily from the Baroque period.	February	1,085
2 Ronald Radford, Flamenco guitar	One of the few American masters of the Flamenco guitar shares Spanish gypsy music with you through performance and dialogue.	April	1,085
3 Michael Lorimer, guitarist	A protégé of Andres Segovia, Lorimer has carved an enviable reputation as a classical guitarist.	May	1,085

*Guitarists usually perform in the 1,700 seat hall, but some 600 of these seats are not made available for sale.

EXHIBIT 4 JAZZ

Name	Description	Month available	Seating capacity
1 New England Conservatory Ragtime Ensemble with Gunther Schuller	The toe-tapping sounds of Joplin, Morton, Marshall, Hampton, and others are played by this very famous ensemble. Gunther Schuller himself will be at the podium, conducting and discussing this marvelous period in our country's musical history.	October	1,700
2 Richard Stoltzman, clarinet	Consistently acclaimed as "an artist of indescribable genius." Often compared to the legendary Reginald Kell. Pianist/bassoonist Bill Douglas will perform with Stoltzman.	October	720
3 Billy Taylor Trio	Jazz pianist, composer, arranger, teacher, and actor, Billy Taylor performs in company with a drummer and bassist. Taylor is among those musicians who have elevated jazz to new heights of recognition and appreciation.	December	1,700
4 Toshiko Akiyoshi/ Lew Tabackin Big Band	An outstanding jazz orchestra in the tradition of the great Duke Ellington: each musician's individual sound and style becomes an integral part of the ensemble's musical identity. Akiyoshi is composer, conductor, pianist. Tabackin plays tenor sax and flute and is the principal soloist.	February	1,700
5 Sonny Rollins, tenor saxophone	"A giant speaking. A man who has altered the course of music to which he still contributes mightily." Hear the musician who has converted a new generation to the meaning and joys of jazz!	February	720
6 Dizzy Gillespie, trumpeter	Revered throughout the world as one of the giants of jazz, an artist with absolute mastery of his instrument and seemingly unlimited musical ideas.	March	1,700

EXHIBIT 5 OTHER ARTISTS

Name	Description	Month available	Seating capacity
Theater			
1 Edward Albee, playwright	Edward Albee is one of the world's most important contemporary playwrights. A cast chosen and directed by Albee will present *The Zoo Story* and *The American Dream*. The former was Albee's first play and won the Vernon Rice Award in 1960; the latter was written in 1960 and won the Foreign Press Association Award in 1961.	October	1,700
2 The World of Gilbert & Sullivan	Artists from the famous D'Oyly Carte Opera Company present in concert some of Gilbert & Sullivan's finest tunes and patter. Produced in cooperation with the university chorus and orchestra.	October	1,700
3 The Acting Company	Presenting the *White Devil*, a work by John Webster, author of the Elizabethan classic, *The Duchess of Malfi*.	January	1,700
4 Ruby Dee & Ossie Davis, theater	Two of America's foremost black performers share their love of stories, poems, legends and experiences in *Inside/Out*, a project of personal love and dedication that has become one of our nation's theatrical riches.	April	720
Soloists and Duets			
1 Elly Ameling	Truly one of the foremost masters of the art of song in the world.	October	720
2 Igor Kipnis, harpsichordist	The foremost harpsichordist of today. "He need bow to no one in the intelligence and scrupulousness with which he approaches the various stylistic requirements of Renaissance, Baroque, and classical music."	November	720
3 Misha and Cipa Dichter, pianists	Husband and wife, Misha and Cipa Dichter win accolades wherever they perform for their assurance, virtuosity, and unique sense of musical spirit.	January	720
4 Nicanor Zabaleta, harp	The harp virtuoso of our era. A veteran of more than 4,000 concerts around the world and a sellout at every previous Lively Arts concert.	February	720
5 Charles Rosen, piano	"His playing is all one could wish for. It has taste, intelligence, and artistic insight."	April	720
6 Robert Cohen, cello	Winner of the 1978 Gregor Piatigorsky Award, Cohen is known for his combination of high virtuosity and genuine eloquence.	May	720
Groups			
1 Sour Cream	Frans Brueggens' avant garde recorder trio. Join him, Kees Boeke, and Walter van Hauwe for an informal session of music making, featuring works from the Renaissance to the present.	October	720
2 Il Divertimento	Eight master woodwind players performing on 18th-century instruments. Hear Haydn, Beethoven, and Mozart played the way the composers themselves heard it.	November	720
3 Greenwood Consort	Music of the late Middle Ages and Renaissance delivered with verve, enthusiasm, humor, and top-notch musicianship. The Boston-based Greenwood brings early music to life by combining voices with flute, recorder, lute, pipe and tabor, krummhorns, and viols.	April	720
4 Waverly Consort	Hear gentle pastorales and madrigals, ribald drinking songs, delicate airs for the recorder, and sedate minuets—all played on original instruments.	May	720

asked a marketing faculty member at Hanson University for help. By employing a statistical technique known as regression analysis, a fairly accurate attendance forecasting system was developed. Moreover, the professor and a student assistant were able to transform the technical statistical analysis into a "user-friendly" computer system, called "ARTS PLAN," that LAH management had used to help plan a season. The remainder of this appendix describes briefly the development and usage of the system.

Development of a Forecasting Model

A number of factors beyond the distinctive appeal of an individual performer could influence the attendance at any given performance. The first step was to determine these factors and to measure their importance via the use of regression analysis. The resulting model forms a preliminary base case forecast for a planning model. The manager can override the forecast, if necessary, because of factors not captured in the model.

Data were available on attendance by performances for 93 LAH performances over three years. Preliminary analyses of these data revealed that there were seasonal effects in attendance. An average performance drew 85 percent of capacity in the fall, 60 percent in the winter, and 50 percent in the spring. Similarly, there were effects by type of performance. Chamber music performances drew 80 percent of capacity, dance 60 percent, guitar 105 percent (seats on the stage or tickets for standing room were sometimes sold), and jazz 75 percent. Performers classified as Young Concert Artists (YCA) drew 50 percent of capacity. These five performance types accounted for 81 of the 93 performances. The remaining 12 events averaged 60 percent of capacity. It was also believed, although not specifically tabulated, that performances on Friday nights drew better than performances during the week. There are too few Saturday night or Sunday performances to examine other weekend nights.

Approximately 15 percent of the performers who were booked appeared for more than one perfor-

mance. There were a number of reasons for multi-performance bookings. Some groups had a varied repertoire and fairly broad appeal. Dance groups were generally booked for multiple performances because of the fixed costs involved in bringing such a group to campus. The number of performances for some groups was determined by their availability or the availability of auditoriums on campus. Because of the various reasons for having multiple performances, the effect on attendance was problematical. Multiple performances could spread out a limited audience over several days, provide opportunities for word of mouth to build second or third day audiences, and allow devotees to attend several times.

Examination of the data revealed that there was only one group that appeared more than five times over the three years. A specific variable was set up to represent this group.[2] Although no dance group appeared more than five times, there appeared to be a subset of dance groups that were particularly well known. A specific variable was established for dance groups belonging to this subset.

The performances were held (with 3 exceptions in 93 performances) in three different halls on campus with capacities of approximately 350, 720, and 1,700 seats. Thus, the capacity of the hall could be a factor in the actual attendance obtained; however, the hall chosen was dictated by the musical and technical requirements of the performance type and not by an estimate of attendance. Thus, for example, chamber music concerts usually are held in a 720 seat hall, and dance groups always perform in a 1,700 seat hall. Because of the direct association between type of performance and capacity of hall, it was not possible to separate the effect of capacity from performance type. Thus the performance type "dance" actually refers to dance held in a 1,700 seat auditorium; if a dance performance were to be held in a 2,000 seat auditorium, some extrapolation would be required.

Data on several other potentially important factors

---

[2]Code named the Gala Quartet in the computer analysis, this group is actually the Guarneri String Quartet.

(such as competing events being held on the same night and different weather conditions) were not readily available in LAH records. For example, attendance might suffer if a basketball game were being played that night. Also, the effect of any special promotion was not included. However, to account for any temporal shift, variables to represent year were included.

Statistical Modal The mathematical model tested was the following:

$$Y = a_0 + a_w W + a_s S + a_{T1} T_1 + a_{T2} T_2$$
$$+ a_{T3} T_3 + a_{T4} T_4 + a_{T5} T_5 + a_{F1} F_1 + a_{M1} M_1$$
$$+ a_{G1} G_1 + a_{G2} G_2 + a_{Y1} Y_1 + a_{Y2} Y_2$$

where Y = attendance

W = 1, if held in winter, 0 otherwise,

S = 1, if held in spring, 0 otherwise,

T_1 = 1, if chamber music, 0 otherwise,

T_2 = 1, if dance, 0 otherwise,

T_3 = 1, if guitar, 0 otherwise,

T_4 = 1, if jazz, 0 otherwise,

T_5 = 1, if young concert artist, 0 otherwise,

F_1 = 1, if held on Friday, 0 otherwise,

M_1 = 1, if part of a series of multiple performances, 0 otherwise,

G_1 = 1, of by group performing more than five times, 0 otherwise,

G_2 = 1, if by well-known dance group, 0 otherwise,

Y_1 = 1, if held during year 1, 0 otherwise,

Y_2 = 1, if held during year 2, 0 otherwise.

The independent variables are all 0,1 dummy variables in order to represent different effects and, as is usual, are defined to omit one class in order to preserve the nonsingularity of the independent variables.

Statistical Results When regression analysis was run, five variables, Y_1 for year 1, M for multiple performances, F for Friday, W for winter, and T_1 for chamber music were not statistically significant at the 0.05 level. When these variables were deleted, all the remaining variables were significant at the 0.05 level. The regression results are shown in *Exhibit 6*. The adjusted R^2 was 0.79. When a split-half double crossover validation was run, the R^2 turned out to be 0.70. These results are considered to be very good and are superior to what has been expected by both management and the analyst. All the significant effects were in the expected direction.

There was a clear effect for performance type, four of the five dummy variables for performance type were significant and, in addition, were significantly different from each other. Although the dummy variable for chamber music did not achieve significance, this only implies that its attendance is

EXHIBIT 6
REGRESSION RESULTS FOR PREDICTING ATTENDANCE

	Coefficient	Beta weight	Value of F*
Variable:			
S (Spring)	− 127	− 0.12	5.5
T$_2$ (Dance)	231	0.22	12.3
T$_3$ (Guitar)	481	0.26	27.0
T$_4$ (Jazz)	732	0.46	79.6
T$_5$ (YCA)	− 400	− 0.30	33.0
G$_1$	178	0.10	4.1
G$_2$	804	0.50	74.1
Y$_2$ (Year 2)	− 113	− 0.12	6.0
Constant	647		

*As discussed in the text, all coefficients are significant at the 0.05 level or above.

not significantly different from that for the 12 non-classified performances. The attendance estimate for chamber music is significantly different than that for the other four performance types.

Year 3 was the base case for the annual effects. No particular explanation for the comparative drop-off in year 2 attendance, but not in year 1, has been developed. In the absence of an apparent trend, it was decided to assume $Y_2 = 0$ in the forecasting model.

Forecasting Rule In brief, the forecasting model was:

$$
\begin{aligned}
\text{Attendance} = 647 \\
- 127 \ (\text{if spring}) \\
+ 231 \ (\text{if dance}) \\
+ 481 \ (\text{if guitar}) \\
+ 732 \ (\text{if jazz}) \\
- 400 \ (\text{if YCA}) \\
+ 178 \ (\text{if Guarneri}) \\
+ 804 \ (\text{if popular dance group})
\end{aligned}
$$

For example, the base case forecast for a dance event to be held in the spring is $647 - 127$ (Spring) $+ 231$ (Dance) $= 751$; the forecast for jazz in the fall would be $647 + 732$ (Jazz) $= 1,379$.

Planning Model

The planning model is designed to help the manager determine whether a tentative or planned schedule will meet attendance objectives for the year and what the impact of promoting certain events would be on the attendance predictions.

The model has three main stages. The first stage establishes a base case forecast for the season being planned, using the forecasting model discussed in the previous section. The second stage allows the manager to *override* the regression forecast because of unique factors of which the manager is aware. For example, although the expected attendance for jazz groups booked in the fall was 1,379 people, one group may be expected to do particularly well at the university because of its local reputation or a previous successful appearance. The manager may wish

to test alternative estimates for groups falling in the "other" category. When this stage is completed, a forecast of attendance by performance, season, or year is available.

In the third stage, the manager can then test the impact of alternative strategies. The strategic options are to make scheduling changes (add, omit, or substitute a performance) and to promote particular performances. For example, if the manager wants to schedule a dance company instead of a guitarist as the second performance of the season, the impact of this scheduling change on attendance can be assessed.

Implementation Experience

The ARTS PLAN system has been used at LAH as an aid in the management of an on-going season and in the planning of a future season. Before the start of the last season, attendance forecasts were made for the 26 performance schedule. A few adjustments were made to the regression analysis forecast to account for several factors that the manager thought were important. Selected performances in the winter and spring were scheduled for intensive promotion. At the end of the season, the actual and predicted attendances were compared. An R^2 of 0.80 between actual and predicted was obtained. Further, the total attendance prediction was within 5 percent of the actual attendance.

Sample Application of Usage

Exhibit 7 is an illustration of the usage of the ARTS PLAN system. The number of options considered is relatively small because of space limitations, and fictitious names are used for the performances. The exhibit is largely self-explanatory. The following comments briefly describe the use of the model in this example.[3]

After identifying the time period to be examined and setting the number of performances, the program

---

[3]Note that display format may vary according to the version of computer program used. However, all statistical relationships remain the same.

EXHIBIT 7
EXCERPTS FROM A SAMPLE RUN

ARTS PLANNING MODEL
DO YOU WISH TO INVESTIGATE AN ENTIRE SEASON, OR A SINGLE QUARTER?
(S = SEASON; Q = QUARTER)? Q
WHICH QUARTER DO YOU WISH TO INVESTIGATE
    (FALL = 1, WINTER = 2, SPRING = 3)   ? 3
NO. OF PERFORMANCES PLANNED FOR QUARTER (MAX = 17)? 4
THE FOLLOWING TABLE PRESENTS THE BASE-CASE ATTENDANCE
PERCENTAGES WHICH WILL BE USED IN GENERATING THE FIRST-ROUND
ATTENDANCE PROJECTION

ESTIMATED ATTENDANCE PERCENTAGES (HISTORICAL)*

	FALL	WINTER	SPRING
(1) CHAMB MUSIC	90	90	72
(2) DANCE	52	52	44
(3) GUITAR	104	104	92
(4) JAZZ	81	81	74
(5) YCA	71	71	34
(6) OTHER-(720)	90	90	72
(7) OTHER-(1700)	38	38	31

*IN ADDITION THE FOLLOWING SUPPLEMENTARY EFFECTS HAVE BEEN
OBSERVED

    (G) GALA QUARTET   +22 PERCENT
    (P) POPULAR DANCE GROUP +47 PERCENT

AT THIS STEP YOU ARE ASKED TO PROVIDE SPECIFIC INFORMATION ON
THE PROGRAM YOU ARE PLANNING.
****

PERFORMANCE NUMBER 1
ENTER PERFORMANCE NAME (MAXIMUM 12 CHARACTERS)? BETH
ENTER PERFORMANCE TYPE (USE CODE NUMBER:)

    1 = CHAMBER MUSIC   3 = GUITAR   5 = YOUNG CONCERT ARTISTS (YCA)
    2 = DANCE   4 = JAZZ   6 = OTHER-(720)   7 = OTHER-(1700)
?2
ENTER CAPACITY OF HALL? 1700
    POPULAR DANCE GROUP   (Y = YES, N = NO)? Y
****

† (Remainder of initial input deleted)

ATTENDANCE PREDICTIONS FOR SPRING QUARTER

PERFORMANCE NUMBER	PERFORMANCE NAME	PERCENTAGE ATTENDANCE	CAPACITY OF HALL	ATTENDANCE
1	BETH	91	1700	1547
2	SARI	74	1700	1258
3	AMY	34	350	119
4	MICHELLE	72	720	518
TOTALS	*	77	4470	3442

****

(Continued on next page)

EXHIBIT 7 *(continued)*

DO YOU WISH TO MAKE ANY CHANGES? (Y = YES, N = NO)? <u>Y</u>
ENTER NUMBER OF PERFORMANCE YOU WISH TO CHANGE? <u>2</u>
CURRENT STATUS OF PERFORMANCE NUMBER 2

NAME	SARI
TYPE	(4) JAZZ
PCT ATTEND	74
CAPACITY	1700
ATTENDANCE	1258

INDICATE BY CODE NUMBER THE PARAMETER YOU WISH TO CHANGE

ENTER ONE ONLY 1 = PERFORMANCE   3 = PERCENTAGE ATTENDANCE
                     NAME   EXPECTED
                2 = PERFORMANCE   4 = CAPACITY OF HALL
                     TYPE

?<u>3</u>
OLD PERCENTAGE ATTENDANCE IS: 74
NEW PERCENTAGE ATTENDANCE EXPECTED: <u>85</u>
ANY OTHER CHANGES TO THIS PERFORMANCE (Y = YES, N = NO)? <u>N</u>

ATTENDANCE PREDICTIONS FOR SPRING QUARTER

PERFORMANCE NUMBER	PERFORMANCE NAME	PERCENTAGE ATTENDANCE	CAPACITY OF HALL	ATTENDANCE
1	BETH	91	1700	1547
2	SARI	RV 85	1700	1445
3	AMY	34	350	119
4	MICHELLE	72	720	518
TOTALS	*	81	4470	3629

prints out the historical record. The program then requests the user to identify each performance by name and type, give the capacity of the hall it is in, and indicate any special effects that may exist. When all the required information has been submitted, the program provides a forecast of attendance.

An option is then provided to override the base case projections because of additional information that the manager has available. For example, the jazz group Sari may be particularly well-known and consequently may be expected to do better than the average jazz group, even without special promotion. The adjustment may either be upward or downward. The manager can also examine the impact of adding, deleting, or replacing a performance with another. When all the adjustments are completed, a planning base forecast for the quarter is established.

Using the *Marketing Challenges* Personal Computer Disks

John D. Claxton

This appendix is written for people who have beginner-level familiarity with the use of personal computer spreadsheets such as VP Planner or Lotus 1-2-3. Users with no spreadsheet experience should see their instructor for information on getting started with these disks.

The Decision Support Package (DSP) is an option that accompanies this book. The @START spreadsheet lists the cases that are available on the DSP. To get started quickly, just load @START (see *Exhibit 1*) onto your computer and follow the directions on the screen. The @START spreadsheet also describes any updates and revisions made to the disk following publication of this book.

EXHIBIT 1
GETTING STARTED

The following steps should be used to gain initial familiarity with this DSP:
1. Make a back-up copy of all DSP diskettes.
2. Load spreadsheet software.
3. Assuming you use the "B" disk drive for your working files, place DSP disk in B-drive.* (Alternatively remove the spreadsheet disk from the A-drive, insert disk in the A-drive, and skip to step 5.)
4. Make sure the spreadsheet active directory is B: by typing:
   /F D B: <ENTER>
5. Retrieve the spreadsheet named @START by typing:
   /F R <ENTER>
6. The @START spreadsheet provides a listing of the spreadsheets available. You can move to the spreadsheet for the case of interest by typing:
   /F R {select spreadsheet via arrow keys} <ENTER>

---

*Users with a hard disk drive may want to load the disk onto the hard disk drive and then use C-drive.

System Requirements

The use of the DSP requires the following hardware and software:

1. An IBM-compatible personal computer with MS-DOS 2.1 or later
2. Spreadsheet software: VP Planner or Lotus 1-2-3

Description of the Spreadsheets

The DSP spreadsheets have the following characteristics:

1. A title page with the following instructions: HIT ⟨ENTER⟩ to begin . . .
2. User instructions contained on a screen that is accessed from anywhere in the spreadsheet by the following keystrokes:

While holding the "Alt" key, tap the "I" key. In other words, type: ⟨Alt-I⟩

3. Every screen has an instruction suggesting a next step to take.
4. The spreadsheets generally follow a marketing decision focus by using a setup that emphasizes the flow of three major decision-making components:

Marketing decisions: Major decisions of concern in the case.

Estimates: The market trends and market responses of concern.

Outcomes: Calculations such as contribution and profitability.

5. Many of the spreadsheets are set up with "Protection Enabled." This means that only entry areas indicated by braces, { }, can be altered.